Early eighteenth-century literary critics thought the King James Bible had 'all the disadvantages of an old prose translation'. But from the 1760s on criticism became increasingly favourable. In the nineteenth century it welled into a chorus of praise for 'the noblest monument of English prose'. This volume, the second of a two-volume work, traces how that reversal of opinion came about and helped to shape the making and reception of modern translations such as the Revised Version and the New English Bible. At the same time the story of the development of modern literary discussion of the Bible in general is told. From the Augustan discovery of Longinus' comments on Genesis through such major figures as Robert Lowth to modern critics such as Frank Kermode and Robert Alter, this story reveals a fascinating world of original insights and repetitions of received opinions. It shows not only how criticism has shaped understanding of the Bible, but how the Bible has shaped literary criticism.

A history of the Bible as literature

VOLUME 2

A history of
the Bible as literature

VOLUME TWO

From 1700 to the present day

David Norton

Senior Lecturer in English, Victoria University of Wellington,
New Zealand

CAMBRIDGE UNIVERSITY PRESS

Published by the Press Syndicate of the University of Cambridge
The Pitt Building, Trumpington Street, Cambridge CB2 1RP
40 West 20th Street, New York, NY 10011-4211, USA
10 Stamford Road, Oakleigh, Melbourne 3166, Australia

First published 1993

Printed in Great Britain at the University Press, Cambridge

A catalogue record for this book is available from the British Library

Library of Congress cataloguing in publication data

Norton, David.
A history of the Bible as literature.
Includes bibliographical references and indexes.
Contents: v. 1. From antiquity to 1700 – v. 2. From 1700
to the present day.
1. Bible as literature.   2. Bible – Criticism, interpretation,
etc. – History.
3. Bible – Versions.   1. Title.
BS585.N67 1992   809'93522   92–1034

ISBN 0 521 33398 9 (v. 1) hardback
ISBN 0 521 33399 7 (v. 2) hardback

For Aaron, Isaac and Benny – one day.

And for Ruby

Contents

ix

Abbreviations

AV	Authorised Version or King James Bible, 1611
ASV	American Standard Version, 1901
CHB	*The Cambridge History of the Bible*
DNB	*Dictionary of National Biography*
KJB	King James Bible or Authorised Version, 1611
NEB	The New English Bible, 1970
NKJV	The New King James Version, 1982
NT	New Testament
OED	*Oxford English Dictionary*
OT	Old Testament
PB	The Book of Common Prayer
RSV	Revised Standard Version, 1952
RV	Revised Version, 1885

CHAPTER I

The early eighteenth century and the KJB

'All the disadvantages of an old prose translation'

The superior language

Yet how beautiful do the holy writings appear, under all the disadvantages of an old prose translation? So beautiful that, with a charming and elegant simplicity, they ravish and transport the learned reader, so intelligible that the most unlearned are capable of understanding the greater part of them. (P. 30)

So exclaims in 1731 the very minor poet and critic, John Husbands (1706–32). He seems to be saying that the KJB, in spite of being rather bad by his standards, is, after all, very good. This curious combination of praise and dispraise is one of a line of such remarks that reflects conflicting forces among the literati of Augustan England. Before exhibiting these remarks, some of the forces need to be sketched.

The phrase 'an old prose translation' suggests the three main negative elements. The disadvantage of being a translation needs no comment – everybody believed that translation must necessarily be inferior to the original, especially if that original was divinely inspired – but we are accustomed to admiring prose and do not think of the language of a hundred years ago or less as particularly old. We certainly do not think it worse than present-day English: quite the reverse (see below, p. 434). The world of Dickens and George Eliot may be very different from ours, but their language is not. In contrast, the eighteenth century was vividly aware that the English it used for literature (to look no further) was very different from – and, most thought, far better than – that of pre-Restoration literature: 'the language of the present times is so clean and chaste, and so very different from our ancestors, that should they return hither they would want an interpreter to converse with us'.[1] Rewritings of the

---

[1] Blackmore, *Essays*, p. 99.

best old authors such as Chaucer and Shakespeare abounded. Dryden, prefacing his adaptation of *Troilus and Cressida* (1679), had this to say of Shakespeare's language:

> it must be allowed to the present age that the tongue in general is so much refined since Shakespeare's time that many of his words and more of his phrases are scarce intelligible. And of those which we understand, some are ungrammatical, others coarse, and his whole style is so pestered with figurative expressions that it is as affected as it is obscure.[2]

This is criticism as much of the time as of its greatest author. Comments such as this are not, so far, to be found on the KJB's language, but they represent what must have been in people's minds when they dismissed it as old. In the dedicatory epistle to the same play, Dryden anticipates much that will be characteristic of the early eighteenth century. He believes English is still barbarous. Like Palmer nearly three centuries earlier (see volume 1, pp. 63–4), he complains of its sound, for 'we are full of monosyllables, and those clogged with consonants, and our pronunciation is effeminate, all which are enemies to a sounding language' (p. 223). But the weaknesses are more than just aesthetic. It lacks a standard, so he translated his own English into Latin, 'a more stable language', in order to judge its quality (p. 222). Indeed, one must have a perfect knowledge of Greek, Latin, Old German, French and Italian, and of the most faultless English authors, if one is to judge English style. Though Old German is mentioned, pre-Renaissance forms of English are not: the emphasis is squarely on classical and romance languages. Only a few people looked to the native roots of the language, roots so strong in the KJB; most looked to the very different Latin. The ardent classicist Anthony Blackwall is as explicit as anyone. He looks forward to 'the dawn of a Reformation' when 'men of elevated spirit shall arise to drive out the barbarous Goths and Vandals' through recourse to the classics, in which 'there are unexhausted stores of noble sense and suitable expression ... By supplies drawn from them, gentlemen of happy talents and industry may ... fill up the defects and smooth the roughness of their mother tongues' (*An Introduction*, pp. 4–5).

Dryden wanted 'a perfect grammar' of the language as the foundation for 'an exact standard of writing and of speaking' (p. 225). The eighteenth century did its best. Dictionaries helped standardise meaning, spelling and, consequently, pronunciation; grammars, modelled on Latin grammar, not on observation of English in use, fixed themselves on the tongue like marriage, for better or

---

[2] *The Works of John Dryden*, 20 vols., ed. Alan Roper and Vinton A. Dearing (Berkeley, Los Angeles and London: University of California Press, 1961 etc.), XIII: 225.

worse. What is more, the century believed it was doing well. Leonard Welsted (1688–1742) illustrates this with all the enthusiasm so characteristic of minor critics. Though others might disagree, he believes that 'the English language does at this day [1724] possess all the advantages and excellencies, which are very many, that its nature will admit of, whether they consist in softness and majesty of sound, or in the force and choice of words, or in variety and beauty of construction'.[3] Sound, vocabulary and grammar, if that is what the last phrase means, are all as perfect as can be. Further, the language has only recently reached this aesthetic excellence: 'it is not, unless I mistake, much more than a century since England first recovered out of something like barbarism with respect to its state of letters and politeness ... we have laid aside all our harsh antique words and retained only those of good sound and energy; the most beautiful polish is at length given to our tongue, and its Teutonic rust quite worn away'.[4] Again the prejudice against the native element in the language is rampant. The very term 'Augustan' expresses both the prejudice and the contentment that so quickly took over from Dryden's reservations. Initially it was used for the writers of Charles II's reign (1660–85), but Welsted and others used it as it is still used, for their own time, the time of Pope and Addison, with extension back to Dryden. It suggests a self-satisfied comparison with the time of Virgil, Horace and Ovid. In such a situation, the KJB was doubly disadvantaged. Not only was it old, but its linguistic roots were, in vocabulary, largely Teutonic, and, in form, often Hebraic.

The nearest we can get to detail of how this sense of the Augustan perfection of English affected reading of the KJB comes from a Roman Catholic source. An Irish priest, Cornelius Nary (1660–1738), made a new translation of the NT from the Vulgate, ('diligently compared' with the Greek and other translations (Dublin, 1719)). He claims in the title that he is working 'for the better understanding of the literal sense', yet his preface points not to revision of Gregory Martin's scholarship but of his language, which 'is so old, the words in many places so obsolete, the orthography so bad, and the translation so very literal, that in a number of places it is unintelligible, and all over so grating to the ears of such as are accustomed to speak, in a manner, another language, that most people will not be at the pains of reading [it]' (fol. A2 v). Except that people did read it, much of this could apply to the KJB, and the comment is notable for combining aesthetic and practical objections, as well as looking to a

---

[3] 'A Dissertation Concerning the Perfection of the English Language, the State of Poetry, etc.' (1724); in Elledge, I: 320–48; p. 324.

[4] Pp. 321–2. 'Politeness' was much used in this century; as an adjective it corresponds to our 'cultivated', and is often used interchangeably with 'polished'.

standard in the objection to the spelling. Nary's work was unsuccessful, but deserves to be remembered as the first English prose version of a Testament to be made with open care for the aesthetic quality of its English: the Bible was to be 'in a style and dress less obscure and somewhat more engaging than it has been' (fol. B2 v). The one commendatory letter again bespeaks the Augustans in praising Nary for 'reconciling a literal translation with the purity of the English tongue'. 'Purity' here means anything but the historic purity of the native strain in the language.

The disadvantage of prose reflects the fact that interest in literary aspects of the Bible at this time concentrated on the poetic parts. Wither had already argued that prose was a poor substitute for verse translation (see volume 1, p. 279), and now the much-pilloried John Dennis (1657–1734) thought along similar lines, arguing this way in his most representative work, *The Grounds of Criticism in Poetry* (1704):

> it is ridiculous to imagine that there can be a more proper way to express some parts and duties of a religion which we believe to be divinely inspired than the very way in which they were at first delivered. Now the most important part of the Old Testament [the prophecies] was delivered not only in a poetical style, but in poetical numbers ... because they who wrote them believed that the figurative passionate style and the poetical numbers ... were requisite to enforce them upon the minds of men.
>
> (Pp. 139, 140)

The divine precedent demands that a proper (here probably meaning 'appropriate' rather than 'accurate') translation be in verse. Consequently, when Dennis cites a biblical passage for its literary quality he uses his own verse paraphrase, but when he cites the Bible for its meaning alone he uses the KJB. 'Poetry', he argues, 'is the natural language of religion, and ... religion at first produced it as a cause produces its effect' (p. 131). Prose is a later and lesser invention, 'by no means proper' for religion (p. 132). Referring to the ancient Greeks, he explains that 'the wonders of religion naturally threw them upon great passions, and great passions naturally threw them upon harmony and figurative language, as they must of necessity do any poet' (p. 132). Turning to Christianity, he elaborates: 'because if the ideas which these subjects afford are expressed with passion equal to their greatness, that which expresses them is poetry; for that which makes poetry to be what it is is only because it has more passion than any other way of writing' (p. 139). The quality of poetry lies in its power to move the passions, and the passions are most moved by religious subjects given appropriate poetic expression. In other hands this could be an argument that divorced the idea of poetry from the technical idea of 'poetic numbers', but Dennis has no doubt that verse form is essential to expressive power.

Dennis wanted to restore modern poetry to its true role by returning it to religion (Milton's example was of major importance). Others disagreed. Inheriting the Puritan distrust of art, they thought poetry irredeemable and shrank from any suggestion that the Bible might be literary. Isaac Watts (1674–1748), best remembered for hymns such as 'When I Survey the Wondrous Cross', closely echoes Dennis, but offers this reminder of the opposite view:

> This profanation and debasement of so divine an art has tempted some weaker Christians to imagine that poetry and vice are naturally akin, or at least that verse is fit only to recommend trifles and entertain our looser hours, but it is too light and trivial a method to treat anything that is serious and sacred. They submit, indeed, to use it in divine psalmody, but they love the driest translation of the Psalm best. They will venture to sing a dull hymn or two at church in tunes of equal dullness, but still they persuade themselves and their children that the beauties of poesy are vain and dangerous. All that arises a degree above Mr Sternhold is too airy for worship, and hardly escapes the sentence of 'unclean and abominable'.[5]

Among those willing to admire literature and to think of the Bible as poetry, some began, as we shall see, to think along lines more conducive to admiration of the KJB. These lines owe a real debt to the most powerful new force in critical thought in this time, Longinus' treatise *Peri Hupsous*.

Longinus and Boileau

Peri Hupsous was translated into English as *Of the height of eloquence* by John Hall in 1652, then, from the French of Boileau, as *Of the loftiness or elegancy of speech* by J. Pulteney in 1680. In 1698, also from the French, came an anonymous translation entitled *An essay upon sublime*. These changes encapsulate an important shift in literary attitudes. In a general way, 'eloquence' and 'sublime' evoke the same thing, a sense of what is best in writing, but they have a basic difference. 'Eloquence' points towards all the rhetorical devices of a piece of writing and indicates a technical judgement of literature: its main purpose is persuasion, and there had of course been many arguments mounted that the Bible fulfilled this purpose in spite of its apparent lack of eloquence. Such arguments tried to shift the basis for judgement from technical qualities to effectiveness. With the advent of 'sublime' as a key word for literary quality this

---

[5] Preface to *Horae Lyricae* (1709); in Elledge, 1: 148–63; p. 150. The whole preface is of interest but contains nothing that cannot be found elsewhere.

shift in basis became widely accepted. Not only did effectiveness become a primary criterion for quality, but a new kind of effectiveness came to be admired, not the power to persuade but the power to move, particularly to move to heights of emotion.

Pulteney's intermediate title, *Of the Loftiness or Elegancy of Speech*, shows the change taking place. 'Loftiness' and 'elegancy' are coupled uneasily, the new idea struggling to take over from the old (as indeed it continued to struggle: interest in eloquence did not disappear). Moreover, true to the predominantly technical nature of Longinus' work, the emphasis remains on language. But underlying Longinus' technical discussion is a sharp critical sense of the effect of language, so he defines sublimity as a quality which pleases, rather than persuades, all men at all times. It uplifts souls, filling them 'with a proud exaltation and a sense of vaunting joy' (ch. 7, p. 107), or, in Hall's phrase, 'a transport of joy and wonder'.[6] This is the aspect of his work that meant so much to the eighteenth century, even if it was at odds with Augustan ideas of a polished, regulated, neo-classical perfection. If sublimity of effect was a criterion for aesthetic quality, then any writing – indeed, any object – which produced this effect could be admired whether or not its style appeared admirable. This was of great importance for literary estimation of the Bible in translation, if not always as a cause of that estimation, then certainly helping to legitimise it and to make it fashionable.

There is a second crucial element for biblical appreciation in Longinus' idea of the sublime, its religious dimension. He identifies the two prime sources of the sublime as 'the ability to form grand conceptions' and 'the stimulus of powerful and inspired emotion' (ch. 8, p. 108); the latter Hall calls 'fierce and transporting passion' (p. XII), while both Pulteney and Smith understand this as the pathetic, 'by which is meant that enthusiasm and natural vehemency which touches and affects us' (Pulteney, p. 24). Longinus pushes both these sources towards divinity. Sublimity is not just 'the echo of a noble mind' (ch. 9, p. 109); it 'carries one up to where one is close to the majestic mind of God' (ch. 36, p. 147). Pulteney puts this most interestingly: it has in it 'something supernatural and divine, two qualities which almost equal us to the gods themselves' (pp. 134–5). Hall, who is weak at this point, elsewhere pushes it furthest. In his dedication he writes that the sublime 'must therefore have somewhat I cannot tell how divine in it',[7] and, now translating, he proclaims

---

[6]   P. XI. For ease of reference I have used Dorsch's translation, and then selected among Hall, Pulteney and Smith, whose version predominated after 1739.

[7]   Fol. B3 v. He goes on to explain that such works must possess outstanding knowledge of man, sciences, history and nature, but yet that all these things are trivial without the

that 'there is nothing nearer divine inspiration' (p. XIV; similarly the modern version, ch. 8, p. 109). Sublimity bespeaks divinity. So too does the Bible. It was difficult, following Longinus, not to think of the Bible as sublime, especially as he himself, in a famous passage, had taken one of his examples of sublimity from the Bible.[8] After a Homeric example of passages 'which represent the divine nature as it really is, pure, majestic and undefiled', Longinus observes: 'so too the lawgiver of the Jews, no ordinary person, having formed a high conception of the power of the Divine Being, gave expression to it when at the very beginning of his laws he wrote: "God said" – what? "Let there be light, and there was light; let there be land, and there was land"' (ch. 9, p. 111). If an honoured pagan could find sublimity in the Scripture, how much more might the Christian find? Longinus' most important translator, one of the founding fathers of French literary criticism, Nicolas Boileau-Despréaux (1636–1711), spelt out the point: 'Longinus himself, in the midst of the shades of paganism, did not fail to recognise the divinity that there is in these words of Scripture' (III: 443). For a facile repetition wherein the single instance of Longinus has become an all-embracing plural, there is this by the controversialist Charles Leslie (1650–1722) – it is of added interest as it is also an example of the phrase we will be following: 'the heathen orators have admired the sublime of the style of the Scriptures. No writing in the world comes near it, even with all the disadvantage of our translation, which, being obliged to be literal, must lose much of the beauty of it.'[9]

Boileau seized on Longinus' remark. Misrepresenting what Longinus says but true to the underlying tendency of his work, Boileau argues that Longinus does not mean by 'sublime' what orators call the sublime style, but the extraordinary and marvellous which elevates and ravishes:

> The sublime style always seeks great language, but the sublime can be found in a single thought, in a single figure, in a single turn of phrase. A thing can be in the sublime style and yet not be sublime, that is, may have nothing extraordinary or

inexpressible something: 'there must be somewhat *ethereal*, somewhat above man, much of a soul separate, that must animate all this and breathe into it a fire to make it both warm and shine' (fol. B4 r–v). Hall's running title reflects this emphasis: it is 'of height' rather than 'of eloquence'.

[8] Since it is so rare for a Greek author to cite the Bible, the authenticity of this passage is often questioned. However, it was accepted as genuine by most people in the eighteenth century (Smith, who takes the passage as an occasion for a discourse on biblical simplicity and sublimity, reports some dispute (pp. 128ff.)). The most recent translation of Longinus, that of James A. Arieti and John M. Crossett (New York and Toronto: the Edwin Mellen Press, 1985), summarises the discussion, p. 57.

[9] *The Truth of Christianity Demonstrated* (London, 1711), p. 153.

astonishing in it. For example, 'the sovereign disposer of nature in one word created light': that is in the sublime style, yet it is not sublime because there is nothing particularly marvellous in it ... But, 'God said, Let there be light, and there was light': this extraordinary turn of expression which marks so well creation's obedience to the creator is truly sublime and has something divine in it.   (III: 442)

Opposition to these claims led Boileau to elaborate them in his posthumous tenth reflection on some passages of Longinus (1713). Much of this contains familiar arguments for the literary power of the Bible, but what is particularly important is his insistence that there is no opposition between simplicity and sublimity (III: 409). Simple language can create, can even enhance, sublimity. So 'God said, Let there be light, and there was light' 'is not only sublime, but all the more sublime because, the words being very simple and taken from ordinary language, they make us understand wonderfully, and better than all the finest words, that it is no more difficult for God to make light, heaven and earth than for a master to say to a servant, "bring me my cloak"' (III: 412). The point is well made. If the Bible is all the more sublime for not trying to match the grandeur of its content with grandeur of style, then the language of ploughboys may be the very means for conveying its sublimity, that is, its power to elevate the soul. But, just as few English critics were able to match Boileau's nice perception of the relationship between expression and meaning, so none of them, except in the most general terms, was able to bring out the potential for appreciation of the Tyndalian tradition of translation.

The growth of a commonplace

The tension between Longinian or pseudo-Longinian ideas and the time's hostility to the old, the prosaic and the translation helped to produce observations such as that by Husbands. By the time he wrote, it had become a commonplace to appreciate the KJB with reservations. Mostly what was praised could be found in any version; the reservations applied particularly to the form of the KJB, but only because that was now the generally used version. This note was first sounded by the much-admired essayist, defender of the ancients against the moderns and patron of Swift, Sir William Temple (1628–99). It follows a discussion in his essay 'Of poetry' (1690) that usefully develops the tussle between Longinian ideas and the age's sense of decorum. The essence of true poetry is

that elevation of genius which can never be produced by any art or study, by pains or by industry, which cannot be taught by precepts or examples, and therefore is agreed by all to be the pure and free gift of heaven or of nature, and to be a fire kindled out of some hidden spark of the very first conception.   (P. 179)

So it is the power to move rather than technical ability that distinguishes a true poet:

> Whoever does not affect and move the same present passions in you that he represents in others, and at other times raise images about you, as a conjurer is said to do spirits, transport you to the places and to the persons he describes, cannot be judged to be a poet, though his measures are never so just, his feet never so smooth, or his sounds never so sweet.   (P. 183)

This is not to dismiss technical merit but to put it in its proper place. At this time, especially in France, there was a good deal of discussion of rules for good writing: they are the period's opposite pole from unbridled admiration of sublimity. Temple will have little to do with them – 'there is something in the genius of poetry too libertine to be confined to so many rules' (p. 182) – yet he still holds that the elevation of genius must be accompanied by a severe artfulness.[10] Poetry, like a child, 'must be nourished with care, clothed with exactness and elegance, educated with industry, instructed with art, improved by application, corrected with severity, and accomplished with labour and with time before it arrives at any great perfection or growth' (p. 179). Here speaks the neo-classicism of the time, and it is this voice that produces the reservations.

Having turned his back on giving rules for poetry, Temple gives a history of it, dealing first with its antiquity. Biblical poetry merits discussion not as being superior to the classics but as an example of how poetry is older than prose in many nations. Job is discussed as the most ancient book of the Bible and allowed to be an 'admirable and truly inspired poem'. But its origin is not Jewish, so he turns to the most ancient Hebrew poem, Deborah's song (Judges 5). Here he launches the commonplace, remarking that he never read this 'without observing in it as true and noble strains of poetry and picture as in any other language whatsoever, in spite of all disadvantages from translations into so different tongues and common prose' (p. 185). An obviously genuine Longinian response to literary power is tempered by dislike of the translations. Implicitly, some poetic quality is independent of poetic form. Temple does not develop this; rather, it lies in his work like a grain of mustard seed accidentally sown.

The next occurrence of this kind of remark comes ten years later from the

---

[10] To some it seemed that here he contradicted himself. Gildon, normally an admirer of Temple, argues just this, though a careful reading of the passage shows that two different ideas of 'rules' are involved (*Complete Art*, I: 117–19): Gildon sees no difference between artfulness and rules, whereas Temple rejects the implication that there is a correct way to manage each kind of writing.

much-maligned minor poet, Queen Anne's physician, Sir Richard Blackmore (1658?–1729), in the preface to his *Paraphrase on the Book of Job* (1700). Though the following paragraph makes the point twice, it is worth giving in full because it suggests several important connections:

> The language in which this book is written is Hebrew, and considering the obscurity of the style or manner of expression in the eastern parts of the world, their eloquence as well as their customs and habits being very different from ours, 'tis very strange that a literal translation of this book, as it is now found in the Bible, especially considering how long since it was written, how little the language is at present known, and how much the idiom of it is lost, should not be found more harsh, and be less capable of being understood than it is. I am confident that if several of the Greek poets should be verbally translated, they would appear more obscure, if not altogether unintelligible. As if in a literal translation the book of Job written in an eastern language does so much affect us and raises in our minds such an admiration of its beauty and majesty, what a wonderful and inimitable kind of eloquence must be supposed in the original when we cannot translate verbatim a good poet from one modern language into another, though it be that of our nearest neighbours, without a great diminution of its excellence.   (Pp. xlii–xliii)

To begin with, it is typical that the remark should accompany praise of the originals. This is hardly surprising, but the way the effectiveness of the translation is used to bolster a sense of their perfection is. That the Bible seems to survive translation, even in a poor old medium, better than any other writings is used as a new argument for the old point that the Bible is superior to the classics. Now, one of the most important literary debates of this time, in France as well as England, concerned the relative merits of classical and contemporary literature – the ancients versus the moderns. One might well expect the conviction of the Bible's literary superiority, with this new and commonly repeated argument supporting it, to have widened that debate into a three-sided contest, but it did not. Temple had found it convenient to use the Bible in the time's other great debate, on the issue of laws for poetry, but it is typical of the time that he found no place for the Bible in the discussion when he defended the classics in 'An essay upon the ancient and modern learning'. Opinion on the relative merits of the Bible and the classics, rather than being a part of 'the battle of the books', was a counter-current to it. The majority of those who voiced an opinion gave the palm to the Scriptures, but, as in the past, this was usually for religious rather than literary reasons. The Bible was edging its way into literary discussions, but only in a few works did it claim the spotlight.

Blackmore's passage points to a second new way of thinking in his recognition of different standards of eloquence.[11] He recurs to this in explaining why he has 'not attempted a close translation of this sacred book [Job], but a paraphrase' (p. lxxiv). The original does not meet modern European standards of literary method; rather, it is repetitious and irregular; it has broken and obscure connections, and it neglects transitions (pp. lxxv–lxxvi). Such candid recognition of 'faults' is rare in an advocate of biblical literature who believes in the divine inspiration of the Bible,[12] but Blackmore prevents his observations from being a reproach to the style of the Bible by using the idea of different tastes:

> I would not peremptorily condemn their taste, for the opinion of beauty and ornament seems not to be capable of being determined by any fixed and unalterable rule... What we censure as careless, wild and extravagant, strikes them with more admiration, and gives them greater pleasure than all our elaborate and orderly contrivances. All that can be said is that our tastes are different, and if they are barbarous to us, we are so to them...
>
> We in this part of the world are also full of Homer and Virgil, and so bigoted to the Greek and Latin sects, that we are ready to account all authors heretical that are without the pale of the classics.   (Pp. lxxvi–lxxvii)

Admiration for the Bible has pushed him to a sharp piece of criticism.[13] As we

---

[11] The freshness of some of Blackmore's points should not be allowed to obscure his indebtedness, particularly to Cowley (see p. lxxxii). Moreover, though Dennis had made what Johnson describes as 'insolent and contemptuous' animadversions on the first of his many epic poems, Blackmore was later a friend of Dennis and regarded him as 'equal to Boileau in poetry, and superior to him in critical abilities' (as given in Johnson, *Lives*, II: 15). He is one of many writers still trying to wean Christian poets from their love for pagan writings, and so to break down 'the total neglect of the inspired writings' (p. xxxix). It may be that he continued the effort to the end of his life: I have not seen his posthumous *The Accomplished Preacher, or an Essay upon Divine Eloquence*' (1731).

[12] He explicitly connects divine inspiration with 'eloquence and the right art of persuasion' in the preface to *Essays* (pp. xxxiii–xxxiv).

[13] Stennett published similar remarks in the same year, though they lack Blackmore's acuity (his subject is the Song of Songs):

> If any are shocked at the style and manner of composure, as thinking the figures some of them too bold and not natural, the transitions too abrupt, etc., let 'em consider that the gust of all ages and nations is not the same, and that that is a very graceful expression in one language which seems very mean in another. They that would judge accurately of the style of this poem should be well acquainted with the language in which it was originally written, and with the genius and customs of the age and nation in which it was first published. These none can now pretend to be thoroughly versed in: therefore 'tis more modest and becoming to lay the fault on our own ignorance if we don't see that beauty and elegancy which the ancient Hebrews did in a piece composed by one who, by the testimony of God himself, had the highest intellectual accomplishments of any man in the world, and who wrote it by the special inspiration

shall see when it is echoed by Husbands (below, p. 28), this is capable of making any age look at its own standards.

Given such novel candour, we can hardly criticise Blackmore for failing to cultivate more Hebraic tastes in himself, or for electing to paraphrase, even if we cannot admire the results. These are worth illustrating since there will be many references to Augustan verse translation, and it is useful to see what the Augustans typically thought they wanted. Here is part of what Blackmore makes of Job 3: 11 ('why died I not from the womb? why did I not give up the ghost when I came out of the belly?'), unkindly chosen if the intention was to do Blackmore justice as a poet as well as as a critic:

> Why did a false conception not elude
> My parents' hopes, and breath from me exclude?
> Why was I shaped and fashioned as a man?
> Or why, when first the vital work began,
> Did not the genial active spirits cease
> My green unfolded members to increase?
> Would an abortion, while the quickening strife
> My mother felt, had quenched the spark of life
> When first it kindled in the tepid vein,
> Glowed in the heart and glimmered in the brain.   (P. 13)

If, as a statement of his taste, this underlines just how much scorn could lie behind the concessions to power even in the KJB, it also makes unsurprising the reaction against Augustan poetification and the fading-away of the scorn in some critics.

Two better remembered figures, Edward Young (1683–1765), author of *Night Thoughts on Life, Death and Immortality*, and James Thomson (1700–48), author of *The Seasons*, are, compared with Blackmore, mere echoers, showing that what Temple and Blackmore were initiating was indeed becoming a general idea. Writing in the *Guardian*, Young compares Job's description of the horse (Job 39: 19–25, given from the KJB with two minor variations) with a description in Virgil:

> Now follows that in the book of Job, which under all the disadvantages of having been written in a language little understood, of being expressed in phrases peculiar to

> of the Holy Spirit too; and, instead of puzzling ourselves and others by too nicely criticising on its external form, to seek a more useful and agreeable entertainment in getting a solid and experimental knowledge and relish of those spiritual mysteries it contains.   (Pp. xii–xiii)

> Again inspiration is an essential part of the idea. It assures the beauty and elegance of the original, while cultural relativity explains the present dissatisfaction with the form and the unnatural boldness of the figurative language.

a part of the world whose manner of thinking and speaking seems to us very uncouth, and, above all, of appearing in a prose translation, is nevertheless so transcendently above the heathen descriptions that hereby we may perceive how faint and languid the images are which are formed by mortal authors when compared with that which is figured, as 'twere, just as it appears in the eye of the creator.[14]

Thomson, taking Temple's view of the relative merits of the Bible and the classics, supplies an interesting new adjective for the KJB. Discussing the best poets' happiness in singing the works of nature, he drops in this aside before going on to praise Virgil: 'the book of Job, that noble and ancient poem, which, even, strikes so forcibly through a mangling translation, is crowned with a description of the grand works of nature, and that too from the mouth of their almighty author'.[15] Comments such as these point to a growing use of the KJB, the beginning of a Longinian willingness to judge it by its effect, and yet a persistent prejudice against it over a period of some forty years (1690–1731).[16]

Even less remembered than Blackmore is the critic Henry Felton, DD (1679–1740), yet his *A Dissertation on Reading the Classics* (1713) was popular enough to reach a fifth edition in 1753. He picks up Blackmore's point about the relative effectiveness of the KJB as a translation and gives another example of the commonplace:

> Take the best and liveliest poems of antiquity, and read them, as we do the Scriptures, in a prose translation, and they are flat and poor. Horace and Virgil and Homer lose their spirits and their strength in the transfusion to that degree that we have hardly patience to read them. But, my lord, the sacred writings, even in our translation, preserve their majesty and their glory, and very far surpass the brightest and noblest compositions of Greece and Rome. (Pp. 128–9)

But what comes after might make one wonder if 'even in our translation' is not a deliberately ironic invocation of the commonplace, were it not that such subtlety is alien to Felton. He explains that the Bible's superiority to the classics even in translation comes not from 'the richness and solemnity of the eastern

---

[14] The *Guardian* 86 (Friday 19 June 1713); in the *Guardian*, p. 313. This essay is sometimes attributed to Sir Richard Steele.

[15] Preface to the second edition of *Winter* (1726).

[16] Though most expressions of the idea concentrate in this time, there are at least two later examples, the preface to *Choheleth*, ascribed to J. Dennis Furley (London, 1765), pp. xii–xxiii, and, ninety-five years later, Le Roy J. Halsey's declaration that 'there is no stronger proof of the indestructible character of the poetry of the Bible, and of its inherent sublimity and beauty, than this fact, that through all the disadvantages and disguises of a literal prose translation, many passages of the poetical books, and nearly all the Psalms, still retain the spirit and rhythm and very music of the bard' (p. 74).

eloquence',[17] since no other oriental writings come across well in translation, but from 'the divine direction and assistance of the holy writers'. This is the familiar argument from inspiration, but what he adds is extraordinary:

> For, let me only make this remark, that the most literal translation of the Scriptures, in the most natural signification of the words, is generally the best; and the same punctualness which debaseth other writings preserveth the spirit and majesty of the sacred text: it can suffer no improvement from human wit, and we may observe that those who have presumed to heighten the expressions by a poetical translation or paraphrase have sunk in the attempt, and all the decorations of their verse, whether Greek or Latin, have not been able to reach the dignity, the majesty and solemnity of our prose, so that the prose of Scripture cannot be improved by verse, and even the divine poetry is most like itself in prose.   (Pp. 129–31)

This has suddenly moved far from prejudice, and we might seize on it as evidence that the English of the KJB, 102 years after its publication, has taken its place as literature. But Felton is contradicting most of his contemporaries, and he does not take the simple, apparently unavoidable next step of giving the KJB itself explicit praise. He is a harbinger, well in advance of the main company. He has jumped to a point the age was not ready for, arriving there because he is arguing less from the experience of reading the KJB against verse translations than from a peculiar application of the common idea that God's poetry can receive no improvement from human wit. This had never before been taken as proving that a literal prose translation is best ('punctualness' means 'literal precision of translation'). Few people who thought about the qualities of the original poetry considered poetic translation as an attempt to improve it; rather, with Dennis, they saw it as an attempt to convey some fuller idea of the original than could be given by an unnaturally literal version in the inferior medium of prose. To take one example from the beginning of the century, Joseph Collet, sometime governor of Madras, commended *A Version of Solomon's Song of Songs* (1700) by his fellow Seventh-day Baptist, the minister Joseph Stennett (1663–1713), in the following terms:

> But all these beauties were to us obscured
> By distant time and place (yet just secured
> Of the true sense in rough unpolished prose)
> Till you, preacher and poet too, arose
> To storm the heights of sacred poetry . . .   (P. xxiv)

Yet, however much we may question whether Felton writes from a genuine appreciation of the KJB, it must have helped his many readers towards an

---

[17] Addison had urged this point in the previous year (see below, p. 31), but Felton's work was written in 1709, which suggests that the point had been made before.

esteem for both the originals and the translation to read his assertions under the dogmatic running heads, 'the Scripture only sublime', and 'above all improvement'.

More outspokenly than any of his contemporaries, Felton is taking the Scriptures as 'a very masterpiece of writing', and 'as absolutely perfect in the purity and justness either of style or composition'. These phrases were first published two years before Felton's work, but they are the more significant because they are part of an objection to such ideas by the Earl of Shaftesbury.[18] That such ideas could provoke moderating comment suggests how strong they were becoming.

Though Felton's resounding claims could not be further removed from Dennis's ideas on biblical poetry and translation, his starting-point is Dennisian: 'the thoughts which are natural to every sacred theme are so far exalted above the heathen poetry or philosophy that the meanest Christian, however he may fail in diction, is able to surpass the noblest wits of antiquity in the truth and greatness of his sentiments' (pp. 165–6). This underlines just how much his conclusions are theoretic rather than experiential, and so in essence belong with the arguments from divine inspiration. Others managed to bring to their comments a greater sense of authentic response, and tried to take up the challenge Blackmore had recognised and rejected, of adapting their tastes and critical ideas to the Hebraic. The most interesting of these is another follower of Dennis (he had more followers than is generally realised), Charles Gildon (1665–1724), as he presents himself in *The Laws of Poetry Explained and Illustrated* (1721).[19] He too echoes the commonplace in his observation that the reader will find in 'some of the songs or odes of the Hebrew poets . . . that heat, that divine enthusiasm, that true sublime, which is nowhere else to be met with, at least in that perfection which even our vulgar translations give us' (p. 115). Yet he also shows the prejudice against the KJB dwindling towards insignificance. True to the spirit of Longinus-through-Boileau, he rests his literary judgements on the

---

[18] II: 302. This is not the only time Shaftesbury touches on the Bible and literature. Notably, he is the one writer to dissent from the idea that biblical stories and poetry are good sources for modern literature (I: 229–31).

[19] Aaron Hill, admired by Gildon and portrayed as Laudon in *The Complete Art*, but described by the *DNB* as 'absurd, and a bore of the first water, deserves to be remembered here. He prefaces his poem *The Creation* (1720) with a discussion of 'the sublimity of the ancient Hebrew poetry' that mixes received ideas with praise of the 'divine spirit', 'terrible simplicity' and 'magnificent plainness' of the Hebrew poetry (p. 4), condemnation of the contemporary concern with form ('our poetry has been degenerating apace into mere sound or harmony' (p. 5)), and good practical demonstration of the quality of Ps. 104: 3 (ed. Gretchen Graf Pahl (Los Angeles: Augustan Reprint Society, series 4, March 1949), pp. 7–8).

power to move; he depreciates the importance of technical proficiency,
especially as some of the poets, so it seemed to him and a few of his
contemporaries such as Hill, had gone too far with rhyme.[20] To demonstrate
that 'wherever there is force and genius expressed in numbers and harmony, we
shall find there is not the least occasion for rhyme' (p. 65), he sets Dennis's
Miltonic paraphrase of Hab. 3: 3–10 against an elaborately rhymed version by
'the famous, ingenious and justly-admired Mrs Singer' (p. 66; her fame extends
no further than this remark).[21] Gildon is wrong to suggest that rhyme has led
Mrs Singer to paraphrase where Dennis has not. Dennis does not go the length
of turning the passage into a kind of national anthem – Mrs Singer concludes
with reference to William of Orange's wars with Louis XIV, 'So now, great
God, wrapped in avenging thunder, / Meet thine and William's foes, and tread
them grovelling under' – but he too paraphrases and elaborates in his pursuit of
a sublime style: it is not the quest for rhyme that makes the difference between
these two mediocre efforts. To see Gildon praising Dennis's version for 'the
force, vehemence and energy of a true poetic enthusiasm, conveyed in a lofty

---

[20] Behind these attitudes to rhyme lies Milton's note on the verse prefaced to *Paradise Lost*.
   For another instance of rhyme being attacked in the context of a biblical poem, there is
   Prior's preface to his *Solomon on the Vanity of the World* (1708; *The Literary Works of
   Matthew Prior*, ed. H. Bunker Wright and Monroe K. Spears, 2nd edn (Oxford:
   Clarendon Press, 1971), p. 309).
[21] This is Dennis's version:

> When the almighty from mount *Paran* came,
> The brightness of his glory, with its blaze,
> Expanding, fill'd the vast abyss of heaven,
> And the whole earth resounded with his praise.
> The burning pestilence before him march'd,
> And from his feet a fiery whirlwind flew.
> He stood and measur'd the extended earth,
> Scattering the trembling nations with a look,
> At which the everlasting mountains fled,
> And, shaking, the perpetual hills did bow.
> Against the floods was thy fierce anger then,
> Against the sea the burning of thy wrath,
> That thou didst thro' it, with thy flaming steeds,
> And with thy chariots of salvation, drive.
> The rocks their summits beetled o'er their base,
> To view the terrors of thy wondrous march;
> Then, shivering, shrunk from the amazing sight:
> The floods divided, show'd a fearful chasm;
> And as thy sounding horses, all on fire,
> Thro' heaps of congregated waters flew,
> The deep his roaring voice at all his mouths
> Utter'd, and lifted all his arms on high.

diction and a perfect harmony of numbers' (p. 68) seems not to augur well for the KJB.

However, though a connoisseur of metre and diction, Gildon is still more attached to sublimity of effect. Discussion of the sublimity of Pindaric odes leads him back to biblical poetry, for too much of Pindar's quality depends on his diction and is lost in translation. So it is as a substitute for Pindar that he invites his reader, in the remark already quoted, to admire the true sublime of the Hebrew odes. He gives three examples, Moses' song (Exod. 15: 1–18), and Psalms 18 and 127, and refers to others, confident that they need no commentary to produce 'the highest transport and pleasure' in readers with 'any soul or genius for poetry' (p. 116). Moses' song is given from the KJB, Psalm 127 from the PB, and this leads him to a passage as fascinating as Felton's:

> I have chosen to give two of these songs ... in the diction of our translators of the Bible, because it is more strong and close than any of those paraphrastic efforts in rhyme ... The public translators had only in their view the rendering the Hebrew text as fully and close as they possibly could, without endeavouring at the smooth and polished expression that should give their words a numerousness and an agreeable sound to the ear. By this means they have retained a much more valuable quality, that is, the sense, the spirit, the elevation and the divine force of the original; whereas those gentlemen, who have attempted any part of the Old Testament in rhyme, have ... lost the force and energy of the divine song in the weak ornaments of modern poetry: at least, this I can say for myself, that I never found my soul touched by the best of these performances ... though it has been scarce able to support the violent emotions and excessive transports raised by the common translation.   (P. 120)

At last the moving power of the poetry as given in the KJB and the PB is allowed full weight. It touches Gildon's soul with violent emotions. The possibilities in Longinus as presented by Boileau have become quite explicit. The KJB and PB are being read as superb literature, and men of taste are invited to admire them. But still there are limitations. The two translations are not appreciated as achievements in their own right, nor is the Hebrew poetry presented as necessarily the best poetry. Rather, the KJB and the PB are the most affecting translations of any ancient poetry, classical or biblical, in instances where a Milton or a Dennis has not given a superior version. Psalm 18 is given for preference in 'that sublime diction with which Mr Dennis has clothed it' (p. 117). As in Felton, the quality most admired in the KJB and PB is their literal fidelity to the originals. The frequent emphasis on literalness at this time suggests that the alien nature of their English was more obvious to the Augustans than to later readers.

In a sense Gildon is doing no more than repeat Felton's argument 'that the prose of Scripture cannot be improved by verse, and even the divine poetry is most like itself in prose', and adding to it testimony to the experience of reading the prose translations. No doubt he knew Felton's passage (Gildon read widely, and, like many at this time, was not averse to plagiarism). But the effect of his arguments is of a quiet correction of Felton's excesses. The Scripture is not the 'only sublime'; it is perhaps not even the pinnacle of sublimity, and the translation is not 'above all improvement'. If Gildon is an outspoken enemy of rhyme, still he is an admirer of Augustan diction, so elevated in Dennis's versions, and Augustan 'numerousness', that is, command of poetic harmony. He encourages literary admiration of the Bible *through* the KJB, but, however close it may seem, this is not the same as encouraging admiration *of* the KJB. Only when the writing is as abstract and theoretical as Felton's does it *seem* that the KJB itself is to be admired.

Longinus' gift of the word 'sublime' to critical vocabulary opened up a major new way of thinking about poetry, but the Augustan critic still lacked that crucial word, 'literature'. In his earlier *The Complete Art of Poetry*, this leads Gildon into severe difficulties which he only half realises, for he is trying to write a complete art of literature rather than of poetry. Though he attempts to give 'poetry' the wider force of 'literature' by distinguishing it from 'verse', the attempt is largely a failure, in part because it contradicts his real tastes, in part because the idea of sublimity has not broken down the over-rigid form/content duality of the rhetorical idea of literature. Gildon often writes as if a critic has to choose between form and content, and so should make the choice Tyndale made of the pith over the husk. The first dialogue, 'of the nature, use, excellence, rise and progress of poetry', concludes with this Sidneian point: 'though number and harmony have been allowed likewise one of the causes of poetry, yet imitation is the most valuable part, for there may be just imitations, that is, true poems, without that most known kind of number and harmony which we call verse'.[22] He never moves on from this to suggest that there are other verbal qualities that a critic might admire in prose; the kind of argument Boileau had made for the sublime power of simple prose appropriately used is totally lost on him.

To leave Gildon for a moment: only one critic was able to make this kind of move, the non-conformist clergyman Samuel Say (1676–1743), in his posthumous 'An essay on the harmony, variety and power of numbers, whether in prose or verse' (1745).[23] The title alone is sufficiently striking in its willingness to

---

[22] 1: 88; see Sidney, pp. 10–11.
[23] In Elledge, 1: 456–83.

consider prose not only as a literary medium, but as one capable of 'numbers'. Say argues against the dominant view of the time that metrical regularity was an essential quality of good verse, which is a very significant step further than Hill and Gildon's arguments against the necessity of rhyme. His method is not prescriptive but deductive and relativistic ('the genius of one language [is not] to be measured by another' (p. 467)). Like many later critics, he believes that the sound must reflect the sense, and he analyses passages to show wherein their quality lies. At one point he turns to the Bible for examples. He argues that there exist what he calls expletive particles and also expletive sentences which 'are necessary to the ear where they are not necessary to the sense' (p. 467). Thus he observes that 'do' is present in Luke 10: 11 ('even the very dust of your city ... we do wipe off against you') to prevent the disagreeable grouping of sounds, 'we wipe'.[24] This attributes a taste and artistry to the translators such as the seventeenth-century sermons of Tillotson, the source of his main example, exhibit. As examples of expletive sentences, that is, sentences 'that are not necessary to the sense ... and yet may be necessary to the hearer, that he may receive with delight and retain forever the truths so artfully and strongly impressed upon his mind', he gives the beginnings of Psalm 78 and Isaiah, quoting the KJB exactly bar one omission in the Isaiah. The Psalm he gives thus:

1. Give ear, O my people, to my law:
    Incline your ears to the words of my mouth.
2. I will open my mouth in a parable:
    I will utter dark sayings of old.   (P. 467)

What he seems to have in mind is the synonymous parallelism, which he notes 'appears to be the perpetual practice of heavenly wisdom in the Psalms and in the Prophets'. It is a matter for regret that he did not develop the point. More startling, though, is his presentation of the quotations as free verse. The Psalm is exactly as the RV was to set these words 140 years later, and his setting of Isaiah's words was not followed until 1936, in Bates's *The Bible Designed to be Read as Living Literature*. He makes no comment on this procedure, and it is such

---

[24] P. 468. If Say is right, the literary credit goes to the makers of the Bishops' Bible, then to Gregory Martin. Coverdale has 'do we wipe', while the RV and RSV, not sharing Say's sensitivity, revert to Tyndale's 'we wipe off against you'. It does not matter if Say's example is wrong: it is a possible way of understanding the choice of words, and his thought is enlightening. 'Do' and 'did' are particularly common before verbs beginning with vowels.

a fleeting instance that we cannot grant it any historical importance. Yet, if we interpret his action favourably (there seems no reason not to), we may say that one eighteenth-century critic was able to read the KJB's prose as verse; his is a truly exceptional mind, jumping from the muddled quarrel with the technical implications of 'poetry' to what, on a minuscule scale, looks like a modern perception. Moreover, he shows the unrealised potential in lesser, more industrious critics like Gildon.

A different but important theoretical consequence of Gildon's separation of form and content is that what he takes to be the essence of poetry – its content, including its images – is translatable and 'may be in all languages' (1: 77). Though this falls well short of Felton's idea of the translatability of biblical poetry, it helps to show how some Augustans, reacting against their age's polish, were moving, in one sense, towards a non-textual idea of the Bible, and, in another, towards appreciation of biblical poetry translated into prose. The first sense remains undeveloped, and the furthest Gildon can go with the latter in *The Complete Art* is to comment on Jesus' use of fiction in his parables (1: 56), and to reproduce, sometimes verbatim, Sidney's discussion of Nathan's parable to David (2 Sam. 12: 1–4; Sidney, p. 25): his purpose is Sidney's, to prove that 'the feigned images of poetry' are more efficacious than 'the regular instruction of philosophy' (1: 56), and so to defend fiction. Again it is striking that he has to call these parables 'poetry'. He seems not to have known 'fiction' in its modern sense, though, unlike 'literature', it was beginning to be used at this time. Richard Daniel, dedicating his version of the Psalms to the King, contrasts the *Odyssey* and the *Aeneid* with the story of David, and remarks that 'the adventures of that brave prince, without the beauties of fiction to support them, are much more entertaining than anything we can meet with in the heathen story'.[25] However, it is revealing that Johnson did not record this sense of 'fiction' in his dictionary. The limitation of vocabulary is, in Gildon, a limitation of thought. However much he may stretch 'poetry' as his word for literature, he is still locked in to a way of thinking that does not recognise prose as a worthy medium. The 'collection of the most beautiful descriptions, similes, allusions, etc., from Spenser and our best English poets, as well ancient as modern' which makes up volume II contains no prose and only one brief, forgettable biblical paraphrase ('Tis Zion then, 'tis Zion we deplore'). This is another statement of Gildon's taste and a fair reflection of the real taste of so many Augustans: in spite of their theoretical gropings away from the formal connotations of poetry and towards new ideas that were eventually to help recognition of the KJB as

---

[25] *A Paraphrase on Some Select Psalms* (London, 1722), fol. A4 r.

literature, they still did not appreciate literal prose as found in the KJB. The commonplace we have been following is the natural expression of this situation.

Voices from France

All Gildon's biblical passages come in the context of his argument against rhyme, but he had read a work of the rationalistic Arminian scholar Jean Le Clerc (1657–1736), which argued that the Hebrew poetry rhymed. This presented Gildon with a major problem, for he regularly justifies things by divine precedent. For instance, opening the defence of poetry in *The Divine Art*, Morisina, 'the perfect image of modesty, the characteristic of womanhood' (1: vii), observes that 'that which determines me entirely for poetry is that God has made use of it in the Sacred Scripture' (1: 31). This way of arguing would invalidate his opposition to rhyme if Le Clerc were right. Probably because of Le Clerc's argument, which he twice reports in *The Complete Art* (1: 74, 179), he does not argue against rhyme there. But in *The Laws of Poetry* he is determined to attack rhyme, so he dismisses Le Clerc's conclusion as 'a conjecture, a mere guess' (p. 121). The importance of this is that it underlines just how important the old pre-scientific ideas of divine inspiration and divine precedent were to writers who voiced our commonplace. If scholars, for whatever reason, reached conclusions that seemed inconsistent with the premise of inspiration, then those conclusions had to be dismissed. Yet the commonplace also represents the essentially scientific spirit that reaches conclusions from observation of the text and of its effect. It would be too simple to say that the combination of praise and dispraise comes from the clash of theological premise and scientific observation, but this clash seems to be an essential condition for the commonplace.

Gildon's difficulties with Le Clerc show the mixed situation of the Augustans in conflict with a purer form of the scientific spirit. Le Clerc's 'An essay upon critics, wherein it is endeavoured to show in what the poesy of the Hebrews consists' (1692)[26] takes a rational if not necessarily sound approach to Hebrew poetics. His specific conclusions do not matter much (he does have his presuppositions and his limitations) but his general view of the people and the poetry does. He stresses that the Hebrews, 'who were not extraordinary polite [parum cultam], took little pains to reduce poetry to an art' (p. 296): they were primitives, and their poetry is primitive. As so often with the Bible, it is remarkable how conclusions from the same evidence can be so different, according to the premises used. Gomarus had seen much the same irregularity that Le Clerc draws his conclusions from, and taken it as the statement of

---

[26] First published in French in *La Bibliothèque universelle* 9 (Paris, 1688). A Latin version is reprinted in Ugolino, cols. 991–1020.

metrical perfection (see volume I, p. 242). Le Clerc, making no *a priori* assumption of the quality of the poetry, presents it as a human achievement of mixed success. The critic is not compelled to admire, and so need not be surprised at finding in himself a mixed response to the text. Moreover, to move beyond Le Clerc, he may find that an unharmonious prose version of the Bible is even more faithful to the rough, uncultivated original than Felton had imagined in arguing that 'the divine poetry is most like itself in prose'.

The work had little immediate effect on English ideas. One has to look to another French work significant enough to be translated into English to find repeated Le Clerc's sense of the poetry as artistically primitive, *Antiquities Sacred and Profane* (London, 1724–7) of the Benedictine Dom Augustin Calmet (1672–1757). Calmet, who does not believe the poetry was either rhymed or metrical, concludes his 'Dissertation concerning the poetry of the ancient Hebrews' thus:

> It is then very credible that the poetry of the ancient Hebrews consisted wholly in the grandeur, nobleness and sublimity of the thoughts and style, in the daringness of the figures, in lively and pathetic expressions, in a brief and concise manner of discourse, in a turn more florid, more enlivened, more expressive, more proper to paint and display the images of things before our eyes than the common forms of speech; that their poems were the productions of a happy genius, animated and inspired by the spirit of God, which being carried by the divine impulse above the restraints of the rules of a methodical poetry, expressed its thoughts and sentiments in a sublime and poetical manner. The Hebrews were never very fond of novelty, nor were they of so nice a taste as the Greeks and Romans, but, satisfied with their ancient poetry and music, which was grave, solemn, affecting, agreeable and seldom made use of but in religious matters, they took no pains to polish and refine them.　　　　(P. 36)

What is so striking about this passage is that it is first cousin to our commonplace in combining a very high opinion of the Bible with reservations about its form. But where the commonplace attached the high opinion to the originals and the reservations to the translation, here both attach to the originals. The idea of inspiration is still explicit, but in the more moderate form that sees the poetry not as directly dictated but as written by men 'inspired by the spirit of God', and that makes possible the inclusion of Le Clerc's sense of an unpolished, unrefined art.

The kind of empiricism that Le Clerc represents leads towards understanding of the form of Hebrew poetry from observation of its characteristics but without reference to known standards. The beginning of this important move – important for appreciation of the originals and the KJB – is to be found in the first essay of *Antiquities*, 'A discourse concerning poetry in general and concerning that of the Hebrews in particular' by a church historian, the Cistercian Abbot Claude Fleury (1640–1725). He observes that the poetry 'abounds with repetitions, and the same thoughts are expressed twice over in different terms'. After speculating as to the cause, he adds that 'these repetitions are the most obvious and common mark of the poetic style' (p. 5). Calmet, believing 'that the art of versifying alone no more makes the poet than the numbers and measures make the poetry' (p. 29), builds a little on this. In terms that could fit the KJB, he argues that

> this natural poetry ... consisted altogether in the style and not at all in the measure of the syllables. The whole was nothing else but figurative, sublime and sententious expressions, wherein they generally affected a kind of repetition of the same thing in different terms in the two parts of the same sentence, and sometimes we find a sort of rhyme and cadence which are so obvious and remarkable that we need not be at much pains to discover them.   (Pp. 30–1)

Just what he means by 'a sort of rhyme and cadence' is left unspecified: the very vagueness opens a possibility that was developed later, that there could be a kind of rhyming of sense rather than sound.

Neither man goes further than what is quoted here: the point is not stressed, but the seed is sown. Several Englishmen at this time took note of the repetitions. Luke Milbourne, one of the many would-be reformers of Sternhold and Hopkins, remarks that 'the repetitions in the Hebrew are so charming that I could not but think they would be very beautiful in English, as particularly in the 118th Psalm',[27] but the remark is unique and undeveloped, and it does not occur to him that these repetitions might already be found in the English of the KJB. Blackmore's contrary view is probably more representative. He 'avoided the immediate repetition of the same thought in words little different from the first, which is so very common in' Hebrew poetry, because it is contrary to present ideas of eloquence (p. lxxv). Wither had earlier adopted the same attitude (see volume 1, p. 280). Repetition was all too easy to see in the poetry, even if the full extent of the parallelism was not, and, with the occasional exception of a man like Milbourne, was not admired. This is probably why it is so little commented upon. As long as it was possible to believe that the form of the poetry was metrical and, perhaps, rhymed, there was no need to attend to formal characteristics that were distasteful.

The kind of cultural relativity evident in Blackmore and Stennett – they have one standard of eloquence, we another – was only just beginning to be developed in England. One English writer noted something like this idea, and

---

[27] *The Psalms of David in English Metre* (London, 1698), preface (unpaginated).

gave it the kind of turn that was being developed by Le Clerc, Fleury and Calmet, observing that 'no book can be so plain but that it is requisite for the perfect understanding of it that men should be acquainted with the idioms and proprieties of the original language and the customs and notions which were generally received at the time when it was written'.[28] Rather than encouraging one to appreciate what one can without being put off by the rest, this encourages one to read Hebrew poetry as a Hebrew would have. The significance lies less in the intrinsic interest of the idea – it is no more than a brief generalisation – than in its author, William Lowth: his son Robert developed this passing hint, Felton's notion of the appropriateness of literal translation for Hebrew poetry, some of the French ideas noted here, and the preoccupation with the sublime into the century's most famous English work on Hebrew poetry, *De Sacra Poesi Hebraeorum*.

John Husbands

One of the few Englishmen before Robert Lowth willing to bring together many of the time's ideas of biblical poetry was John Husbands, who began this chapter. His importance is twofold. In part he summarises Augustan attitudes, in part he pushes them forwards. Yet he would be quite unknown did not his only work, *A Miscellany of Poems by Several Hands* (1731), contain Samuel Johnson's earliest publication, a Latin translation of Pope's 'Messiah'.[29] The poems themselves open with several biblical paraphrases, including Habakkuk 3 done into Latin verse, and a lengthy comparison between Solomon and

[28] *Directions for the Profitable Reading of the Holy Scripture* (1708). As given in Thomas R. Preston, 'Biblical criticism, literature, and the eighteenth-century reader', in Isabel Rivers, ed., *Books and their Readers in Eighteenth-Century England* (Leicester: Leicester University Press, 1982), pp. 97–126; p. 100. Perhaps the best-known statement the time has to offer of this idea comes in Pope's 'Essay on Criticism' (written 1709), lines 118–23:

> You then whose judgement the right course would steer,
> Know well each Ancient's proper character;
> His fable, subject, scope in ev'ry page;
> Religion, Country, genius of his Age:
> Without all these at once before your eyes,
> Cavil you may, but never criticise.

[29] Ronald S. Crane has argued that Husbands 'deserves a larger place in literary history than has so far been accorded him' ('An early eighteenth-century enthusiast for primitive poetry: John Husbands', *Modern Language Notes* 37 (1922), 27–36; p. 27). Since 1961, extracts from the preface have been available in Elledge's anthology (1: 416–31). Because Husbands's preface is unpaginated, I have used the printer's letters as a guide, counting the first page as 1; so, b = 7, c = 15, d = 23, etc.

Virgil's 'sacred pastorals'; a few biblical or religious poems are to be found later amid quite different subjects. 'A Hymn to the Creator' is followed by 'A Night-Piece: to Eliza'. The paraphrases are typical Augustan efforts at expansive poetification of the Bible: Ps. 57: 9 stretches to twenty-eight lines. Nothing in them so much as hints at liking for the KJB. The manner is what one would expect, an implicit rejection of literal prose. These four lines about the Song of Songs confirm the attitude (they are a variant of our commonplace):

> The numbers winged with holy rapture seem,
> While promised glory warms the sacred theme.
> Even through translators' language and abuse
> We trace the footsteps of an heavenly Muse. (P. 42)

However little merit one may find in the poems, the lengthy preface, 'containing some remarks of the beauties of the Holy Scriptures, more especially of the Old Testament', is of real interest. Husbands admires both eloquence and sublimity, believing that 'the essence of poetry consists in a just and natural imitation and illustration of things by words, tending at once both to improve and please; it consists moreover in a lively and affecting manner of writing, adorned with figures, varying according to the greatness, nature and quality of the subject' (p. 18). This combines the Horatian ideal, so dear to the Augustans, of 'dulce et utile', a Longinian glance at effect and the rhetorical notion of decoration, and it leads to contradictions according to whether he is thinking of the form or the content of a piece. Thus he writes at one point that 'the foundation of all beauty in composition is truth' (p. 47), apparently setting up an aesthetic of content, but later praises the perfect unity and entertaining variety of Job, and calls these qualities of form 'the two great essentials to beauty' (p. 74). Like Gildon, he has trouble thinking of form and content together, and more trouble where two aspects of content, truth and affective power, are involved.

He represents also a mix of old and new ideas of the literary quality of the Bible. Though he builds on most of the new ideas already sketched, he takes his starting-point from yet another French critic, Fleury's patron the Archbishop of Cambrai, François Fénelon (1651–1715), who essentially represents the old ideas. Fénelon argues from divine inspiration and, though he often mentions the sublime, his stress is on eloquence. He is also a champion of the Scripture against the classics, but he does make two points that are rare at this time. Literary merit, he argues, is not confined, as most people think, to the OT:

C. I easily conceive that the Old Testament is written with that magnificence and those lively images you speak of. But you say nothing of the simplicity of Christ's words.

A. That simplicity of style is entirely according to the ancient taste. 'Tis agreeable both to Moses and the Prophets, whose expressions Christ often uses. But though his language be plain and familiar, it is however figurative and sublime in many places.[30]

Gildon and Blackwall, who will be discussed later, both hold this view, but not many others. Again poetic power is found in simple prose. Second, unlike other commentators of this time, Fénelon believes in the qualities of the whole, a belief that was to lead writers in the next century to proclaim the literary quality of the whole Bible. His particular reason is the interconnectedness of the Bible:

C. We find that preachers do choose those passages they think most beautiful.

A. But it mangles the Scripture thus to show it to Christians only in separate passages. And however great the beauty of such passages may be, it can never be fully perceived unless one knows the connection of them: for, everything in Scripture is connected, and this coherence is the most great and wonderful thing to be seen in the sacred writings.   (Pp. 158–9)

Rather than these two points, Husbands quotes Fénelon's praise of the divine superiority of the Scriptures to the classics, and then casually remarks that 'as I don't remember to have seen this subject handled *ex professo* by anyone, I shall fling together some loose remarks upon it' (p. 14). This will not be the last time the false claim of novelty for a literary discussion of the Bible is made. In fact, he does know works such as Boyle's, Boileau's, Le Clerc's and Calmet's, and is familiar with most of the current ideas. He begins his 'loose remarks' by presenting Hebrew poetry as one kind of primitive poetry; like several of his predecessors he wants the English to develop divine poetry, and he offers this 'natural poetry' – as he calls it, using Calmet's phrase – as the model:

To praise Him however in the worthiest manner, we must copy after those representations we have of Him in the Holy Scriptures, where He has been pleased to descend in some measure to human eyes, and is become more familiar to mankind. There the inspired authors have left us the noblest examples of this divine kind of writing. We have not only a religion but a language from heaven. There poetry is the handmaid to piety, and eloquence sits beside the throne of truth. What innumerable beauties might our poetry be furnished with from those sacred repositories? What a pleasing variety of Godlike sentiments, what noble images, what lofty descriptions might from thence be transplanted into our tongue? These are the writings which far

---

[30] *Dialogues Concerning Eloquence in General*, trans. William Stevenson (London, 1722), pp. 156–7.

surpass all human compositions. No other books, however useful or excellent, can stand in competition with them. (Pp. 9–10)

What is so curious here is that he offers up this supreme poetry for imitation as if no-one had yet transplanted it into English – as if not only the prose translations but all the verse translations and even Milton were failures – and his own ordinary collection of verse paraphrases were a first step to this new poetry. Husbands's conceit of novelty is enormous, yet it should not blind us to the typicality of what he says: even the neatness of his use of the idea of divine inspiration, 'we have not only a religion but a language from heaven', looks like plagiarism of Joseph Spence: 'we are not only blessed with instructions but favoured too with language from heaven'.[31]

Sadly, Husbands makes only limited progress in describing this natural poetry. He admires it – to the point of adoration – along with all the other primitive poetry he knows of, but the limitedness of his description of it shows, like Gildon's remarks, the limits of this un-Augustan movement of the Augustans:

> For the strength and energy of the figures and the true sublimity of style are a natural effect of the passions. No wonder therefore that their diction is something more flourished and ornamental, more vigorous and elevated, more proper to paint and set things before our eyes than plain and ordinary recitals. This sort of poetry is more simple, and at the same time worthy of the majesty of God, than that which is regular and confined, which must with difficulty express the dictates of the Holy Spirit, and would be apt to give some alloy to the sublimity of the sense. (P. 19)

Felton could move from this to advocation of literal translation. Husbands, however, turns to a review of opinion on the form of the poetry. Accepting that the Hebrews 'were very inaccurate in the art of numbers' (p. 24), indeed, that their numbers 'are no more than Aristotle thinks requisite in a good oration', he suddenly adds, 'in other respects the style of their poetry, to speak a little paradoxically, seems to have been prose' (p. 27). So often the history of criticism seems to be a tale of lost opportunities. This suggests so much for an understanding of the originals, of the relationship between form and content, and for an appreciation of the KJB's prose as the appropriate form of translation, but Husbands can go no further. His practical notion of appropriate

---

[31] *An Essay on Pope's Odyssey* (Oxford, 1726), p. 57. This comes as part of a digression on 'orientalism' (Spence antedates the *OED*'s examples of this word) which notes a few biblical examples, one of which, Hab. 3: 10, specifically refers to the KJB and is presented as being more sublime than his examples from Homer and Virgil (pp. 71–2). Spence longs 'to expatiate on so glorious a subject', and believes that as criticism it would 'make any other kind look poor and insipid' (p. 58).

translation is exactly the 'regular and confined' method he argues is inappropriate. So, critically, he resorts to the limitations of translation and an appeal, much
stronger than William Lowth's, to adopt new critical standards and read not as a
neo-classicist but as the Hebraic standards themselves dictate.

The first of these ideas, the limitations of translation, leads him to an explicit
statement of the perennial sense that the Scriptures are so much better as poetry
than they appear: 'a modern reader of the Holy Scriptures ought to make great
allowances since many beauties must be lost to him' (p. 29). To this he adds
Blackmore and Gildon's argument that 'a strictly literal version' of even so
'regular' an author as Virgil would be unreadable, and the commonplace
observation of the ravishing beauty of 'an old prose translation' follows
immediately.

The appeal for different critical standards is worth careful attention even if
much of it is very like Blackmore (above, p. 11):

> It may be considered farther that the eastern people differ something from us in their
> notions of eloquence. We condemn them for being too pompous, swelling and
> bombast; perhaps they despise us for being languid, spiritless and insipid. People are
> apt to form their notions of excellence from their own perfections, and their notions
> of things from objects with which they are most conversant. Our art of criticism is
> drawn from the writers of Rome and Athens, whom we make the standard of
> perfection. But why have not the Jews as much right to prescribe to them as they
> have to prescribe to the Jews? Yet to this test we endeavour to bring the Sacred
> Books, not considering that the genius and customs of the Israelites were in many
> things very different from those of the Greeks and Romans.   (P. 32)

To place 'pompous, swelling and bombast' against 'languid, spiritless and
insipid' is an instructive caricature, on the one hand rough, sublime intensity,
on the other refined restraint such as most of the Augustans practised with their
polished numerousness, and admired through their criticism by rules. But what
is most significant is that Husbands's argument does not apply just to his time.
The effort from Josephus to the Renaissance to understand Hebrew poetics in
terms of classical metre, and now the effort to transform the poetry into
Miltonic blank verse, or Cowleian Pindarics or Augustan heroic couplets – all
are attempts to make it conform to 'notions of excellence' drawn from each
time's 'own perfections'. The effort still continues, even if it seems to us that our
poetic forms in particular can be very close to the Hebrew. The insistence in
most modern versions, especially those made with a deliberately literary
attitude to the originals, on presenting all the acknowledged poetic parts in
some kind of free verse is often nothing more than a visual statement that we

should regard the writing as verse rather than prose. We are no more capable than the Augustans of distinguishing the technical form, verse, from the vague notion of certain qualities designated 'poetry'. 'Prose' and 'poetry' are still antithetical, as if there is more difference between the two than the merely formal. Given the flexibility of our literary appreciativeness, this usually matters little, but it may be that the presentation of the supposed poetic parts in truncated lines of print that at least look like verse is a masquerade of the same sort, if not to the same degree, as presenting them in heroic couplets or Sternholdian common metre. It is easy to be literal and give the appearance of verse; moreover, that appearance draws out the only obvious formal quality, parallelism, without necessarily imposing what might be a falsifying metre or an even more falsifying rhyme, but it still implies that a kind of poetic form such as we are familiar with is everywhere to be found in the poetry. Too often the parallelism does not accommodate itself in the literal translations to our notion of the right sort of visual length for a line of poetry, with the result that line endings either impose a new structure or become meaningless. Too often, also, there is no evident parallelism, and then the line endings are, again, a masquerade. Our notions of poetic form could hardly be further removed from those of the Augustans, yet the way Husbands puts Blackmore's argument should make us question ourselves and wonder whether Felton's claim that the poetry is most like itself in literal prose does not retain a truth that our Bible makers have forgotten.

Where Husbands is at his best as a critic of the text is not with the poetry but with the prose. Ideas of poetry do not interfere, and he develops Longinus and Boileau's perception of sublimity in simplicity to good effect, eliciting much that is powerful in the KJB – which, for this part of his discussion, he uses regularly. The following is typical of his ability to find original and persuasive examples, and of the way he discusses them:

> How concisely, how emphatically is Jacob's love for Rachel comprised in one verse? 'And Jacob served seven years for Rachel, and they seemed unto him but a few days, for the love he had unto her' [Gen. 29: 20]. There is more of nature, of expressiveness, of affection in that simple passage than in all the motley descriptions of a French or Italian romance. The whole passion of love is crowded into a few words. The beauty of such passages as these, where the affections are to be described and made, as it were, visible to us, does not consist in a flourish of words or pomp of diction, not in the *ambitiosa ornamenta* of rhetoric, but in a natural and easy display of tender sentiments, and in opening those softnesses which are supposed to arise in the bosoms of the persons introduced. For this purpose nothing is more effectual than a decent simplicity of language. 'Tis this simplicity which in such instances constitutes

the just, proper and sublime more than all the glittering descriptions and little prettinesses which a modern author might probably use on such occasions.

(Pp. 59–60)

The example is better than the discussion; he is more interested in criticising current literary practice than in locating the power of the verse, which indeed 'does not consist in a flourish of words', but in the briefest possible presentation of facts. It is an example of what, following Blackwall (see below, p. 35), we may call the translatable sublime, for the mind and imagination dwell on these facts, realising just how powerful a love must be to make a man serve seven years and think them but a few days. The facts are as eloquent as the language is inconspicuous. It is not the particular diction of the KJB that creates the sublimity, for it is to be found in any unelaborated translation: in such examples a distinction between form and content *is* helpful. Not all the sublimities Husbands identifies are as independent of the language, but none of them depend on qualities peculiar to the KJB. The power is *in* rather than *of* the KJB.

The section Husbands most particularly evokes admiration for is Joseph's story. If, like many of his contemporaries, he works too much by exclamation,[32] nevertheless there is enough of example and discussion to sustain his opinion that 'never was any story, from the beginning to the end, contrived more artfully, never was any plot for the stage worked up more justly, never any unfolded itself more naturally than this of Joseph' (p. 66). Here he has escaped the preoccupation with poetry and found power where few of his contemporaries thought to find it. Lukin in the previous century (see volume 1, p. 246) and Blackwall (*Sacred Classics*, 1: 3) thought to mention this story, while Pope in a note to book XVI of his translation of the *Odyssey* remarked the superiority of Joseph's discovery of himself to his brothers (Gen. 45: 1–15) to Ulysses' discovery to Telemachus, and went on to a few general comments on the power of the story.[33] Steele devoted one issue of the *Tatler* to it partly to prove 'that the greatest pleasures the imagination can be entertained with are to be found there,

---

[32] Gibbon describes this method as using 'an idle exclamation, or a general encomium, which leaves nothing behind it'. Until he read Longinus he thought there were only two ways of criticising a beautiful passage, this, and 'to show by an exact anatomy of it the distinct beauties of it and from whence they sprung'. Longinus, however, 'tells me his own feelings upon reading it; and tells them with such energy that he communicates them'. Such an observation from 1762 fairly suggests the commonness of the exclamatory and the anatomical methods (*Gibbon's Journal*, ed. D. M. Low (London: Chatto & Windus, 1929), p. 155).

[33] *Poems*, x: 131. He also refers his reader to Longinus' comment on Genesis and concludes that Job, 'with regard both to sublimity of thought and morality, exceeds beyond all comparison the most noble parts of Homer'.

and that even the style of the Scripture is more than human'.[34] However, he does not go beyond plot summary and exclamation at a few beauties. Such remarks furnished Husbands with the hint, if he needed one, for discussion; what is new is the length and quality of the discussion. By following Boileau's perception of the relationship between sublimity and simplicity, and by reading the Bible for himself, Husbands has come to a modern perception – and something like a modern demonstration – of literary qualities in a biblical narrative.

Though what Husbands finds to admire in the stories of Genesis has little to do with the unique qualities of the KJB, he elsewhere suggests a critical awareness of them. His taste for literal Hebraisms perhaps owes something to Addison's briefly expressed enthusiasm for them – certainly Addison's comparison between Hebrew energy and the 'elegant and polite forms of speech which are natural to our tongue' in the *Spectator* 405 anticipates Husbands. There Addison gave his opinion that 'our language has received innumerable elegancies and improvements from that infusion of Hebraisms which are derived to it out of the poetical passages in Holy Writ'.[35] Husbands gives examples of these admirable Hebraisms such as dawn being expressed as 'the eyelids of the morning'.[36] He also shows himself willing, as no one before him had been, to comment on both literary success and failure in the KJB. He finds 'an uncommon grandeur and solemnity of phrase in the English version' of Deborah's song (Judges 5; p. 43), but by contrast the KJB shares in the general failure to render Job adequately: 'that unaffected majesty, that comprehensive brevity, that lovely simplicity in which consists its beauty never have been preserved in the version. In the version generally the thoughts are wire-drawn or ... distilled and quite drawn off till the spirit evaporates and nothing remains but a *caput mortuum*' (p. 75). In these fleeting remarks and in his exposition of the quality of Genesis, Husbands shows himself something better than a representative and synthesising figure, worthy to be remembered for more than his connection with Johnson, his pioneering enthusiasm for primitive poetry or his version of the age's most frequent comment on the KJB. Had his work been better known, or, perhaps, had he lived to develop the

---

[34] 233 (5 October 1710). *The Tatler*, ed. Donald F. Bond, 3 vols. (Oxford: Clarendon Press, 1987), III: 204.

[35] Ed. Donald F. Bond, 5 vols (Oxford: Clarendon Press, 1965), III: 514.

[36] P. 39; Job 41: 18. It may be that the KJB translators disliked this Hebraism (if that is what it is: it occurs only in Job and is not included in Rosenau's thorough list of Hebraisms), for it is relegated to the margin earlier in Job (3: 9), and perhaps is only used here to preserve the closeness of the simile, 'his eyes are like the eyelids of the morning'. The KJB margin is the source for most of Husbands's information on Hebraisms.

perceptions, he might have hastened on literary appreciation not only of the Scriptures but of their English representatives.

Anthony Blackwall

The classical scholar Anthony Blackwall (1674–1730) also deserves separate recognition, largely but not only because of the size of his work: he devotes the whole of volume I and some of volume II of *The Sacred Classics Defended and Illustrated* (1725, 1731) to praise of the Bible as literature, and earlier he had given the public a substantial foretaste of his views in *An Introduction to the Classics* (pp. 81–124). There he places the Scriptures ahead of the classics, though the latter are his subject. He argues 'that the Bible is the most excellent and useful book in the world, and to understand its meaning and discover its beauties 'tis necessary to be conversant in the Greek and Latin classics' (p. 82). To prove the point he gives some thirty pages of parallel passages where the classics are indebted to both Testaments, but he does not use biblical examples for the second part of the book, which is on rhetoric.

Many critics lamented both the general profanity of the age and its neglect of the Scriptures.[37] Blackwall's intention in *The Sacred Classics* is to remedy the neglect (if not the profanity) by demonstrating the purity of the Greek of the NT and imbuing a love for its perfections. A major cause of the neglect is that young scholars such as he addresses take 'the charge of solecisms, blemishes and barbarisms' in the NT Greek for granted and so either neglect it or read it 'with careless indifference and want of taste' (1: 13). Like a latter-day Broughton, he will admit no blemish in the Scripture. He argues, as so many in the previous century had, from divine inspiration:

> Now for this reason that the holy writers were under the influence and direction of the spirit of infinite wisdom, who does all his wondrous works in proportion, harmony and beauty, I am fully persuaded he would not suffer improprieties and

---

[37] The pithiest expression comes from an early scientist who was also particularly well versed in theology and had pertinent remarks to make on literary aspects of the Bible, Nehemiah Grew (1641–1712):

> No book was ever so well writ but through ill will or misunderstanding it has been undervalued. And so it fares with the Bible itself. As bad men take it to be their interest, so witty men their reputation to make it a fable. And they who are weak learn to say as others do. Some from the matter, others from the style, method, or on some other account, either tax it with falsehood or think meanly of it. And some, only because it is become cheap and common. As most people admire the tail of a glow-worm, which is a rare sight, more than they do the sun, which shines upon them every day.   (*Cosmologia Sacra* (London, 1701), p. 162)

violations of the true and natural reason and analogy of grammar to be in writings dictated by himself, and designed for the instruction and pleasure of mankind to the end of the world. If we consider God, says an excellent person, as the creator of our souls, and so likeliest to know the frame and springs and nature of his own workmanship, we shall make but little difficulty to believe that in the book written for and addressed to men he hath employed proper language and genuine natural eloquence, the most powerful and appropriated mean to work upon them. But solecism and absurd language give an offence and disgust to all people of judgement and good sense, and are not appropriate means to work and prevail upon human minds. (1: 160–1)

This is not just a familiar argument rolled out with striking candour and simplicity: the idea of the divine purpose has undergone a subtle shift. Where previously perfect, or at least appropriate, eloquence had been a characteristic of the inspired writing, now God is imagined as deliberately writing literature: it is 'designed for the instruction and pleasure of mankind'.

Blackwall could not be at a further remove from the developing idea of the OT poetry as primitive and artless, and one might instantly dismiss him as archaic and uncritical. Yet his emphasis on the NT as literature is novel for this time, and, within limits, he does give his ideas critical demonstration. He begins by agreeing with the deprecators of NT Greek that it contains Hebraisms, but defends them on two grounds, that they invigorate the Greek and conform to Greek grammar. Few critics were persuaded by the latter argument, but the former connects with Addison and Husbands's brief observations and must have helped his readers to appreciate English Hebraisms. His first example is typical:

> To do things acceptable to God is common language. To do things acceptable before, or in the presence of God is a Hebraism; but does it not enlarge the thought, and enliven and invigorate the expression? And is it any breach of the rationale of grammar, or does it any ways trespass upon concord or government? It places every serious reader under the inspection and all-seeing eye of the most highest, and therefore is apt to inspire him with a religious awe for that immense and adorable presence. (1: 6–7)

The last sentence could give the reader of the KJB a sharpened appreciation of 1 Tim. 2: 3 and 5: 4, but, more often than Husbands's, Blackwall's discussion of his examples is limited to the exclamatory, as in the two rhetorical questions here. It is not persuasive to read that 'St Luke is indeed admirable for the natural eloquence and easiness of his language. And don't the rest write with a wonderful perspicuity and a very beautiful and instructive plainness?' (1: 43), unless one already agrees, and then persuasion is hardly necessary. For the reader who thinks only of the English NT, the book is a kind of guided tour, Blackwall a Cicerone who says no more than 'look!' By the end he appears to have invited his young acolyte to admire everything in the NT indiscriminately – but, given his belief in the inspired perfection of the writing, he could hardly have encouraged discrimination.

'I must desire the friends of this sacred book', he writes at the end of the volume, 'to read it carefully and study it in the original, and to esteem it as an immense treasure of learning that requires all their abilities and all their reading' (1: 367). His method makes it inevitable that he should think he is writing for the Bible's friends – it is preaching for the converted – and the volume of praise from other writers in the years preceding his work makes it likely he found a substantial audience even if he made few converts. They would have been encouraged as never before to join appreciation of the NT as literature to their growing taste for Hebrew poetry. An account survives of one of these converts' reactions, but, alas, the convert exists only in fiction: it is the villainous Lovelace's somewhat less villainous correspondent, Robert Belford in Samuel Richardson's *Clarissa* (1747–8). Immediately after finding the first of Clarissa's four meditations from the Bible, Belford comes across *The Sacred Classics*:

> I took it home with me, and had not read a dozen pages when I was convinced that I ought to be ashamed of myself to think how greatly I have admired less noble and less natural beauties in pagan authors, while I have known nothing of this all-excelling collection of beauties, the Bible! By my faith, Lovelace, I shall for the future have a better opinion of the good sense and taste of half a score parsons whom I have fallen in with in my time and despised for *magnifying*, as I thought they did, the language and the sentiments to be found in it in preference to all the ancient poets and philosophers. And this is now a convincing proof to me, and shames as much an infidel's presumption as his ignorance, that those who know least are the greatest scoffers. A pretty pack of would-be wits of us, who censure without knowledge, laugh without reason, and are most noisy and loud against things we know least of![38]

Richardson himself needed no converting, and the passage is not dramatically persuasive; it has the character of a reference to authority and suggested further reading, since it follows Belford's surprised comments on the power and quality of the Bible. Lovelace confirms that Belford is right to admire the 'beauty and noble simplicity' of the Bible, and reproves him for having been ignorant of it.[39]

[38] Ed. Angus Ross (Harmondsworth: Penguin, 1985), p. 1126.
[39] P. 1146. Clarissa's meditations consist of biblical extracts, unlike the pastiche her predecessor, Pamela, indulges in (*Pamela* (1740); 2 vols. (London: Dent, 1914 etc.), 1: 284–7). Richardson later added to Clarissa's meditations and published them separately,

Whether Lovelace, or Richardson-through-Lovelace, means the KJB is uncertain – probably, like so many casual commentators, he means the originals as they happen to be represented by the KJB – but Blackwall constantly directs his readers' talent for sublime admiration to the Greek, even though, echoing ideas of the Bible's translatability, he claims that 'the true sublime will bear translation into all languages, and will be great and surprising in all languages, and to all persons of understanding and judgement' (1: 277). In *An Introduction* Blackwall gave his examples from the KJB, but here he rarely uses it: Greek examples predominate, and the English is usually his own. Thus the cause of the Bible as literature is given a solid nudge towards the NT and towards the idea of uniform excellency, but the cause of the KJB is only advanced in so far as his Greekless readers can see the excellence of the originals in it.

Revision canvassed

Blackwall, rounding off this period of discussion of the Bible as literature, directs us away from rather than towards the KJB, but there are two more areas to be surveyed. After half a century of quiet, the demand for a new translation was again beginning to be heard, though as no more than the first rumbles of a far distant army. The way was led by a somewhat disreputable Church of England minister, Hugh Ross, disreputable in that his *An Essay for a New Translation of the Bible* (1701) is a translation, sometimes badly adapted to English Bibles, of Charles Le Cène's *Projet d'une nouvelle version française de la Bible* (Rotterdam, 1696); Ross's second edition (London, 1702), which has a new preface and adds a second part from Le Cène, hides the fact that it is a translation and presents itself as an original work. Consequently the one remark in the first edition that praises the KJB, that 'it has a great many passages better rendered than they are to be found in some other languages' (fol. A2 v), is omitted from the second as it implies that Ross is translating a work discussing other Bibles. There remain a large number of complaints of inaccuracy and obscurity in the KJB, though often these should not have impressed the careful reader. For instance, arguing that translations should adhere to what the original ought to say rather than what it says, he gives this: 'it is said "that the Egyptians could not eat bread with the Hebrews" [Gen. 43: 32]; we should translate, "that it was not lawful for", etc. For these things were not absolutely impossible, but were contrary to the rules either of justice or decency, and therefore not to be done' (2nd edn, pp. 176–7). The KJB and Geneva both obviate the point, reading

one of his aims being to raise 'in the minds of the contemners of religion a due estimation of the Sacred Books' (*Meditations Collected from the Sacred Books* (London, 1750), p. ii).

'because the Egyptians might not eat bread with the Hebrews'. He has translated Le Cène (p. 510) without checking against his English versions. Ross himself warrants no closer examination, except to note that he suggests, this time not translating Le Cène, that there is a spirit of discontent with the KJB. 'Ministers in their pulpits', he says, 'often complain of the translations of their texts; nay, some make the most part of their sermons consist of various readings, diverse acceptations and of nice criticisms and grammaticisms.'[40]

Ross had few successors in this half of the century. Edward Wells, mathematician, geographer and divine (1667–1727), complains in a voluminous commentary on the Bible that some of the literalism of the KJB makes it 'so very uncouth and harsh as not readily to be understood by any reader, on account of its being so very different from our common way of speaking in like cases'.[41] He joins action to complaint, 'quite altering or at least explaining the terms in our common version' until, about half way through the work, the consequent bulk and price led him to desist. Later the highly esteemed preacher Zachariah Mudge (1694–1769) looks forward to 'when the wisdom of the Church shall think the time come to authenticate a new translation of the Bible'.[42]

Not surprisingly, the one writer to add some real detail to the case for a new translation is Blackwall. In the preface to the second volume of *The Sacred Classics*, he argues for 'the necessity and usefulness of a new version of the sacred books' (from the title). Le Cène through Ross had argued that a new translation would help to unite Christendom by resolving controversies. Blackwall sees this as a primary benefit of revision, arguing that 'such a work resolved on and vigorously carried on by any one church would soon engage the imitation of most of the rest, and would produce a happy agreement and uniformity amongst them, and consequently mutual charity and Christian endearment, and so would give strength and additional ornament to our common faith and most holy religion' (II: xxiv). There is a literary as well as an ecumenical concern here. A new translation, he believes, ought to be followed by 'a comment and exposition', proving before all else 'the propriety and beauty of the phrase and language' (II: xxi–xxii). So it is perhaps to the commentary rather than the translation that one should look for the beauty of the original. This is confirmed by a chapter which he describes as 'an account of several

---

[40] 2nd edn, fol. Aa3 v. The same point is made by Collins, *Grounds and Reasons*, p. 20, and Shaftesbury, II: 302.

[41] *An Help for the More Easy and Clear Understanding of the Holy Scriptures*, NT, 2 vols. (London, 1714–19), OT, 4 vols. (Oxford, 1724–7); preface to OT, vol. 2 (1725), p. II.

[42] *An Essay Towards a New English Version of the Book of Psalms* (London, 1744), p. iii.

places in the New Testament which are misrepresented and weakened either as to their sense, or their beauty and vigorous emphasis, in our translation; though I believe it is the best of the modern versions of the same standing'. He goes on:

> It is with pleasure and a just veneration to the memory of our learned and judicious translators that I acknowledge their version in the main to be faithful, clear and solid. But no man can be so superstitiously devoted to them but must own that a considerable number of passages are weakly and imperfectly, and not a few falsely, rendered.
>
> (II: 161)

This situation he finds unsurprising, given the advancements in knowledge of antiquities and critical learning achieved in the study of the classics, 'and a diligent comparing of them with the language and manner of the divine classics' (II: 161–2). Here is another straw in the wind: eventually a sense of advanced knowledge, though particularly of advances in textual criticism, was to be a major cause of the demand for revision.[43]

His, then, is a call for greater accuracy in the new translation, but accuracy now means not just fidelity, in whatever way, to the truth of the original, but fidelity to its literary quality. Two examples show just what he had in mind. He criticises the KJB's rendering of 2 Cor. 4: 6, although it 'sounds well in English and makes a good sense', because 'it does not accurately come up to and represent the Greek construction' (II: 191). Discussion of the figurative sense of some words in the Hebrew and Greek leads him to quote Rev. 14: 8, 'Babylon is fallen, is fallen, that great city, because she made all nations drink of the wine of the wrath of her fornication.' 'How harsh and unnatural!' he exclaims at the last part of this, and offers a revision: 'how proper and easy would a translation run thus: "the wine of the poison – *poisonous wine* – of her fornication". That would be an allusion to the custom of lewd and profligate women, who give poisonous

---

[43] Wells's work in place was an advance in textual criticism, as was the Presbyterian Daniel Mace's. Though Mace attempted a colloquial English, the predominant character of his work is clear from the title, *The New Testament in Greek and English. Containing the original text corrected from the authority of the most authentic manuscripts: and a new version formed agreeably to the illustrations of the most learned commentators and critics: with notes and various readings* . . . (London, 1729). A useful outline of Mace's work is given by H. McLachlan, 'An almost forgotten pioneer in New Testament criticism', the *Hibbert Journal* 37 (1938–9), 617–25, but Kenyon says all that is needed about both the achievement and the insignificance of Wells and Mace: 'both of these editors introduced many emendations which have been accepted by modern criticism, but in their own day their work had no effect. General opinion regarded the "received text" as sacrosanct, and any attempt to alter it as sacrilegious, while even the collection of various readings was deprecated as tending to throw doubt on the authenticity of the Scriptures. The policy of the ostrich held the field' (F. G. Kenyon, *The Text of the Greek Bible* (1936); 3rd edn, revised A. W. Adams (London: Duckworth, 1975), p. 176).

draughts, which they call love potions, to their gallants, to enflame and enrage their lust' (II: 188–9). He documents the point with a footnote and then demonstrates that his reading is supported by the Hebrew and the Septuagint. In this way his comments show a literary awareness of the KJB subordinated to his sense of the precise literary meaning of the originals. The commentary that he looks forward to would do exactly the job he has done of pointing up the allusion. The English would be more accurate and, where possible, better, and appreciation of the original would be fostered.

Jessey pleading for revision had wanted chapter and verse divisions changed in order, as he put it, to 'illustrate the texts' (see volume 1, p. 221). Blackwall also complains of them, but seems to want them eliminated. He gives enough detail to make the point of real interest. Yet, though he did not know Jessey's work, the point is still not original: it comes from the major philosopher John Locke (1632–1704), whom he both cites and plagiarises. One passage merits quotation at length, since it couples the criticism of presentation with analysis of the consequences for the reader's (and hearer's) sense of the text. Locke identifies a major difficulty in understanding Paul's sense in his Epistles as

> the dividing of them into chapters and verses ... whereby they are so chopped and minced, and, as they are now printed, stand so broken and divided that not only the common people take the verses usually for distinct aphorisms, but even men of advanced knowledge in reading them lose very much of the strength and force of the coherence and the light that depends on it. Our minds are so weak and narrow that they have need of all the helps and assistances [that] can be procured to lay before them undisturbedly the thread and coherence of any discourse, by which alone they are truly improved and led into the genuine sense of the author. When the eye is constantly disturbed with loose sentences that by their standing and separation appear as so many distinct fragments, the mind will have much ado to take in and carry on in its memory an uniform discourse of dependent reasonings, especially having from the cradle been used to wrong impressions concerning them, and constantly accustomed to hear them quoted as distinct sentences, without any limitation or explication of their precise meaning from the place they stand in and the relation they bear to what goes before or follows. These divisions also have given occasion to the reading these Epistles by parcels and in scraps, which has further confirmed the evil arising from such partitions.
>
> (P. vii; plagiarised by Blackwall, II: 126)

Now, Locke's concern, as was Jessey's, is the old, old theological concern with understanding the true meaning ('nobody', he observes, 'can think that any text of St Paul's Epistles has two contrary meanings' (p. x)). Yet the kind of reading he wants to promote by eliminating the misleading divisions is only to be distinguished from a literary reading by its purpose. His description of how he had to read the Epistles to understand them properly would have won approval from the author of *Practical Criticism*, I. A. Richards:

> I concluded it necessary, for the understanding of St Paul's Epistles, to read it all through at one sitting and to observe as well as I could the drift and design of his writing it. If the first reading gave me some light, the second gave me more; and so I persisted on reading constantly the whole Epistle over at once till I came to have a good general view of the apostle's main purpose in writing the Epistle, the chief branches of his discourse wherein he prosecuted it, the arguments he used and the disposition of the whole.
>
> This, I confess, is not to be obtained by one or two hasty readings: it must be repeated again and again, with a close attention to the tenor of the discourse and a perfect neglect of the divisions into chapters and verses. (P. xv)

The tiny shift needed to make reading both theological and literary is accomplished by Blackwall putting Locke's point in the context of a care for 'pleasure and advantage'. He is as concerned with 'the beauty and strength of the period' as with 'the conclusiveness of the reasoning and the connection and dependence of the context' (II: 124–5, immediately preceding his use of Locke, p. vii).

The kind of presentation Locke and Blackwall want (save that neither would eliminate commentary) is that which Tyndale had given his NT, continuous prose ordered only by paragraph breaks and occasional larger divisions, and poetry distinguished visually. In a very important way, the pure religious text and the pure literary text are identical. It is the *practical* religious text that is so different from the literary text. Tyndale's insistence on 'the process, order and meaning of the text' is exactly Locke's insistence on reading Paul whole. Yet it was historical accident rather than choice that led him to present the pure text (see volume 1, p. 164). The utility of verse division for study and reference outweighed its disadvantages. Hardly anybody before Locke, especially as publicised by Blackwall, was aware that there were disadvantages, and all the cogency of Locke's argument was insufficient to persuade the world that the disadvantages outweighed the utility. Most KJBs and other versions have retained them, though ways have been found to minimise their interference with the text. Even Roland Mushat Frye's relatively recent *The Bible: Selections from the King James Version for Study as Literature* keeps the numbers within the text.

The few calls for revision went unheeded. If the age was not in love with the KJB, it was becoming thoroughly accustomed to it. Locke observes that 'Paul's Epistles, as they stand translated in our English Bibles, are now by long and constant use become a part of the English language, and common phraseology, especially in matters of religion' (p. xi). The greatest Augustan poet, Alexander Pope (1688–1744), refers to 'those general phrases and manners of expression which have attained a veneration even in our language from being used in the Old Testament'.[44] Though this is a variation on the commonplace discussed earlier and looks more to the originals than to the KJB (Pope, though Catholic, did sometimes use the KJB), the jump from familiarity to 'veneration' is striking. Yet it is veneration for Hebraisms in English rather than a general veneration for the KJB's English. Another of the age's great writers, Jonathan Swift (1667–1745), uses the observation in a strikingly original way. It comes as part of an argument for that great eighteenth-century goal of 'ascertaining and fixing our language for ever' for fear that it will 'at length infallibly change for the worse'.[45] In his view it is better to fix the language in an imperfect state than not to fix it at all. There are many qualities of classical and romance languages that he could wish English possessed, but, showing abundant scorn for his contemporaries, he is more afraid that the language will be changed for the worse. Indeed, thoroughly uncharacteristically for an Augustan, though few moderns would disagree, he sees English as having received most improvement between 1558, the accession of Elizabeth 1, and the rebellion of 1642 (p. 9). He builds on what he presents as the Earl of Oxford's 'observation, that if it were not for the Bible and Common Prayer Book in the vulgar tongue, we should hardly be able to understand anything that was written among us an hundred years ago':

> which is certainly true: for those books, being perpetually read in churches, have proved a kind of standard for language, especially to the common people. And I doubt whether the alterations since introduced have added much to the beauty or strength of the English tongue, although they have taken off a great deal from that simplicity which is one of the greatest perfections in any language ... no translation our country ever yet produced hath come up to that of the Old and New Testament ... I am persuaded that the translators of the Bible were masters of an English style much fitter for that work than any we see in our present writings, which I take to be owing to the simplicity that runs through the whole. Then, as to the

---

[44] Preface to The *Iliad*, *Poems*, VII: 18.

[45] 'A proposal for correcting, improving and ascertaining the English tongue' (1712); in Herbert Davis, ed., *The Prose Works of Jonathan Swift*, 14 vols. (Oxford: Blackwell, 1957), IV: 14.

greatest part of our liturgy, compiled long before the translation of the Bible now in use, and little altered since, there seem to be in it as great strains of true sublime eloquence as are anywhere to be found in our language; which every man of good taste will observe in the Communion Service, that of Burial, and other parts.

(Pp. 14–15)

The claim that the KJB and the PB are the best of English translations is probably an echo of the argument made by Felton, Gildon and others that they are the best English translations from any source, but the idea that they are stylish in their own right is new (Swift is writing a third of a century before Say). Even so, one cannot be sure whether Swift, if pressed, would have claimed the KJB as a great work of English literature. He holds that the translators were artists of a sort, 'masters of an English style', and he qualifies by adding, 'much fitter for that work'. Explicit praise, redolent of Longinus and Boileau, is reserved for the liturgy – here Swift achieves an honourable critical first. Some dozen years later the freethinking deist Anthony Collins (1676–1729) refers sarcastically to the English being charmed with 'the beauty of holiness in our Common Prayer Book' (*Grounds and Reasons*, p. 2), so it seems likely that Swift was articulating a view that was beginning to be generally held. Certainly the biblical 'beauty of holiness' had been used in connection with biblical sublimity as early as 1713. Steele, writing in the *Guardian* 21, uses it to sum up 'the effect which the sacred writings will have upon the soul of an intelligent reader' (pp. 103–4). He had just praised, though without reference to the KJB, the story of Jesus on the road to Emmaus (Luke 24). The only praise of the PB I have found which antedates Swift does admire the language but goes no further than this: 'considering the plainness and perspicuity, the soundness and propriety of speech which is used in it, the least that can be said of the Common Prayer is that all things in it are so worded as is most for the edifying of all those that use it'.[46]

Swift is a useful witness, a stimulating and original figure, but hardly an influence on his time in his desire to elevate the KJB and the PB as standards for the language. That they went on operating as standards owes nothing to his argument – he was arguing to a select group of political and literary leaders – and everything to their continued intensive use by the people. This intensive, and, for the most part, exclusive use was leading the people to a feeling that the KJB was verbally inspired. Beveridge, whose conservatism of taste exceeds Swift's, credibly reports that 'most people reading the Scripture no otherwise

---

[46] Beveridge, 'The excellency and usefulness of the Common Prayer', sermon preached 27 November 1681; *The Theological Works of William Beveridge*, 12 vols. (Oxford, 1844–8), VI: 377.

than it is translated into their own language ... look upon everything which they find in such a translation as the word of God, especially if it be publicly owned and commonly used as such among them' (*A Defence*, p. 34).

Other comments can be found that praise the KJB, but they do not refer to its qualities as English. In the first of the many, many books on English Bible translations, Anthony Johnson, thinking of the KJB's merits as a true revelation of the originals, calls it 'this glorious work'.[47] This is his enthusiastic conclusion:

> Happy! thrice happy! hath our English nation been since God hath given it learned translators to express in our mother tongue the heavenly mysteries of his holy word delivered to his church in the Hebrew and Greek languages; who although they may have in some matters of no importance unto salvation, as men, been deceived and mistaken, yet have they faithfully delivered the whole substance of the heavenly doctrine contained in the Holy Scriptures without any heretical translations or wilful corruptions.   (P. 100)

Though there is a slight recognition of faults here, the outspokenness of the praise is not as characteristic of the time as the following comment which appeared in the short-lived *Bibliotheca Literaria* in 1723:

> The other English translations are now antiquated and difficult to be procured, there having been no editions of any of them, I am persuaded, since the publication of the last version; which seems to have made its way by a general consent and approbation without the interposition of authority to enforce it: a sure argument that it is generally esteemed the best we have, though it has still many considerable faults, and very much needs another review.[48]

The KJB is best but far from perfect. The ignorance of the political, religious and printing history of Bible translation, to say nothing of the KJB's close linguistic ties with its predecessors, is very striking. So is the consequence: it allows the beginning of the myth that the KJB was instantly successful through its own intrinsic qualities.

The popular front

'*A great prejudice to the new*'

The people and the literati were perhaps as far apart in the early eighteenth century as they had been at any time since the Reformation, and all that has been

---

[47] *An Historical Account of the Several English Translations of the Bible and the opposition they met with from the Church of Rome* (London, 1730); in Watson, *Tracts*, III: 60–100; p. 97.

[48] Newcome, pp. 116–17; he gives the following reference: 'Bibliotheca Lit. N. iv. p. 72'.

surveyed so far comes from the literati. Appreciation of the sublimities of Hebrew poetry, or even of OT narrative and the NT in general, was no issue for the people. Nor even was the KJB, if we set aside the absorption in Bible language of some of the dissenters so maliciously caricatured by Swift in *The Tale of a Tub*, section XI. The KJB was not under threat, but the people's own treasured possession in the worship of the Church, the Sternhold and Hopkins Psalter, was. It was at last losing its battle against rival versions, particularly in the face of competition from Tate and Brady's Psalter (1696). This sparked some debate that not only anticipates arguments about the KJB but at times involves it. Sternhold and Hopkins was more obviously antiquated than the KJB, thoroughly open to aesthetic objection, but much more loved. In the early eighteenth century it was the sharpest focus of the issues of the old and the familiar versus the new, and of religion versus art, both issues that were to be increasingly important for the KJB.

Bishop William Beveridge (1637–1708), whom the *DNB* quietly describes as 'not in advance of his age', spells out the arguments with engaging intransigence in his posthumous defence of Sternhold and Hopkins against Tate and Brady. It is his dogmatic view – by no means indefensible though perhaps never so bluntly expressed – that 'it is a great prejudice to the new that it is new, wholly new; for whatsoever is new in religion at the best is unnecessary' (p. 3). In other days he would have been a great defender of the Vulgate, or of the Old Latin against the Vulgate, and it is instructive to see the same kind of conservatism that opposed vernacular translation manifesting itself in relation to those very translations: so many ideas broadly connected with the language of the Scriptures repeat themselves. His paternalistic reason is one that Augustine, having made a very similar point to Jerome, would have sympathised with (see volume 1, pp. 35–6):

> when a thing hath once been settled, either by law or custom, so as to be generally received and used by [the people] for a long time together, it cannot be afterwards put down and a new thing set up in its stead without giving them great offence and disturbance, putting them out of their road and perplexing their minds with fears and doubts which way to take, and inclining them also to have an ill opinion of the Church they live in. (P. 4)

The line of defence for the Sternhold and Hopkins Psalms is obvious, simply that they are old. But, besides this, they belong to a time that, though less artful and learned, surpassed the present in 'wisdom, piety and devotion' (p. 16). The people love them and 'ye never hear them ... complain that ... [they] are too plain, too low or too heavy for them'; rather, 'the plainer they are, the sooner they understand them, the lower their style is, the better it is suited to their capacities, and the heavier they go, the more easily they can keep pace with them' (pp. 42–3). Beveridge builds on this a very important claim for both Sternhold and Hopkins and the KJB, that they have established an individual style that is ecclesiastical, unliterary English:

> the style of the Scripture, of which the Psalms are part, is all such. There are no enticing words of man's wisdom there, no flights of wit, no fanciful expressions, no rhetorical, much less poetical, flourishes. But everything necessary for mankind to believe and do is delivered there in such a plain and familiar style that all sorts of people may understand it. When Almighty God Himself speaks of Himself, He condescends so low as to use such words and expressions as we commonly use among ourselves. And seeing the whole Scripture is written in such a style, all translations of it must be so too, or else they cannot be true translations. And, therefore, this is so far from being a fault that it is one of the greatest excellencies of this old translation of the Psalms that it doth not only keep to the sense of the text but to the same manner of expressing it which is there used. (Pp. 43–4)

It would be untrue to Beveridge to insist that he is describing the originals or that he is prescribing a method of translation rather than a style. The paragraph started as it finishes, with the translations as its subject. God, it seems, did not so much speak vulgar Hebrew or Greek as the same language 'as we commonly use among ourselves'. Indeed, the translations, Sternhold and Hopkins and the KJB, are inspired. Only when a translation disagrees with the original is it 'not of divine inspiration but human invention'. This, as noted above, pp. 41–2, is how the people regard the Bible.

Zeal to defend Sternhold and Hopkins leads Beveridge into a flat contradiction of the Augustan admiration for French and Latin. As he understands it, the main objection to Sternhold and Hopkins is 'that there are many old words in it which are now grown obsolete and out of use' (p. 49). He concedes there may be a few, but the people 'still use those words, or, at least, understand them as well as any that are in common use among them'. This may be dubious, but he adds pertinently that 'it is, we know, among the common people that the language of every nation is best preserved' (p. 50). So he challenges the Augustans: 'what exception, then, can be taken against those old words? Are they not all true English words? And is it any fault that they are not Latin or French? It must come to that at last, for ye can scarce find any better English' (p. 51). This is not just rhetoric. He discusses a number of examples, of which none is more interesting than 'the word that most stumble at ... at the very threshold in the first verse of the first Psalm', for this is an example where not only does he admit misunderstanding but he documents it from the alteration made in some editions:

> The man is blest that hath not bent
>   To wicked rede his ear,
> Nor led his life as sinners do;
>   Nor sate in scorner's chair.

That which they find fault with here is the word 'rede', which they say is now grown out of use, so that many do not know the meaning of it. But must the word be blamed for the people's ignorance? This is not only the best but the only English word I know of in all our tongue that signifies that which we otherwise call 'advice' or 'counsel'. For these two words, the one is taken from the French, the other from the Latin, but 'rede' is truly and originally an English-Saxon word, commonly used to this day in Germany, from whence our language came ... And therefore 'rede', as it is written in the translation of the Psalms (not 'read', as in some later editions) is properly a true English word, and was always used in the same signification as we now use 'counsel' and 'advice', words plainly of foreign extraction. And, therefore, I can see no reason why it should give place to them. It is very hard that a native of our own country should be cast out only to make way for a foreigner, and that too for no other reason but because he is old.[49]

'Counsel' goes back to Middle English, and 'advice' has a long history; Tyndale used the former, while the KJB has both. This and the last comment betray Beveridge's bigotry, but still the argument is of real importance: adulation of the vernacular translations keeps natural company with a highly un-Augustan reverence for the Teutonic roots of the language. In a sense, the battle between the inkhorn and the native strain is being fought again: on the one side is the predominantly native biblical English inherited from Tyndale and the language of the common people, on the other the educated and literary English of the Augustans. What one may call the popular front, with the KJB playing a dominant role, was before long to exert its power. Extreme conservative though he is, Beveridge is another of the harbingers. And, in a larger view, he will come to seem one of the most representative figures of this history.

Several anecdotes confirm the accuracy of Beveridge's portrait of popular attitudes. From the other side of the fence, Nahum Tate himself (1652–1715), known not just as a Psalm translator but as the gallant rescuer of Cordelia from her Shakespearian fate, tells this story:

[Simon Patrick,] the late Bishop of Ely, upon his first using of his brother Dr

---

[49] Pp. 74–5. The same mistake, 'read' for 'rede', is noted by the antiquary Thomas Hearne and used as an occasion to lambaste modern corruptions of the text (Hearne, ed., *Robert of Gloucester's Chronicle*, 2 vols. (Oxford, 1724), II: 698–9).

Patrick's new version [of the Psalms] in his family devotion, observed, as I heard himself relate the passage, that a servant-maid of a musical voice was silent for several days together. He asked her the reason, whether she were not well or had a cold? adding that he was much delighted to hear her because she sang sweetly and kept the rest in tune. 'I am well enough in health', answered she, 'and have no cold; but, if you must needs know the plain truth of the matter, as long as you sung Jesus Christ's Psalms, I sung along with ye; but now you sing Psalms of your own invention, you may sing by yourselves.'   (Pp. 20–1)

Here is a new 'mumpsimus' (see volume 1, pp. 60–1). The degree of the ignorance may be exceptional,[50] but it is a salutary reminder that affection and knowledge can be as separate as the two trees in the Garden of Eden. One wonders if the good Bishop did anything for the maid's soul by turning to the title page and showing her the translators' names. The tale also shows how easily the people could do as Beveridge did, attribute divine authorship to a translation.

Tate gives another vivid illustration of the popularity, and the religious and cultural efficacy, of Sternhold and Hopkins. He quotes the outstanding churchman of the time, principal founder of the Society for Promoting Christian Knowledge (SPCK) and the Society for the Propagation of the Gospel in foreign parts (SPG), the saintly Thomas Bray,[51] who writes 'that through the fondness of people for Psalm-singing many have recovered their reading, which they had almost forgot, and many have learned to read for the sake of singing Psalms where it has been practised to some advantage in the performance'. Tate adds:

'Tis likewise certain that in his own country parish the young men that used to loiter in the churchyard, or saunter about the neighbouring grounds and not come into the church till the divine service was over, upon his ordering a Psalm to be sung before prayers began, they came flocking into the church, where, by this means, he had 'em present both at the prayers and preaching.   (Pp. 6–7)

Bray, the great spreader of Christian culture, could turn into reality the theory that literary appreciation (of a sort) would make people more religious. There is a precedent here that many familiar with the use of soul and pop music in

---

[50] But not unique: perhaps about the beginning of the present century, a young curate declared to his congregation, 'if the King James Version was good enough for St Paul, it is good enough for me' (as given in Newton, p. 53).

[51] Bray, Tate and the two Patricks seem to have had considerable connections. Simon Patrick was a co-founder of the SPCK, and a prominent supporter of the SPG, while John Patrick was involved in the Tate and Brady Psalter (his comments on popular attitudes to Sternhold and Hopkins were noted in volume 1, p. 288).

modern congregations will recognise, though in his time the lure of a contemporary idiom was unnecessary. Sternhold and Hopkins was a kind of classical pop music to thousands upon thousands.

A basis for love

The coming of the vernacular Bible made readers of many such as William Maldon (see volume 1, p. 86), and the association between the Bible and learning to read is both ancient and continuing. What Maldon did by choice generations of children have done of necessity, having not only religious material but the text of the KJB as a central element in their growth to literacy and piety. This, coupled with the hearing of the text in the family, in school and in church, gave the KJB, once it was the established version, a unique place in their literary and linguistic consciousness. It was nursery story, primer, adolescent and adult reading, present from the alpha to the omega of verbal consciousness. In a fragmentary way its language, imagery, story and poetry, to say nothing of its faith, was the highest common factor in the mental environment of millions over many generations. Home is not always loved, but, as anyone who has ever been homesick knows, there is a close link between the familiar and love, and, as anybody, astonished that other people can love a place that seems so awful, knows, that love has little to do with objective merit. Such love created a new basis for literary opinion of the Bible, the basis of sentiment. It was independent of scholarly ideas of inspiration and of fashionable literary standards, hitherto the prime forces in moulding opinion, and it begins to give its own stamp to opinion of the KJB by the middle of the eighteenth century.

The development of Bible primers and family and school Bibles at first reflected and then promoted the educational use of the Bible. The Reformation brought the Bible into the family before it came into the church. Doubtless whole households read the Lollard Bible together. In the early 1540s a draft proclamation seems to envisage family reading, exhorting that every man 'use this most high benefit quietly and charitably every of you to the edifying of himself, his wife and family' (Pollard, p. 114). Benjamin Franklin tells a tale of such reading from a few years later:

> This obscure family of ours was early in the Reformation, and continued Protestants through the reign of Queen Mary, when they were sometimes in danger of trouble on account of their zeal against popery. They had got an English Bible, and to conceal and secure it, it was fastened open with tapes under and within the frame of a joint stool. When my great great grandfather read in it to his family, he turned up the joint

stool upon his knees, turning over the leaves then under the tapes. One of the children stood at the door to give notice if he saw the apparitor coming, who was an officer of the spiritual court. In that case the stool was turned down again upon its feet, when the Bible remained concealed under it as before. (*Autobiography*, p. 50)

Persecution was a great encourager of home religion.

From the beginning of the seventeenth century Thumb Bibles and other verse presentations of biblical material were published for children, but family Bible reading differs in that it presents the child with the text as well as the content. Publishers began deliberately to present children with the text later in the century, the first notable example being *The King's Psalter* (London, 1670). The title continues: 'containing Psalms and hymns, with easy and delightful directions to all learners, whether children, youths or others, for their better reading of the English tongue'; the work is dedicated 'to the instructors of youth'. It is a religious miscellany, complete with illustrations, ranging from a rhymed alphabet through a version of Herbert's 'The Altar' and Psalms from the PB to passages from the KJB, 'all which', the title concludes, 'are profitable, plain and pleasant'. If this is not just a cliché or a pious wish, the coming together of learning to read, the KJB and delight ('delightful directions') nicely suggests how such early reading led some to a love that might be literary.

School (rather than family) Bibles began to appear in 1737 with an NT published in Glasgow, and in eighteenth-century Scotland 'children were generally taught to read in country schools, by first using the Shorter Catechism, then the Proverbs, afterwards the New Testament, and lastly the Bible'.[52] One curious anecdote from Daniel Defoe affords a glimpse of the use of the KJB text in schools early in the eighteenth century. With good reason,[53] he shows no surprise at it being so used, but what happens to the text intrigues him. Going into a school in Somerset, he writes,

> I observed one of the lowest scholars was reading his lesson to the usher, which lesson it seems was a chapter in the Bible, so I sat down by the master till the boy had read out his chapter. I observed the boy read a little oddly in the tone of the country, which made me the more attentive because on enquiry I found that the words were the same and the orthography the same as in all our Bibles. I observed also the boy

---

[52] J. Lee, *Memorial of the Bible Societies in Scotland* (Edinburgh, 1826), p. 195n. Quoted by Herbert in his entry for the 1737 NT (Herbert 1037).

[53] By this time the Bible was long established in schools. Foster Watson give samples from school statutes that specify Bible reading as long ago as 1552 (*The English Grammar Schools to 1660* (1908; London: Cass, 1968), pp. 57–62).

read it out with his eyes still on the book and his head like a mere boy, moving from side to side as the lines reached cross the columns of the book; his lesson was in the Cant 5: 3, of which the words are these, 'I have put off my coat, how shall I put it on, I have washed my feet, how shall I defile them?'

The boy read thus, with his eyes, as I say, full on the text. 'Chav a doffed my cooat, how shall I don't, chav a washed my veet, how shall I moil 'em?'

How the dexterous dunce could form his mouth to express so readily the words (which stood right printed in the book) in his country jargon, I could not but admire.[54]

The modern reader might also admire. Was 'the dexterous dunce' translating the KJB's English into his English as he read (Defoe believes he was), or was the text sufficiently familiar, and his literacy sufficiently weak, that this was how he knew the KJB? Is this another 'mumpsimus'? The anecdote is unique, but it does suggest a real familiarity with the text, if not a fidelity to it (if the learned could misquote, why should not a dunce misread?): the boy had made it his own.

The Geneva Bible, containing not only the text but the understanding of the text given in prefaces, notes and diagrams, was the first great English Bible for home religion. However, the first Bible to *describe* itself as a family Bible was S. Smith's *The Complete History of the Old and New Testament: or, a Family Bible* (London, 1735; NT 1737).[55] In the spirit of *The King's Psalter*, Smith writes in the preface, 'how laudable it is for a parent, and what a fine amusement for a child, to hear the holy writ read? It confirms the former in his religion, and at the same time initiates the other into the sacred mysteries.' His title continues, 'with critical and explanatory annotations, extracted from the writings of the most celebrated authors, ancient and modern. Together with maps, cuts, etc., curiously designed and engraved in copper'. This gives a fair sense of his and later family Bibles. They are usually large volumes well suited to reading out loud or to sitting impressively on a table in the centre of the living room of a middle-class or would-be middle-class family: in this respect they are the ancestors of coffee-table books. They are copiously illustrated and full of information, sometimes theological, sometimes not. In Smith's case, for instance, the Geneva arguments are used along with the headings from the KJB and annotations from many sources. The desire to provide information beyond mere commentary went so far that Thomas Bankes's family Bible of ?1790 even recorded that there are 3,566,480 letters in the two Testaments (nowadays this is

---

[54] *A Tour Through Great Britain* (1724–6), 2 vols. (London: Dent, 1928), 1: 219.
[55] Herbert's general index gives a substantial if not complete list of family Bibles.

mere useless information, but such facts were useful to the Masoretes checking the accuracy of their handwritten copies of the text).[56]

The first NT for children published in England seems to have been Joseph Brown's 1766 *The Family Testament, and Scholar's Assistant: calculated not only to promote the reading of the Holy Scriptures in families and schools, but also to remove that great uneasiness observable in children upon the appearance of hard words in their lessons, by a method entirely new* (London). This contains 'an introduction to spelling and reading in general ... and directions for reading with elegance and propriety'. Other attempts to present parts of the Bible in a form attractive to children followed. One of the most notable was *A Curious Hieroglyphic Bible; or, select passages from the Old and New Testaments, represented with emblematical figures, for the amusement of youth: designed chiefly to familiarize tender age, in a pleasing and diverting manner, with early ideas of the Holy Scriptures* (London, 1784; Dublin, 1789). The 'emblematical figures' are engravings representing particular words, and this popular little book is dedicated 'to the parents, guardians, and governesses, of Great Britain and Ireland'.[57]

---

[56] Here is more such useless information from Bankes:

	OT	(Apoc.)	NT	Total
Books	39	—	27	66
Chapters	929	(183)	260	1,189
Verses	23,214	(6,081)	7,959	31,173
Words	592,439	(152,185)	181,253	773,692
Letters	2,728,100	—	838,380	3,566,480

'And' occurs 35,543 times in the OT and 10,684 in the NT, while 'Jehovah' occurs 6,855 times. The middle and shortest chapter of the Bible is Psalm 117, the middle verse Ps. 118: 8, and the middle time 2 Chr. 4: 16. Ezra 7: 21 has all the letters of the alphabet (in old editions it begins 'And J, euen J'). The identical information is reproduced by J. I. Mombert, *English Versions of the Bible* (London, 1883), pp. 372–3n, with minor variations due to transcription errors rather than making an independent count. He gives his source as *Notes and Queries*, 2nd series, vii, 481, but Bankes, whether or not he is original, is much older. In awe of the labour of older and more diligent scholars, I have not checked this information. But the figure for 'Jehovah' does not easily stand up to examination ...

[57] Hieroglyphic Bibles go back to 1687 in Germany, while the use of hieroglyphics for teaching reading is a little older. The *Orbis Pictus* of J. A. Comenius (Nuremberg, 1657), using illustrations reminiscent of the diagrams of the Geneva Bible, was adapted into English by Charles Hoole in 1658. Such works were of course associated with religion, so the *Nolens volens: or, you shall make Latin whether you will or no* of Elisha Coles (London, 1658) was published with *The Youth's Visible Bible*. Hieroglyphic Bibles were available in England and America from about 1780 (see W. A. Clouston, *Hieroglyphic Bibles: Their Origin and History* (Glasgow, 1894), also Virginia Haviland and Margaret N. Coughlan,

Not everybody was happy with the general use of the Bible to teach reading. Sarah Trimmer (1741–1810), known as 'Good Mrs Trimmer', argued in the preface to the third edition of her *Sacred History* (1796) that 'every part of early instruction ought to be held in subordination to the study of religion'.[58] The Bible should not be used without this end in mind. So she declares:

> The opposite customs which have, of late years, prevailed in many schools and families, of either suffering the Scriptures to be read by children in a promiscuous manner, or totally neglected, may be justly regarded as principal causes of the profaneness and libertinism of the age ... it is presumptuous to suppose we can educate youth properly without them; and it may justly be considered as an irreverent act to make use of God's Holy Word with no further end in view than to the improvement of pupils in the art of reading.   (1: vii)

Needless to say, this lengthy work supplements its selections from the KJB, 'with annotations and reflections, particularly calculated to facilitate the study of the Holy Scriptures in schools and families' (subtitle).

The successors to these books are still published, and reading programmes based on the Bible continue to be created,[59] but the story does not need pursuing here; the inescapable familiarity with the KJB (and then with more recent versions) that the whole story both reflects and promotes is the crucial point. The consequences of familiarity we have seen before, not only in feelings towards Sternhold and Hopkins, or in the 'mumpsimus' anecdote, but in the difficulties Jerome faced in revising the Old Latin Bible, dangerously presuming 'to change the language of an old man', destroying 'the sweet flavour he once drank' (see volume 1, p. 35). What Augustine wrote of the Bible of his time is now true of the KJB, 'as the child grows this book grows with

Yankee Doodle's Literary Sampler of Prose, Poetry and Pictures (New York: Crowell, 1974), pp. 18–19).

There is another aspect of family Bibles which has little to do with familiarity with the text or with their expository role, but emphasises the special nature of the Bible within the family, their role as heirloom and the place to record family history. This latter practice goes back to the seventeenth century if not further (see volume 1, p. 119n10), and became well established in the eighteenth century (see C. J. Mitchell, 'Family trees in eighteenth-century Bibles', *Factotum* 11 (1981), 16). Jane Austen parodies the practice at the beginning of *Persuasion* (1818), and Thackeray sourly shows it continuing as a form without substance in chapter 24 of *Vanity Fair* (1848). In the mining household of D. H. Lawrence's parents, the family Bible lay centre-table in the living room with, I am told, an aspidistra on it. So one could go on.

[58] *Sacred History* (1782 etc.); 3rd edn, 6 vols. (London, 1796), 1: viii.

[59] A recent example is the American Bible Society's programme, 'Good news for new readers', 'a multi-national, multi-language endeavour to encourage literacy throughout the world through the use of Scripture Literacy Selections' (ABS leaflet).

him' (see volume 1, p. 5). The KJB in relation to Augustan literary standards was something like the Old Latin Bible and then the Vulgate in relation to the Ciceronian standard. Just as the Bible's Latin, kept alive by the vitality of religion and its consequent familiarity, could replace the literary standard for men such as Aldhelm and Bede, so now the KJB's English is in a position to challenge the much less stable literary standard of the Augustans.

CHAPTER 2

Mid-century

Religion and literature kept apart

The idea of the Bible as a literary work became so strong in the latter half of the eighteenth century that there is a danger of forgetting that, as in all periods, there were many who kept religion and literature separate. Some did so for the familiar reason that literature was inseparable from vice; others admired literature but shied away from religion: for them the Bible was obviously associated with religion and so they ignored it as literature. There is abundant testimony to the endurance of this latter prejudice. To take but one example from the period we are entering on, the novelist and cleric Laurence Sterne believed that the 1760s was a 'licentious age . . . bent upon bringing Christianity into discredit' (IV: 420). He states baldly that 'men of taste and delicacy . . . turn over those awful sacred pages with inattention and an unbecoming indifference . . . so far has negligence and prepossession stopped their ears against the voice of the charmer' (IV: 413). Where Richardson had believed that a rake like Belford might be freed from this negligence by chancing on a work like Blackwall's, another remedy occurred to some in the latter part of the century, that the Bible – or parts of it – might be appreciated as literature by these men if it could somehow be separated from its religious context. The biographer James Boswell (1740–95) was one of the first to hit on this notion, incidentally showing the KJB's ability to affect an eighteenth-century reader through its own merits. He writes in his journal:

Sunday 20 February 1763
This forenoon I read the history of Joseph and his brethren, which melted my heart and drew tears from my eyes. It is simply and beautifully told in the sacred writings. It is a strange thing that the Bible is so little read. I am reading it regularly through at present. I dare say there are many people of distinction in London who know nothing about it. Were the history of Joseph published by some genteel bookseller as an

eastern fragment and circulated amongst the gay world, I am persuaded that those who have any genuine taste might be taken in to admire it exceedingly and so by degrees have a due value for the oracles of God.[1]

This repeats the idea first noted from Dennis that literary enjoyment may lead to proper religious feelings. Anecdotes of questionable authenticity exist which seem to prove the point. Johnson is supposed to have presented the story of Ruth as a newly found pastoral, and then told his listeners that it was 'from a book called the Bible, that they affected to despise', and Benjamin Franklin (1706–90) is supposed to have done the same in Paris with Habakkuk (Pattison, p. 205). Both anecdotes have been attributed elsewhere to Franklin (Eckman, p. 18), but I have been unable to confirm either. They seem out of character for Johnson but they fit Franklin, who practised a similar deception with a brilliantly done spurious chapter of Genesis in the style of the KJB, now usually published as 'A parable against persecution' (a topic dear to his heart).[2] The chapter concerns Abraham's intolerance of a stranger's religious ideas and God's reproof of Abraham. Franklin's editor writes that 'it was his practice ... when conversations turned to religious intolerance and persecution, to call for a Bible and, pretending to read a chapter from Genesis, to recite his verses to the astonishment of the company and his own enjoyment of their comments'

---

[1] *Boswell's London Journal, 1762–1763*, ed. Frederick A. Pottle (London: Heinemann, 1950), pp. 196–7. Boswell's notion continued to find occasional expression. For instance, the Hancock professor of Hebrew at Harvard, George Rapall Noyes, waxing lyrical on the Psalms, put it this way:

> What a sensation would be produced in the literary world by such a collection of poetry as is presented in the book of Psalms, could it come recommended by the attraction of novelty! But the truth is that, in general, the ear is accustomed to these admirable productions before the mind can comprehend their meaning or feel their beauty; so that, in maturer life, it requires no inconsiderable effort to give them that attention which is necessary for the reception of the impressions they are adapted to impart.   (*A New Translation of the Book of Psalms*, 2nd edn (Boston, 1846), p. 6)

A somewhat similar anecdote comes from the present century:

> Dr R. Newton Flew used to recall that as a young minister he read Ephesians 1: 3–23 in the Moffatt version at a devotional meeting. He did not mention Moffatt or give the reference to Ephesians. When the meeting was over an elderly minister asked him, 'What great work of devotion was it that you read from this evening?' Had the name 'Moffatt' been mentioned before the passage was read, the reaction would have been hostile; but anonymity made a favourable judgement possible.

(George Anderson, 'James Moffatt: Bible translator', in David F. Wright, pp. 46–7)

[2] *The Papers of Benjamin Franklin*, vol. VI, ed. Leonard W. Labaree (New Haven and London: Yale University Press, 1963), pp. 114–24. The parable is reproduced in the appendix. Labaree dates it perhaps from 1755. Franklin wrote another piece of the same

(p. 114). Whether this is an instance of Franklin, ever tactful, reminding God of something he had meant to put in the Bible but forgotten, or merely an instance of the great American's teasing wit, its spirit is akin to that of the anecdotes. If we accept that they have a truth to them, they do suggest that parts of the Bible could be enjoyed by men of taste if the prejudice against it were neutralised.

It is worth noting that this idea is a particular form of the general situation of the Bible being read with fresh eyes, a situation that takes us back to early readers such as Augustine and Tatian, or a Reformation reader such as Bilney (see volume 1, pp. 4–5, 18, 88). The first two came to the Bible for religious reasons and their literary sensibilities were shocked; the last came to it for its literary merits and was converted. There are few other accounts of literary first impressions of the Bible. Indeed, I know of only one that concerns the KJB, so it may be recorded here as a warning against optimistic reliance on the Bible speaking for itself. Randolph Churchill, son of Winston, was as ill-read as he was talkative. Evelyn Waugh and Lord Birkenhead were stuck with him on a mission in wartime Yugoslavia. They each 'bet him £10 that he will not read the Bible right through in a fortnight. He has set to work but not as quietly as we hoped. He sits bouncing about on his chair, chortling and saying, "I say, did you know this came in the Bible, 'bring down my grey hairs with sorrow to the grave'?" [Gen. 42: 38, 44: 29]. Or simply, "God, isn't God a shit."' This has been retailed as if it were a condemnation of the Bible,[3] but Churchill, still well short of the ten commandments, was very obviously enjoying his reading. The profane exclamation probably reflects no more than simple engagement with the story and its characters.[4] Randolph Churchill would be few people's choice

sort at the same time, but it was unsuccessful. The parable was published several times and was apparently quite well known from 1764 onwards, though Eckman is, until now, the only writer on the Bible to notice it. Franklin, it is worth noting, had seen a parodic treatment of the Bible. An ingenious but irreligious Dr Brown, whom he met during his youthful escape from apprenticeship to his older brother, 'wickedly undertook some years after to travesty the Bible in doggerel verse... By this means he set many of the facts in a very ridiculous light, and might have hurt weak minds if his work had been published: but it never was' (*Autobiography*, p. 74).

[3] Mordecai Richler, loosely retelling Christopher Sykes's already loose account, says 'Randolph only made it halfway before he slammed his Bible shut and exclaimed...' (Richler, 'Deuteronomy', in Rosenberg, p. 54, referring to Sykes, *Evelyn Waugh* (Harmondsworth: Penguin, 1977), p. 363).

[4] The end of the story is less suggestive. Over the next few days, escaping allied prisoners of war, told they would find a military mission commanded by the Prime Minister's son, found 'Churchill in bed, a cigar in one hand and a glass of *rakija* in the other, reading Lord Birkenhead's very large family Bible'. A week after the first diary entry, Waugh records that Birkenhead, 'having doubled his bet, is now anxious to win it, so that instead of purchasing a few hours' silence for my £10 I now have to endure an endless

as guineapig in a Bible-reading experiment, but it is a pity that nothing more of his reactions is recorded, not even at what point he bogged down.

To return to the matter in hand. Between the two extremes of those prejudiced against literature and those prejudiced against religion were many who kept their religion and their ordinary life distinct, a situation that can but does not necessarily produce hypocrisy. The seventeenth-century diarists John Evelyn (1620–1706) and Samuel Pepys (1633–1703) are useful here, for, although they record their lives intimately, they make almost no reference to religion or the Bible. Evelyn appears to have known the Bible quite well, but his diary gives no evidence of other than scholarly interest in old Bibles. If he read the Bible and had an opinion of it, he did not think this relevant for his diary. Pepys has only two relevant entries. In 1660 he had some silver bosses put on his Bible,[5] and three years later he writes that he collected 'several books ready bound for me; among others, the new Concordance of the Bible, which pleases me much, and is a book I hope to make good use of' (p. 200). It seems that he not only took pride in the possession of the Bible but also studied it. If his resolution of making good use of the concordance was not an idle one, the absence of further reference suggests that he kept his Bible reading and religion quite divorced from the everyday life and intrigue his diary revels in.

Samuel Johnson (1709–84), the foremost English literary critic of the eighteenth century, is a particularly helpful example of the way literature and religion can be kept apart, since he was both a literary and a religious man. Moreover, he was familiar with the work of most of the advocates of the literary quality of the Bible: his work had appeared in Husbands's miscellany, he wrote a life of Watts, knew the work of Dennis and Lowth, frequently cited the KJB in his dictionary,[6] and of course saw much of Boswell, who was very positive towards the Bible.

Johnson's separation of religion and literature is seen most clearly in his life of Milton:

Pleasure and terror are indeed the genuine sources of poetry; but poetical pleasure must be such as human imagination can at least conceive, and poetical terrors such as

campaign of interruption and banter, both reader and heckler drunk'. With the fortnight running out, 'Randolph got drunk at midday and abandoned his Bible reading' (*The Diaries of Evelyn Waugh*, ed. Michael Davie (London: Weidenfeld & Nicolson, 1976), pp. 591–3).
[5] *The Diary of Samuel Pepys*, ed. G. Gregory Smith (London: Macmillan, 1924), p. 54.
[6] See, for instance, *Boswell's Life of Johnson*, pp. 46, 382, 745, 1306.

human strength and fortitude may combat. The good and evil of eternity are too ponderous for the wings of wit; the mind sinks under them in passive helplessness, content with calm belief and humble adoration.[7]

Clearly he found it as impossible to respond with literary sensitivity to the sacred things of religion as to let his mind sink under literature in passive helplessness. Yet this was not an unthinking attitude. He objected to the presence of religious elements in literature on the grounds that they were incapable of evoking a literary response. Immediately prior to the opinion just noted, he writes of the religious truths in *Paradise Lost* that 'they have been taught to our infancy; they have mingled with our solitary thoughts and familiar conversation, and are habitually interwoven with the whole texture of life. Being therefore not new, they raise no unaccustomed emotion in the mind; what we knew before, we cannot learn; what is not unexpected, cannot surprise.'

Johnson values that in literature which is new, capable of raising an 'unaccustomed emotion in the mind', teaching and surprising. The truths of religion are so familiar that *for him* they lack this quality of newness (it is a sign of the degree to which he kept religion and literature apart that he never addresses the question of whether the literature that he has been familiar with all his life is aesthetically dead). Such an opinion might be revised if the reader is suddenly struck by something new in what had seemed fully familiar. One may call this an aesthetic or a religious experience (though the definition of 'religion' needs to be a wide one), as is suggested by the current Joycean use of 'epiphany'. The philosopher and psychologist William James makes this important if far from novel point thus:

> The simplest rudiment of mystical experience would seem to be that deepened sense of the significance of a maxim or formula which occasionally sweeps over one. 'I've heard that said all my life', we exclaim, 'but I never realized its full meaning until now.' 'When a fellow-monk', said Luther, 'one day repeated the words of the Creed: "I believe in the forgiveness of sins", I saw the Scripture in an entirely new light; and straightway I felt as if I were born anew. It was as if I had found the door of paradise thrown wide open.'[8]

Here James associates an experience of words with a religious experience. He goes on to argue that this experience 'is not confined to rational propositions', and then makes a key point about the arts:

[7] 'John Milton', in *Lives*, 1: 107,
[8] *The Varieties of Religious Experience* (1901–2; London: Collins, 1960), p. 369.

Most of us can remember the strangely moving power of passages in certain poems read when we were young, irrational doorways as they were through which the mystery of fact, the wilderness and the pang of life, stole into our hearts and thrilled them. The words have now perhaps become mere polished surfaces for us; but lyric poetry and music are alive and significant only in proportion as they fetch these vague vistas of a life continuous with our own, beckoning and inviting, yet ever eluding our pursuit. We are alive or dead to the eternal inner message of the arts according as we have kept or lost this mystical susceptibility.

When religious or literary experiences contain the elements of freshness and illumination, there is no real difference in kind between them, whatever the difference in degree may be. Religious *experience* and literary *experience* can be analogous. Whether they will in fact *be* analogous for an individual is a different and private thing. The separation of religion and literature can indicate a limitation, either in the individual in his or her response to one or the other, or in the quality of the religion or the literature.

Johnson of course knew the KJB, but when, at the age of fifty-six, he recommenced reading the Bible, he read predominantly in the Greek NT. In his will he left a Polyglot Bible, Mill's Greek Testament, Beza's Greek Testament, 'all my Latin Bibles', and a Greek Bible by Wechelius (Boswell, *Life*, p. 1381). Yet he was an advocate of biblical translation, in part because he was a scholar of languages and believed translations to be an excellent means of preserving language (pp. 374–5). In his preface to the dictionary (1755) he expresses the opinion that 'from the authors which rose in the time of Elizabeth, a speech might be formed adequate to all the purposes of use and elegance' (fol. c1 r), but gave the use of the KJB as being, with Hooker, the appropriate source for the language of theology. Following the preface he gives 'the history of the English language', which consists largely of examples. Among these is Luke 1 in the Anglo-Saxon and Wyclif's versions, prefaced by the following comment:

> Translations seldom afford just specimens of a language, and least of all those in which a scrupulous and verbal interpretation is endeavoured because they retain the phraseology and structure of the original tongue; yet they have often this convenience, that the same book, being translated in different ages, affords opportunity of marking the gradations of change, and bringing one age into comparison with another.   (Fol. D1 r)

This is perhaps the closest Johnson comes to giving his opinion on the language of English translations of the Bible as literature: he seems to take them as being literal and unnatural, and therefore not good models of the language, even if they are a good quarry for evidence of language change. He does not give Tyndale, the KJB or other later versions in his history, which suggests that he found other sources preferable as exemplars of the language after the fourteenth century.

In keeping with his separation of religion and literature, Johnson shows little sympathy with Dennis's argument that poetry is the necessary language of religion and that the best poetry must be religious. In his life of Watts he allowed that Watts showed the dissenters 'that zeal and purity might be expressed and enforced by polished diction', but still held that 'his devotional poetry is, like that of others, unsatisfactory. The paucity of its subjects enforces perpetual repetition, and the sanctity of the matter rejects the ornaments of figurative diction' (*Lives*, II: 296, 298). Again he is wary of associating literature and religion; here he also shows himself sharing Gell's sense (see volume 1, p. 262) that it is inappropriate to adorn religious truth.

Robert Lowth's *De Sacra Poesi Hebraeorum*

Johnson is a salutary side-track. The most substantial and significant figure in the history of the Bible as literature in the eighteenth century, arguably the most important critic after Johnson, Robert Lowth (1710–87), takes us in a quite opposite direction. For nine years he was the Oxford Professor of Poetry,[9] and later his eminence in the Church was such that he was offered the Archbishopric of Canterbury. His influence was wide and benevolent. Translators and scholars as different as Kennicott, Harwood, Geddes and Merrick[10] testify to the practical help, advice and encouragement he gave them,

[9] This, the first literary chair in England, was founded by Henry Birkhead and first occupied in 1708. Saintsbury gives a history of it through to the end of the nineteenth century (III: 615–29). It is a matter of minor pedantry that the chair of rhetoric and belles-lettres at Edinburgh, founded in 1762 and first held by Hugh Blair, is often claimed (by Scots especially) as the first chair of English. Neither chair was specifically concerned with English, but from the beginning the lectures at Edinburgh were in English. A Cambridge man may leave the alumni of the two schools to dispute the precedence with indifference.

[10] Lowth encouraged Kennicott to doubt the integrity of the Hebrew text. Kennicott writes that he 'became convinced in the year 1748 that our Hebrew text had suffered from transcribers at least as much as the copies of other ancient writings, and that there are now such corruptions in this sacred volume as affect the sense greatly in many instances. The particular chapter which extorted from me this conviction and which was benevolently recommended to my perusal for this very purpose by the Reverend Dr Lowth ... is' 2 Sam. 23 (*The Ten Annual Accounts of the Collation of Hebrew Mss of the Old Testament* (Oxford, 1770), p. 7). Harwood acknowledges his indebtedness to *De Sacra Poesi* and adds that Lowth 'condescended to offer me every assistance in his power' (*A New Introduction to the Study and Knowledge of the New Testament* (1767); 2nd edn, 2 vols. (London, 1773), pp. xxvii–xxviii). Geddes is warm in his memory of such assistance, even though he did not always agree with Lowth. He quotes Lowth's kindly note of

and his own work did more to shape ideas of biblical poetry and poetics than anyone's in the century. The influence continues: no discussion of the form of Hebrew poetry can proceed without reference to Lowth. From our point of view his work divides into two parts which span the most crucial period in the development of the KJB's literary reputation, the first and most substantial part being his greatest achievement, *De Sacra Poesi Hebraeorum Praelectiones*. This belongs with the many discussions of the originals as literature but nevertheless has significant, if varied, consequences for attitudes to the KJB. The less substantial part, his work on the English language and his opinions of the KJB, will need consideration later.

De Sacra Poesi Hebraeorum consists of thirty-four Latin lectures given in his capacity as the Oxford Professor of Poetry between 1741 and, at the latest, 1750. They were published in 1753, and the extensively annotated English translation by George Gregory, *Lectures on the Sacred Poetry of the Hebrews* (1787), continued to be published until 1847.[11] Moreover, the chief arguments were repeated and, in some instances, developed, in his highly respected *Isaiah* (1778). Perhaps the greatest immediate importance of the lectures lay in their choice and valuation of their subject. Lowth's exhortation at the very end of the lectures to the Oxford students to pursue Hebraic studies makes the crucial point:

> consider it as a work worthy of your utmost exertions to illustrate and cultivate this department of literature. You will find it no less elegant and agreeable than useful and instructive, abounding in information no less curious for its extent and variety than for its great importance and venerable sanctity, deserving the attention of every liberal mind, essential to all who would be proficients in theology .   (II: 434)

Thirty-four lectures composed with a scholarship and elegance that must

encouragement for the manuscript of his *Prospectus*, 'which he has read with some care and attention, and with the fullest approbation ... he doubts not but it will give universal satisfaction. He cannot help wishing that Dr Geddes would publish it...' (*Address to the Public* (London, 1793), pp. 7–8). Earlier Geddes had written of Lowth that 'never were the gentleman, the scholar, the grammarian and the theologue more happily united' (*Prospectus*, p. 99). Merrick, the most minor of these figures, composed *The Psalms, translated or paraphrased in English verse* (Reading, 1765). Lowth, 'having read a part of the work, was pleased to express a desire of seeing the whole' (fol. A2 r), and offered advice and revisions. The last work in which he had a personal hand was Thomas Wintle's *Daniel, an improved version* (Oxford, 1792), for which he designed the plan (p. ii).

11 Gregory translated from Lowth's revised edition with notes by the German scholar J. D. Michaelis. The lectures were also published in monthly instalments in *The Christian's Magazine* in 1767 and Hugh Blair gave a brief account of some of the key ideas (mixed with some original examples), in lecture XLI of his popular *Lectures on Rhetoric and Belles Lettres* (1783).

have appealed to all who heard or read them[12] constituted a discovery of 'a few of the more delightful retreats of this paradise' (ii: 435), and an argument for the supremacy of the Hebraic poetry of unparalleled thoroughness. They are a milestone in the long history of preference for the Bible over the classics. What had been a minority, shakily founded opinion became a demonstrated truth for many. Moreover, the demonstration that large parts of the OT were of great literary quality and susceptible to rational literary criticism set a seal on the growing literary sense of the Bible. Lowth finished the work of critics such as Blackwall, making it all but impossible for the unprejudiced not to think of the Bible as a literary as well as a religious work. None of the translators and few of the annotators in the latter part of the century could work without recognising that they were dealing with literary as well as sacred texts, and in some of them this recognition was paramount.

Even to make these two points about Lowth is to show at once that there is continuity as well as originality in *De Sacra Poesi Hebraeorum*. Many of its attitudes and points are old. To begin with, it seems to reinforce the old prejudice that only poetry is worth consideration as literature, and the opening lecture is a standard Augustan exposition of the nature of poetry: its object is utility, its means pleasure (i: 6–7). But, if pleasure is subservient to moral purpose, it is the pleasure that most interests Lowth:

> For what is a poet destitute of harmony, of grace and of all that conduces to allurement and delight? or how should we derive advantage or improvement from an author whom no man of taste can endure to read? The reason, therefore, why poetry is so studious to embellish her precepts with a certain inviting sweetness ... is plainly by such seasoning to conciliate favour to her doctrines... (i: 10)

This is the old ornamental theory of poetry, and at once he speaks of 'all the decorations of elegance' (i: 11). One might expect Lowth to be about to continue the sixteenth- and seventeenth-century search for classical figures in the Scriptures, but his description of criticism suggests something different. First, it is 'a particular department of science' (i: 4): the suggestion of scientific method is apt, for one of the characteristics of the lectures is the 'cautious

---

[12] Their reputation is shown by the *Monthly Review*'s comment on the occasion of the publication of the translation that 'the well-earned celebrity of Bishop Lowth's *Lectures* renders any commendation of them on the present occasion superfluous, if not impertinent' (78 (April 1788), 311). Gibbon also gives memorable testimony. Amid his scathing attack on the indolence and intellectual poverty to be found at the English universities, he pauses to describe what lectures should be, and adds, 'I observe with pleasure that in the university of Oxford Dr Lowth, with equal eloquence and erudition, has executed this task in his incomparable *Praelections* on the poetry of the Hebrews' (*Memoirs of My Life*, ed. Betty Radice (Harmondsworth: Penguin, 1984), p. 79).

reserve' (II: 311) with which Lowth examines his evidence. Suggestions of scientific method continue in his description of the high value of criticism:

> Nothing surely can be more worthy of a liberal and accomplished mind than to perceive what is perfect and what is defective in an art, the beauties of which frequently lie beneath the surface; to understand what is graceful, what is becoming, in what its excellencies consist, and in a word to discover and relish those delicate touches of grace and elegance that lie beyond the reach of vulgar apprehension. From these subtle researches after beauty and taste there is also the fairest reason to apprehend that the judgement itself will receive some accessions of strength and acuteness which it may successfully employ upon other objects and upon other occasions.
>
> (I: 5)

This is the patrician voice of Augustanism, immensely confident of the value of criticism and obviously looking to the establishment of rules of taste. The pursuit of the aesthetic is a worthy occupation in itself, but, like poetry, it has its utility. If this seems unexciting, at least Lowth is, as so often, candid that he is repeating the ideas of another, in this instance the founder of the Oxford lectures on poetry, Henry Birkhead. What leaves open the possibility of something quite different from the quest for figures is the insistence on discovering excellencies without pre-defining what an excellency is.

The point is developed crucially in the second lecture. Lowth declares in his own authentic voice that, 'as in all other branches of science, so in poetry art or theory consists in a certain knowledge derived from the careful observation of nature' (I: 45), and he insists that rules come from art, not art from rules. Moreover, if we are to understand the power of art 'in exciting the human affections ... we must consider what those affections are and by what means they are to be excited' (ibid.). His scientific criticism, then, is not only to be deductive but to have a foundation in psychology.

To return to the first lecture: Lowth's idea of poetry seems to be based on the classics and is high to the point of absurdity – the dominion of the Caesars would have been ended once for all if the killers of Caesar had spoken poetry of quality to the people after the Ides of March (I: 26). Now, however, perhaps with a glance at the Puritan distrust of literature, he makes a turn reminiscent of Dennis: 'but after all we shall think more humbly of poetry than it deserves unless we direct our attention to that quarter where its importance is most eminently conspicuous, unless we contemplate it as employed on sacred subjects and in subservience to religion' (I: 36). Here he seems to be one of those who argue from content to quality. He is at once an aesthete and a religious moralist, an open-minded investigator and a representative of the old positions.

The period he worked in is one of important development in ideas of the originals as literature and fundamental change in ideas of the KJB. The seemingly contradictory attributes he displays place him as the perfect representative of this time.

Lowth repeats the familiar views that the original purpose of poetry was religious and that only when serving this purpose does it appear 'to shine forth with all its natural splendour, or rather to be animated by that inspiration which on other occasions is spoken of without being felt' (1: 36). As is evident elsewhere, he does not distinguish between divine and poetic inspiration,[13] though he does allow individuality to the sacred authors and always treats the writings as if they are human productions (1: 347). He holds two other old views, that oldest is best and that biblical poetry is superior to classical poetry; these come out as he claims that his observations on poetry and religion

> are remarkably exemplified in the Hebrew Poetry, than which the human mind can conceive nothing more elevated, more beautiful or more elegant; in which the almost ineffable sublimity of the subject is fully equalled by the energy of the language and the dignity of the style. And it is worthy observation that as some of these writings exceed in antiquity the fabulous ages of Greece, in sublimity they are superior to the most finished productions of that polished people. (1: 37)

Here is yet another familiar notion, sublimity. Just as it transformed the old rhetorical ideas of writing (ideas we have seen still alive in Lowth's thinking), so it is a key to how Lowth will transform his compendious baggage of received ideas. He remarks in a footnote to lecture 14 concerning Burke's distinction between the beautiful and the sublime that 'after all that has been said, our feelings must be the only criterion' (1: 302), and this, out of context, summarises how his idea of sublimity operates: he works from the intensity of his feelings. Though we have often seen the ideas in the passage just given issue from theory rather than feeling, in Lowth they issue from the deepest conviction: he loves the sacred poetry with a passion second to none, and everywhere the lectures tell of this love. If this is a prejudice, still it is open-eyed, and one old idea that he does not share is of the total undifferentiated perfection of the Scriptures. His critical empiricism forbids this. Hebrew poetry is the best, but is uniform neither in kind nor in achievement.

In such ways Lowth begins to build for his lectures a framework redolent of Augustanism and received ideas, yet containing promise of something new

---

[13] One of the proofs he offers for the connection between prophecy and poetry is that 'they had one common name, one common origin, one common author, the Holy Spirit' (11: 18).

even in its repetition of the old: he will develop old ideas so methodically, fully and intelligently that some of them become new. What is most striking about this opening is that, more than any other work we have yet seen, it enforces an aesthetic approach: if harmony and grace and all that conduces to allurement and delight are essential to poetry, then biblical poetry, being the best, must show them at their best. The lectures are indeed to be a 'subtle research after beauty and taste'.

Lowth's taste is principally for the sublime. He never tackles the relationship between sublimity and his sense of the utility of poetry as philosophy in pleasing dress. Indeed, as soon as he starts to consider the origin of poetry, ideas of utility disappear into the background:

> The origin and first use of poetical language are undoubtedly to be traced into the vehement affections of the mind. For what is meant by that singular frenzy of poets which the Greeks, ascribing to divine inspiration, distinguished by the appellation of 'enthusiasm', but a style and expression directly prompted by nature itself and exhibiting the true and express image of a mind violently agitated? when, as it were, the secret avenues, the interior recesses of the soul are thrown open, when the inmost conceptions are displayed, rushing together in one turbid stream, without order or connection.
>
> (1: 79)

'The inmost conceptions' this poetry displays were religious conceptions. The attitude here is thoroughly Longinian, and Lowth acknowledges Longinus when he turns explicitly to the sublime. Sublimity is 'that force of composition, whatever it be, which strikes and overpowers the mind, which excites the passions and which expresses ideas at once with perspicuity and elevation, not solicitous whether the language be plain or ornamented, refined or familiar' (1: 307). Passion and poetry belong together, and sublimity is the essence of poetry. It comes from and works on the passions. He draws this distinction, echoing what we have already read:

> The language of reason is cool, temperate, rather humble than elevated, well arranged and perspicuous, with an evident care and anxiety lest any thing should escape which might appear perplexed or obscure. The language of the passions is totally different: the conceptions burst out in a turbid stream, expressive in a manner of the internal conflict; the more vehement break out in hasty confusion, they catch, without search or study, whatever is impetuous, vivid or energetic. In a word, reason speaks literally, the passions poetically.
>
> (1: 309)

Though the way the point is made sounds thoroughly mid eighteenth century, the idea itself looks so far forward that we can find D. H. Lawrence expressing it in 1918 as if it is new:

> free verse is ... direct utterance from the instant, whole man. It is the soul and the

mind and body surging at once, nothing left out. They speak all together. There is some confusion, some discord. But the confusion and the discord only belong to the reality as noise belongs to the plunge of water ... in free verse we look for the insurgent naked throb of the instant moment.[14]

The image of a turbid stream or the plunge of water is the same, as is the fascination with the passions of the moment and the acceptance of confusion in the form of the utterance. Lowth and Lawrence have in common a high sense of the value of revealing the true feelings of a moment and an awareness that the appropriate form of expression differs from accepted poetic standards. The latter point must be returned to; for now it is enough to see the fundamental tendency of Lowth's idea of the sublime, and how fine the dividing line is in his work between the derivative, the typically Augustan, and something very modern.

One of the most striking aspects of the *Lectures* is that they drastically widen the sense of poetry in the OT. Until now the poetic parts had been reckoned to be the Psalms, the Song of Songs, the bulk of Job, the various interposed poems from Moses' song (Exodus 15) on, including a few passages from the Prophets such as Habakkuk 3, and, sometimes, Proverbs. The Prophets in general, if they were considered in literary terms, had been thought of as orators – Ambrose Ussher had called them the 'most perfect orators and the very prime' (see volume 1, p. 216). Lowth extended poetry to include the Prophets,[15] and devoted lecture 18 to arguing that 'the writings of the Prophets [are] in general poetical'. Indeed, he gives 'the first rank' (II: 4) among the kinds of Hebrew poetry to the prophetic, and in many places declares that Isaiah is 'the first of all poets for sublimity and eloquence' (I: 166; see particularly II: 84–7). There is no need to follow his arguments closely: as he remarks in lecture 18, the many examples he has already given demonstrate the point (II: 4). The arguments depend on the nature of the language, historical evidence about the Prophets, the fact that Hebrews used the same word for a prophet, a poet and a musician (II: 14), and the very effect of the Prophets. Lowth observes that all the arguments he had used at the outset for the presence of metre in Hebrew poetry are applicable to the Prophets save only the argument from the alphabetic poems, and the aside he makes at this point clearly demonstrates why he assigns the prophetic poetry first place: 'such an artificial arrangement' as alphabetic

---

[14] 'Poetry of the present' (1918); in Vivian de Sola Pinto and Warren Roberts, eds., *The Complete Poems of D. H. Lawrence* (London: Heinemann, 1964), pp. 184–5.

[15] Kugel has called this 'Lowth's great contribution' (p. 172), which is to overstate the case. Roston writes that 'the realisation that Isaiah did, in fact, write in poetry, and that his poetry was filled with passion, fire and moral vision, gave to the preromantics that model for which they had been searching' (p. 13). *Prophet and Poet* is of general interest here.

poetry, he argues, 'would be utterly repugnant to the nature of prophecy; it is plainly the effect of study and diligence, not of the imagination and enthusiasm [the very word he had used for inspiration]; a contrivance to assist the memory, not to affect the passions' (II: 10–11). The prophetic poetry fits most closely with his preference for the sublime.

Lowth's arguments are scholarly and persuasive, but still more persuasive is the first thing he referred to, his multiplication of examples. They are eloquent in themselves and are given with such evident love. But, strong as the examples are, Lowth's discussion of them is not. He only occasionally rises to good close commentary, and indeed he notes in this same lecture that 'it was my wish and intention rather to point out and recommend to your own consideration, than minutely to investigate and explain' (II: 3). Often his commentary consists of the same exclamation at beauties that we saw from critics such as Blackwall, and his remark on Gen. 1: 3, that 'the understanding quickly comprehends the divine power from the effect, and perhaps most completely when it is not attempted to be explained' (I: 350), is only a pale reflection of Boileau.

Another important general argument connects closely with Lowth's positive idea of confusion as an aspect of poetic sublimity. Throughout *De Sacra Poesi Hebraeorum* Lowth adheres to his father's point 'that it is requisite for the perfect understanding of [any book] that men should be acquainted with the idioms and proprieties of the original language and the customs and notions which were generally received at the time when it was written' (above, p. 24). By insisting that 'we must see all things with their eyes, estimate all things by their opinions; we must endeavour as much as possible to read Hebrew as the Hebrews would have read it' (I: 113), the younger Lowth was not only establishing a major point about the need for a historical imagination but setting the foundation for the new standards that we have just observed. Several times he warns his audience against the error 'of accounting vulgar, mean or obscure passages which were probably accounted among the most perspicuous and sublime by the people to whom they were addressed' (I: 167), so cajoling his audience to accept his idea of Hebraic literary taste. Augustan standards are neither the only ones nor the best ones, he is telling the next generation of youth 'addicted to the politer sciences and studious of the elegancies of composition' (I: 51). There is of course an element of faith in this move – the Hebrews must have felt this way and, implicitly, their judgement must have been the best – but it is essentially healthy and sane.

The emphasis on historical imagination is highly important, but even more important for the development of taste and for changing attitudes to the KJB is the way Lowth uses what was pejorative language. He has just juxtaposed the kind of language often used for the KJB's English – 'vulgar, mean' – with key Augustan words for literary excellence. His frequent acknowledgement of passages in the Bible which 'appear to us harsh and unusual, I had almost said unnatural and barbarous' (1: 321) turns such terms into something like praise. This is only due in part to his arguing, as others had done before him, for the effectiveness of such apparently bad writing; he has this to say of Jer. 25: 30 and Hos. 13: 7–8: 'from ideas which in themselves appear coarse, unsuitable and totally unworthy of so great an object, the mind naturally recedes, and passes suddenly to the contemplation of the object itself and of its inherent magnitude and importance' (1: 364).

In part his transformation of such terms is due to the way he uses them. In one of the best pieces of close demonstration Lowth has to offer, Job 3: 3 is compared with Jer. 20: 14–15. Just to write that 'the meaning is the same, nor is there any very great difference in the phraseology, but Jeremiah fills up the ellipses, smoothes and harmonises the rough and uncouth language of Job' (1: 315), in the context of a preference for the Job passage ('the Hebrew literature itself contains nothing more poetical' (1: 313)) is to give 'rough and uncouth' a new meaning.

The *Lectures* are best remembered for their exposition of parallelism. Though Lowth does not develop this until quite late, it grows out of the first subject he treats in detail, not the metre of Hebrew poetry but the fact that the poetry is metrical. The distinction is typical of his caution. His opening observation, 'that scarcely any real knowledge of the Hebrew versification is now to be obtained' (1: 52), is not a prelude to yet another attempt on the secret of Hebrew verse, but exactly what it appears, a statement of limitations he will stay within. He has the highest opinion of the importance of metre, so it is important to him to show that the Hebrew poetry was metrical even if he cannot recover the secret. Here he argues from theory to literature rather than the other way round:

> But since it appears essential to every species of poetry that it be confined to numbers and consist of some kind of verse (for indeed, wanting this, it would not only want its most agreeable attributes but would scarcely deserve the name of poetry), in treating of the poetry of the Hebrews it appears absolutely necessary to demonstrate that those parts at least of the Hebrew writings which we term poetic are in metrical form. (1: 56)

Once he has satisfied himself of this he has, of course, established one area in which the originals are necessarily more beautiful than can now be appreciated. This idea, again a familiar one, is frequently apparent in the lectures, and he constantly writes of lost beauties. So, having shown parts of the Song of Songs than which 'nothing can ... be imagined more truly elegant and poetical', he adds that 'the discovery of these excellencies ... only serves to increase our regret for the many beauties which we have lost, the perhaps superior graces which extreme antiquity seems to have overcast with an impenetrable shade' (II: 340). This is not his typical method, but it does permit him and his audience to assume that whatever can be demonstrated scientifically is yet less than what was originally there. The poetry was indeed metrical but 'he who attempts to restore the true and genuine Hebrew versification erects an edifice without a foundation' (I: 67). And what can be demonstrated is the form of the sentences. Here is how he embarks on what he is later to call parallelism:

> as the poems divide themselves in a manner spontaneously into periods, for the most part equal, so the periods themselves are divided into verses, most commonly couplets, though frequently of greater length. This is chiefly observable in those passages which frequently occur in the Hebrew poetry in which they treat one subject in many different ways, and dwell upon the same sentiment; when they express the same thing in different words, or different things in a similar form of words; when equals refer to equals, and opposites to opposites: and since this artifice of composition seldom fails to produce even in prose an agreeable and measured cadence, we can scarcely doubt that it must have imparted to their poetry, were we masters of the versification, an exquisite degree of beauty and grace.   (I: 68–9)

Lowth does not develop the discussion here; rather, he adds a comment on the translatability of the poetry that appears, in Gregory's translation, to refer to the KJB:

> a poem translated literally from the Hebrew into the prose of any other language, whilst the same forms of the sentences remain, will still retain, even as far as relates to versification, much of its native dignity, and a faint appearance of versification. This is evident in our common version of the Scriptures, where frequently
>
> > 'The order chang'd, and verse from verse disjoin'd,
> > 'Yet still the poet's scattered limbs we find.'   (I: 71)

The original Latin for 'in our common version of the Scriptures' is simply 'in vernacula' (p. 32). The idea has major implications for appreciation of the KJB as a representation of the original poetry, but Lowth himself did not make the point until much later.

The observation of parallelism and the realisation of its implications for literal translations are no more original than was the description of criticism in the first lecture. Fleury and Calmet had already pointed to parallelism (above, pp. 22–3), and Lowth knew some of Calmet's work, but there is another, older source which only now makes its appearance in an English environment, the *Meor Enajim* (1574) of Rabbi Azarias de Rubeis (or Azariah dei Rossi).[16] Lowth quotes him as an authority for the point about translation in a footnote, and later, again as an authority, for his main discussion of parallelism (II: 54–6). He reserves the fullest discussion of Azarias for *Isaiah* (pp. xxxiii–xli – it is to these pages that anyone wanting a full account of Azarias's views should turn), noting that he 'has treated of the ancient Hebrew versification upon principles similar to those above proposed, and partly coincident with them' (p. xxxiii). The principles are similar but not identical, and Lowth concludes by distinguishing the essential difference between himself and the Rabbi:

> I agree therefore with Azarias in his general principle of a rhythmus of things, but, instead of considering terms or phrases or senses in single lines as measures, determining the nature and denomination of the verse as dimeter, trimeter or tetrameter, I consider only that relation and proportion of one verse to another which arises from the correspondence of terms and from the form of construction, from whence results a rhythmus of propositions and a harmony of sentences.   (P. xl)

Here he defines not only the essence of his own view but the relation his work has with the past: he has read widely and judiciously, he has no wish to claim undeserved originality, he is willing to allow others' views to play against his own, but, crucially, he is capable of building on what he has received, overturning old standards and establishing new ones. Because parallelism is a necessary characteristic of Hebrew poetry, it is a beauty rather than 'a superfluous and tiresome repetition', as it would seem by any other standards. Here is how he puts the point:

> Each language possesses a peculiar genius and character on which depend the principles of the versification, and in a great measure the style or colour of the poetic diction. In Hebrew the frequent or rather perpetual splendour of the sentences and the accurate recurrence of the clauses seem absolutely necessary to distinguish the verse, so that what in any other language would appear a superfluous and tiresome repetition, in this cannot be omitted without injury to the poetry.   (I: 101)

The primary exposition of parallelism comes in lecture 19. There he writes that

> The poetical conformation of the sentences, which has been so often alluded to as characteristic of Hebrew poetry, consists chiefly in a certain equality, resemblance, or parallelism between the members of each period; so that in two lines (or members of

---

[16] Kugel notes that there is a tradition behind this work (p. 172), but Lowth sees Azariah's views as original.

the same period) things for the most part shall answer to things, and words to words, as if fitted to each other by a kind of rule or measure. This parallelism has much variety and many gradations; it is sometimes more accurate and manifest, sometimes more vague and obscure.   (II: 34)

Three kinds are distinguished, synonymous, the commonest, in which 'the same sentiment is repeated in different but equivalent terms' (II: 35), antithetic, in which 'a thing is illustrated by its contrary being opposed to it' (II: 45), and 'synthetic or constructive parallelism', 'in which the sentences answer to each other not by the iteration of the same image or sentiment, or the opposition of their contraries, but merely by the form of construction' (II: 48–9); this last is confessedly a catch-all category, covering anything that does not fit into the first two. There is nothing rigid in all this; as he makes explicit in *Isaiah*, 'sometimes the parallelism is more, sometimes less exact, sometimes hardly at all apparent' (p. xx). He is as flexible as his material warrants in his description of the categories (indeed, too flexible for some such as George Buchanan Gray, who reanalyses synthetic parallelism,[17] but then it is characteristic that he errs on the side of caution). Antithetic parallelism, for instance, 'is not confined to any particular form, for sentiments are opposed to sentiments, words to words, singulars to singulars, plurals to plurals, etc.' (II: 45), and the point is confirmed with a persuasive variety of examples.

'Sometimes hardly at all apparent' raises a major point often forgotten in restatements and revisions of Lowth. It must be painfully apparent to anyone who has tried to read the poetic parts of the K JB using parallelism as a guide to the true form that it is often no help. But to try to read this way is to apply Lowth's ideas simplistically, as if what he had really said was that 'the unvarying element in the Hebrew poetry is the constant balance of lines of about equal length' (Gardiner, p. 109). He not only admits that there are places where parallelism is hardly apparent, but suggests that parallelism may work over larger structures than simple pairs, and these larger structures may involve unparalleled lines. There may be triplet parallelisms in which 'the second line is generally synonymous with the first, whilst the third either begins the period or concludes it, and frequently refers to both the preceding' (II: 42). Next he observes that 'in stanzas (if I may so call them) of five lines, the nature of which is nearly similar, the line that is not parallel is generally placed between the two distichs'. He gives Isa. 31: 4 as an example:

> Like as the lion growleth,
> Even the young lion over his prey;

[17] *The Forms of Hebrew Poetry* (1915; New York: Ktav, 1972).

Though the whole company of shepherds be called together
                              against him:
At their voice he will not be terrified,
Nor at their tumult will he be humbled.   (ii: 42–3)

The pattern is less obvious in the K JB, but we may let that pass. Lowth does not explore the implications of this pattern (and so perhaps contributes to the simplification of his ideas). Nevertheless, if there are unparalleled lines, and parts of the poetry where parallelism is not apparent, it would seem that parallelism is not to be found everywhere in the poetry: consequently parallelism cannot be taken as the general system it is often thought of as being.

While this suggests that some of the poetry has no perceptible form, the idea of stanzas suggests larger units of form. Lowth points out one other stanza-like pattern, groups of four lines with alternate parallelisms, like a quatrain rhyming ABAB, and then, once more, leaves things tantalisingly in the air. He goes no further in *Isaiah*. How often, one might ask, does what could be called couplet parallelism simply break down, and how often, and in what ways, is it developed into more sophisticated structures? The questions go to the heart of the sense of formal artistry in Hebrew poetry. As such, they are likely to be answered according to the critic's willingness or unwillingness to discover such artistry. At least two critics, John Jebb in the mid nineteenth century, and Richard Moulton at the end of that century, were willing, and their conclusions will be seen later. No one has taken the opposite line: Lowth's ideas of parallelism have proved to be so generally helpful for appreciation of the poetry that, however much his analysis of the kinds of parallelism may have been questioned, the fundamental observation has not been. The seed of doubt sown by the suggestion of unparalleled lines and of parts where parallelism is hardly apparent has fallen on stony ground.

Lowth thought that parallelism might 'appear light and trifling to some persons, and utterly undeserving any labour or attention'; this is his answer:

> let them remember that nothing can be of greater avail to the proper understanding of any writer than a previous acquaintance with both his general character and the peculiarities of his style and manner of writing; let them recollect that translators and commentators have fallen into errors upon no account more frequently than for want of attention to this article; and indeed I scarcely know any subject which promises more copiously to reward the labour of such as are studious of sacred criticism than this one in particular.   (ii: 57)

Parallelism certainly seemed, like other systems, to be a tool for textual scholarship,[18] and we can go beyond Lowth's reminder of the importance of the character and manner of the writing. Unlike previous attempts on the secret of Hebrew verse, Lowth's description of parallelism is sufficiently cautious to be applicable to most of the poetry (and to some of the prose, though he does not proceed so far). Now something of the formal artistry of the poetry was open to all. Moreover, it was artistry that could be perceived to some extent in literal translation, and this opened the door to new appreciation of such translations. It also provided a basis for a new idea of translation: the Hebrew poetry might be most literally translated by combining fidelity to its words with fidelity to the one aspect of its poetic form that remained apparent.[19] It could appear as poetry without adopting the alien ornaments of neo-classical verse. Where Say had hinted at the possibility of seeing the prose of the KJB as free verse, Lowth, in his version of Isaiah, introduced free verse into English. As we shall see, a number of translators followed his example in the short term, and the many modern versions that give the poetry the appearance of poetic form owe something to Lowth. What is more, in one narrow area of poetry, Lowth broke the mould of English verse and anticipated the verse of Whitman and Lawrence. And he did this not by being an avant-garde radical but by pursuing the implications of his cautious scholarship.

In lecture 27 Lowth links parallelism, sublimity and translations. 'Brevity of diction', he argues, is 'conducive to sublimity of style' (II: 250), and this brevity is everywhere evident in the poetry. Yet it goes with a copiousness and fullness.

---

[18] Lowth is explicit in *Isaiah*: 'it will be of great use ... and will often lead ... into the meaning of obscure words and phrases; sometimes it will suggest the true reading where the text in our present copies is faulty, and will verify and confirm a correction offered on the authority of MSS or of the ancient versions' (p. xxx). Le Clerc had been much less cautious about the potential of his own system, claiming that difficult passages in the poetry could be reconstructed according to his principles so that 'the sense of them becomes not only fine and clear, but also the rhyme very good' ('Essay upon critics', p. 299). In recent times Bishop Francis Hare had produced a system of Hebrew metre in the 'dissertatione de antiqua Hebraeorum poesi' prefaced to his *Psalmorum Liber in Versiculos Metrice Divisus* (London, 1736; reprinted in Ugolino). This openly looked back to Le Clerc, Meibomius and Gomarus. Lowth himself confuted it (*Lectures*, II: 436–46). The Hebraist William Green thought that Hare's system would 'clear up more difficulties in the poetical parts of Scripture than all other helps without it put together' (*The Song of Deborah Reduced to Metre* (Cambridge, 1753), p. iv), and he maintained this view even after Lowth had dealt with Hare (*Poetical Parts of the Old Testament* (Cambridge, 1781), p. vi). The most convenient English summary of Hare's theories is to be found in the introduction to Thomas Edwards's *A New English Translation of the Psalms* (Cambridge, 1755).

[19] 'But this strict attention to the form and fashion of the composition ... is ... useful and even necessary in the translator who is ambitious of preserving in his copy the force and spirit and elegance of the original' (*Isaiah*, p. xxx).

Part of the effect of parallelism is that the Hebrew poets 'amplify by diversifying, by repeating, and sometimes by adding to the subject; therefore it happens that it is frequently, on the whole, treated rather diffusely, but still every sentence is concise and nervous in itself. Thus it happens in general that neither copiousness nor vigour is wanting.' He adds that 'the most literal versions therefore commonly fail in this respect, and consequently still less is to be expected from any poetical translations or imitations whatever' (II: 251). This is sharp. The *Lectures* constantly suggest the need for translation that responds to the literary character of the texts and so, on the surface, are close to the desires of all the translators who attempted to match their notions of the original beauties with contemporary beauties, invariably expanding and regularising the originals. Such translators of course applied their own standards of elegance. Lowth is suggesting that the true way to achieve the end of an appropriately effective literary translation is to match the parallelistic brevity of the originals. Prose translations such as the KJB might match the brevity and retain, as he had noted earlier, 'a faint appearance of versification' (I: 71), but his ideal of translation is to couple the literal brevity with a clear appearance of versification that reveals the parallelism. He was to give the world an example with *Isaiah* in 1778. In the mean time his ideas filtered slowly through to translators. The chief of them was the conviction that the Bible could not be translated without a sense that it was literature as well as truth.

Uncouth, harsh and obsolete

Anthony Purver and archaic words

For a century and a half following the making of the KJB, the field of biblical translation was dominated by versifiers. Verse translation did not stop, but in the latter half of the eighteenth century prose versions break this domination. Important among the many reasons for this was a shift in critical focus from Sternhold and Hopkins to the KJB. Battles similar to those that had been fought over the Psalter were now fought over the much more vital territory of the whole English Bible, and the army that had lost a campaign if not a war by the time of the Restoration, and then had begun to rumble distantly in the first half of the eighteenth century, took on substantial proportions. In its vanguard were the makers of new versions: they had to attack the KJB to justify their efforts. Yet it was a peculiar war, for the attacks in due course conceded more and more to certain strengths in the KJB.

The KJB's increasing age was its greatest weakness yet also one of its strengths. Study of the Greek and Hebrew texts had advanced. Scholars believed they had a better understanding of the texts and that they had improved on the texts available to the KJB translators. Moreover, much of their scholarship now involved the explicit literary awareness of the texts that Lowth did so much to foster. The question was not just whether the KJB had translated the truest texts but whether it was accurate in the sense of being an appropriate rendering of the literary characteristics of the originals. Yet advances in scholarship were as nothing compared to the continuation of the Augustans' sense of improvements in the English language. The arguments about the KJB's language had been foreshadowed by the attacks on Sternhold and Hopkins, by Nary's complaints about Gregory Martin's language, Wells's complaints of the uncouthness, harshness and incomprehensibility of the KJB, and, on the other side, by Pope and Swift suggesting that the language was not only venerated but becoming 'a kind of standard' (above, p. 40). But such foreshadowings give little idea of the detail and interest of the criticism that was to come, especially in the 1760s: that decade produced the most fascinating criticism of the language of the KJB ever to appear.

The central figure is one of only two men who made complete independent English versions of the Bible in this century, Anthony Purver (1702–77).[20] Prefaced to this work is a discussion of principles of translation that includes both detailed hostile criticism of the KJB's English and substantial lists of faulty words and phrases. Since Purver is almost totally forgotten (he is rarely granted notice in histories of English Bible translation), came from a very different background from most of the scholars of the Bible, and received, at

---

[20] The other, who signs himself J. M. Ray but seems to have been one David Macrae (1750–1816), licentiate preacher of the Church of Scotland (Herbert, p. 320), deserves only a footnote, in spite of all his eccentric labours. The full title gives some sense of the work: *Revised Translation and Interpretation of the Sacred Scriptures, after the eastern manner, from concurrent authorities of the critics, interpreters and commentators, copies and versions; showing that the inspired writings contain the seeds of the valuable sciences, being the source whence the ancient philosophers derived them; also the most ancient histories and greatest antiquities: with a philosophical and medical commentary; the use of the commentary is not to give the sense of the text, as that is done in the interpretation, but to describe the works of nature, showing the connection of natural science with revealed religion.* In the preface to the second edition (Glasgow, 1815), dated 1802, Ray tells how he has cleared the Bible of absurdities and obscurities, and so reconciled many deists to the Bible (p. iii; for an account of deistic objections to the Bible in this time, see below, pp. 124ff.); he also tells – quite unconvincingly, given the appalling obscurity with which he writes – of his 'great delicacy of expression', which is intended to remove the aversion to the Bible of youths of unprincipled minds (p. iv). He is yet another of the translators to refer frequently to Lowth, and there are a number of remarks on the superiority of the Scriptures as literature to all other writing in both the preface and the notes: the reader who struggles sufficiently with the preface will find, for instance, that 'there is no book or history, real or romantic, so entertaining and instructive as the Bible, or that has so great a variety' (p. iv).

best, a mixed press in his own time, his credentials need establishing before this
important material is discussed. He was from neither the upper classes nor the
universities (not that either guarantees soundness). Like Bunyan, Purver was an
artisan. While apprenticed as a shoemaker in Hampshire, he read Fisher's
Rusticus ad Academicos and found himself called and commanded by the divine
Spirit to translate the Scriptures. He became a Quaker and an occasional
teacher; he studied Hebrew, Chaldee, Syriac, Greek, Latin and, probably, other
languages, and he read as widely as anyone in biblical translations and in
scholarly (including Rabbinic) and literary commentary on the Bible. From
about 1733 he laboured at his translation, finishing it in 1763. A year later it was
published in two volumes as *A New and Literal Translation of all the Books of the
Old and New Testament*, but became known as the Quakers' Bible. He did not
depend on scholarship alone, for, 'on arriving at a difficult passage, he would
shut himself up for two or three days and nights, waiting for inspiration. He
accepted the theory of the divine inspiration of the scriptures in its most literal
form' (*DNB*). He was, then, an exceptionally industrious autodidact, but not,
on the face of it, a person to whom one should give unreserved credence.

Certainly his contemporaries were reserved. John Seddon, a staff member of
the dissenting academy at Warrington, was the least unsympathetic in a notice
for the *Monthly Review*, observing 'no small share of erudition. This is a work to
which we should have thought very few individuals equal, however great and
extensive their abilities: and we cannot help admiring the man who hath had
intrepidity enough to attempt it' (32 (March 1765), 194). This is praise for the
attempt rather than the result. The *Critical Review*, in a lengthy two part article,[21]
also managed to praise the attempt and the use of the Masoretic text, but
otherwise panned the result. All the critics who discuss Purver at all deplore his
English as it appears in this 'rude, incondite and unshapely pile, without order,
symmetry or taste'.[22] Even the mildly sympathetic Seddon remarks that 'some
passages ... lead us to hope he is better acquainted with [the original languages]
than he seems to be with his native tongue, in which he is often ungrammatical,
improper and obscure' (p. 203). The *Critical Review* reasonably connects this
with his criticisms of the KJB's English, and later John Symonds fills out the
point:

> It might well be expected that so desperate a critic should be perfectly skilled in his
> native tongue, but the following specimens of his taste will show that he boldly
> usurped a province for which he was totally unqualified. Matt. 5: 22: 'blockhead'.

---

[21] Vol. 19 (April, May 1765), 241–50; 331–9.
[22] Geddes, *Prospectus*, p. 97.

Mark 8: 11: 'began *to query* with him'. 12: 4: 'And him they stoned, *nay, broke his head*' ...

Such are the flowers with which Purver has so liberally adorned his boasted translation. From a vicious affectation of what is natural and easy he sometimes falls into very gross indecencies.   (Pp. 91–2)

One might say that Purver's sin was that he attempted, in places, an English for cobblers, and then wonder whether the greatest of self-taught translators, writing an English for ploughboys, might not have suffered similarly at the hands of critics who demanded a stylish as well as a scholarly translation. But that is a false track. New Bibles are rarely acclaimed. It is no matter whether Purver was a Tyndale born out of his time or an upstart with audacity and tenacity that outran his ability, or even that the examples of his writing that will be given do sometimes appear 'ungrammatical, improper and obscure'. The contemporary reaction must make us treat him with caution, but it does not destroy him as a critic and as a collector of examples, and it is in these roles that he is important here.

However much the critics who noticed him might denigrate his work, all of them agreed that the literary style of a translation was a major issue, and most agreed that faulty or obsolete English was inappropriate. So Symonds might rubbish Purver, but he gives a whole chapter to 'obsolete and harsh expressions' (ch. VIII) in the KJB, including ten pages of examples. It is not any subjective response to Purver's own language but the kind of correlation there is between the examples he gives and examples given by others that establishes him as a major figure.

The first in this period to publish a list of uncouth and obsolete expressions in the KJB, also the first to publish a work devoted to the need for a new translation, was a man of very different pedigree, the Cambridge-educated divine, Matthew Pilkington (1705–65). Pilkington knew nothing of Purver, and Purver appears to have known nothing of Pilkington's *Remarks*, yet there is a remarkable harmony to their criticisms of the KJB's language. *Remarks upon Several Passages of Scripture: rectifying some errors in the printed Hebrew text; pointing out several mistakes in the versions; and showing the benefit and expediency of a more correct and intelligible translation of the Bible* (1759) is primarily concerned with the 'primitive purity' of the Hebrew text and 'the translators misunderstanding the true import of the Hebrew words and phrases',[23] but it includes remarks whose tone and tendency are very similar to Nary's and Wells's:

The uncouth and obsolete words and expressions that are met with in our English

---

[23] From 'two general remarks' placed before the contents page.

version of the Bible are generally intelligible and convey the ideas the writers had in view; but as our language is very much improved in politeness and correctness since that version was made, it may properly be wished that the Scriptures might receive every advantage which the improvement of our language can give them, especially as the delicacy of some people's ears is pretended to be disgusted with every uncouth sound.   (P. 114)

In its attitude to the English language, this is Welsted's view. It is no accident that it makes us look back. Pilkington, like Purver, formed his ideas on language while Augustan attitudes were at their strongest.

In support of his argument Pilkington gives the earliest example of the unhistorical idea that the KJB was a literary rather than a scholarly revision. He alleges that improvement of the language was one of the main motives which led King James to order a new translation, for the earlier translators 'appeared so well to have understood the Scriptures that little more than the language of it was altered by the translators in King James's time' (p. 114). In order to convince his reader of this, he lists (p. 115) 'some of those words and expressions, which would certainly be altered by persons of such learning and judgement as would, undoubtedly, be appointed to undertake a new translation' (pp. 114–15). The following entries are also given by Purver:

Advisement	Afore	Albeit	Aliant
Ambushment	Anon	Ate	Bestead
Bettered	Bewray	Blains	Chaws
Days-man	Discomfiture	Fet	Fray
Haply	Holpen	Hosen	Kerchiefs
Lade	Laden	Leasing	Leese
Listed	Listeth	Magnifical	Marishes
Mete	Meted	Munition	Nurture
Poll	Polled	Purtenance	Seethe
Seething	Servitor	Silverlings	Sith
Sod	Sodden	Tablets	Trow
Unwittingly	Wastness	Wench	Wert
Wist	Wotteth		

Hough and houghed their horses and chariots
We do you to wit.[24]

What is particularly interesting is that although there are many words here

---

[24] Here are the remaining entries: chode, cracknels, doleful creatures, folk, habergeon, his strength shall be hunger-bitten, issues of life and death, lad, list, mufflers, outer darkness, peeled, searchings of heart, silver shrines, stature, strew, strewed, swolen, terrises, twain, unpatient, wot.

which a present-day reader would readily agree are obsolete, there are also some which would not be assented to, such as 'albeit', 'ate', 'discomfiture', 'laden', 'nurture' and 'unwittingly'. Yet the coincidence of two independent writers citing the same words gives a real likelihood that these words were obsolete at that time. The greater detail of Purver's work will allow us to take this observation further.

Pilkington then attacks another area which should not be ignored though it has no direct relevance to Purver. The KJB may be improved in 'those expressions which, though delivered in words of common use, may be called uncouth from their being in some measure unintelligible' (p. 115). Here are two of his examples and his conclusion:

> Isa. 27: 8. 'In measure, when it shooteth forth, thou wilt debate with it: He stayeth his rough wind, in the day of the east wind.' Here are words, intelligible, and in common use; but when they are thus connected the sentence is no more intelligible than it was in the former version . . . Nahum 2: 7. 'Her maids shall lead her as with the voice of doves, taboring upon their breasts.' The sentiment is evidently, as the Latin, Greek and Chaldee versions give it, that the maids of her that was led away captive should mourn as doves and beat upon their breasts, as persons in the utmost distress; and 'taboring' was certainly very injudiciously put for 'smiting', which was the word in our former version. – These instances are here mentioned farther to show the benefit and expediency of a more correct and intelligible translation of the Bible than we have at present, and that a translator should not too strictly adhere to any of the former versions.   (Pp. 117–18)

The point is well made, and it is curious that few other critics in any period have ventured to give examples of incomprehensibility in the KJB. Pilkington's general call for revision was to be much echoed over a long period, but hostile discussion of 'words and expressions' belongs mostly to this time.

Like Pilkington's, Purver's attitude to language is full of Augustan pride:

> Language was anciently rude and unpolished, and it was proper even for the inspired writings to be delivered in that of the times: hence nouns are frequently repeated in the original where they may much better be rendered by pronouns, according to the improvements of grammar and manner of speech now, especially in this part of the world, without any diminution or alteration of the sense at all. In such a case certainly our language is to be like it self, and not made uncouth to no manner of purpose.
> (1: viii)

He maintains this view about developments in the English language. Addison 'is justly esteemed the best writer or our language' (1: xii), and Purver asks his reader to compare the preface to the KJB with Addison's writings, 'and see what difference of language there is in a hundred years' (1: v). He is careful not to let this appear a merely personal opinion. Though he takes a just pride in thinking for himself, he also knows where he is in relation to scholarship and opinion (see, for example, 1: xvi), and here, as in many places, he cites authorities who express the same view. This helps to identify him, where English is concerned, as a man who applied the standards of the age he grew up in to the KJB.

Four pages of the 'introductory remarks' are given to the axiom that 'a translation ought to be true to the original', eleven to the axiom that 'a translation should be well or grammatically expressed in the language it is made in', and fourteen to an appendix giving lists of various faults in the KJB. There are further remarks and lists prefaced to the NT. The emphasis thus falls squarely on what is most interesting to us, issues of language. On the one hand, Purver believed that a translation should be literal; on the other, as already noted, that 'our language is to be like itself'. Though he also believed the language 'ought to be plain and suited to common capacities' (1: vi), this represents a major difference from Tyndale's desire to present the Bible in simple contemporary prose that everyone could understand. The desire is, within limits, to show the language at its best, and he frequently writes of ways the translation may be given an elegant turn. Moreover, he works with a literary awareness. To quote his own version of Eccles. 12: 10, 'he endeavoured to find agreeable words; however, what is written is right, the words of truth'. His note to this reads, 'by Sandys, worthy to be transcribed for the poetry, "He found out matter to delight the mind; / And every word he writ, by truth was signed."' This attitude reflects both the growing literary awareness of the Bible and the Augustan sense of the perfection of English. The long discussion of principles equally reflects the general eighteenth-century desire to set down rules for this perfection. Yet, in attacking the KJB from this point of view he provides strong evidence of the hold the KJB was gaining on the popular mind, as well as of the sense that there is an appropriate biblical English that is different from current English:

> Yet the obsolete words and uncouth ungrammatical expressions in the sacred text pass more unheeded as being oftener read and heard, especially when the mind is filled with an imagination, that a translation of the Scriptures must be so expressed . . .
> There ought to be the greatest exactness even in spelling the Scripture because our children learn to read by it. (1: v, vi)

He is in fact testifying to important factors which will make the KJB seem less obsolete, uncouth and ungrammatical than it appears to him, and the obvious difference from Selden's picture of the common people (see volume 1, p. 229) shows such a change already taking place.

Purver then gives some examples of obsolete English; it is, as with Pilkington's list, the presence of a number of words in this paragraph that are now standard English which is of particular interest:

> The following preterperfect tenses and participles are become old, viz. baken (baked) bitten (bit) folden (folded) holden (held) holpen (helped) laden (loaded) lien (pret. lay, part. lain) mowen (mowed) ridden (rid) slidden (slid) spitted (spit) stricken (struck) unwashen (not washed) wakened (awaked) waxen (become) with-holden (with-held) upholden (upheld), but some of *en* in termination sprinkled about, especially when passive, may give an agreeable relish of age, as broken, begotten, forgotten; and other such continue, i.e. done, given, gone, known, seen, slain, taken, chosen, spoken, thrown, written, smitten, fallen, born, torn, sworn, stolen, shewn, hewn, driven, drawn, lain, risen, forsaken, striven, sown, shaken, etc., and for a participle rotten; *a* is also obsolete where *o* is used now, in the preterimperfects bare, brake, drave, forgat, gat, spake, sware, ware, ate, laded, slang, spat, strake; but swore and begot sound too vulgar to be used of God.[25]

In the last two examples, one should note in passing that, despite his principles, Purver has some sense of a special religious English that differs from the English he advocates. He too has some 'imagination that a translation of the Scriptures must be so expressed'.

Purver's three categories, which one may call the archaic, the familiarly archaic and the familiar, are useful, but the words now need redistributing. Only 'smitten' and 'lain' need moving from the familiar to the familiarly archaic. 'Stricken' is now familiarly archaic rather than archaic (the main KJB use is 'stricken in age' or 'years', which Johnson finds antiquated and the *OED* archaic, yet 'stricken' survives in other uses such as 'the stricken ship'; 'stricken in years', though it would not be used, is well known). 'Bitten', 'laden', 'mowen' (mown),[26] 'ridden' (of horses) and, of course, 'ate' are all familiar, not archaic. Familiar also are two of his three familiarly archaic words, 'broken' and 'forgotten'.

The bulk of Purver's evidence comes in the lists appended to the

---

[25] I: vi–vii. In *A Short Introduction* Lowth gives a substantial list of 'irregulars in *en*' that contains some of the words given here. Mostly they are asterisked; by this Lowth means there are regular as well as irregular forms (p. 48n). The asterisks generally correspond to obsolete forms (pp. 50–5), and so support Purver.

[26] 'Mowen' is the spelling used in 1611, but this was altered sometimes in the printing history of the KJB to 'mown'. Purver's feelings about the spelling of the KJB were universally shared.

'introductory remarks' and to the 'additional remarks' that preface the NT. Three of these concern language, while the others deal with consistency and accuracy of translation. One list gives words beginning in A and B which are 'base or misapplied', a second gives samples from the rest of the alphabet, and the third gives instances of 'badly-joined' words. On the whole these lists appear to be soundly compiled: most of the entries are indeed obsolete or awkward, and it is clear that Purver did not just go by his own taste, but made much use of Johnson's recently published dictionary. He notes 'that several words of the common translation were not found in any other English books by Johnson in his great dictionary; a sign of their wanting the currency requisite even when that translation was made' (1: vi).

In examining these lists I have also used Johnson, as well as the *OED*; the most authoritative nineteenth-century commentary on the vocabulary of the KJB, Eastwood and Wright's *The Bible Word Book* (London and Cambridge, 1866) and its successor, Bridges and Weigle's *The Bible Word Book* (New York: Nelson, 1960); lastly, the RV and RSV. The comparison of Purver's criticisms with the vocabulary of the RSV confirms his general reliability as a commentator on vocabulary: the RSV, like the RV a revision of the KJB, adhered to 'our present understanding of English' and tried to 'embody the best results of modern scholarship as to the meaning of the Scriptures, and express this meaning in English diction which is designed ... [to] preserve those qualities which have given to the King James Version a supreme place in English literature'.[27]

Among the words which would not now be regarded as obsolete but which are listed by Purver is 'unwittingly' (which Pilkington also gives). Purver, who gives alternatives for all the words he lists, gives 'unawares'. The *OED* states clearly, 'in very frequent use c 1380–c 1630, and from c 1815', and refers to 'unwitting', which it says was 'rare after c 1600 until revived (perhaps after UNWEETING ...) c 1800'. Eastwood and Wright felt it was still 'either obsolete or archaic', but it appears to have been thoroughly acceptable to the makers of the RV: they once change 'unwittingly' to 'unawares' (Josh. 20: 5), once reverse the

---

[27] From the preface. I have discussed the OT lists in more detail and presented the most significant of the evidence in 'The Bible as a reviver of words: the evidence of Anthony Purver, a mid-eighteenth century critic of the English of the King James Bible' (*Neuphilologische Mitteilungen* 86 (1985), 515–33). The correlation with the RSV is shown in detail. Harold A. Guy's 'An English eighteenth century N.E.B.' (*Expository Times* 81 (February 1970), 148–50) is a brief evaluation of Purver which praises him not only because many of his renderings 'have a charm of their own', but also because 'he sometimes anticipates the renderings and even the critical findings of recent translations'.

two words, and thirteen times use 'unwittingly' where the KJB has 'ignorance' or 'unawares'. Bridges and Weigle does not give it. By the twentieth century it needed no comment.

'Unwittingly', then, quite clearly demonstrates that a word could be archaic in the eighteenth century yet current in the nineteenth. It also shows that Purver and Pilkington's evidence is sound enough to bring this to light (how many such entries are there in the *OED*?). Perhaps the evidence of the KJB and RV combined suggests that 'unwittingly' was losing currency in 1611 (two of the KJB's uses go back to Tyndale and Coverdale),[28] but was fully meaningful and usable by 1885, for the KJB in fact only uses it three times to the RV's fourteen. These last figures make another point: the KJB's three uses are, in the absence of a famous context, obviously not the reason the word regained its familiarity. As Shakespeare only uses it twice, he too must be discounted. Is 'unwittingly' an example of changing fashions in vocabulary?

I have given 'unwittingly' first because of the clarity of the *OED*'s evidence. The remaining examples are a few particularly interesting words which seem to have become obsolete and then been revived primarily through their use in the KJB. The first three are words which probably owe much to famous contexts in the KJB, 'heritage', 'laden' and 'ponder'.

'Ponder', for which Purver gives 'consider', may have survived or revived through one famous verse: 'but Mary kept all these things and pondered them in her heart' (Luke 2: 19). This comes from Tyndale. The *OED* has among many examples only one from the eighteenth century, from Cowper, 1791. The revival was probably helped by a mid-nineteenth-century hymn, 'Ponder anew / What the Almighty can do' (*Hymns Ancient and Modern*, 382). Further evidence of this revival is that the RSV once replaces the KJB's 'study' with 'ponder' (Prov. 15: 28).

'Laden' is also given by Pilkington, but Johnson's evidence suggests they are being finicky. 'Lade', he notes, 'is now commonly written *load*', and he gives the past participle for 'load' as 'loaden' or 'laden' but not 'loaded', which is what Purver, in keeping with modern usage, gives. The KJB does not use 'load' or 'loaded' at all, but has 'loaden', which Shakespeare prefers to 'laden', once (Isa. 46: 1, Johnson's only example). 'Laden' is used six times, and 'lade' with variations another eight times. The *OED* suggests a continued *poetic* currency for 'laden', but by the mid nineteenth century, as its absence from Eastwood

---

[28]   I can find no evidence that earlier versions used 'unwittingly' more than twice, but a thorough check is impractical. In no case where the KJB has 'unawares' does an earlier version have 'unwittingly'. The KJB's one use of 'wittingly' (Gen. 48: 14) goes back to Coverdale.

and Wright suggests, it appears to have regained general currency, though without challenging 'loaded' as the ordinary word. Much of this revival or survival must be due to Tyndale's use of it in 'come unto me, all ye that labour and are heavy laden, and I will give you rest' (Matt. 11: 28).

'Heritage' is only used twice by Shakespeare but comes thirty times in the KJB. Geddes classes it among 'words and phrases which, though obsolete in common use, are still intelligible to one acquainted with the scripture style'.[29] As with most of the words considered here, it is not a special coinage for purposes of translation, for the *OED* gives examples going back to Wyclif and earlier. Since the substantial use of it in the KJB does not derive from Tyndale (Coverdale uses it only occasionally), 'heritage' perhaps belongs more to the vocabulary of 1611 than the previous examples. The *OED*'s only example between 1639 and 1810 is from John Wesley's translation of the Psalms (1738) and is clearly biblical. Yet again the word was familiar enough to Eastwood and Wright to need no entry. One verse makes clear how dominant the KJB could be both as a source and a preserver of language: 'lo, children are an heritage of the Lord: and the fruit of the womb is his reward' (Ps. 127: 3). The sentiment and the wording, especially the Hebraism 'fruit of the womb', have made this ring in the English language (I hesitate to judge here between the KJB and Coverdale's version, as preserved in the PB; it supports the point just as readily).

'Eschewed' is a curious variation on this type of example. Purver gives 'refrained from'. The KJB gives it, in various forms, only four times, Shakespeare uses it only once in one of his obscurer plays (*Merry Wives* 5: 5: 237), and Johnson calls it 'a word almost obsolete'. The *OED* quotes this from Johnson but adds, 'it is now not uncommon in literary usage'. George Campbell, another to give examples of peculiarities of vocabulary in the KJB, lists 'eschew' among 'words totally unsupported by present use ... Terms such as some of these, like old vessels, are, I may say, so buried in rust as to render it difficult to discover their use' (*Four Gospels*, 1: 579). In this case the word comes from Tyndale and Coverdale, and it is Coverdale's use of it in the PB Psalter that seems to be crucial: 'eschew evil and do good' (Ps. 34: 14). The KJB echoes this in its usages (especially 1 Pet. 3: 11), yet it alters the words I have just quoted to

[29] *A Letter to the Right Reverend the Lord Bishop of London [Robert Lowth] containing queries, doubts and difficulties relative to a vernacular version of the Holy Scriptures* (London, 1787), p. 2. The other words he gives are worth noting as being mostly words we would not consider obsolete: 'ambushment', 'meet', 'wroth', 'banquet', 'banner', 'bereave', 'bewail', 'portray', 'discomfit', 'marvel', 'obeisance' and 'progenitors'. The *Monthly Review* was sceptical, objecting that 'banquet', 'banner', 'bewail', 'portray' and 'progenitors' 'are still in very frequent use' (new series, 1 (January 1790), 56).

'Depart from evil . . .' This suggests that 'eschew' was of dubious currency by
1611. Nevertheless this is a clear case of a word rescued from obsolescence, but
probably, this time, by the PB.

It may be that sometimes this kind of evidence exists without showing that
the KJB was a cause of revival. 'Warfare', for which Purver has 'war', appears
from the *OED* to have been extensively used in the fifteenth and sixteenth
centuries and then to have revived in the mid nineteenth.[30] Shakespeare, though
war figures so much in his plays, does not use it. The KJB has it five times, once
only going back to Tyndale and once to Coverdale; twice it sounds modern
without going back to either of them: 'the Philistines gathered their armies
together for warfare' (1 Sam. 28: 1), and 'cry unto [Jerusalem] that her warfare is
accomplished' (Isa. 40: 2). Are these strong enough contexts to preserve the
word? Johnson's evidence suggests that 'warfare' was preserved within the
general context of religion, as four of his five examples are religious. Is the KJB
here merely *reflecting* the survival of a now-common word in a religious context?

'Changes' or 'change', which Purver would alter to 'suits' in phrases such as
'changes of raiment' (Gen. 45: 22 etc.), suggests another possibility. 'Change' in
this sense the *OED* records first from Greene in 1592. It then gives two biblical
examples before jumping to 1815, and it records 'a change of clothes' first in
1876. Johnson seems barely familiar with this meaning, his closest definition
being 'that which makes a variety; that which may be used for another of the
same kind', and he quotes 'thirty change of garments' from Judg. 14: 12, 13,
which is modern in meaning. Shakespeare four times uses 'change' with a word
for clothing, but each time as a verb. Does 'change' in this biblical sense enter
the language as a Hebraism (the phrase in fact goes back past Greene to
Tyndale), or has the Bible just by chance picked up a stray usage from its period
and happened to anticipate modern usage?

Lastly, here is one of the words which Purver would argue lacked 'the
currency requisite' even in 1611, since the only examples Johnson has are
biblical, 'avenge'. Purver would amend it to 'revenge'. Johnson suggests that
'avenger' was a little more widely used. The *OED* has nothing between Milton
and Sheridan (1799) bar the phrase 'the avenger of so many treasons' in the
controversial divine Conyers Middleton (1741), but shows a clear history back
to Langland and Wyclif. In the immediate history of the KJB, 'avenge' goes
back to Tyndale, and it is only the linguistically independent Rheims-Douai
version that uses 'revenge' ('avenger' is perhaps less old, since Tyndale does not

---

[30] Symonds includes this in a brief list of words that Purver should not have objected to
(p. 100).

use it; biblically, it originates with Coverdale). Eastwood and Wright comment only on the phrase 'to avenge of', implying the familiarity of the word except in this construction, and it remains familiar, especially in the form 'avenger'. The KJB uses 'avenge' and variants 46 times, 'revenge' only 18. With Shakespeare the position is drastically reversed: he uses 'avenge' and its variants 6 times, 'revenge' 237 times. 'Avenge' therefore does seem to have faded even before 1611, but the KJB has kept it alive not only by the frequency of its use but also by its use in memorable verses: 'out of the mouth of babes and sucklings hast thou ordained strength because of thine enemies, that thou mightest still the enemy and the avenger',[31] and 'how long, O Lord . . . dost thou not judge and avenge our blood?' (Rev. 6: 10).

These few examples can only suggest a case, but they make it appear quite possible that some words and phrases faded from use about the beginning of the seventeenth century, and then reappeared early in the nineteenth. Further, the KJB caused some of these reappearances, acting as a kind of uncrowded Noah's ark[32] for vocabulary for perhaps two hundred years. Certainly the KJB is a good source for testing the progress of vocabulary.

Beyond this specific case about the history of vocabulary, Purver and his fellow-critics show that in their time the language of the KJB appeared more objectionable than it has since. Their standards did not accommodate the standards of the KJB.

Revision gets a bad name

Purver is most interesting in revealing the objections to the KJB: other translators give a better sense of what these late Augustans thought might be appropriate language for the English Bible as a rendering of originals that they now knew were literary. Here the most extreme figure is the much-mocked dissenting minister, classicist and biblical critic Edward Harwood (1729–94).

---

[31] Ps. 8: 2; almost identical in PB; Purver also lists 'suckling' as archaic, but this verse as quoted by Jesus (Matt. 21: 16) has kept it familiarly archaic.

[32] Some time after writing this, I find that the image and something like the point were anticipated some 130 years ago by Le Roy J. Halsey. He declares (rather than argues) that

> This book, universally read as it is, and must be, by a Protestant people, renders it impossible that words thus enshrined in the daily thoughts of the people should ever grow obsolete. And so this version has done for our language what no other influence under heaven could have done – it has been an ark of safety which has borne it across the wide abyss of centuries, and is still bearing it gloriously adown the current of ages.
>
> (P. 40)

His intentions in his 'ridiculous work',[33] *A Liberal Translation of the New Testament* (1768), are

> to exhibit before the candid, the unprejudiced and the intelligent of all parties, the true, original, divine form of Christianity in its beautiful simplicity, divested of all meretricious attire with which it hath been loaded, and solely adorned with its native elegance and charms, which need only be contemplated in order to excite the imagination, transport and love of every ingenuous and virtuous bosom.[34]

Truth matters – and elsewhere (p. iv) Harwood writes of how hard he worked to discover it – but the emphasis is on literary qualities that will affect the reader. This is the furthest an English prose translator has moved from the tradition of literal translation without ceasing to think of himself as a translator. Harwood owns Castellio as 'my precedent and pattern' (p. v), and Blackwall and Lowth also lie behind the work. He treats the NT as a Greek classic and aims not only to reproduce the elegance of the original but 'to translate the sacred writers of the NT with the same freedom, impartiality and elegance with which other translations from the Greek classics have lately been executed' (p. iii). So his idea of a faithful translation, which he freely admits is 'liberal and diffusive' and serves as 'explanatory paraphrase' as well as translation (pp. iii–iv), is to 'clothe the genuine ideas and doctrines of the apostles with that propriety and perspicuity in which they themselves, I apprehend, would have exhibited them had they *now* lived and written in our language' (p. iii). The result of this thoroughly un-Lowthian aim is the greatest loading of the 'meretricious attire' that he claimed to be removing ever seen in an English prose Testament.

His sense of 'our language' is much like Purver's, though the figures he looks to are a little more modern:

> It is pleasing to observe how much our language within these very few years hath been refined and polished, and what infinite improvements it hath lately received. The writings of Hume, Robertson, Lowth, Lyttelton, Hurd, Melmoth, Johnson and Hawkesworth will stand an everlasting monument of what grace and purity in diction, of what elegance and harmony in arrangement, and of what copiousness and strength in composition our language is capable; and the writings of these learned and illustrious authors are not only a distinguished honour and ornament to their country, but in point of true excellence and sublimity will bear the severest critical comparison with the politest writers of Greece and Rome.   (Pp. iv–v)

The familiarity of such remarks suggests little originality, and that is part of

---

[33] *Boswell: The Ominous Years: 1774–1776*, ed. Charles Ryskamp and Frederick J. Pottle (London: Heinemann, 1963), p. 333.

[34] P. viii. All quotations are from volume 1.

Harwood's importance: he represents in an extreme form the late-Augustan attitude to language and the Bible. Here is his conception of how Jesus would have spoken in the 1760s:

> Survey with attention the lilies of the field, and learn from them how unbecoming it is for rational creatures to cherish a solicitous passion for gaiety and dress – for they sustain no labour, they employ no cares to adorn themselves, and yet are clothed with such inimitable beauty as the richest monarch in the richest dress never equalled.
>
> (Matt. 6: 28–9)

This is not an extreme example, yet one can hardly imagine anything less like the KJB. If this is how the untalented thought the Bible should sound, it is no wonder that the KJB appeared 'bald and barbarous' (p. v).

Harwood's translation failed with both the critics and the public, but other versions which tended in the same direction had more success. Another non-conformist, Philip Doddridge (1702–51), best known now as a hymn-writer, began publishing *The Family Expositor: or, a paraphrase and version of the New Testament* in 1739, and it continued to be printed for over a hundred years. He reports that in making the paraphrase he rarely altered the general sense of the KJB but yet found the labour valuable as it enabled him to search 'more accurately into several beauties of expression' and to make changes which 'may yet in some degree do a further honour to Scripture, raising some of those ornaments which were before depressed, and sufficiently proving that several objections urged against it were entirely of an English growth'.[35] Again the beauty of the Bible is a major issue, even if criticism of the KJB is kept as muted as possible: in Doddridge's view it is 'the business and glory of true criticism' to bring out the 'thousand latent beauties' in the NT (1: vi). His method is to place the KJB in relatively small print beside the paraphrase, italicise the parts of his paraphrase that come directly, though with variation, from the KJB, add detailed notes at the foot of the page, and, at the end of each section, to give a kind of précis of the passage. Just the paraphrase of the same two verses from Matthew is sufficient to show how far he goes towards Harwood:

> *And as for raiment, why are you anxious [about that?]* Observe not only the animal but what is yet much lower, the vegetable part of the creation; and particularly *consider* there *the lilies of the field, how they grow; they toil not* to prepare the materials of their covering, *nor do they spin*, or weave them into garments: *yet I say unto you that even* the magnificent *Solomon* in all his royal *glory*, when sitting on his throne of ivory and gold (1 Kings 10: 18) *was not arrayed* in garments of so pure a white and of such curious workmanship *as one of these* lilies presents to your view.

[35] 6 vols. (London, 1761), 1: ii–iii.

Rather than rejecting the KJB outright, this treats it as a bare body waiting to be clothed with its appropriate beauties. It is an attempt to supply what the reader should both understand and imagine, but it does not invite direct admiration of the KJB.

Purver and Harwood represent the peak of the reaction against the KJB, but they also contain within themselves signs of why the attitudes they represent were soon to pass. Purver noted the growing sense that the KJB's language was the appropriate English for the Bible (above, p. 79). Harwood goes further, declaring himself 'conscious that the bald and barbarous language of the old vulgar version hath acquired a venerable sacredness from length of time and custom' (p. v). This pinpoints the clash between the developed standards of the late Augustans and the force of popular feeling which was to do so much to reverse critical attitudes to the KJB's language. Looking to be kings of the earth, the bloated Harwood and the many-toothed Purver stand like dinosaurs at the end of an era, authentic specimens, but grotesque and sterile. They may even have contributed to the demise of the attitudes they represent by showing how unlikely a derivative idea of cultivated taste was to produce acceptable results. Harwood, by reducing taste to absurdity, and Purver, by multiplying examples to excess, helped the literati to revalue the KJB's English along lines that matched both the implications of Lowth's movement towards a positive sense of uncouth and harsh language and, still more importantly, the growing popular feeling for the KJB.

Certainly there was such a revaluation. It coincides with the change in taste neatly captured by Oliver Goldsmith in *The Vicar of Wakefield* (1766). An actor tells the Vicar, '"Dryden and Rowe's manner, Sir, are quite out of fashion; our taste has gone back a whole century, Fletcher, Ben Jonson, and all the plays of Shakespeare are the only things that go down."' The Vicar's puzzled response articulates the passing age: '"How", cried I, "is it possible the present age can be pleased with that antiquated dialect, that obsolete humour, those over-charged characters, which abound in the works you mention?"' (ch. 18). The changing tone of reviews of translations suggests how the translators themselves helped to effect this change. In 1764 Richard Wynne (?1718–99) published an NT. His chief concern was to relieve the confusion caused by the chapter and verse divisions, and he intended to copy the KJB verbatim:

> but, on comparing that version carefully with the original (though it is a good translation upon the whole), I thought it requisite to deviate from it sometimes, and frequently to alter the language. For some of the words and phrases, familiar to our ancestors, are now grown so obsolete as not to be intelligible to the generality of readers: others are too mean, equivocal or inadequate to the original, which perhaps

is owing to the fluctuating state of our language; and some passages are not so exactly rendered by our translators as a work of that kind required. In all these cases I made no scruple of differing from our public translation, endeavouring at the same time to steer in a just medium between a servile literal translation and a paraphrastic loose version; between low, obsolete and obscure language, and a modern enervated style.[36]

There is nothing here that is not found in Purver and Harwood except moderation, and the result is not too far different from the KJB.[37] The *Critical Review* was sympathetic, like Wynne damning the KJB with faint praise, then encouraging further effort to produce 'an accurate and elegant translation':

These divine writings should be translated with accuracy and spirit. Our common version is, indeed, a valuable work, and deserves the highest esteem, but it is by no means free from imperfections. It certainly contains many false interpretations, ambiguous phrases, obsolete words and indelicate expressions which deform the beauty of the sacred pages, perplex the unlearned reader, offend the fastidious ear, confirm the prejudices of the unbeliever and excite the derision of the scorner. An accurate and elegant translation would therefore be of infinite service to religion, would obviate a thousand difficulties and exceptions, prevent a multitude of chimerical tenets and controversial questions, give a proper dignity and lustre to divine revelation, and convince the world that whatever appears confused, coarse or ridiculous in the Holy Scriptures ought to be imputed to the translator.

(18 (September 1764), 189)

---

[36] *The New Testament*, 2 vols. (London, 1764), 1: xii–xiii. Six years later John Worsley writes almost identically in the 'author's advertisement' to *The New Testament . . . Translated from the Greek according to the present idiom of the English tongue* (London, 1770):

The English translation of the Bible . . . is no doubt a very good one, and justly so esteemed to this day, though it be above a hundred and fifty years old; but it is not to be wondered at if some words and phrases, then in use and well understood, should by this time become obsolete and almost unintelligible to common readers, such as 'mote', 'we do you to wit', 'do thy diligence', 'shall' for 'will', 'will' for 'shall', 'quick' for 'living', 'should' for 'would', etc. The principal attempt therefore of this translation is both to bring it *nearer to the original*, either in the text or notes, and to make the form of expression more suitable to our present language. For as the English tongue, like other living languages, is continually changing, it were to be wished that the translation of the sacred oracles could be revised by public authority and reduced to present forms of writing and speaking at least once in a century; but though this be not allowed for public use, it is to be hoped some private persons may receive benefit by that which is now offered.   (Fol. A3 v)

[37] The *Monthly Review* (31 (December 1764), 401–7) claims he largely plagiarised Doddridge, which is to overstate the case. He used many of Doddridge's phrases while avoiding his amplification. If we take the same two verses from Matthew, there is no sign of Doddridge. 'Why take ye thought for' becomes 'why are ye solicitous about', and 'unto' becomes 'to'; otherwise the text is the KJB's.

Clearly Wynne had not gone far enough to satisfy or explode the desire for elegance, so the reviewer looks *for* a new version rather than *to* the old version. Seddon's response in The *Monthly Review* was similar:

> We look upon every attempt to improve and render perfect the translation of the New Testament to be of so much importance to the progress of true religion and to the honour of genuine Christianity that we are disposed to receive every work of this kind with the greatest candour: and it is with peculiar satisfaction and pleasure ... that we see so many of our clergy directing their studies and attention this way.
>
> (31 (December 1764), 406)

Reviews of Purver followed within months in each journal, and thereafter the notes of optimism about new versions and lack of interest in the KJB vanish. The nearest the former came to reviving was when the *Monthly Review* in 1784 looked back to Lowth's *Isaiah* and commented that it had removed 'many prejudices which persons of scrupulous minds had conceived against a general revision of the present translation of the Bible'.[38] It seems probable that these prejudices were the product not just of popular feeling, which the review discusses candidly, but of failed attempts giving new versions a bad name.

If there is something like a *volte-face* here, three years later the more outspoken *Critical Review* seems to have undergone a conversion like Saul on the road to Damascus. Reviewing Geddes's *Proposal*, it claims that 'to reform the text of the Bible would have appeared to the ignorant little less than a change of a national religion' (63 (January 1787), 46). What makes this startling is that the reviewer shares the feeling of 'the ignorant'. The literati and the people come together in a passage of unprecedented warmth:

> [The KJB's] faults are said to be a defect in the idiom, as English ... The defect in idiom we cannot allow to be a fault: it raised the language above common use and has almost sanctified it; nor would we lose the noble simplicity, the energetic bravery, for all the idiomatic elegance which a polished age can bestow. Dr Geddes objects to a translation too literal, but we wish not to see the present text changed unless where real errors render it necessary. The venerable tree which we have always regarded with a religious respect cannot be pruned to modern fashions without our feeling the most poignant regret. Our attachment to this venerable relic has involuntarily made our language warm.
>
> (P. 48)

Still a contrast is maintained between the standards of the KJB and the elegance of a polished age, but the judgement between the two has shifted decisively. Instead of the achievement of a literary Bible being looked forward to, now the KJB is looked back to as the literary standard. The KJB is not merely a relic but

---

[38] Vol. 71 (September 1784), 161. The passage is given more fully below, p. 100.

a 'venerable relic' that has beneficially influenced the language. Its age is still recognised, but no longer disliked. Critical opinion has followed the people, like Wenceslas's page, treading in warm footsteps.

An aside: Higher Criticism

In 1753 appeared an anonymous volume with the title, *Conjectures sur les mémoires originaux dont il parait que Moïse s'est servi pour composer le livre de la Genèse*. It was the work of a physician to the court of Louis XV, Jean Astruc (1684–1766). Because of the way he treated the observation which had been made many times over back into patristic times of the different names used for God, this work is generally taken as the beginning of what, following J. G. Eichhorn in Germany and, later, William Robertson Smith in England, is called Higher Criticism.[39] It is 'higher' by contrast with study of textual variations. Astruc explained the use of 'Yahweh' and 'Elohim' in Genesis on the basis that Moses used two original documents. Such inferences are the basis of all Higher Criticism: what it aims at is distinguishing and dating the different sources, including sources in the human imagination, which have been scrambled together to make either the omelette[40] or the mess (according to whether one wishes to think favourably or unfavourably of the result) that has come down to us as the books of the Bible.

Its central element is the assumption that, at least in their composition and transmission, the books of the Bible are human documents subject to rational criticism such as one might apply to other texts. One can readily see how such work might produce what a literary critic would recognise as valuable insight, for it is a way of study that has the potential to reveal the ways of the imagination as works of art are created. Moreover, it leads to insight into the nature of the text, revealing features of the different strands within a composition. This kind of insight is epitomised by the *Polychrome Bible* (1897 etc.).[41] The different strands of the text are printed against different coloured

---

[39] *CHB* III: 265–89 gives an invaluable outline of the history of Higher Criticism. For Robertson Smith's use of the phrase, see his *The Old Testament in the Jewish Church* (Edinburgh, 1881), p. 105.

[40] I borrow the image from Edmund Leach. He uses it to make witticisms about scholars, that is, Higher Critics, who try to unscramble the omelette, an activity 'at best laborious and ... not likely to improve the taste!' ('The legitimacy of Solomon', *Genesis as Myth*, p. 81). He likes the joke well enough to repeat it elsewhere.

[41] The full title is *The Sacred Books of the Old and New Testaments: A New English Translation*, ed. Paul Haupt (London, 1897–9; Herbert 2088). Only six parts of this ambitious work were published. The same editor's '"Rainbow" edition', *The Sacred Books of the Old Testament* (Leipzig, 1896 etc.), gave the reconstructed Hebrew text prepared on the basis of the new translation.

backgrounds, sometimes making for a curious beauty rather like that of some modernist painting.[42] Whether in the long run such insight can make for better reading is something that has only recently become a matter of debate. However, there is one outcome of this kind of study that does yield something that looks like a unified literary text, the attempt to put together the Yahwist elements as a single book in their own right so that what is argued to be the greatness of the Yahwist as a writer can be seen and appreciated.[43]

Within the world of biblical scholarship, Higher Criticism is often thought of as historical or, more often and more significantly for us, literary criticism. So the *Cambridge History of the Bible* paraphrases 'literary criticism of the Bible' as 'the examination of its contents with a view to determining the date, authorship, integrity and character of the various documents' before explaining that such study is generally called Higher Criticism (III: 270). This is a perfectly legitimate use of 'literary', but is not the use that literary scholars recognise. Most of this kind of literary study has been practised by biblical rather than literary scholars, and has not been aimed towards literary appreciation of the texts. Moreover, though Lowth and, particularly, Geddes were among the early Higher Critics, Higher Criticism had few practitioners and less sympathy in nineteenth-century England before the 1880s. It was developed, often at the

---

[42] The 'explanation of colours' in C. J. Ball's *Genesis* (vol. I of the '"Rainbow" edition') gives a taste of Haupt's editions:

> The combination of *red* and *blue*: PURPLE ... indicates the composite document (JE), commonly known as the *Prophetic Narrative* of the Hexateuch, compiled by an editor or redactor (RJ[E]) about 640 from two independent sources: *viz.* (1) the Judaic document (J) whose various strata seem to have originated in the Southern Kingdom after 850 B.C., and (2) the *Ephraimitic* document (E), written by a native of the Northern Kingdom prior to 650 B.C. The older strata of J (J[1], about 850 B.C.) are printed in DARK RED..., and the later strata (J[2], about 650) in LIGHT RED... E is printed in BLUE... GREEN... is used for the *Deuteronomistic* expansions (D[2]) which were added to JE during the second half of the Exile (560–540), while BROWN ... marks later strata (440–400) of the *Priestly Code* (P), the main body of which (compiled in Babylonia about 500 B.C.) is printed black without any additional colouring. Ch. 14, which seems to be derived from what might be termed an Exilic Midrash, has been printed in ORANGE.

> Further distinctions are made through the use of overlining. (The passage is from a tipped-in sheet; similar explanations are found in the notes to the English-language editions.)

[43] I refer to Harold Bloom and David Rosenberg, *The Book of J*. Bloom summarises this enterprise in terms that suggest an activity like Higher Criticism but are combatively literary:

> To read the Book of J we need to begin by scrubbing away the varnish that keeps us from seeing that the Redactor and previous revisionists could not obliterate the

cost of faith and position, in Germany and, to some extent, France. Only occasionally did one of its products penetrate the xenophobic and reactionary English consciousness. Slowly, of course, it became an accepted critical method, but its protagonists had had to fight so hard for its theological respectability that no attention was given to its possible implications for literary appreciation of the Bible. Moreover, as will become apparent, much of the literary appreciation of the Bible before the twentieth century came from sources that favoured inspirationist ideas and so were temperamentally hostile to Higher Criticism. It is only as recently as the 1970s and 1980s that it becomes an important cause of reaction that helps to shape some contemporary literary discussion of the Bible. So, though it has its ongoing literary interest, it is only at that point that Higher Criticism will be taken up again, and then not so much for its own sake as for its connections with literary criticism.

> original work of the J writer. That varnish is called by many names: belief, scholarship, history, literary criticism, what have you. If these names move or describe you, why read the Book of J at all? Why read the *Iliad*, or the *Commedia*, or *Macbeth*, or *Paradise Lost*? The difference is that those works have not been revised into creeds and churches, with a palimpsestic overlay of orthodox texts obscuring what was there to be revised. Recovering J will not throw new light on Torah or on the Hebrew Bible or on the Bible of Christianity. I do not think that appreciating J will help us love God or arrive at the spiritual or historical truth of whatever Bible. I want the varnish off because it conceals a writer of the eminence of Shakespeare and Dante, and such a writer is worth more than many creeds, many churches, many scholarly certainties. (Pp. 47–8)

CHAPTER 3

The critical rise of the KJB

The influence of popular feeling

The Bible had so long been entrenched in popular culture that it is almost superfluous to recur to the point. Nevertheless, the references to popular feeling in prefaces to and reviews of new translations make a recurrence necessary. Popular feeling was a major factor in the reversal of critical opinion that took place over roughly the span of a generation, 1760–90, but particularly in the 1760s. From the beginning there was an association between the vernacular Bible and the ill-educated: literacy and Bible reading went hand in hand, as in the stories of William Maldon (see volume 1, p. 86) or of Defoe's Somerset schoolboy (above, pp. 48–9). The kind of simple love and faith such as Bishop Patrick's maid had shown for the singing Psalms (above, pp. 45–6) were common responses to the Bible. One Josiah Langdale, born in 1673, recalls that 'I had not time for much schooling ... yet I made a little progress in Latin, but soon forgot it; I endeavoured, however, to keep my English, and could read the Bible and delighted therein.'[1] Such comments are, naturally, infrequent, but they have a representative value, as does this recollection of the 'domestic interiors of the husbandmen or farmers' in the Lothians in the 1760s: 'no book was so familiar to them as the Scriptures; they could almost tell the place of any particular passage, where situated in their own family Bible, without referring to either book, chapter or verse; and where any similar one was situated'.[2]

From the 1760s on such intense and widespread feeling and familiarity among the less educated played an important role in the rise of admiration for

---

[1] Margaret Spufford, *Small Books and Pleasant Histories* (London: Methuen, 1981), p. 30.
[2] George Robertson, *Rural Recollections* (1829), as given in Spufford, p. 47. The same picture is given, more fully and vividly, in Robert Burns's 'The Cotter's Saturday Night' (1785), lines 100–53.

the KJB among the intelligentsia. Just as the opponents of Sternhold and Hopkins had had to take notice of the popularity of that version, so, over a shorter period, the arguers for revision and the revisers themselves tried to discount the popular feeling. But the kind of testimony they give, beginning from Purver's observation that the familiarity of the language made people imagine 'that a translation of the Bible must be so expressed' (above, p. 79), quickly takes a different turn. In spite of their wider reading and their education in Augustan standards, the intelligentsia, also brought up on the KJB, were catching up with the people: they could maintain a distance from their new opinion by attributing it to the people, which is what the *Critical Review* seems to have been doing in its remarks on Geddes's *Proposal* (above, p. 90). Beyond this reluctant admission, though, they were being genuinely influenced, and reference to popular opinion became a common stepping-stone for their arguments.

The cleric and critic Vicesimus Knox (1752–1821) shows this in his youthful *Essays, Moral and Literary* (1778). In his essay 'On simplicity of style in prosaic composition', he reports the post-Longinian view that 'the Bible, the Iliad and Shakespeare's works are allowed to be the sublimest books that the world can exhibit. They are also truly simple' (p. 85). At once this suggests that he will be that most useful sort of literary critic, the representative rather than the original. Then, in his essay 'On the best method of exciting literary genius in boys who possess it', he suggests that the Bible is one of the books most suitable for exciting this genius 'if a little care were taken by the superintendents of education, to select those parts which are so beautifully distinguished for simple sublimity and unaffected pathos',[3] and he adds, 'the poetry of the Bible contributed much to the sublimity of Milton' (p. 356). Whether or not he really means these remarks to refer to the KJB, in practice there is no other version they could refer to; it is only when he writes 'On the impropriety of publicly

---

[3] There were other, more direct attempts to encourage the youth of England to take a literary delight in the Scriptures, most notably by the blue stocking Hannah More (1745–1833), whose *Sacred Dramas, chiefly intended for young persons* (1782) is made up of blank verse playlets on OT subjects and has a verse introduction eulogising the Bible as literature and appealing directly to the taste of the young. Young women were also encouraged to develop their taste from the Bible. Mary Wollstonecraft's anthology, *The Female Reader* (1789), contains a large number of passages from the KJB. Wollstonecraft writes, 'the main object of this work is to imprint some useful lessons on the mind, and cultivate the taste at the same time – to infuse a relish for a pure and simple style, by presenting natural and touching descriptions from the Scriptures, Shakespeare, etc. Simplicity and sincerity generally go hand in hand, as both proceed from the love of truth' (facsimile, intro. Moira Ferguson (Delmar, N.Y.: Scholars' Facsimiles, 1980), p. iv).

adopting a new translation of the Bible' that he deals explicitly with the KJB. He believes its antiquity is a greater source of strength than any correction of its inaccuracies would be (p. 266), and is thus an early, if not the first, champion of its literary virtues against its scholarly defects: 'I cannot help thinking', he writes, 'that the present translation ought to be retained in our churches for its intrinsic beauty and excellence' (p. 267). This is where popular feeling becomes an important part of the argument. He freely associates himself with 'the middle and lower ranks' in reporting that

> We have received the Bible in the very words in which it now stands from our fathers; we have learned many passages of it by heart in our infancy; we find it quoted in sermons from the earliest to the latest times, so that its phrase is become familiar to our ear, and we cease to be startled at apparent difficulties. Let all this be called prejudice, but it is a prejudice which universally prevails in the middle and lower ranks, and we should hardly recognise the Bible were it to be read in our churches in any other words than those which our fathers have heard before us.   (P. 267)

Though Knox was still in his twenties when he wrote this, it has an element of conservatism that might remind us of that champion of the old and the popular, William Beveridge. Beyond Beveridge, it is yet another of the remarks in the line of Augustine's observation that 'as the child grows these books grow with him' (see volume 1, p. 5).

There is another element here that is perhaps less conservative, for the appeal to popular sentiment goes along with a certain aestheticism: familiarity and beauty seem scarcely distinguishable in Knox's thinking, and he values them more than truth or clarity, an almost novel opinion (it might remind us of Gregory Martin's argument for preserving some of the vocabulary of the Vulgate) which has yet maintained its vitality to the present day and which is completely at odds with the minute concern for accuracy so characteristic of biblical translation and criticism even by such aesthetically sensitive men as Lowth. Knox declares roundly that

> The poetical passages of Scripture are peculiarly pleasing in the present translation. The language, though it is simple and natural, is rich and expressive. Solomon's Song, difficult as it is to be interpreted, may be read with delight, even if we attend to little else but the brilliancy of the diction; and it is a circumstance which increases its grace that it appears to be quite unstudied. The Psalms, as well as the whole Bible, are literally translated, and yet the translation abounds with passages exquisitely beautiful. Even where the sense is not very clear nor the connection of ideas obvious at first sight, the mind is soothed and the ear ravished with the powerful yet unaffected charms of the style.   (P. 268)

This unashamed popular aestheticism leads him to conclude that there is a kind of divine providence in the beauty of the KJB – he is very close to claiming that it is divinely inspired: 'it is our duty to inspect it, and it is graciously so ordered that our duty in this instance may be a pleasure, for the Bible is truly pleasing considered only as a collection of very ancient and curious history and poetry' (p. 269).

Taken at large, Knox is doing no more than restating old ideas of the literary quality of the Bible, but in detail there are two things that are very striking and very expressive of the 1770s. First, the idea of the Bible's literary quality is specifically an idea of the KJB's quality. He may have started off in terms vague enough to allow a scholarly reader to think he was doing the right thing and writing of the quality of the originals, but it rapidly becomes clear that for him the Bible is the KJB. There is a sharp contrast with Temple and his echoers in that they felt similar pleasure in translations but retained a sharp sense of their weaknesses: no 'all the disadvantages of an old prose translation' for Knox, as he seems to forget that the KJB is a translation and is not in the least bothered that it is in prose. Secondly, he reaches his conclusions about the quality of the Bible on a basis Lowth used, his own love for it. The conclusions are much the same as those reached by the argument from divine inspiration to literary perfection, but where Lowth bolstered his views with ample critical demonstration, Knox is content to rest on his and the people's love. This is hardly as persuasive as Lowth. Even so, to argue, or, more accurately, assert from experience is more effective than the hypothetical argument. Popular feeling has helped to reshape the old desire to believe that the Bible is the perfection of eloquence.

Lowth and the English Bible

It is difficult to imagine the understanding of Hebrew poetry developing as it did without Robert Lowth. He was also a major figure in the progress of English attitudes to the KJB, but there is every likelihood these attitudes would have developed in the same way had he not existed. Rather than originating opinion in this area, he picked up things already in the air and gave them the weight of his own authority and prestige. Some of his opinions were more than just in the air. For instance, his judgement that 'the vulgar translation of the Bible ... is the best standard of our language' (*Short Introduction*, p. 62) simply makes absolute the tendency of Swift's observation that the KJB and the PB 'have proved a kind of standard of language'.[4] The effect of such

---

[4] Above, p. 40. Lowth knew Swift's 'Proposal', and refers to it approvingly, pp. iii–iv.

authoritative repetition was to establish the opinion. In 1774 James Burnet, Lord Monboddo, repeated it in his voluminous *Of the Origin and Progress of Language*: 'the translators of our Bible, though as I observed before, they may not have perfectly understood the original, did certainly understand their language very well; and accordingly I hold the English Bible to be the best standard of the English language we have at this day'.[5] Five years later the public could read this from Joseph White, Laudian professor of Arabic etc.:

> The English language acquired new dignity by it, and has hardly acquired additional purity since: it is still considered as a standard of our tongue. If a new version should ever be attempted, the same turn of expression will doubtless be employed, for it is a style consecrated not more by custom than by its own native propriety.   (P. 9)

At the end of the century the reactionary George Burges favoured the public with much of the same view:

> The merit of our present received version ... is sufficiently apparent from the universal and almost enthusiastic respect in which it has long been held by all ranks of people among us. The English Bible ... may be justly held up, even in these polished times, as the purest standard of the English language and the best criterion of sound and classical composition.   (P. 9)

Only one critic took Lowth to task for this opinion, John Symonds, yet his opening remark confirms how far it had become a commonplace. 'It will be proper', he notes, 'to inquire into the grounds of an opinion which passes among some persons for an undoubted truth, namely, that the vulgar translation of the Bible is the best standard of the English language' (pp. 6–7). He is willing to accept that it may be a standard for the use of English words 'in preference to those of a foreign growth' (p. 7), but distinguishes between being a standard and being the best standard: he turns Lowth against himself by noting how many corrections he has made of the KJB's grammar in his *Short Introduction*.[6] This is not entirely fair: it is full of examples from the KJB, impartially using it as a model and pointing out some faults, vulgarities and obsolescences. It concludes with a grammatical analysis of an abbreviated

---

[5] 6 vols. (Edinburgh, 1773–92), II: 141; the reference to his earlier observation is to II: 84n.

[6] The point was repeated by Frederick Henry Scrivener in 1845, but more important is that even so long after the appearance of Lowth's work, Scrivener regards it as 'the text book on the subject of which it treats' (*A Supplement to the Authorised English Version of the New Testament* (London, 1845), p. 53).

conflation of Luke 3: 1–22 and Matt. 3: 4–17 (pp. 126–32).[7] Moreover, even as Lowth makes his observation about the KJB as the best standard, he notes corruptions in its English. Yet, if one goes on the balance of the evidence to be found in the last forty years of the century, it is substantially against the KJB. Symonds has good reason to question the basis of the 'undoubted truth', but his protest was as ineffectual as the pleas of reason usually are against an idea whose time has come.

Some of Lowth's opinions develop from the less clearly expressed ideas of others. The new criticism of the KJB and the calls for revision had quickly produced defenders. Among the first was the dissenting minister and Hebrew lexicographer John Taylor (1694–1761). His tract, *A Scheme of Scripture-Divinity... With a vindication of the Sacred Writings* (1762), defends the KJB against criticism of its accuracy on the Beveridgean ground that it is the established translation: one may and should go to the originals for their exact meaning, but the KJB does not need revising:

> In above the space of an hundred years, learning may have received considerable improvements, and by that means, some inaccuracies may be found in a translation more than a hundred years old. But you may rest fully satisfied that as our English translation is in itself by far the most excellent book in our language, so it is a pure and plentiful fountain of divine knowledge. (1: 188)

All Taylor is really saying is that, as he puts it, 'whoever studies the Bible, the English Bible, is sure of gaining that knowledge and faith, which, if duly applied to the heart and conversation, will infallibly guide him to eternal life' (1: 188), which is hardly an original position. Nevertheless, his vagueness has led him to imply that, as literature, the Bible is 'the most excellent book in our language'. That there are aesthetic criteria involved is suggested by another vague claim, that 'the language of Nature is most certainly the language of God, the sole author of Nature' (1: 5). He too comes close to the notion of the divine inspiration of the English translation.

Lowth, who seems to have developed his particular attitude to the KJB in the 1760s, clarified the implications of such woolliness, leading the opinion that resulted in the RV being a revision which sought to maintain the style of its predecessor while improving its accuracy. On the one hand as a cleric he

---

[7] John Ash's *Grammatical Institutes* (1760), in its later editions subtitled *An Easy Introduction to Dr Lowth's English Grammar*, also uses biblical examples (4th edn, 1763; facsimile (Leeds: Scolar, 1967), pp. 97–107). This work was popular on both sides of the Atlantic.

believed that more progress had been made in the knowledge of the Scriptures in the 150 years since the publication of the KJB than in the fifteen centuries preceding. He therefore advocated 'an accurate revisal of our vulgar translation by public authority' in order

> to confirm and illustrate the Holy Scriptures, to evince their truth, to show their consistency, to explain their meaning, to make them more generally known and studied, more easily and perfectly understood by all; to remove the difficulties that discourage the honest endeavours of the unlearned, and provoke the malicious cavils of the half-learned.[8]

On the other hand, as a literary man he developed Taylor's feeling, combining literary judgement with evidence of, and appeal to, popular taste. Defending the closeness with which he has followed the language of the KJB in his *Isaiah*, he observes that 'the style of [that] translation is not only excellent in itself, but has taken possession of our ear, and of our taste'. A revision is therefore more advisable than a new translation, 'for as to the style and language, it admits but of little improvement; but in respect of the sense and the accuracy of inter-pretation, the improvements of which it is capable are great and numberless' (pp. lviii–lix). This, by the end of the century, was to be the dominant opinion.

The example as well as the arguments in *Isaiah* contributed significantly to the acceptance of this opinion in the short term, for

> So judiciously was this great work executed as to remove many prejudices which persons of scrupulous minds had conceived against a general revision of the present translation of the Bible; and as the necessity of it hath appeared more obvious, so the objections to it have been much diminished, and people are more reconciled to the idea of a new translation of the sacred text than they were before the Bishop of London convinced them that such an undertaking would, instead of lessening their reverence for the Bible, increase their veneration for it and give them a juster insight into its contents.[9]

With such a commendation before us, it will be as well to give a specimen of Lowth's work. The first edition is spaciously, even luxuriously, presented[10] (the reader who goes to the facsimile to which I have referred will not perceive the whole effect of the work); verse and chapter numbers are given in the margin, and the copious notes are presented in a solid body after the complete text. The

---

[8] Visitation Sermon at Durham, 1758; *Sermons and Other Remains of Robert Lowth*, ed. Peter Hall (London, 1834), p. 85.

[9] *Monthly Review*, 71 (September 1784), 161–2.

[10] Its price is indicative. At a guinea it was one of the most expensive versions available. Geddes gives a list of prices for various versions (*General Answer*, p. 8).

result is an uninterrupted reading text presented in paragraphs of free verse. Here is a famous passage to which there will be occasion to return, 40: 1–8:

> Comfort ye, comfort ye my people, saith your God:
> Speak ye animating words to Jerusalem, and declare unto
>   her,
> That her warfare is fulfilled; that the expiation of her
>   iniquity is accepted;
> That she shall receive at the hand of Jehovah
> [Blessings] double to the punishment of all her sins.
>
>   A voice crieth: In the wilderness prepare ye the
>   way of Jehovah!
> Make straight in the desert a highway for our God!
> Every valley shall be exalted, and every mountain and
>   hill be brought low;
> And the crooked shall become straight, and the rough
>   places a smooth plain:
> And the glory of Jehovah shall be revealed;
> And all flesh shall see together the salvation of our God:
> For the mouth of Jehovah hath spoken it.
>   A voice sayeth: Proclaim! And I said, What shall I
>   proclaim?
> All flesh is grass, and all its glory like the flower of
>   the field:
> The grass withereth, the flower fadeth;
> When the wind of Jehovah bloweth upon it.
> Verily this people is grass.

Lowth's notes on this passage say much about the principles on which he worked. Typical of the pervasive spirit of rationalism is his insistence that many parts of the prophecy literally refer to Cyrus' delivery of the Jews, not to John the Baptist, even though that is the understanding found in the Gospels. Some readings he defends on the grounds that the KJB's rendering is unpalatable, so he notes of verse 2, 'blessings double to the punishment', that 'it does not seem reconcilable to our notions of the divine justice, which always punishes less than our iniquities deserve, to suppose that God had punished the sins of the Jews in double proportion'; his alternative reading, he argues, fits the original, and he suggests some similar cases. The change in verse 3 that breaks up the words used for John in the NT, 'the voice of him that crieth in the wilderness', is made because it accords with 'the punctuation of the Masoretes, which agrees best both with the literal and the spiritual sense; which the construction and parallelism of the distich in the Hebrew plainly favours; and of which the Greek of the LXX and of the evangelists is equally susceptible'. This leads him to comment on our prepossession with the idea of John living and preaching in the desert. Others of the annotations elucidate the sense of the passage, and they are detailed enough to include the observation in relation to verse 7 that '"a wind of Jehovah" is a Hebraism, meaning no more than a strong wind'.

But, compared with the version and the form it is presented in, these are minor matters. For all the variations, even down to replacing 'surely' with what might be felt to be the more biblical 'verily' in verse 7, the language is substantially that of the KJB. Indeed, Lowth keeps more of the KJB than any of his successors.[11] To some extent he anticipates the RSV in form (the RV uses prose), except that he typically incorporates the two halves of a parallelism in one line whereas the RSV makes a visual distinction, generally giving the second part as an indented line. While this makes the RSV more effective as a presentation of the parallel form, the most important thing is that Lowth demonstrates that a loose verse form combined with the language of the KJB can give an effective sense of versification; the KJB can, in places, be read as verse (in a sense the passage is very close to what Say did with his two brief examples from the KJB (above, p. 19)). Such a demonstration is the more effective because of Lowth's reputation for elegance and erudition. More than any other biblical scholar of the time he could appear as an Augustan and so, as it were, get away with something that so radically revised Augustan standards of language and versification.

One further point about the presentation of the Hebrew poetry in English free verse needs recalling here.[12] Often the line divisions are hypothetical and so, to a degree, represent an unscholarly adaptation of the form of the poetry to something like a familiar English pattern. This is less of a falsification than the addition of rhyme and metre but still has its dangers. Only Blayney is candid on this point:

> In those cases, therefore, where neither the initial letter nor the constructive form or sense of the passage afforded any more probable means of distinguishing, I have adopted an appeal to the eye instead of to the ear upon the following principle of analogy: having remarked a certain determinate medium in the length of those verses

[11] The *Monthly Review* complained of the chief of Lowth's followers, Benjamin Blayney, in his *Jeremiah and Lamentations* (a work, like his later *Zechariah*, presented in a form identical to that of the first edition of *Isaiah*), that he erred in both directions, sometimes sounding too modern and vulgar, sometimes too refined and obscure (71 (September 1784), 162).

[12] The point is made more fully above, pp. 28–9.

whose measure was capable of being ascertained, with a variation of seldom more than a syllable or two either in excess or defect, I have divided the rest according to the like proportion... A method, it must be owned, sufficiently inaccurate and precarious, and admitted only because there appeared little chance of a better.[13]

Such appeals to the eye, often with little apparent justification in the actual form of the words, persist, unremarked, in most modern versions.

Myths arise

The 1760s were the crucial years of change in the literary fortunes of the KJB, but it would be naive to think that the change was absolute. Just as there were forerunners of the favourable view, so the sense of the perfection of modern letters and the accompanying hostility to the KJB's antiquated English did not vanish on the instant. It is a useful reminder to find in the midst of a characteristic statement from 1790 of the kind of favourable, indeed sentimental, opinions that we are now following the comment that 'it is fashionable, we know, to talk of the superiority of our own age, particularly in biblical literature, over those ages which preceded it'.[14] Nevertheless, it is the development of the favourable ideas rather than the sterile self-satisfied hostility that is of interest.

Even in tracing the story of favourable opinion this far we have come across suggestions of two myths, that the translators were divinely inspired, and that the KJB was a literary revision. While the first of these develops little for the time being, a period so concerned with translation was fertile ground for the second myth, and it will be as well to show this before going on. I call the idea that the KJB was a literary revision a myth because, in the form that Pilkington gives it (above, p. 77), it has little to do with the facts. Yet this is not to say that all versions of the idea are mythical, only those expressions of it which forget just how much the work of the translators was dominated by the demands of scholarship and the care to keep as close as possible to the words and structure of the originals. Now that the KJB was admired as English, it was difficult not to argue backwards from a perception of achievement to a belief in conscious artistry: the translators, it seems, must have engaged in literary rubbing and polishing of the sort that was such a priority with some of the later eighteenth-century translators. Clement Cruttwell, for instance, comments that

More than common care seems to have been taken by Miles Coverdale in the

---

[13] *Jeremiah and Lamentations. A new translation* (Oxford, 1784), p. v.
[14] *Monthly Review*, new series, 1 (January 1790), 66.

language of his translation: we have some, but they are very few, instances of barbarism, and none which are not authorised by the writers of the times in which he wrote. To him and other translators of the Scriptures, especially of the present Bible by the authority of King James, our language owes perhaps more than to all the authors who have written since ... they preserve their ancient simplicity pure and undefiled, and in their circumstance and connection perhaps but seldom could be exchanged for the better.   (Fol. AI v)

Earlier Hugh Blair, one of the prominent members of the mid-century Edinburgh circle, had helped to spread such ideas by remarking in his well-known lectures 'that our translators ... have often been happy in suiting their numbers to the subject'.[15] This envisages the kind of deliberate attention to prose rhythm that the translator Nathaniel Scarlett describes in commending his revision of Matt. 22: 21, 'render therefore the *things* of Caesar to Caesar, and the *things* of God to God': 'this closes with a double iambic preceded by an anapaest, all which are allowed to be the best concluding feet'.[16] Yet, whatever the KJB translators achieved, there is no evidence that they applied this sort of consideration to their work. Nor, indeed, is there any evidence in the Bible translations that such consciousness produces better prose than the constraints under which the KJB translators worked. So much of beauty lies in the accustomed eye of the beholder.

A third myth of the sort that we have already seen in connection with the Septuagint (see volume 1, p. 8) sprang up just as easily, that the KJB was an immediate success. Joseph White, one of our echoers of the commonplace about the KJB being the 'standard of our tongue', seems to have been the first to put forward this tenacious notion, observing simply that 'it was a happy consequence of this acknowledged excellence [of the KJB] that the other versions fell immediately into disrepute, are no longer known to the generality of the people, and are only sought after by the curious' (p. 9). Now, when the KJB was first offered to the public, the translators were well aware of the truth

---

[15] Blair continues:

> Grave, solemn and majestic subjects undoubtedly require such an arrangement of words as runs much on long syllables, and, particularly, they require the close to rest upon such. The very first verses of the Bible are remarkable for this melody: 'in the beginning God created the heavens and the earth. And the earth was without form, and void; and darkness was upon the face of the deep. And the spirit of God moved upon the face of the waters.' Several other passages, particularly some of the Psalms, afford striking examples of this sort of grave, melodious construction.
>
> (*Lectures on Rhetoric and Belles Lettres*, XIII; intro. Thomas Dale (London, 1853), pp. 148–9)

[16] *A Translation of the New Testament from the Original Greek* (London, 1798), p. viii.

that 'he that meddleth with men's religion in any part meddleth with their custom, nay, with their freehold' (preface, p. 2). With prescient pessimism, they anticipated a very different reception from that accorded them by this myth: 'was there ever any thing projected that savoured any way of newness or renewing, but the same endured many a storm of gainsaying and opposition?' (p. 1). If there is irony in this contrast, there is more irony when another expression of the myth comes in context of the same pessimism about the reception of a new version. Geddes laments that

> He who undertakes a new translation of the Sacred Scriptures lies under disadvantages, in any country, which no other translator has to encounter, and there are circumstances which make them lie peculiarly heavy on an English translator. The idea that has for almost two centuries prevailed of the super-excellence of our public version is alone an almost insuperable difficulty. Mankind are naturally unwilling to see, and ashamed to acknowledge, not only their own faults but even the faults of those whom, from their earliest years, they have been taught to admire and revere. James's translators have been so long in possession of so high a reputation, and their work has been considered as such a pattern of perfection, that the smallest deviation from their standard is by many deemed a species of literary felony which admits not of benefit of clergy. (*General Answer*, pp. 1–2)

The bases for such remarks are palpably simple. First, it is a happy reinforcement of an opinion to believe that it has always been held – here it would detract from either the KJB or the English people if *it* had not been an instant success or if *they* had not recognised it as such. Second, in ignorance of the historical evidence, White and Geddes have generalised backwards from the present dominance of the KJB and ideas of its quality. What has been true for twenty or thirty years can easily be thought to have been true 'for almost two centuries'. So myths arise out of opinion and desire; in due course they influence opinion further and reinforce the desire to attribute perfection to what was once seen as a very human and distinctly imperfect production.

The KJB as a literary example

The reputation of the KJB developed most through the increasingly common literary discussion of the Bible and the ongoing debate on the question of revision. Before these are examined, a third area is of some significance, the continuing use of the Bible, now in the form of the KJB, as an example in general literary discussion. Two popular and influential works are of use here, Henry Home, Lord Kames's *Elements of Criticism* (1762), and George

Campbell's *The Philosophy of Rhetoric* (1776). Home (1696–1782) and Campbell (1719–96) were both leading figures in what is usually called 'the Scottish enlightenment', an intellectual flowering in the mid-eighteenth century. Adam Smith, himself one of this group, refers to Home as 'after all the master of us all',[17] and Campbell thought *Elements of Criticism* the furthest advanced work of its sort (p. li). Home was Campbell's elder by twenty-three years but they grew up in substantially similar intellectual environments and both wrote on religious as well as literary and philosophical matters; Home made his name in the law, and Campbell, who had studied law for a time, entered the ministry and became a theologian, educator and Bible critic and translator. This common background and the younger man's admiration for the older are of some importance, for they direct us towards their relative ages, the later date of Campbell's work and the particular qualities of Campbell's mind as the major sources of difference between them. These differences help to show changes that took place in attitudes to the KJB in the 1760s.

Both men were deeply religious and liberal-minded, both knew the Bible intimately, and both thought the Bible had literary quality, but Home's sense of this is muted compared with Campbell's. Although he could quote the Bible readily and with accuracy,[18] he uses it only six times in *Elements of Criticism*, and then usually in versions that alter the wording of the KJB. Five of his examples are intended to indicate quality in the Bible, though, one suspects from the alterations, not necessarily in the KJB. For instance, on the subject of comparisons between dissimilar things, he remarks that

> There is little resemblance between fraternal concord and precious ointment, and yet observe how successfully they are compared with respect to the impressions they make:
>
>> Behold how good and how pleasant it is for brethren to dwell together in unity. It is like the precious ointment upon the head, that ran down upon Aaron's beard, and descended to the skirts of his garment.   (P. 312)

The first sentence follows the KJB, but the second is rewritten from, 'it is like the precious ointment upon the head, that ran down upon the beard, even Aaron's beard: that went down to the skirts of his garments' (Ps. 133: 2). Home has smoothed out the sentence structure, implying that, although the simile is good, the expression of the English translation is not what it should be.

This particular biblical quotation perhaps needs no more commentary than Home has given it, but it is characteristic of his work as well as of what we can

---

[17] Quoted in Lehmann, *Henry Home*, p. xvi.
[18] See, e.g., ibid., p. 134.

now begin to think of as older literary discussion that general observations are garnished with illustrative passages but little if any detailed comment. It will be one of Campbell's main marks of distinction that he can develop detailed discussion of his examples. Three of Home's other biblical passages are given without comment, but of Ps. 80: 8–15 he observes that there is not 'a finer or more correct allegory' (p. 354). These five examples, then, hint that the Bible can be used as a source for literary examples, but they hardly promote the KJB or illuminate the passages.

Home's one other use of the Bible gives the truest sense of his attitude to it as literature. Near the beginning of his chapter on comparisons he writes:

> When a nation emerged out of barbarity begins to think of the fine arts, the beauties of language cannot long lie concealed; and, when discovered, they are generally, by the force of novelty, carried beyond moderation. Thus, in the early poems of every nation we find metaphors and similes founded on slight and distant resemblances which, losing their grace with their novelty, wear gradually out of repute; and now, by the improvement of taste, none but correct metaphors and similes are admitted into any polite composition.   (Pp. 310–11)

In illustration of this Augustan sense of present refinement, he gives a loose version of parts of chapters 4 and 7 of the Song of Songs, and a similar passage from Macpherson's 'Fingal'.[19] Parts of the Bible, it seems, are primitive literature of human rather than divine authorship; nevertheless, literature is much improved, and so one finds in Home a freethinking attitude towards the Bible combined with the Augustan sense of literary improvement through to the present time.

Home's work, then, shows some signs of recognition that the Bible is literature and could be discussed as such, but the rarity of his examples suggests that the recognition is weak. His amendments of the KJB show that he did not accept it as great English writing, and his reservations about the Song of Songs suggest that, in spite of his belief in the historical, doctrinal and moral truth[20] of the Scriptures, he did not consider them great literature. In these respects he is

---

[19] Here is Home's Macpherson:

> Thou art like the snow on the heath; thy hair like the mist of Cromla, when it curls on the rocks and shines to the beam of the west; thy breasts are like two smooth rocks seen from Branno of the steams; thy arms like two white pillars in the hall of the mighty Fingal.

This is no more accurate than his biblical quotations (see Macpherson, *Fragments*, pp. 62–3; the passage was revised, but not to the form Home gives).

[20] Cf. Lehmann, p. 276.

characteristic of the middle part of the eighteenth century: a coming idea has made its way into his work without reaching full conviction.

Campbell, too, has little of a general nature to say about the Bible in his *Philosophy of Rhetoric*, but again uses biblical examples to illustrate points about language. It is in the number and use of the examples that the two men differ, and out of this comes a different attitude towards the Bible, both in the original languages and in English. Campbell habitually (and, for one section of his argument, exclusively) turns to the KJB for examples. In part this is because from 1750 he had been collecting criticisms on the text of the NT[21] and so was especially familiar with details of the KJB's language, but there is also a less personal reason: his interest is in 'reputable, national, and present' uses of English (p. 151), which he defines primarily in terms of English Augustan prose writers, and a rather wider range of poets. He is concerned 'that there may be no suspicion that the style is superannuated' (pp. 150–1) in the writers he chooses, but exempts 'the vulgar translation of the Bible' because 'the continuance and universality of its use throughout the British dominions affords an obvious reason for the exception' (p. 151). This takes the KJB as a standard for language (though not as a model of contemporary English) on the sound basis of its achieved popular position, so establishing Campbell as a critic who acted on Lowth's commonplace.

The section where he uses biblical examples exclusively serves as a convenient introduction to his work. He is discussing word order in sentences and arguing

> that though the most usual, which is properly the artificial order, be different in different languages, the manner of arranging, or (if you like the term better) transposing, above specified, which is always an effect of vivacity in the speaker and a cause of producing a livelier conception in the hearer, is the same in all languages. It is for this reason, amongst others, that I have chosen to take most of my examples on this topic, not from any original performance in English, but from the common translation of the Bible, and shall here observe once for all that both in the quotations already made and those hereafter to be made, our translators have exactly followed the order of the original. And, indeed, all translators of any taste, unless when cramped by the genius of the tongue in which they wrote, have in such cases done the same. (P. 358)

The KJB is used solely for its qualities as an accurate representation of the rhetorical quality to be found in other languages possessing a different 'artificial order'. The promise of careful scholarship to demonstrate the point is kept as

---

[21] See *Four Gospels*, 1: ii.

Campbell takes examples from both OT and NT, giving the original, Latin and modern language translations. Here is one example, which I give at length to show the quality of Campbell's practical criticism:

> The third example shall be of an active verb preceded by the accusative and followed by the nominative ... we are informed by the sacred historian that when Peter and John ordered the cripple who sat begging at the beautiful gate of the temple to look on them, he looked at them very earnestly, expecting to receive something from them. Then Peter said, 'Silver and gold have I none, but such as I have, give I thee; in the name of Jesus Christ of Nazareth, arise and walk' [Acts 3: 6]. Here the wishful look and expectation of the beggar naturally leads to a vivid conception of that which was the object of his thoughts, and this conception as naturally displays itself in the very form of the declaration made by the apostle. But as everything is best judged by comparison, let us contrast with this the same sentence arranged according to the rigid rules of grammar, which render it almost a literal translation of the Italian and French versions quoted in the margin, 'I have no gold and silver; but I give thee that which I have: in the name of—' The import is the same, but the expression is rendered quite exanimate. Yet the sentences differ chiefly in arrangement, the other difference in composition is inconsiderable.
>
> There is another happy transposition in the English version of the passage under view which, though peculiar to our version, deserves our notice, as it contributes not a little to the energy of the whole. I mean not only the separation of the adjective 'none' from its substantives 'silver' and 'gold', but the placing of it in the end of the clause which, as it were, rests upon it. 'Silver and gold have I *none.*' For here, as in several other instances, the next place to the first, in respect of emphasis, is the last. We shall be more sensible of this by making a very small alteration in the composition and structure of the sentence, and saying, 'Silver and gold are not in my possession', which is manifestly weaker. (Pp. 358–9)

Campbell has drawn out the special quality of the order of the words as creators of more than they are saying. This he calls 'the energy of the whole', and it is common in his work for him to illustrate this energy (or 'vivacity', as he usually terms it) by comparison with other possible renderings. Here the contrast with Lowth is striking. Perceptive and convincing as Lowth often is, he cannot match the precise demonstration of quality that Campbell gives here, but rather suggests to the reader how he can come through to the kind of perception Campbell creates. Further, Lowth is not discussing the KJB, and, unlike Campbell, he confines himself to the OT, if not entirely to its poetical parts. Campbell, however, lacks Lowth's wide-ranging commitment to exposition of Hebrew poetry: it was not part of his purpose.

Campbell's ability to push beyond his particular point and note also the force of 'have I none' is particularly striking because he presents it as 'a happy transposition peculiar to our version'. Such awareness of a unique literary quality in the KJB, implicitly an improvement on the Greek, could be used as evidence of literary intention and taste on the part of the translators. He characteristically does not draw such a conclusion; nor does he conclude that what he shows proclaims the literary quality of the KJB,[22] but his readers might easily reach both conclusions. Without saying so, he is helping to build the conviction that the KJB was a masterpiece of English literature.

The remarks on the English refer only to the KJB: for all Campbell's knowledge of translations in other languages, he shows no awareness of older English translations. He implies that 'have I none' was the creation of the KJB translators, whereas it is Tyndale's. A knowledge of the other translations could have strengthened his final point, for it would have been more instructive to have Gregory Martin's 'silver and gold I have not' in place of his invented alternative, 'silver and gold are not in my possession'.[23]

The quotations are usually but not always accurate. In a footnote to the passage, he gives the Greek and Latin correctly, but the KJB reads 'rise up' rather than 'arise', which does not affect his point but suggests that he shares Home's sense of infelicity in the KJB; indeed, one of the reasons for collecting criticisms of the KJB NT was to find translations that expressed 'the meaning with more perspicuity or energy' (*Four Gospels*, 1: ii). However, only once does he make a clear attempt to improve the KJB: he substitutes 'perfume the air' (pp. 292–3) for 'give a good smell' (S. of S. 2: 13). Since the rest of the quotations only vary insignificantly, his work in relation to Home's suggests a movement towards literal adherence to the KJB.

Campbell sums up some of what has been inferred of his attitudes in commenting on 'prolixity in narration, arising from the mention of unnecessary circumstances'; he begins with an invented example:

'On receiving this information, he arose, went out, saddled his horse, mounted him

---

[22] By no means all of his examples are favourable to the KJB. Like Lowth in *Short Introduction*, he is as ready to observe faults as he is to observe strengths; see e.g., pp. 189 and 210.

[23] Knowledge of the history of translations of the Bible into English was kept alive by Cruttwell, and revived by the publication in 1841 of *The English Hexapla*. Cruttwell's preface to *The Holy Bible* (1785 – sometimes known as Bishop Wilson's Bible after Thomas Wilson, who provided the notes) gives an external history of translations followed by a chronological list of English versions, complete and incomplete. The edition itself is a variorum Bible, taking note of all the versions before the KJB as well as several later versions, including Purver's; it even includes readings by commentators such as Henry Hammond.

and rode to town.' All is implied in saying, 'on receiving this information, he rode to town'. This manner, however, in a certain degree, is so strongly characteristic of the uncultivated but unaffected style of remote ages that in books of the highest antiquity, particularly of the sacred code, it is not at all ungraceful. Of this kind are the following scriptural phrases, 'He lifted up his voice and wept.' 'She conceived and bore a son.' 'He opened his mouth and said.'[24] For my own part, I should not approve the delicacy of a translator who, to modernise the style of the Bible, should repudiate every such redundant circumstance. It is true that in strictness they are not necessary to the narration, but they are of some importance to the composition, as bearing the venerable signature of ancient simplicity. And in a faithful translation there ought to be not only a just transmission of the writer's sense, but, as far as is consistent with perspicuity and the idiom of the tongue into which the version is made, the character of the style ought to be preserved. (P. 352)

Campbell implies that the KJB translators consciously tried to meet these criteria for 'a faithful translation' and that they frequently succeeded. He shows too that their work is capable of improvement: for him the KJB was not unerringly great literature. Further, some of his observations of inaccuracies, as well as of infelicities, suggest that he is writing with an eye open to the possibility of revision. In the example just given, he anticipates the nineteenth-century view that the KJB should be revised for accuracy but that 'the character of the style ought to be preserved'. He means the character of the originals, but implies what he demonstrates elsewhere, that the KJB preserves this character.

There is another contrast with Home. Like him, Campbell sees the Bible as 'uncultivated' literature, and he too implies subsequent improvement, but, in keeping with critics such as Husbands and Lowth, his dominant sense of this literature of 'antiquity' is positive. It may be 'uncultivated', but it is also 'unaffected', and is often worthy of favourable commentary as being 'not at all ungraceful'. So, where Home cites the Song of Songs to show defects in primitive literature, Campbell responds to it positively in his capacity as a close and sensitive reader. It is in passages such as the following (which contains the revision already noted) that he does most to advance a recognition of quality both in the Scriptures and in the KJB:

in composition, particularly of the descriptive kind, it invariably succeeds best for brightening the image to advance from general expressions to more special, and thence again to more particular. This, in the language of philosophy, is descending. We descend to particulars; but in the language of oratory it is ascending. A very beautiful climax will sometimes be constituted in this manner, the reverse will often have all the effect of an anticlimax. For an example of this order in description, take

[24] All these phrases and variations on them are used frequently in the KJB.

the following passage from the Song of Songs: 'My beloved spake and said to me, Arise, my love, my fair, and come away; for lo, the winter is past, the rain is over and gone, the flowers appear on the earth, the time of the singing of birds is come, and the voice of the turtle is heard in our land; the figtree putteth forth her green figs, and the vines, with the tender grape, perfume the air. Arise, my love, my fair, and come away' (S. of S. 2: 10–13). The poet here, with admirable address, begins with mere negatives, observing the absence of every evil which might discourage his bride from hearkening to his importunate request: then he proceeds by a fine gradation to paint the most inviting circumstances that could serve to ensure the compliance of the fair. The first expression is the most general, 'the winter is past'. The next is more special, pointing to one considerable and very disagreeable attendant upon winter, *the rain*, 'the rain is over and gone'. Thence he advanceth to the positive indications of the spring, as appearing in the effects produced upon the plants which clothe the fields, and on the winged inhabitants of the grove. 'The flowers appear on the earth, and the time of the singing of birds is come.' But as though this were still too general, from mentioning birds and plants, he proceeds to specify *the turtle*, perhaps considered as the emblem of love and constancy; *the fig-tree* and *the vine*, as the earnest of friendship and festive joy, selecting that particular with regard to each which most strongly marks the presence of the all-reviving spring. 'The voice of the turtle is heard in our land, the fig-tree putteth forth her green figs, and the vines with the tender grape perfume the air.' The passage is not more remarkable for the liveliness than for the elegance of the picture it exhibits. The examples are all taken from whatever can contribute to regale the senses and awaken love. Yet reverse the order and the beauty is almost totally effaced.   (Pp. 292–3)

Campbell's work, then, is striking in its use of the KJB as a major source of examples for discussion both of literary effects and English literary and grammatical usage, in the quality of the demonstrations of these literary effects and in the treatment of the KJB as a literary text without prejudice against either the NT or the prose parts of the OT. Though *The Philosophy of Rhetoric* is not specifically about the KJB, it contributes importantly to the eighteenth-century literary understanding of the KJB. The difference between it and Home's *Elements of Criticism* also reflects the rapidly changing attitudes to the KJB in the 1760s: Campbell, the best practical critic of his day, both represents and helps to create the new orthodoxy.

The KJB in literary discussions of the Bible

The movement towards increased use and increased accuracy of use of the KJB in general literary discussion is also to be found in literary discussions of the originals. Though the scrupulous and scholarly Lowth leaves his reader in no doubt that his subject is the originals, most other critics use the KJB with a minimal sense that it is a translation. For instance, in the 1750s English readers might have been forgiven for thinking that Longinus had been reading the KJB, for he brings together a substantial catalogue of beauties from the KJB and PB that have convinced him not only of the frequent superiority of the KJB to the Greek classics but also of its divine inspiration. Longinus confesses that he is

> greatly astonished at the incomparable elevation of its style and the supreme grandeur of its images, many of which excel the utmost efforts of the most exalted genius of Greece.
> ... With what majesty and magnificence is the Creator of the world ... introduced making the following sublime inquiry! 'Who hath measured the waters in the hollow of his hand, and meted out heaven with a span, and comprehended the dust of the earth in a measure, and weighed the mountains in scales, and the hills in a balance?' [Isa. 40: 12] Produce me, Terentianus, any image or description in Plato himself so truly elevated and divine! Where did these barbarians learn to speak of God in terms that alone appear worthy of him? How contemptible and vile are the deities of Homer and Hesiod in comparison of this Jehovah of the illiterate Jews! before whom, to use this poet's own words, all other gods are 'as a drop of a bucket, and are counted as the small dust of the balance' [Isa. 40: 15].   (Pp. 51–2)

Longinus has clearly not just undergone a critical conversion but has learnt the Augustan trick of exclamatory criticism; he has also read the OT closely and found a great deal to admire, not only in the imagery, especially the personification (which 'may be justly esteemed one of the greatest efforts of the creative power of a warm and lively imagination'), but also in the narrative of Joseph's story and in the picture presented in Job.

This Longinus is the creation of the critic Joseph Warton (1722–1800) in the *Adventurer* 51 and 53.[25] Warton pretends that a new manuscript of Longinus has been found in which Longinus comes across the Septuagint and then writes in the vein we have seen.[26] Apart from this opening reference, there is nothing to suggest that the subject of 'Longinus'' praise is anything other than the KJB or

---

[25] 1 and 22 May 1753; in *The British Essayists*, ed. Lionel Thomas Berguer, 45 vols. (London, 1823), xxiv: 50–6, 86–92.

[26] Such a pretence was more than merely a witty pretext. Readers of Longinus in Smith's popular translation knew that there was a manuscript in the Vatican Library in which Longinus included Paul among the greatest orators; Smith, though he reports the view that this was a Christian forgery, inclined to think it genuine (pp. xxiii–xxiv). Smith's extensive annotations may have helped furnish the hint for Warton's piece, for he adds biblical examples to the Longinian text, frequently extolling them, in their KJB form, as the highest literature.

the PB except that they are not always accurately quoted; so, where the careless reader would take 'Longinus' to be lauding the KJB, the careful reader would think not of the originals – or the Septuagint – but of Warton praising what the English reader can find in the English Bible without absolutely committing himself to the qualities of the translation. In either case attention to the originals has dwindled and there is little to suggest that the literary Bible is not the KJB.

The implication is the same in two other discussions of the Bible as literature from the 1770s, the first of which has special significance less through its intrinsic merits than through being the first American discussion of the subject, 'A dissertation on the history, eloquence and poetry of the Bible' (1772) by the twenty-year-old Timothy Dwight (1752–1817) on the occasion of his taking his master's degree at Yale. Dwight, as others before and since, thought his subject had 'novelty to recommend it', for no one had ever attempted to entertain the Yale audience by 'displaying the excellencies' of the Bible as 'fine writing' (p. 3). In the local context who would wish to deny the youth his claim of originality?[27] Not only was his dissertation an American first, but, for so young an author, it reveals a considerable confidence and flair in the choice of examples for admiration. For instance, building on Longinus' supposed opinion of Paul's excellence as an orator, he sets Paul against the classical orators and himself against the classicists who hear him 'boldly, unconcernedly prefer St Paul's address to Agrippa [Acts 26: 2–27] for himself before Cicero's to Caesar for Marcellus' (p. 10), and then hear him

> trespass still farther in a declaration that [Paul's] farewell to the Ephesians [Acts 20: 18–35] is much more beautiful, tender and pathetic than the celebrated defence of Milo. Never was the power of simplicity in writing so clearly, so finely demonstrated as in this incomparable speech. Not a shadow of art is to be found in it – scarce a metaphor, and not one but the most common, is used – nothing but the natural unstudied language of affection; and yet I flatter myself no person can read it attentively without a profusion of tears.   (P. 11)

This is typical Dwight, exclamatory, challenging and personal in his preferences. He does not often quote, but when he does he sticks close enough to the KJB to persuade the reader that the numberless beauties he finds are all in that version.

---

[27] Vincent Freimarck notes the range of relevant works to be found in the Yale library at that time and rightly concludes that Dwight's speech is a synthesis ('Timothy Dwight's *Dissertation* on the Bible', *American Literature* 24 (1952), 73–7). It is interesting that Lowth's *Praelectiones* appear not to have been held, and certainly Dwight shows no close familiarity with them. Nevertheless, the idea of the Prophets as poets is present in the speech, so one at least of Lowth's ideas had made the transatlantic journey.

He is too much the enthusiast and too little the scholar to allow himself or his audience to remember that the Scriptures were not originally written in English, except perhaps near the beginning where he accounts for the special perfection of the Bible in terms of the climatic situation of the Hebrews and divine inspiration: 'born in a region which enjoyed this advantage [nearness to the sun] in the happiest degree, and fired with the glorious thoughts and images of inspiration, can we wonder that the divine writers, though many of them illiterate, should so far transcend all others as well in style as in sentiment?' (p. 4). This inspired style, it seems, is fully visible in English, and again we come close to the implication that the KJB is inspired.

It is apt that the American response to the Bible as literature should start with such youthful enthusiasm and with such a close connection with the KJB. Yet it is hardly a declaration of independence, and it may be as well to use Dwight to make a point that might be made about many of the critics of this time. The distinction between Longinian ideas and the old idea of the flowers of rhetoric that had seemed so important at the beginning of the century has all but disappeared. Dwight is at once a thorough admirer of Longinus and the sublime, and a searcher after beauties. In his dissertation or in Warton's new Longinus we have writings not substantially different from the sixteenth- and seventeenth-century exemplifications of the figures of rhetoric from the Bible. Enthusiasm has replaced method, but the idea of identifiable beauties and figures remains. What were the old and the new have now become the familiar together.

There is one respect in which Dwight points forwards. Others had praised narrative parts of the Bible, and Dwight notes that 'the story of Joseph is too universally admired to allow a comment' (p. 8), but he moves on to something near-allied to this, the Bible's presentation of character. The sacred penmen, he remarks,

> have yet inserted an endless variety of incidents and characters... Convinced that human manners are the most delightful as well as the most instructive field for readers of the human race, they have exhibited them in every point of view – where are characters so naturally drawn? where so strongly marked? where so infinitely numerous and different? (P. 6)

This is less modern than its generality makes it sound. Dwight continues rhetorically, 'to what can the legislator so advantageously apply for instructions as to the life and laws of Moses? – Whom can the prince propose for examples so properly as Solomon and Jehoshaphat? – In Joshua and Joab the general, the hero are magnificently displayed' (p. 6) – and so on. What he is remarking on is not complexity or depth of characterisation but the wide range of exemplary types visible in the Bible; rather than being the first in what was to become a major line of discussion in the next century, he gives an idea of what might be to come.

Dwight's dissertation reappeared in 1795 as a supplement to a New York edition of the other work of this sort from the 1770s, Samuel Jackson Pratt's *The Sublime and Beautiful of Scripture*. This too is an early work: the young Pratt (1749–1815), eventually to be the author of a large number of miscellaneous works under the pen-name Courtney Melmoth, composed with romantic ardour and enthusiasm a series of essays on literary aspects of the Bible 'in the animated moments of feeling when their author was destined to holy orders, and while the impression made by each passage was yet glowing on the imagination and the heart' (1: vii); he then gave some of them as public lectures in the Edinburgh winter of 1776 before such luminaries as Home, David Hume and Hugh Blair. Among the more significant aspects of these essays is that Pratt is the first of our critics to use 'literary' in its modern sense: he describes his subject as 'the *literary* excellence of the Holy Bible' (his italics), and links 'literary' with 'entertaining'. Here is the passage at length:

> And I am thus particularly earnest to display in this work the *literary* excellence of the Holy Bible because I have reason to apprehend it is too frequently laid by under a notion of its being a dull, dry and unentertaining system, whereas the fact is quite otherwise: it contains all that can be *wished* by the truest intellectual taste, it enters more sagaciously and more deeply into human nature, it develops character, delineates manner, charms the imagination and warms the heart more effectually than any other book extant; and if once a man would take it into his hand without that strange prejudicing idea of flatness, and be willing to be pleased, I am morally certain he would find all his favourite authors dwindle in the comparison, and conclude that he was not only reading the most religious but the most *entertaining* book in the world.
>
> (11: 81–2)

Besides the use of 'literary', and the familiar, indeed perennial, complaint of literary prejudice against the Bible, this is notable for developing Dwight's hint at a modern sense of character. Soon afterwards Pratt writes that

> Whoever examines the Scriptures will find the nicest preservation of character, each delicately discriminated, and so admirably contrasted that nothing which marks one is given heterogenously to another. This also has been considered among the first excellencies of composition: its beauty is manifested in Shakespeare much, but in the Bible more.
>
> (11: 100)

Besides confirming the new emphasis in criticism, this gives Pratt the honour of another first. We have long seen the Scriptures battling with the classics;

recently Knox grouped the Bible, the *Iliad* and Shakespeare together as the sublimest books (above, p. 95), and now Pratt awards the Bible the palm over Shakespeare. All that was needed for this to happen was for Shakespeare's reputation to have risen far enough to make him worthy yardstick and for the Bible to be thought of as a literary work.

This would be peculiarly significant if Pratt had the KJB specifically in mind, for that would make it tantamount to a claim that the KJB is the greatest piece of English literature. Pratt does not make this claim, yet it is implicit in his essays because, as usual, one can hardly believe that he is not writing about the KJB. In this important description of the emotional, personal approach taken to the Bible one may well wonder what Bible Pratt means as, in a ringing phrase, 'the noblest composition in the universe':

> The genuine effusions of the author's mind in the progress of perusing the noblest composition in the universe – indulging himself now and then in a moral comment upon passages of particular beauty; or, in a tender illustration of some of the most striking and pathetic narratives, are now offered to the reader, in the hope of recommending, and still of *more,* [*sic*] endearing to him the original.   (1: viii–ix)

He has almost used Lowes's phrase for the KJB from a century and a half later, 'the noblest monument of English prose', and the odd thing is that 'the original' is, for the first time, not necessarily used to refer to the Hebrew (Pratt keeps to the OT); rather, Pratt uses it in distinction from his own 'effusions' – *they* will send the reader to the work that originally caused them. That work is of course the KJB, whose language he rarely ever modifies. Now, his normal method is to base his essays on one or two verses and then to expatiate as the spirit takes him, and there are occasions when the comments depend on the particular language of the version. This is especially evident when he discusses Gen. 1: 3; whereas Boileau's comments on this verse depended on a quality of sense that might be found in any literal version, Pratt's comments do not necessarily survive the transfer to a different form of words (he gives the KJB verbatim but adds his own italics):

> 'And God said, *let* there be *light*, and there *was* light.' It is altogether *inimitable* and *incomparable*, being infinitely sublime and sacred in itself, and expressed in words exactly suitable. The sentence consists wholly of monosyllables, and those short, smooth and, as it were, insisting upon a rapid pronunciation. The celerity of the words assist in and echo to the command they convey. 'Let there be light' – can anything flow faster or with more facility from the lip? 'And there was light.' If the reader can manage his articulation, the image, the tone and everything else will correspond. Here again we have fresh reason to complain of our great epic poet

[Milton], since the five lines he hath employed on this subject contain a great many polysyllables, each demanding a slow, sluggish, reluctant delivery – the sublimest thought may be destroyed by using improper symbols to express it, since every word should, according to a judicious critic [Home], resemble the motion it signifies.

(Pp. 9–11)

Pratt does more than imply to the average reader that the KJB is *the* Bible: he not only believes himself that it is, but he applies to the KJB the kind of opinions that have frequently been applied to the originals. Often the attribution of perfection to the originals had had a distinctly hypothetical element to it – the version we read has obvious shortcomings, but the original, which we cannot read, being inspired, must have been perfect. Pratt is taking the KJB as perfect and supporting his opinion with demonstration; the hypothetical argument comes a little later. A passage such as the following, which for the most part sounds like an Augustan repetition of the argument from inspiration, becomes remarkable when one realises from the nature of the surrounding discussions that it must refer to the KJB:

the God who created human nature knew intimately the method by which that nature was most forcibly attracted; he knew consequently what mode of address was best adapted and would most readily be admitted into the bosom and work its way into the soul. For this very reason it is obvious he directed a language likely to answer such ends, and this accounts for the remarkable majesty, simplicity, pathos and energy, and indeed all those strokes of eloquence which distinguish the Bible... *Religious eloquence* and the rhetoric of the Scriptures are, in the highest degree, favourable to the cause of truth. Nor can they, surely, ever suffer by any critical observations on the splendour, correctness or purity of the diction.   (Pp. 18–19)

Once again there is a strong implication that the KJB is divinely inspired, but adoration of the KJB is not yet full-blown. Where Pratt stops short is in never naming the KJB; he has made one crucial shift by ceasing to distinguish between the KJB and the originals, but he has not made the shift of saying consciously to himself that the Bible is the KJB. If throughout he had used phrases such as 'our authorised version' instead of 'the Scriptures' or 'the Bible', he would not have changed his sense one whit, but would have forced himself to recognise more of the implications of his thought.

At the end of the century George Burges takes us closer to a full recognition of these implications. Developing his view of 'the merit of our present received version' (above, p. 98), he claims that 'every page ... of the inspired writings is conspicuous for some grace of composition or other' (p. 9). 'Inspired writings' is a parallel phrase for 'our authoritative version' in the previous sentence. Were it not that he is attempting to preserve some distinction between the original and the translation, this would be a direct claim of inspiration for the translation. Having made such a remark, he 'cannot debar [him]self the pleasure of a few extracts', and presents four of them.[28] However, he has no specific comment to offer that would direct the reader exclusively to the KJB, although he has given its text unaltered. Instead, he reminds his reader that these passages are representations of originals by beginning, 'if a mere English reader . . . may be allowed to form a judgement'. Without this the judgement would be a declaration of the literary perfection of the KJB:

> instances of sweeter or sublimer composition, of softened melancholy that fills the mind with sorrow, or of awful grandeur that raises it to adoration are nowhere to be found; and if I did not read my Bible to make me wise unto salvation, I would at least peruse it as the greatest treat to the fervency of imagination and as the best standard for the expression of my thoughts. (P. 11)

Readers did not necessarily have to go outside their Bibles to find remarks and implications of these kinds. The well-off or pretentious, for instance, might find them in a handsome folio Bible replete with engravings and annotations, significantly entitled *An Illustration of the Holy Bible* (Birmingham: Boden, 1770). The title of the second edition (1771) goes on significantly: *the notes and comments are selected from the best annotators, whereby the sublime passages are pointed out and some mistranslations rectified.* Never before had readers been able to read annotations of this sort to the KJB text: 'this is as grand a piece of poetry as ever was composed. The descriptions are so lively, the transitions so quick, the ideas so sublime and the apostrophes so noble that it might, exclusive of its being inspired, be considered as the noblest ode that ever the world produced'. The subject is Deborah's song and the sentiment is very much Temple's from eighty years earlier, except that any suggestion of the old cliché about the disadvantages of translations and prose is totally missing. In fact this Bible goes almost as far in the opposite direction as Pratt, only stopping short of commentary that would be specific to the language of the KJB. The reader about to embark on Exodus 15 is commanded to admire it, for 'he who can read it without being enraptured must be harder than the rock which gushed out a river and more impenetrable to beauties than the hearts of the Israelites were'.

There is a major novelty here. For all the large amount of literary discussion of the Bible and the increasing frequency of the use of the KJB in such discussion, never before has the Bible of worship contained within itself the invitation to a literary reading. In a narrow sense of the phrase, this is the first

---

[28] Ruth 1: 15–17, Job 29: 11–16, Ps. 104: 1–4 and 1 Cor. 15: 51–4.

Bible as literature. It is thoroughly true to the developments we have been following, and has open debts to commentators such as South, Locke and Lowth,[29] yet one must beware of overplaying its importance: there is not a large amount of annotation, and one can read for long stretches without coming across any sign of literary praise; moreover, though it went to a second edition in 1771, this was not a widely used Bible. It helps to mark the arrival of the sense of the KJB as literature but not the arrival of the Bible presented as literature: that arrival is still over a century away.

Revision or 'superstitious veneration'

Of the many rival translators and would-be revisers of the KJB in the latter part of the century we may take the one-armed[30] Archbishop of Armagh, William Newcome (1729–1800) as the most representative and influential. He was more successful than anyone, including the livelier and more provocative Geddes,[31] in formulating ultimately acceptable principles of revision. Moreover, he made a major attempt to shape the reputation of the KJB. In perhaps his best work, the Lowthian *Twelve Minor Prophets* (1785), he distils the problem of Bible translation to this: 'whether we shall supply Christian readers and Christian congregations with new means of instruction and pleasure by enabling them to understand their Bible better' (p. xli). Obviously a new version is needed, both for understanding and literary pleasure. Among the reasons for this are 'the mistakes, imperfections and many invincible obscurities of our present version, the accession of many helps since the execution of that work, the advanced state of learning, and our emancipation from slavery to the Masoretic points and to the Hebrew text as absolutely uncorrupt' (pp. xvi–xvii); further, the KJB's qualities are not 'as uniform as the rules of good writing and the refined taste of the present age require' (*Historical View*, p. 238). In short, he is a scholarly and a literary critic, wanting revision in both areas, and unlikely to overpraise the KJB. Yet he cannot avoid the KJB and it has as strong an

---

[29] See, for instance, the preface to Lamentations, and the notes to Habakkuk 3 and 1 Corinthians.

[30] While he was a tutor at Oxford his left arm was crushed in a door because, it is said, of the boisterousness of one of his pupils, Charles James Fox; the arm was amputated (*DNB*).

[31] The several references I have made to Geddes are less than he deserves. For a full treatment, see Reginald C. Fuller, *Alexander Geddes...: A Pioneer of Biblical Criticism* (Sheffield: Almond Press, 1984).

influence on the rules he draws up for revision as does the time's literary consciousness.[32]

The first rule balances the literal and the literary, for 'the translator should express every word in the original by a literal rendering where the English idiom admits of it, and where not only purity but perspicuity and dignity of expression can be preserved' (p. xvii). Rule IV revives the old principle of uniform rendering for the same word in the original and criticises the KJB translators for varying 'their terms not only unnecessarily but so as to mislead the reader' (p. xxvii); here he echoes Broughton and anticipates the RV.[33] Rule V addresses style:

> The collocation of the words should never be harsh and unsuited to an English ear. An inverted structure may often be used in imitation of the original, or merely for the sake of rhythm in the sentence, but this should be determined by what is easy and harmonious in the English language, and not by the order of the words in the original where this produces a forced arrangement or one more adapted to the license of poetry than to prose.
>
> (Pp. xxx–xxxi)

Such a rule is likely to tip the balance from the literal to the literary, but what is more interesting is that it leads to a particular kind of attention to the KJB: discussing the rule, Newcome notes that 'our translators ... sometimes give a pleasing turn to their clauses by conformity to the order of the words in the original' (p. xxxi), as in Ezek. 23: 37, 'and with their idols have they committed adultery'. This is the kind of consciousness of style that attributes stylishness to the KJB. Newcome's other main stylistic rule is that 'the simple and ancient turn of the present version should be retained' (p. xxxii). 'This simplicity', he adds, 'arises in a great measure from the preference of pure English words to foreign ones'; 'modern terms and phrases, and the pomp and elegance of modernised diction' (p. xxxiii) are to be avoided, as is degeneration 'into familiar idiom'; Hebraisms that are compatible with English or which have become familiar should be retained (p. xxxiv). All this means 'that a translation of the Bible should be a classical book to a foreigner' (p. xxxiii), a notion which

---

[32] I have used the rules given in *Twelve Minor Prophets* rather than the later version in chapter v of *Historical View*.

[33] Since this is not as simple a matter as I have made it appear, it may be of interest to give Newcome's formulation: 'the same original word and its derivatives, according to the leading different senses, and also the same phrase, should be respectively translated by the same corresponding English word or phrase, except where a distinct representation of a general idea, or the nature of the English language, or the avoiding of an ambiguity, or harmony of sound, requires a different mode of expression' (p. xxiv).

is nowhere repeated but which shows the extent to which literary consciousness goes in Newcome.

This is enough of Newcome's rules to show how far he was in tune with the thinking that eventually produced the RV, enough too to establish a fundamental contrast with the KJB translators and their predecessors. One and three-quarter centuries after the publication of the KJB, a literary consciousness of the business of translation has added itself to the quest for the truth, indeed, has become so significant that at times it seems to be more important than the original quest for truth. This is the consciousness that gave rise to the myth that the KJB was a literary revision.

It would have been surprising if Newcome had not given space to literary praise of the originals carefully distinguished from the KJB – such praise, openly indebted to Lowth, is to be found in the preface to his *Ezekiel* (Dublin, 1788) – but what is of more interest is the way he deals with the KJB. In 1792 he produced a valuable introduction to eighteenth-century opinion, indeed, the only work before the present to treat the development of critical opinion of the KJB as a matter of importance, *An Historical View of the English Biblical Translations: the expediency of revising by authority our present translation and the means of executing such a revision.* After a chapter on the history of translation which is a digest of a work by John Lewis,[34] he collects 'authorities respecting the received version of the Bible'. These include extracts from many of the figures we have met and are quite sufficient to establish how highly the KJB was thought of in the latter part of the century. Nevertheless, though Newcome claims to have quoted impartially (p. 185), there is a leaning towards authorities that advocate revision. In effect, his tactic is to concede the present high view of the KJB and then to modify it. The reader who knew nothing of the history Newcome partially reveals would first find his established ideas confirmed and then be taught to question them. Many of the later extracts have this qualifying effect, and Newcome then builds on it by considering the objections to an improved version, arguing that such a version is expedient and presenting his rules for its conduct.

Newcome's various works are the soundest advocation of revision the

---

[34] *A History of the Several Translations of the Holy Bible,* prefixed to *The New Testament . . . by John Wyclif* (London, 1731). This dry, largely bibliographical work is accurately described by Newcome as 'too minute and sometimes too indistinct to invite a perusal' (p. iv). Part of the motive for republishing the Lollard Bible was linguistic: the advertisement characterises it as 'a valuable curiosity and of great use to those Englishmen who are desirous to understand their mother tongue'. The dedication notes that 'it serves to explain the meaning of a great many words still retained in the English translations of the Bible and Psalter now in use' (p. iii).

century has to offer, and there is historical justice of a sort in the fact that his *An Attempt towards Revising our English Translation of the Greek Scriptures*, 2 vols. (Dublin, 1796) was adopted by the SPCK in 1808 as the basis for their 'improved version', which was intended 'to supply the English reader with a more correct text of the New Testament than has yet appeared in the English language, and to give him the opportunity of comparing it with the text in common use'.[35] By this time the SPCK had become Unitarian and there was objection from his family to the good Archbishop's work appearing in sectarian company. Whatever Newcome himself would have thought of this, he would have been saddened to see the larger failure of his work and argument: the version he looked to was still almost a century away.

As the reputation of the KJB rose, there was increasing resistance to change. The danger of unsettling the fragile faith of the people was much canvassed. John Parsons, future Bishop of Peterborough and Master of Balliol, approved Newcome's rules but objected to 'the authoritative substitution of a new version in the room of that which custom has familiarised to the ears and hallowed in the imaginations' because the people 'would lose their veneration for the old version without acquiring sufficient confidence in the new', and so be a prey to doubt and even atheism.[36] It was a very different kind of French influence from those noted in the earlier part of the century that helped produce this failure of the revision movement, the revolution and the Napoleonic wars. In face of the horrors across the channel, England turned neophobic. George Burges (?1764–1853), whom we have already met as a reactionary voice, was the prime spokesman for this feeling as it affected the Bible. France he considered to be 'an awful spectacle to surrounding nations of the dreadful effects which must ever necessarily result from a revolution of government preceding a revolution of mind' (p. 25). He argues that

> if ever an almost superstitious veneration for our excellent version of the Bible required to be inculcated and enforced, it is in a period like the present when the relaxations of society are of such a nature that the wisest men can scarce conjecture upon what basis it will hereafter subsist or by what laws it will be regulated, and when the spirit of revolution, driving rapidly through the world, assimilates in one discordant and heterogeneous mass the sentiments of the philosopher, the Christian and the infidel.   (P. 34)

---

[35] *The New Testament in an Improved Version* (London: SPCK, 1808), p. v. The Society regarded Newcome's use of Griesbach's Greek text as the key to his correctness. Newcome also worked towards a full revsion of the OT: his four volume interleaved OT is in the Lambeth Palace Library.

[36] *Monthly Review* 76 (January 1787), 46, 44.

So minor a pamphlet from the little-known Vicar of Halvergate would have had no influence on the public, especially if set against the weight of the Archbishop of Armagh, but the sentiment it reveals took hold on the country, and the 'almost superstitious veneration for our excellent version' continued to grow as the attempt to procure official revision foundered.

The fairest summary of the position the reputation of the KJB had reached is given by an anonymous advocate of revision in 1788:

> The present version certainly has to a high degree the qualities of beauty, simplicity and force; and we are taught from our infancy to look upon it with such affection and respect that we not only perhaps give it credit, where it does possess those excellencies, for a greater share of them than it actually has, but frequently persuade ourselves of their existence without any real grounds, and are blind to all but very glaring defects. This opinion of the scripture style, though in part ill-founded, is very conducive to our religious improvement: it may be unfavourable to us as critics, but it tends to make us good Christians.[37]

Rancorous reason and brouhaha

Although I have been careful to point out any tendencies towards the idea that the KJB was an inspired translation, one of the more obvious aspects of later-eighteenth-century literary discussion of the Bible is the decline of the idea of inspiration and the growth of the sense that the OT especially is a human product fully open to rational examination. This is not to say that the idea of inspiration disappeared[38] – very few of the general ideas about the Bible do ever disappear, and behind all the developments that so clearly take place there is always a sense of the durability of basic human opinions. For instance, the 1780s, in spite of the strength of the scientific and aesthetic approach to the Bible, provide one of the baldest statements ever of the argument from inspiration to literary perfection:

> When the maker of the world becomes an author, His word must be as perfect as His work: the glory of His wisdom must be declared by the one as evidently as the glory of His power is by the other: and if nature repays the philosopher for his experiments,

---

[37] *Reasons for Revising by Authority Our Present Version* (Cambridge, 1788), pp. 53–4.

[38] In a sense, it had been legally enforced since 1698, when a statute included the penalty of being barred from public office on first offence, and three years' imprisonment on second offence for anyone who 'shall deny the Holy Scriptures of the Old and New Testament to be of divine authority' (*CHB* III: 241–2).

the Scripture can never disappoint those who are properly exercised in the study of it.[39]

This at least shares with writers such as Lowth a favourable literary sense of the Bible, and it is an important reminder just how far from dead the absolutist idea of inspiration was. Nearly half a century later Coleridge was to report its continued strength. At meetings of the British and Foreign Bible Society,

> I have heard the same doctrine – that the Bible was not to be regarded or reasoned about in the way that other good books are or may be – that the Bible was different in kind and stood by itself. By some indeed this doctrine was rather implied than expressed, but yet evidently implied. But by far the greatest number of the speakers it was asserted in the strongest and most unqualified words that language could supply. What is more, their principal arguments were grounded on the position that the Bible throughout was dictated by Omniscience, and therefore in all its parts infallibly true and obligatory, and that the men, whose names are prefixed to the several books or chapters were in fact but as different pens in the hand of one and the same Writer, and the words the words of God himself.   (*Confessions*, pp. 317–18)

In rampant opposition to this idea came 'a shocking and insulting invective ... as mischievous and cruel in its probable effects as it is manifestly illegal in its principles' (Erskine, pp. 8, 10), *The Age of Reason*,[40] by that notorious companion of revolutions, best known for *The Rights of Man*, Thomas Paine (1737–1809). 'My own mind is my own church', he declares (I: 4), 'my endeavours have been directed to bring man to a right use of the reason that God has given him' (III: v). Now, 'the age of reason' might seem to sum up the time and the spirit of a Lowth and a Geddes, yet Paine was ignorant of their work and is using the phrase to proclaim the arrival of reason, represented by his work, in opposition to the inspirationists.[41] Where Lowth and Geddes, particularly, were pioneers moving towards Higher Criticism, Paine, for all that his work is full of a sense of personal discovery, is squarely in the atheist or deist tradition of rationalistic debunking of the Bible that stretches back through

---

[39] So begins William Jones's *A Course of Lectures on the Figurative Language of the Holy Scripture ... Delivered in the Parish Church of Nayland in Suffolk in the year 1786* (Oxford and London, 1848), p. 1. The book itself is only of further interest in showing how broadly the sense of the Bible as a literary work was spreading itself.

[40] Part I (Paris, 1793), II (Paris, 1795), III (New York, 1807). I have used the text given in *The Theological Works of Thomas Paine* (London, 1819). This numbers the pages afresh for each part, and includes some minor works in the numbering of part III.

[41] Prosecuting Paine's bookseller, Erskine remarks sarcastically, 'but it seems this is an age of reason, and the time and the person are at last arrived that are to dissipate the errors which have overspread the past generations of ignorance' (pp. 11–12).

figures such as Collins, Aikenhead and Rochester to Marlowe. This is to name only those who have already appeared here rather than to call the roll of those who might have appeared: atheism and deism provide a constant background of turbulence to religious discussion in the eighteenth century that varies little in its essentials and so does not need exhaustive coverage here. Paine, the most lively and provocative of them all, writing in France, where deism was a stronger force than in England, is the culmination of English deism and may, somewhat loosely, be allowed to stand for his predecessors.

There are additional reasons for focussing on Paine. First, he makes a large number of literary judgements; second, because of the extreme yet popular nature of his work, he provoked a considerable number of replies, of which the most interesting, in the short term, is by Richard Watson (1737–1816), Bishop of Landaff, Regius Professor of Divinity at Cambridge, collector of theological tracts and receiver of an almost universally bad press from historians for his role as spokesman for the establishment. *An Apology for the Bible* (George III is supposed to have commented that he 'was not aware that any apology was needed for that book' (*CHB* III: 251)) was his most popular work. It circulated widely in both England and America, having the usual effect of publicising what it opposed.[42] The poet William Blake made some significant annotations concerning Watson and Paine, and much later that even more important figure, Samuel Taylor Coleridge, developed his subtle and balanced discussion of inspiration in response to both Paine and the inspirationists, observing succinctly that 'this indeed is the peculiar character of the doctrine [of inspiration], that you cannot diminish or qualify it but you reverse it'.[43]

The essence of Paine's deism, which he calls 'the only true religion', is 'the belief of one God, and an imitation of his moral character, or the practice of what are called moral virtues' (II: 74). In this he is not only thoroughly sincere, but as dogmatically pious as Jones has just been in his argument from inspiration to literary perfection. As Paine writes in a pamphlet, 'What! does not the Creator of the Universe ... know how to write?',[44] but he locates this writing outside the Bible: 'the word of God is the creation we behold: and it is in *this* word, which no human invention can counterfeit or alter, that God

---

[42] See Erskine, p. 19. Three quarters of a century earlier Franklin recalls that 'some books against deism fell into my hands ... It happened that they wrought on me quite contrary to what was intended by them: for the arguments of the deists which were quoted to be refuted appeared to me much stronger than the refutations. In short, I soon became a thorough deist' (pp. 113–14).

[43] *Confessions*, p. 318. I have not explored Coleridge's ideas in their own right, since they do not add significantly to his literary sense of the Bible.

[44] 'A letter to ... Thomas Erskine', in *Complete Writings*, II: 732.

speaketh universally to man' (1: 22). Revelation, he argues, cannot consist in writing, principally because it is given to the individual. The individual can report his own experience of revelation, but it is not revelation for any person to whom it is reported; rather, it is hearsay, and that person is entitled freely to decide for himself what is revelation (1: 5). So he regards the theology that is studied in the place of 'natural philosophy' (which is 'the true theology') as 'the study of human opinions, and of human fancies *concerning* God' (1: 26). 'The Christian system of faith' appears to him 'as a species of atheism – a sort of religious denial of God' (1: 26). Having thus rid the Bible of its claims to be the revealed word of God, Paine examines it in the light of reason, 'the choicest gift of God to man' (1: 21).

Part 1 was written without Paine having access to a Bible, so most of the detailed criticism appears in part 2, written after his release from the Bastille, when he had procured a Bible and found its contents 'to be much worse books than I had conceived' (11: vi). He finds it historically uncertain and generally fabulous (cf. 11: 16, 28), and thus to be treated only as a kind of literature. Further, he finds the God portrayed in, especially, the OT, a hideous travesty of his idea of God, absolutely shocking to humanity:

> There are matters in that book, said to be done by the *express command* of God, that are as shocking to humanity and to every idea we have of moral justice, as anything done by Robespierre, by Carrier, by Joseph le Bon, in France, by the English government in the East-Indies, or by any other assassin in modern times . . .
>
> Whenever we read the obscene stories, the voluptuous debaucheries, the cruel and torturous executions, the unrelenting vindictiveness with which more than half the Bible is filled, it would be more consistent that we called it the word of a demon than the word of God. It is a history of wickedness that has served to corrupt and brutalize mankind. (11: 7–8, 1: 13)

This, of course, reverses the view that takes whatever God has written or done as the best, and it also refuses to take the historical perspective that Lowth had begun to develop and which Herder had already argued for so strongly in Germany. Moreover, it is capable of an ironic turn if one takes a Darwinian view of the laws of nature, for Paine's equating of God, nature and moral law is highly optimistic: God's 'work is always perfect, and His means perfect means'.[45]

Of those in the Christian community, only Geddes was able to take Paine's point while rejecting his final position:

> we have no intrinsic evidence of inspiration, or anything like inspiration, in the

---

[45] 'Extracts from a Reply to the Bishop of Llandaff', in *Complete Writings*, 11: 785.

Jewish historians. On the contrary, it is impossible, I think, to read them, devoid of theological prepossessions [and] not to discover in them evident marks of human fallibility and human error... As uninspired historians they claim the same indulgence as we grant to other historical writers: we estimate their abilities, genius, style, judgement and veracity by the same rules of comparative criticism... Whereas the admission, once, of a perpetual and unerring sufflation not only, in my mind, destroys their credibility throughout, but is, moreover, highly injurious to the Supreme Being, as it makes him the primitive author of all that they relate: so the abettors of this delusive doctrine, so far from consulting the honour of God and defending the cause of religion, seem to betray and expose both to contempt and ridicule.[46]

This is to yield the battle and to win the war: Paine's view of the OT as fallible human writings is accepted, but its force against Christianity is shattered by the rejection of what Geddes takes to be a quite unnecessary, not to say pernicious element in Christianity, the belief in inspiration. For Geddes as for Paine the OT is 'a poetical history' (II: xii); what is more, he is convinced that if such a view of the Scriptures were generally accepted, they

would be more generally read and studied, even by fashionable scholars, and the many good things which they contain, more fairly estimated. For what chiefly deters the sons of science and philosophy from reading the Bible and profiting of that lecture, but the stumbling block of absolute inspiration, which, they are told, is the only key to open their treasures? Were the same books presented to them as human compositions, written in a rude age, by rude and unpolished writers, in a poor uncultivated language, I am persuaded that they would soon drop many of their prejudices, discover beauties where they had expected nothing but blemishes, and become, in many cases, of scoffers, admirers.   (II: xiii)

In one respect this line of arguing is a foretaste of the attitudes of Higher Criticism and an indication of their literary implications. In another respect it has come down to a statement of the idea noted from Boswell at the beginning of chapter 2, that an unprejudiced reading would show the Bible to be an admirable literary work.

Geddes's rationalistic optimism might have appealed to Lowth were he still living, but he was ten years dead and much of his spirit had passed to Germany. Bishop Watson's more simplistic refutation, taking ground that the deistic Voltaire had made his own in *Candide*, was to claim that Paine is inconsistent by not similarly condemning the death of innocents in earthquakes, which is equally death by the command of God (pp. 17–18 etc.). This is to miss the point

---

[46] *The Holy Bible ... faithfully translated*, 2 vols. (London, 1792, 1797), II: v.

of Paine's argument even if it is fair comment on the unthinking heart of his deism. Blake would have none of such tangential silliness: 'to me who believe the Bible and profess myself a Christian, a defence of the wickedness of the Israelites in murdering so many thousands under pretence of a command from God is altogether abominable and blasphemous'. He argues that the Jewish Scriptures 'are only an example of the wickedness and deceit of the Jews and were written as an example of the possibility of human beastliness in all its branches'.[47]

Much of Paine's detailed argument consists in close examination of the Bible in order to show inconsistencies which refute its claim to historical truth, and which show that some parts, for instance, the early chapters of Genesis, could not have been written by their supposed authors and are therefore, in his simplistic view, forgeries. Some of his arguments, particularly those aimed at dating passages and determining authorship, anticipate later textual scholarship, although the conclusions he comes to about the value of the books are naturally different.

The creation story, the story of Satan and of the fall and the story of Jesus' supernatural origins are all, Paine argues, 'sprung out of the tail of the heathen mythology' (i: 6), a point that those familiar with discussions of the relationships between other ancient near-eastern texts such as the epic of Gilgamesh and the early chapters of Genesis would find hard to dismiss absolutely, however distasteful they might find the tone and implications. He ridicules these stories in some of his wittiest writing as absurd and extravagant fables (i: 8). Here is part of his mocking argument:

> The Christian mythologists, after having confined Satan in a pit, were obliged to let him out again, to bring on the sequel of the fable. He is then introduced into the Garden of Eden in the shape of a snake or a serpent, and in that shape he enters into familiar conversation with Eve, who is no way surprised to hear a snake talk; and the issue of this tête à tête is, that he persuades her to eat an apple, and the eating of that apple damns all mankind.
>
> After giving Satan this triumph over the whole creation, one would have supposed that the church mythologists would have been kind enough to send him back again to the pit; or, if they had not done this, that they would have put a mountain upon him (for they say that their faith can remove a mountain) or have him put *under* a mountain, as the former mythologists had done, to prevent his getting again among

---

[47] *Complete Writings*, p. 387. Blake's annotations to Watson were written in 1798, using a 1797 edition of Watson with different pagination from that used here. They are discussed at length – and with obvious prejudices – in Bernard Blackstone, *English Blake* (Hamden, Conn.: Archon, 1966), pp. 349–66.

the women and doing more mischief. But instead of this, they leave him at large, without even obliging him to give his parole – the secret of which is, that they could not do without him; and after being at the trouble of making him, they bribed him to stay. They promised him *all* the Jews, *all* the Turks by anticipation, nine-tenths of the world beside, and Mahomet into the bargain. After this, who can doubt the bountifulness of the Christian mythology? (I: 9)

Watson offers only blunt unargued contradiction of this: 'as to the Christian faith being built upon the heathen mythology, there is no ground whatever for the assertion; there would have been some for saying that much of the heathen mythology was built upon the events recorded in the Old Testament' (p. 223). He suggests that if the story of Adam and Eve is not history, it is 'an allegorical representation of death entering into the world through sin, through disobedience to the command of God' (p. 363). Some willingness, characteristic of the defenders of the Bible against deistic objections, to concede that not all the Bible is historically true is evident here. Allegory was the frequent recourse of the defenders, without their showing any desire to go further towards literary interpretation.

Paine's view of Genesis as a whole is in keeping with his opinion of the fall story, and shows his idea of authenticity:

> Take away from Genesis the belief that Moses was the author, on which only the strange belief that it is the word of God has stood, and there remains nothing of Genesis but an anonymous book of stories, fables, and traditionary or invented absurdities, or of downright lies. The story of Eve and the serpent, and of Noah and his ark, drops to a level with the Arabian Tales, without the merit of being entertaining. (II: 18)

Thus the Bible is made bad literature, but again some of the possibilities that modern criticism is now exploring without seeking to diminish the Bible are anticipated. At the end of David Damrosch's *The Narrative Covenant* (1987) there is a stimulating comparison between the Bible and the *Thousand and One Nights*. Paine distinguishes the literature of the OT from, say, the writings of Plato and Homer, in that their poetic merit remains whether the author be known or not; they are works of genius and the Bible is not (II: 9). Though Watson rightly points out that 'anonymous testimony does not destroy the reality of facts' (p. 37), Blake's retort to Watson is still sounder: 'of what consequence is it whether Moses wrote the Pentateuch or no? If Paine trifles in some of his objections it is folly to confute him so seriously in them and leave his more material ones unanswered' (p. 392).

In similar vein Paine dismisses the story in Joshua of the sun standing still as 'a tale only fit to amuse children', but backhandedly concedes that 'as a poetical figure the whole is well enough' (II: 22).[48] Ruth is 'an idle bungling story, foolishly told, nobody knows by whom, about a strolling country girl creeping slyly to bed to her cousin Boaz; pretty stuff, indeed, to be called the word of God'.[49] The Song of Songs he considers 'amorous and foolish enough', but sneers that 'wrinkled fanaticism has called [it] divine' (II: 42). Ecclesiastes is 'the solitary reflections of a worn-out debauchee, such as Solomon was', and 'a great deal of the metaphor and of the sentiment is obscure, most probably by translation' (II: 40–1). It may be that this is a reflection of the pious attribution of apparent imperfections in the text to translations, but the likelihood is that Paine is taking an opportunity to disparage the Bible in any form. Living so much out of England and being so little in touch with current trends of reverence, he may well not have been aware of the K JB's advancing reputation: he surely would have developed the point if he had known how much it was likely to offend the Christian establishment.

Rather like an accidental caricature of Lowth, Paine argues that the Prophets were not seers into the future, but 'Jewish poets and itinerant preachers, who mixed poetry, anecdote and devotion together' (I: 14). His proof that the writings were composed in poetical numbers is about as far removed from Lowth's punctilious scholarship as one could imagine; careless of logic and forgetting that he is attacking the originals, he takes ten syllables inaccurately from the K JB and adds a rhyming line. Isaiah's 'Hear, O ye heavens, and give ear, O earth!' (Isa. 1: 2) is shown to be poetical by the addition of: ''Tis God himself that calls attention forth' (I: 15). Turning to Isaiah at large, he finds it 'one of the most wild and disorderly compositions ever put together; it has neither beginning, middle nor end', but, with exceptions, 'is one continued incoherent, bombastical rant, full of extravagant metaphor, without applica- tion, and destitute of meaning; a school-boy would scarcely have been excusable for writing such stuff'. He adds to this one of his very rare gestures

---

[48] Illustrating how some of the more advanced scholars were treating the Bible as a literary work, Gilbert Wakefield takes up this concession:

> The words before us are of a poetical complexion in the original language ... and the detached manner in which the passage is exhibited, neither interfering with the former nor the subsequent parts of the surrounding narrative, gives great countenance to the supposition of its insertion in later times from the book of Jasher to adorn this feat of heroism. On such an acceptation, therefore, this entire passage is nothing more than a sublime exaggeration of an enthusiastic poet indulging those fervours of rapturous invention conceded to his art.
>
> (*A Reply to Thomas Paine's Second Part of the Age of Reason* (London, 1795), pp. 28–9)

[49] As given by Watson, pp. 106–7.

towards the KJB: 'it is (at least in translation) that kind of composition and false taste that is properly called prose run mad' (II: 42). Watson picks this up to observe sniffily that Paine's taste for Hebrew poetry 'would be more correct if you would suffer yourself to be informed on the subject by Bishop Lowth' (p. 167). Of course there was no chance of Paine suffering himself to be so instructed. Going on, he dismisses Jeremiah as 'a medley of detached unauthenticated anecdotes, put together by some stupid book-maker under the name of Jeremiah' (II: 50), and he argues that Jonah was 'written as a fable, to expose the nonsense and satirise the vicious and malignant character of a Bible Prophet, or a predicting priest' (II: 57).

Only Job and Psalm 19 escape this malicious onslaught, and the reason is simple: he has condemned where he does not believe, but he finds in these some conformity with his deistic views. In his 'reply to the Bishop of Llandaff', he writes that, 'as to the precepts, principles and maxims in the book of Job, they show that the people abusively called the heathen in the books of the Jews, had the most sublime ideas of the Creator and the most exalted devotional morality. It was the Jews who dishonoured God. It was the Gentiles who glorified Him' (*Complete Writings*, II: 776). Presumably the possibility of taking this book out of the Jewish context helped Paine to praise it. The result is praise as high as anyone has to offer, couched in terms that show him very much the second-hand neo-classicist as a straight literary critic:

> As a composition, it is sublime, beautiful and scientific, full of sentiment and abounding in grand metaphorical description. As a drama, it is regular. The dramatis personae, the persons performing the several parts, are regularly introduced, and speak without interruption or confusion . . . the unities, though not always necessary in a drama, are observed here as strictly as the subject would admit.   (II: 776–7)

Paine is back to his old provocative self when he demolishes the NT. He argues initially against the fable of Jesus and 'the wild and visionary doctrine raised thereon' (II: 61). Later he becomes bolder, declaring that 'so far from his being the Son of God, he did not exist even as a man – that he is merely an imaginary or allegorical character, as Apollo, Hercules, Jupiter, and all the deities of antiquity were' (III: 47). He continues to see the Bible in literary terms, so that the NT 'is like a farce of one act, in which there is not room for very numerous violations of the unities' (II: 62) compared with the OT. The story of the crucifixion and the resurrection 'is most wretchedly told' (II: 80): 'it is . . . impossible to find in any story upon record so many and such glaring absurdities, contradictions and falsehoods, as are found in [the Gospels]' (II: 74). To this Watson's reply is simply to return to the old patristic argument and read the evidence in an opposite way: 'had [the evangelists] been imposters, they would have written with more caution and art, have obviated every cavil and avoided every appearance of contradiction. This they have not done, and this I consider as a proof of their honesty and veracity' (p. 290). What is lacking here is any close consideration of the text. As so often, Watson is merely dogmatic, and illuminating discussion is thereby avoided. It is also worth noting that Watson's reply takes Paine's charge of lack of literary quality as evidence of authenticity, and so moves to an anti-literary reading of the NT. Finally, Paul's rhetoric, particularly his statement that 'one star differeth from another star in glory' (Paine comments, 'instead of distance') is denigrated as 'nothing better than the jargon of a conjuror' (II: 85), and Revelation is dismissed as 'a book of riddles that requires a revelation to explain it' (I: 11).

The most obvious point to come out of all this is the familiar one that literary estimation of the Bible can be thoroughly dependent on preconceived religious attitudes. Paine is a Marlowe[50] or an Aikenhead writ large, and he was lucky that his time, compared with theirs, was an age of reason, but still luckier that he lived out of reach of English justice: the representatives of authority might not be able to attack him personally, but they could attack his printer, Thomas Williams, who was found guilty of publishing a blasphemous work, fined £1,500 and jailed for three years (later, with more mercy than God showed in the flood, so Paine might have sneered, commuted to one),[51] and they could attack his reputation. After Paine's death the story that he had recanted his teaching in *The Age of Reason* was circulated in an effort to further discredit the book, but Paine remained proud of his opinions.[52] What is most interesting, though, beyond the general point about preconceived ideas, is the tone of the responses: Geddes might successfully meet Paine on his own ground, and others thought they ought to be able to do so, the Bible translator Gilbert Wakefield, for instance, declaring roundly that 'if I should prove unable to vindicate my faith in Christianity upon principles truly rational and unambiguously explicit, I will relinquish it altogether and look for an asylum in the deism of Thomas Paine and the calm philosophy of Hume'.[53] Even Bishop Watson, for all that he is so often content with contradiction, is still arguing with Paine rather than burning his book and, like an Ayatollah, issuing an execution order.

---

[50] Marlowe had claimed he could write something much better than the NT (see volume 1, p. 205); now Paine remarks 'I can write a better book myself' (*Complete Writings*, II: 737).

[51] Shelley, hearing of the trial in Italy, was roused to write a fine letter condemning it (to Leigh Hunt, 3 November 1819, *Complete Works*, x: 105–19).

[52] See Audrey Williamson, *Thomas Paine: His Life, Work and Times* (London: Allen & Unwin, 1973), pp. 276ff.

[53] *An Examination of The Age of Reason* (London, 1794), p. 20.

At times there is even something approaching concession in his arguments, as in this part of his summary of Paine's arguments against the OT:

> In plain language, you have gone through the Old Testament hunting after difficulties, and you have found some real ones; these you have endeavoured to magnify into insurmountable objections to the authority of the whole book. When it is considered that the Old Testament is composed of several books, written by different authors, and at different periods, from Moses to Malachi, comprising an abstracted history of a particular nation for above a thousand years, I think the real difficulties which occur in it are much fewer, and of much less importance, than could reasonably have been expected.   (Pp. 209–11)

Although argument is again avoided, one feels that Watson might be willing to investigate, or to allow someone else to investigate, some of the problems raised. The proviso would of course be that the investigation be carried out within the reverent overview he sets down. Certainly, he is prepared to read the Bible as a composition having a human element. His overall view of the Bible, given during an exhortation to Paine to become a believer, makes still clearer the concession to the human element:

> Receive but the Bible as composed by upright and well-informed, though, in some points, fallible men (for I exclude all fallibility when they profess to deliver the Word of God), and you must receive it as a book revealing to you, in many parts, the express will of God, and in other parts, relating to you the ordinary history of the times. Give but the authors of the Bible that credit which you give to other historians, believe them to deliver the word of God when they tell you that they do so, believe, when they relate other things as of themselves and not of the Lord, that they wrote to the best of their knowledge and capacity, and you will be in your belief something very different from a deist: you may not be allowed to aspire to the character of an orthodox believer, but you will not be an unbeliever in the divine authority of the Bible, though you should admit human mistakes and human opinions to exist in some parts of it.   (Pp. 110–11)

From Watson's point of view, the concessions and moderation evident here are not the most important element in his work. His prime concern is that Paine's views should be stopped from spreading, and here he speaks with the voice of the establishment:

> In accomplishing your purpose you will have unsettled the faith of thousands, rooted from the minds of the unhappy virtuous all their comfortable assurance of a future recompence; have annihilated in the minds of the flagitious all their fears of future punishment; you will have given the reins to the domination of every passion, and have thereby contributed to the introduction of the public insecurity and of the

private unhappiness usually and almost necessarily accompanying a state of
corrupted morals.   (Pp. 3–4)

This, of course is a misrepresentation of Paine's views, but it is a clear reminder
of the reactionary spirit of the times. Yet for many, such moderate conservatism
was far from sufficient and likely to have the very effect Watson feared. The
ordinary inspirationist in the street could not let such heresy pass challenged
only by inadequate reason, so one Michael Nash, who had experienced all the
doubts of reason but then had been converted back to Christianity and love of
the Bible, believed that critics who conceded ground to Paine were no better
than Paine himself:

> If the foundations be destroyed, what can the righteous do? . . . Take away the Bible
> from the believer (or make him think it an amphibious fraud, which is all one), and
> you rob him of more than all that earth can give. And thus languishingly he pines.
> What! says the true Christian, have I forsaken all the delights of life, its riches,
> honours, pleasures, and everything the flesh holds dear, in pursuit and expectation of
> that eternal state of felicity which the Bible unfolds, and that book a fable after all . . .
> Avaunt, Satan! let my God be true, who is truth itself! Tom Paine and every man that
> contradicts his word are *liars*.[54]

Such protest, with which one may have some sympathy, suggests that *The Age
of Reason*, by producing an inspirationist backlash, may have made it more
difficult to think about the Bible with freedom, and so may have hindered the
English development of both Higher Criticism and understanding of the Bible
as literature.

[54] *Paine's Age of Reason . . . Wakefield's Examination of, and a Layman's Answer to The Age of
Reason, both weighed in the balance and found wanting* (London, 1794), pp. 82–3.

CHAPTER 4

Romantics and the Bible

Forerunners and the influence of the KJB

'Nunc est bibendum' or 'eat, drink and be merry'

Blake, perhaps, Wordsworth, Coleridge, Byron, Shelley and Keats – these are the central figures of English romantic poetry. As far as their religious views are concerned they are as diverse a group as one could wish to find – profound and indifferent, orthodox and unorthodox, Christian and non-Christian – yet they share a biblical upbringing in a time when a favourable literary opinion of the KJB had become established. They are the first major literary group to have this in common, so it is of particular interest to see how they responded to the Bible, whether it influenced their work, and whether this heritage produced an attitude to the Bible that, in spite of their religious variety, was more or less shared by them all.

Two other factors of interest to us lie behind their work: a few of their predecessors had already moved towards new ways of writing poetry that had some indebtedness to the KJB (from our point of view, Blake belongs with these poets rather than with the romantics: he is the central pre-romantic poet of the Bible). Less obviously significant but still relevant is a somewht new way of quoting the Bible which has its origins in both the alehouses and the classics ('nunc est bibendum'). As the language of the KJB gained in respect, so the scornful profanity of the alehouse mockery took on a new character, though still one capable of arousing indignation among the pious.[1] Sterne, for instance,

---

[1] Since this is the last time alehouses will be mentioned, three other uses of the Bible in this kind of setting are worth recording. Christian says of Talkative in *The Pilgrim's Progress* that 'as he talketh now with you, so will he talk when he is on the ale-bench; and the more drink he hath in his crown, the more of these things he hath in his mouth: religion hath no place in his heart, or house, or conversation; all he hath lieth in his tongue, and his religion is to make a noise therewith' (Roger Sharrock, ed., *Grace Abounding* and *The Pilgrim's Progress* (London: Oxford University Press, 1966), p. 202). Empty profession

at the end of his life identified a set of people who 'upon all occasions
endeavour to make merry with sacred Scripture, and turn everything they
meet therein into banter and burlesque' (IV: 414–15; 'eat, drink and be merry').
At first sight, this appears to describe the same kind of mockery we have seen
in the previous two centuries, but a difference becomes apparent in other
observations. Taylor, contemporaneous with Sterne, complains that 'it is with
some reckoned a turn of wit to introduce Scripture phrase into common
conversation, and to provoke pleasantry by quoting the Bible', and asks
rhetorically, 'what is this but burlesquing the word of God and raising a laugh
at the expense of the greatest blessing of heaven?' (I: 208). Boswell is still more
specific in his journal:

> 7 April 1773. I mentioned Burke's using Scripture phrases, such as, in describing that
> the same sentiment will have quite a different effect when it comes from the Treasury
> bench from what it has when it comes from the side of Opposition, he said when I
> heard him, 'it is sown in weakness here, it is raised in power there' [1 Cor. 15: 43]. Mr
> Johnson said, 'I'm afraid Burke sacrifices everything to his wit. 'Tis wrong to
> introduce Scripture thus ludicrously.'[2]

Johnson's reaction is unsurprising, given what we have already seen of his
attitudes, but Boswell's private counter is more illuminating: 'I am not clear
that Scripture is hurt by being introduced in the manner Burke did it here. It is
like using a highly classical phrase. It has its effect at once, and very good
Christians have not scrupled to use Scripture phrases so' (ibid). The link with
classical quotation (which Johnson declared to be 'the *parole* of literary men all

of religious knowledge was obviously not out of place in this setting. Somewhat
different is an incident in Henry Fielding's *Tom Jones* (1749). The landlady of an inn has
found her maid in a compromising position on the stage of a puppet show that had been
held in the inn, and she berates 'her husband and the poor puppet-mover': 'I remember
when puppet-shows were made of good Scripture stories, as Jephthah's Rash Vow, and
such good things, and when wicked people were carried away by the devil. There was
some sense in those matters' (book 12, ch. 6). No doubt there was plenty of use of such
sensational biblical stories, but just how long they survived, how closely they connected
with miracle plays or ballads (see Hamlet's use of a ballad on Jephthah in connection
with acting, act 2, scene 2), and what their true character was must remain conjectural.
An engraving of Bartholemew Fair in 1721, about the time the landlady refers to, shows
a booth with the story of Judith and Holofernes being presented by actors. Adjacent
booths have peep shows, rope dancing, tumbling, magic tricks and, perhaps, boxing or
wrestling (the engraving is reproduced in *The Oxford Illustrated History of English
Literature*, ed. Pat Rogers (Oxford: Oxford University Press, 1987), pp. 242–3). Such
subterranean exploitation of biblical narrative may be seen as continuing in popular
adaptations for the cinema.

[2] William A. Wimsatt, Jr, and Frederick A. Pottle, eds., *Boswell for the Defence: 1769–1774*
(London: Heinemann, 1960), p. 178.

over the world')[3] pinpoints the difference between this 'burlesquing' of Scripture and the earlier alehouse mockery: that was scornful of biblical English, but this, impious as it may seem, shows biblical language becoming accepted intellectual currency, instantly recognisable as an enrichment of secular language and thought. Implied is a favourable literary sense of the Bible that can be independent of religious assent or dissent.

The faker and the madman

While biblical allusion had long been a source of religious enrichment in literature, until now there have been only a few instances of the language of the KJB being used for literary effect, and fewer still of it being an influence on literary style. Such a situation was bound to change in a time when the KJB was coming to be loved and respected as English. The witty use of it by conversationalists and orators is a straw in the wind for literature, yet the poets it leads to are hardly to be described as wits. In 1760 an extraordinary collection of 'poems' appeared purporting to be a translation of much the same sort as the KJB. Part of its preface very nearly describes biblical poems and their translation:

> They are not set to music nor sung. The versification in the original is simple, and to such as understand the language, very smooth and beautiful. Rhyme is seldom used, but the cadence and the length of the line varied so as to suit the sense. The translation is extremely literal. Even the arrangement of the words in the original has been imitated; to which must be imputed some inversions in the style that otherwise would not have been chosen.

No one reading this with a knowledge of Lowth and an awareness of the KJB's literalness could fail to see the parallels – significantly, the author of the preface was Hugh Blair, later to publicise Lowth's ideas. This is the kind of poetry he is describing:

FRAGMENT 1.
SHILRIC, VINVELA

Vinvela.

My love is a son of the hill. He pursues the flying deer. His grey dogs are panting around him; his bow-string sounds in the wind. Whether by the fount of the rock, or

---

[3] *Boswell's Life of Johnson*, p. 1143. Johnson was responding to John Wilkes's censure of such quotation as pedantry, and Wilkes's reply is of some interest: 'upon the continent they all quote the Vulgate Bible. Shakespeare is chiefly quoted here; and we quote also Pope, Prior, Butler, Waller, and sometimes Cowley.' Though it is odd that the KJB is not mentioned (this conversation postdates the comments on its use), the largely Augustan literary company that the Bible is keeping speaks of its literary rise. It is much the same company that the Bible keeps in Johnson's dictionary.

by the stream of the mountain thou liest; when the rushes are nodding with the wind, and the mist is flying over thee, let me approach my love unperceived, and see him from the rock. Lovely I saw thee first by the aged oak; thou wert returning tall from the chase; the fairest among thy friends.[4]

Pratt found this 'not much unlike the scriptural manner of writing', having 'an almost scriptural sublimity' (1: 155–6). It is of course the opening of that very successful forgery, *Fragments of Ancient Poetry* (Edinburgh, 1760), by the Scot James Macpherson (1736–96), a work soon to be developed into 'Ossian's' *Fingal*. The passage is biblical in ways nothing before it had been. It is prose poetry, cadenced but unmetrical; simplicity is at once apparent in the brevity of the sentence structures and the general reliance on unsubordinated statements; there is parallelism and even that oddity of some parts of the Bible, a seemingly illogical switching between second and third person. Though the content is occasionally reminiscent of the Song of Songs, this differs from all previous biblical imitations in being an imitation of style rather than of content. Where paraphrase, like commentary, functions in part as an exposition of meaning, this kind of imitation, like criticism, is an exposition of style, capable of sending the reader back to the KJB with insight into its literary nature. Moreover, it suggests that parts of the style of the KJB can be used for poetic effect, though the suggestion would have been muted by the contemporary perception of the fragments as translations.

Macpherson was an oddity, but the time was right for him in part because of the increasingly favourable sense of the KJB and in greater part because of the developing taste for antiquities that had been evident some thirty years earlier in Husbands's work. Also an oddity, but in an important respect, less of one, was that much-troubled poet Christopher Smart (1722–71); he is less of an oddity because, like so many before him, he was more concerned with the matter than the manner of the Bible. Nevertheless, his work also shows a movement towards poetry that depends to some extent on the style of the KJB. Four of his works relate more or less directly to the Bible, the posthumously published *Jubilate Agno*, written during his confinement to a madhouse, 1758–63, *A Song to David* (1763), *A Translation of the Psalms of David* (1765) and *The Parables of Our Lord* (1768). By far the best known is *A Song to David*,[5] a work eloquent of

[4] P. 9. Blair's passage is from pp. vi–vii.
[5] In the background to this poem lies a substantial debate on the character of David, an outline of which can be found in Arthur Sherbo's *Christopher Smart: Scholar of the University* (East Lansing, Mich.: Michigan State University Press, 1967), pp. 172–4; Sherbo quotes a summary of David's life from the opposition side that anticipates Paine in its general tone. It is not clear that this debate is to be seen in terms of the coming interest in character since a major factor in it was the question of whether David was the

Smart's love for biblical poetry. He describes David's characteristics as a poet in this way:

> Sublime – invention ever young,
> Of vast conception, tow'ring tongue,
>   To God the eternal theme;
> Notes from yon exaltations caught,
> Unrival'd royalty of thought,
>   O'er meaner strains supreme.   (x)

This is unmistakably neo-classical in thought and expression, and has nothing that might send the reader to the KJB rather than any other version. The same is true of *A Translation of the Psalms of David*. Here are the opening two verses of Psalm 23:

> The shepherd Christ from heav'n arriv'd,
>   My flesh and spirit feeds;
> I shall not therefore be depriv'd
>   Of all my nature needs.
>
> As slop'd against the glist'ning beam
>   The velvet verdure swells,
> He keeps, and leads me by the stream
>   Where consolation dwells.

There is nothing to distinguish this, in quality or kind, from the common ruck of paraphrase: the excesses of poetic diction lead it far from the still waters of the KJB or the PB. Like so many other versions, it implies that literary quality is not to be found in the English Bible. So far Smart is just another Augustan, only slightly unusual in devoting so much of his effort to the biblical.

Unfinished, unpublished and extraordinarily uneven, *Jubilate Agno* presents a different and by no means simple picture. If it is a poem at all, it is a poem without rhyme or metre, consisting of a long series of lines beginning with either 'let' or 'for', including one substantial section in which these beginnings alternate. Such a form is inescapably repetitious or parallelistic, and Smart was not only familiar with Lowth's *De Sacra Poesi Hebraeorum*, but had publicly characterised it as 'one of the best performances that has been published for a century'.[6] Roston, who sees the discovery of parallelism as crucial to poetry's release from the shackles of neo-classicism, presents this work as an exploitation of 'biblical parallelism for original verse-writing' (p. 148). The poem begins:

model king, and therefore whether it was appropriate to use him as such in eulogies on George II.

6 The *Universal Visiter* (January 1756), 56; quoted in, e.g., Roston, p. 148.

Rejoice in God, O ye tongues; give the glory to the Lord, and the Lamb.
Nations, and languages, and every Creature, in which is the breath of Life.
Let man and beast appear before him, and magnify his name together.
Let Noah and his company approach the throne of Grace, and do homage to the Ark
of their Salvation.

Roston writes:

> Not merely is this parallelism, but the poem has captured the excited pulsation of
> Hebrew poetry. The latter half of each line seems to lean back on its haunches before
> leaping forward with the next thought; and the subject-matter, too, takes us back to
> the world of the Old Testament, revitalising it as though Abraham and Isaac were
> standing beside Smart ready to participate in this universal thanksgiving. (P. 149)

Perhaps the point is pressed too hard: the accumulative but unprogressive
echoing of form from one line to the next is certainly a kind of parallelism, but
such synonymity of phrases is not often to be found within the lines, and the
effect is quasi-biblical rather than biblical.

Here is an example of the poem at its most characteristic, taken from
fragment B before the poem degenerates into notebook jottings that yet have
occasional flashes of power:

> Let Shimron rejoice with the Kite, who is of more value than many sparrows.
> *For I this day made over my inheritance to my mother in consideration of her age.*
> Let Sered rejoice with the Wittal – a silly bird is wise unto his own preservation.
> *For I this day made over my inheritance to my mother in consideration of her poverty.*
>
> (B47–8)

Parallelism is used primarily in the way the pairs of lines echo each other in
form, but the latter halves of the 'let' lines add description rather than parallel
the first halves, and the 'for' lines are single statements. Just as the
subject-matter is a mixture of the biblical and the personal that depends to a
considerable extent on their incongruity, so is the form, with the result that it is
less likely than Macpherson's *Fragments* to send one back to the KJB with
insight into its style.

As well as using an idea of biblical form, these lines use the Bible in other
ways: Shimron and Sered, like many of the names at the beginnings of the 'let'
lines, are biblical; Matt. 10: 29 and Luke 12: 6 are alluded to in the second half of
the first line, and 'wise unto his own preservation' elegantly varies 2 Tim. 3: 16
and Prov. 26: 5. None of this is more than use of the Bible, and some of it, that is,
the use of names, is only confirmed as biblical by the use of a concordance.

In sharp contrast with Macpherson's work, *Jubilate Agno* remained unknown until this century and so had no influence on ideas of how the Bible might be used in poetry. Indeed, none of Smart's four main biblical works, not even *A Song to David*, achieved much success for many years. *The Parables of Our Lord* had a dismal reception. Smart designed these parables 'for the use and improvement of younger minds' (title) and dedicated them to a three-year-old boy. The *Monthly Review* sneeringly found 'great propriety' in this, and the *Critical Review* damned them by comparing them to Sternhold and Hopkins (*Poetical Works*, II: 201). Such remarks have an element of justice, but from this distance they seem to promise something different from most of the century's paraphrases, and therefore perhaps something better. It is indeed in these parables (the word is used in a wide sense) that Smart comes closest to the style of the KJB while demonstrating just how difficult it is for regular English verse to be like the KJB. Rather than the audacious experiment of *Jubilate Agno* with a quasi-biblical technique, *The Parables of Our Lord* attempts to use the words of the KJB as far as possible, and to keep necessary alterations to its text within the range of its vocabulary. This is a major departure for Smart, since, eccentrically, he believed that Greek and Latin were 'the consecrated languages spoken by the Lord on earth' (*Jubilate Agno*, B6). His one direct comment on the English Scriptures comes in his hymns:

> We give the glory for thy word,
> That it so well becomes our tongue:
> And that thy spirit is transferr'd
> Upon the strains of old in Hebrew sung.   (Hymn XVII: 73–6)

He also declares that

> The muse at length, no more perplext
> In search of human wit,
> Shall kneel her down, and take her text
> From lore of sacred writ.   (XI: 5–8)

The Parables seems to fulfil this prophecy. The results can be peculiarly pleasing, and, an important contrast with *A Translation of the Psalms of David*, it often invites comparison with the KJB. Here is the main part of the thirty-eighth parable, 'The Beam and the Mote', preceded by the KJB:

> Judge not, that ye be not judged. For with what judgement ye judge, ye shall be judged: and with what measure ye mete, it shall be measured to you again. And why beholdest thou the mote that is in thy brother's eye, but considerest not the beam that is in thine own eye? Or how wilt thou say to thy brother, Let me pull out the mote out

of thine eye; and, behold, a beam is in thine own eye? Thou hypocrite, first cast out
the beam out of thine own eye; and then thou shalt see clearly to cast out the mote out
of thy brother's eye.

> Judge not, lest ye be judg'd for pride:
> For with what judgement you decide,
> Ye shall be censur'd like for like;
> And the same measure that ye strike,
> That shall be measured you again.
> And why beholdest thou with pain
> The mote that's in thy brother's eye,
> And thine own beam canst not descry?
> Thy brother, how canst thou reprove,
> 'From thee let me that mote remove,
> 'That I may set thy vision right';
> When, lo! a beam obstructs thy sight.
> Thou hypocrite with canting tone,
> First cast the beam from out thine own:
> And then shalt thou distinctly note
> Thy brother's eye, and clear the mote.

Preservation decisively outweighs change: not only do the key words remain,
but several phrases survive as complete lines. Moreover, there is little
incongruity of style between the changed and the unchanged. Rather than the
Bible neo-classified, this is the KJB lightly tailored to a verse whose rhythm it
seems readily adapted to.

In one sense there is a long tradition behind such versification of the Bible,
even if few poets of stature had attempted this degree of fidelity, but, coming
after a period in which a very different idea of paraphrase held sway, this is
significantly new: literature of a sort is not only being found but being shown in
the KJB. Moreover, these parables are novel in treating the 'unpoetic' NT in
this way. Lowth had been a traditionalist in keeping to the poetic parts of the
OT; Smart shows that something like poetry can be found still more widely
distributed. In doing so, he helps to create new ways of writing that inevitably
attract to themselves those so-common epithets for the style of the Bible, plain
and simple.

Similar effects are sometimes to be seen in the nearly contemporaneous *Olney
Hymns* of William Cowper (1731–1800). In the following two verses from hymn
III, direct quotation is tempered with adaptation: the KJB's 'help thou mine
unbelief' (Mark 9: 24) might have fitted the verse as well as 'O help my
unbelief':

Remember him who once apply'd
   With trembling for relief;
'Lord, I believe', with tears he cry'd,
   'O help my unbelief.'

She too,' who touch'd thee in the press,
   And healing virtue stole,
Was answer'd, 'Daughter, go in peace,
   Thy faith hath made thee whole.'

However, close paraphrase was not Cowper's prime aim. Where he does take a biblical passage, as in hymn xvi, 'The Sower', the result is much less close to the Bible than Smart's version of the same passage in the first of his parables.

For all that Cowper was deeply religious and a lover of the Bible, his work is surprisingly slight in its implications for the Bible. When he praises it, as in hymn xxx, it is for its truth. His dialogue poem, *Table Talk*, written after *Olney Hymns*, suggests a reason for this slightness. Although he looks back to a magnificent purity of poetry in Eden, 'elegant as simplicity, and warm / As ecstasy, unmanacled by form' (lines 588–9), he does not think of the prose-poetry of the Bible as a possible model for creating anew such poetry, even though, being 'unmanacled by form', it might seem to fit this description particularly well. He knows what he would like to see:

'Twere new indeed to see a bard all fire,
Touch'd with a coal from heav'n, assume the lyre,
And tell the world, still kindling as he sung,
With more than mortal music on his tongue,
That He, who died below, and reigns above,
Inspires the song, and that his name is love.   (Lines 734–9)

However, he is scathing of the 'flowing numbers and . . . flow'ry style' (line 741) of modern poetry, and this prompts his interlocutor to exclaim with attempted sarcasm, 'Hail Sternhold, then; and Hopkins, hail!' (line 760). The sarcasm falls flat. This is his point: if it is a choice between them and 'Butler's wit, Pope's numbers, Prior's ease' (line 764), then 'Amen' to Sternhold and Hopkins. For us, concentrating on the KJB and looking now for *its* influence, it is too easy to forget that the poets of the late eighteenth and early nineteenth centuries, when they turned to divinity, thought of that old Psalter as a model at least as readily as they thought of the KJB. Their critics too were likely to think – unfavourably – in this way, as the *Critical Review* did with Smart's *Parables*.

William Blake, 'bard all fire'

Poet, engraver, designer, printer, thinker and prophet, William Blake (1757–1827) seems not only a natural step from Smart, but in some respects the incarnation of Cowper's 'bard all fire'. The plainness and simplicity of his best-known collections of poems, *Songs of Innocence* (1789) and *Songs of Experience* (1789–94), seem to grow out of the childlike directness of Smart's *Parables*. The constantly religious nature of his poetry – even if it is, in Iago's phrase, a 'divinity of hell' – is a somewhat ironic fulfilment of Cowper's vision, especially in its constantly prophetic aspect.[7] And the poetry shows Blake's perpetual absorption in the Bible. Like Smart, Blake was little known in his own time, and must be taken more as a figure reflecting, however idiosyncratically, the changing sentiments of his time than as one who immediately shaped ideas. Yet, in the longer perspective, he is a shaper of literary attitudes to the Bible: once Alexander Gilchrist's *Life*, published in 1863 began to bring his work the fame it had always deserved, his sense and use of the Bible became public property.

That he knew his Bible intimately almost goes without saying. In some fanciful (not a slight word where Blake is concerned) lines enclosed in a letter to the painter John Flaxman, he reminisces, 'Milton lov'd me in childhood & shew'd me his face. / Ezra came with Isaiah the Prophet, but Shakespeare in riper years gave me his hand.'[8] Presumably he takes Ezra as the compiler of the historical books of the OT: his meaning is that he loved much of the OT as literature from childhood.[9] Something of his later contact with the Bible may be glimpsed when, in his late thirties, he observes blithely:

I go on merrily with my Greek and Latin; am very sorry that I did not begin to learn languages early in life as I find it very easy; am now learning my Hebrew אב ג

---

[7] The equation between prophecy and poetry is largely Lowth's but is also to be found, without reference to the Bible, in Cowper's *Table Talk*. Following a description of the power of an inspired poet that has its aptness for Blake, he writes:

> Hence, in a Roman mouth, the graceful name
> Of prophet and of poet was the same;
> Hence British poets, too, the priesthood shar'd,
> And ev'ry hallowed druid was a bard.　　　　　　(Lines 500–3)

[8] 12 September 1800, *Complete Writings* (hereafter *CW*), p. 799.

[9] Tannenbaum gives an alternative reading, stating that Ezra is the Esdras of the Apocrypha, and suggesting that Blake names Ezra and Isaiah because of their influence on his prophetic writings (Leslie Tannenbaum, *Biblical Tradition in Blake's Early Prophecies: The Great Code of Art* (Princeton: Princeton University Press, 1982), p. 124). Tannenbaum's book takes an understanding of the influence of the Bible and of current ideas about it on Blake far beyond what is encompassed here. The first three chapters especially are of interest for a student of literary ideas of the Bible.

[alphabet]. I read Greek as fluently as an Oxford scholar and the Testament is my chief master: astonishing indeed is the English translation, it is almost word for word, and if the Hebrew Bible is as well translated, which I do not doubt it is, we need not doubt of its having been translated as well as written by the Holy Ghost.

(To James Blake, 30 January 1803: *CW*, pp. 821–2)

His pleasure is as obvious as his diligence. Moreover, in this, his only explicit comment on the KJB, he clearly admires that Bible well enough to think it inspired in its literal fidelity to the originals. Almost redundantly, his biographer, J. T. Smith, recalls that 'his greatest pleasure was derived from the Bible, – a work ever in his hand, and which he often assiduously consulted in several languages',[10] and William Hayley found Blake, like Cowper, 'a most fervent admirer of the Bible, and intimately acquainted with all its beauties' (*Blake Records*, p. 106). Indeed, the Bible was the most thumbed from use of his English books (*Blake Records*, p. 527). Blake himself writes that he and a friend 'often read the Bible together'. But this friend was an imaginary angel become a devil, and they read the Bible 'in its infernal or diabolical sense'.[11] There is a warning here: however representative he is, in general terms, of turn-of-the-century love for the Bible as literature, he is no orthodox figure.

Sometimes Blake's absorption in the Bible shows in the same way as Smart's use of obscure biblical names in *Jubilate Agno*: biblical figures appear freely intermixed with figures from Blake's own private mythology and seem to be as much the creatures of his imagination as they are. But at other times his work does take us, and perhaps took some of his contemporaries, back to the Bible. One of his best known poems, 'The Tyger' from *Songs of Experience*, inescapably invokes the book of Job. Not only does it appear to belong with the descriptions of the creatures of God's creation in Job 40 and 41, especially the superficially similar questioning description of Leviathan in Job 41: 1–7, but the compressed form of the questioning echoes Job's earlier 'why did the knees prevent me? or why the breasts that I should suck?' (3: 12). The questions in Job 41 reflect man's impotence against Leviathan, but Blake's questions concern God. Perhaps, disturbingly, they ask whether any creator is powerful enough to dare to frame the frightful symmetry of the imagined beast. Such undercurrents run through Blake's work: if he is a Christian, he is a peculiar one,[12] but this

[10] J. T. Smith, as given in *Blake Records*, p. 467.
[11] 'A memorable fancy', in 'The Marriage of Heaven and Hell' (c. 1790), *CW*, p. 158.
[12] He was interested enough in the Swedenborgian New Jerusalem Church to attend its general conference in 1789 and sign its manifesto, which includes several propositions about the Bible. However, his attitude to Swedenborg and to this church became ambiguous; he did not join the New Jerusalem Church, and from this time did not attend any church (see *Blake Records*, pp. 35–8).

does nothing to lessen the obviousness of the strength of his literary response to the Bible. Biblical allusion pervades the *Songs*. Moreover, particularly in *Songs of Innocence*, there is an un-Augustan simplicity that has, as I have suggested, much in common with Smart's *Parables*.

Where the *Parables* are versifications that draw out qualities in the Bible, Blake's simplicity comes in original poems that are less directly connected with the Bible,[13] and so, in their style, make a more muted statement about it. However, there is nothing muted about Blake's claim in the first poem of *Songs of Experience*, 'Introduction':

> Hear the voice of the Bard!
> Who Present, Past, & Future, sees;
> Whose ears have heard
> The Holy Word
> That walk'd among the ancient trees,
>
> Calling the lapsed Soul,
> And weeping in the evening dew;
> That might controll
> The starry pole,
> And fallen, fallen light renew!

Like a prophet, the poet both sees through all time and has heard God's voice direct, specifically the voice that was heard in Eden after the fall. Blake implies that, like a prophet, the bard will deliver the word of God: his readers are alerted to expect something biblical.[14]

The link between prophecy and poetry pervades Blake. His early statement of principles, 'All religions are one' (c. 1788; p. 98), has for epigraph the synoptic Gospels' version of Isa. 40: 3, 'the voice of one crying in the wilderness'. In Mark's version this invokes exactly the point of 'Introduction': 'as it is written in the prophets, Behold, I send my messenger before thy face, which shall prepare thy way before thee. The voice of one crying in the

---

[13] The closest Blake comes to verse paraphrase of the Bible is in a series of notebook drafts known as 'the everlasting gospel'; there he is freer with the language of the KJB than Smart was. According to the diarist Henry Crabb Robinson, Blake made a version of Genesis 'as understood by a Christian visionary' in 'a style resembling the Bible'; if Robinson is right, the work is lost (see *Blake Records*, p. 322, also p. 547).

[14] The illuminated version of this poem (of course available to only a very few readers of the time) can be seen as adding to these suggestions. The poem appears celestial, being inscribed on a cloud against a starry background, as if imagined by the naked figure at the foot of the picture. This figure reclines on something that might be a scroll; though sometimes taken as female, it is likely to be the bard, and in some versions Blake underlines the divine aspect by giving it a halo.

wilderness, Prepare ye the way of the Lord, make his paths straight' (Mark 1: 2–3). Principle five announced under this prophetic banner is that 'the religions of all nations are derived from each nation's different reception of the poetic genius, which is everywhere called the spirit of prophecy'. Principle six follows logically: 'the Jewish and Christian Testaments are an original derivation from the poetic genius'.

This is, as it were, from the unknown Blake, but it leads to the most famous of all his poems, known as the hymn 'Jerusalem'.[15] It will be best to consider it first as it commonly appears, removed from its Blakean context:

> And did those feet in ancient time
> Walk upon England's mountains green?
> And was the holy Lamb of God
> On England's pleasant pastures seen?
>
> And did the Countenance Divine
> Shine forth upon our clouded hills?
> And was Jerusalem builded here
> Among these dark Satanic Mills?
>
> Bring me my Bow of burning gold:
> Bring me my Arrows of desire:
> Bring me my Spear: O clouds unfold!
> Bring me my Chariot of fire.
>
> I will not cease from Mental Fight,
> Nor shall my Sword sleep in my hand
> Till we have built Jerusalem
> In England's green & pleasant Land.

It seems to be a magical, barely understood call to exert one's faith to the uttermost. The language seems to have a biblical simplicity, and that impression is reinforced by the obvious references to the lamb of God and to Jerusalem, and by images such as 'chariot of fire', which is directly biblical, and 'arrows of desire', which one feels ought to be biblical since the Bible sometimes uses 'arrows' metaphorically, as in Ezekiel's 'evil arrows of famine' (5: 16). Even the sword might well be the sword of Scripture. As much as any of the *Songs of Innocence and Experience*, it takes one into the world of the Bible and suggests literary power in the Bible. These impressions do not disappear when the poem is read in context, yet a different poem emerges.

---

[15] Sir Hubert Parry's setting was published in 1916, and one can readily imagine how inspirational the hymn would have seemed in wartime. The date helps to suggest just how modern Blake's popularity is.

Blake wrote the poem as part of the preface to his epic, 'Milton' (1804), a preface in which he takes his idea of the Bible as poetry further than we have seen so far:

> The stolen and perverted writings of Homer and Ovid, of Plato and Cicero, which all men ought to contemn, are set up by artifice against the sublime of the Bible;[16] but when the new age is at leisure to pronounce, all will be set right, and those grand works of the more ancient and consciously and professedly inspired men will hold their proper rank, and the daughters of memory shall become the daughters of inspiration. (*CW*, p. 480)

The old ideas that the classics stole from the Scriptures and that the Bible is sublime and inspired (there is no difference here between religious and literary inspiration) lead to a vision of a new world in which the Scriptures are rightly estimated supreme and there will be a new, inspired poetry. 'Rouse up, O young men of the new age', cries Blake: 'we do not want either Greek or Roman models if we are but just and true to our own imaginations, those worlds of eternity in which we shall live for ever in Jesus our Lord.' In part this is a rejection of classical for biblical models, since no difference is made between being true to one's imagination and being true to the Scriptures: they are the books of the imagination. It is here that the song comes, still prefacing the poem proper, and it is followed by the last line of the preface, a slightly adapted quotation, with the reference fully given, from Num. 11: 29: 'would to God that all the Lord's people were prophets'. In this context, the poem is an exhortation to create the new world of the imagination, transforming England into a kingdom of God which is also a kingdom of the imagination, all its people true poets as the poets of the Bible had been in the past. In this way it is a central poem for a literary sense of the Bible and for a religious sense of literature. That this sense should have escaped the public is testimony to the inspiring strength the poem has beyond its specific concern; to return to its Blakean meaning is to underline how far his essential ideas about the Bible, religion and poetry have remained hidden.

Blake's is not the Bible of morality and theology but one of poetry and energy, a Bible that has little to do with common ideas. For him 'the whole Bible is filled with imagination and visions from end to end and not with moral

---

[16] Interestingly, where the quarrel between the Bible and the classics had been a matter of the Bible versus the classics, now the footing is reversed: for Blake it is the classics versus the Bible. Returning to this subject in 1827, he declared roundly, 'the Greek and Roman classics is the Antichrist' ('Annotations to Dr Thornton's "New translation of the Lord's Prayer"', *CW*, p. 786).

virtues'; it is 'not allegory, but eternal vision or imagination of all that exists'.[17] In the same vein, 'Jesus and his apostles and disciples were all artists', and 'the Old and New Testaments are the great code of art'.[18] This is not, as it might appear, unadulterated aestheticism, but part of what we might call a moral conception of man that values the imagination ahead of reason and abhors the mechanical limitedness of conventional morality. In a relatively early letter that sets out the essence of his views, Blake asks rhetorically, 'why is the Bible more entertaining and instructive than any other book?', and answers at once, 'is it not because [it is] addressed to the imagination, which is spiritual sensation, and but mediately to the understanding or reason?'.[19] Perhaps this is no more than the English discovery of the Bible as literature run wild. Yet, as with so much of Blake, it remains a challenge, a challenge aimed at one's response to the Bible in general.

William Wordsworth and the possibility of a new literary sense of the Bible

Nature rather than the Bible was the 'great code of art' and true source of inspiration for William Wordsworth (1770–1850), so it is not surprising to find only a little in his work (and nothing in his sister Dorothy's journals) that relates to the Bible. Of course he alludes to the Bible and occasionally uses biblical phrases so naturally that the sense of their source is almost lost, as when he describes how one becomes 'a living soul' (Gen. 2: 7) under the influence of 'that serene and blessed mood' ('Tintern Abbey'). Moreover, he says enough to make it clear that he loved his Bible, but not enough to suggest that this perhaps lukewarm love was of central importance to him: here his silences are more impressive than his utterances. *Ecclesiastical Sonnet* II: xxix hails the Bible in English as a 'transcendent boon', and in *The Prelude* he mentions vaguely 'the voice / Which roars along the bed of Jewish song' in a passage that characteristically returns to Nature, 'which is the breath of God' (1805 version, V: 202–3; 222).

---

[17] 'Annotations to Berkeley's "Siris"', '[A vision of the Last Judgement]', *CW*, pp. 774, 604.

[18] 'The Laocoön', *CW*, p. 777. The latter statement is now a favourite with critics. It is something like a translation of Augustine's phrase for the Bible, 'legum artium' (see volume 1, p. 58). Stephen Prickett has suggested that Blake is responding to Lowth's description of Aristotle's *Poetics* as 'the great code of criticism' (*Isaiah*, p. xlviii; *Words and the Word*, p. 117). Prickett, occasionally misrepresenting Lowth (e.g. p. 42), brings out some aspects of his influence on criticism and ideas about the Bible at large that I have not dealt with.

[19] To Dr Trusler, 23 August 1799, *CW*, p. 794.

Wordsworth's most significant piece for the Bible is his preface to *Lyrical Ballads* (1800) and the appendix on poetic diction added in 1802.[20] There he suggests that the best demonstration of what he means by poetic diction would be to put eighteenth-century metrical paraphrases against the KJB. The example he chooses is Johnson's version of Prov. 6: 6–11, after which he remarks with effective simplicity, 'from this hubbub of words pass to the original' (1: 163). Implicitly the KJB shows the affecting and 'genuine language of passion' (1: 160). In the context of the argument of the whole preface this brief example is highly suggestive. The crux of the preface is to justify his decision to focus on 'low and rustic life', and to use the language of common rural men 'purified indeed from what appear to be its real defects' (1: 124). In general terms this is a justification of something like the language Tyndale chose to use for his translation, and Wordsworth does seem to have been aware of Tyndale's intentions, writing in the same *Ecclesiastical Sonnet*, 'Translation of the Bible',

> And he who guides the plough, or wields the crook,
> With understanding spirit now may look
> Upon her records, listen to her song,
> And sift her laws...

Tyndale's language, too, was close to being an artful variation of common language: where Wordsworth varied to avoid 'real defects', Tyndale varied because of the demands of his originals. Wordsworth goes on to argue 'that there neither is nor can be any essential difference' 'between the language of prose and metrical composition', because 'the same human blood circulates through the veins of them both' (1: 134). Indeed, he adds to these observations a footnote on the confusions caused in criticism by treating 'poetry' and 'prose' as antonyms; for him, metre, with or without rhyme, is not the defining characteristic of poetry. This is an often-forgotten rather than a new idea,[21] and it usefully develops Lowth's points that a literal translation of biblical poetry will retain some semblance of versification and that the passions speak irregularly. Though Wordsworth chose to remain a versifier as well as a poet, his preface promotes a recognition that prose can be as powerful as verse. A reader going from this preface to the KJB could take its language, in places at least, as achieved literature without having to see in it a muted appearance of versification. Had he wished, Wordsworth might have written powerfully on

---

[20] *The Prose Works* gives both the 1800 and 1850 texts, with variants; throughout I have used the earliest readings in order to keep the evidence as historical as possible.

[21] The commentary gives a recent antecedent for this point in the *Monthly Magazine* 2 (1796), 456 (1: 174).

the poetry of the KJB. That he did not suggests that, in spite of the affinities between his ideas and ideas of the Bible, the Bible fitted with rather than generated his thought.

One further argument, added in 1802, can be read in a way that is favourable to literary appreciation of the Bible. Just as the Bible is the book of truth, so 'poetry is the breath and finer spirit of all knowledge'; it 'is the first and last' – might one not say, the alpha and omega? – 'of all knowledge' (1: 141). Wordsworth brings this part of his argument to a climax in religious language that, in Blake's hands, would explicitly invoke *his* supreme poet, Jesus: 'if the time should ever come when what is now called science . . . shall be ready to put on, as it were, a form of flesh and blood, the poet will lend his divine spirit to aid the transfiguration, and will welcome the Being thus produced as a dear and genuine inmate of the household of man' (1: 141). Wordsworth's 'sublime notion of poetry' (1: 141) is plainly religious. Little imagination is needed to reverse the coin and see the Bible as supreme poetry. Yet it is a reversal. Cowper had revived Dennis's argument that poetry should become religious, and the result, in a sense, had been Blake. The difference lies in the idea of what is religious. For Cowper and Blake, Christ, in their different conceptions of him, is the soul of poetry; for Wordsworth poetry is the soul of religion.

In this distinction lies a change that will be important to some ideas of the Bible as literature. Just as Wordsworth takes imagery from religion to describe his aesthetic, so literature adopts characteristics of religion – and higher education takes on some of the characteristics of a church. Where literature was once synonymous with lying, it has become, and remains in many respects, an art of truth. Indeed, though Wordsworth emphasises pleasure equally with knowledge, there are times when literature seems, like religion, to value truth ahead of pleasure. The significance for the Bible of the change Wordsworth suggests is that it helps to make possible reverence for it as literature rather than as religion. By virtue of the pleasure it gives, particularly in its poetic insight into man and his passions, but also in the felt beauty of its language, it changes from being the canon of Christian writing to being part of the canon of literature. The Bible may now be religion because it is literature. Wordsworth, of course, does not make such a claim, but it will be the basis of Shelley's view of the Bible. What he does, quite incidentally to his own purposes, is to suggest the possibility of such a change in a way that is more obvious than in any previous writer.

Samuel Taylor Coleridge

It is natural to bracket together Samuel Taylor Coleridge (1772–1834) and Wordsworth and unsurprising to find at least one opinion on the KJB's English attributed to them both: they are reported to have

> thought the bad taste in writing which now prevails, is owing to works of two celebrated authors, Pope's translation of Homer and the Odyssey, and Johnson's *Lives of the Poets*. These models of art and an inflated style have been imitated to the destroying of all simplicity. – The Old Testament, they say, is the true model of simplicity of style.[22]

Almost all of this fits Wordsworth's argument in the preface to *Lyrical Ballads* and its appendix, but it has one peculiarly Coleridgean aspect, the restriction to the OT. Late in his life, Coleridge declared,

> I think there is a perceptible difference in the elegance and correctness of the English in the versions of the Old and New Testament. I cannot yield to the authority of many examples of usages which may be alleged from the New Testament version. St Paul is very often most inadequately rendered, and there are slovenly and vulgar phrases which would never have come from Ben Jonson or any good writer of the times.   (*Table Talk*, 17 August 1833, *CW* 14, 1: 430)

This makes it probable that the remark was principally Coleridge's, and it immediately shows that he had a qualified respect for the KJB.

His few other remarks on the KJB's English fit with the idea of it as 'the true model of simplicity'. He once observed that 'intense study of the Bible will keep any writer from being vulgar in style' (*Table Talk*, 7 June 1830, 1: 165). This may be traced in part to the impression made on him by Henry More's observation that 'constant reading of the Bible' was one of the causes of power in the language of David George, and that an intelligent but illiterate man will naturally acquire a 'winning and commanding rhetoric' from it (see volume 1, p. 250). In his notebooks for 1808–9 he contemplated writing an essay to test the truth of Gray's lines, 'Full many a flower is born to blush unseen, / And waste its sweetness on the desert air'; he began his note:

> To examine what and whether there be truth in this – take the present age. Every boy who strongly wished it might learn to read – three out of four are now taught reading – it is scarce possible that he might not procure the Bible, and many religious books,

---

[22] Joseph Farington, *Diary*, ed. James Greig (8 vols., 1922–8), v: 132 (28 March 1809). As given in Coleridge, *Biographia Literaria, Collected Works* 7, 1: 39n. Hereafter *Collected Works* is abbreviated to *CW*; references to the volume number in *CW* is given when a work is first referred to, then the volume number within that work is given.

which at all events would give him the best and most natural language – here quote Dr H. More.[23]

Moreover, he viewed the KJB not just as a model but as a beneficial influence on the language, remarking, again in *Table Talk*, that 'our version of the Bible [is] most valuable in having preserved a purity of meaning to many of the plain terms of natural things; without this our vitiated imaginations would refine away the language to mere abstractions' (24 June 1827, 1: 75), as indeed he thought had happened with French and Spanish. He went so far as to suggest in one of his lectures on Shakespeare that its English affected the passionate expressions of the people: 'if a mother had lost her child she was full of the wildest fancies, the words themselves assuming a tone of dignity for the constant hearing of the Bible and Liturgy clothed them not only in the most natural but most beautiful forms of language'.[24]

There is much that is familiar in these remarks: they have a lineage that goes back through Lowth proclaiming the KJB to be 'the best standard of our language' (above, p. 97) to Swift's observation that the KJB and PB 'have proved a kind of standard for language, especially to the common people' (above, p. 40). Nevertheless, there is a sense of freshness and discovery that distinguishes them from mere repetitions of received ideas, and, in Coleridge's last observation particularly, there is a larger aesthetic dimension. Swift's concern was for the stability of English; Coleridge's (and Wordsworth's) is with quality of language, for he sees the KJB as an influence towards beauty: the KJB is not just a conservative force, but a shaping influence on the language of the people.

A somewhat similar observation is reported from the next lecture, but this time Coleridge seems to be thinking directly of poetic quality in the KJB, and a new, peculiarly Coleridgean idea begins to emerge:

> When Coleridge read the song of Deborah he never supposed that she was a poet, although he thought the song itself a sublime poem. It was [as] simple [a] dithyrambic poem as exists but it was the proper effusion of a woman, highly elevated by triumph... When she commenced, 'I Deborah the mother of Israel', it was poetry in the highest sense.   (1: 310)

Here he may be following Wordsworth, who described the song as a 'tumultuous and wonderful poem', and had cited it to show that 'repetition and

---

[23] *Notebooks*, III: 3415. Though the essay remained unwritten, Coleridge returned to More's passage in *Biographia Literaria*, *CW* 7, II: 44.

[24] From John Payne Collier's account of Coleridge's lecture 6, 1811–12. The account seems somewhat muddled; the observation itself is apparently part of a larger nexus of ideas (*Lectures 1808–1819 on Literature*, *CW* 5, I: 292).

apparent tautology are frequently beauties of the highest kind'.[25] Coleridge was
to repeat this in *Biographia Literaria* (*CW* 7, II: 57), and certainly the idea seems
to fit Wordsworth's willingness to find poetry in prose more easily than it does
Coleridge, for the two part company on the question of poetry and prose.
Coleridge did not agree that there was no essential difference between poetry
and prose (*Biographia Literaria*, II: 55), believing rather that 'wherever passion
was, the language became a sort of metre'.[26] He demonstrated the point at some
length in the same lecture in his most detailed commentary on the KJB as
literature. Tomalin reports:

> So closely connected ... was metre with passion that many of the finest passages we
> read in prose are in themselves, in point of metre, poetry – only they are forms of
> metre which we have not been familiarised to and not brought forwards to us and
> other English readers in the shape of metre – Coleridge had paid particular attention
> to the language of the Bible and had found that all persons had been affected with a
> sense of their high poetic character – not merely from the thoughts conveyed in them,
> but from the language enclosing those thoughts – from the stately march of the
> words, which had affected them in a degree and kind altogether different from that of
> common writing, and different from the narrative and preceptive parts of the same
> books. It had been his business to discover the cause, and he found that in almost
> every passage brought before him as having produced a particular effect there was
> metre and very often poetry – not indeed regular – not such as could be scanned on
> the fingers – but in some cases fragments of hexameter verses ... of dactyls and
> spondees, forming sometimes a complete hexameter verse ... [here he gave two
> examples from the Psalms].
>
> Thus taking the first chapter of Isaiah, without more than four or five
> transpositions and no alteration of words, he had reduced it to complete hexameters.
>
> (I: 222–3)

Jerome lives! we might exclaim, though there seems to be no indebtedness to
that master: Coleridge is pursuing his own theory to the point of idiosyncrasy,
and, one has to admit, with even less success than Jerome, for nobody cared to
take up this idea. Further, since Coleridge knew Lowth's work,[27] this seems a
deliberate rejection of his ideas of parallelism.

Tomalin reports the illustrations from the Psalms with reasonable accuracy,

---

[25] Note on *The Thorn*, *The Poetical Works of William Wordsworth*, ed. E. De Selincourt, 5
vols. (Oxford: Oxford University Press (1944) 1952), II: 513.

[26] J. Tomalin's notes on lecture 3 of the 1811–12 lectures on Shakespeare (*Lectures
1808–1819*, I: 223).

[27] He used *Isaiah* in 1795 (see below, p. 158n.35). It is one of the many teasing curiosities of
Coleridge's mind that it seems not to have responded to Lowth.

but the development of the idea may be followed more closely elsewhere. Coleridge concluded a letter of 1799 to his brother George, 'we were talking of hexameters while with you. I will for want of something better fill up the paper with a translation of one of my favourite Psalms into that metre which, allowing trochees for spondees as the nature of our language demands, you will find pretty accurate in scansion' (*Letters*, 1: 532). There follows the paraphrase of Psalm 46 reprinted in *Poems* as 'Hexameters'. Here are two lines from it:

> Thĕre ĭs ă | rīvĕr thĕ | flōwĭng whĕre | ōf shāll | glāddĕn thĕ | cītў,
> Hāllē|lūjăh thĕ | cīty ŏf | Gōd Jē|hōvăh hăth | blēst hĕr.

The scansion (and reading) is as Coleridge gave it near the end of his life when he returned to these two lines as an example of hexameters 'from the Psalms'.[28] What is most striking about the lines is how different they are from the KJB's 'there is a river, the streams whereof shall make glad the city of God, the holy place of the tabernacles of the most high'. Divine intervention would be needed to make this scan as hexameters. Yet, according to Tomalin he used this example in the lecture to show how the KJB naturally fell into hexameters. The letter to his brother suggests that his interest in hexameters and the Bible began from a technical interest in hexameters ('he was quite an epicure in sound').[29] We may guess that the idea of finding hexameters in the KJB itself followed from this, for he did indeed claim to find 'a rare instance of a *perfect* hexameter ... in the English language':

> Gōd cāme | ūp wĭth ă | shōut: oūr | Lōrd wĭth thĕ | sōund ŏf ă | trūmpĕt.

This is much closer to the KJB, which reads, 'God is gone up with a shout, the Lord with the sound of a trumpet' (Ps. 47: 5). As long as one is willing to give 'the' different quantities in different places, this is scannable. But what is most striking is that the one surviving instance of Coleridge finding a perfect hexameter in the Bible still is not verbatim, and it is quickly followed with the two lines of paraphrase already noted.

All this makes it seem unlikely that Coleridge really thought the point through. If he did indeed render Isaiah 1 as hexameters in the lecture,[30] it must have been a virtuoso performance, impossible to be reproduced by ordinary mortals. That Coleridge was aware of the flimsiness of his argument is

---

[28] Note prefixed to 'Hymn to the Earth', *Poems*, p. 327.
[29] Wordsworth, quoted in Coleridge, *Poems*, p. 511n.
[30] The reports are ambiguous: he may have done no more than *say* that he had reduced it to hexameters.

suggested by its omission from *Biographia Literaria*. He contradicts Wordsworth without offering any proof, and earlier had contented himself with
reducing his appreciation of Isaiah 1 to the comment that it 'is poetry in the
most emphatic sense'; this follows what seems to be an acceptance of
Wordsworth's point in his admission that 'poetry of the highest kind may exist
without metre, and even without the contradistinguishing objects of a poem'
(II: 14–15).

In so far as he maintained the point, one has, reluctantly, to class Coleridge as
an English Gomarus and say that he was no more successful in scanning the
English than that worthy in scanning the Hebrew. He obviously believed that
metrical qualities were to be found in the KJB's passionate utterances, and he
had the advantage of working with a known language of which he was a poetic
master. Hexameters might not be readily demonstrable in Isaiah 1, but
quasi-poetic rhythms are: had he not been preoccupied with hexameters, he
might have produced insights into some of the rhythms of the KJB that would
have been a real addition to Lowth's insights.[31]

Two copies of the KJB belonging to Coleridge survive. The second of these
contains a substantial number of notes written between 1826 and 1829, of which
a few record literary responses. Occasionally he notes difficulties, for he
concurred with Gregory the Great 'that even in the Scriptures there are parts
where the elephant must swim, as well as others which the lamb may ford'.[32] So
he remarks after Job 21, 'I seem, through great part of this most precious as
most ancient poem,[33] to feel that the clue of the argument is yet to be given'
(*Marginalia*, *CW* 12, I: 426). Slightly more often he records admiration. In
chapters 50 and 51 of Isaiah he found 'a sublimity only to be fitly acknowledged
by adoration' (I: 435). Psalm 50 prompted a remark that might have come from
many a commentator in the previous century, 'what can Greece or Rome
present worthy to be compared with the 50th Psalm, either in sublimity of the
imagery or in moral elevation?' (I: 430). This may not represent an absolute
judgement between the classics and Scripture, for soon after he observes that
the 'majestic, profound and pregnant' eighth chapter of Proverbs is directly
comparable with Aeschylus' *Prometheus* (I: 432). Only in his *Table Talk* does he
appear to take sides with finality in this old debate, asking there, 'could you ever

---

[31] There is another metrical area in which he tantalises: late in life he thought seriously of
making a metrical translation '(if I find it practicable)' of Revelation, but nothing came
of this (*Letters*, VI: 867–8).

[32] *The Friend*, *CW* 6, II: 61n. I have seen this remark attributed to 'a French writer'
(Eckman, p. 51).

[33] This fairly standard opinion echoes *Biographia Literaria*, I: 202: Job is 'the sublimest, and
probably the oldest book on earth'.

discover anything sublime, in our sense of the term, in the classic Greek literature? I never could. Sublimity is Hebrew by birth' (25 July 1832, II: 180).

Though these comments were all made in his KJB, there is nothing in them that applies particularly to that version. When he deals specifically with the words in front of him, it is either to remark on the accuracy of the translation, or to consider a scholarly point – as when he notes the apparent anachronism of David referring to the temple in Ps. 27: 4, and resolves the problem by suggesting that 'a Psalm of David must often mean no more than a Davidic Psalm: as we say, a Pindaric ode' (*Marginalia*, 1: 428). Particularly significant is his note on Job 5: 7, 'yet man is born unto trouble, as the sparks fly upward': 'one is sorry to disturb a rendering which has passed into a proverb, but the context requires a different translation, viz., "man is born for the trouble (of man) as the birds of prey to a high flight". I.e., to soar in order to pounce' (1: 425). As befits a scholar of the meaning, even one so conscious of the poetic qualities of the originals, he would sacrifice felicity for accuracy. Indeed, he was sufficiently aware of limitations in the KJB and the PB to want both revised, so, in similar vein, he finds the PB version of Psalm 49 'erroneous throughout', and remarks that it 'is admirably suited to devotional purposes, but this is not accurate enough to compensate for its inferiority in all other respects'; 'a new translation of the Psalms is a great desideratum' (1: 429). In *Table Talk* he repeated the idea, implying that both the PB and the KJB Psalms lack some of the poetical power of the originals because they are insufficiently literal: 'the Psalms ought to be translated afresh; or, rather, the present version should be revised. Scores of passages are utterly unmeaning as they now stand. If the primary visual images had been preserved, the harmony would have been perceived.'[34] Such criticism is not confined to the Psalms: most of the notes on the NT concern the inaccuracy of the KJB, and many years earlier, in the third of his *Lectures on Revealed Religion*, he had prefaced his quotation of Isa. 52: 13–53: 12 thus: 'the passage is well known yet as it is in some parts falsely rendered in our translation, I shall repeat it as collected from later and more accurate versions'.[35]

Coleridge considered one other kind of revision of the Bible, this time involving the presentation of Paul's Epistles. Confronting the difficulty of

---

[34] 27 May 1830, 1: 148. As with several of these passages, Henry Nelson Coleridge's editing made his uncle seem less critical of the translations (cf. II: 99). Coleridge noted in his copy of the PB, 'I think the Bible version [of Psalm 104] might with advantage be substituted for this, which in some parts is scarcely intelligible' (*Marginalia*, 1: 708).

[35] *Lectures 1795 On Politics and Religion*, *CW* 1: 153. He chose to use only one version, Lowth's, somewhat adapted.

following Paul's arguments (the same problem that had led Locke to formulate his criticisms of the chapter and verse form of the KJB), he suggests that 'if we could now arrange this work [Romans] in the way in which we may be sure St Paul would himself do, were he now alive and preparing it for the press, his reasoning would stand out clearer. His accumulated parentheses would be thrown into notes, or extruded to the margin.'[36] Here he speaks as a different kind of revisionist from the one he usually appears to be, imagining Paul as a prose writer such as himself and presuming to know how he would have presented his work had he lived in the early nineteenth century. Such thinking is essentially the same as Harwood's, though one would hope that such a version of Paul, had Coleridge ever acted on his own suggestion, would have been more illuminating than that worthy's efforts.

All these criticisms of the KJB were made privately: Coleridge never joined the public campaign for a new version, but he clearly belongs with the many scholarly critics whose demands for a new version were to lead to the making of the RV. This is a significant alignment, not only because he lived at a time when conservative attachment to the KJB was very strong but because he had been closely and lovingly familiar with it from earliest childhood (by the age of four he 'could read a chapter in the Bible' (*Letters*, I: 312)), and because he studied it all his life. In a less scholarly and profound man these facts would have been a sure basis for an overriding attachment, but the truth is that he was a scholar and lover of the Bible rather than of the KJB. He knew enough Hebrew to work regularly through parts of the OT in later life,[37] enough even to form the judgement that Hebrew was 'in its height in Isaiah' (*Table Talk*, 24 February 1827, I: 64); his Greek was better than his Hebrew, and he frequently extended his reading to the Septuagint. When he declares himself to be 'passionately fond of the Hebrew poetry' (*Notebooks*, I: 1749), one takes him at face value. Unlike so many of the praisers of the Bible who attached their praise to the texts they imagined behind their English text, he could always move behind the KJB. His decision to prefer revision over retention is as meaningful – though of course lacking the historical significance – as the early translators' decision to be scholarly rather than literary.

---

[36] *Table Talk*, 15 June 1833, I: 388. The identical point is made in *Marginalia*, I: 459. There he draws a parallel with his own practice of occasionally subjoining a note to a note. He considered Romans 'the most profound work in existence' (*Table Talk*, I: 387). Although Coleridge read widely, one wonders whether he would have made this argument in the same way had he read – or remembered – Locke; the same kind of question might be raised in connection with some of his other arguments.

[37] See Henry Nelson Coleridge's note in *Table Talk*, II: 99. A useful account of his knowledge and reading is to be found in *Marginalia*, I: 415–16.

The relationship between Coleridge the literary critic, Coleridge the textual critic and Coleridge the religious thinker is complex. His marginal annotations, for instance, sometimes show a literary response, sometimes a text-critical response, sometimes a religious response, sometimes two or even all of these responses mixed. In works such as *Aids to Reflection, Confessions of an Inquiring Spirit, The Statesman's Manual* and his lectures on religious subjects, he appears as a religious rather than a literary thinker about the Bible, and he frequently describes the Bible in terms many an unliterary divine would use. So *The Statesman's Manual* is subtitled 'the Bible the best guide to political skill and foresight', and he presumes that his reader 'will indeed have directed your *main* attention to the promises and the information conveyed in the records of the evangelists and apostles... Yet not the less on this account will you have looked back with a proportionate interest on the *temporal* destinies of men and nations, sorted up for our instruction in the archives of the Old Testament.'[38] There is no hint of aesthetic interest here. Yet the links between his literary and his religious thought constantly assert themselves: they were bound to, for he believed poetry to be 'the blossom and the fragrancy of all human knowledge, human thoughts, human passions, emotions, language' (*Biographia Literaria*, II: 26). This is exactly Wordsworth's idea that 'poetry is the breath and finer spirit of all knowledge', but Coleridge pushes well beyond Wordsworth into the religious implications. Trying to read the Scriptures as he would any other work (*Confessions*, p. 294), he finds he cannot, because they are 'are distinguishable from all other books pretending to inspiration ... in their strong and frequent recommendations of truth. I do not here mean veracity, which cannot but be enforced in every code which appeals to the religious principle of man, but knowledge.'[39] The essence of this knowledge – common to his idea of poetry and his idea of the Bible – lies not in the reason but in the feelings. He writes in *Aids to Reflection*, 'in wonder all philosophy began: in wonder it ends: and admiration fills up the interspace. But the first wonder is the offspring of ignorance: the last is the parent of adoration. The first is the birth-throe of our knowledge: the last is its euthanasy and apotheosis' (p. 156). This is largely secular language (grandiose too – the KJB was hardly an influence on the style of this latter-day inkhornist) for the mystic experience of insight, at once a religious and an aesthetic experience. It is far removed from the previous century's emphasis on reason, yet close in temper to that century's rediscovery of sublimity, for one may say that wonder is the response aroused by the sublime, and we have already seen that 'sublime' was an essential critical

---

[38] *Lay Sermons, CW* 6: 8. A similar passage comes in *Confessions*, p. 322.
[39] Both *The Friend*, I: 104, and *The Statesman's Manual, Lay Sermons*, pp. 47–8.

term in Coleridge's vocabulary, and that he believed sublimity to be Hebrew by birth. It is this wondering response that he describes, almost as if it is so obvious as to go without saying, in *Confessions*:

> And need I say that I have met everywhere [in the Bible] more or less copious sources of truth, and power, and purifying impulses; – that I have found words for my inmost thoughts, songs for my joy, utterances for my hidden griefs, and pleadings for my shame and my feebleness? In short whatever *finds* me bears witness for itself that it has proceeded from a Holy Spirit, even from the same Spirit, 'which remaining in itself, yet regenerateth all other powers, and in all ages entering into holy souls maketh them friends of God, and prophets'.[40]

The wondering experience of being *found* by the Bible is precisely what he describes in the opening aphorism of *Aids to Reflection*: 'in philosophy equally as in poetry, it is the highest and most useful prerogative of genius to produce the strongest impressions of novelty while it rescues admitted truths from the neglect caused by the very circumstances of their universal admission' (p. 1). In this essential respect, philosophy – and, of course, religion – and poetry are united. The effect produced by the Bible is not different in kind from that produced by other writing or, in Coleridge's case as in Wordsworth's, by nature, only different in extent, as he underlines at the beginning of the next letter in *Confessions*: 'more ... than I have experienced in all other books put together ... the words of the Bible find me at greater depths of my being' (p. 296).

The Bible is inseparably bound up with Coleridge's complex ideas of the imagination. When, in a memorable phrase, he described Scripture histories as 'the living educts of the imagination',[41] he was making an early statement of the idea that they find him: they bring out the essential imagination within him. But that imagination must be present in the individual to begin with. So he looks for a quality of the imagination in the individual to match the original creative imagination, and exclaims later in *The Statesman's Manual*:

> O what a mine of undiscovered treasures, what a new world of power and truth would the Bible promise to our future meditation, if in some gracious moment one solitary text of all its inspired contents should but dawn upon us in the pure untroubled brightness of an IDEA, that most glorious birth of the God-like within us which, even as the light, its material symbol, reflects itself from a thousand surfaces and flies homeward to its parent mind enriched with a thousand forms, itself above form and still remaining in its own simplicity and identity! (P. 50)

---

[40] Wisd. 7: 27, paraphrased. Pp. 294–5.
[41] *The Statesman's Manual, Lay Sermons*, p. 29.

This is a reworking of part of one of his finest poems, 'Dejection: An Ode':

> O Lady! we receive but what we give,
> And in our life alone does Nature live:
> Ours is her wedding garment, ours her shroud!
>   And would we aught behold, of higher worth,
> Than that inanimate cold world allowed
> To the poor loveless ever-anxious crowd,
>   Ah! from the soul itself must issue forth
> A light, a glory, a fair luminous cloud
>   Enveloping the Earth –
> And from the soul itself must there be sent
>   A sweet and potent voice, of its own birth,
> Of all sweet sounds the life and element!

The joy that he laments the loss of in this poem is essentially the same as the wonder he writes of in *Aids to Reflection*. In the poem he can no longer feel that joy in the world of nature; if there is a hint of a similar dejection in the passage from *The Statesman's Manual*, it is nevertheless clear from most of his declarations of his response to the Bible that he did recover something of the joy and wonder in that world, if not in the world of nature. 'The primary imagination' that he held 'to be the living power and prime agent of all human perception, and as a repetition in the finite mind of the eternal act of creation in the infinite I AM' (*Biographia Literaria*, I: 304), remained active and responsive in his study of the Bible.

There is a further link here, between God the creator and the artist as creator. So, on the one hand, he can image the supreme human artist as the creator: 'in Shakespeare one sentence begets the next naturally; the meaning is all inwoven. He goes on kindling like a meteor through the dark atmosphere – yet when the creation in its outlines is once perfect, then he seems to rest from his labour and to smile upon his work and tell himself it is very good' (*Table Talk*, 5 April 1833, I: 356–7); on the other, he can hint at the familiar idea of the Bible being a perfect work of art because it has the supreme author: 'the content of every work must correspond to the character and designs of the workmaster; and the inference in the present case is too obvious to be overlooked' (*The Statesman's Manual*, p. 5). However, he did not care to develop the artistic part of the inference because of his awareness of the dangers of absolute ideas of inspiration (see above, p. 125). Even so, he saw the same quality of literary genius in the Bible that he saw in Shakespeare. A key element in Shakespeare is that 'in all his various characters we still feel ourselves communing with the same human nature ... that just proportion, that union and interpenetration of the universal and the particular which must ever pervade all works of decided genius and true science' (*The Friend*, 1: 457), and he found the identical quality in the Bible, where 'every agent appears and acts as a self-subsisting individual: each has a life of its own, and yet all are one life' (*The Statesman's Manual*, p. 31).

In spite of this fundamental identity in his religious and aesthetic ideas, Coleridge did make some separation of kind between the Bible and literature. He asks explicitly at the beginning of essay II of 'The Landing-Place' whether 'is it ... most important to the best interests of mankind ... that [the Bible] ... should be distinguished from all other works not in degree only but even in *kind*?', and noted in one copy that he was, with reservations, 'on the affirmative side'.[42] His observation in *Biographia Literaria* that 'the first chapter of Isaiah ... is poetry in the most emphatic sense' comes almost immediately after his almost hedonistic definition of a poem as 'that species of composition which is opposed to works of science by proposing for its *immediate* object pleasure, not truth' (II: 13), so he adds, 'yet it would be not less irrational than strange to assert that pleasure, and not truth, was the immediate object of the Prophet' (II: 15). The apparently pure aestheticism of his definition of a poem must be qualified by the poetry of the book of truth: there pleasure is the signature of truth, but truth is the key. Coleridge's sense of the unsurpassed beauty of the Bible is, at the last, grounded not on aesthetics but belief. Yet if that truth did not arouse pleasure, it would not be truth. The Bible, particularly the NT, is the yardstick of truth by which to measure the quality of other books. Like a Tyndale expounding the necessity of reading the Bible with a baptismal predisposition to believe in the heart, he would advise 'a nephew or son about to enter into Holy Orders' to read the NT 'with a prepared heart', which is as much as to say, with the primary imagination active. He adds, 'did you ever meet any book that went to your heart so often and so deeply – are not other books ... wonderfully efficacious in proportion as they resemble the New Testament?' (*Notebooks*, III: 3440).

Percy Bysshe Shelley and 'Scripture as a composition'

Hellenist, probably atheist, perhaps deist, but definitely not Christian, Percy Bysshe Shelley (1799–1822) pursues the implications of Wordsworth's sense that poetry is the soul of religion (above, p. 152). For him, almost mirror-like reversing Coleridge, the Bible is literature, and this is what makes it religious. This may seem strange for one who was so notoriously anti-christian

---

[42] *The Friend*, 1: 135. His reservations came principally from his reading of Chillingworth, for he recognised the importance of church authority and tradition (see *Table Talk*, 1: 231).

– surely the position of a Paine would have been more natural, rejection of the
Bible at once as religion and as good literature? But Shelley, admirer as he was of
Paine, distinguished sharply between the practice of Christianity and Christianity 'in its abstract purity',[43] between the teaching of Jesus and its interpretation
or corruption: he could abstract Jesus from the institutional religion he so
reviled. He knew his Bible as well as most of the orthodox and he read it to the
end of his life,[44] even if he had Keats's poems in his pocket rather than a Bible
when he drowned. Evidently there had been a rumour to this effect: Byron set
the record straight, adding significantly, 'however, it would not have been
strange, for he was a great admirer of Scripture as a composition'.[45] The
importance for us of the comment is that it is almost[46] the first use of a phrase
analogous to 'the Bible as literature'. That it should come in connection with a
literary man who was not a Christian anticipates a major aspect of ideas about
the Bible as literature, that very often they come either from unbelievers or are
directed towards them.

Shelley never wrote at length on the Bible, or rather, he wrote nothing
substantial that has survived: his lost 'Biblical Extracts' may have been
preceded by an essay, but it is not clear whether this would have been presented
as a literary, a philosophical or a religious anthology.[47] Nevertheless his
scattered remarks on parts of the OT and his more connected discussions of
Jesus confirm that he was indeed 'a great admirer of Scripture as a composition'.
The essence of this admiration is summarised in 'A defence of poetry': 'it is
probable that the astonishing poetry of Moses, Job, David, Solomon and Isaiah

---

[43] 'A defence of poetry', *Complete Works*, VII: 127.

[44] Among the books he and Mary read in 1820 was 'the Bible until the end of Ezekiel'; he
also reread the NT in that year (Newman Ivey White, II: 544).

[45] Letter to Thomas Moore, 27 August 1822, *Letters and Journals*, IX: 198.

[46] Byron had used the phrase, 'as compositions' in the previous year (see below, p. 167).
Earlier, Knox had considered the Bible 'as a collection of ... poetry' (above, p. 97).

[47] The following probably refers to what became 'Biblical Extracts', and is all we know of its
character: 'I have met with some waverers between Christianity and deism. I shall attempt
to make them reject all the bad, and take all the good, of the Jewish books. I have often
thought that the moral sayings of Jesus Christ might be very useful, if selected from the
mystery and immorality which surrounds them; it is a little work I have in contemplation'
(Letter to Elizabeth Hitchener, 27 February 1812, *Complete Works*, VIII: 285). The
'immorality' may not be confined to the corruptions he finds in Christianity, for he was
quite prepared to play with Paine-like criticism of the Bible, as when he puts this
observation in the mouth of his deist, Theosophus: 'the loathsome and minute
obscenities to which the inspired writers perpetually descend, the filthy observances
which God is described as personally instituting, the total disregard of truth and
contempt of the first principles of morality, manifested on the most public occasions by
the chosen favourites of Heaven, might corrupt, were they not so flagitious as to disgust'.
His note refers to Hosea 1 and 9, and Ezekiel 4, 16 and 23 ('A refutation of deism', VI: 34).

had produced a great effect upon the mind of Jesus and his disciples. The scattered fragments preserved to us by the biographers of this extraordinary person are all instinct with the most vivid poetry' (vii: 126). In a similar passage he supposes that

> The sublime dramatic poem entitled Job had familiarised [Jesus'] imagination with the boldest imagery afforded by the human mind and the material world. Ecclesiastes had diffused a seriousness and solemnity over the frame of his spirit glowing with youthful hope, and made audible to his listening heart
>
> > The still, sad music of humanity
> > Not harsh or grating but of ample power
> > To chasten and subdue.   ('Essay on Christianity', vi: 229)

Finally, in a letter he refers to Job and the Song of Songs as 'models of poetical sublimity and pathos'.[48]

Like and unlike Blake, he views Jesus as a poet, indeed, he seems to make him the supreme poet of the Bible, but he does this partly on the basis of his morality. Again 'A defence of poetry' makes the essential point:

> Plato, following the doctrines of Timaeus and Pythagoras, taught ... a moral and intellectual system of doctrine comprehending at once the past, the present and the future condition of man. Jesus Christ divulged the sacred and eternal truths contained in these views to mankind, and Christianity, in its abstract purity, became the exoteric expression of the esoteric doctrines of the poetry and wisdom of antiquity.   (vii: 127)

Central to these ideas of the Bible as poetry and Jesus as poet is Shelley's idea of poetry. The climactic passage of 'A defence of poetry' begins in this way:

> Poetry is indeed something divine. It is at once the centre and circumference of knowledge; it is that which comprehends all science, and that to which all science must be referred. It is at the same time the root and blossom of all other systems of thought; it is that from which all spring, and that which adorns all; and that which, if blighted, denies the fruit and the seed, and withholds from the barren world the nourishment and the succession of the scions of the tree of life. It is the perfect and consummate surface and bloom of things; it is as the odour and the colour of the rose to the texture of the elements which compose it, as the form and the splendour of unfaded beauty to the secrets of anatomy and corruption.   (vii: 135)

The equation with divinity is essential, and it is perhaps not surprising that the passage as a whole reminds one of Paul on charity: charity, the vital essence of meaning, is a supreme quality for Paul, as poetry is the supreme element for

---

[48] To Leigh Hunt, 3 November 1819, x: 110.

Shelley. There is another familiar quality in this passage: it echoes Wordsworth's claim that 'poetry is the breath and finer spirit of all knowledge', and
Coleridge's that poetry is 'the blossom and the fragrancy of all human
knowledge'. Shelley is playing a cadenza on his predecessors' ideas and images.
The difference from them comes not in his sense of poetry or in his literary sense
of the Bible, but in his sense of religion. He remains apart from Christianity, but
poetry is religion and the Bible is, in parts, poetry. So linking poetry and belief
in the 'Defence', he declares that

> it exceeds all imagination to conceive what would have been the moral condition of
> the world if neither Dante, Petrarch, Boccaccio, Chaucer, Shakespeare, Calderón,
> Lord Bacon nor Milton had ever existed; if Raphael and Michelangelo had never been
> born; if the Hebrew poetry had never been translated; if a revival of the study of
> Greek literature had never taken place; if no monuments of ancient sculpture had
> been handed down to us; and if the poetry of the religion of the ancient world had
> been extinguished together with its belief.   (VII: 133–4)

In the same vein, he included the Bible in his catalogue of the 'few well-chosen
titles' that might make up a good library. The list starts with Greek drama and
Plato, and finishes 'last, yet first, the Bible'.[49] What was suggested by
Wordsworth's ideas has indeed happened: the Bible has become part of the
canon of literature.

An infidel and the Bible: Lord Byron

Lord Byron (1788–1824), for all his notoriety, was neither an enemy of
the Bible nor especially interested in religious truth. Lacking the intellectual
urgency and subtlety of Coleridge or Shelley, he is more like a representative
figure. He was brought up – as who was not before the twentieth century? –
with the Bible before him. Though he lapsed as a Christian, he remained a
literary admirer of the Bible. In 1821 he asked his publisher, John Murray, to
send him

> A common Bible of good legible print (bound in Russia) I *have* one – but as it was the
> last gift of my Sister – (whom I shall probably never see again) I can only use it
> carefully – and less frequently – because I like to keep it in good order. – Don't forget
> this – for I am a great reader and admirer of those books – and had read them through
> and through before I was eight years old – that is to say the *Old* Testament – for the

---

[49] Thomas Medwin, *Revised Life of Shelley* (London, 1913), p. 255, as given in Newman
   Ivey White, II: 234.

New struck me as a task – but the other as a pleasure – I speak as a *boy* – from the recollected impressions of that period at Aberdeen in 1796.[50]

This surely describes the experience of many. More specifically, he noted, 'of the Scriptures themselves I have ever been a reader and admirer as compositions, particularly the Arab-Job – and parts of Isaiah – and the song of Deborah'.[51] He passed the occasional favourable literary comment on the Bible in his conversation, observing once,

> Since we have spoken of witches, what think you of the witch of Endor? I have always thought this the finest and most finished witch-scene that ever was written or conceived; and you will be of my opinion if you consider all the circumstances and the actors in the case, together with the gravity, simplicity and dignity of the language. It beats all the ghost scenes I ever read.[52]

Byron composed two works that connect with the Bible, *Hebrew Melodies* (1815) and the drama *Cain* (1821), but the connection is too slight to make them genuine contributions to a literary sense of the Bible. They are a further reflection of the growing literary rather than religious feeling for the Bible, and of the taste for poetic antiquities that had been slowly developing from the time of Husbands's work through that of Macpherson and Bishop Percy. That Byron wrote *Hebrew Melodies* at all was an accident: as he remarked, 'it is odd enough that this should fall to my lot, who have been abused as "an infidel"'.[53] He was approached by a Jewish musician (later to become the 'father of Australian music' (Ashton, p. 59)), Isaac Nathan, who was working on a collection of old Hebrew melodies and wanted a marketable poet to compose verses for them. Byron – with Scott, who had declined Nathan's invitation – was pre-eminently marketable; in agreeing to provide Nathan with lyrics he became involved in the twin fashions for ancient national poetry and music, the fashions that Byron's friend the Irishman Thomas Moore (1779–1852) was cultivating so successfully in his *Irish Melodies*. At first Byron gave Nathan a few lyrics he had on hand, but once the project was underway he turned to the Bible for some subjects. This is what he made of Job 4: 13–21:

> A spirit passed before me: I beheld
> The face of Immortality unveiled –

---

[50] Letter of 9 October 1821 (*Letters and Journals*, VIII: 238).
[51] Letter to Annabella Milbanke, 15 February 1814; as given in Ashton, p. 67.
[52] From James Kennedy's *Conversations on Religion with Lord Byron* (1830, p. 154), as given by Ashton, p. 174n.
[53] Letter to Annabella Milbanke, 20 October 1814, as given in Ashton, p. 14.

> Deep sleep came down on ev'ry eye save mine –
> And there it stood,– all formless – but divine:
> Along my bones the creeping flesh did quake;
> And as my damp hair stiffened, thus it spake:
>
> 'Is man more just than God? Is man more pure
> Than he who deems even Seraphs insecure?
> Creatures of clay – vain dwellers in the dust!
> The moth survives you, and are ye more just?
> Things of a day! you wither ere the night,
> Heedless and blind to Wisdom's wasted light!'

However kindly or unkindly one may judge this, it does not take one with renewed appreciation to the language of the KJB; rather, it functions like the multitude of exclamations at gems in the Bible, as an identification of an excellence. The taste that produces it may be more romantic (and in keeping with the liking for the witch of Endor) than the taste which produced the eighteenth-century paraphrases, but the result, though less expansive, is hardly more biblical. Sternhold and Hopkins obviously were not Byron's model, yet here he may be in the line suggested by Cowper's *Table Talk* in that Sternhold and Hopkins was still a byword for the bad lyrics that get made from the Bible. He indeed hoped to do 'a little better than Sternhold and Hopkins', but was judged by some not to have succeeded (Ashton, pp. 14, 46).

Hebrew Melodies scooped a project Moore had been working on, *Sacred Songs* (1816); many of these are paraphrases of the Bible, and sometimes they show a greater fidelity to the KJB, as in his version of Isaiah 60, which begins:

> Awake, arise, thy light is come;
>   The nations, that before outshone thee
> Now at thy feet lie dark and dumb –
>   The glory of the Lord is on thee!
>
> Arise – the Gentiles to thy ray,
>   From ev'ry nook of earth shall cluster;
> And kings and princes haste to pay
>   Their homage to thy rising lustre.

As so often in versifications, the pursuit of regular metre removes the felicity, and there are other typical signs of the pressure of verse form in additions that smack of poetic diction such as 'thy rising lustre', and in the omissions. In particular, the parallelism that is so striking in the prose version is diminished: one has to perceive it across the interruption of two lines in the first verse, and between pairs of lines in the second. A couple of phrases survive more or less intact, so one is certainly reminded of the KJB. Nevertheless, by comparison with the prose parallelism of Macpherson sixty years earlier, and the slightly more recent work of Smart and Blake, this sounds less biblical. The cause is the fundamental incompatibility between regular lyric versification and the almost free verse form of the parallelistic prose. The movement towards a more biblical style that was occasionally evident in pre-romantic and early romantic poetry has faded out.

There is, then, plenty of evidence from Wordsworth through to Byron (with the exception of Keats) that the major romantic poets admired the Bible as literature, indeed, that some of them regarded it as literature rather than as religion, but, with the possible exception of Wordsworth, little evidence that it affected their writing. This is not just because they rarely turned to the Bible for subjects but also because their styles, both in verse and prose, are fundamentally un-biblical. Coleridge, of them all the most devoted to the Bible, was also the one who wrote least like it, not only in his verse but in his extraordinarily erudite and convoluted prose. In the long perspective, perhaps the most striking thing to emerge is the beginning of the idea of the Bible as literature in the way Shelley and Byron take pleasure in the Bible without accepting the framework of institutional religion that usually surrounds it.

A Bible for the romantic reader

Here is part of a report of a conversation that perhaps took place about 1829:

> Something was observed about Byron and Tom Paine as to their attacks upon religion; and I said that sceptics and philosophical unbelievers appeared to me to have just as little liberality or enlargement of view as the most bigoted fanatic. They could not bear to make the least concession to the opposite side. They denied the argument that because the Scriptures were fine they were therefore of divine origin, and yet they virtually admitted it; for, not believing the truth, they thought themselves bound to maintain that they were good for nothing. I had once, I said, given great offence to a knot of persons of this description by contending that Jacob's dream was finer than anything in Shakespeare, and that Hamlet would bear no comparison with, at least, one character in the New Testament. A young poet had said on this occasion, he did not like the Bible because there was nothing about flowers in it; and I asked him if he had forgot the passage, 'Behold the lilies of the field', etc? 'Yes', said Northcote, 'and in the Psalms and in the book of Job there are passages of unrivalled beauty. In the latter there is the description of the warhorse that has been so often referred to, and of the days of Job's prosperity; and in the Psalms I think there is that passage, "He openeth his hands, and the earth is filled with plenteousness; he turneth

away his face, and we are troubled; he hideth himself, and we are left in darkness"; [cf. Ps. 104: 28–9] or, again, how fine is that expression, "All the beasts of the forests are mine, and so are the cattle upon a thousand hills!" [Ps. 50: 10, PB]. What an expanse, and what a grasp of the subject! Everything is done upon so large a scale, and yet with such ease, as if seen from the highest point of view. It has mightily a look of inspiration or of being dictated by a superior intelligence. They say mere English readers cannot understand Homer because it is a translation; but why will it not bear a translation as well as the book of Job, if it is as fine?'

The author is the voluminous essayist and critic William Hazlitt (1778–1830).[54] He does not guarantee the accuracy of his reports but hopes they have a verisimilitude, and this one, especially in the haziness of the quotations, certainly does. The literary virtues of the Bible were a subject of conversation among the intelligentsia, and the mixture of standard and personal examples of excellence is characteristic of what we have seen; so is the rivalry with Shakespeare and with the classics. As would have been so in the two preceding centuries, most of the comments seem to be vaguely referred to the originals, but the superiority of the KJB as a translation to translations of all other literary works is also taken for granted. One aspect of the conversation, however, distinctly belongs to this late romantic time. Indeed, it takes the idea of the Bible as part of the canon of literature further than we have seen in Shelley, the explicitly stated idea 'that because the Scriptures were fine they were therefore of divine origin': the divinity of the Scriptures is shown by their literary superiority. This superiority bespeaks inspiration, and who should inspire if not God? Literary and divine inspiration seem to have become indistinguishable, though they are not coupled quite as Blake had coupled them; for him divine inspiration was literary inspiration, but here it is the other way round.

It makes no difference whether this was really Northcote's idea or whether Hazlitt was using him as a stalking-horse. Thought about the Bible as literature was clearly developing in this direction from Wordsworth on, and Hazlitt was helping that development, here going beyond the praise he had accorded the Bible in his *Lectures on the English Poets*[55] or his *Lectures on the Dramatic Literature of the Age of Elizabeth*. In these latter comes a phrase that epitomises the movement towards reading the Bible as literature rather than religion, 'leaving religious faith quite out of the question'.[56] This is part of what is, as always in Hazlitt, a long passage. Description of the Bible's impact in Elizabethan times

---

[54] *Conversations with James Northcote*, *Complete Works*, XI: 245–6. For the comments on accuracy referred to in the next sentence, see p. 350.
[55] 'On poetry in general', *Complete Works* V: 16–17.
[56] 'General view of the subject', *Complete Works*, VI: 183.

becomes an account of its literary excellence, and herein lie two ideas that were gradually to become important, first, that the English Bible was a literary influence, and second, an idea closely akin to the myth that the KJB was an instant success, that it had had this kind of influence almost from the time it first appeared:

> But the Bible was thrown open to all ranks and conditions 'to run and read', with its wonderful table of contents from Genesis to the Revelations ... I cannot think that all this variety and weight of knowledge could be thrown in all at once upon the mind of a people and not make some impressions upon it, the traces of which might be discerned in the manners and literature of the age. For to leave more disputable points and take only the historical parts of the Old Testament, or the moral sentiments of the New, there is nothing like them in the power of exciting awe and admiration, or of rivetting sympathy. We see what Milton has made of the account of the Creation from the manner in which he has treated it, imbued and impregnated with the spirit of the time of which we speak. Or what is there equal (in that romantic interest and patriarchal simplicity which goes to the heart of a country and rouses it, as it were, from its lair in wastes and wildernesses) equal to the story of Joseph and his brethren, of Rachel and Laban, of Jacob's dream, of Ruth and Boaz, the descriptions in the book of Job, the deliverance of the Jews out of Egypt, or the account of their captivity and return from Babylon? There is in all these parts of the Scripture, and numberless more of the same kind, to pass over the Orphic hymns of David, the prophetic denunciations of Isaiah or the gorgeous visions of Ezekiel, an originality, a vastness of conception, a depth and tenderness of feeling, and a touching simplicity in the mode of narration which he who does not feel need be made of no 'penetrable stuff'. There is something in the character of Christ too (leaving religious faith quite out of the question) of more sweetness and majesty, and more likely to work a change in the mind of man by the contemplation of its idea alone, than any to be found in history, whether actual or feigned. This character is that of a sublime humanity.
>
> (VI: 182–3)

What is of most significance here is the way that the idea is formed: the Bible is so excellent a creation that it must have exercised a literary influence, and this is to be proved not by showing that influence but by exclaiming at the beauty of the Bible in terms that are redolent of romantic sensibility. The passage is rhetoric rather than literary criticism or history: it is a powerful persuasion to a literary opinion, but it neither proves that opinion to be right nor draws out a true history. Nevertheless, it is important. If Coleridge (with Swift behind him) was the first to argue that the KJB had influenced the English language (and influenced it for the better), Hazlitt is the first to argue that the English Bible has been a literary influence.

The terms and the items Hazlitt selects suggest one more thing, the gradual replacement of poetry by the novel as the predominant literary mode. If the highest English literary achievements between 1790 and 1820 belong to the poetry, still it is a close-run thing; in Victorian times they belong to the novel. Where, say, Lowth had unhesitatingly confined himself to the poetry of the OT, Hazlitt, without in any way denying the power of the poetry, passes over it, as if the securest demonstration of quality can now be made from examples which take, by and large, the territory of the novel, moving histories, moral sentiments, and character. He is creating a Bible for the readers of Sir Walter Scott's novels.[57]

Charlotte Brontë and the influence of the KJB

In spite of what we have seen from Say and from Lowth among the critics, and Smart, Macpherson and Blake among the poets, there are good grounds for thinking that signs of the influence of the KJB's language are more likely to be found in prose than in verse – at least until the establishment of free verse – and one novel shows that influence in a particularly useful way, Charlotte Brontë's *Jane Eyre* (1847). It not only shows the obvious distinction between use of and influence by the KJB, but it suggests distinctions between kinds of influence, distinctions which will allow us to cut through the difficulties that would arise if we took the whole field of the influence of the Bible (itself a subject to generate at least one large book) as part of the present subject.

In *Jane Eyre*, romanticism, religion and the KJB come together to create important artistic effects, and the result is sometimes insight into the KJB. It contains many examples of quotation or allusion (the line is a fine one) that differ from the example from Burke given at the beginning of this chapter only in their lack of witty intention. When Rochester, analysing Jane's character, says, '"strong wind, earthquake-shock, and fire may pass by: but I shall follow the guiding of that still small voice which interprets the dictates of conscience"' (II: 4; p. 203), the biblical echo would have been obvious enough: he is both alluding to and quoting 1 Kgs. 19: 11–12. What makes this different from most biblical allusions in works that pre-date the literary rise of the KJB is the inescapable presence of its language in 'still small voice'. Such quotation needs no quotation

---

[57] In passing, Scott's well-known love for the Bible is worth recording. As he lay dying he asked his future biographer, John Gibson Lockhart, to read to him, 'and when I asked from what book, he said, "Need you ask? There is but one." I chose the 14th chapter of St. John's Gospel' (*Memoirs of Sir Walter Scott* (1837–8), 5 vols. (London: Macmillan, 1900), V: 423).

marks or typographical distinction because it is fully integrated with the language of the novel. Familiarity with both content and language of the KJB is used in a straightforward but unostentatious manner to enrich the text.

But Charlotte Brontë does not just use the KJB; her language is in a number of respects shaped by it: it is an influence on her as well as a source for her to draw on. This mixture of use and influence in her language is clearest at the end of volume II, as the desolation following the broken wedding overwhelms Jane:

> My eyes were covered and closed: eddying darkness seemed to swim round me, and reflection came in as black and confused a flow. Self-abandoned, relaxed and effortless, I seemed to have laid me down in the dried-up bed of a great river; I heard a flood loosened in remote mountains, and felt the torrent come: to rise I had no will, to flee I had no strength. I lay faint; longing to be dead. One idea only still throbbed life-like within me – a remembrance of God: it begot an unuttered prayer: these words went wandering up and down in my rayless mind, as something that should be whispered; but no energy was found to express them:–
>
> 'Be not far from me, for trouble is near: there is none to help.'
>
> It was near: and as I had lifted no petition to heaven to avert it – as I had neither joined my hands, nor bent my knees, nor moved my lips – it came: in full, heavy swing the torrent poured over me. The whole consciousness of my life lorn, my love lost, my hope quenched, my faith death-struck, swayed full and mighty above me in one sullen mass. That bitter hour cannot be described: in truth, 'the waters came into my soul; I sank in deep mire: I felt no standing; I came into deep waters; the floods overflowed me.' (P. 299)

In important ways this is similar to Bunyan's description of Christian and Hopeful wading into the river of death (see volume I, pp. 308–9): both are climactic passages, and both quote or adapt the Psalms, including, in both cases, Ps. 69: 2. Moreover, neither passage is written in a purely biblical style: just as one could distinguish Bunyan from the Bible, so one can distinguish Brontë. The crucial difference between the two passages becomes apparent when one recognises that, by contrast with the Bunyan, the Brontë is typical of the style of the whole novel, and that the Brontë not only uses but is influenced by the Bible. Where the Bunyan uses the Bible for a local effect, and so suggests little in the way of a literary sense of the language of the KJB, the Brontë rings with admiration for the KJB.

The quotations (Ps. 22: 11 and Ps. 69: 1–2) adapt the originals in two ways, to the grammatical demands of the local context and for rhythmic effect. The latter is the significant change: Brontë has eliminated linking words to heighten the drumbeat parallelism of clause against clause. This is how the second quotation reads in the KJB, with Brontë's omissions italicised:

Save me, O God; for the waters are come in unto my soul. I sink in deep mire, *where* there is no standing: I am come into deep waters, *where* the floods overflow me.

Yet the effect is not of a departure from the style of the KJB, for the rhythm is still biblical, as the next verse of Psalm 69 shows:

I am weary of my crying: my throat is dried: mine eyes fail while I wait for my God.

The first three clauses, balancing on colons, have the same drumbeat. Brontë's quotations, in their adapted but still biblical rhythm, are at one with the dominant rhythm of her prose, which is based on parallel phrases and, a development beyond the Bible, parallel words. The rhythm of the quotations is matched by the rhythm of 'my life lorn, my love lost, my hope quenched, my faith death-struck', or 'to rise I had no will, to flee I had no strength'. That there are other effects and influences in the language besides the biblical, or that there are other biblical turns of phrase, need not bother us here: the crucial point is that a major element in the style proclaims its origin in the KJB, and the language of the KJB is shown to be like the artful language of the novel. This demonstrates literary quality in the KJB as surely as good practical criticism: *Jane Eyre* creates literary appreciation of the Bible in a way that Bunyan's work does not.

Brontë's characteristic accumulation of synonymous words into triplets or, occasionally, longer units (mentioned above but only evident in the passage in 'self-abandoned, relaxed and effortless'), leads to an important distinction. In her prose this parallelism of words is stylistically at one with the biblical parallelism of phrases, yet it is not, in itself, a characteristic of the KJB. It may well be that such non-biblical parallelism was influenced by the Bible, but, unlike the parallelism of phrases, it does not send one back to the Bible. Such instances of influence, or of the possibility of influence, should not concern us here: they are covert, and so do not help to create an attitude to the Bible.

One last example may make the distinction still clearer. Brontë's idea of love is intensely religious and constantly expressed in religious language. When Rochester first proposes (II: 8) in an 'Eden-like' setting, it is a call 'to the paradise of union' (pp. 250, 258). Jane describes their relationship as 'communion'; to have it broken would be 'to have my morsel of bread snatched from my lips, and my drop of living water dashed from my cup'. Essential to this love is a sense of equality. Moving towards the avowal of love, Jane develops her sense of communion: '"I have talked, face to face, with what I reverence; with what I delight in,– with an original, a vigorous, an expanded mind. I have known you, Mr Rochester"' (p. 255). Only 'reverence' here explicitly sustains the religious idea of love. 'Face to face' is too ordinary a phrase to invite us to treat it as an allusion, but, if we do, the result is surprising. Twice the KJB uses the phrase in an everyday way, but six of the seven OT uses of it describe man and God together (the seventh, Judg. 6: 22, concerns Gideon and the angel of the Lord), and the novel several times presents the love relationship as a relationship with God, or with a god. The most striking use of 'face to face' comes in Paul:

> For now we see through a glass, darkly; but then face to face: now I know in part; but then shall I know even as also I am known. And now abideth faith, hope, charity, these three; but the greatest of these is charity.   (1 Cor. 13: 12–13)

Brontë's 'face to face' links with knowledge just as this passage does, and the aptness of the passage becomes still greater if one substitutes 'love' for 'charity', for love is Brontë's greatest. This is enough to show that 'face to face' might be an allusion, but not to prove that it is or to demonstrate that Brontë herself was aware of the connection. Indeed, the probability is otherwise: if she seeks an effect, she seeks it openly. Nevertheless, the aptness of the connection shows just how far Brontë's idea of love was created by her religious upbringing: the Bible has influenced her even more than she is aware, and more than any ordinary reader could realise. Now, influence of this sort is common: it shows a writer's absorption in the Bible and religion, but it neither tells of the writer's attitude to the Bible nor helps to create an attitude to the Bible in the reader. For both reasons, such influence lies outside the scope of this book.

CHAPTER 5

Literary discussion to mid-Victorian times

The pious chorus

> If to adore an image be idolatry,
> To deify a book is bibliolatry.

This *bon mot*, the *OED*'s first example of 'bibliolatry', comes from John Byrom (d. 1763) in the course of an argument against the idea that the Holy Spirit is present in the Bible, for 'Books are but books; th' illuminating part / Depends on God's good spirit, in the heart'.[1] Nearly a century later the English opium-eater, Thomas De Quincey (1785–1859), defined 'bibliolatry' as 'a superstitious allegiance – an idolatrous homage – to the words, to the syllables and to the very punctuation of the Bible'.[2] The invention of the word, though overdue, was particularly appropriate for the latter part of the eighteenth century and the nineteenth century, but what is most striking about De Quincey's engaging and witty discussion of bibliolatry is that none of it concerns literary attitudes. A new word is needed to denote not just literary bibliolatry but its English form, already so thoroughly evident, reverence for the KJB. 'AVolatry' (in preference to 'KJBolatry') has been rife since the 1760s. Typically it emerges in a pious chorus of adoration that is more often an exercise in rhetoric than criticism. Commentators seem to vie to produce the most resounding and memorable praise of the KJB, and it is a nice irony that, if this was a competition, the palm would most likely go to a Roman Catholic lamenting the hold of the KJB on the English.

The greatest spur to the chorus was the pressure of rival versions, and the chorus increasingly takes on a polemic aspect as argument for an official

---

[1] 'A stricture on the Bishop of Glocester's doctrine of grace', in Samuel Johnson, ed., *The Works of the English Poets*, 21 vols. (London, 1810), XV: 267.
[2] 'Protestantism' (1847), *The Collected Writings of Thomas De Quincey*, ed. David Masson (London, 1897), VIII: 263.

176

revision made it more and more possible that the revered old treasure would be left to moulder in the vault of antiquities. Yet it would be wrong to view the chorus as mere political agitation spurred by reactionary nostalgia. There may be an element of unthinking overstatement, but there is no hypocrisy in stating what, in common with most of your peers, you believe, nor is rational examination necessary to make that belief sincere. Indeed, though a De Quincey might debunk bibliolatry, the first half of the nineteenth century was a time when it was difficult to question AVolatry, so fashionable had it become. At least one critic, the literary historian Henry Hallam (1777–1859), recognised the difficulty and raised mild but ineffectual protest:

> The style of this translation is in general so enthusiastically praised that no one is permitted either to qualify or even explain the grounds of his approbation. It is held to be the perfection of our English language. I shall not dispute this proposition; but one remark as to a matter of fact cannot reasonably be censured, that, in consequence of the principle of adherence to the original versions which had been kept up ever since the time of Henry VIII, it is not the language of the reign of James I. It may, in the eyes of many, be a better English, but it is not the English of Daniel, or Raleigh, or Bacon, as any one may easily perceive. It abounds, in fact, especially in the Old Testament, with obsolete phraseology, and with single words long since abandoned, or retained only in provincial use. On the more important question, whether this translation is entirely, or with very trifling exceptions, conformable to the original text, it seems unfit to enter. It is one which is seldom discussed with all the temper and freedom from oblique views which the subject demands, and upon which, for this reason, it is not safe for those who have not had leisure or means to examine it for themselves, to take upon trust the testimony of the learned.[3]

This fairly accounts for the unsatisfactoriness that one may find in the declarations of AVolatry and is sufficient warning of political motivation in some of the arguments.

The typical – and not unfamiliar – sound of the chorus can be heard in three remarks from the first twenty years of the century. Citing Swift and Monboddo, Thomas Rennell, Dean of Winchester, later Master of the Temple, declared 'that the grandeur, dignity and simplicity of [the KJB] is confessed even by those who wish eagerly to promote a revision, and by the most eminent critics, and masters of style it is allowed to exhibit a more perfect specimen of the *integrity* of the English language, than any other writing which that language can boast'.[4] Reverence for the translators and the belief that their work was an

---

[3] *Introduction to the Literature of Europe in the Fifteenth, Sixteenth, and Seventeenth Centuries*, 4 vols. (1837–9; sixth edn, London, 1860), II: 464.

[4] *Discourses on Various Subjects* (London, 1801), p. 240.

instant success of the sort the Septuagint was supposed to have been are natural corollaries of this judgement. Both were voiced in response to another new version, John Bellamy's (1818). The *Quarterly Review* declared that

> He has no relish or perception of the exquisite simplicity of the original, no touch of that fine feeling, that pious awe which led his venerable predecessors to infuse into their version as much of the Hebrew idiom as was consistent with the perfect purity of our own; a taste and feeling which have given perennial beauty and majesty to the English tongue.[5]

Creation implies a creator, art an artist. It is a kind of atheism to deny that beauty was created deliberately. Evidently the good taste of the translators led them to adopt aesthetic criteria, criteria which perfected their language and made it either a monument of the 'perennial beauty and majesty of English', or an influence for beauty and majesty in English. It is a confirmation of beauty to believe that it has always been appreciated. So another critic responding to Bellamy, John William Whittaker, was full of confidence:

> it may safely be asserted, without fear of contradiction, that the nation at large has always paid our translators the tribute of veneration and gratitude which they so justly merit . . . Their version has been used ever since its first appearance, not only by the Church, but by all the sects which have forsaken her, and has justly been esteemed by all for its general faithfulness and the severe beauty of its language.[6]

The ease with which this is tossed off confirms that recognition of the linguistic merits (at least) of the KJB was thoroughly well established. Now, these three pieties together form a small part of a collection of authorities modelled on Archbishop Newcome's *Historical View of the English Biblical Translations*, section VIII of Henry John Todd's *A Vindication of our Authorised Translation and Translators of the Bible* (1819). However, where Newcome was prepared to let contrasting voices produce a debate that eventually became an argument for revision, the arch-conservative Todd's purpose is sufficiently indicated by his title.[7]

---

[5] 38: 455; as given in Henry John Todd, *A Vindication of our Authorised Translation* (London, 1819), p. 80.

[6] Whittaker, pp. 92–3.

[7] In another work prepared while he was keeper of manuscripts and records at Lambeth Library, Todd gave absolute proof of his conservatism by defending Sternhold and Hopkins with considerable recourse to Beveridge (*Observations upon the Metrical Versions of the Psalms* (London, 1822)). Earlier Samuel Horsley had also defended Sternhold and Hopkins as 'the best and most exact [Psalter] we have' (1798 sermon; quoted in the preface to his *The Book of Psalms*, 2 vols. (London, 1815), p. xi). Though the praise is more for accuracy than literary merit, we may see in Horsley and Todd's attitude to that Psalter a reflection of the spirit that was glorifying the KJB.

Nationalism is implicit in Whittaker's reference to 'the nation at large'. In the following year a chauvinistic nationalism that far outstrips any previous comparisons with the Bibles of other nations was added to the chorus in the conclusion of a work defending the textual basis and scholarly accuracy of the KJB:

> The language of our present version has the full tide of popular opinion strongly in its favour; it exhibits a style appropriately biblical, and is distinguished by a general simplicity of expression, which the most uncultivated mind may comprehend, and the most cultivated admire. It is a translation in possession of characteristical merits, which might be extinguished, but cannot be augmented, by principles of transitory taste and ephemeral criticism; a translation which, with all its imperfections in whatsoever part of Scripture the comparison be made, is superior to every other in our own, and inferior to none in any foreign language.[8]

The meaningless concession to imperfections in no way disguises the fact that this is AVolatry rampant: the KJB is supreme. Of special interest is the circularity of one part of the comment, that 'it exhibits a style appropriately biblical'. The translators, as I argued in volume 1, chapter 6, had no special biblical English available to them. Time has made their language appear the only possible English for the Bible.

The best-known pre-Victorian nugget of AVolatry comes from the enormously popular historian, critic and poet Thomas Babington Macaulay (1800–59). He proclaimed of 'the English Bible' that it was 'a book which, if everything else in our language should perish, would alone suffice to show the whole extent of its beauty and power'.[9] In its pithiness and excess of a truth many would like to believe (is the beauty and power of English confined to a vocabulary of some 6,000 words?[10] Is Shakespeare's English to be confined

---

[8] Anon (Archbishop Richard Lawrence), *Remarks upon the Critical Principles, and the Practical Application of those Principles, Adopted by Writers, who have at Various Periods Recommended a New Translation of the Bible as Expedient and Necessary* (Oxford, 1820), pp. 161–2.

[9] 'John Dryden', *Edinburgh Review* (January 1828); *The Life and Works of Lord Macaulay Complete*, 10 vols. (London: Longman, 1903), v: 101.

[10] This is the general estimate (see, e.g., W. J. Heaton, *Our Own English Bible, its Translators and their Work*, 3 vols. (London: Griffiths, 1905–13), III: 331). Heaton estimates that 93 per cent of these words are native English, while Muir puts the figure at 97 per cent (William Muir, *Our Grand Old Bible* (London: Morgan and Scott, 1911), p. 134). Both rely on George P. Marsh. He had found that 60 per cent of the total vocabulary of the KJB was of native origin, about the same as in Shakespeare (by contrast, in Milton's poetry the proportion was less than one third). Turning to 'the proportions in which authors actually employ the words at their command', he found John 1, 4 and 17 to be 96 per cent Anglo-Saxon, Matthew 7, 17 and 18 93 per cent, Luke 5, 12 and 23 92 per cent

within the range of the Bible? Is the beauty and power of subordinated sentence structures to be lost?), this has not only made its way into the *Oxford Dictionary of Quotations* but may be found repeated from time to time in any newspaper that offers its readers not only a daily verse from the Bible and a dose of comic strips but a quotation from anyone from Aristotle to Zsa Zsa Gabor. What was it that prompted the magnificent and incisive Macaulay to such a remark? It was not just his 'talent for saying what is ordinary and familiar in impressive language'.[11] The remark comes as an aside in an elaborate argument that the imaginative and the critical faculties cannot flourish together; he has extolled Shakespeare to the skies (like so many, he is a bardolater before he is an AVolater) when Shakespeare is, as it were, writing naturally, but scorned him when he attempts to write to the critical standards of his time, especially the standards for prose. Herein lie two important factors beyond his personal response to the KJB. He has argued that times are more important than capacities to the productions of genius or the making of discoveries, and the English Bible belongs to the most fertile time in English literary history: did not that time produce Shakespeare? Secondly, he sees a key factor in the quality of the Bible as its independence from the critical tastes of the time, a quality it shares with Shakespeare. He observes in the next sentence that 'the respect which the translators felt for the original prevented them from adding any of the hideous decorations then in fashion'. Though this stops short of AVolatrous acclaim for the genius of the translators, the logic is still not compelling. Moreover, it is instructive to see bardolatry and AVolatry coming together in what we may call an imaginative truth. The Bible's reputation probably did little for Shakespeare's, but his certainly helped the Bible's, and together they are the key to seeing the late Elizabethan and early Jacobean period as the greatest in English literature.

Macaulay never elaborated on his literary sense of the Bible, but he did tell his beloved sister Hannah Macaulay that 'a person who professed to be a critic in the delicacies of the English language ought to have the Bible at his finger's ends'.[12] Had this been a public pronouncement, it would have commanded instant assent not just from AVolaters but from the critical public at large.

An echo of Macaulay's brand of AVolatry appeared shortly afterwards at the

and Romans 2, 7, 11 and 15 90 per cent. The proportion drops to 80 per cent in *Paradise Lost* vi (pp. 91–3). It is characteristic of AVolatry – as of any conspiracy to admire – that the figure that is highest should be picked, and that no heed should be taken of the careful distinction between total vocabulary and usage.

[11] Margaret Cruickshank, *Thomas Babington Macaulay* (Boston: Twayne, 1978), p. 20.

[12] Letter to Hannah Macaulay, 30 May 1831. *The Letters of Thomas Babington Macaulay*, ed. Thomas Pinney, 6 vols. (Cambridge: Cambridge University Press, 1974–81), II: 22.

end of Hartley Coleridge's brief and sympathetic account of Anthony Parver (as he calls Purver); observing that his Bible has received less attention than it merited, he adds presciently,

> We doubt, indeed, whether any new translation, however learned, exact or truly orthodox, will ever appear to English Christians to be the real Bible. The language of the Authorised Version is the perfection of English, and it can never be written again, for the language of prose is one of the few things in which the English have really degenerated. Our tongue has lost its holiness.[13]

This expresses so exactly how many people now think that it is easy to forget what a massive change it represents from Augustan attitudes; easy to forget, too, just how many magnificent writers of prose were yet to delight the world. Swift's idea that the KJB should be a standard for language has reached its apotheosis: the KJB is more than the standard: it is perfection. The rise of AVolatry is part of that idealisation of the past and contempt for the present that is so typical of our own age.

AVolatry and the desire for rhetorical flourish were potent forces. They undermine the substantial and scholarly 'Historical account of the English Versions of the Scriptures' prefixed to *The English Hexapla* (London, 1841). This was the work of the young Samuel Prideaux Tregelles (1813–75), soon to become widely known as a scholar of the Bible, particularly of the text of the NT. The *Hexapla* was prepared primarily in order to promote the best possible comprehension of the Scriptures. Tregelles brings out his lack of concern with possible literary qualities of the English translations in his regret that, because the KJB 'has too entirely superseded all those [translations] which were formerly in use ... the advantage which was enjoyed during the reign of Elizabeth has been let go, namely that of comparing the various renderings of the same passage as a help to the true understanding of what the Scripture teaches' (p. 160). Two pages later, in 'plan of the English Hexapla', he proves the point by showing from John 10: 16 that Tyndale could be more faithful to the Greek than his successors, and by showing from Heb. 10: 23 that the KJB could use a word not in its predecessors which damages the meaning of the verse. Such scholarly nicety does not prepare one for AVolatry, especially as the whole work is factual rather than critical. Tregelles concludes with the reception of the KJB and at first appears to be maintaining his admirable soundness, observing that 'the Bishops' Bible had been the translation read in churches previously, and this became wholly superseded by the new version: the Geneva Bible, which was the *household* version, maintained its ground for

---

[13] *Biographia Borealis* (London, 1833), p.718.

some time, but *gradually* gave way; so that this translation soon became the only one in general use' (p. 60). The force of *'gradually'* is much reduced by 'soon', and the next paragraph, the last of the 'historical account', quite obscures the general historical accuracy: 'if a testimony were needed to the general excellence of this version, an appeal need only be made to the fact that it has maintained its ground for two hundred and thirty years. It has been as highly esteemed by the learned as by the unlearned'. It is the work of a thoughtless moment to turn this into a belief that the KJB had, from the moment of its first appearance on, been universally acclaimed a masterpiece. In his final sentence AVolatry suddenly sounds its trumpet. Like others, Tregelles allows that there are 'minor particulars [which] might ... be corrected to advantage', but concludes:

> It is impossible to form any estimate of the blessing in result which has flowed from this version: the translators acted in their labour as being the servants of Christ; they knew that it was vain to trust in themselves, and thus, like Tyndale and Coverdale before them, they laid their work before the Lord in prayer, and found, in so doing, that He to whom they trusted was indeed faithful.

So it seems that the translators were inspired, and a careful work of scholarship at the last encourages the most uncritical AVolatry.

In the same year the public was treated to this thoroughly familiar version of the chorus:

> so inimitable, as an entire production, is the English version, so deep and extensive is the hold it has acquired of the public mind, so sacred has it become by our earliest associations and by a hallowed prejudice, almost amounting to superstitious attachment, that no new translation materially differing from it is ever likely to become acceptable and popular.
>
> (P. iv)

Thus the man-midwife John Tricker Conquest (1789–1866), best known for his *Outlines of Midwifery* and *Letters to a Mother on the Management of Herself and her Children in Health and Disease*, in the preface to his *The Holy Bible, Containing the Authorised Version of the Old and New Testaments with Twenty Thousand Emendations* (London, 1841). Even would-be revisers had not only to acknowledge AVolatry but to restate it.

Others besides these gentle enemies lent their voices to the chorus. The sweetest voice of all, frequently elevated to solo by later writers, belonged to a man Calvinistically reared who became an Anglican priest and consummated his rise to the heights by converting to Catholicism, Father Frederick William Faber (1814–63):

If the Aryan heresy was propagated and rooted by means of beautiful vernacular hymns, so who will say that the uncommon beauty and marvellous English of the Protestant Bible is not one of the great strongholds of heresy in this country? It lives on in the ear like a music that never can be forgotten, like the sound of church bells which the convert hardly knows how he can forego. Its felicities seem often to be things rather than mere words. It is part of the national mind and the anchor of the national seriousness. Nay, it is worshipped with a positive idolatry, in extenuation of whose grotesque fanaticism its intrinsic beauty pleads availingly with the man of letters and the scholar. The memory of the dead passes into it. The potent traditions of childhood are stereotyped in its verses. The power of all the griefs and trials of a man is hidden beneath its words. It is the representative of his best moments, and all that there has been about him of soft, and gentle, and pure, and penitent, and good, speaks to him forever out of his English Bible. It is his sacred thing which doubt never dimmed and controversy never soiled. It has been to him all along as the silent, but O how intelligible voice, of his guardian angel; and in the length and breadth of the land there is not a Protestant, with one spark of religiousness about him, whose spiritual biography is not in his Saxon Bible. And all this is an unhallowed power! The extinction of the Establishment would be a less step towards the conquest of the national mind, than, if it were possible (but we are speaking humanly and in our ignorance), to adopt that Bible, and correct it by the Vulgate. As it is, there is no blessing of the Church along with it, and who would dream that beauty was better than a blessing?[14]

Perhaps the argument that the aesthetic qualities of the KJB have been basic to the hold Protestantism has on England could only have been made by one who knew from experience the power of the KJB but now had to explain why his adopted Church was not dominant in England. In a sense, Faber gives the other side of the much-repeated idea that pleasure in the Scriptures will lead to religious enlightenment: seeing this enlightenment as heresy frees him from the obligation to regard the KJB's aesthetic qualities as subservient to its qualities as religious truth. The same freedom could only begin to be possible for English Protestants when a new version of the Bible, the RV, became available as a more authoritative representative of religious truth.

Faber's passage was pounced on: it was not only powerful; it was the enemy admitting much that the AVolaters believed. Among the pouncers was the then Dean of Westminster, later to be Archbishop of Dublin, a man of wide scholarly accomplishment who originated the scheme for the *OED*, Richard Chenevix Trench (1807–86). Discussing the relationship between the Latin and the Saxon

---

[14] 'An essay on the interest and characteristics of the Lives of the Saints', in F. W. Faber, *The Life of S. Francis of Assisi* (London, 1853), pp. 116–17.

elements in English, he refers to the KJB since he can find no 'happier example of the preservation of the golden mean in this matter'.[15] The translators, he declares, steered a middle course with 'happy wisdom' and 'instinctive tact'; instantly wisdom and tact become inspiration as he turns to Faber:

> There is a remarkable confession to this effect, to the wisdom, in fact, which guided them from above, to the providence that overruled their work, an honourable acknowledgement of the immense superiority in this respect of our English version over the Romish, made by one now unhappily familiar with the latter, as once he was with our own.   (P. 33)

And so he cites Faber, diplomatically omitting the sentence beginning, 'nay, it is worshipped with a positive idolatry', and the last three sentences.

Trench develops the argument into a new point: in his view, though the language of the KJB is 'the chief among the minor and secondary blessings which that version has conferred' (p. 32), it has an important religious significance. If the KJB had used the Latin-English of the Rheims-Douai Bible, he suggests, 'our loss would have been great and enduring, one which would have searched into the whole religious life of our people, and been felt in the very depths of the national mind' (p. 35). Then he reverses the point to argue that the golden mean of the KJB's language is at one with the position of the Anglican Church, standing midway between Rome and 'the Protestant communions' (p. 37), a position which 'may yet in the providence of God have a great part to play for the reconciling of a divided Christendom'. This is an extreme idea of the superiority of the KJB as English to all other versions, for, in Trench's view, a united Christendom would have only one Bible, the KJB (suitably revised, for he belonged to the party of the revisers).

In a later work Trench uses a phrase that was to become the essence of AVolatry, 'the first English classic'. The context is plainly literary. Looking to revision and arguing the importance of being able to read the Bible 'with pleasure', he declares that 'the sense of pleasure in it, I mean merely as the first English classic, would be greatly impaired by any alterations which seriously affect the homogeneousness of its style' (*On the Authorised Version*, p. 24). The ease with which the phrase rolls off his pen suggests it was not new, and indeed it had already been used several times in America (see below, p. 264). It seems unlikely that Trench knew this, but he may have known a less close antecedent in George Gilfillan's declaration that the Scriptures are 'the *classics* of the *heart*' (see below, p. 214). The phrase was picked up by the American scholar, AVolater and originator of statistics about the KJB's vocabulary, George P.

---

[15] *English, Past and Present* (1855; 4th edn, London, 1859), p. 32.

Marsh, in the twenty-eighth of his influential *Lectures on the English Language*: the KJB 'has now for more than two centuries maintained its position as an oracular expression of religious truth, and at the same time as the first classic of our literature – the highest exemplar of purity and beauty of language existing in our speech' (p. 441). Later Talbot W. Chambers, one of the members of the American Revision Committee, wrote an essay entitled 'The English Bible as a classic' (1879), but the phrase's most significant use came in the preface to the RV OT (1885): there the revisers, riding roughshod over history, describe the KJB as a translation 'which for more than two centuries and a half had held the position of an English classic' (pp. v–vi). This was enough to make the phrase a cliché and to prompt the celebrated author of *The Golden Bough*, Sir James George Frazer, to begin the preface to his *Passages of the Bible Chosen for their Literary Beauty and Interest* (1895) thus: 'that our English version of the Bible is one of the greatest classics in the language is admitted by all in theory, but few people appear to treat it as such in practice'. As so often in religious and quasi-religious matters, practice falls short of dogma. Viewed with a rigour few of us would survive, that falling-short is an index of hypocrisy. One of the fascinations of ideas of the Bible as literature is the spectacle of attempts to correct that hypocrisy.

For all his caution and learning, Trench leans towards AVolatry. It is, therefore, thoroughly understandable that he should have omitted from Faber's remarks the charge of AVolatry ('it is worshipped with a positive idolatry'), and yet Faber's charge is only a little removed from a comment Trench himself was to make, that the English of the KJB 'has been very often, and very justly, the subject of highest commendation; and if I do not reiterate in words of my own or of others these commendations, it is only because they have been uttered so often and so fully, that it has become a sort of commonplace to repeat them' (*On the Authorised Version*, p. 9). Trench implies the lack of thought needed to iterate such praise. Hallam had previously hinted that critical thought about the KJB was becoming difficult, and now Faber has made the accusation explicit. Such suggestions and accusations were as drops of water on a forest fire.

The chorus still sounds its song, but only one more of its notes needs recording at this point. Spenser had described Chaucer as a 'well of English undefiled' (*The Faerie Queene* 4: 2, 32), and the phrase was too good to ignore. Johnson, for instance, writes in the preface to his dictionary of 'the writers before the Restoration, whose works I regard as "the wells of English undefiled"' (fol. c1 r). Prompted by either Spenser or Johnson, the Unitarian advocate of revision, John R. Beard, attempting to diminish AVolatry and magnify Tyndale, argues that the KJB translators attenuated the force and injured the expressiveness and unity of the Bible by their use of Latinisms. So, 'whenever a proper revision of our English Bible is undertaken, reference for improvements should be made to the learned and cultured yet thoroughly English William Tyndale, from whose "well of English undefiled" may be drawn many words and phrases of the true old English flavour'.[16] The argument for Tyndale as 'the first and, it may be added, the best translator of the Bible into English' (p. 17) perhaps had some effect, but the mixture of sensible and prejudiced criticism of the KJB did not. Possibly spurred by Beard,[17] three of the makers of the RV picked up Spenser's phrase. Joseph Barber Lightfoot almost uses it in describing the KJB as 'not only the storehouse of the highest truth, but also the purest well of their native English' (p. 191), and the Americans Philip Schaff and Chambers both call the KJB '"the pure well of English undefiled"'.[18] Just as the phrase 'an English classic' sealed the KJB's literary status, this phrase sealed its linguistic status.

Todd's *A Vindication* was a collection of authorities proclaiming the quality of the KJB, and I have several times alluded to the practice of quoting passages from the pious chorus. Inevitably what might, in the present context, be called chorus-books began to appear.[19] The American Methodist George P. Eckman's Mendenhall Lectures at DePauw University, published as *The Literary Primacy of the Bible* (1915), have substantially this character: in them is to be found a very wide range of authorities assembled as the primary building blocks to prove the assertion in his title. It is useful to take one of his examples, for it shows the same kind of editorial manipulation that Trench applied to Faber. T. H. Huxley,

---

[16] *A Revised English Bible the Want of the Church and the Demand of the Age* (London and Manchester, 1857), pp. 53–4.

[17] I have already noted the apparently independent and contemporaneous use of the phrase 'as a classic' in England and America. Halsey probably had not read Beard (their books appeared a year and an ocean apart). He writes that the KJB, 'this grand old English Bible ... has come down to us with every quality and attribute that could make any book a "well of English undefiled"' (p. 36). When the time is right more than one person can invent or discover the same thing, as Darwin and Alfred Wallace found.

[18] Schaff, p. xx, Chambers, 'The English Bible as a classic', p. 40. Chambers opens the quotation at 'well'.

[19] Perhaps the best of these are Jane T. Stoddart's two volumes, *The Old Testament in Life and Literature* and *The New Testament in Life and Literature* (London: Hodder, 1913, 1914). Each is an anthology some 500 pages long of passages relating to individual books of the Bible. The first volume begins with a section called 'Lovers of the Bible'. Stoddart notes that the general outline of the work was suggested to her 'some years ago', the idea being to build up an entirely new collection 'with a narrative connecting as far as possible the passages of Scripture illustrated' (1: vii).

Among more recent efforts is *In Praise of the Bible: An Anthology of Thanksgiving*, comp. Geoffrey Murray (London: Muller, 1955). This is part of a series 'in praise of' such things as Westminster Abbey, ballet, Bernard Shaw, cats, golf, cricket and flowers.

redoubtable champion of Darwin and inventor of the word 'agnostic', was, to popular perception, as unlikely a champion of the Bible as Faber was of the KJB. Yet he did advocate the use of the Bible in schools, and Eckman, like several others such as Newton and Chambers, enlists part of what he wrote in the ranks of bibliolatry. Eckman twice quotes part of Huxley's passage, the second time introducing it with the remark that 'Huxley will not be regarded as a prejudiced witness for the Bible, yet he could say . . .' (p. 162). Huxley appears first as an AVolater, second as a bibliolater. So, in a paragraph that goes on to quote Macaulay and Green, we read: 'it is almost impossible to exaggerate the influence of the English Bible upon our language. Of the Authorised Version Huxley says: "it is written in the noblest and purest English, and abounds in exquisite beauties of a merely literary form"' (p. 39). Later a longer quotation is given as one of four testimonies that 'the Bible is the supreme guide for conduct' (p. 162).

In context, Huxley is more reserved. William Forster's Education Bill of 1870 attempted to establish State schools free of sectarian teaching. Huxley, who was standing for the Metropolitan School Board, gave the issue careful and often witty consideration in 'The School Boards: what they can do, and what they may do' (1870). The question of the Bible's place in primary education was central to the issue, and we will see later that it prompted Matthew Arnold to work of major significance for this history. Huxley defined his own position, beginning thus:

> I have always been strongly in favour of secular education, in the sense of education without theology; but I must confess I have been no less seriously perplexed to know by what practical measures the religious feeling, which is the essential basis of conduct, was to be kept up, in the present utterly chaotic state of opinion on these matters, without the use of the Bible. The pagan moralists lack life and colour, and even the noble Stoic, Marcus [Aurelius] Antonius, is too high and refined for an ordinary child. (P. 397)

Clearly he would rather not recommend the Bible if that were possible, for it is too closely associated with theology (Huxley it was who declared that he would rather be descended from a humble monkey than a man such as Bishop Wilberforce). But religious feeling, by which he means neither sectarian belief nor Christianity at large but 'love of some ethical ideal' (p. 396), and the responsive ability of an ordinary child are key points for Huxley. It is after these points that Eckman (and Newton and Chambers) begin to quote:

> Take the Bible as a whole; make the severest deductions which fair criticism can dictate for shortcomings and positive errors; eliminate, as a sensible lay-teacher

would do, if left to himself, all that it is not desirable for children to occupy themselves with; and there still remains in this old literature a vast residuum of moral beauty and grandeur. And then consider the great historical fact that, for three centuries, this book has been woven into the life of all that is best and noblest in English history;[20] that it has become the national epic of Britain, and is as familiar to noble and simple, from John-o'Groat's House to Land's End, as Dante and Tasso once were to the Italians; that it is written in the noblest and purest English, and abounds in exquisite beauties of mere literary form; and, finally, that it forbids the veriest hind who never left his village to be ignorant of the existence of other countries and other civilisations, and of a great past, stretching back to the furthest limits of the oldest nations in the world. By the study of what other book could children be so much humanised and made to feel that each figure in that vast historical procession fills, like themselves, but a momentary space in the interval between two eternities; and earns the blessings or the curses of all time, according to its effort to do good and hate evil, even as they also are earning their payment for their work?

Here the quotations end. Huxley was never averse to rhetorical or witty flourishes, but he takes care to remind his reader that his view is carefully qualified: 'on the whole, then, I am in favour of reading the Bible, with such grammatical, geographical, and historical explanations by a lay-teacher as may be needful, with rigid exclusion of any further theological teaching than that contained in the Bible itself' (pp. 397–8). Shortly afterwards he remarks in a Boswellian spirit (see above, pp. 53–4) that 'if Bible-reading is not accompanied by constraint and solemnity, as if it were a sacramental operation, I do not believe there is anything in which children take more pleasure'. He adds a personal testimony that might have been included in chorus-books but for its scorn of religious teaching:

> At least I know that some of the pleasantest recollections of my childhood are connected with the voluntary study of an ancient Bible which belonged to my grandmother... What comes vividly back on my mind are remembrances of my delight in the histories of Joseph and of David; and of my keen appreciation of the chivalrous kindness of Abraham in his dealing with Lot. Like a sudden flash there returns back upon me my utter scorn of the pettifogging meanness of Jacob, and my sympathetic grief over the heartbreaking lamentation of the cheated Esau, 'Hast thou not a blessing for me also, O my father?' And I see, as in a cloud, pictures of the grand phantasmagoria of the book of Revelation.

[20] Eckman omits from here to 'By the study'. Newton and Chambers begin from 'consider the great historical fact', and conclude with 'the oldest nations in the world'. Newton, perhaps deliberately (but it is not the only alteration), misquotes later in the passage, 'exquisite beauties of literary form'. Eckman simply got the phrase wrong when he quoted it earlier.

I enumerate, as they issue, the childish impressions which come crowding out of the pigeon-holes in my brain, in which they have lain almost undisturbed for forty years. I prize them as an evidence that a child of five or six years old, left to his own devices, may be deeply interested in the Bible, and draw sound moral sustenance from it. And I rejoice that I was left to deal with the Bible alone; for if I had had some theological 'explainer' at my side, he might have tried, as such do, to lessen my indignation against Jacob, and thereby have warped my moral sense for ever.

(Pp. 401–2)

We may take these last remarks as clear testimony just how widespread youthful pleasure in the Bible was at this time, even if it was not translated into adult reading (the reference to forty years and the misquotation of Gen. 27: 38 show this was Huxley's situation). And, taking this passage and the way it has been used as a whole, we can see that there was a real desire both to enlist as many voices as possible in the choir and to ensure that they sang in harmony.

An inspired translation

Tregelles had implied that the translators were inspired. In 1832 an advocate of translation, James Scholefield, had described the translators as 'those venerable men who were raised up by the providence of God and endowed by his spirit to achieve for England her greatest blessing in the authorised translation of the Scriptures'.[21] At about the same time a 'learned commentator' linked inspiration with Swift's idea of the translation as a standard of the language (I give the point as it was quoted in an American work):

The English tongue in [the translators'] day was not equal to such a work. But God enabled them to stand as upon Mount Sinai, and *crane up* their country's language to the dignity of the originals; so that after the lapse of two hundred years, the English Bible, with very few exceptions, is the standard of the purity and excellence of the English tongue.

(Spring, p. 64)

The idea of inspiration naturally attaches itself to the established version of Scripture in the minds of the faithful. Explicit statements that, in the words of an anonymous critic, the KJB was regarded as having 'a sort of inspiration belonging to it'[22] began to appear. The strongest comes in *The Translators Revived; A Biographical Memoir of the Authors of the English Version of the Holy Bible* (New York, 1853) by the prominent American evangelist Alexander Wilson

---

[21] *Hints for an Improved Version of the New Testament* (Cambridge, 1832), pp. vi–vii.
[22] *Will the Version by the Five Clergymen Help Dr. Biber?* (London, 1857), p. 5.

McClure (1808–65; he was associated with the Presbyterian, Congregational and Dutch Reformed Churches. The subject of the work is significant, for it is one that is rarely tackled,[23] and yet it is natural that a reverence for the KJB should lead to a curiosity about its creators. McClure notes that his curiosity about 'the personal qualifications for their work possessed by King James's translators' (p. iii) was aroused more than twenty years before the book was published. By offering the fruits of his curiosity 'to all who are interested to know in regard to the general sufficiency and reliableness of the Common Version' (p. iv), he makes clear the sequence from reverence for the version to reverence for the translators. He continues with a declaration of assurance that

> these biographical sketches of its authors . . . will afford historical demonstration of a fact which much astonished him when it began to dawn upon his convictions,– that the first half of the seventeenth century, when the translation was completed, was the *Golden Age* of biblical and oriental learning in England. Never before, nor since, have these studies been pursued by scholars whose vernacular tongue is the English with such zeal and industry and success. This remarkable fact is a token of God's providential care of his word as deserves most devout acknowledgement.

Such an assertion goes against the long-repeated argument that the KJB needed revising because of the great advances in scholarship, and in this McClure is a rare voice. Yet, from a different point of view, this is but another aspect of the kind of period-worship exhibited by Macaulay (above, p. 180).

From period-worship and AVolatry, the idea of 'God's providential care of his word' (implied earlier by Scholefield and Tregelles) is a short move that has been made with considerable dogmatism by some twentieth-century fundamentalists (see below, pp. 313ff.). The line between 'providential care' and plenary inspiration is a thin one. This is how McClure crosses it:

> Taking into account the many marked events in divine providence which led on to this version and aided its accomplishment and necessitated its diffusion . . . we are constrained to claim for the good men who made it the highest measure of divine aid short of plenary inspiration itself . . .
>
> But we hold that the translators enjoyed the highest degree of that special guidance which is ever granted to God's true servants in exigencies of deep concernment to his kingdom on earth. Such special succours and spiritual assistances are always vouchsafed where there is a like union of piety, of prayers and of pains to effect an object of such incalculable importance to the church of the living God. The necessity of a supernatural revelation to man of the divine will has often been argued in favour

[23] The other two works devoted to the subject are both recent, Gustavus S. Paine's *The Men Behind the King James Version* and Olga S. Opfell's *The King James Bible Translators* (Jefferson and London: McFarland, 1982).

of the extreme probability that such a revelation has been made. A like necessity, and one nearly as pressing, might be argued in favour of the belief that this most important of all the versions of God's revealed will must have been made under His peculiar guidance, and His provident eye. And the manner in which that version has met the wants of the most free and intelligent nations in the old world and the new may well confirm us in the persuasion that the same illuminating Spirit which indited the original Scriptures was imparted in rich grace to aid and guard the preparation of the English version. (Pp. 247–9)

As so often, the hedging with which an extreme point is made is ineffectual. McClure's readers would have been in no doubt that the KJB was as inspired as the originals, and that is the view taken by the later exponents of this line of argument.

McClure's interest in the KJB is religious rather than literary, but nothing in his argument excludes the literary point of view. He is openly arguing backwards from the present perception of achievement to an inspiration inherent in both translators and the period. Though going further than most would, especially in England, he expresses the tendency of both literary and religious AVolatry.

Yet this is not quite as far as the idea of the inspiration of the KJB can go. Some people thought it more inspired than the originals. Benjamin Jowett, Regius Professor of Greek at Oxford, seems to have been one of these. His response to the RV NT was to observe that the revisers 'seem to have forgotten that, in a certain sense, the Authorised Version is more inspired than the original'.[24] If he did indeed say this as reported (on the face of it, it seems unlikely from the controversial author of 'The interpretation of Scripture' in *Essays and Reviews*), then others must have held the view at the time, for it is treated as a truth that has been forgotten. At all events, it has been picked up at least once and accepted as reasonable. Eckman cites the remark and explains it with what we may call a cumulative theory of inspiration:

> this startling statement is not the rash thing that some would suppose. It is to be presumed that the translators in 1611, being very devout men, constantly invoked the blessing of God upon their work, and that infinite wisdom was pleased to grant their request, so that upon the inspiration originally given to the Bible writers there was added the inspiration which God gave to the revered translators of the ancient tongues into the English vernacular. (P. 197)

In short, the KJB is the most inspired Bible ever given to humanity.

---

[24] As reported in Evelyn Abbott and Lewis Campbell, *The Life and Letters of Benjamin Jowett*, 2 vols. (London, 1897), 1: 406.

Parallelism revisited

With the pious chorus singing so loud and long (more of the song will have to be listened to later), it may seem odd that there was little substantial literary discussion of the Bible in general and even less of the KJB through much of the nineteenth century. Absolute praise succeeds best uncluttered by particulars, but there were other factors, the most important of which will be the subject of the next chapter, the preoccupation with the question of revision. Nevertheless, there are a number of works which have little or no connection with the KJB that need to be considered before taking up the story of the revision. A mixed lot, they develop familiar issues such as parallelism, or develop new interests such as the Bible's literary influence.

Lowth's work on the poetry of the Old Testament remained magisterial for many years. Only one English work before mid-century sought to extend it and, gently, to criticise it, John Jebb's *Sacred Literature; Comprising a Review of the Principles of Composition Laid Down by the late Robert Lowth...: and an Application of the Principles so Reviewed to the Illustration of the New Testament; in a Series of Critical Observations on the Style and Structure of that Sacred Volume* (1820). Jebb's purpose is 'to prove by examples that the structure of clauses, sentences and periods in the New Testament is frequently regulated after the model afforded in the poetical parts of the Old' (p. 1). He anticipates the usual advantages from such a proof, including correction of the text, resolution of grammatical difficulties, general clarification and a sharpened awareness of some of the proprieties and beauties of conception and style. Behind the undertaking lies a belief in the unified inspiration of the whole Bible, for

> design pervades the whole matter of both Testaments; and unity is the soul of that design; but the matter and manner of Scripture are, beyond the matter and manner of any other body of writings, most intimately connected; so intimately connected that unity of matter demands and implies, in this divine book, a correspondent unity of manner. And, on this ground alone, we may reasonably conclude that a manner largely prevalent in the Old Testament cannot be relinquished in the New.
>
> (P. 77)

He has other reasons for this belief, notably that most of the writers of the NT were steeped in the OT and so would naturally have followed its manner of writing. Such thinking set him to searching the NT for passages 'which bear evident marks of intentional conformity to the Hebrew parallelism' (p. 79).

Before embarking on these passages he outlines Lowth's theories and proposes a modification to them that shows not only a desire to think as highly as possible of the Scriptures but also a critical conservatism that compares unfavourably with Lowth. He dislikes the idea of synonymous parallelism because it implies 'gross tautology' (p. 39), and so he proposes an alternative, 'progressive parallelism' (p. 38), observing that 'in the parallelisms commonly termed synonymous, the second or responsive clause invariably diversifies the preceding clause; and generally so as to rise above it, forming a sort of climax in the sense' (p. 35). Some of his examples are persuasive, but the argument as a whole is flawed by a confusion between grammar and effect: synonymity describes the grammatical relationship, progression its common effect. Repetition, even of the identical words, commonly produces an effect of intensification or progression. Consequently the result of his argument is not a correction of Lowth but a change of emphasis that points to a quality in most parallelisms, whether synonymous or not. The new emphasis is on a sense of the mind and imagination moving forward. His objection to 'synonymous' is that he believes it implies stasis, not movement.

Jebb has one other development of Lowth's ideas to offer, a development that became quite well known through John Kitto's admiring summary in his popular *Daily Bible Illustrations*.[25] A close attention to parallelism, he argues, will reveal in some places a stanza form for which he suggests the term 'introverted parallelism'; in this form, 'whatever be the number of lines, the first line shall be parallel with the last, the second with the penultimate, and so throughout' (p. 53). Here is one of his more complex examples, Isa. 27: 12–13, using the words of Lowth's translation:

> And it shall come to pass in that day;
>> Jehovah shall make a gathering of his fruit:
>>> From the flood of the river;
>>> To the stream of Egypt:
>> And ye shall be gleaned up, one by one;
> O ye sons of Israel.

> And it shall come to pass in that day;
>> The great trumpet shall be sounded:
>>> And those shall come, who were perishing in the land
>>>> of Assyria;
>>> And who were dispersed in the land of Egypt;
>> And they shall bow themselves down before Jehovah;
> In the holy mountain, in Jerusalem.

He argues that this shows not only the stanzaic form he has suggested but also

---

[25] 1850–4. 1901 edn, reprinted as *Kitto's Daily Bible Illustrations*, 2 vols. (Grand Rapids, Mich.: Kregel, 1981), II: 136–43.

an 'utmost precision of mutual correspondence, clause harmonising with clause, and line respectively with line' as the second stanza repeats in literal terms what is figured in the first (pp. 54–5). He has changed Lowth's presentation, adding indentations and dividing some lines into two, but the result is not the complete success that would justify his affectation of surprise at Lowth's failure to see this pattern. Some of the correspondences he elicits, as between the second and fifth lines of the first stanza ('Jehovah shall make a gathering of his fruit / And ye shall be gleaned up, one by one') and between the opening lines of the two stanzas, appear quite persuasive, but there is as much appearance of parallelism in 'And it shall come to pass in that day / The great trumpet shall be sounded' as there is in the parallelism Jebb substitutes, 'And it shall come to pass in that day / In the holy mountain, in Jerusalem.' Moreover, if we retreat a verse in Lowth, it becomes obvious that Jebb could not be proposing stanza form as a regular organising principle:

> When her boughs are withered, they shall be broken:
> Women shall come, and set them on a blaze.
> Surely it is a people void of understanding;
> Wherefore he, that made him, shall not have pity on him;
> And he, that formed him, shall show him no favour.

Here two obvious pairs of lines straddle a line that has no parallel, and we may be justified in wondering if a stanza scheme that is unsustained is any more a real experience for a reader than the infinite variety of Gomarus' scansion. There are several difficulties, then, with Jebb's scheme, but also some profit.

The latter part of the book is devoted to showing how parallelism, as Jebb understands it, is to be found in the NT. First he argues that the NT writers preserve the parallel form as well as the meaning of their quotations from OT poetry ('no trifling evidence that they were skilled in Hebrew poetry' (p. 97)), and then without difficulty demonstrates that original parallelisms, such as 'my soul doth magnify the Lord; / And my spirit hath rejoiced in God my saviour' (Luke 1: 46–7; p. 143), are to be found in the NT. He is at his most interesting with longer passages, as with the following 'tremendous apostrophe to the unbelieving Jews [which] is in the grandest style of Hebrew poetry' (p. 258; as with all his NT passages, he gives the Greek first):

> Come now, ye rich men, weep, howl,
> For the stunning afflictions which are coming upon you;
> Your riches are putrefied;
> And your robes are moth-eaten:
> Your gold and silver are cankered with rust;

And their rust shall be a witness against you;
And shall eat your flesh as fire:
Ye have laid up treasures for the last days!

Behold! the hire of the labourers who have reaped your
                                                    fields
Fraudfully kept back by you, crieth:
And the outcries of those who have gathered in your
                                                    harvest,
Have entered into the ears of the Lord of Hosts:
Ye have lived delicately upon the earth; ye have been
                                                    luxurious;
Ye have pampered your hearts, as for a day of slaughter:
Ye have condemned, ye have slain the Just One;
He is not arrayed against you!   (Jas. 5: 1–6)

What attracts Jebb's particular attention is the passage's use of climax, first in the ascending scale of 'weep, howl ... stunning afflictions', then in the poetic amplification of the three kinds of wealth, '1. stores of corn, wine, oil, etc., liable to putrefaction; 2. wardrobes of rich garments ... proverbially the prey of the moth; ... and 3. treasures of gold and silver, liable to rust or, at least, to change of colour' (pp. 259–60). Only one parallelism is specifically mentioned, 'Your riches are putrefied; / And your robes are moth-eaten', but the attention to climax in this example (or descending scales in other examples) is, in his view, at one with his sense of progressive parallelism. Others might be less inclined to see the passage in terms of parallelism. Jebb's comments are reasonable, but there is little that makes them different in kind (a difference of quality might be distinguished) from Augustine's analysis of Rom. 5: 3–5 (see volume 1, p. 46): they take us back to the world of classical criticism. As if to underline the point, Jebb concludes his discussion with similar passages from Menander and Horace, declaring that 'St James, in his poetry, is at least equal to the finest of the classics', and asking, 'am I deceived, or is not this worthy of Aeschylus or Pindar?' (pp. 260–1). One might have suspected such a tendency from his unhappiness with tautology: for all that he recommends an experimental acquaintance with the texts, Jebb is more bound by preconceptions than Lowth was.

One might also have suspected this tendency from the style of the passage which shows a greater desire for neo-classical English than Lowth exhibited – 'ye have lived delicately upon the earth; ye have been luxurious' rather than 'ye have lived in pleasure on the earth, and been wanton'. Jebb is, of course, writing as a critic of the originals, and his relationship with the KJB is ambiguous. His quotations usually vary from it (or, sometimes in the Psalms, from the PB), and it is not always possible to apply his observations to the KJB. He mentions the KJB rarely: sometimes it is no more than a faint reflection of the originals (for example, p. 63), sometimes it is fit to demonstrate the 'cadence of well-modulated prose' (p. 21), and once he quotes approvingly two sentences from the pious chorus.[26]

There are three more general ways, each connected with the other, in which Jebb's work is significant. He is the first to use 'literature', in its modern sense, for the Bible in the title of a work.[27] This striking variation from Lowth's 'Sacred Poetry' was probably prompted by the focus on the prose of the NT as well as the need for a different but related title, but it shows almost as conclusively as the changing titles of the early translations of Longinus a change in values. Just as 'sublime' replaced 'eloquence' as the key word for literary quality, so 'literature' replaces 'poetry' as the key word for itself. Criticism is beginning to recognise that the highest achievements of writing are not necessarily to be found in poetry. Secondly, the distinction between poetry and prose becomes redundant in Jebb's discussion: now the essential qualities of OT poetry are matched by the prose of the NT, which Jebb does not hesitate on occasions to call poetry. Matching the substitution of 'literature' for 'poetry' is the application of 'poetry' to prose. The prose is literature if you are looking forward, poetry if you are looking back; either way, the old position of poetry and its association with verse is broken down. Lastly, matching the extension of 'poetry' to the point where 'literature' is the better word, Jebb has taken a large step towards seeing literary excellence in the whole Bible. In this as much as in his ideas of parallelism he is a successor to Lowth. What Lowth did for the Prophets in relation to the Psalms and other songs of the OT, Jebb does for the NT in relation to the OT. Yet *Sacred Literature* is not the major work *Sacred Poetry* was: it shows movements happening, but is not their cause.

---

[26] Thomas Fanshawe Middleton, *The Doctrine of the Greek Article* (London, 1808), p. 328; Jebb, p. 350.

[27] In the following year James Townley published his huge *Illustrations of Biblical Literature*, 2 vols. (London, 1821), and later, as a second edition of his 1813 *Biblical Anecdotes, An Introduction to the Literary History of the Bible* (London, 1828). His subject throughout is what we would call the external history of the Bible, 'exhibiting the history and fate of the Sacred Writings from the earliest period to the present century, including biographical notices of translators and other eminent biblical scholars', and even 'curious ecclesiastical events connected with the history of the Sacred Volume' (*An Introduction*, p. vi). Nowhere is he concerned with literary qualities in the Bible; rather, he uses 'literary' because he is writing about a book. In this sense even a telephone directory has a literary history.

Herder's theological aesthetic

Standing apart from the purely English progression of ideas is a work that might have claimed attention in either or the last two chapters except that it made almost no impression on the English-speaking world until it was translated in 1833. This was *The Spirit of Hebrew Poetry* by the German romantic critic and thinker Johann Gottfried von Herder (1744–1803). Originally published in 1782 and 1783, and of major influence in Germany, it became well known in America through James Marsh's translation.[28] It had been commended to American readers in an 1829 edition of Lowth in terms which suggest much of Herder's distinctiveness:

> If you would ascertain the great principles on which you must judge of the Hebrew poetry and become acquainted with its characteristic features, study Lowth; if you desire to know more of the precise idea which the Hebrew poets intend to express and to trace with philological accuracy the sources of their language and imagery, follow the criticisms of Michaelis; but if you would lay aside the philosopher and critic and give yourself up to intellectual enjoyment, if you would have the same sensations and the same thoughts, while chanting the Hebrew poetry, which the ancient Hebrews themselves had, catch the tuneful notes of Herder.[29]

The intellectual pleasure of thinking and feeling like a Hebrew is central: Herder develops Lowth's historicism rather than his technical insights. His emphasis is on appreciating the Hebrew poetry as the product of particular men at particular times, often, but not always, writing under divine inspiration. This makes his work a vigorous antidote to attempts to judge the poetry by exterior standards, whether classical or contemporary, and also to the bibliolatrous approach.

The book's first volume is cast in the form of dialogues between the right-thinking Euthyphron and the sharp-thinking Alciphron, who voices many of the prejudices against Hebrew poetry and is characterised as speaking 'very much such sentiments as are uttered by the public with its hundred heads' (1: 21). Gradually he is converted by Euthyphron's enthusiasm. They quickly define Herder's general position. Euthyphron remarks that 'it was long before I acquired a taste for [Hebrew's] beauties, and only by degrees that I came to

---

[28] An earlier translation of selections from volume 1, *Oriental Dialogues* (London, 1801), seems to have gone unnoticed.

[29] Calvin E. Stowe, in Robert Lowth, *Lectures on the Sacred Poetry of the Hebrews*, trans. C. Gregory, new edition, with notes by Calvin E. Stowe (Andover, Mass., 1829), p. xii; as given in Robert T. Clark, Jr, *Herder: His Life and Thought* (Berkeley and Los Angeles: University of California Press, 1955), p. 294.

consider it, as I do now, a sacred language, the source of our most precious knowledge and of that early cultivation which, extending over but a small portion of the earth, came to us gratuitously and unsought'. Alciphron at once suspects bibliolatry, suggesting that Euthyphron is 'driving at an apotheosis', but Euthyphron rebuts the implication: 'at no such thing: we will consider it as a human language, and its contents as merely human' (1: 26–7).

Now, this sounds like the approach if not the language of any number of recent literary critics of the Bible. But much of Herder's interest lies in the way he builds up an aesthetic that is different from what one finds in recent critics. A central issue in literary discussion of the Bible is the relationship between religion and literature. Herder's work is one of the most thorough discussions of the connections, even the identity, between the two. Blurring the lines between theology, literature and history, Herder argues that he who would read the Bible as literature must give as much credence to God as he would to a successful character in literature; he must willingly suspend his disbelief if much of what he reads is not to fail as literature (we have seen what sort of outcome failure to suspend disbelief can produce in, say, Marlowe and Paine). At the least he must believe that the writers believed, must sympathise with that belief, and so must adopt a quasi-religious viewpoint.

Herder's approach to Hebrew poetry is founded on the idea that there is an immanent will that unites all living things in a moral relationship, because they are all manifestations of the same will. So he sees man as part of nature, and there is much in his attitude to appeal to romantic – or transcendental – temperaments nurtured by Wordsworth and Coleridge. To Herder 'man is a moral being, and should learn to view everything under its moral aspect' (1: 201). That this does involve a sense of the 'one life' (to pick up a phrase associated with Coleridge) or immanent will is clearest when he writes that 'relations of feeling and moral duties cease where I conceive nothing in a living being analogous to my own being' (II: 12). Moreover, 'in nature all things are connected, and for the view of man are connected by their relation to what is human' (1: 97). Poetry develops this sense of analogous life, and Herder emphasises that in his view the ethical and the aesthetic are indivisible, that, in Keats's phrase, 'beauty is truth, truth beauty'. Euthyphron couples the two words in his observation that 'we shall find in Job more sublime pictures of the formation of the earth; more true or beautiful are scarcely possible'. Alciphron, here helping express right views, adds, 'and in truth whatever is most consonant to nature is most perfect in beauty. What are all the mythologies to me, if they teach me nothing? ... Poetry, in order to affect the heart and the understanding, must combine beauty with truth, and animate both with sympathetic feeling' (1: 73).

Fundamental to this moral sense of relationship between man and nature, and between beauty and truth, is a sense of God the creator, giver of life to all things. Poetry reveals the God-given oneness of life, and it reflects it by being the word of God through man. Although one may believe in the oneness of life without believing it is God-given, Herder is quite clear about the relationship: the unity in Hebrew poetry is inseparable from monotheism:

> From the idea of one creator the world came to be considered as a united whole ($\chi\acute{o}\sigma\mu\sigma\varsigma$); the mind of man was directed to its combined glories, and learned wisdom, order and beauty. The contributions of philosophy and poetry to the same end have also produced the most beneficial effects, especially the poetry, of which we are treating. It was the most ancient obstacle to the progress of idolatry of which we have any knowledge, and it poured the first bright beam of unity and order into the chaos of the creation. (1: 57)

The Hebrew poetry has this effect principally through 'the parallelism of the heavens and the earth' (1: 58), a parallelism which contrasts 'the boundlessness of the heavens with the nothingness of the earth, their elevation with our abasement'. Moreover, unlike the idols of other religions, 'the God of Israel was without a sensuous representation' (II: 99), so the Hebrew poetry praises God 'in his deeds, in the perfections of his works' (II: 43).

Herder expresses the essence of his religious view of poetry and the world in this way:

> Can there be any more beautiful poetry than God himself has exhibited to us in the works of creation? poetry, which He spreads fresh and glowing before us with every revolution of days and of seasons? Can the language of poetry accomplish anything more affecting than with brevity and simplicity to unfold to us in its measure what we are and what we enjoy? We live and have our being in this vast temple of God; our feelings and thoughts, our sufferings and our joys are all from this as their source. A species of poetry that furnishes me with eyes to perceive and contemplate the works of creation and myself, to consider them in their order and relation, and to discover through all the traces of infinite love, wisdom and power, to shape the whole with the eye of fancy and in words suited to their purpose – such a poetry is holy and heavenly. (1: 95)

The beauty of the natural world is poetry, and the words of poetry reveal this beauty. Moreover, the order, coherence, meaning and beauty of a work of art expresses the similar order, coherence, meaning and beauty of the world. For him, the highest poetry reveals the moral relationship between what man is and the world he lives in, 'what we are and what we enjoy'. Poetry emphasises life in the surrounding world: 'it makes the objects of nature to become things of life, and exhibits them in a state of living action' (I: 93). So 'it awakens a love, an interest and a sympathy for all that lives' (I: 96), and it does this through 'three leading qualities, ... animation in the objects for awakening the senses, interpretation of nature for the heart, a plan in the poem, as there is in creation, for the understanding' (I: 97).

Such an intermingling of belief and aesthetic leads Herder to a more subtle distinction between the divine and the human in poetry than he had suggested in promising to treat the poetry as a merely human production:

> It was God who created the fountain of feeling in man, who placed the universe with all its numberless currents setting in upon him and mingled them with the feelings of his own breast. He gave him also language and the powers of poetical invention, and thus far is the origin of poetry divine. It is human in respect to the measure and peculiarity of this feeling, and of the expression which is given to it; for only human organs feel and utter the emotions and conceptions of the poet. Poetry is a divine language, yet not in the sense that we understand by it what the Divine Being in himself feels and utters: whatever was given to the most godlike men, even through a higher influence, to feel and experience in themselves, was still human.   (II: 6)

In keeping with this distinction, Euthyphron says, 'do you not believe that mere earthborn poetry, however refined, must be necessarily poor and grovelling? All elevating and sublime poetry is by an influence from above' (I: 60). Further, since poetry is 'a divine language', revealing God's creation and the interconnectedness of all life, there is a direct connection between the poet and God: in 'ordering all from the impulse of his own inward feeling, and with reference to himself, [the poet] becomes an imitator of the Divinity, a second Creator, a true ποιητής, a creative poet' (II: 7). The poet is of course *re*-creating and revealing what God has created. This reverence for the spirit within the man, for what is usually subjective and intuitive, leads him to argue that 'every emotion contains its own law ... also its characteristic aim in itself ... Every emotion has its perfect sphere in which its action may be contemplated as a whole' (II: 25, 241). There is a major link with one of Lowth's more innovative ideas here. Lowth had argued that poetry was the language of the passions, bursting out unstudied (above, p. 64), and now Herder also, locating the poetic impulse in the emotions, is moving towards an idea of free verse. Such a way of thinking fits particularly well with the informality of Hebrew poetry.

Herder's theological aesthetic, viewed in these general terms, is the most thorough and rational development of the basic position noted from Dennis onwards, that there is a necessary connection between poetry and religion. His specific sense of Hebrew poetry is based on sympathy with its historical circumstances, observations on the peculiar qualities of the Hebrew language, and close reading. He begins his discussion with the language. The verb is fundamental and gives it a special vitality: 'the noun always exhibits objects only as lifeless things, the verb gives them action, and this awakens feeling, for it is itself as it were animated with a living spirit' (I: 29). Hebrew therefore reflects the common life, for 'every thing in it proclaims "I live and move and act"' (I: 30). This is 'the spirit of the Hebrew language' (cf. I: 35).

Two further characteristics help to make Hebrew different from modern languages: first, 'in the Hebrew a single word, easily uttered and agreeable in sound, expresses the whole sentiment. In ours ten are often necessary; and though they express it with more logical distinctness, it is with less ease and eloquence' (II: 25); second, it is full of puns or 'verbal conceits'. This renders much of Hebrew poetry untranslatable (II: 210), and, without denying Lowth's sense of the translatability of the parallelistic form, is an important corrective to the idea of the translatableness of Hebrew poetry. It emphasises that there are qualities in the originals that cannot be represented in, for instance, the KJB. Jebb, overplaying Lowth, argued that Hebrew is 'a poetry not of sounds or of words but of things', and that as such it 'is universal poetry, the poetry of all languages and of all peoples' (Jebb, p. 20). Herder, however, maintains the connection between poetry and language, in effect reminding us that even the best of versions cannot represent all the qualities of the original.

When he deals with the form of the poetry, Herder defends 'the celebrated parallelisms' (the phrase is used sarcastically by Alciphron) as being 'the most simple proportion and symmetry' (I: 39) and having a natural expressive power. Poetry is the language of the feelings, and Herder argues in this way:

> So soon as the heart gives way to its emotions, wave follows upon wave, and that is parallelism. The heart is never exhausted, it has forever something new to say. So soon as the first wave has passed away, or broken itself upon the rocks, the second swells again and returns as before. This pulsation of nature, this breathing of emotion, appears in all the language of passion, and would you not have that in poetry which is most peculiarly the offspring of emotion? (I: 41)

This is precisely the kind of insight that the unpoetic formalist Jebb missed. Alciphron, who starts from something like Jebb's position, objects that, as far as understanding is concerned, 'when one is under the necessity of saying every thing twice he shows that he had but half or imperfectly expressed it the first time' (1: 39). Pursuing the physiological metaphor, Euthyphron counters that this 'systole and diastole of the heart and breath – the parallelism' (11: 23) – 'changes the figure and exhibits the thought in another light. It varies the precept and explains it or impresses it upon the heart' (1: 41). Thus Herder develops Lowth's relatively technical account of parallelism by showing how it may be appreciated.

Although Herder's approach insists upon a historical understanding of the poetry, he is not concerned with historical truth, but with human truth; here, if not in his more general theorising, he does keep to the human position. It does not matter whether Job is founded on historical fact because 'its powerful and profound poetry makes it a history such as we have few examples of. It becomes, by the depth and truth of its exhibitions, a history of afflicted and suffering innocence all over the world' (1: 114). This willingness to accept the truth of fiction is evident throughout. His treatment of the patriarchs is characteristic: theirs

> is in a word the poetry of herdsmen, a poetry breathing the spirit of their covenant relation, that is, of the family bond by which they were united, and the relation of friendship in which the patriarch of the race stood to God; in a word it is the poetry of Canaan as the land of promise. Read it in this spirit and it will no longer be unmeaning.
>   (1: 236–7)

The Spirit of Hebrew Poetry is unfinished. Herder intended to go on to write about the Prophets, the apocryphal writings and Revelation, but the loss is probably not a great one, since he is comparatively poor as a practical critic.[30] The quality of his work lies in the freshness and freeness of spirit in which it is written, a spirit capable of bringing readers to the Hebrew poetry with sympathetic critical intelligence unhampered by doctrine. Further, however little *The Spirit of Hebrew Poetry* may have been read in the United Kingdom, it remains an important model of a theological aesthetic.

The KJB as a literary influence

In the 1830s there was sufficient interest in the question of the Bible as a literary influence for discussion to begin to appear on both sides of the Atlantic. Earlier Hazlitt had broached the subject in England, and in a sense it

---

[30] He believed that the critic should as far as possible allow the poetry to speak for itself, for 'what is beautiful in it [the youthful reader] will love without noisy commendation' (11: 229).

derives from Addison's comment that 'our language has received innumerable elegancies and improvements from that infusion of Hebraisms which are derived to it out of the poetical passages in Holy Writ' (above, p. 31). By 1819 this comment was beginning to turn into an explicitly literary idea, as a passing remark by John William Whittaker shows: 'the great number of Hebraisms in the English Bible have had a powerful effect upon our language, more particularly observable in our national poetry' (pp. 113–14).

A more general background to American interest in the subject may be glimpsed in an 1839 work by the prominent Pastor of the Brick Presbyterian Church, New York, Gardiner Spring (1785–1873), *The Obligations of the World to the Bible*. The title itself indicates an interest in the Bible as the foundation of all things, an interest that must have been natural in a country so highly conscious of its biblical foundations. Included are lectures on the Bible's influence on 'oral and written language – upon history and literature – upon laws and government' (p. 16), and on 'social institutions', 'slavery', 'the extent and certainty of moral science' and 'moral happiness' (table of contents). Spring's design, 'my young friends, is to call your attention to the Bible, and to exalt and honour, in your estimation and my own, this Great Book' (p. 14). So the book is eulogistic in character; moreover, it has a sense not only of learning but of conversation behind it, as in this: 'it was the remark of a sensible and thinking layman, many years ago made to the writer, that "it sometimes seemed to him that the Bible is as much greater than all other books as its author is greater than all other authors"' (p. 15).

Among all these large questions of influence, the proposition that 'English literature is no common debtor to the Bible' (pp. 61–2) perhaps gets no more attention than it deserves, two pages. In them Spring includes a passage from 'an anonymous writer' supporting the point, and notes that

> At the suggestion of a valued friend, I have turned my thoughts to the parallel between Macbeth and Ahab – between Lady Macbeth and Jezebel – between the announcement to Macduff of the murder of his family, and that to David of the death of Absalom by Joab – to the parallel between the opening of the Lamentations of Jeremiah and Byron's apostrophe to Rome as the Niobe of nations – to the parallel between his ode to Napoleon and Isaiah's ode on the fall of Sennacherib – and also to the resemblance between Southey's chariot of Carmala in *The Curse of Kehama* and Ezekiel's vision of the wheels; and have been forcibly impressed with the obligations of this class of writers to the sacred Scriptures. (P. 63)

This bespeaks both the desire to discover the Bible as a prime source of English literary excellence, and a literary sense of the Bible, if not specifically of the KJB.[31] It is a fair hint for others to work on. More important, though, is the sense it gives of interest in the Bible as a literary influence being in the air by the 1830s.

The first sustained discussion of the subject seems also to come out of a background of interest, for this is the likeliest cause of the fellows of Trinity College, Cambridge, setting it, as I presume they did, as a subject for their annual prize. It is the only work of William Thomas Petty (later FitzMaurice), Earl of Kerry, *An Essay upon the Influence of the Translation of the Bible upon English Literature, which Obtained the Annual Prize at Trinity College* (1830). Considering the Bible 'only as a literary work' (p. 2n), Petty sets up camp immediately with the AVolaters by exclaiming, 'what beauties are not united in its pages! beauties almost incompatible with one another' (p. 2). He intends

> to examine the influence which the translation of this truly great work into our language has produced upon English literature; a subject than which none could have been selected of more importance, or of greater difficulty; which embraces the consideration of the effects which the most interesting work ever committed to the hands of mankind has produced upon that language.   (Pp. 2–3)

In spite of this, he has little to say about influence on language, and nowhere does his discussion become specific enough for it to matter what version he is writing about: he is a bibliolater masquerading as an AVolater.

One of his major positions is 'that from the very nature of these compositions, which are adorned with all the flowery style and dazzling imagery of the East, it was to be expected (and it will be found upon examination to be true) that they should exercise a far greater influence upon poetry than upon prose' (p. 19). The extent of the logic is to associate imagery with poetry, but all logic disappears when he later declares, in the kind of extending spirit we have seen in Jebb, that 'the very nature of the Book of Holy Writ' is poetical, and this prevents it from being an influence on prose; he immediately adds a qualification that seems all-embracing, 'except as far as it has contributed to the general purity of the language, by having served as a standard of style' (p. 74). These assertions combine the position that runs back through Lowth to Swift with the even older tendency to think of poetry as the highest literature and the present tendency to think of the whole Bible as great literature.

---

[31] Spring only attends to 'our common *English Bible*' (p. 63; his italics) as a standard for the language (see above, p. 189). In this connection he does quote Addison on the influence of Hebraisms on English.

Not without repetition, he spells out his view of the KJB's influence:

We may . . . justly infer that the vulgar translation has probably exercised a beneficial influence upon our literature: first, as being a standard of the purity of our language; secondly, as having naturalised in our country foreign idioms and words, and having thereby enriched our tongue; thirdly, as having thrown open the gate of the Holy Scriptures to all persons, and having thereby conferred on every one the power of profiting by the beauties which they contain. (P. 22)

The opening statement is of historical importance as being the first clear, *published* expression of this idea. Only in the explicitness of its generalisation is it new. What follows already sounds familiar, and when he moves to detail the result is disappointing. His method is 'to quote from the most distinguished authors of this age a few of those passages which appear to have been most indebted to the English translation of the Holy Bible' (pp. 52–3). Milton is particularly used, but the proof of influence rests on no more than the discovery of sources for allusions, phrases and figures. The KJB is treated as a source-book rather than as an influence, and there is no demonstration of how it has operated as 'a standard of the purity of our language'.

In spite of such failings, Petty's conclusion picks up his main points in a strong and original claim for the KJB's literary importance: it is

that the translation of the Bible into our language is a most remarkable event in the history of English literature: that the influence it has exerted upon our writers has been more fully developed in our poetical than our prose authors; but that it has, in general, been great and beneficial, whether the translation be considered as a book of reference, or a standard of style. (P. 81)

That he had only shown the Bible functioning as 'a book of reference' matters little. This claim for the publication of the KJB as a major event in English literary history is important, and was only slowly picked up.

As a historical first – but on no other grounds – Petty's work does not deserve the total oblivion into which it fell. The one other British work on literary aspects of the Bible to appear before 1850, John Murray McCulloch's *Literary Characteristics of the Holy Scriptures* (1845), was a little more successful. It too touches on the question of influence. The first of the supplementary notes in the second edition, 'Obligations of English poetry to the Scriptures', contains this:

some intimate connexion there must be between the Bible and English poetry – otherwise the fact of their contemporaneous prosperity and contemporaneous decline would not meet us so frequently in the course of our literary annals. The Bible is doubtless far from being the only influence to which English poetry owes its peculiar mould; but it may be confidently affirmed to be one of the chief influences. At all events the two have hitherto invariably flourished and faded together. Our English eolian-harp, it would seem, yields its peculiar music freely and abundantly only when the wind that sweeps over its strings is the breath of the Lord.

(Pp. 129–30)

McCulloch here develops Petty's sense of the Bible's importance to English literature by adding to it a vague suggestion that divine inspiration then operated at large. Though this is rather like the idea of the importance of their time as a major factor in Shakespeare's and the KJB's greatness, the claim that poetry and the Bible have flourished and faded together requires some ingenuity to make sense of. Does he simply mean that the best English poetry comes from the most pious times? Or is he casting aspersions on the eighteenth century? He does not say, perhaps because he could not: such statements are cosmic dust.

McCulloch's work as a whole reflects the progress of the idea of the KJB as literature and as a literary force, but contributes little in the way of new understanding. It is an attempt 'simply to present such a sample of the beauty and fruitfulness of "the good land" as may induce the student to "go up" and explore it for himself' (p. 5), and has two main parts. The first deals with characteristics of subject-matter: originality, which, illogically for one who claims the Bible as the first and best work of literature, he says 'displays itself either in throwing out new thoughts, or in re-casting old thoughts into new and striking forms' (p. 14 – here he is applying accepted criteria of literary quality thoughtlessly); depth of thought, sublimity, spirituality, 'a singular reserve on all subjects of mere curiosity', the 'miscellaneous and unsystematic manner in which [the Scriptures] convey religious instruction', and 'harmony with itself'. The second section deals with characteristics of style, and McCulloch, in keeping with Tyndale and Addison, comments that 'the disadvantage of estimating an author's style from a translation [he means the KJB], is happily much less in the case of the Bible than of any other book' because of its '*translatableness* . . . with little loss of its original colour and energy' (p. 56). This allows that the originals are best while suggesting that the KJB loses nothing significant of their quality.

McCulloch's work is suggestive of his time rather than either a contribution to scholarship or a moulder of opinion. Perhaps its single most interesting declaration is an echo of Petty's determination to consider the Bible 'only as a literary work': 'irrespective of its peculiar claims and character as the record of divine truth, the Bible stands, *as a mere book*, apart and aloft from all others' (p. 12). That he should italicise 'as a mere book' shows just how acceptable it was becoming to think of the Bible as literature, but the complete statement is blatantly a literary judgement arrived at for religious reasons. The Bible is 'apart and aloft' because it is God's book, 'the earliest and the brightest star in the literary heavens' (p. 12). This was now the dominant view of the Bible, and its natural corollary was the claim that the KJB is 'the first English classic'.

George Gilfillan's *The Bards of the Bible* touched on the subject of the Bible's literary influence in 1851 but will need separate discussion; the last work signalling the arrival of interest in the subject takes us back to America and is redolent of Gardiner Spring, 'The influence of the Bible on literature' (1853) by the Reverend J. A. Seiss of Baltimore. Largely an exercise in panegyric, it begins with seven pages of bibliolatry acclaiming the Bible as 'the oldest of all books' (p. 1), 'the most *original* of books' (p. 3), 'the Daguerreotype of the universe', 'the *sublimest and most beautiful* of books' (p. 5), and as 'a literary *aereolite*, with characteristics kindred to nothing earthly; and whose own superior attributes demonstrate that it has come down from some high and holy place' (p. 3). Then Seiss makes a turn which shows just how closely interest in the Bible's literary influence is linked with bibliolatry: 'since the Bible is the most ancient, original and sublime of books . . . it must needs have made its deep broad marks upon the entire world of letters' (p. 8). This opens up a vast range – anything written about the Bible, all theology and most works of science, archaeological, geological or natural, all are influenced by the Bible – so vast a range that at last he stands back and asks, 'what is modern learning and the march of intellect and the reading million but one great monument of the quickening power of sacred truth upon the human mind?' (p. 15). This is literary influence so broadly conceived as to be meaningless: everything is biblical.

In between these last two remarks, Seiss surveys a wide range of literature and, given the confines of an article, the result is better than such a setting would lead us to expect. Much of what he writes does no more than show what Spring had suggested, that a large range of poets from Spenser to Byron used the Bible as a source, but some of it indicates a stricter idea of influence. So two sentences lauding Milton are followed with this:

> But the great thoughts of this illustrious epic and the great mass of its enrapturing imagery have been derived from the Bible. So much of the Bible spirit fills his pages that he seems like some great Hebrew bard belated in his birth. And had there been no Prophets in Israel, the world should have had no *Samson Agonistes*, no *Paradise Lost*, no *Paradise Regained*, no towering Milton. (P. 11)

This suggests more than the Bible acting as a source. With Shakespeare he goes a little further:

look at the unbelieving Shakespeare. Hear that admired and much quoted passage in his *Tempest*:

> The cloud-capp'd towers, the gorgeous palaces,
> The solemn temples, the great globe itself,
> Yea, all which it inherit, shall dissolve
> And, like this insubstantial pageant faded,
> Leave not a wrack behind. We are such stuff
> As dreams are made on, and our little life
> Is rounded with a sleep.

This certainly is but another edition of the Scripture sentiments, 'the heavens shall pass away; the elements shall melt; the earth also, and all the works that are therein shall be burned up; these things shall be dissolved' [2 Pet. 3: 10–11, adapted]. 'For what is your life? It is even a vapour that appeareth for a little time, and then vanisheth away' [Jas. 4: 14].   (Pp. 13–14)

The sentiments and a little of the imagery are close enough for the connections to be enlightening, but not close enough to account for the quality of Shakespeare's passage or to demonstrate antecedent excellence in the Bible; nevertheless, Seiss's fundamental point, that there are parallels, holds good, and the Bible may have helped shape the passage. He goes on to show more substantial parallels in Portia's speech on 'the quality of mercy'; within the scope of a short paper this is impressive. Perhaps more impressive still is one part of his remarks on Byron, that

the language used by the startled Abbot in *Manfred* [III: iv] is very moving:

> I see a dark and awful figure rise,
> Like an infernal god from out the earth,
> His face wrapt in a mantle, and his form
> Robed as with angry clouds.

But it is only a poetic account of Samuel and the witch of Endor, along with Job's vision of the night.[32]   (P. 15)

Seiss perhaps knew of Byron's admiration for the scene with the witch of Endor (above, p. 167), and he goes on to mention *Hebrew Melodies*, which contains the paraphrase of the Job passage (above, pp. 167–8), but this in no way detracts from the sharpness of the observation: whether Byron was imitating or was influenced by these, Seiss has made real connections that give substance to his

---

[32] There may be two printer's errors here, 'dark' for 'dusk' and 'Samuel' for 'Saul'.

largely general remarks and go beyond mere identification of use with influence.

Minor and little known as it must have been, Seiss's article takes us beyond Petty and McCulloch: *they* signal the arrival of an awareness; *it* shows ways the awareness might be explored.[33] Exploration was not long in coming. The first of many books on individual authors and the Bible was T. R. Eaton's *Shakespeare and the Bible* (London, 1858). Eaton declares his purpose to be 'to show, by new evidence, the vastness of Shakespeare's Bible lore' (p. 2), but the real effect of the book is to bring bardolatry and religion together. He sketches the Bible's dramatic mode of teaching, remarks that this 'must have had an irresistible charm to one of Shakespeare's peculiar bent' (p. 3), and finds it 'pleasant to fancy the delight with which young Shakespeare must have feasted upon these and like divine lessons, unconscious the while that he was strengthening his pinions for loftier flights than had ever been attained by uninspired man' (p. 4). His drift is clear, that Shakespeare's quality comes from the Bible even before it comes from God's creation or inspiration: 'in storing his mind, Shakespeare went first to the word and then to the works of God. In shaping the truths derived from these sources, he obeyed the instinct implanted by Him who had formed him *Shakespeare*' (p. 4). With the addition of a touch of AVolatry, he pictures Shakespeare and the KJB as having the same fundamental qualities:

> Shakespeare perpetually reminds us of the Bible, not by direct quotation, indirect allusion, borrowed idioms, or palpable imitation of phrase and style, but by an elevation of thought and simplicity of diction which are not to be found elsewhere. A passage, for instance, rises in our thoughts, unaccompanied by a clear recollection of its origin. Our first impression is that it *must* belong *either* to the *Bible* or to *Shakespeare*.   (Pp. 4–5)

This is as much general argument as Eaton offers, but it is sufficient to show how Shakespeare and the KJB's reputations have come together. For the rest of the book he pursues his aim of demonstrating the wealth of Shakespeare's knowledge of the Bible by accumulating sometimes sharp examples of passages in Shakespeare which refer or allude to the Bible, and by suggesting some more general similarities.

Six years later appeared Bishop Charles Wordsworth's *On Shakespeare's*

---

[33] The awareness was well enough established by 1873 to produce a variation on the cliché noted earlier: the KJB 'has formed the style and taste of the English classics' (Schaff, p. xx).

Knowledge and Use of the Bible (London, 1864). Wordsworth thought himself the first to undertake this subject, which suggests that bardolatry, AVolatry and literary studies had come together sufficiently by this time for such works to be inevitable. Though this is a better book than Eaton's, Wordsworth's purpose is the same, and he adds only one point of real significance here, the passing suggestion 'that our translators of 1611 owed as much, or more, to Shakespeare than he owed to them' (p. 9). Later he notes that the KJB has 'well stricken in years' (Luke 1: 7) where Tyndale and the Great Bible had 'well stricken in age', and asks,

> Is it possible that our translator of St Luke altered the expression out of deference to the following passage of Shakespeare?

> We speak no treason, man; we say the King
> Is wise and virtuous: and his noble Queen
> Well struck in years.   (*Richard III*, 1: 1)
>   (P. 42)

Such an argument, though in this instance unsustainable,[34] if developed, would complement the idea that the Bible is central to Shakespeare's strength: did Shakespeare's mastery of language contribute to the literary strength of the KJB? In an age which could produce fantastic arguments that Shakespeare was not the author of the plays attributed to him, it will be no surprise to find this question taken up as a way of accounting for the quality of the KJB without resorting to the argument from divine inspiration (see below, pp. 323ff.).

George Gilfillan and 'the lesson of infinite beauty'

George Gilfillan's (1813–78) *The Bards of the Bible* (1851) is a fine example of extended bibliolatry. Gilfillan, a Scots Presbyterian minister and noted literary critic and editor, thought of the book as repaying 'in a certain measure, our debt to that divine volume which, from early childhood, has hardly ceased for a day to be our companion – which has coloured our imagination, commanded our belief, impressed our thought and steeped our language' (p. 11). Many people evidently shared this sense of indebtedness, for, though it has been ignored by subsequent writers on the Bible as literature,

---

[34] 'Well stricken in years' is used by Tyndale and most subsequent translators in Luke 1: 18. Moreover, the KJB uses 'stricken in age' almost as often as it uses 'stricken in years'. The reason is a matter of accuracy, not aesthetics: 'age' and 'years' represent different Hebrew words. Occasionally, where the context demands, 'years' is used for the word generally translated 'age', but not the other way round. Comparison with the Geneva Bible, especially Josh. 13: 1, might suggest that the KJB was stricter than its predecessor.

Bards was a popular book, going through at least seven British editions by 1888, as well as several American editions. It not only reflects its time, but, by its popularity, helped to form and confirm attitudes.[35]

Though familiar with some of his scholarly predecessors (he regards Lowth, Herder and Heinrich Ewald as the chief of these), Gilfillan did not aim to make his work scholarly. Rather, he intended that it should be 'a prose poem or hymn in honour of the poetry and poets of the inspired volume' (p. iii), because 'every criticism on a true poem should be itself a poem'. He goes on:

> We propose, therefore, to take up this neglected theme – the bards of the Bible, and in seeking to develop their matchless spirit as masters of the lyre, to develop, at the same time, indirectly, a subordinate though strong evidence that they are something more – the rightful rulers of the belief and the heart of man. Perhaps this subject may not be found altogether unsuited to the wants of the age. If properly treated, it may induce some to pause before they seek any longer to pull in vain at the roots of a thing so beautiful. It may teach others to prize that Book somewhat more for its literature which they have all along loved for its truth, its holiness and its adaptation to their nature. It may strengthen some faltering convictions, and tend to withdraw enthusiasts from the exclusive study of imperfect, modern and morbid models, to those great ancient masters. It may, possibly, through the lesson of infinite beauty, successfully insinuate that of eternal truth into some souls hitherto shut against one or both; and as thousands have been led to regard the Bible as a book of genius, from having first thought it a book of God, so in thousands may the process be inverted.
>
> (Pp. 10–11)

This bibliolatrous linking of 'infinite beauty' and 'eternal truth' places him in the line traced from Dennis to Herder. His intention is to praise the beauty, leading those who believe to a wider appreciation of the Bible, and leading those who do not to the beauty, and thence the truth. These too are familiar

---

[35] A cutting which I found in my second-hand copy nicely suggests the kind of response it was capable of arousing. It is a letter signed 'Dublanensis' to the editor of the *British Weekly*, dated 24 March, year unknown. Referring to a recent leader on 'the spiritual and literary worth of the Bible', the writer recalls how, as a student at St Andrews in 1850, he heard Gilfillan read a chapter as a popular lecture:

> Our youthful blood danced within us by the bold figures of speech, and the bold figure of the speaker, with his massive head of brown hair, his broad, massive face, his two eyes like lamps of fire glaring through spectacles, his fine round voice with sough and cadences as of covenanting days, pouring forth his glowing sentences and periods, each of which, as it escaped his lips, was followed by a strange ventriloquist hum, like the smoke of the powder after it has discharged the shot. The *tout ensemble* gave a captivating impression to young minds of the rich combination of physical and intellectual force of the lecturer, and the vivid reproduction of the old Hebrew Prophet.

desires, and the desire to divert enthusiasts from modern literature suggests that he wants to take on the role of Euthyphron, though his book lacks the argued-out aesthetic of Herder's work.

Less familiar is the extent to which Gilfillan sees the Bible as literature. His chapter headings indicate that he will touch on the whole Bible, not just the obviously poetic parts of the Old Testament. This is a natural consequence of the growing enthusiasm for the Bible and of his close linking of beauty and truth, for he sees poetic beauty in the quality of thought. So:

> 'God is a spirit', or 'God is love', contains, each sentence, a world of poetic beauty, as well as divine meaning. Indeed, certain prose sentences constitute the essence of all the poetry in the Scriptures... Truly the songs of Scripture are magnificent, but its statements are 'words unutterable', which it is not possible for the tongue of man to utter!
>
> (P. 58)

In other words, the statements are such as only God could make. The argument moves from divine authorship through divine meaning to poetic beauty. Where it differs from Dennis's position that religion produces poetry (see above, p. 4.) is that Dennis believes that the ideas which come from religion have to be expressed 'with passion equal to their greatness', whereas Gilfillan believes that the quality of the idea alone is the essence of poetry: the highest poetry can be embodied in the plainest statement. In keeping with this, he uses (or, perhaps, invents) the term 'prose-poetry',[36] noting that this 'abounds in the historical books, and constitutes the staple of the entire volume' (p. 56). He also calls this 'seed poetry' (p. 57), perhaps meaning statement that is capable of growing into poetry, having the essence but yet to take the form. If this is indeed what he means, he has put his finger on a major element in appreciation of the Bible as literature: it has the potential for growing within the minds of believers into great literature.

On the basis of this idea of seed poetry, Gilfillan 'would arrange Hebrew poetry under the two general heads of song and poetic statement' (pp. 56–7). Song he divides into exulting, insulting, mourning, worshipping, loving, reflecting, interchanging, wildly luxuriating, narrating (this includes 'the simple epic – Psalm 78, Exodus, etc.') and predicting. His four kinds of statement are:

---

[36] Shaftesbury had used 'prose-poets' scathingly in 1711, and the *OED* traces 'prose-poem' back to Poe in 1842 and Kingsley in 1850, but there are no entries for 'prose-poetry'. Vocabulary was lagging behind the writers, but there is a historical aptness to these words emerging in the middle of the nineteenth century.

1st, Of poetic facts (creation, etc.).

2nd, Of poetic doctrines (God's spirituality).

3rd, Of poetic sentiments, with or without figurative language (golden rule, etc.).

4th, Of poetic symbols (in Zechariah, Revelation, etc.).   (P. 57)

This is nearly all-embracing, as he realises:

> Song and statement appear to include the Bible between them, and the statement is sometimes more poetical than the song. If aught evade this generalisation, it is the *argument*, which is charily sprinkled throughout the Epistles of Paul. Even that is logic defining the boundaries of the loftiest poetical thought. All else, from the simple narrations of Ezra and Nehemiah up to the most ornate and oratorical appeals to the Prophets, is genuinely poetic, and ought by no means to be excluded from the range of our critical explication and panegyric.   (P. 57)

The circularity of this consists in finding 'literary' categories to cover all parts of the Bible, and then saying all of the Bible is literature, whilst the importance is that it brings into the open the inclusive tendency of bibliolatry. The size of the move makes Jebb's extension of parallelism to the NT look modest indeed.

It is difficult for someone who defines poetry so broadly and who sees the whole Bible as expressive of divine meaning to make any critical judgement other than that, while some parts are higher than others, all are beyond mortal literature, and therefore open only to explication and panegyric. This is naked bibliolatry, but Gilfillan himself would reject the charge: he comments that 'there is, or was till lately, extant, a vulgar bibliolatry, which would hardly admit of any preference being given to one scripture writer over another, or of any comparison being instituted between its various authors' (p. 292), but the point is only that he has favourites among the bards of the Bible.

The emphasis on meaning leads away from discussion of any particular version of the Bible, which is why I have referred to bibliolatry rather than AVolatry. He usually quotes from the KJB or the PB, though without a consistent preference between the two, but his comments are never specific to their form of words. This is in spite of the answer he gives to those who ask

> why he has not conformed to the common practice of printing his poetical quotations from Scripture, *as poetry*, in their *form* of parallelism. His answer is merely that he never could bring himself to relish the practice, or to read with pleasure those translations of the Bible where it was used. Even favourite passages, in this guise, seemed new and cold to him. This, of course, was, in some measure, he knew, the effect of associations; but such associations, he knew also, were not confined to him. He may say this the more fearlessly as translations of the great masterpieces of foreign literature into plain English prose are becoming the order of the day. (Pp. iii–iv)

This seems to be the now normal testimony to pleasure in the familiar, but there is sufficient inaccuracy in his quotations for one to wonder whether verbal precision mattered to him (as an editor of the older English poets he was notoriously careless in textual matters). Consequently, *The Bards of the Bible*, like many of its eighteenth-century predecessors, appears to be about the originals. Gilfillan's philosophical basis for this is the same extreme version of the idea of the translatableness of the Bible that Jebb subscribed to. Rather than observing a compatibility between Hebrew and English, he sees the Bible as written in a kind of universal language, what he calls 'the oldest speech', which is independent of any particular form of words:

> This beauty, too, is free of the world. It passes, unshorn and unmingled, into every language and every land. Wherever the Bible goes, 'beauty', in the words of the poet, 'pitches her tents before it'. Appealing, as its poetry does, to the primitive principles, elements and 'all that must eternal be' of the human mind – using the oldest speech, older than Hebrew, that of metaphors and symbols – telling few, but life-like stories – and describing scenes which paint themselves easily and forever on the heart – it needs little more introduction than does a gleam of sunshine. It soon domesticates itself among the Caffres, or the Negroes, or the Hindoos, or the Hottentots, or the Chinese, who all feel it to be intensely human before they feel it to be divine. What heart but must palpitate at the sight of this virgin daughter of the Most High, going forth from land to land, with no dower but innocence, and with no garment but beauty; yet powerful in her loveliness as light, and in her innocence safe as her Father who is in heaven?   (P. 356)

The image of the Bible as 'this virgin daughter of the Most High' helps to link this idea of a universal language with the voice of God. Gilfillan's view of the Bible, then, is essentially this: it is the voice of God, anterior to all languages and so speaking through all languages direct to the human heart; it is felt as poetry, and, coming from truth, it is beautiful. The books of the Bible are 'the *classics* of the *heart*' (p. 42).

Gilfillan's 'prose-poems' have something in common with the paraphrases of the previous century. Here is how he treats the passage from Habakkuk already given in Dennis's version (above, p. 16 n21):

> Amidst the scenery of Sinai there was heard, at the crisis of the terror, a trumpet waxing gradually very loud, giving a martial tone to the tumult, drawing its vague terror into a point of war, and proclaiming the presence of the Lord of Hosts. Could we conceive that trumpet to have been uttering words descriptive of the scene around, they had been the words of Habakkuk's song: 'God came from Teman, the Holy One from Paran; his glory covered the heavens, and the earth was full of his praise.'

But the description is not of Sinai alone, nor, indeed, of any single scene. It is a picture of the divine progress or pilgrimage throughout the Jewish economy, formed by combining all the grand symbols of his power and presence into one tumult of glory. It were difficult for a thunderstorm to march calmly and regularly. There must be ragged edges in the darkness, and wild flashes and fluctuations in the light; and so with Habakkuk's song. Its brightness is as the sun's; but there is a hiding or veil over its might. Its figures tremble in sympathy before the trembling mountains it describes. Its language bows before its thoughts, like the everlasting mountains below the footsteps of Jehovah.

Where begins this procession? In the wilderness of Paran. There, where still rise the three tower-like summits of Mount Paran, which, when gilded by the evening or morning sun, look like 'horns of glory', the great Pilgrim begins his progress. He is attired in a garment woven of the 'marvellous light and the thick darkness'. Rays, as of the morning sun, shoot out from his hand. These are at once the horns and the hidings of his power. Like a dark raven, flies before him the plague. Wherever his feet rest, flashes of fire (or 'birds of prey!') arise. He stands, and the earth moves. He looks through the clouds which veil him, and the nations are scattered. As he advances, the mountains bow. Paran begins the homage; Sinai succeeds; the giants of Seir and Moab and Bashan fall prostrate – till every ridge and every summit has felt the awe of his presence. (Pp. 210–1)

The intention is to rouse admiration, and to demonstrate by repetition and elaboration the quality of the passage. Gilfillan reminds his reader of the KJB's words, but gives them inaccurately. He seems to be trying to improve the KJB, for 'God came from Teman, the Holy One from Paran', by omitting 'and', emphasises the parallelism between 'God' and 'the Holy One'; the omission of 'mount' before 'Paran' has the same effect. The KJB's 'God ... and the Holy One' misleadingly implies two figures, not one. Gilfillan goes on to give some sense of the passage's intent, and then throws out descriptive similitudes at the passage, not elucidating but, like an advertising agent, applying an aura of quality to it.

The last part of the passage elaborates the meaning and associations of the KJB by adding geographical detail such as 'the three tower-like summits of Mount Paran', associations with other biblical phrases ('"marvellous light and the thick darkness"', for instance, is an amalgamation of two biblical phrases), and his own imagination of the scene. Dennis, a century and a half earlier fitting the passage to metre, also added his own imagination of the scene. The KJB has: 'He stood and measured the earth: he beheld, and drove asunder the nations.' Metricising, Dennis adds, 'the *extended* earth', then alters the meaning so that the beholding causes the driving asunder, and adds his sense of how the nations felt: 'scattering the trembling nations with a look'. Gilfillan, though free from the demands of metre, also works as if he is growing real poetry from the seed. The KJB's dramatic 'He stood and measured the earth' is transformed into a philosophical truth: 'He stands, and the earth moves.' Then he imagines Jehovah like the sun looking through the clouds: 'He looks through the clouds which veil him.' Gilfillan is hardly more content with the KJB as poetry than Dennis was.

Dennis's dissatisfaction was conscious; Gilfillan's was not. Critics had changed the ways they thought they thought, yet the fundamental attitude that there is more poetry in the Bible than its mere English words contain has changed only in the sense of just what constitutes poetry. Gilfillan's emphasis on a universal language behind the text and his willingness to supply what is not in the text from his own imagination align him with the eighteenth- and nineteenth-century critics of Shakespeare who endowed the characters of the plays with a reality and life of their own beyond the text (see below, pp. 375ff.). In both cases the words are taken to be the mediators of an *independent* reality. Once readers have received that reality, it is free of the words, and they are similarly free to go on creating the character or meaning or image or action. They are then reporting on their own imagination, not on the text.

This is not necessarily an invalid process – indeed, it may seem distinctly attractive when set against some modern attitudes. It helps Gilfillan achieve his aim of infecting the reader with his own enthusiasm. Further, it can reach insights that are true to the text. Gilfillan's 'rays, as of the morning sun, shoot out from his hand' helps to elucidate the difficulty of 'horns' in 'and his brightness was as the light; he had horns coming out of his hand'. One may also see this elaborative process as reflecting the centuries-old habit of expanding on a single text in the making of a sermon. Gilfillan's practice as a critic reflects both his time and his calling.

The last three chapters move beyond 'the bards of the Bible'. They deal with 'the poetical characters in Scripture', 'comparative estimate, influences, and effects of Scripture poetry', and the 'future destiny of the Bible'. He begins the first of these chapters: 'beside the authors and poets of the Old and New Testaments, there are, in the course of both, a number of characters depicted teeming with peculiar and romantic interest, and who are abundantly entitled to the epithet poetical' (p. 309). 'Poetical' here means that they live in his imagination, again as if independent of the text. In this chapter his method is at its clearest. For instance, he correctly notes of Cain that 'we can hardly judge accurately or distinctly, apart from the many poetic shapes which, since the account of Moses, he has assumed' (p. 312). This he follows with a key statement for understanding his method: 'yet our idea of him may be uttered'.

And so he imagines the life behind the text:

> Born amid great expectations, called by his mother 'the man, the lord', he grew up, disappointing every fond hope and becoming a somewhat sullen drudge, 'a tiller of the ground'. Meanwhile, his younger brother is exhibiting the finer traits of the pastoral character. The 'elder is made to serve the younger'. Fiercely does the once-spoiled child kick against the pricks, till at last the fury of conscious inferiority breaks out in blood – the blood of Abel. Conscience-struck, hearing in every wind the voice of his brother's gore – nay, carrying it in his ear, as the shell carries inland the sound of ocean's waters – he flees from his native region, and a curse clings to him, and the whole story seems to prove – first, the evil of over-excited and disappointed hopes; secondly, the misery of the murderer; and, thirdly, how God can deduce good from evil, and mingle mercy with judgement. (Pp. 312–13)

This readiness of critics to find the life behind the text is crucial to the growth of literary admiration for the Bible. Yet Gilfillan does not pause to ask what creates the life. Is it (narrowing the possibilities to two) the text, or is it the reader's imagination, left to its own devices by a text that is both skeletal and totally familiar?

The chapter entitled 'Comparative estimate, influences and effects of Scripture poetry' concludes with a section that names a large range of writers who have been influenced by the Bible. The effect is to suggest the ubiquity of the Bible's influence on modern authors, and the general respect with which writers have regarded the Bible. He claims that 'even in "the godless eighteenth century" – we find numerous traces of the power of the Bible poetry' (p. 362), and that 'in the nineteenth century, all our great British authors have more or less imbibed fire from the Hebrew fountains' (p. 365). Finally he notes that 'our living writers have, in general, shown a sympathy with the Hebrew genius' (pp. 368–9). His claims throughout lack proof, but they fulfil the intention of suggesting the importance of the Bible to literature and providing a starting-point for his readers to develop. This too is typical: the book is an emotional spur to regard the Bible as literature, and to see its influence in every possible place. As such it was popular, and gave a strong stimulus to bibliolatry, though not specifically to AVolatry.

CHAPTER 6

The Revised Version

Rules for the revision

By far the most important new English version of the Bible to appear in the 350 years between 1611 and 1961, when the New English Bible was published, was the Revised Version (NT 1881, OT 1885, Apocrypha 1895), yet its significance here lies not so much in its achievement as in the insight it gives into the business of translation, its effects on opinions of the KJB and, to a minor extent, its role in generating the multitude of twentieth-century versions. This is not to belittle its achievements or to gloss over its weaknesses, but to recognise that, even though a literary welcome was given to its work on some of the OT books, it has not become a significant work of English literature. In spite of – and even because of – the RV, the KJB's general reputation continued to grow, and it remained the paramount Bible for English writers: nowhere in English literature does the text of the RV become a significant factor.

As a revision, the RV has much in common with the KJB. Both were committee revisions undertaken at the behest of parliament. If the decision to make the RV was taken tardily as against the almost indecent haste of the decision to make the KJB, if political and sectarian motives had their role in generating the KJB while the RV was the result of scholarly agitation, nevertheless each revision proceeded with exemplary care and thoroughness. Both were conducted by leading churchmen and scholars of the day; moreover, in terms of their scholarship and their own literary achievements outside their translation, there is nothing to choose between the two groups (unless one were to argue for the preface to the KJB or for Lancelot Andrewes's sermons). The later revisers were as well qualified for the work as their predecessors.

The essentials of the background to the RV have all, with one exception, been seen. There is no need to follow here the long sequence of nineteenth-century criticism of the KJB's scholarly accuracy, since it adds nothing to the story of literary attitudes and is a continuation of the kind of discussion that had received a temporary setback through the conservative temper induced by the Napoleonic wars. The one exception – and it is a major one – is the renewed criticism of the language of the KJB, but it will be more convenient to examine this in connection with the RV's linguistic revisions. In the meantime it will be best to look at the kind of evidence which parallels that available for the KJB, and then to move on to other kinds of evidence. In this way it is possible to see whether similar evidence leads to similar conclusions, and then whether other evidence modifies those conclusions.

The similar evidence is, of course, the instructions to the revisers and the revisers' prefaces to their work. Supplementing this, there is a wealth of discussion by the revisers of their work, of which the most important for present purposes are *Addresses on the Revised Version of Holy Scripture* (1901) by Charles John Ellicott (1819–1905), Bishop of Gloucester and Bristol, and chairman of the NT committee, *Some Lessons of the Revised Version of the New Testament* (1897) by Brooke Foss Westcott (1825–1901), biblical scholar and Bishop of Durham, and *A Companion to the Revised Old Testament* (1885) by the American reviser Talbot W. Chambers. Ellicott's book is close to being an official history of the revision, while Westcott and Chambers's books give very detailed and somewhat contrasting accounts of the reasons for changes. Such discussions take us beyond the evidence available for the KJB: for a historian, one of the major differences between the two translations is that there is a wealth of commentary from the revisers, to say nothing of a similar abundance of reviews, whereas almost nothing survives from the earlier version.

The task undertaken by the Jacobeans and the Victorians was substantially the same, to revise the previous official version in the light of the best scholarship of the day. Here are the instructions issued to the makers of the RV:

1. To introduce as few alterations as possible into the text of the Authorised Version consistently with faithfulness.

2. To limit, as far as possible, the expression of such alterations to the language of the Authorised and earlier English versions.

3. Each company to go twice over the portion to be revised, once provisionally, the second time finally, and on principles of voting as hereinafter is provided.

4. That the text to be adopted be that for which the evidence is decidedly preponderating; and that when the text so adopted differs from that from which the Authorised Version was made, the alteration be indicated in the margin.

5. To make or retain no change in the text on the second final revision by each company, except *two thirds* of those present approve of the same, but on the first revision to decide by simple majorities.

6. In every case of proposed alteration that may have given rise to discussion, to defer the voting thereupon till the next meeting, whensoever the same shall be required by one third of those present at the meeting, such intended vote to be announced in the notice for the next meeting.

7. To revise the headings of chapters and pages, paragraphs, italics and punctuation.

8. To refer, on the part of each company, when considered desirable, to divines, scholars and literary men, whether at home or abroad, for their opinions.

(RV NT preface, p. viii)

The first and chief of these is identical to the first rule for the KJB, 'the ordinary Bible read in the Church, commonly called the *Bishops' Bible*, to be followed, and as little altered as the truth of the original will permit'. Most of the remaining instructions concern the method of working, and they have the same aim as the KJB rules, to ensure that the revision is as carefully made as possible. It would be hard to say which is the better set of instructions. Those for the KJB envisage consultation between the different companies, whereas the RV was made by two companies, one for each Testament (the Apocrypha was undertaken later), and the companies worked separately (Ellicott several times remarks that he cannot speak directly of the work done on the OT). As the work developed, each company consulted with an equivalent American company, so that both the KJB and the RV were made with substantial consultation. Only in one area of practice did the two revisions differ to a significant extent: the RV as a whole was not given a final revision by a small group of revisers. If that final revision had made a significant difference to the literary quality of the KJB, the method adopted for the RV might be judged significantly inferior. On the other hand, the revisers saw one distinct advantage in their method, the use of only one committee for the whole of the NT (implicitly the same advantage existed for the OT). The KJB's division of the NT between two companies is seen by the writer of the preface to the RV NT as being 'beyond all doubt the cause of many inconsistencies' (p. vii).

In large part, then, the task set the Victorian revisers was the same as that set their Jacobean predecessors, and their way of working was not significantly different. Since there is nothing to choose between the two groups of men as far as their qualifications for the work is concerned, we might expect a version of broadly similar quality to result. But we have seen that the perception of the quality of the KJB depended principally on historical circumstances, and the circumstances of the Victorian revision were quite different from that of its predecessor. The chief of these differences is pointed to in the second rule for the RV, to keep to the language of the KJB and earlier English versions.

Nothing in the rules for the KJB corresponds to this. The KJB translators (I call them translators to distinguish them from their Victorian successors, not to make a distinction between the two versions) worked with a nearly established biblical English, sometimes altering the largely Anglo-Saxon tone of the Tyndale tradition by bringing in Gregory Martin's Latinate vocabulary, and they worked with an English that was not too far removed from their own. The RV revisers had before them not only an absolutely established biblical English, but one which they revered and which was substantially different from their own language. If they wished to make changes, they had often to write pastiche. Only rarely were they able to return to renderings given in earlier versions. Ellicott says these were always before the revisers but that he does not remember them often being used (p. 29), and Westcott and Chambers give only three examples, John 10: 16, Heb. 10: 23 (Westcott, pp. 120, 196–7) and Gen. 49: 9 (Chambers, p. 82); in each case the explanation is that the older renderings are more accurate than those of the KJB. Further, although the KJB translators worked with a largely established language, they still worked in a situation in which the English text of the Bible was not generally felt to be fixed: not only were there competing versions, but the habit of verbal fidelity to the English text had not yet become ingrained, especially among the clergy. By the 1870s the KJB had had no significant rivals for generations, and its precise phraseology was not only thoroughly well known but had acquired an aura of holiness. In effect the KJB was to the Victorians what the Vulgate was to the pre-Reformation Church. Far more than their predecessors, the RV revisers were 'meddling with men's religion' (KJB preface, p. 2). Rather than standing at the end of an era of textual instability, they stood at the beginning of a new era of instability – an era which they inaugurated and which shows no sign of coming to an end for most Christians outside those sects that continue to adhere reverently and dogmatically to the KJB. The KJB finished a process, and this was a key to its eventual success. The RV began a new process, and this put it in a position where it was unlikely to gain the monopoly that a version needs to conquer the hearts of the people.

One more major difference shows up in rule 8: this reproduces rule 11 for the KJB, to consult with 'any learned man in the land' on obscure places, but, where the KJB rule envisages only scholarly consultation, that for the RV adds 'literary men' to divines and scholars. Although the rule was only once acted on,[1] its spirit is crucial. The revisers were charged with more than preserving

---

[1] Ellicott remembers that the NT company consulted with the First Sea Lord as to the correctness of the nautical terms used in Acts 27 (pp. 31–2). However, there was at least one instance of a scholar communicating with the revisers to good effect (see Blaikie,

the language of 'the first English classic': they had to remember that they were translating a great work of literature and that the result of their labour should be a stylistic achievement as well as the most faithful rendering of the book of truth yet achieved. Was this rule a hint that they should rub and polish – to give those words now a fully literary turn – the language of the KJB, not only removing archaisms and purging grammatical faults, but improving its cadences and diction wherever improvements, consistent with faithfulness, might be made? At least one advocate of revision, taking a swipe at AVolatry, had argued this very point, claiming that the KJB 'is impaired by manifold literary blemishes which any one moderately acquainted with English literature may easily detect', and so, 'even in its character *as* an English composition ... is capable of extensive improvement' (Johnston, p. 190). In short, it seems they were to work with the kind of literary consciousness that their time commonly imputed to their predecessors but for which almost no evidence can be found apart from one's sense of the fineness of the KJB. Here the tasks set before the two groups of translators and their sense of their work really diverge. It will be a crucial matter for this study to see whether such a task and consciousness did affect the work.

AVolatry (inseparably linked with a mumpsimus conservatism) and the conviction that the Bible was literature were the forces behind the rule for the style of the RV and the theoretical though never actual consultation with literary men. Had AVolatry been the only force, there would of course have been no revision: by itself the idea that the KJB could be improved as a literary version would never have been sufficient motivation for an official revision. The RV was a compromise between the irresistible need to revise and the immovable monument of the KJB.

The remaining rules all reflect the fundamental reason for making the RV, the certainty among scholars stretching back to Hugh Broughton that the KJB did not perfectly represent the truth of the originals.[2] The key word is 'faithfulness' in the first rule. Moving beyond the kind of evidence available for the KJB, we can be absolutely certain how the revisers understood 'faithfulness'. Ellicott recalls

a very full discussion on the true meaning of the word at one of the early meetings of

---

p. 230).

[2] Nevertheless, it is curious that Chambers, in his account of 'The need of a revision' (chapter title), gives first 'the progress of the language', second 'infelicities in the form of the common version', and third 'the progress of sacred learning' (pp. 18–24). If this reflects his priorities, it separates him from most of the revisers and most of the agitators for revision.

the [NT] Company. Some alteration had been proposed in the rendering of the Greek to which objection was made that it did not come under the rule and principle of faithfulness. This led to a general and, as it proved, a final discussion. Bishop Lightfoot, I remember, took an earnest part in it. He contended that our revision must be a true and thorough one; that such a meeting as ours could not be assembled for many years to come, and that if the rendering was plainly more accurate and more true to the original, it ought not to be put aside as incompatible with some supposed aspect of the rule of faithfulness. (Pp. 98–9)

The highly scholarly Joseph Barber Lightfoot had been more specific:

the most important changes in which a revision may result will be due to the variations of reading in the Greek text. It was not the fault, it was the misfortune of the scholars from Tyndale downward, to whom we owe our English Bible, that the only text accessible to them was faulty and corrupt ... the permanent value of the new revision will depend in a great degree on the courage and fidelity with which it deals with the questions of readings [of the Greek]. (Pp. 19, 32)

The result was a clear understanding on the NT committee that, in Ellicott's words, 'faithfulness' meant fidelity 'to the original in its plain grammatical meaning as elicited by accurate interpretation' (p. 98).

This is precisely what the KJB translators aimed at, yet it is not what the public in general had been led to expect. The debate on 'faithfulness' was a crucial step in shaping the RV NT, but such scholarly adherence to the original was not the inevitable step that the history of translation as a whole might lead us to expect. Just as the Vulgate had come to be thought of as truer than the Greek and Hebrew, so some people thought the same way about the KJB. The anonymous critic who noted that the KJB is regarded as having 'a sort of inspiration belonging to it' (above, p. 189) was reviewing one of the predecessors of the RV. He adds, 'the result has been that we are apt to take it as a standard, and then to try the Greek by it'.[3] As the NT reviser Robert Scott put it, 'there might be more inspiration in the received version than in the original Greek'.[4]

One might not expect such extreme AVolatry to affect scholars, but it did, if only for the good reason that Bible translation was not just a question of scholarship; it was also for the people. Ellicott himself and two other future revisers, George Moberly and William G. Humphry, were involved in making *The Gospel According to St John, after the Authorised Version. Newly Compared with the Original Greek, and Revised*, by Five Clergymen (London, 1857), and it was

---

[3] *Will the Version by the Five Clergymen Help Dr. Biber?*, p. 5.
[4] As given in Allen, II: 318.

this that led to the first of the observations of AVolatry just given. This version, which gives the KJB and its revision in parallel columns, was intended as a stalking-horse for the RV. It paid scrupulous attention to the beauty of the KJB and to the language of its predecessors, and it provides a significant example of concession to the language of the KJB:

> We have constantly rejected words which presented themselves as the most exact equivalents of the words of the Greek because they wanted the biblical garb and sound which we were anxious to preserve. The verb 'seize', for instance, which seemed to render the Greek word πιάσαι [John 7: 30] with much correctness, has been dropped upon finding that its archaic or biblical use is always in combination with the word 'on', and that it is never used as a simple transitive verb as in our modern English.   (P. viii)

No examples of this sort are to be found in the records of the RV, and it does use 'seize' without 'on'. Although Ellicott, as chairman of the NT revision committee, was later, as we have seen, to enunciate unreservedly the principle of faithfulness, he continued to advocate what we may call light (or AVolatrous) revision right up to the time work began on the RV, declaring 'that no revision in the present day could hope to meet with an hour's acceptance if it failed to preserve the tone, rhythm and diction of the present Authorised Version'. He adds a footnote that is crucial:

> Nothing is more satisfactory at the present time than the evident feelings of veneration for our Authorised Version, and the very generally-felt desire for as little change as possible. In a recent leading article on this subject in the *Times* of May 6 the writer very properly presses on the revisers a salutary caution – 'that it should be their aim not to make as many, but to make as few alterations as possible', and justly remarks that 'it will often be much better to sacrifice a point of strict grammatical accuracy than to jar the ear and lose the sympathy of readers'.[5]

This is more than a political statement, though such a placing of the KJB ahead of the cavils of scholarship helped to make revision acceptable.

Light revision of this sort is all that was contemplated in the five resolutions adopted by the Convocation of Canterbury at the beginning of May 1870, that is, before the rules were settled:

> 1. That it is desirable that a revision of the Authorised Version of the Holy Scriptures be undertaken.
>
> 2. That the revision be so conducted as to comprise both marginal renderings and such emendations as it may be found necessary to insert in the text of the Authorised Version.

[5] *Considerations on the Revision of the English Version of the New Testament* (London, 1870), p. 99.

3. That in the above resolutions we do not contemplate any new translation of the Bible, or alteration of the language, except where in the judgement of the most competent scholars such change is necessary.

4. That in such necessary changes, the style of the language employed in the existing Version be closely followed.

5. That it is desirable that Convocation should nominate a body of its own members to undertake the work of revision, who shall be at liberty to invite the co-operation of any eminent for scholarship, to whatever nation or religious body they may belong. (RV NT preface, p. viii)

'Faithfulness' does not appear: the echoing word here is 'necessary'. Nothing more than correction of errors is envisaged, and the qualities of the KJB seem to be more important than the exact truth of the originals. The rules for the RV were agreed less than three weeks later, and it may have seemed at the time that they embodied no significant change. Yet, by reducing the repeated 'necessary's to 'as few alterations as possible' and qualifying this with 'consistently with faithfulness', Convocation crossed a line and made the originals the touchstone. The issue of faithfulness was opened up and the revision of the NT became a heavy one (though not as heavy as it might have been): by one count the revisers made 36,191 changes (Hemphill, p. 71n), that is, four and a half for each verse. The warnings in *The Times* that Ellicott only a few years earlier had found so proper were ignored.

The preface to the New Testament

Because the RV NT and OT were made and published separately, the RV has two prefaces. 'The present Revision is an attempt, after a long interval, to follow the example set by a succession of honoured predecessors' (NT, p. v), and so the NT preface begins by looking briefly at the KJB and its predecessors. Apart from this beginning, both prefaces explain the principles on which the committees worked, and this gives them a different character from the preface to the KJB: that was largely polemical in purpose and rhetorical in style, and gave scant detail of the work; these avoid any flourish and are full of sober facts. Where one may read the KJB preface with real pleasure in its verbal and argumentative energy, and glean from it an impression of the translators' attitudes, no such pleasure is afforded by the RV prefaces, but they are invaluable repositories of information.

In the words of the NT preface, the task was to produce 'a version that shall be alike literal and idiomatic, faithful to each thought of the original, and yet, in the expression of it, harmonious and free' (p. xv); the OT preface states more simply that the 'leading principle [was] the sincere desire to give to modern readers a faithful representation of the meaning of the original documents' (p. x). Faithfulness to the meaning or, more ambiguously, thought, of the original is indeed fundamental. Deliberately echoing the KJB preface, the NT preface says earlier, 'to render a work that had reached this high standard of excellence still more excellent, to increase its fidelity without destroying its charm, was the task committed to us' (p. vii).

Discussing the KJB and taking matters in order of importance, the NT preface deals first with the Greek text the translators used. Quietly it makes the point that the scholarship of the translators was as good as it could have been at that time, but that advances in scholarship and the discovery of 'nearly all the more ancient of the documentary authorities' mean that 'it is but recently that materials have been acquired for executing [a revision] with even approximate completeness' (pp. v–vi).

Next the general character of the KJB is outlined through a commentary on the major rules for its conduct and the degree to which they were followed. One major criticism is made, that the 'studiously adopted ... variety of expression ... would now be deemed hardly consistent with the requirements of faithful translation' (p. vi). This would have brought a grim smile of satisfaction to the face of Hugh Broughton, but that worthy would have been less amused by this very important statement:

> We have had to study this great version carefully and minutely, line by line; and the longer we have been engaged upon it the more we have learned to admire its simplicity, its dignity, its power, its happy turns of expression, its general accuracy and, we must not fail to add, the music of its cadences and the felicities of its rhythm.
>
> (P. vii)

As so often, the order matters. This is critical AVolatry wherein the KJB's general qualities of language are admired ahead of its accuracy, and yet cadence and rhythm come last. The definition of the task as increasing fidelity without destroying charm follows. Literary admiration for the KJB is balanced against scholarly reservation. There is no sign that the revisers felt that they could or should improve the language.

The real interest of the preface lies in the explanation of the changes. The revisers found themselves 'constrained by faithfulness to introduce changes which might not at first sight appear to be included under the rule' of introducing as few alterations as possible (p. x). Five classes of scholarly change are specified in the following order: changes required by a changed reading of the Greek, changes where the KJB is wrong or chooses 'the less probable of two possible renderings', clarification of obscure or ambiguous renderings, corrections of inconsistencies and, finally, subsequent alterations necessitated by these changes (p. x). On the face of it, none of these classes involves literary alteration – indeed, the shunning of ambiguity may well result in placing doctrinal considerations ahead of literary ones – but the preface allows that the consequential alterations may be literary, for sometimes they are made 'to avoid tautology, sometimes to obviate an unpleasing alliteration or some other infelicity of sound, sometimes, in the case of smaller words, to preserve the familiar rhythm' (p. xi).

Language is discussed separately. The revisers 'have faithfully adhered' to rule 2 prescribing the language of the KJB and its predecessors:

> We have habitually consulted the earlier versions; and in our sparing introduction of words not found in them or in the Authorised Version we have usually satisfied ourselves that such words were employed by standard writers of nearly the same date, and had also that general hue which justified their introduction into a Version which has held the highest place in the classical literature of our language. We have never removed any archaisms, whether in structure or in words, except where we were persuaded either that the meaning of the words was not generally understood, or that the nature of the expression led to some misconception of the true sense of the passage. The frequent inversions of the strict order of the words, which add much to the strength and variety of the Authorised Version and give an archaic colour to many felicities of diction, have been seldom modified. Indeed, we have often adopted the same arrangement in our own alterations; and in this as in other particulars we have sought to assimilate the new work to the old.
>
> In a few exceptional cases we have failed to find any word in the older stratum of our language that appeared to convey the precise meaning of the original. There, and there only, we have used words of a later date; but not without having first assured ourselves that they are to be found in the writings of the best authors of the period to which they belong. (Pp. xii–xiii)

Nothing could be more explicit. Revision of language, except where dictated by the classes of scholarly change, is only made where there was a question of either 'the meaning of the words', or 'the true sense of the passage', or 'the precise meaning of the original' (these are the key phrases) being misunderstood or misconceived. Modernisation for its own sake is not even contemplated; archaism is tolerated and even cultivated. By one count, the RV NT is more archaic than the KJB in at least 549 places (Hemphill, p. 85). Moreover, the introduction of new words is fenced in by pedantry rather than subject to taste.

Two further matters are of importance. First, following the arguments of Locke and his successors, the text is presented in paragraphs, and verse numbers are relegated to the margin. This is 'after the precedent of the earliest English versions, so as to assist the general reader in following the current of narrative or argument' (p. xiv). Nevertheless, the text is given in boxed double columns and so remains manifestly biblical rather than returning to the standard prose presentation of Tyndale's work. References to the margin still interrupt, and the verse and chapter numbers remain very obvious, printed hard up against the text. The result is a sensible compromise between a genuine reading and a reference text, though the retention of double columns reduces the effect of the paragraphing and seems unnecessary except for conservation of space in the poetic parts. The visual impression is of workmanlike biblical formality: nothing tends towards visual pleasure.[6]

The second matter is one that was to be more important in the OT. Quotations from OT poetry and the poems in Luke 1 and 2 are printed as verse lines: 'such an arrangement', the preface declares, 'will be found helpful to the reader, not only as directing his attention to the poetical character of the quotation, but as also tending to make its force and pertinence more fully felt' (p. xiv). In other words, it is to 'ensure a clear and intelligent setting forth of the true meaning of the words' (p. xv), which is the way the revision of the punctuation is described. The visual representation of parallelism, then, is regarded by the NT revisers as a scholarly rather than a literary device. Oddly, the OT preface is less detailed, simply remarking that 'in the poetical portions ... [the revisers] have adopted an arrangement in lines so as to exhibit the parallelism which is characteristic of Hebrew poetry', and adding that 'they have not extended this arrangement to the prophetical books, the language of which, although frequently marked by parallelism, is, except in purely lyrical passages, rather of the nature of lofty and impassioned prose' (p. viii). This is a retreat from Lowth and his followers, and one can only presume that it stems from the revisers' caution since Lowth's argument that the prophetic books were poetical had nowhere been refuted. One of the American revisers, Chambers, is more explicit, arguing that the old uniform printing of verse and prose is unfortunate 'not only in that many readers fail to see that the Scriptures are in part poetical, but also in that the parallelisms, which are so important a part of Hebrew verse and which often do so much to facilitate the understanding of difficult passages, are greatly obscured'. He makes no claim that the division is perfect but thinks even an incorrect division is better than none at all because it draws the reader's attention to the form and allows him, if he wishes, to make corrections (pp. 23–4). The appearance of verse form, then,

---

[6] Even these sensible and conservative changes were capable of arousing ire as a 'further external *assimilation of the Sacred Volume to an ordinary book*' (Burgon, p. 224).

is no more than an appearance, designed to remind the reader of the literary nature of the text and to help him to perceive the meaning. It is an aid to what Chambers so often calls 'perspicuity'. The implication of the NT preface that this apparently literary device is really employed as a rather approximate scholarly aid is confirmed.

The NT preface as a whole produces an effect entirely in keeping with the presentation of the work. At every point the sober scholarship of 'a company of earnest and competent men'[7] predominates. Literary awareness is there, but it operates as a restraining rather than as a constructive principle except where change has to be made. The degree of explicit literary awareness goes well beyond that found in the KJB preface, yet it is everywhere subordinated to the scholarly purpose.

Evidence from the New Testament revisers

The recollections of the revisers reinforce this conclusion. Ellicott makes the key statement of their position. Of rule 8, to consult with 'divines, scholars and literary men', he observes:

> It has sometimes been said that it would have been better, especially in reference to the New Testament, if this rule had been more frequently acted on, and if matters connected with English and alterations of rhythm had been brought before a few of our more distinguished literary men. It may be so; though I much doubt whether in matters of English the Greek would not always have proved the dominant arbiter.
>
> (P. 32)

This is exactly what we have been taught to expect by Jerome and the English translators from Tyndale to the KJB, and it is exactly in keeping with the RV NT preface. The two Cambridge professors, Westcott and Fenton John Anthony Hort, formidable scholars and joint editors of the Greek NT, were chief influences in the committee; with Lightfoot, they vigorously promoted 'linguistic accuracy' over 'literary picturesqueness'.[8] Westcott puts the matter thus: 'faithfulness, the most candid and the most scrupulous, was the central aim of the revisers . . . And the claim which they confidently make – the claim which alone could justify their labours – is that they have placed the English reader far more nearly than before in the position of the Greek scholar' (*Some Lessons*, pp. 18, 4). In the end, the RV NT accommodates but does not cater for

---

[7] So described by one of the company, Charles J. Vaughan, *Authorised or Revised?* (London, 1882), p. ix.

[8] *DNB* account of William F. Moulton.

the aesthetic reader. Scholarship – the truth of fact, not the truth of beauty – is the essence of truth. This is fully in keeping with the complaint Henry Thomas Day made in pleading for a revision:

> I am constrained to allege that no man can fully and truthfully expound the Holy Scriptures if he depends altogether upon the Authorised Version. One stands aghast at the frightful emphasis which ignorant or incautious preachers and expounders are accustomed to lay upon words and texts for which we seek in vain in the original. With the pure gold of the Authorised Version unrefined and unseparated from the alloy, 'the wisest master builder builds upon the sand'. I dare not preach from any text in the Authorised Version without first comparing it with the original, and revising or re-translating it if it be unfaithful.   (Pp. 5–6)

It is almost equally in keeping with the attitude of that 'radiant spiritual athlete' (*Dictionary of American Biography*), Phillips Brooks, Episcopal Bishop of Boston, preacher to Harvard and professor of Christian Ethics (but not one of the American revisers; the Episcopal Church of America declined an invitation to take part in the revision). Objections to the newly published RV NT's 'sacrifice of rhythm in style and of familiar expressions which had become dear' provoked him to this:

> The thing that is really upon trial ... is not the Revised Version but the Church. If a man is going to translate a book for me, the one thing I demand is scrupulousness – the most absolute fidelity to details, the absolute binding of themselves to the simple question how they could most completely represent the Greek in English, letting the question of literary merit take care of itself.[9]

Such thinking dominated the revisers, even if they did not go as far as Henry Alford had advocated in his *The New Testament* (London, 1869 – a continuation of the work of the Five Clergymen): 'a translator of Holy Scripture must be absolutely colourless, ready to sacrifice the choicest text and the plainest proof of doctrine, if the words are not those of what he is constrained in his conscience to receive as God's testimony' (p. viii). Yet, as Ellicott had, a substantial number of the revisers took different views, even if this rarely affected the outcome. The early discussion of 'faithfulness' had a binding power: it led to what one of the revisers, David Brown, regretfully called 'the itch of change'. In his own words, Brown 'was one of those who saw that the changes which were being made were not only far too many, but, out of a desire to squeeze out the last shred of the sense, were destroying the purity of the English and all hope of our version being accepted by the public'.[10] Similarly, 'no member of the

---

[9] Allen, II: 317–18.
[10] As given in Blaikie, p. 222. Blaikie continues with an account of two changes to the Greek text, one opposed and one suggested by Brown.

Company regretted more than [Archdeacon Frederick George Lee] the number of changes which altered the rhythm of the Authorised Version where the sense was fairly correct. Here, though submitting loyally to the majority, he retained as usual his conservative convictions.'[11]

For the most part, then, faithfulness defeated popular aestheticism and religious conservatism, but this is not to say that those forces did not find a voice in the committee. Westcott points out that all the arguments against their conclusions were made there (p. 3), and describes the revision as exhibiting 'no preponderance of private opinion. It is, so to speak, the resultant of many conflicting forces. Each reviser gladly yielded his own conviction to more or less serious opposition. Each school among the revisers ... prevailed in its turn' (p. 9). For instance, Robert Scott, of Liddell and Scott's Greek lexicon, recalls that

> On one occasion when the English word which had to be used, according to our principle, for the Greek, brought out what seemed to him most objectionable English, the member who was looked up to as the master of lexicography [Trench][12] exclaimed, 'we are impoverishing the English language', in response to which a whisper of 'Hear, hear' was heard across the table.[13]

We do not know what decision was made in this case, but there were times when AVolatry won through. Hort recalls Dean Arthur Stanley 'fighting for every antique phrase which can be defended', and Ellicott says of Stanley that 'the Revised Version bore many marks of the culture and good taste of the Dean, and graceful diction and harmonious numbers found in him a constant friend. The Dean, too, defended the retention of some innocent archaisms which had become honoured in the minds of the people, and they were spared accordingly.'[14]

There is more direct evidence still of the NT revisers preserving KJB readings. Copies of proofs of the 'First and Provisional Revision' are preserved in the Cambridge University Library.[15] One of these contains annotations by that leading proponent of heavy revision, Hort. Not all his annotations

---

[11] J. P. Mahaffy, *Athenaeum* (19 May 1883); as given in Hemphill, p. 73.

[12] Scott does not identify this reviser as Trench, but his association with the *OED*, his published opinions on the RV (see, e.g., Hemphill, pp. 72–3, 104–5), and Hemphill's description of him as 'the only English specialist amongst the revisers' (p. 104) all make the identification probable.

[13] David Brown, *Expository Times* 4: 64; as given in Hemphill, p. 79.

[14] Hort, letter of 7 July 1870; Ellicott, *The Times* (20 July 1881); both as given in Hemphill, p. 78.

[15] So too are proofs of the second revision. A copy of the first revision of Matthew contains the criticisms and suggestions of the Americans.

correspond to the final text, but it is significant that some of them are restorations of KJB readings which the final text did indeed retain. Mark 2: 23 in the KJB reads, 'and it came to pass, that he went through the corn fields on the Sabbath day, and his disciples began as they went, to pluck the ears of corn'. The first revision changed the latter part of this to 'and his disciples began to make their way plucking the ears of corn'. Hort crosses out 'to make their way plucking', restores 'as they went, to pluck', and relegates the revision to the margin, 'Gr: *to make* their *way plucking*'. Whether this represents his considered judgement in preparation for the appropriate meeting or his record of the committee's discussion does not matter: it confirms that the familiar was sometimes retained at the expense of what was considered a more correct reading.[16] Such testimony and examples make it clear that the NT revision was not as heavy as it might have been: faithfulness was tempered with respect for the KJB's language, but it is no more than a tempering.

An English account of changes in the New Testament

Westcott's is by far the best account of changes made in the NT, and, as a corollary, is also the best detailed account of the scholarly weaknesses of the KJB translators (such is its thoroughness and suggestiveness that the need to summarise and simplify is more than usually regrettable). Yet, for all the authority of tone that Westcott characteristically adopts, it represents throughout a personal view of the changes, and that view is from one of the extremes of the committee. Westcott was probably the chief proponent of what he himself calls 'heaviness of rendering' (p. 25), and he frequently comments on renderings in the RV which he considers did not go far enough. At the furthest remove from Dean Stanley, whom Ellicott regarded so benevolently, he reserves his last and sharpest barb for the advocates of aesthetic translation, claiming that the experience of the student who has 'learnt to interrogate [the text] with intelligent patience ... will teach him to look with something more than suspicion upon the criticisms of scholars who appear to find nothing better than solemn music in the English version of words of life, and to admit no hope of riper knowledge from the discipline of two centuries and a half' (p. 222).

---

[16] One other small group of alterations warrants notice in passing. Sometimes added archaisms were rejected. The revisers initially altered 'endure' in Mark 4: 17 to 'dure', but then returned to 'endure', which had been the reading from Tyndale onwards. On other occasions archaisms are added, as in Matt. 28: 11: the first revision retained the KJB's 'things that were done', but Hort alters this to the typically biblical 'that were come to pass', which is the reading eventually adopted.

Westcott assumes that his 'readers are anxious to use to the best purpose the fresh materials which the Revised Version offers for the understanding of the apostolic writings', and so gives 'typical illustrations ... of the purpose and nature of the changes which the revisers have introduced' (p. 1). The book is therefore a guide for the English reader wanting to approach as nearly as possible the position of the Greek scholar; particularly, it is an aid 'for him to trace out innumerable subtleties of harmonious correspondence between different parts of the New Testament which were hitherto obscured' (p. 4). Consequently Westcott, who again and again stresses faithfulness, gives this telling description of a translator's duty: he

> is bound to place all the facts in evidence, as far as it is possible for him to do so. He must feel that in such a case he has no right to obscure the least shade of expression which can be rendered; or to allow any prepossessions as to likelihood or fitness to outweigh direct evidence, and still less any attractiveness of a graceful phrase to hinder him from applying most strictly the ordinary laws of criticism to the determination and to the rendering of the original text.   (Pp. 5–6)

Going on, he raises the question that is so important here, what are 'the relative claims of faithfulness and elegance of idiom when they come into conflict'? We already know his answer, but it is an important piece of evidence for the view of the work of the K JB translators that has been offered here that this leader in the new effort at revision should appeal to the K JB as a precedent for his own adhesion to faithfulness:

> the example of the Authorised Version seems to show that it is better to incur the charge of harshness than to sacrifice a peculiarity of language which, if it does nothing else, arrests attention and reminds the reader that there is something in the words which is held to be more precious than the music of a familiar rhythm.
>
> (Pp. 6–7)

This is to take the K JB as a literal version which places faithfulness ahead of beauty. Westcott does not criticise the K JB for unfaithfulness through a desire for beauty: his arguments are always that it has been insufficiently faithful,[17] and that the revisers, with the benefit of accumulated scholarship, have been able to bring out more of the truth of the original. He makes these points without denying beauty to the K JB; he is well aware of the lure of its language, and

---

[17] Elsewhere he makes this judgement on the translators; 'but when every deduction is made for inconsistency of practice and inadequacy of method, the conclusion yet remains absolutely indisputable that their work issued in a version of the Bible better – because more faithful to the original – than any which had been given in English before' (*General View*, p. 274).

eager to point out occasions where the RV's fidelity produces renderings that may be responded to with more than a scholarly pleasure.

Westcott's heads of discussion are significant. With a methodicalness similar to that of the NT preface, he deals first with 'exactness in grammatical details', then the related questions of marking uniformities and differences of language. After a section on the restoration of vivid details through faithfulness of rendering, he develops the discussion into an exposition of the way the changes shed light upon theological matters. Only at the end does he deal with changes due to alterations of the Greek text. Most of the book, therefore, is about how the received text should be translated, and this adds to its value (in response to critics of the RV NT, he observes that only about one-sixth of the revisions are occasioned by changes in the Greek text (p. 14)).

The essential nature of the book is best illustrated by a discussion that turns on the precise rendering of two prepositions and leads directly to a theological truth:

> Two alterations ... each of a single syllable, are sufficient to illuminate our whole conception of the Christian faith. How few readers of the Authorised Version could enter into the meaning of the baptismal formula, the charter of our life; but now, when we reflect on the words, 'make disciples of all the nations, baptising them into (*not* in) the name of the Father and of the Son and of the Holy Ghost' (Matt. 28: 19), we come to know what is the mystery of our incorporation into the body of Christ. And as we learn this we enter into St Paul's words, 'the free gift of God is eternal life in (*not* through) Christ Jesus our Lord' (Rom. 6: 23). It is indeed most true that the Son of God won life for us, but it is not anything apart from Himself. We live, as He has made it possible for us to realise life, only in Him ... Am I then wrong in saying that he who has mastered the meaning of these two prepositions now truly rendered – '*into* the Name', '*in* Christ' – has found the central truth of Christianity? Certainly I would gladly have given the ten years of my life spent on the revision to bring only these two phrases of the New Testament to the heart of Englishmen. (Pp. 62–3)

Precision in even the smallest details, the result the closest possible apprehension of the truth of the Bible – the one is Westcott's method, the other his aim: in such a passage he encapsulates the school of translation that includes not only the RV, but the KJB, and behind that the work of Gregory Martin (to some extent), the Bishops, the Geneva translators, Coverdale, Tyndale and the Wyclif translators; and, still further back, the Vulgate and the Septuagint.

In this context Westcott's evidence on matters of vocabulary, English construction and rhythm is particularly interesting. He gives, as one would expect, many examples of places where familiar rhythms are sacrificed or new roughnesses tolerated in the interest of faithfulness. Attention to the Greek article changes 'the seats of them that sold doves' to 'the seats of them that sold the doves' (Matt. 21: 12), and he remarks, 'if at first hearing [this] sounds harsh, the pointed reference to the common offering of the poor is more than a compensation' (p. 59). This is not just a gain in accuracy for the sake of accuracy: it is also a gain in meaningfulness. Westcott often brings out such gains of literary vividness (here, as opposed to literary rhythm): many of the examples in chapter IV, 'vivid details: local and temporal colouring', show how the English reader is 'able to catch the fresh vigour of the original language' (p. 147). In such examples he often implies a literary artistry in the original. Showing the RV's fidelity to the Greek tenses, he notes how the KJB failed to mark the force of the imperfect in some parts of John's Gospel where the verb 'to stand' is used. He gives seven examples of the RV's amendment of the KJB's 'stood' to 'was standing', and concludes: 'in all these places the Authorised Version has "stood", for which the Revised Version has substituted the strict rendering, except in 7: 37, where the combination "was standing, and he cried" seemed unhappily (I think) to many too harsh. The detail is perhaps a small one; but still is it not just the master-touch which kindles each scene with life?' (pp. 46–7). Impatient readers who dismiss such changes as trivial or pedantic will 'lose a lesson on the vivid power of the Gospel narrative' (p. 43). These examples do not show the revisers aiming at artistic effect (even if collectively and against Westcott's better judgement they refuse to make a change that seems too harsh); rather, Westcott has no objection if the result happens to be aesthetically pleasing. Once, indeed, he claims that the change of 'His dear Son' to 'the Son of His Love' (Col. 1: 13), a change made to bring out the use of a genitive, 'is an enrichment of English scriptural language which cannot fail to pass into common use' (p. 33).

It seems that aesthetic matters hardly entered Westcott's mind while he worked at the Greek text and the English revision. He was happy to recognise gains in this area if they chanced to occur, but is quite unapologetic for losses. Only in discussing changes he would have preferred but which were not made does he show aesthetic judgement entering into the business of the revision; in such cases it was the collective judgement of the committee that the proposed change was too harsh or that 'the power of association was too strong to allow the disturbance of a familiar phrase' (p. 57n).

Taking Westcott's evidence with the slightly more liberal evidence from the rest of the committee and from the preface, we have found no more than might have been expected, that scholarship ruled, but that the literary consciousness of the time and AVolatry affected the committee, even if it often did so only after scholarship had produced its verdict. This is of major importance, for it allows two possible ways of viewing the evidence from the KJB. We may speculate that, if that evidence had been fuller, it would have shown something like the literary consciousness that affected the RV. Alternatively, we may refuse to speculate and conclude that no more literary consciousness went into the KJB than the absolute minimum that we have seen from Bois's notes. Either way, the result is the same: scholarship – or faithfulness – was bound to be the decisive force, as it was with the RV NT. There is no need to reinterpret the evidence from the KJB.

The reception of the New Testament

In absolute contrast to the dearth of evidence for the reception of the KJB, the RV NT may well have been the most-discussed English translation of them all. This is because it occupies a unique position in the history of English translations by being both the first ecclesiastical revision in two and a half centuries and the first made at a time when there was an ample structure for public discussion. Moreover, it was greeted with an unsurpassed eagerness. If the English were keen for it, the Americans were keener still, and its reception outdid even the famous occasion when the episode of *The Old Curiosity Shop* containing Little Nell's death was awaited by crowds on the dockside calling to the ship's passengers, 'Is Little Nell dead?' More than 300,000 copies were sold on the first day, daily newspapers (having had the text wired to them) serialised it, and reprints sprang up everywhere.[18]

Unprecedented interest did not guarantee success. Favourable response largely ignored questions of the English literary quality of the revision, and was confined to the likes of Phillips Brooks, that is, to scholarly Churchmen who shared Westcott's desire to know the truth of the Greek as closely as possible. Some of the negative criticism also confined itself to scholarly grounds: the revisers' mastery of Greek was questioned, and the principles on which the Greek text had been constructed were the subject of more serious objections. But it is the literary response that concerns us, particularly because its central element is a rooted dislike of the new such as we have seen on many occasions and which will continue to appear to the present day. Its archetypal anecdote is the 'mumpsimus' story and its archetypal figure William Beveridge declaring that 'it is a great prejudice to the new that it is new, wholly new; for whatsoever is new in religion at the best is unnecessary' (above, p. 43). This is not to pass

---

[18] See Hemphill, pp. 86–9. Hemphill's summary of the criticism – it takes over fifty pages, yet is far from complete and treats everything with admirable brevity – is invaluable.

judgement on the rightness or otherwise of the response but to keep clearly in mind the close link between familiarity and literary preference.

The *Edinburgh Review* may be allowed to stand for the generality of responses. Back in 1855 it had advocated a revision on several grounds, scholarship, presentation and archaism, and concluded that 'neither the researches of the clergy nor the intelligence of the laity have remained stationary. We have become desirous of knowing more, and they have acquired more to teach us.'[19] Whether or not the review of the RV NT is by the same author, by referring to this article, it begins from a position of sympathy perhaps representative of the expectations and hopes of many serious Christians. Nevertheless, a confession of disappointment comes quickly. The first effect of comparing the new with the old 'has been to enhance in no small degree the high estimate which we had previously formed of the merits of a work which ... may well be regarded as unsurpassed in the entire range of literature, whether sacred or profane'.[20] Disappointment with the RV and reinforced AVolatry lead to this very important distinction:

> we cannot read a chapter of the Gospels without perceiving the diametrically opposite principles which govern the procedure of the revisers of 1611 and of 1881. The former coveted earnestly, as the best gifts of translators, forcible English. They determined to make their version flexible and rhythmical; they cared but little for precision and minute accuracy; and literal reproduction of their original they utterly ignored, even to the verge of the limits prescribed to faithful rendering from one language to another. Our revisers strive, with undoubted learning and almost incredible industry, to reproduce the very order and turn of the words, the literal force of each tense and mood, and the rendering of each Greek term by the same English equivalent as far as practicable. They have obtained their ends, but at too great a price ... Every phase of New Testament scholarship was represented in the New Testament Company, but the niceties of idiomatic English appear to have found no champion, and no voice was raised to warn these eminent scholars of the dangers that threatened their work from over-refinement. (P. 173)

What a turnaround is here: the RV is exactly the same kind of literal translation that Selden in particular had characterised the KJB as being. Selden, whose comments had been noted in the *Review*'s 1855 article, had complained that 'the Bible is translated into English words rather than into English phrase', and added that this was 'well enough so long as scholars have to do with it, but

---

[19] Review of paragraph Bibles, vol. 102, no. 208 (October 1855), 418–35; p. 429.
[20] Vol. 154, no. 315 (July 1881), 157–88; p. 158. Hemphill does not include this article in his survey.

when it comes among the common people, Lord what gear do they make of it' (see volume 1, p. 229). The people's reaction may have changed, but what a defence of their work could the revisers have found here. The *Edinburgh Review* shows both how far the response to the KJB's language had changed and how far perception of literary quality can mould the perception of intentions. The KJB translators, creators of the familiar and loved, were supreme artists; the revisers, creators of the new and destroyers of the loved, were supreme pedants. The pedantry has its value, yet 'we are left with another critical commentary on the New Testament, but not with a new version which will mould our thoughts and afford a dignified vehicle for the great truths of revelation' (p. 188). So, in sorrow, the article concludes.

Cutting as all this is, it comes from a moderate critic predisposed to be friendly to the revision. There is no need to survey the enemies of the revision except to note that the most outspoken of them all, John William Burgon, Dean of Chichester, leaves no doubt that he is at least as much a Beveridge reborn as the Broughton he was so often dismissed as (see Hemphill, p. 101): 'we never spend half an hour over the unfortunate production before us without exclaiming with one in the Gospel, "the old is better" [Luke 5: 39]. Changes of *any* sort are unwelcome in such a book as the Bible, but the discovery that changes have been made *for the worse*, offends greatly' (p. 145).

The strength of the hostile criticism may have affected the OT revisers, and it is worth noting that some of the reservations were expressed by revisers currently working on the OT. To take the earliest example, the future bishop, John Perowne (like many Cambridge scholars, he achieved the immortality of having a street of that city named after him), found many of the new renderings praiseworthy, but objected to the practice of uniform rendering of single words as 'mere pedantry ... the surest way to destroy all freedom and all dignity of language', to that 'uncouth literalism' as a perpetual reminder to the reader 'that he is reading a translation', and to the 'inversion of the natural order of words in English' as 'construing rather than translating'.[21] Such views would have made themselves heard in the OT committee, and the vehemence with which they were expressed would have been all the stronger for the distaste caused by the NT. Despite the facts that the NT revisers were also critical and that the negative criticisms were all made within the committee while it was at work – facts which might be taken as negating the points just made – it seems probable that the NT's often extreme adherence to its sense of faithfulness helped to make the OT a somewhat different kind of translation. At all events, another of

---

[21] *Contemporary Review* (July 1881); adapted from Hemphill, pp. 93–4.

the OT revisers, Frederick Field, proposed an alternative understanding of faithfulness while discussing the NT, 'faithfulness to the sense and spirit of the original', not to its 'grammatical and etymological proprieties'.[22]

The preface to the Old Testament

Nothing in the preface to the Old Testament contradicts that to the New, yet it leaves a different impression and, without saying so directly, leads one to expect a lighter revision. One basic reason for this is that the OT revisers did not have to establish a new text of the original; rather, they 'have thought it most prudent to adopt the Masoretic Text as the basis of their work, and to depart from it, as the Authorised translators had done, only in exceptional cases' (p. v). Though Westcott had played down the importance of changes in the Greek text of the NT, this means that there was less scholarly pressure to revise the OT. There is another reason why the pressure was less, though the preface does not imply it: the NT is the theological heart of the Bible and there was less sense of significant errors in the KJB OT. The OT (and the Apocrypha) was revised because the NT was being revised rather than because there was an overwhelming need for it. So, referring to rules 1 and 2, the preface makes its already-quoted reference to the KJB as 'an English classic' and, rather than stressing faithfulness, says simply that 'the revisers have borne in mind that it was their duty not to make a new translation but to revise one already existing' (p. v). This is more in keeping with the stress on *necessary* changes in the original resolutions of Convocation, and may well have been influenced by the consequences of the NT revisers' strict sense of faithfulness. The preface goes on to describe what looks like light revision: the revisers

> have therefore departed from [the KJB] only in cases where they disagreed with the translators of 1611 as to the meaning or construction of a word or sentence; or where it was necessary for the sake of uniformity to render such parallel passages as were identical in Hebrew by the same English words, so that an English reader might know at once by comparison that a difference in the translation corresponded to a difference in the original; or where the language of the Authorised Version was liable to be misunderstood by reason of its being archaic or obscure; or, finally, where the rendering of an earlier English version seemed preferable, or where by an apparently slight change it was possible to bring out more fully the meaning of a passage of which the translation was already substantially accurate. (P. vi)

All bar the last of these describe what would have been thought of as necessary

---

[22] *Otium Norvicense*, as given in Hemphill, p. 99.

changes, but it is what is not said that is truly eloquent. Not only has 'faithfulness' – as a word though not as a general idea – disappeared, but so has the NT preface's criticism of the KJB's 'variety of expression'. The very next paragraph explains that the revisers have generally followed the KJB's use of 'Jehovah' rather than inserting it uniformly, and then, two paragraphs later, attention is drawn to one distinction that has 'been introduced with as much uniformity as appeared practicable or desirable'. The distinction is between 'tabernacle' and 'tent' 'as the renderings of two different Hebrew words', and is given as an example of the treatment of 'some words of very frequent occurrence'. This seems like an exception to prove the rule, and the explanation given for it confirms the difference of principle: it is not to promote scholarly perception of uniformities in the original (a tricky if not impossible task in the OT), but to avoid the confusion caused by the KJB's inconsistency.

A paragraph remarkable for its vagueness comes at the end of the general discussion: 'in making minor changes, whether in translation or language, the revisers have followed the example of the translators of the Authorised Version, who allowed themselves in this respect a reasonable freedom, without permitting their liberty to degenerate into license' (p. viii). The vagueness is surely there to avoid making it too obvious that the OT revisers dissented from their NT brethren. There can only be one thing, with respect to language, that they can mean by following the example of the KJB, that 'reasonable freedom' is 'the studied avoidance of uniformity' that the NT preface declared to be 'one of the blemishes' of the KJB. A glance at what must be the greatest concordance ever compiled, Strong's *Exhaustive Concordance*, shows that the OT revisers did not strive for uniformity in rendering individual words.[23] Perowne's objection to uniform rendering as 'mere pedantry' was heard in the OT committee – or, it may have sprung from decisions they had already taken. At all events, it is clear that the OT preface dissents from the practice of the NT revisers. Part of this dissent emerges as a stress on the example of the KJB rather than the truth of the original. This is not to say that accuracy was not the OT revisers' first principle – it clearly was – but that, in modern political slang, they were wet to Westcott's dry: consideration of English weighed more strongly against, but did not

---

[23] Strong has numbered all the Hebrew and Greek words so that one can tell immediately which original word the English word renders; moreover, the concordance is fully correlated with both the RV and the ASV. One of the few deliberate changes of vocabulary which are recorded in Wright's notes (discussed below) is 'ground' for 'earth'. Two Hebrew words are involved, and the concordance shows that the RV made some changes but remained almost as inconsistent as the KJB.

outweigh, consideration of the original. The OT preface announces, as softly as possible, a revision such as the majority of critics had wanted.

It is no surprise, then, that most of this preface is concerned with questions of language. A nice example of the desire to conform to the KJB is given in the discussion of the need to be consistent and to avoid misleading language:

> In consequence of the changes which have taken place in the English language, the term 'meat offering' has become inappropriate to describe an offering of which flesh was no part; and by the alteration to 'meal offering' a sufficiently accurate representation of the original has been obtained with the least possible change of form. (P. vi)

However, what is most interesting from the present point of view is the general discussion of archaism:

> In regard to the language of the Authorised Version, the revisers have thought it no part of their duty to reduce it to conformity with modern usage, and have therefore left untouched all archaisms, whether of language or construction, which though not in familiar use cause a reader no embarrassment and lead to no misunderstanding. They are aware that in so doing they will disappoint the large English-speaking race on the other side of the Atlantic, and it is a question upon which they are prepared to agree to a friendly difference of opinion. (P. vii)

Following an outline of principles similar to those given in the NT preface, 'two typical examples' are given:

> The verb 'to ear' in the sense of 'to plough' and the substantive 'earing' for 'ploughing' were very reluctantly abandoned, and only because it was ascertained that their meaning was unknown to many persons of good intelligence and education. But it was easy to put in their place equivalents which had a pedigree of almost equal antiquity, and it would have been an excess of conservatism to refuse to substitute for an unintelligible archaism an expression to which no ambiguity could be attached. On the other hand the word 'bolled' (Exod. 9: 31), which signifies 'podded for seed' and is known in provincial dialects, has no synonym in literary English. To have discarded it in favour of a less accurate or more paraphrastic expression would have been to impoverish the language; and it was therefore left, because it exactly expresses one view which is taken of the meaning of the original. (P. viii)

This is eloquent of care for the language: accuracy is consulted, ambiguity is removed wherever possible, but changes are only made in the most pressing cases, and then both dialect and literary English are consulted. Evidently the American revisers desired a fuller revision of the language, and the preface returns to this near the end, observing that many of the changes in the American appendix are 'changes of language which are involved in the essentially different circumstances of American and English readers' (p. x).

In a sense this revision of language, though it had an aesthetic purpose, was not an aesthetic matter. The revisers were not guided by taste in making their decisions; rather, they had a standard prescribed to them, and they followed it scrupulously. Only when 'the final review, which was in reality the completion of the second revision', is described does it appear that taste played a part: 'the company employed themselves in making a general survey of what they had done, deciding finally upon reserved points, harmonising inconsistencies, smoothing down roughnesses, removing unnecessary changes and generally giving finish and completeness to their work' (p. x). Smoothing roughnesses and giving finish, which sounds like the rubbing and polishing of the KJB preface, is here certainly a matter of style. And again there is the care that no unnecessary changes should be allowed to remain.

The OT preface points us towards language, and it is a happy chance that material exists which allows the OT changes of language to be examined more closely than the NT changes. There is Chambers's detailed account and there is a set of notes recording all the changes to the first six chapters of Genesis suggested at the first revision. First, though, we must return to critical discussions of the KJB.

Noah Webster, obsolescence and euphemism

With eighteenth-century critics and translators such as Pilkington and Purver almost totally forgotten, several mid-nineteenth-century critics took up the challenge of examining the KJB's language. Noah Webster (1758–1843), the great American lexicographer, was the first and most important. His *The Holy Bible ... in the Common Version. With Amendments of the Language* (1833), the fruit of lifelong biblical and linguistic studies,[24] is primarily a linguistic revision of the KJB, though 'a few errors in the translation, which are admitted on all hands to be obvious, have been corrected' (p. iv). What is more, it is done not in the refining spirit of a Harwood but in a spirit of reverence for the KJB that is compatible with the spirit of the RV. Webster regards the KJB's language as,

---

[24] Webster knew both Hebrew and Greek (and some eighteen other languages). Among other things, he had compared the KJB NT with the Greek in order to test Lowth's grammatical rules. His revised Bible eventually became widely used in America (see Harry R. Warfel, *Noah Webster: Schoolmaster to America* (1936; New York: Octagon, 1966), ch. xviii).

'in general, correct and perspicuous; the genuine popular English of Saxon origin; peculiarly adapted to the subjects; and in many passages uniting sublimity with beautiful simplicity'. He adds that in his view 'the general style of the version ought not to be altered' (p. iii). This makes him an ideal stalking-horse for approaching the way the RV as a whole deals with the language of the K JB, but there is a further very important reason for concentrating on him: from the evidence of the American appendices to both Testaments, it is clear that Webster substantially influenced the American revisers. Many of his suggestions find their way into these lists and were incorporated in the American Standard Version (ASV; 1901). So, whether or not the British committees were directly aware of Webster's work, many of his suggestions were made to them. Though the British revisers were aware of other discussions of the language of the K JB,[25] Webster's, if indirectly, was the one they had most to deal with.

In Webster's opinion,

> The language of the Bible has no inconsiderable influence in forming and preserving our national language. On this account the language of the common version ought to be correct in grammatical construction and in the use of appropriate words. This is the more important as men who are accustomed to read the Bible with veneration are apt to contract a predilection for its phraseology and thus become attached to phrases which are quaint or obsolete. This may be a real misfortune, for the use of words and phrases, when they have ceased to be a part of the living language and appear odd or singular, impairs the purity of the language and is apt to create a disrelish for it in those who have not, by long practice, contracted a like predilection. It may require some effort to subdue this predilection, but it may be done, and for the sake of the rising generation it is desirable. The language of the Scriptures ought to be pure, chaste, simple and perspicuous, free from any words or phrases which may excite observation by their singularity, and neither debased by vulgarisms nor tricked out with the ornaments of affected elegance.
> (P. iv)

Purver had made the same point, but Webster is neither as ambitious nor as eccentric as the poor Quaker. His alterations are of three main kinds:

> 1. The substitution of words and phrases now in good use for such as are wholly obsolete, or deemed below the dignity and solemnity of the subject.

[25] As well as the eighteenth-century material, criticisms were available from, among others, John Tricker Conquest, *The Holy Bible* (1841), Samuel Hinds, *Scripture and the Authorized Version of Scripture ... with ... a Glossary of Words which have become Obsolete in the Sense which they Bear in the Translation of the New Testament* (London and Dublin, 1845), and David Johnston, *Plea for a New English Version*. All of these give words Webster does not deal with. Hinds's is the most substantial list, and most of his words are not in Webster. A few of them are changed in the RV, and a few more in the ASV.

2. The correction of errors in grammar.

3. The insertion of euphemisms, words and phrases which are not very offensive to delicacy, in the place of such as cannot with propriety be uttered before a promiscuous audience.   (P. iv)

Consideration of 'the dignity and solemnity of the subject' smacks of Harwood, but otherwise the first two kinds of alteration were explicitly attempted by the revisers. Of the third kind they make no mention. Nevertheless, such corrections might clarify the meaning and remove any difficulties caused by apparent improprieties like that of Webster's own now unfortunate use of 'promiscuous'.

Webster not only gives a substantial list of the changes he has made to the language but discusses the reasons for them (pp. vii–xvi). Some concern tenses and other matters of grammar, some matters of scholarship and geography, but it will be sufficient to concentrate on the changes to vocabulary. There are familiar, obvious examples, and the RV in due course makes the appropriate changes. Among these are 'trow', for which he substitutes 'suppose', 'leasing' ('falsehood') and 'tache' ('button'). But he gives surprisingly few such examples, probably because his list is of 'principal alterations' and quite a few of the obsolete words are used only once or twice, as are 'trow' and 'leasing'. Other examples, apparently just as obvious, lead to mixed responses from the revisers. Webster would change 'wist', 'wit' and 'wot' to 'know' or 'knew', and the RV regularly changes the latter two but leaves 'wist' unchanged more often than it alters it. There are archaisms such as 'sodden' ('boiled') and 'fray' ('terrify' or 'drive away') which the RV leaves untouched. Finally there are archaisms such as 'travail', 'peradventure' and 'yea' which the RV sometimes alters but more often adds. One of the more extraordinary of these is 'ensample' (not given by Webster), which the RV twice changes to 'example' but once substitutes for 'example'. This confirms how conservative the revisers were. Where a choice of synonyms alone is concerned they keep revision to a minimum and they show a real desire to make their work sound more like the KJB than the KJB itself.

Webster's arguments are often very precise. Here are two discussions of meaning that anticipate (or may indeed have caused) changes in the RV. 'Coast', he observes, 'is never used to express the border, frontier or extremity of a kingdom or district of inland territory . . . Its application in the Scriptures is, in most cases, to a border of inland territory' (p. viii). It is therefore 'improper' and needs changing. Similarly,

In Daniel 3: 22 we read that the flame of the fire 'slew' the men that threw Shadrach and his companions into the furnace. This use of 'slew' is improper, so much so that the most illiterate man would perceive the impropriety of it. 'Slay' is used to denote killing by striking with any weapon whatever; but we never say a man is 'slain' by poison, by drowning or by burning. This distinction proceeds from the original signification of 'slay', which was to 'strike'. (P. viii)

The sharpest of these points turns on the distinction between 'shadow' and 'shade'. Webster speculates that this was not known at the time of the KJB, and argues that 'shadow of death' should be 'shades of death', but only the Americans, a little less loath to tinker with famous phrases, followed him.

The concern for 'the dignity and solemnity of the subject' only occasionally appears. Webster reduces the use of words such as 'wherein' and 'thereon' which 'are not wholly obsolete but are considered, except in technical language, inelegant' (p. vii), and substitutes 'afflict' for 'plague' as a verb because 'it is now too low or vulgar for a scriptural word' (p. viii), but most of his other changes of this sort concern possible indecencies. Only occasionally does the RV change 'wherein' and similar words; the one use of 'plague' as a verb becomes 'smite' (Ps. 89: 23), but only one of the six uses of 'plagued' is changed, to 'smote'. Appropriate dignity of language appears in practice to have had little effect on Webster and none on the revisers. The occasional addition of archaisms was the only means by which they sought to heighten the KJB's language.

Phrases such as 'would God', 'would to God' and 'God forbid' incur Webster's censure on two grounds, scholarly – 'they are not authorised by the original language, in which the name of the Supreme Being is not used' – and censorious – 'the insertion of them in the version has given countenance to the practice of introducing them into discourses and public speeches with a levity that is incompatible with a due veneration for the name of God' (p. ix). Some two centuries earlier Henry Jessey had made the identical point (see volume 1, p. 222). The Americans were inclined to agree, particularly over 'God forbid',[26] but the British make two changes only to these phrases. Here it seems that adherence to the idiom of the KJB, that is, AVolatry, outweighed both scholarship and concern over profane use of biblical language.

Levity was a major concern for Webster as it had been for many others before him, but only twice before had it been made an explicit issue for translators, in the instruction to the makers of the Bishops' Bible to find 'more convenient terms and phrases' for 'all such words as soundeth in the old translation to any offence of lightness or obscenity' (see volume 1, p. 117), and by Hugh Ross, who, following his French original (pp. 583–4), objected to the use of 'naked' in the Bible since 'none can read these texts [1 Sam. 19: 24, Isa. 20: 2–4, Mic. 1: 8

---

[26] See appendix to OT, 'classes of passages' VII.

and John 21: 7] without imagining that the persons spoken of in them were altogether *naked*' (p. 179). It was a matter both of inappropriate responses and of offensive language. Webster observes that 'many words and phrases are so offensive, especially to females, as to create a reluctance in young persons to attend Bible classes and schools, in which they are required to read passages which cannot be repeated without a blush, and containing words which, on other occasions, a child could not utter without rebuke' (p. xvi). This point was not new.[27] It had been made, far more provocatively, in 'a novel on the sofa or toilet of every woman of quality of all immoral books the most disgusting',[28] Matthew Lewis's *The Monk* (1797): Antonia's prudent mother,

> while she admired the beauties of the sacred writings, was convinced that unrestricted no reading more improper could be permitted a young woman. Many of the narratives can only tend to excite ideas the worst calculated for a female breast: everything is called plainly and roundly by its name, and the annals of a brothel would scarcely furnish a greater choice of indecent expressions. Yet this is the book which young women are recommended to study, which is put into the hands of children able to comprehend little more than those passages of which they had better remain ignorant, and which but too frequently inculcates the first rudiments of vice and gives the first alarm to the still sleeping passions . . . She had in consequence made two resolutions respecting the Bible. The first was that Antonia should not read it till she was of an age to feel its beauties and profit by its morality; the second, that it should be copied out with her own hand, and all improper passages either altered or omitted.[29]

It was this Websterised Bible that Antonia perused 'with an avidity, with a delight that was inexpressible', and it was this passage which particularly aroused Coleridge's ire.

Webster thought such revisions the most pressing of all, though 'difficulties occurred which I could not well remove' (p. xvi). He gives a list of offensive verses and passages (the longest are Ezek. 16 and 23) and regularly changes

---

[27] A reviser of similar ilk to Webster, Benjamin Boothroyd, observes that 'many offensive and indelicate expressions obtain' (*A New Family Bible and Improved Version* (Huddersfield, 1824), 'prospectus', unpaginated), but goes no further (he is almost as vague about general improvements needed in the language). William Alexander, in his *The Holy Bible . . .: Principally Designed to Facilitate the Audible or Social Reading of the Sacred Scriptures* (3 vols. (York, 1828)), remarks that there are passages which are not 'adapted to modern views of propriety' (1: vi). In America the *Knickerbocker* thought the KJB used 'language too foul to be uttered in decent society' (7 (April 1836), 355; as given in Allen Walker Read, 'Noah Webster as a euphemist', *Dialect Notes* 6: viii (1934), 385).

[28] From John Payne Collier's account of Coleridge's lecture 6, 1811–12, Coleridge, *Lectures 1808–1819, CW* 5, 1: 296.

[29] Ed. Howard Anderson (London: Oxford University Press, 1973), pp. 259–60.

'womb', 'teat', 'stones', 'privy member', 'piss', 'prostitute', 'whore' and 'stink', as well as Gen. 38: 9, 24, describing Onan, and 'her young one that cometh out from between her feet' (Deut. 28: 57).[30] Further examples are given in Henry Thomas Day's *Bible and Ritual Revision.* Noting that the KJB 'is obnoxious to the charge of offensive unseemliness', he cites half a dozen of the same verses and passages as Webster, and adds ten others.[31] Several of these are passages of narrative or denunciation, and, though Day believed that 'every versicle and word both in the Old and the New Testament can be rendered into English faithfully and without the least shock to the most sensitive decorum' (p. 19), it is difficult to know what he wanted if it was not censorship. The most striking example is Hab. 2: 15–16. The KJB reads,

> Woe unto him that giveth his neighbour drink, that puttest thy bottle to him, and makest him drunken also, that thou mayest look on their nakedness! Thou art filled with shame for glory: drink thou also, and let thy foreskin be uncovered: the cup of the Lord's right hand shall be turned unto thee, and shameful spewing shall be on thy glory.

Webster substituted 'vomiting' for 'spewing'. The RV thought more was needed:

> Woe unto him that giveth his neighbour drink, that addest thy venom thereto, and makest him drunken also, that thou mayest look on their nakedness! Thou art filled with shame for glory: drink thou also, and be as one uncircumcised: the cup of the Lord's right hand shall be turned unto thee, and foul shame shall be upon thy glory.

'Let thy foreskin be uncovered' is retained in the margin. The real solution in these cases is either to omit or to resort to vagueness, but then one is paraphrasing rather than translating. The Good News Bible, for instance, reads,

> You are doomed! In your fury you humiliated and disgraced your neighbours; you made them stagger as though they were drunk. You in turn will be covered with shame instead of honour. You yourself will drink and stagger. The Lord will make you drink your own cup of punishment, and your honour will be turned to disgrace.

Phil. 1: 8 is objectionable because of the phrase, 'how greatly I long after you all in the bowels of Jesus Christ'. The RV, similarly sensitive here and in some other places, changes 'bowels' to 'tender mercies'. From a contemporary point

---

[30] Here is Webster's full list: Gen. 20: 18; 29: 31; 30: 22; 34: 30; 38: 9 and 24; Exod. 7: 18; 16: 24; Lev. 19: 29; 21: 7; Deut. 22: 21; 23: 1; 28: 57; Judg. 2: 17; 1 Sam. 1: 5; 1 Kgs. 14: 10; 16: 11; 21: 21; 2 Kgs. 9: 8; 18: 27; Job 3: 10–12; 40: 17; Ps. 22: 9–10; 38: 5; 106: 39; Eccles. 11: 5; Isa. 36: 12; Ezekiel 16 and 23; John 11: 39; Eph. 5: 5. He adds an etcetera.

[31] Gen. 9: 20–7; 19: 30–8; Numbers 25; 1 Sam. 25: 22; Hab. 2: 15–16; Rom. 1: 24–32; 1 Corinthians 7; 1 Thess. 4: 1–6; Phil. 1: 8 and 2 Pet. 2: 22 (pp. 18–19).

of view, the most necessary of these changes to a Hebrew idiom is to S. of S. 5: 4, 'my bowels were moved for him'. Perhaps the most curious objection is to 'stink'. The *OED* notes of it in the sense 'to emit a strong offensive smell', 'now implying violent disgust on the part of the speaker: in ordinary polite use avoided as unpleasantly forcible'. It may be that 'stink' was too closely associated with 'fart' for delicate ears, and in this respect American ears were more delicate than English. Typical of Webster's changes is Gen. 38: 9: 'and Onan knew that the seed would not be his: and it came to pass, when he went in to his brother's wife, that he frustrated the purpose, lest he should give seed to his brother'.[32]

Though the American revisers agreed with Webster about 'stink', both sets of revisers were less squeamish than the lexicographer. They do change 'piss' to 'water'; 'whore' they generally change to 'harlot', and 'whoremonger' to 'fornicator', but they keep 'went a whoring'. They change the one use of 'prostitute', but retain 'womb', 'stones' and 'privy member'.[33] Evidently propriety mattered a little, but not to the extent that we can say the revisers wished to raise the literary tone of the Bible. It is one thing to change a few words with obscene associations (even 'stink' is in this category), another to undertake a general elevation of language.

What Webster's evidence as a whole confirms is that, with some differences between the English and the Americans, the revisers were exceedingly conservative in their approach to the language of the KJB. They modernised as sparingly as possible, they refined only where obscenity was an issue, and they did indeed accept archaism wherever they felt it did not seriously interfere with comprehension. These observations, it should be remembered, are made in relation to a reviser who was himself conservative, only rarely choosing more elegant words and, for the most part, treading a judicious path between his admiration for the KJB and his knowledge of contemporary proprieties of language and grammar.

Notes from the first revision of Genesis

This is not to say that the British revisers (and presumably the Americans) did not think about literary improvements to the language. Not

---

[32] H. L. Mencken, ignoring the continuity of such worries about the Bible, places these changes in the context of what he calls the American 'Golden Age of euphemism', the 1830s and 1840s (*The American Language*, 4th edn (1936; New York: Knopf, 1980), p. 303).

[33] I presume the alteration of 'stone' to 'thighs' in Job 40: 17 is a question of meaning, not euphemism. One might add 'teats' to the list. The British revisers alter one of its three occurrences, the Americans all of them.

only did they consider many, if not all of Webster's suggestions, but direct evidence survives from the British OT committee that they made their own suggestions for more felicitous phrasings. William Aldis Wright, secretary of that committee, scrupulously recorded all the changes proposed to the first six chapters of Genesis during the initial consideration of these chapters.[34] The notes are headed 'proposed alterations in the Authorised Version'. Against every verse where alterations were proposed Wright records the original reading, the proposed change or changes and a number or numbers which correspond to 'the members of the Company in the order in which they stand in the printed list'. An *m* after a number 'indicates that the translation is to be placed in the *margin*' (p. 1). Unfortunately these numbers, which range from one to twenty-seven, cannot be reconciled with any printed list I have seen, so anonymity is preserved. Six of the twenty-seven either made no suggestions or did not attend these discussions. Altogether some 455 words or phrases were considered and 1,470 suggestions made. Translator nineteen was the most active, contributing to or agreeing with 174 suggestions. What is missing from the notes is any record of the reasons for the suggested changes. In this they differ somewhat from Bois's notes for the KJB, and they differ further in being a record of first rather than last discussions. Though correspondence with America and later discussions produced further changes, it seems that the most substantial work was done in the first revision. Wright's notes, then, give us a unique glimpse of a committee of revisers at the beginning of their work.

In the KJB, Gen. 3: 6 reads:

> And when the woman saw that the tree *was* good for food, and that it *was* pleasant to the eyes, and a tree to be desired to make one wise, she took of the fruit thereof, and did eat, and gave also unto her husband with her; and he did eat.

The original KJB had two marginal notes (it is not clear which edition the revisers worked from, and their references to marginal notes do not always correspond to the original); one is to 'pleasant', '*Heb. a desire*'; the other adds two references to 'fruit thereof'. The RV changes the verse to:

> And when the woman saw that the tree was good for food, and that it was a delight to the eyes, and that the tree was to be desired to make one wise, she took of the fruit thereof, and did eat; and she gave also unto her husband with her, and he did eat.

A note follows 'that the tree was', 'Or, *desirable to look upon*'. All the changes

---

[34] A hectographic, bound reproduction of the unpublished and previously undiscussed notes is held by the Cambridge University Library. Wright's handwriting, though neat, is sometimes too small for legibility, and legibility is also sometimes impaired by the binding.

except for the deletion of the KJB's notes appear in Wright's notes (he uses a square bracket to denote the end of the KJB's phrases, and a dash for the start of a new phrase):

> And when the . . . she took] and the . . . and she took 4. 16. – pleasant to] a lust of (1 John 2: 16) 5. desirable to 27. a delight (or, desire) to 7. 27*m.* – and a tree . . . wise] yea, delightsome was the tree to contemplate 19. and a tree] and that the tree was 11. 16. 21. 22. 27. – to be desired to make one wise] to be desired to make one sagacious 11. desirable to look upon 4*m.* to be desired to look upon 2*m.* 13*m.* to be desired to make wise (& in marg. many of the versions have *desirable to behold*) 6. pleasant to regard (or, contemplate) 7. 27. desirable to behold 8. – the fruit thereof] its fruit 19. – and gave] and she gave 16.   (Pp. 5–6)

Some of the considerations are scholarly – the suggested link with 1 John's 'the lust of the flesh' and the suggested marginal note to 'many of the versions' – but more are literary. To change 'wise' to 'sagacious', or 'look upon' to 'behold', would be to raise the literary tone of the passage. 'Yea, delightsome was the tree to contemplate' shows both the desire to increase the archaic flavour ('yea', as we have seen, was frequently added) and the desire for elegance. In the end only one of the changes adopted is clearly made for the sake of the language, the substitution of 'and that the tree was' for the more awkward 'and a tree to be desired'. Other phrases that appear awkward by modern standards such as 'her husband with her' are left unaltered. This one verse, then, shows that literary considerations did enter into the work and affect the result, but also that the revisers resisted the temptation some of them felt to make substantial 'improvements'.

In one important respect this verse is atypical of the work on the first six chapters. Taken as a whole, the chapters are lightly revised and the revisers' restraint is very evident. Wright's notes on the verse are also atypical in showing so many changes that were eventually adopted. If one takes the first chapter only, the RV makes twelve alterations (not counting repetitions of the same kind of alteration), of which five do not appear in his notes, including the most substantial and felicitous alteration, 'and there was evening and there was morning, one day' (etc.). In reaching these seven accepted alterations, the revisers considered some 55 readings in the KJB (not counting repetitions and suggested deletions from the margin), and made some 105 suggestions, including no fewer than 12 suggestions for 'bring forth abundantly the moving creature that hath life' (1: 20), one of which was adopted for the margin while the text remained unchanged.

The progress of this last, very minor change can be traced still further.

Wright's copy of the printed 'second revision' is also preserved at the Cambridge University Library (Adv b 100 41). It contains the printed preferences of the American company and Wright's notes, made in 1875, as to final decisions. The British revisers had opted for 'swarm with the moving creature that hath life', while the Americans preferred another of their suggestions, 'swarm with swarms of living creatures'. Wright struck through the first, indicating approval of the latter reading, which was placed in the margin while the KJB reading was restored to the text. This bespeaks both diligence and eventual restraint. Every jot and tittle of the text was considered, and it is worth bearing in mind that the notes from the first revision only represent those occasions when, after consideration, at least one of the revisers contemplated a change. Yet, even having worked so carefully, the revisers remained open to further thoughts, whence the alterations that did not occur to them at this time, and they often rejected change when, at the last, they felt it was insufficiently justified.

An American account of changes in the Old Testament

After these notes, the closest we can get to the OT revisers at work is a very substantial account of the reasons for some of the changes given by one of the American revisers, Talbot W. Chambers (1819–96), minister of the Collegiate Dutch Church of New York, in his *A Companion to the Revised Old Testament*. His purpose is 'to furnish a tolerably fair conception of the revisers' work, both in amount and character'. He is careful to point out that he is working from memory, but thinks it unlikely that errors have crept in for the curious reason that 'the revision never contemplated novelties, but only a summing up of the results of criticism during the last two centuries' (p. 80). Since the English revisers did not communicate the reasons for their decisions to the Americans,[35] Chambers's account cannot be taken as speaking for the British revisers. Nor, given that it is based on memory and 'the results of criticism', can it be taken as a properly authoritative account of the Americans' reasons. Even so, it is uniquely informed, as indispensable for any student of translation as Westcott's account of the NT revisions, and as biassed: Chambers constantly stresses the aesthetic side of translation.

Archaism is his first reason for revision, but he gives it little discussion (pp. 19–22 contain a selective list of archaisms that were changed). His emphasis

---

[35] The surviving records, as I have shown, suggest that reasons were not recorded. Westcott writes of 'the general and perfectly independent concurrence of the American revisers' (p. 13).

is on matters of scholarship and style. Among the scholarly changes most accessible to general readers are what we may call logical changes. The simplest example is the change of 'wine bottles' to 'wine-skins', 'of which alone it could be said that they were "rent and bound up"' (Josh. 9: 4, 13; p. 98). Similarly logical are the changes that demythologise the KJB. One of these shows something that could not have been inferred from the OT preface, which observes that 'terms of natural history have been changed only where it was certain that the Authorised Version was incorrect and where there was sufficient evidence for the substituted rendering' (p. vi). Unicorns become wild-oxen, displacing 'a mythological creature for a real animal well known in the East' (p. 89). What Chambers, who often simplifies, does not add is that the revisers made this alteration tentatively, putting in the margin of Num. 23: 22 'or, *ox-antelope* Heb. *reem*', and referring back to this note when the word is used again.

Often such changes are made with the general aim of removing ambiguity from the text (and consequently using the margin to indicate other possibilities). Sometimes, however, ambiguity or obscurity are simply inescapable. Chambers notes a logical and demythologising change which is also to be found in Wright's notes. Num. 13: 33, 'and there we saw the giants', becomes 'and there we saw the Nephilim', with 'or, *giants*' in the margin. He explains that '"Nephilim" (which is merely the Hebrew word in English letters) is substituted for "giants", as in Gen. 6: 4, because the meaning of the word is uncertain, and the ordinary reader is as well able as the scholar to gather it from the connection' (p. 88). Wright's notes show that the revisers also considered the following possibilities, 'the giants were', 'there were men of violence', 'there were Nephilim (men of violence)' and 'there were marvellous men of violence'. To put Wright with Chambers is to show the complexities behind final decisions.

Many of the changes combine scholarly and stylistic considerations. In Gen. 49: 5 the KJB's margin (slightly altered, though Chambers does not mention this) is used 'as being both more literal and more expressive' (p. 82). Lev. 17: 11 is changed from 'for it is the blood that maketh an atonement for the soul' to 'for it is the blood that maketh atonement by reason of the life' because this 'is at once more faithful and expressive than the Authorised Version' (p. 86). 'The voice of one speaking' (Num. 7: 89) becomes 'the Voice speaking', 'which is more literal and more vivid' (p. 87).

So far, though the changes are examined with less scholarly thoroughness and without method, there is nothing out of keeping with the changes Westcott details. However, Chambers does not hesitate to give reasons that are principally aesthetic. The change to Num. 24: 2–3 and 15–16, 'representing the seer [Balaam] in the first instance with eyes closed and in the second with eyes opened, is quite agreeable to the original, and at the same time much more poetic and striking than the Authorised Version, since it conveys the conception of one whose bodily vision is closed against all outward things, while his inner sense, on the contrary, is divinely illumined' (p. 89). This is a change for felicity of meaning that is neither justified nor forbidden by the original, but rather 'quite agreeable to' it. Many similar examples contain no reference to the originals, but rest on an assertion of some kind of superiority to the KJB, with faithfulness to an ambiguous original being taken for granted.

In most cases the literary aspect of the changes is a matter of poetic force and clarity. Only in one instance does sound come close to playing a part, the change from 'be merciful, O Lord, unto thy people Israel, whom thou hast redeemed, and lay not innocent blood unto thy people of Israel's charge, and the blood shall be forgiven them' (Deut. 21: 8) to 'forgive, O Lord, thy people Israel, whom thou hast redeemed, and suffer not innocent blood *to remain* in the midst of thy people Israel. And the blood shall be forgiven them.' Taking the tone of a reviewer rather than a reporter, Chambers says this is more accurate and smooth (p. 93).

Chambers makes no attempt to arrange his comments according to type; rather, he works steadily through the Bible. Job, by common consent, was the most successfully revised of the OT books. Here, complete and characteristic, is what Chambers reports on Job 30 and 31:

> In ch. 30 many obscurities are removed. In v. 20 'thou regardest me *not*' is properly changed to 'thou lookest at me' – i.e., in silent indifference, as the sense requires. In 31: 31 an obvious error that disturbs the sense and the connection is amended; and in 35, instead of the prosaic and incorrect, 'Oh that one would hear me! Behold, my desire is that the Almighty would answer me', the revision reproduces the vigour of the original,
>
> > Oh that I had one to hear me!
> > (Lo, here is my signature, let the Almighty answer me;)
> > And that I *had* the indictment which my adversary hath written!
>
> Job offers to affix his sign manual to the protestations of innocence already made, and prays to see the charge against him, which is very different from the AV's absurd rendering, 'Oh that mine adversary had written a book!'　　　　(Pp. 116–17)

Particularly significant is the sense of the literary quality of the original and the pleasure in having been able to reproduce some of it.

Such examples are sufficient to confirm that the OT revisers worked with a literary awareness and to suggest that sometimes it was their primary motive. This is not to say that questions of scholarship do not predominate but that Chambers is particularly keen to show changes where an increase in accuracy – and often in literalness – has literary benefits. In part he can do this because he makes, at best, a blurred distinction between scholarly and stylistic matters, constantly seeing gains in clarity, that is, improvements in the faithful rendering of the original, as literary gains. Nevertheless, the emphasis he repeatedly gives to these literary gains and the emphasis the OT preface gives to questions of language show that the character of the OT revision was somewhat different from that of the NT revision. The relative infrequency of pressing matters of scholarship made the OT a comparatively light revision wherein necessity was more often a deciding factor than faithfulness: the bulk of the suggestions recorded by Wright were rejected, and many of those suggestions were stylistic. Where the NT revisers found themselves considering questions of the Greek ahead of questions of English, the OT revisers, though just as attentive to their original, found that their decisions much more often depended on questions of English. Accordingly there is a larger, though still subordinate, aesthetic dimension to their work.

Conclusion

Many people have imagined that the KJB was a stylistic revision made to capture the English language at its best and to give an appropriate aura of beauty to the English Bible. The revised OT is the closest an official translation has come to giving direct evidence of something like these concerns, so we must speculate as to whether we would have found the same aesthetic dimension if notes such as Wright's had been preserved and if a Chambers had been found among the KJB translators. The first point has to be negative. Although Wright and Chambers take us further than the OT preface, they are consistent with its discussion of questions of language and its implications that stylistic matters were considered. These aspects are missing from the KJB preface, so we have no basis for supposing that a record of the initial discussions of the first Westminster company would have shown the interest in style exhibited by the OT revisers. Rather, if we have to make a supposition, it would go the other way, since the only bases for it are the implications of the preface and the example of Bois's notes.

However, this is not to close the matter. The revised OT does show that a group of scholarly translators making an official revision under a primary rule of faithfulness could still bring an aesthetic dimension to their work, at least in circumstances where style was a real issue and where the truth of the original was not an overwhelming issue. Did these circumstances exist for some or all of the companies that made the KJB? We can give a reasonably firm negative to the first on several grounds. First, literary translation of the Bible until, at the earliest, the end of the eighteenth century produced very different results from the KJB. It is only when one comes to a Webster in the nineteenth century that something not too far removed from a literary revision produces a result similar to that produced by the great sequence of translations, and that result is of course a product of admiration for the KJB as a masterpiece of language and literature. Second, literature and religion were quite separate through the time of the great translations, whereas for the Victorians and their counterparts in America the separation hardly existed. Not one of the KJB translators could have elided literary and scholarly considerations as Chambers did. Third, there is no evidence that the KJB translators thought highly of the style of their work, and substantial evidence in their preface that their sense of good style was very different from the language in which the demands of the original and the ideal of being understood even by the very vulgar forced them to translate.

It is difficult to be as clear about the second circumstance, especially as 'the truth of the original' is a complex matter. Much of the literalism of the RV NT comes from a belief that every jot and tittle of the Greek is ascertainable and significant, and ought to be rendered if at all possible. Mostly the truth can be determined; where it is uncertain, the doubt can and should be recorded. Here truth seems to be an almost scientific matter, attainable by exact scholarship. But the OT revisers seem to have had a more poetic conception of the truth of the original, perhaps because it was more often uncertain, perhaps also because it was often less theologically urgent. We simply do not know how difficult a matter all the groups of KJB translators found this question. Bois and his fellow-workers certainly laboured just as hard as Westcott at the truth of the Greek, but at other stages and in other parts of the work the translators may have felt differently, though in just what way is uncertain. It seems that the greater a translator's sense of the theological importance and precision of the original, the less freedom he has to consider the quality of the translation as language. The probabilities, therefore, are against our hypothetical lost evidence proving that something like the literary consciousness that went into the making of the revised OT did indeed go into the making of parts, at least, of the KJB.

An aside: dialect versions

Much of the history of Bible translation from, say, the Syriac Peshitta or the Old Latin to Tyndale and Coverdale in English is a history of attempts to open the Bible to the people in their own language. All such translations in a sense are dialect versions, and many of them were made into languages that had no established register into which to cast the Bible. The effort to make such versions continued and continues, from the making of the Welsh Bible (1567) and the attempts to make Gaelic Bibles (an Irish Gaelic NT was published in 1602) through the multitudinous efforts of the Bible Societies to contemporary efforts such as the present work on a new Maori Bible.[36] The purpose of almost all these versions is evangelistic.

Another purpose began to appear in some mid-nineteenth-century dialect versions, the preservation of language. The projected new Maori version of the Bible, though it is essentially evangelical, points in this direction, for it is intended in part as a 'book for students studying the language'.[37] Bible translation could be used as a way of preserving endangered languages or dialects, or as a way of demonstrating linguistic variation. This latter philological interest seems to have been the motivation for a series of versions of the Song of Songs, many of which were made especially for Prince Louis Lucien Bonaparte, who paid for their publication in editions of 250 between 1858 and 1860.[38] One set formed the *Celtic Hexapla, Being the Song of Solomon in all the Living Dialects of the Gaelic and Cambrian Languages* (London, 1858), but of greater interest is the dialect series: it contains, for instance, four different Yorkshire versions, North, West, Craven and Sheffield. In a different format – and so perhaps not directly associated with Bonaparte, but from the same time – was a series which included Cumberland, Central Cumberland and Craven, West Riding. Each of these is preceded with notes on the dialect, spelling, punctuation, and so on. Here is part of one of the Bonaparte series, Henry Scott Riddell's version in Lowland Scotch (1858):

> Pu' me, we wull rin efter thee: the King hes brung me intil his chammers; we wull be gladsome an' rejoyce in thee; we wull mind thy loefe mair nor wyne: the leal an' aefauld loe thee. I am blak but bonnie, O ye douchters o' Jerusalem, as the sheilins o'

[36] Basic information on Welsh, Gaelic and Manx translations may be found in *CHB* III: 170–4. A more detailed account of Scottish Gaelic work is given by Donald Meek, 'The Gaelic Bible', in David F. Wright, pp. 9–23.

[37] *Evening Post* (Wellington, NZ) (15 April 1985).

[38] A brief account of Bonaparte is to be found in Graham Tulloch's *A History of the Scots Bible: With Selected Texts* (Aberdeen: Aberdeen University Press, 1989), pp. 19–20.

Kedar, as the coortins o' Solomon. Glowerna at me becaus I am blak, becaus the sun hes shaine on me: my mither's childer wer angrie wi' me; thaye maede me keepir o' the vyneyairds, but mine ain vyneyaird I haena keepet. Acquant me, O thou wham my saul loeist, wi' whare though feedist, wi' whare thou mak'st thy hirsel til rest at nuun: for wharefor shud I be als ane that gangs danderin' agley efter the hirsels o' thy cumrades?   (1: 4–7)

A Sassenach is under almost as much difficulty in commenting on this as a Pakeha on a Maori version, yet it seems hardly likely to commend itself as a felicitous version with its triple uncertainty of tone – the Hebraic elements seem more alien in such a setting, and the idiom of the KJB jars against the occasional energetic colloquialism such as 'gangs danderin' agley'. But such commentary probably misses the point: what Riddell has produced is the mirror image of Rolle's Psalter or the early Wycliffite version, a version that is the equivalent of an interlinear gloss, but as a guide to the Lowland Scotch rather than a guide to the meaning of the translated version, the KJB. Now, knowing the meaning of the passage, one can go to Riddell's version and discover that the Lowland Scotch for 'flock' is 'hirsel'. If there is a lesson for translators, it is essentially that of versions like Rolle's: the energy of a new language is vitiated by adherence to the form of another language – until, that is, that form becomes sufficiently familiar to be accepted as a special form of the new language.

These versions not only take the KJB as a perennial standard against which to reflect their dialect, but also show the Bible becoming a book of linguistic as well as literary interest. Descended from them are versions of less purely philological interest and, often, greater literary success. Skipping over versions such as P. Hately Waddell's *The Psalms in Scots* (1871), two twentieth-century versions have illustrative value here. In the 1930s a Methodist local preacher, 'Jim Cladpole' (James Richards), made and printed Sussex versions of various parts of Scripture. His version of Psalm 23 (1937) retailed for a penny and contained this:

> Yea, though I walk 'tween hills
> De shaades of death all through;
> Of evil I wunt be afeardt
> Acos I walk wid You.

> Your kind of Sussex bat,
> Your kind of Pyecombe crook,
> Dey comfort me; (and 'sure me I
> To You for help can look.)

Sternhold and Hopkins could do no worse than the last line and a half, but there is a pleasing and seemingly apt country energy and simplicity to the rest that suggests that dialect translation has a potential vividness lacking in versions that try to use biblical or standard English. Though Cladpole worked from the KJB or the RV, there is little sense of its English working against his, and the results can be charmingly convincing:

> While He was talking a messenger come to de head one of de synagogue, from he's home, who said, 'Your daughter be dead, why trouble de Teacher any more?' But Saver heard what was said, and He said to de head one of de synagogue, 'Dunt be afraid, onny believe!' And He wuddent let any of de oders goo wid Him except Rockman, James and John de broder of James. And when He got to de house He see'd de folk maaking a gurt adoo, crying and wailing a lot. And when he was inside, He said, 'Why do you cry and maak so much noise? De child beant dead, onny asleep. And dey laughed and jeered at Him. Den He turned hem all out, and took de fader and moder of de girl and He's three prentices wid Him into de room where de girl was laid out. Den He took holt of her hand, and said, '*Talitha cumi*' which means 'come along liddle gel get up!' And drackly minute de gel got up and walked, for she was twelve yeers old. And dey was astonished and reglar overjoyed. And He told hem not to goo on talking about it; but to give her summat to eat.
>
> (*De Good News according to Mark*, 5: 35–43)

Similar effects are gained by a pioneer of interracial farming in Georgia, USA, who held a doctorate in NT Greek from Southern Baptist Theological Seminary, Clarence L. Jordan (1912–69). His 'Cotton Patch Versions' of parts of the NT were intended

> to help the modern reader have the same sense of participation in [the Scriptures] which the early Christians must have had . . . By stripping away the fancy language, the artificial piety and the barriers of time and distance, this version puts Jesus and his people in the midst of our modern world, living where we live, talking as we talk, working, hurting, praying, bleeding, dying, conquering, alongside the rest of us. It seeks to restore the original feeling and excitement of the fast-breaking *news* – good news – rather than musty history.
>
> (Pp. 9–10)

Cladpole had had something of this effect, and we have seen his daring use of 'Sussex' and 'Pyecombe'. Jordan takes such translation still further, often with rather comic – yet not, one feels, irreverent – effect.[39] A longer passage is needed

---

[39] While Jordan and Cladpole do not deal with this issue, two other makers of dialect versions do. Carl Burke's *God is for Real, Man* (1967) has illustrations by the cartoonist Papas; observing that 'some, no doubt, will find this book amusing', he replies that 'it was done in almost deadpan seriousness' (p. 135). By contrast, Frank Shaw is unashamed of perhaps appearing irreverent, for 'irreverence could be like beauty: in the eye of the beholder', and he goes on to suggest that the Gospels have a comic element in them (Dick Williams and Frank Shaw, *The Gospels in Scouse* (1967; rev. edn, London: White Lion, 1977), pp. 11–12).

to give a proper sense of the character – weakness as well as strength – of his work.

> When Jesus came into the region of Augusta, he asked his students, 'Who do people think the son of man is?'
>
> They said, 'Some say John the Baptizer, others say Elijah, and still others, Jeremiah or one of the famous preachers.'
>
> 'But you, who do you think I am?' he asked.
>
> Simon the Rock spoke right up and said, 'You are the Leader, the Living God's Man.'
>
> 'You are beautiful, Simon Johnson!' exclaimed Jesus. 'This isn't human reasoning, but divine revelation. And I want to tell you, you are Rock, and on this rock I will build my fellowship, and the doors of death will not hold out against it. I will give you the keys of the God Movement, and whatever you bind in the physical realm shall have been bound in the spiritual realm, and whatever you loose in the physical realm shall have been loosed in the spiritual realm.' Then he strongly warned them to tell no one that he was the Leader.
>
> From then on Leader Jesus began to make clear to his students that he had to go to Atlanta and to go through terrible things at the hands of the leading church people – to be killed, and three days later to be raised! But Rock collared him and began to take him to task. 'Not on your life, sir', he said, 'Be dadblamed if this will ever happen to you.' Jesus whirled on Rock and said, 'Get away from here, you devil; you are gumming up the works for me, because you're not following God's ideas but human reasoning!' Jesus then said to his students, 'If a man wants to walk my way, he must abandon self, accept his lynching, and share my life. For the person who aims to save his life will lose it, and the one who loses his life for my cause will find it. What's a man's advantage if in getting the whole world he loses his life? Indeed, what shall a man trade in his life for?'
>
> (Matt. 16: 13–26)

To some extent it is as if Uncle Remus or Huck Finn had set out to tell the Bible story: Jordan is in their tradition of semi-literate slang story-telling. The accent is closer to Uncle Remus than to Huck, but Joel Chandler Harris framed Uncle Remus with standard English narrative; like Twain, Jordan uses a colloquial narrator. However, he does not exploit varying levels of language as, say, Scott and James Hogg did in their portrayals of a variety of Scottish religious characters. Jordan's idiom is, as far as he can make it, homogeneous. Like the geography of his translation, his narrator, his Jesus and the disciples, his Jews, Gentiles, publicans and pharisees are all Georgian; all speak a language spiced with slang. The result is, by and large, a real sense of homely humanity. It is even a sense of universal humanity. Like Scott, exploiting varieties of Scottish English, or Twain, exploiting Huck's Mississippi idiom, or Lawrence, exploiting Nottinghamshire working-class language – so one could go on –

Jordan is writing in a language all English speakers can read. William Laughton Lorimer's *The New Testament in Scots* (Edinburgh: Southside, 1983) confirms the point. Only a Scots reader can understand, 'syne he stricklie chairged the disciples no tae mouband a wurd til onie-ane at he wis the Christ' (Matt. 16: 20), most particularly because of 'mouband'. Lorimer has crossed the line between accessible slang and a partly separate and therefore exclusive language.

For all Jordan's efforts, his is not a pure slang: the tug of standard English is often felt, as in 'then he strongly warned them to tell no one that he was the Leader', but such phrases emerge as flatness in the prose rather than inconsistency, as in Riddell's version. The flavour is weakened rather than destroyed. Occasionally too there are failures of imagination in the rendering of images, as in the retention of the image of binding and loosing. But such failures are rare and serve rather to underline just how successful Jordan usually is in his adaptations. He comments on one of the bolder changes, the use of 'lynching', in the introduction:

> there just isn't any word in our vocabulary which adequately translates the Greek word for 'crucifixion'. *Our* crosses are so shined, so polished, so respectable that to be impaled on one of them would seem to be a blessed experience. We have thus emptied the term 'crucifixion' of its original content of terrific emotion, of violence, of indignity and stigma, of defeat. I have translated it as 'lynching', well aware that this is not technically correct. Jesus was officially tried and legally condemned, elements generally lacking in a lynching. But having observed the operation of Southern 'justice', and at times having been its victim, I can testify that more people have been lynched 'by judicial action' than by unofficial ropes. Pilate at least had the courage and the honesty publicly to wash his hands and disavow all legal responsibility. 'See to it yourselves', he told the mob. And they did. They crucified him in Judea and they strung him up in Georgia, with a noose tied to a pine tree.[40]

This is a powerful statement of method and purpose. As Jordan concludes his introduction, Jesus 'may come alive. And we too'. The effect is neither to produce a version that sounds appropriately biblical nor a banal everyday version, but to show that it is possible to translate the Bible so as to give it the energetic immediacy normally associated with some fiction, and to make one feel that the original had something of this quality.

[40] Pp. 10–11. Burke regularly uses this kind of alteration. *God is for Real, Man* 'represents a search for a way in which spiritual truths can be taught in frames of reference that are real and vivid, in language and thought patterns that are understood and that have meaning. It is an attempt to permit the so-called inner-city adolescent to speak to us, rather than us to him' (pp. 134–5), and he gives an interesting account of how the beginning of Psalm 23 came to be paraphrased as 'the Lord is like my probation officer' (pp. 136–7).

In a sense this is literary translation, but it could hardly be further removed from such 'literary' efforts as Harwood's. In that work a conception of literary supremacy led to a disastrous elaborate paraphrase, but here a conviction of the text's imaginative presence, a conviction that is both religious and literary, produces a translation of genuine literary quality. One might ordinarily think of Jordan's work as paraphrase, yet, by comparison with most paraphrases, verse such as Dennis's or prose such as Harwood's, it is a translation, not just carrying the words across to a new language but carrying the people, the places and the frame of reference across to the new environment. The passage shows Jerusalem translated as Atlanta, and this literal transference (the verbal root is the same) is applied throughout. Moreover, for all that the language seems so casual, there lies behind it a sharp awareness of the Greek. The passage has one of Jordan's rare footnotes after 'on this rock':

> A literal translation of the Greek goes like this: 'You are *petros* [rock, masculine gender] and on this *petra* [rock, feminine gender] I will build ...' Obviously the masculine form refers to the disciple. The feminine cannot refer to Rock himself, but possibly to his 'revelation' (feminine gender in the Greek) that Jesus is the Living God's Man. (P. 58)

Jordan's willingness to translate names has produced here a translation that preserves the pun of the original in a way that few English versions manage. It is the kind of small triumph that so boldly imaginative a translation deserves to meet with now and then.

The effect of *The Cotton Patch Version* may, in some respects, be similar to the effect Tyndale's version had on some of his early readers. Though, as I have suggested, Tyndale's work would have seemed to his earliest readers to have a difficult, inkhorn element, it also had the effect of putting the Bible in plain clothes, and only a version such as Jordan's or Cladpole's can reproduce that kind of effect for a modern reader. The Vulgate was more occult than the KJB, Jordan is more colloquial than Tyndale, but Jordan in relation to the KJB is not too far removed from Tyndale in relation to the Vulgate. As a result, *The Cotton Patch Version* helps point a larger lesson about translation than just an insight into the effect of Tyndale. By the nineteenth century the KJB had taken on a major characteristic of the Vulgate: it had become the revered biblical standard of language. To attempt a version in its language was not to attempt Tyndale's kind of translation or even to attempt the KJB's kind of translation. The RV might preserve much of the linguistic character of the older version, but it could not have the same kind of effect on its readers and hearers. Cladpole and Jordan show that a genuine vitality can be achieved by ignoring the biblical English of the fixed version and avoiding both standard and high literary English.

CHAPTER 7

'The Bible as literature'

The Bible 'as a classic': Le Roy Halsey

Byron noted that Shelley 'was a great admirer of the Scripture as a composition', and he described himself in the same terms (above, pp. 164, 167; earlier Knox had used a similar phrase, above, p. 97). The phrase is an almost exact equivalent of 'the Bible as literature', which I have used for any seemingly literary response to the Bible, even where that response is no more than a fleeting aspect of quite different concerns. Such a broad usage is the inevitable fate of an easy phrase. But strictly it designates a narrowed approach to the Bible: the most obvious approach, the Bible as religion, is set aside. Moreover, it signals an awareness of this narrowed focus that is rarely to be found in discussions prior to the middle of the nineteenth century. To some extent it is a new phrase for a new phase. Though the new phase easily runs into AVolatry, it needs to be treated separately for two reasons: it often takes little notice of the KJB, and it often involves a non-religious approach to the Bible. These are the very things implied by the phrase: the Bible, not the KJB, as literature, not as religion.

The idea of the Bible as literature is closely associated with school Bible reading, a common enough practice but by no means universal in the British Isles: attempts to promote wider reading of the Bible in schools occurred periodically in the nineteenth century (to look no further). There was, for instance, an ecumenical effort to improve Irish education, *Extracts from the Old and New Testaments, for the Use of Schools in Ireland, According to the Respective Translations of the Church of England and the Church of Rome* (Dublin, 1814). This, as the preface explains, took its starting-point from 'the Fourteenth Report of the Commissioners of Education in Ireland'. The Report disclosed that the books adopted in most of the 4,600 schools 'for the instruction of children of the lower orders . . . too often, "instead of improving, corrupt the mind, being calculated to incite to lawless and profligate adventure, to cherish superstition and to lead to dissension and disloyalty"' (p. iii). Consequently it recommended

> for the use of schools, the selection of 'extracts from the Sacred Scriptures, an early acquaintance with which we deem of the utmost importance, and indeed indispensable in forming the mind to just notions of duty and sound principles of conduct. The study of such a volume would, in our opinion, form the best preparation for ... more particular religious instruction.'   (P. iv)

There is no trace of literary purpose here: the Bible is to be the antidote to depravity caused by secular literature. Nevertheless, the anonymous editor of the volume allows something like literary response as a contributing factor in the Bible's ability to improve. He concludes his preface with a paternalistic, not to say patronising, reference to 'the vacant minds and mental leisure of our peasantry'; the well educated, he declares, are unaware 'of the manner in which the first disclosure of the histories of the Old and New Testament have been found to captivate their imaginations and to excite the best passions of their nature' (p. v). Rudimentarily, this is an argument for the utility of the literary pleasure the Bible gives, but the moral point is paramount. In such basic form, no special value is given to *literary* pleasure: churches commonly lure potential converts to the truth through the provision of pleasurable activities such as singing or sport.

The choice of extracts allows narrative portions of the OT to predominate, but 'passages from the Psalms, the Proverbs and Ecclesiastes are added to convey juster ideas of the Supreme God and useful directions for the moral conduct of mankind' (p. iv); the selections from the NT give the Gospel story, Paul preaching before Agrippa, and the doctrine of the Resurrection. In this bias towards narrative there is a more even balance between literary and religious considerations, but the presentation of the extracts, though free of editorial material other than titles, is unsurprisingly biblical, being in single-column numbered verses. The one real peculiarity of the book is that it presents the KJB and the Rheims-Douai versions on facing pages.[1] This, 'a mere experiment of the editor's' (p. v), is a far cry from Fulke's 1601 adoption of the same presentation for controversial purposes. In this ecumenical context nothing can be said of the relative merits of either version, so the question of the merits of the language of the KJB for forming style does not arise.

The real use for present purposes of this pious and laudable (but, one judges from the lack of further editions if not from the continued sectarian divisions of

---

[1] The exhibition slip in the Bible Society's copy describes the work as 'an interesting example of a co-operative venture between Protestants and Roman Catholics in Ireland'.

Ireland, unsuccessful) book is its similarity to, yet difference from, the books that usher in the phrase 'the Bible as literature'. A literary consideration is allowed to creep in for its pedagogical usefulness in leading to moral improvement, but there is no question of literary enjoyment for its own sake.

With the phrase 'the Bible as a classic' we come closer to 'the Bible as literature'. We also cross the Atlantic. The statement that 'the Bible [is] the best of the classics' goes back at least as early as 1837, when it was made by a North Carolina lawyer, Thomas Grimkee, in an article in a school reader.[2] It was picked up by a Presbyterian American Doctor of Divinity, Le Roy J. Halsey (1812–96),[3] first for an 1855 discourse at Louisville, Kentucky, 'Thoughts for the time: or the Bible as a classic', then for a work that shows the next stage of the movement towards the Bible as literature, *The Literary Attractions of the Bible; or, a Plea for the Word of God Considered as a Classic* (1858). Though it is unfair to write it of him and of none of the other figures in this history, Halsey is a windbag, and much of his book is an exercise in rhetoric and assertion, with the word 'belief' constantly substituting for demonstrated argument. In short, his book is second-rate (to distinguish no more finely). Yet it is one of those marvellously revealing bad books: leaning heavily and openly on Herder (this is one of the book's several distinctively American qualities) and Gilfillan, it mixes their ideas with dogmatism in a way that leads to something that looks like originality. It shows how diligent exploitation of a few current ideas can give those ideas new turns that anticipate developments still to come from far more substantial figures.

In spite of his title, Halsey's purposes are as religious as those of the anonymous editor of *Extracts*, and he is even more hostile towards popular literature than the Irish commissioners of education. Just as *Extracts* attempts to bring Irish children to the Bible through its narrative appeal, so Halsey is trying to sell the Bible through advocation of its literary merits set against the horrors of fiction. He explains that

> The object of these pages is to tell, at least in part, what [the Bible] contains; to gain the eye of those who, under an impression that there is nothing in the Bible but religion, really do not know how much there is in it; to bring out to their view some of its many treasures; and to present them in such a way that they shall desire to see more, and so be attracted to the book itself.   (P. vi)

Implicit in this object is a sense that the Bible has two aspects. Halsey wants to

---

[2] McGuffey's *Eclectic Fourth Reader* (Cincinnatti, 1837); cited in Westerhoff, p. 30.
[3] Catalogues generally give Halsey's first name as Leroy; I have followed his spelling on the title page of *Literary Attractions*.

bring his readers to the Bible 'as a book of religion' by setting forth 'what may be called [its] incidental attractions, or, in other words ... its claims both as a classic and as a book of general education' (p. 13). It is an inevitable consequence of this division that he should use the word 'as', and clearly 'the Bible as literature' lurks round the corner, especially with the use of 'literary' in the title. But his opposition to contemporary literature dictates his preference for the Bible 'as a classic': he would rather see the Bible in relation to the Greek and Latin classics. Moreover, by treating the Bible also 'as a book of general education', he is keeping his view wider than 'the Bible as literature' would allow.

Here is part of the way he develops his sales pitch:

> But whilst it is chiefly as a book of religion, and especially of religious education, that the Bible has spread civilisation among the nations, still, it is true that, regarded simply as a book of learning, of taste and genius, of history and eloquence, it has exerted an influence which cannot be too highly estimated. As such, it has claims which commend themselves to every cultivated understanding. Independently of all its higher glories – the knowledge which it gives us of the way to heaven and the hope with which it inspires us of a blessed immortality – there are attractions which may be felt and appreciated even by the irreligious and the worldly-minded.   (P. 14)

These people as well as the youth of the country may be led to 'peruse [the Bible] with growing interest until, advancing from the less to the greater, and from the outer to the inner sanctuary, they find for themselves that other attraction which is its chief glory – even a Saviour who is God over all blessed forever' (pp. 16–17). Blatant in this is one of the main aspects of presentations of the Bible as literature: they involve unbelievers. Halsey, presenting the Bible as a classic in order to bring unbelievers to its truth, shows the commonest but not the only form of this involvement.

One section of Halsey's first chapter is devoted to the topic of the Bible 'as a classic'. This is how it begins:

> It is greatly to be desired that our children and youth should grow up with the conviction firmly fixed in their minds that the Bible is a classic of the very highest authority in all matters of education, taste and genius; that it holds the same place of pre-eminence in the republic of letters which it holds in the church of God. It is exceedingly important that the public mind should be made to understand what the most eminent scholars of all ages and all lands have always understood and confessed – that there is no book in the world which can stand before the Bible as a classic. Such an impression, early implanted and generally received, would do much to save our

young people from the evils of that flimsy, superficial literature which, in the form of the wild, extravagant romance, the lovesick novel and the run-mad poem, is coming in upon us like a flood. It would do much to rescue the rising generation from that deluge of fiction which now threatens to overlay the learning of this boasted nineteenth century with a deeper detritus of trash than that of all the geological epochs.   (Pp. 18–19)

This is *Extracts* writ large, and writing large is Halsey's forte. The whole section is so full a collection of assertion that it reads rather like parts of the index to this book: the Bible is 'at once the most ancient, the most substantial, the most wonderful of all the classics'; it 'is as truly a classic as Homer or Virgil, Xenophon or Cicero, Milton or Addison' (p. 19); 'it stands without a rival at the head of all human literature' (p. 20), and is 'classical and indigenous on every soil, in every era'; 'it bears its own credentials; it carries a self-evidencing power, not only of religious truth but of classic beauty. It is true to nature and true to man' (p. 21); it 'is the truest cosmos. And of all students, the Bible student is the most thorough cosmopolite' (p. 23). At the back of all these grandiosities lies the idea of inspiration, divine or human, whichever one cares to believe in. Halsey concludes:

> Call it what you will, a divine revelation or a human production – an inspiration from God or an inspiration of genius; still it must be admitted to be the most remarkable book in the world, and to exhibit the most remarkable achievement that has ever been made by man, or for man, in his advance towards perfection ... We hold it to be the greatest of classics because it is inspired of God – the most perfect work of the human mind because a mind more than human is everywhere at work in it. 'Thy testimonies are wonderful' [Ps. 119: 129].   (Pp. 24–5)

The quotation at the end is the only evidence given: it is the Bible evidencing itself. The blatant circularity of this is the essence of Halsey's position.

This is as far as we need to go to show the way bibliolatry, as soon as it admits divine *and* human attractions in the Bible, opens up phrases that begin, 'the Bible as...'. It is also as far as we need go in showing that such thinking connects easily and naturally with thought about the Bible's role in education. The ground for 'the Bible as literature' is thoroughly prepared. But it is useful to follow Halsey one step further. So far he has been writing about the Bible either in the originals or as transcending any particular language, and he does maintain both these positions, declaring on the one hand that 'it ought to be studied in its original tongues just as our youth study the Greek and Latin authors' (pp. 32–3) and, on the other, that it is 'designed to be translated into all the languages of the earth' (p. 83).[4] It is the perfect book,[5] most perfect in the originals, but still perfect in any language and any translation: 'translate it, however badly', he declares, 'dilute it, however much with paraphrases, still it is almost impossible to hide the native beauty of its imagery or the original lustre of its thoughts' (pp. 20–1). The reader can readily guess the way in which Halsey writes about the KJB. Having turned to this version, he makes another significant use of 'as': 'it is chiefly as an English classic, the best and most important in our language, that we advocate its claims' (p. 33). 'Its' refers to the Bible in general, though the sentence as a whole refers to the KJB, 'a translation ... which, simply as an English book, is as classical to our language as it is faithful and true to the original' (p. 36).

The American Constitution and school Bible reading

There are some particularly American forces behind Halsey's work, and they lead directly to some contemporary aspects of the Bible as literature. America's especially intense biblical heritage does not need rehearsing here. Its early schools centred on Bible reading and Protestant belief. A lawyer in an 1869 case could 'not refrain from saying that the common schools of this country owe their existence to [the] Bible – that they were organised and are principally maintained by men who adhere to its teachings'.[6] By this time, however, the American conception of the role of the Bible, and of religious education generally, in public schools was changing. The reasons were both Constitutional and demographic. In the 1840s, the arrival of large numbers of Roman Catholics, mostly of Irish or German background, challenged Protestant dominance and spurred debate about the value of Bible reading.[7]

---

[4] Here he is, with open approval, drawing on Kitto's *Daily Bible Illustrations* (1849). Some of Jebb's analysis and demonstrations of parallelism, as given by Kitto, is also reproduced here, and attributed to Kitto.

[5] Halsey does admit that there are apparent dullnesses, but these are quickly transformed into things 'hard to be understood, deep things of God which have not yet given up their secrets to any human explorer' (p. 31).

[6] *The Bible in the Public Schools*, p. 57. In addition to the use of the Bible in schools, it is worth remembering that between the American Revolution and the Civil War, Bible societies made vast efforts to make sure everyone had a Bible. For example, the Monroe County (New York) Bible Society gave a Bible to the 1,200 households in the county that an 1824 census had shown to be without it (Mark A. Noll, 'The image of the United States as a biblical nation, 1776–1865', in Hatch and Noll, pp. 39–58; p. 40).

[7] See, for example, Boles, pp. 32–8.

The lawyer I have just quoted was arguing in a Cincinnati Superior Court case that has representative value. The Cincinnati Board of Education had resolved 'that religious instruction, and the reading of religious books, including the Holy Bible, are prohibited in the common schools of Cincinnati, it being the true object and intent of this rule to allow the children of the parents of all sects and opinions, in matters of faith and worship, to enjoy alike the benefit of the Common School fund' (pp. 6–7). A group of Cincinnati citizens sought to have this rule nullified. Behind the Board's rule lay the First Amendment to the Constitution, adopted in 1791; it states that 'Congress shall make no law respecting an establishment of religion, or prohibiting the free exercise thereof'. Eventually this was taken to mean that, in the words of a crucial 1963 Supreme Court judgement, 'in the relationship between man and religion the State is firmly committed to a position of neutrality' (*Abington School District* v. *Schempp*, p. 861). Consequently religious practice or teaching, including reading of the Bible, in State schools came to be seen as unconstitutional. In 1870 the Cincinnati Superior Court judged otherwise, but it is not so much the judgement as some of the arguments that are of real interest here.

Among the exhibits at the trial was the series of readers that contained the first use of the idea of the Bible as 'the best of classics', *McGuffey's Eclectic Readers*. Little remembered now in the United States, and never known in the United Kingdom, they sold in numbers which must be the envy of all commercial authors. By the time their use declined in the 1920s, some 122 million had been published, and most of these had gone through several sets of hands. Their influence was enormous. In the *Eclectic First Reader* young children were given plentiful references to biblical teaching as well as stories such as that of Mr Post, who finds a baby on his doorstep. He brings her up. She loves him. The tale, with some words divided for ease of reading, concludes: 'Mr. Post taught her to read, and at night Ma-ry would read the Bi-ble to her fa-ther; and when Mr. Post got so old that he could not work, Ma-ry took care of him.'[8] The fifth and sixth readers contained a substantial number of biblical passages, often given without the source being specified. William Holmes McGuffey, the chief but not the sole compiler, included this note about his use of the Bible in most of the early editions:

> From no source has the author drawn more copiously in his selections than from the Sacred Scriptures. For this he certainly apprehends no censure. In a Christian country

---

[8] Stanley W. Lindberg, ed., *The Annotated McGuffey* (New York: Van Nostrand Reinhold, 1976), p. 11.

that man is to be pitied who, at this day, can honestly object to imbuing the minds of youth with the language and spirit of the Word of God.

The student of the Bible will, it is believed, be pleased to find a specimen of the elegant labors of Bishop Jebb, and some specimens of sacred poetry, as arranged by Dr. Coit, in which the exact words of our authorised translation are prescribed, while the poetic order of the original is happily restored.[9]

In later editions, however, the KJB was not always followed verbatim. Even so, to find a lesson headed 'Song of Moses at the Red Sea', given as verse lightly revised from the KJB, following an extremely enthusiastic article by Gardiner Spring on 'the poetry of the Bible' would have been a strong spur to appreciation of the KJB.[10] From such lessons many millions of Americans must, over the years, have become familiar with the idea that biblical passages could be presented in a literary way and keep equal company with passages from Shakespeare.

Now, McGuffey's readers had been used in the schools of Cincinnati for upwards of twenty years 'as the regular and only authorised text books for lessons in reading' (*The Bible in the Public Schools*, p. 19). Stanley Matthews, a Presbyterian elder, argued for the rule banning Bible reading. He sought to distinguish different ways in which passages from the Bible might be read:

> When the Bible is read in the morning as a part of the opening exercises of the school, when singing accompanies it, that is instruction in religion because it is an act of worship, because the exercises are devotional, because the necessary implication is that you are listening to the inspired and revealed will of God. But when the class takes up the Fifth Reader and reads the fifth chapter of Matthew – and I don't think any better reading could be found – it is done ... not as the words that fell from the second person in the Godhead, when incarnate on earth, but as a beautiful specimen of English composition – fit to be the subject of the reading of a class – and stands, as far as that exercise is concerned, on the same footing precisely as a soliloquy from Hamlet, or the address of Macbeth to the air drawn dagger. (P. 211)

Devotional use of the Bible is unacceptable (because it constitutes State support of religion and because it is sectarian), but the Bible's literary qualities exist separately, so it can be used elsewhere in the curriculum.

The reply to this was twofold. First, McGuffey's readers consist 'not merely

[9] Ibid., p. 316. Lindberg gives only one example of a biblical passage, Psalm 37, set as verse, with some omissions and rearrangements (pp. 315–16).

[10] *McGuffey's Newly Revised Rhetorical Guide; or Fifth Reader, Revised and Improved* (New York: Clark, Austin and Smith, 1853), pp. 294–8. Westerhoff notes that the *Eclectic Fifth Reader* from 1879 on contained a lesson headed with Grimkee's phrase, 'The Bible: the best of the classics'. He shows – but cannot explain – that the successive revisions reduced the amount of biblical material, and he gives a detailed account of the biblical passages used.

of extracts from the Bible, but some of the most beautiful lessons of religion and morality ... compiled, arranged and adorned ... for laying the foundation of religious character, virtue and morality broad and deep throughout the country' (p. 294; see also p. 323). Second, the Bible is inescapably a religious book, so 'if the Bible is not thus read as an act of worship, it must be by way of religious instruction' (p. 129).

Matthews's point is the nearest approach to AVolatry in the trial, but it is worth noting that he does not rest his argument on the qualities, literary or scholarly, of the KJB. Neither side, especially that advocating Bible reading, emphasised versions, for there the sectarian issue comes in. So, in the opinion of one of the judges, 'we do not suppose there is any very essential difference between the versions' (p. 383). In general, the parties (often including Roman Catholics) who wished Bible reading to continue were willing, like the Irish editor of *Extracts*, to admit the Rheims-Douai Bible (or other versions), as desired by the individual readers.[11] At heart what they wanted was the Bible behind the versions.

Arguments of this sort were heard in and out of court rooms in nineteenth- and twentieth-century America.[12] The Constitutional separation between the State and religion made Americans especially used to seeing a distinction between sacred and secular. Seeing the Bible in different aspects is a spur to the central element implied in phrases beginning, 'the Bible as ...'. For an American Christian there might therefore be real advantages in demonstrating qualities of secular importance in the Bible since the Bible considered only as a religious book might be removed from public schools.

The 1963 Supreme Court ruling on the matter took the position the Cincinnati School Board had unsuccessfully anticipated: public-school reading from the Bible, associated with prayers at the beginning of the school day, was found to be unconstitutional. Nevertheless, all parties in the case, and the Court

[11]   Such a picture of inter-denominational harmony is necessarily a simplification. An 1842 Roman Catholic attempt to have the Rheims-Douai Bible read by children of their faith in Philadelphia schools led to the formation of anti-Catholic organisations, the burning of two Catholic churches and a number of deaths (Gerald P. Fogarty, 'The quest for a Catholic vernacular Bible in America', in Hatch and Noll, pp. 163–80; pp. 165–6).

[12]   See, especially, Boles, chapters 3 and 4. Boles's book as a whole is of considerable interest. The same author's *The Two Swords: Commentaries and Cases in Religion and Education* (Ames, Ia.: Iowa State University Press, 1967) has an account of the crucial Schempp case and of reactions to it, pp. 102–17. A more detailed analysis of the Schempp decision and a history of pedagogical responses to it can be found in Peter S. Bracher and David L. Barr, 'The Bible is worthy of secular study: the Bible in public education today', in Barr and Piediscalzi, pp. 165–97; see especially pp. 167–71 and 190–1.

itself, agreed that 'the Bible was of great moral, historical and literary value' (p. 851), and the Court did not accept the contention that to ban such readings was to institute a 'religion of secularism'. Part of its decision reads as follows:

> It is insisted that unless these religious exercises are permitted a 'religion of secularism' is established in the schools. We agree of course that the State may not establish a 'religion of secularism' in the sense of affirmatively opposing or showing hostility to religion, thus 'preferring those who believe in no religion over those who do believe'... We do not agree, however, that this decision in any sense has that effect. In addition, it might well be said that one's education is not complete without a study of comparative religion or the history of religion and its relationship to the advancement of civilisation. It certainly may be said that the Bible is worthy of study for its literary and historic qualities. Nothing we have said here indicates that such study of the Bible or of religion, when presented objectively as part of a secular programme of education, may not be effected consistently with the First Amendment.   (P. 860)

This was what Matthews had tried to argue, only to be let down by McGuffey's readers. And the failure of those readers is of course significant. As the Court acknowledged, 'the line which separates the secular from the sectarian in American life is elusive' (p. 863). The long history of Bible reading in schools is consistently an attempt to take pupils across this line; books such as Halsey's attempt to win their readers to the religious qualities of the Bible through advocation of its literary qualities. In effect, the Supreme Court decision told religious communities that if they wanted to have the Bible in schools at all, it must be the Bible as something other than religion: consequently the Court gave religious educators a major encouragement to present the Bible as literature.

In a sense this was encouragement to camouflage. Not all books on the Bible as literature are genuinely literary studies. John B. Gabel and Charles B. Wheeler's *The Bible as Literature: An Introduction* (1986; 2nd edn, New York, Oxford University Press, 1990) starts from a position that appears to be dictated by the Constitutional situation. It is addressed to 'college undergraduates enrolled in a Bible course offered by a department of literature' (p. xi), and the authors hasten to define what they are not doing:

> It is not a commentary on the Bible... Nor is the book an attempt to impose an interpretive scheme or point of view on the Bible, for that would usurp the function of religion. Nor, finally, does it advocate or presume the value of the Bible as a vehicle of moral instruction or as a provider of religious insights or as a source of inspiration for the conduct of daily life. We do not deny these values, but we shall not take them into account either. It is sufficient for our purposes that the Bible be – as it were – a

fascinating human document of enormous importance to the culture and history of
the modern world, a document that can speak volumes to humans about their own
humanity ... everything beyond [this view] is in the area of personal beliefs and is
subject to sectarian controversy.   (Pp. xi–xii)

Such tiptoeing neutrality appears throughout, from anxiety about the use of
'BC' or 'BCE' to the sectless conclusion to the last chapter, 'the religious use and
interpretation of the Bible':

In a sense the Bible has no religious meaning until we see it through religious eyes.
Our religious eyesight has been developed through the lenses of our catechism and
creed; we have learned how to see at Sunday School, Hebrew School, Daily Vacation
Bible School, parochial school, youth group, Bible conference, synagogue, church.
Not surprisingly, what we see when we look at the Bible through our religious eyes is
what we expect to see – the customary, the familiar. This is not the least of the
miracles associated with this remarkable book.   (P. 267)

The point is thoughtful but tinged with bibliolatry: what is most significant is
the use of 'we': the reader is assumed to be religious. This assumption, coupled
with the need to be non-sectarian and non-religious, shapes the book, which
contains almost nothing of what ought to be basic to a literary discussion of the
Bible, reading of the text. The chapter on the Pentateuch, for instance, deals
with questions of its composition and makes no attempt to give its
college-student reader insight into the nature or quality of any of the narratives
contained therein. A further indicator of the nature of this introduction to 'the
Bible as literature' is that only once do the suggestions for further reading at the
ends of the chapters contain a reference to a work specifically on literary aspects
of the Bible, and then it is to Kermode's article on the canon in *The Literary
Guide to the Bible*. In short, this book is not what it appears to be: it provides a
commendable unbiassed background for study of the Bible (of whatever kind),
but it is not a 'systematic general introduction to the study of the Bible as
literature' (p. xi). The idea of the Bible as literature it embodies need not trouble
us again.

Matthew Arnold

The phrase, 'The Bible as literature' was first used by one of Lowth's
successors as both Oxford Professor of Poetry and as a reviser of Isaiah, the poet
turned literary, social, educational and religious critic, Matthew Arnold
(1822–88). It was a logical outcome not only of his time and the British
educational context but also of his own work. In *Culture and Anarchy* (1869) and

in *Literature and Dogma* (1873), he had argued at length for the importance of culture, associating it particularly with poetry and religion. He also argued that the language of the Bible was literary rather than scientific, 'that is, it is the language of poetry and emotion, approximate language thrown out, as it were, at certain great objects which the human mind augurs and feels after, and thrown out by men very liable, many of them, to delusion and error' (*Complete Prose*, VII: 155). Developing these views in *God and the Bible* (1875), he declared 'that no one knows the truth about the Bible who does not know how to enjoy the Bible' (*Complete Prose*, VII: 148). This is not aestheticism for its own sake; rather, it is a deeply held view of the role the feelings and the imagination, along with the intellect, have in religion.[13]

Arnold was a school inspector. Though it turned out not to be William Forster's intention,[14] Arnold feared that his Education Bill of 1870 might remove the Bible from State schools altogether, so he prepared a revision of Isaiah 40–66 for school use. The original introduction to this is crucial.[15] The argument as he mounts it does not start from either the religious question or from the Bible, but from Arnold's 'conviction of the immense importance in education of what is called *letters*; of the side which engages our feelings and imagination' (VII: 499). By 'letters' he means 'poetry, philosophy, eloquence' (VII: 500); these are 'a beneficent wonder-working power in education' (VII: 503), and they make themselves felt by 'the apprehension ... of a single great literary work as a connected whole' (VII: 501). A work from the Bible is the most appropriate choice because there is only 'one great literature for which the people have had a preparation – the literature of the Bible' (VII: 503). He then quotes his own 1868 report on the Wesleyan Training College at Westminster:

> Chords of power are touched by this instruction which no other part of the
> instruction in a popular school reaches, and chords various, not the single religious

13 Arnold has often been charged with aestheticism. James C. Livingston gives an account of such objections in *Matthew Arnold and Christianity: His Religious Prose Writings* (Columbia. s.c.: University of South Carolina Press, 1986), pp. 8–12 etc. Though it does not deal in detail with Arnold's work on Isaiah, Livingston's book as a whole is of considerable interest for its analysis of theological ideas that constantly relate to literary ideas of the Bible.

14 Forster himself had 'the fullest confidence that in the reading and explaining of the Bible, what the children will be taught will be the great truths of Christian life and conduct, which all of us desire they should know, and that no effort will be made to cram into their poor little minds theological dogmas which their tender age prevents them from understanding' (as quoted by Huxley, p. 388n).

15 *A Bible-Reading for Schools. The Great Prophecy of Israel's Restoration (Isaiah, Chapters 40–66) Arranged and Edited for Young Learners* (London, 1872). The work was revised for general readers. Some of the passages to which I refer were omitted, but may be found in the textual notes to *Complete Prose*, VII: 499ff.

chord only. The Bible is for the child in an elementary school almost his only contact with poetry and philosophy. What a course of eloquence and poetry (to call it by that name alone) is the Bible in a school which has and can have but little eloquence and poetry! and how much do our elementary schools lose by not having any such course as part of their school-programme. All who value the Bible may rest assured that thus to know and possess the Bible is the most certain way to extend the power and efficacy of the Bible. (VII: 503–4)

Thus he is advocating the Bible as a school literary text without feeling any of the pressure there was in America to set aside the Bible's religious role. Indeed, the opposite pressure may have been at work. Whereas in America the Bible as literature became a disguise for the Bible as religion, in Arnold there is a sense that the Bible as religion is a disguise for the Bible as literature, for his recommendation of the Bible as a school reader is not as evangelical as would appear from what has just been quoted. The stress of his argument is on literature: in itself the discovery 'of a single great literary work as a connected whole' is a sufficient aim; it is a religious aim only in so far as his literary ideas are part of his religious ideas. So the last twenty-seven chapters of Isaiah are argued for not because they are part of the Bible but because they are a great and accessible literary work.

Two problems make the phrase, 'the Bible as literature' inevitable. First, 'the Bible stands before the learner as an immense whole', and that is too much to grasp: 'this is one reason why the fruitful use of the Bible, as literature, in our schools for the people, is at present almost impossible'. Second, there are 'defects of our translation, noble as it is; defects which abound most in those very parts of the Bible which, considered merely as literature, might have most power' (VII: 504). Specifically, the KJB often does not make sense (it later becomes clear that the same may be said of the originals). Out of these difficulties comes his version, presenting the last part of Isaiah as a coherent whole, which means isolating it, arranging it and correcting some of the translation.

To put a comma in the phrase – 'the Bible, as literature' – is to suggest a restricted aspect of something larger, and that suggestion is emphasised in 'considered merely as literature'. This is careful writing. Arnold is aware of potential difficulties, so he goes to the heart of the matter, whether it is legitimate to treat the Bible in this way. 'We must make a distinction', he argues:

There is a substratum of history and literature in the Bible which belongs to science and schools; there is an application of the Bible and an edification by the Bible which belongs to religion and churches. Some people say the Bible altogether belongs to the

Church, not the school. This is an error; the Bible's application and edification belong to the Church, its literary and historical substance to the school. Other people say that the Bible does indeed belong to school as well as Church, but that its application and edification are inseparable from its literature and history. This is an error, they *are* separable.   (VII: 510)

He goes on to distinguish between the beliefs that are built on texts and the historical or literary sense: the texts' 'application and edification are what matter to a man far most' (VII: 510–11), but they are a source of religious differences, whereas there can be little dissent about the other, less important, sense. Arnold, then, would admit that the Bible can be read without being read as religion. On the one hand, this is pragmatic: the Bible has various aspects; on the other, it is an insignificant distinction because of the ethical and religious weight he gives to 'culture' and 'literature'. Such views are by no means universally held: this first full use of the idea of the Bible as literature mounts a solid case for the concept, but much of the solidity rests on Arnold's idea of the literary nature of the Bible and of the religious nature of literature. Other ideas of religion and literature give different meanings, favourable and unfavourable, to the idea of the Bible as literature.

The argument was part of the aim of the work in its character as a school text. It disappeared when Arnold cut parts of the introduction for the general public. The stress in this later version falls back on AVolatry, but, coming from Arnold, so often a resolutely independent thinker, it is hardly mindless. The central passage now becomes a lead-in to his discussion of the kind of changes he has made in the text:

> I want to enable the reader to apprehend, as a whole, a literary work of the highest order. And the book of Isaiah, as it stands in our Bibles, is this in a double way. By virtue of the original it is a monument of the Hebrew genius at its best, and by virtue of the translation it is a monument of the English language at its best. Some change must be made for clearness' sake, without which the work cannot be apprehended as a whole; but the power of the English version must not be sacrificed, must, if possible, be preserved intact. And though every corrector says this and pays his compliment to the English version, yet few proceed to act upon the rule or seem to know how hard it is to act upon it when we alter at all, and why it is hard.
>
> (VII: 58)

Such a rule stands in contrast to the kind of rule for 'a body of Bible-revisers . . . acting by public authority': they probably ought 'to take much more latitude, and to correct the old version not only where it is unintelligible, but also wherever they think it in error' (VII: 58). That work had started on the RV lies behind some of this discussion: the emphasis on the Bible 'as literature' is in part a prescient reaction to that work. Arnold has recognised, very early in the piece, that literary and scholarly revision are two different things. He implies that it will be impossible for the revisers to preserve the literary qualities of the KJB satisfactorily, and this makes his argument the more important, for he is aware that the public revision is likely to diminish those literary qualities of the English Bible that he takes to be so central a part of its religious effect.

In 1883, with the RV NT to hand and the OT imminent, Arnold published *Isaiah of Jerusalem*. No new arguments are offered in its introduction, but the emphases have become firmer because of the RV. So he begins:

> The time approaches for the revised version of the Old Testament to make its appearance. Before it comes, let us say to ourselves and to the revisers that the principal books of the Old Testament are things to be deeply enjoyed, and which have been deeply enjoyed hitherto. It is not enough to translate them accurately; they must be translated so as also to be deeply enjoyed, and to exercise the power of beauty and of sentiment which they have exercised upon us hitherto.   (x: 100)

With what he sees as the failure of the RV NT in front of him, that it has sacrificed 'the force of beauty and sentiment residing in the old version'[16] to the quest for accuracy, he wonders how Isaiah may be revised more successfully. The discussion itself does not need following. His first remark on the question not only summarises his attitude to literature and his judgement of the Bible, but again places before the public the issue of the Bible as literature:

> Such is the question which ... I keep asking myself about Isaiah. Taking him merely as poetry and literature – which is not, I will readily add, to take him in his entirety – I consider the question very important. I rate the value of the operation of poetry and literature upon men's minds extremely high; and from no poetry and literature, not even from our own Shakespeare and Milton, great as they are and our own as they are, have I, for my own part, received so much delight and stimulus as from Homer and Isaiah.   (x: 102)

Richard Moulton and literary morphology

Though Arnold invented the phrase, 'the Bible as literature', its subsequent use may not depend on his work, especially since, as we have seen, he used it in a school rather than a general edition of his *Isaiah*. The phrase came

---

[16] x: 558. Again the passage from which this phrase comes was deleted from later versions. Arnold's criticism of the RV would have needed reworking after the appearance of the RV OT.

naturally from his way of thinking, much of which can be paralleled in other writers on the Bible, and it owed a good deal to his contemporary situation. In short, 'the Bible as literature' was a phrase waiting to be invented. Yet it did not begin to establish itself until the final year of the century, when a book of that title was published. This was one of a succession of works by the most energetic populariser of a literary approach to the Bible there has ever been, Richard Green Moulton (1849–1924). Son of a Wesleyan Methodist minister, he became one of Cambridge's first and most successful University Extension lecturers; in 1892 he was appointed Professor of Literature in English at the University of Chicago; nine years later, doubtless at his instigation, his title was changed to Professor of Literary Theory and Interpretation. As well as work on Shakespeare and classical drama, he produced a school syllabus entitled *The Literary Study of the Bible*, and in 1895 used the same title for a substantial 'account of the leading forms of literature represented in the sacred writings; intended for English readers' (subtitle). Also in 1895 he began publishing *The Modern Reader's Bible* in twenty-one volumes; this was to be collected into a single, densely printed volume, and to be published in a school edition and in selections, and it remained in print until at least 1952. Then, in 1899, he published, with various collaborators, a collection of essays, *The Bible as Literature*, and in 1901, aiming at a more general readership, *A Short Introduction to the Literature of the Bible*. Such industry (the list I have given is incomplete), applied to both presentation and appreciation of the text, would give him a fair claim to be considered the father of modern literary study of the Bible if such study needed a father, and indeed (though it is unfashionable to quote any critic between Augustine and Auerbach, especially any critic from the first half of this century), he is the most quoted of the period's literary critics of the Bible.

The *Literary Study of the Bible*, popular enough to be reprinted until 1935, is representative of his work.[17] Moulton was a structuralist before his time, and this leads to some peculiarities. First, he is not interested in style, remarking that 'questions of style seem to me to belong to the study of language rather than to the study of literature' (p. 263), and so, bibliolater that he manifestly is, he is no AVolater. He bases his study, as he based his *Modern Reader's Bible*, on the RV, 'with choice between the readings of the text and margin, and such slight changes of wording as are involved in the adaptation to modern literary structure'.[18] This does not represent a judgement on the usual grounds of

---

[17] I have used the revised and partly rewritten second edition (1899). This was the form in which the book was best known, and Moulton gives more developed expression to his ideas of literature in it.

[18] *Modern Reader's Bible*, p. xi.

magnificence of style versus accuracy. Discussion of stylistic merits, he argues, has

> been conducted on a wrong footing. The critics will take single verses or expressions and, as it were, test them with their mental palate to see whether the literary flavour of the old or the new be superior. But comparisons of this kind are a sheer impossibility. No one, least of all a cultured critic, can separate in his mind between the sense of beauty which comes from association, and the beauty which is intrinsic; the softening effect of time and familiarity is needed before any translation can in word and phrase assume the even harmony of a classic.   (*Literary Study*, pp. 91–2)

Others had suggested that the RV needed time before a fair judgement could be made, but nobody else had seriously suggested that comparative stylistic judgement was an impossibility. A Saintsbury would have laughed Moulton out of court, but the point has some sense to it when he suggests that there is little to choose between the three versions currently in use, Coverdale's Psalms in the PB, the KJB and the RV, 'in respect of phraseology and single verses' (p. 85). In Moulton's view, the right basis for discussion is the question of the coherence of the text. Only the RV, he argues, is reliable if one wishes to attend 'to the connection between verse and verse, to the drift of an argument and the general unity of a whole poem' (p. 85). The medieval attention to verses in isolation, he goes on, is thoroughly evident in Coverdale and stands behind the KJB, so that the difference between the KJB and the RV is 'a difference of kind and not of degree, and one which is as wide as the distinction between the words "text" and "context"' (p. 91). The argument, like many of Moulton's, is idiosyncratic, but it is not allowed to stand or fall as mere generalisation. He sets Coverdale's version of Psalm 18 against the KJB and the RV, showing first the continuity of argument that appears in the later versions, and then bringing out the indiscriminate mingling of tenses in Coverdale. He concludes that

> Coverdale formed a different conception of the literature he was translating from that which both ourselves and the later versions assume. It did not belong to Coverdale's age to look upon a Psalm as a poem with a unity running through it; he understood it simply as a collection of pious thoughts, and he used all his skill to make each thought as beautiful as the English language would permit. He has succeeded in his attempt, and given us in the eighteenth Psalm a chaplet of very pearls; but it is a chaplet with the string broken.   (P. 88)

With admirable thoroughness, he follows this with a similar comparison between the KJB and the RV in their rendering of Job 28. We may reasonably object to his ideas of the translators' intentions, and recollect that it was Tyndale, the founder of the English tradition of translation, who insisted again and again on 'the process, order and meaning' of the text, but his main point remains: differences in coherence can be found between the RV and its predecessors. In his view, and here surely few would disagree, coherence is of real importance (provided, as he assumes, that this continuity is present in the originals). Though his book is resolutely untheological, he reminds the reader 'that an increased apprehension of outer literary form is a sure means of deepening spiritual effect' (p. xiv), and that 'form is the foremost factor in the interpretation of matter' (p. 75; cf. pp. 207, 463). He concludes his argument with this resounding challenge: 'speaking from the literary point of view, I make bold to say that the reader who confines himself to the Authorised Version excludes himself from half the beauty of the Bible' (p. 92).

It would be reasonable to assume from this kind of argument that Moulton's literary treatment of the Bible will be, in effect, a treatment of the originals, taking the RV as their best representative. The opposite turns out to be true. The subtitle concluded, 'intended for English readers', and throughout he treats the RV, as he has edited it, as an autonomous anthology of literature: his criticism is always directed towards the text the reader reads rather than the text behind it. This is implicit in his declaration that, 'whoever may be responsible for the Sacred Scriptures as they stand, these are worthy of examination for their own sake; and the literary study of the Bible brings to bear on these writings the light that comes from ascertaining the exact form they are found to present' (p. vi). Few literary discussions of the Bible do this, and yet it is an essential position if the Bible is to be appreciated as English literature. Even John Hays Gardiner (discussed below, pp. 320ff.), who might have been expected to take this position, especially with Moulton's example before him, manages it to a very limited extent. The value of this approach, however, is vitiated by his choice of the RV as text, since this is not the text that has, historically speaking, been the Bible in and of English literature. Much but not all of Moulton's discussion illuminates the KJB, but that is only because the two versions have so much in common. Moreover, his refusal to deal with style means that the discussion is, at best, partial. Idiosyncrasy has its strengths and weaknesses.

Moulton's idiosyncrasies come in large part from his view of himself as a pioneer. He argues that what he means by the literary study of the Bible is something new and that its newness is connected with the fact 'that the study of literature, properly so called, is only just beginning'.[19] It is based on recognising that literature is an entity on its own, with its own unity and its own special focus, the study of form: it is the science, as he more than once calls it (for

---

[19] P. iv. This and several of the following points were not present in the first edition.

example, p. 74), of literary morphology (pp. iv–v). As we have seen, this science (how Arnold would have deprecated the term!) is distinguished from the study of language, which includes the study of style. It is evident from his practice that it is also distinguished from the study of character and of morality (here Arnold would have been more than deprecatory). It is distinguished from older literary studies, which were essentially studies of literatures and stressed the historical side of things; it is also distinguished from textual criticism, and therefore from biblical Higher Criticism, for those are also historic and linguistic studies: 'literary investigation stops short at the question *what* we have in the text of the Bible, without examining *how* it has come to us' (p. vi). Finally, it is not interested in authors: he argues that the study of authors is 'quite a distinct thing', and 'that the study of literature will never reach its proper level until it is realised that literature is an entity in itself, as well as a function of the individuals who contributed to it' (p. 96). This is all quite remarkable in a turn-of-the-century critic and entitles Moulton to a significant place in the history of modern criticism.

The emphasis on morphology as the essence of literary study evidently grew on Moulton as he thought over his book. He acknowledges, in the preface to the first edition, that he has omitted 'other obvious lines of literary treatment' such as discussion of imagery, style or subject-matter (1st edn, p. vii), but the acknowledgement was dropped from the second edition: his sense of the principal difficulty in the way of literary response to the Bible, that it 'is the worst-printed book in the world' (p. 45), led him to work at the elucidation of form, and this in turn became the cornerstone of his idea of literature. 'Nowhere', he argues,

> has literary morphology so important a place as in application to the Sacred Scriptures . . . it comes to most people as a novelty to hear that the Bible is made up of epics, lyrics, dramas, essays, sonnets, philosophical works, histories and the like. More than this, centuries of unliterary tradition have so affected the outer surface of Scripture that the successive literary works appear joined together without distinction, until it becomes the hardest of tasks to determine, in the Bible, exactly where one work of literature ends and another begins. The morphological analysis of Scripture thus urgently required is precisely the purpose to which I have applied myself in the present work . . . its underlying principle is that a clear grasp of the outer literary form is an essential guide to the inner matter and spirit.   (Pp. v–vi)

Moulton's interest in form extends from the minutiae of verse form through to but not beyond the overall structure of the individual books: he shows no desire to treat the Bible as a single book. His treatment of verse form is characteristic. With a brief glimpse at Lowth, he neatly demonstrates the basis of parallelism by taking Psalm 105 and showing that it makes 'excellent historic prose' if the second half of each couplet is omitted, and then how it becomes 'verse full of the rhythm and lilt of a march' if given in full and set out as verse with every second line indented (p. 47). But this is as far as he goes with Lowth. Naming no other commentators, he proceeds to an extraordinary description of the variety of biblical verse form, and later, in an appendix, 'a metrical system of biblical verse', extends things still further. Parallelism may work through couplets or triplets, and through larger units such as quatrains or octets. It may be antistrophic or strophic, and these forms may be inverted or reversed. Refrains are sometimes used, and there may be two other kinds of structure, 'the envelope figure, by which a series of parallel lines running to any length are enclosed between an identical (or equivalent) opening and close' (p. 56), and 'the pendulum figure', which is 'a swaying to and fro between two thoughts' (p. 58).

Moulton's scheme, like Jebb's before him, develops Lowth's suggestions that there are larger patterns to be discovered (see above, especially pp. 70–1), but it is more successful than Jebb's in that it is supported by a larger range of persuasive examples. Yet it is too complex to be properly useful as a scheme: its benefits lie in persuading the reader not that there is a coherent range of interrelated patterns to be discovered, but that it is frequently profitable to attend closely to the progression of thought and language in a poem, because often (Moulton would say *always*) there is a coherent structure to be discovered. This persuasion comes in spite of his characteristically magisterial way of working. Periodically he does stand back and allow that variety of interpretation is possible, as in the conclusion to appendix III, 'a metrical system of biblical verse': 'parallelism belongs to the world of thought, and in the nature of things admits great variability of analysis. Hence, in the systematisation of parallelism there is no right and wrong but only better and worse; and the test will be the amount of symmetry and beauty that a proposed arrangement brings out' (p. 555). So the reader is freed to take the greater eccentricities with the necessary grains of salt.

Moulton demonstrates one of his patterns using Psalm 114, the very Psalm which Lowth took for his initial demonstration of parallelism:[20]

An example of antistrophic inversion is found in the hundred and fourteenth Psalm,

[20] So striking is the synonymous parallelism of this Psalm that it can be used for a demonstration similar to that which Moulton made with Psalm 105. Students new to parallelism have been much impressed by being given it divided into two poems, apparently paraphrases of each other, and then being shown how the two fit together.

which thought and form combine to make one of the most striking of Hebrew lyrics. It is a song inspired not only by the deliverance from Egypt but also by the new conception of Deity which that deliverance exhibited to the world . . . The wonder of this conception the Psalm expresses by the favourite Hebrew image of nature in convulsion; and the effect of inversion in giving shape (so to speak) to the whole thought of the poem may be conveyed to the eye by the following scheme:

> A new conception of Deity!
>   Nature convulsed!
>   Why Nature convulsed?
> At the new conception of Deity.

Those phrases sum up the thought of the successive stanzas, which are so related to one another that the first strophe is followed by a second, and the antistrophe to the second strophe precedes the antistrophe to the first.

>   *Strophe 1*
> When Israel went forth out of Egypt
> The house of Jacob from a people of strange language;
> Judah became his sanctuary,
> Israel his dominion.

>   *Strophe 2*
> The sea saw it and fled;
> Jordan was driven back.
> The mountains skipped like rams,
> The little hills like young sheep.

>   *Antistrophe 2*
> What aileth thee, O thou sea, that thou fleest?
> Thou Jordan, that thou turnest back?
> Ye mountains, that ye skip like rams?
> Ye little hills, like young sheep?

>   *Antistrophe 1*
> Tremble, thou earth, at the presence of the Lord,
> At the presence of the God of Jacob;
> Which turned the rock into a pool of water,
> The flint into a fountain of waters!   (Pp. 54–5)

In several respects this is successful and helpful (and adaptable to the KJB). The division into four visually separate verses is obviously apt, and clearly 'antistrophe 2' picks up 'strophe 2'. What is less persuasive is that 'antistrophe 1' corresponds in the same way with 'strophe 1'. There is some forcing here, and the reader may prefer to see the last verse as a generalised conclusion, exclaiming at the power of the Lord and recalling more of Exodus. The reader is both enlightened and left a little dubious – and that is the general effect of the work.

Though the belief that there is always an admirable form to be drawn out is a shaping premise that rules out of court negative criticism and so disables discrimination, much of what Moulton does has in common with Lowth the willingness to attend open-mindedly to what the text is doing. Central to his method is his comment, near the end of his analysis of Job, that 'he would be a very perverse reader who should cry out against these characteristics of Job as literary faults: on the contrary, they are evidence that the character of the work is insufficiently described by the terms drama and discussion' (p. 40). In other words, Job is *sui generis*, and the task is to understand just what kind of thing the book is through faithful attention. Such attention leads to one of his most valuable insights, introduced in this way:

> We saw that Hebrew rests its verse system not upon metre or rhyme but upon parallelism of clauses. But, as a matter of universal literature, parallelism is one of the devices of prose: the rhetoric of all nations includes it. If then a particular language bases its verse upon something which is also a property of prose, it is an inevitable consequence that in that language prose and verse will overlap: and such is the case with biblical literature. I do not of course mean that the verse literature of the Bible taken as a whole could be confused with the biblical literature of prose ... But while in their extremes they are totally different, yet there is a middle region of biblical style in which verse and prose meet: a high parallelism in which transition can rapidly be made from the one to the other, or even the effects of the two can be combined. It is this overlapping of verse and prose that I call the most important distinguishing feature of Hebrew literature.[21]

For his first example he take Amos 1: 3–15. The first four verses of the passage, in his presentation, show just how close the overlapping can be:

I

Thus saith the Lord:
  For three transgressions of Damascus,
  Yea, for four,

---

[21] Pp. 113–14. Kugel stresses the same point: 'It is not this study's contention that there is no difference between what has been called "biblical poetry" and "biblical prose", nor yet that the very idea of a "biblical poetry" is all one great mistake. Its argument is rather that the concepts of poetry and prose correspond to no precise distinction in the Bible, and that their sustained use has been somewhat misleading about the nature and form of different sections of the Bible, and about the nature of parallelism' (p. 302).

I will not turn away the punishment thereof;

because they have threshed Gilead with threshing instruments of iron:

> But I will send a fire into the house of Hazael,
> And it shall devour the palaces of Ben-hadad.

And I will break the bar of Damascus, and cut off the inhabitant from the valley of Aven, and him that holdeth the sceptre from the house of Eden: and the people of Syria shall go into captivity unto Kir, saith the Lord.

2

> Thus saith the Lord:
>   For three transgressions of Gaza,
>   Yea, for four,
> I will not turn away the punishment thereof...   (P. 115)

He admits that the prose passages could be divided into verses, but offers instead an analysis which depends on the logic of the whole passage, which he designates 'higher parallelism':

> this prophecy against seven peoples is made up of common formulae expressing ideal transgressions and ideal dooms, together with particular descriptions of actual sins and actual sufferings. It is surely in keeping with such a general plan that the formulae and ideal portions should be found to be in verse, and the particular descriptions in prose. Moreover, when we examine the denunciation of Israel, the final climax up to which all the rest leads, we find that it is just here that the description is most difficult to compel into the form of verse: if this goes best as prose then the parts correlated with it should be prose also. Finally, if we look at the whole for a moment simply as a work of art, we must be struck with the superb elasticity of utterance which Hebrew obtains from the power of combining the two styles: the speaker can at any moment suspend rhythm in order to penetrate with unfettered simplicity of prose into every detail of realism, sure of being able to recover when he pleases the rhythmic march and the strong tone of idealisation.   (Pp. 118–19)

Whether or not this is truly the form of the original, the arrangement and explanation illuminate. Where a reader would have struggled to see the whole as a succession of parallel lines, suddenly it has become a marvellously effective pattern. Lowth's analysis of parallelism had been a liberating insight. Moulton has now similarly liberated the reader from some of the limitations of parallelism.

Taken as a whole, *The Literary Study of the Bible* is a strong contribution to one part of literary appreciation of the Bible. And it is made stronger by its unusual willingness to treat an English version as an autonomous work. Since it has no successors as a bold attempt to bring out the forms latent in the English text, it remains a book to be returned to. At times, as when one reads the argument on overlapping prose and verse, even such praise seems lukewarm.

Presenting the text as literature

For both Arnold and Moulton, as for Lowth before them, re-presentation of the text was a major part of their work. This is a characteristic facet of the Bible as literature, and a good deal of this movement is taken up with either biblical anthologies or whole new editions, all designed to encourage literary appreciation of the text. Moulton went further than anybody else, before or since, in *The Modern Reader's Bible*, and this long-lived work is one of the three modern literary presentations of the Bible most worth hunting for in second-hand bookshops. Nevertheless, much of its character may be inferred from the preceding discussion, and, noting that it includes some 358 densely printed pages of introductions and notes tactfully placed at the end of the volume, we may move both backwards and forwards to the efforts of other editors.

First, though, an aside. The following declaration is from an NT published in 1901, by which time the bulk of Moulton's work was well known:

> Unprejudiced treatment of the historical element in Christianity is one of the most immediate needs for faith and truth alike. For if holiness has not its sources in history, the supreme expression of religious thought and conduct has come to us in a historical form, and any intellectual neglect of that form is an error which cannot long be harboured with impunity.

Substitute 'literary' and 'literature' for 'historical' and 'history', and this is so exactly like Moulton that indebtedness is probable. The author is the redoubtable Scots scholar and translator, James Moffatt (1870–1944), the source the preface to his *The Historical New Testament. Being the Literature of the New Testament Arranged in the Order of its Literary Growth and According to the Dates of the Documents. A New Translation* (Edinburgh: Clark), p. xviii. Moffatt's intention had been, like Moulton's, to rearrange the RV, but the basis of the rearrangement was to be chronology. This puts the work in a different category from the Bible as literature, yet Moffatt uses 'literature' and 'literary' in his title, and the general effect he anticipates is a revitalisation just like that aimed for by literary editors: 'writings thus arranged *seriatim* reveal themselves more vividly than before' – but to a somewhat different end, 'as expressions of a contemporary and continuous movement in thought, action and feeling' (p. 3).

The rising Bible as literature movement clearly had its influence on the wider world of biblical scholarship. That influence is further visible in the way Moffatt writes about the new translation which he made because of difficulties in getting permission to reprint the RV.[22] Though 'the one claim of the present version is faithfulness' (p. xix), much of the discussion of translation concerns the effort 'to preserve the freshness of [the originals'] literary charm' (p. xx). Moreover, the presentation of the text is not only chronological but, except in the use of italics, literary, as the careful paragraphing and distinction of the poetic parts on the first page of Luke testifies. This is testimony to the increasingly literary spirit of the time, as well as to the parallels that may be found between literary and other kinds of biblical study.

Moving backwards, in 1895 there appeared something like a direct successor to Arnold's work (some of his notes to Isaiah are cited), *Passages of the Bible Chosen for their Literary Beauty and Interest*, edited by the redoubtable folklorist and anthropologist Sir James George Frazer (1854–1941). Though not the first of a number of such anthologies,[23] it had sufficient popularity to be issued in an enlarged second edition in 1909 and to be reprinted at least until 1932. Its printed life, then, was almost identical with that of *The Modern Reader's Bible*. By contrast with both Moulton and Arnold's work, the prefaces to the two editions are models of brevity. The following passage is fully a third of the preface to the first edition:

> That our English version of the Bible is one of the greatest classics in the language is admitted by all in theory, but few people appear to treat it as such in practice. The common man reads it for guidance and comfort in daily life and in sorrow; the scholar analyses it into its component parts and discusses their authorship and date; and the historian, the antiquary and the anthropologist have recourse to it as a storehouse of

---

[22] It is curious that Moulton should have succeeded in using the RV whereas Moffatt failed. Whatever the reason, it leads to a minor instance of history repeating itself: a project for a historical NT is at present stymied for want of permission to use a suitable version.

[23] The claim has been made by Ackerman, p. 119. Earlier was Cook's *The Bible and English Prose Style* (1892). It gives twenty-nine chapters, selected from both Testaments, and eight Psalms. No attempt is made at a literary presentation and there are no comments. Moreover, there may have been other earlier works. For instance, I have not seen Ezra Sampson's *Beauties of the Bible; Being a Selection from the Old and New Testaments, with Various Remarks and Brief Dissertations, Designed for the Use of Christians in General and Particularly for the Use of Schools and for the Improvement of Youth* (Albany, 1815).

Frazer's later *Folk-Lore in the Old Testament*, 3 vols. (London: Macmillan, 1918) does not connect sufficiently with the Bible as literature to warrant discussion here, though, by associating the Bible with 'savagery and superstition' (1: x), it helped to undermine reverence for the Bible in years following the First World War. Ackerman gives an interesting analysis of its weaknesses and effect (pp. 270–7).

facts illustrative of their special subjects. But how many read it, not for its religious, its linguistic, its historical and antiquarian interest, but simply for the sake of the enjoyment which as pure literature it is fitted to afford? It may be conjectured that the number of such readers is very small. The reason, or, at all events, a chief reason, of this is not far to seek. The passages of greatest literary beauty and interest – those on which the fame of the book as a classic chiefly rests – are scattered up and down it, imbedded, often at rare intervals, in a great mass of other matter which, however interesting and important as theology or history, possesses only subordinate value as literature. It seemed to me, therefore, that a service might be rendered to lovers of good literature by disengaging these gems from their setting and presenting them in a continuous series ... it is noble literature; and like all noble literature it is fitted to delight, to elevate and to console.   (Pp. v–vi, viii)

On the surface, brevity apart, this seems much like Arnold, especially in the insistence on the delight of literature. Nevertheless, there are some significant differences. 'As pure literature' rather than 'as literature' is the most telling. The gems of the Bible may be read as nothing more than literature, that is, in a spirit of pure aestheticism. There is no sign of Arnold's philosophical and religious sense of literature, or of his sense of the religious importance of the Bible, and the preface to the second edition makes clear Frazer's dissociation from devout attitudes (he was later to write privately that he rejected 'the Christian religion utterly as false').[24] He observes with gratification

that the example which I set of treating the Bible as pure literature has since been followed by others who have similarly edited the Old and New Testaments or portions of them in a form divested, as far as possible, of all purely theological import. The publication of such books may be welcomed as a sign that the love of the Bible is not confined to those who accept its dogmas. Though many of us can no longer, like our fathers, find in its pages the solution of the dark, the inscrutable riddle of human existence, yet the volume must still be held sacred by all who reverence the high aspirations to which it gives utterance, and the pathetic associations with which the faith and piety of so many generations have invested the familiar words.   (Pp. ix–x)

Though the gesture to piety is continued in the concluding few sentences, it is clear that Frazer is driving the wedge between the Bible as religion and the Bible as literature that 'the Bible as literature' implies. Arnold's *Isaiah* was for potential Christians; Frazer's anthology is for lapsed Christians. As such, it is the obverse of works such as Halsey's that present the Bible as a classic or as literature in order to bring unbelievers to its religion. It is the Bible without religion, that is, the Bible for unbelievers.

[24] Letter, 18 April 1904; as given in Ackerman, pp. 188–9.

The same impression is given by the notes. These are very much what one would expect from the author of *The Golden Bough*. Parallels from other literatures, ancient and modern, and from other customs abound, and there are pertinent passages from commentators. So the notes to Ruth consist of two passages from his friend William Robertson Smith's *Encyclopaedia Britannica* article describing the book and some of the customs which relate to it, Keats's lines from 'Ode to a Nightingale' and a note on 'a man plucked off his shoe, and gave it to his neighbour' (4: 7), showing parallels in Old German law and Indian custom, with relevant lines from an Indian poem quoted. The few notes on the Gospel passages consist entirely of parallels, several of them classical, and imitations, together with a passage from G. A. Smith's *The Historical Geography of the Holy Land* on 'the grandeur of the shepherd's character' in a country such as Judaea (p. 508). The result is a fascinating mélange of information which often cannot be found elsewhere, but little of it contributes to literary perception and none of it tends to a religious perception of the passages. Frazer's Bible 'as pure literature' is a folklorist's paradise.

Yet to read the anthology itself gives a different impression: it is full of passages of belief, as any liberal sampling of both Testaments cannot help being. Moreover, as a presentation of passages from the KJB, it is exemplary (though, by Moulton's extraordinary standards, conservative). All the passages are titled and referenced. There are no introductory comments or references to the notes, which are tucked away at the end of the volume for readers to take or leave as they wish. Thus the passages are left to make their own impression, religious, literary or other. They appear either as paragraphed prose or, in the poetic parts, as free but not stanzaic verse. Frazer does not intrude on the text, and the result is as good a Bible reader as any of its scale. And it is a scale not often kept to in literary presentations of the Bible. The text runs to 450 pages and the print is generous in size, so the reader is thoroughly accommodated and all signs of traditional Bible presentation have disappeared.

A third of a century later, William Ralph Inge, Dean of St Paul's, published an anthology that is an instructive counterpart to Frazer's, *Every Man's Bible: An Anthology Arranged with an Introduction* (London: Longmans, 1934). The scale is the same, the presentation almost as admirable (the typeface is not as pleasing and the lack of titles and references at the heads of the passages is a small loss), and over a third of the passages chosen are identical. Yet the intention is opposite to Frazer's. The introduction, as long as Frazer's is brief, begins:

> The object of this anthology is to help those who wish to use the Bible as their chief devotional book. For many generations the regular reading of the sacred volume,

chapter by chapter, without explanation and without commentary, brought comfort
and edification to many pious souls. This practice has now so far declined that many
Christians have almost ceased to read their Bibles at all. This is a grievous loss to our
national Christianity.   (P. ix)

Frazer's contrasting starting-point was the fewness of those who read it 'simply
for the sake of the enjoyment which as pure literature it is fitted to afford'. The
similarity of the two anthologies, setting aside the introductions and notes and
Inge's one real piece of shaping within the anthology, his arrangement of the
passages by religious theme, shows how close in practice the Bible as devotion
and the Bible as literature can be. The surrounding beliefs differ, but the texts
themselves stay substantially the same.

   The differences between the anthologists' attitudes to the Bible turn out to be
less absolute than their difference of belief might lead us to expect. Frazer is
more than reserved about Christianity, but Inge has few reservations about the
Bible as literature. Though Inge seems to be attacking that approach by
observing that 'we are on holy ground, and we cannot read the Bible "like any
other book". We read it because for us it is not like any other book' (p. x), he has
no wish to exclude literary appreciation, and notes two sentences later that 'the
literary beauty of many passages can be appreciated only when they are given
entire'. So, with an ambiguity that was not present in the preface to the K JB, he
writes of helping 'some readers to rediscover for themselves the inexhaustible
treasures which are hidden in the most widely read and incomparably the most
important collection of writings in the literature of the world' (p. x), and even
uses one of Frazer's formulations, 'the gems of the Bible' (p. xxxv). For many in
the twentieth century the literary quality of the Bible was less contentious than
its truth. This was not just because it was less important: with exceptions, the
stigma attached to literature had long since disappeared, and most people with
literary opinions, whether or not they were practising Christians, had been
brought up with the language of the K JB as a foundation of their consciousness
and with acclaim for the K JB's literary greatness as an unassailed truth. In some
hands, the Bible as literature, especially the Bible as pure literature, might
exclude the Bible as devotion, but believers, loving the Bible and also desiring
to have it read by everyone, were unlikely to challenge what they took to be
both their literary pleasure in the text and a means of converting the unfaithful.
The problem exposed in Inge's declaration that 'we cannot read the Bible "like
any other book"' greatly exercised critics such as C. S. Lewis, but for many
readers it mattered not a jot.

   So far we have been starting from the Bible and seeing how it is shaped as
literature. But if all the declarations about the Bible being a classic of English

prose were truly believed by literary men, should it not be possible to find literature reaching out to the Bible – would one not expect to find passages from the KJB in anthologies of English prose in the same way that one routinely finds some discussion of the English Bible in histories of English literature? Kenneth Muir, introducing an anthology of English prose, suggests one reason why one should not: 'the Authorised Version is not represented here as it will be accessible to all readers'.[25] If this is only an excuse, it is an excuse for the practice of a good many anthologists. Nevertheless, some anthologists give a taste of the KJB. Herbert Read and Bonamy Dobrée, for instance, include four passages in *The London Book of English Prose* (1931). Two of the passages (S. of S. 7 and Job 3) are generally thought of as poetry, and all four look rather like verse because the verse divisions are preserved as paragraphing. This may suggest some unease on the editors' parts: 'the noblest monument of English prose' is often poetry: could it somehow belong in an anthology of English verse?

Only one compiler that I know of thought so, a literary man of miscellaneous accomplishments, William Ernest Henley (1849–1903). His *English Lyrics*[26] is a magnificent exception among anthologies, giving 42 passages over 53 pages (Shakespeare is given 11 pages for 22 lyrics). The passages range from Exodus 15 through ten Psalms, ten chapters from Job and almost all of the Song of Songs to Habakkuk 3. The opening words of the passages in the Vulgate are used as titles, then the KJB text is given, lineated as free verse. The effect is to remove the biblical appearance of the texts and to allow the poetry of the KJB to stand as the most substantial achievement of English lyric. The poet Francis Thompson's response to this treatment of the Bible is worth recording. He found much to quarrel with in the anthology, but before quarrelling he thanked 'Mr Henley for his tremendous gift of lyrical passages from the Old Testament . . . they appear in this book so unexpectedly as almost to constitute a fresh body of poetry'. Of Henley's arrangement of Psalm 137 he exclaims, 'does it not gain – is not its beauty emphasised – by the new arrangement?', and he thinks the extent of the selection gives the volume 'exceptional interest'.[27]

Henley's rationale for including the Bible is almost as brief as Muir's was for excluding it. First, 'verse in English is, *ipso facto*, English verse'. Second, 'the Authorised Version is a monument of English prose. But the inspiration and effect of many parts of it are absolutely lyrical.' He adds what amounts to a claim that the KJB presents the highest achievement of English lyric: 'on those parts I

[25]   Kenneth Muir, ed., *The Pelican Book of English Prose*, vol. 1, *Elizabethan and Jacobean Prose: 1550–1620* (Harmondsworth: Penguin, 1956), p. xx.
[26]   *English Lyrics: Chaucer to Poe, 1340–1809* (1897; 2nd edn, London, 1905).
[27]   'Mr Henley's anthology' (1897); *Literary Criticisms*, pp. 497–9.

have drawn for such a series of achievement in lyrism as will be found, I trust, neither the least interesting nor the least persuasive group in an anthology which pretends to set forth none but the choicest among English lyrics' (p. vii). He later writes of 'the noble numbers – passionate, affecting, essentially lyrical – from one of the two greatest books in English', and describes the KJB as an 'achievement in art' and as 'an English book' (p. xiii).

This is indeed the kind of conclusion one would expect from sincere AVolaters in the literary world. But Henley, as an anthologist, seems to have been alone in taking this line. Moreover, it was a new line for him. Three years earlier he had compiled an anthology of prose, and the KJB is neither included nor mentioned.[28] We can only guess why this apparent change of heart took place, but it is possible that Frazer's example, coming between these two anthologies, provided the stimulus.

Be this as it may, Frazer did, as we have seen, note with gratification that others had followed his example of treating the Bible as pure literature. He probably had Moulton in mind, but there is a major distinction to be made between their works. Frazer maintains that only some parts of the Bible are literary gems and so gathers together an anthology; Moulton takes the whole Bible as being of literary quality and so makes an edition of the whole, including three books of the Apocrypha, Tobit, Wisdom and Ecclesiasticus.[29] The second of the modern literary presentations most worth hunting for stands between these two positions. It is Ernest Sutherland Bates's *The Bible Designed to be Read as Living Literature* (1936; in England known as *The Bible Designed to be Read as Literature* (1937)). Bates argues that, from a literary point of view, the Bible is full of 'redundancy and irrelevance' that may ruin the finest aesthetic qualities (p. x). The way he describes the difficulties confronting a reader of the OT bears repetition, though the overlap with Moulton will be obvious:[30]

> In following the epic history of the Jews through the first sixteen books of the Old Testament, the reader is hopelessly thrown off his course by the legal codes, the

[28] W. E. Henley and Charles Whibley, eds., *A Book of English Prose: Character and Incident, 1387–1649* (London, 1894).

[29] Another complete version warrants mention here, *The Temple Bible*, 31 vols. (London: Dent; Philadelphia: Lippincott, 1901–3). The aim, described by A. R. S. Kennedy, 'is to lead those that love their Bible to a more intelligent appreciation of its value as literature' (II: v). These pleasing little volumes give the KJB text uninterrupted. Among the supplementary material to each volume are 'passages occurring in the works of well-known writers in English literature [which] have obviously been suggested by the incidents recorded in' the individual books.

[30] Bates willingly acknowledges his debt to Moulton and cites a witty but indirect passage from Quiller-Couch, also indebted to Moulton, on the need to 'clothe the Bible in a dress through which its beauty might best shine' (pp. viii–ix; Quiller-Couch, pp. 165–6).

census reports and genealogies, the beautiful but totally out-of-place fiction of Ruth, the double narrative of the same events in Kings and Chronicles. He then comes upon another piece of prose-fiction in Esther, the poetic drama of Job, the lyrical anthology of the Psalms, the collection of folk Proverbs, the philosophical treatise of Ecclesiastes, and the secular love poetry of the Song of Songs – nearly all of this section being the product of a late highly self-conscious period; after which, without warning, he is whirled back four hundred years to the early group of the Prophets who made their appearance once before in the book of Kings. Then, if he can indeed recognise without difficulty the greatness and appreciate the special quality of the pre-exilic Amos, Hosea and Isaiah, and could even, if he had a fair chance, detect the poignant difference in the post-exilic work of the mighty Unknown Poet at the end of Isaiah, as he goes on from these, Jeremiah and Ezekiel to the later imitative school of minor Prophets, his ears are dinned with endless ever weaker repetitions (always excepting Micah, who belongs among the earlier writers). Also, misplaced amid the prophetical books, he encounters the prose fiction of Daniel and Jonah, similar in type to Ruth and Esther – propagandist fiction all of it, four antithetical works, Ruth and Jonah generous appeals for international tolerance, Esther and Daniel impassioned pleas for patriotism. (Pp. x–xi)

The argument for reorganisation and selection is powerful, and I can testify to the effectiveness of the results Bates achieves (just as I could testify to the power of Tyndale's original, essentially literary, presentation of, say, Genesis, or the power of Frazer's selections). Bates 'is emboldened to proclaim the final heresy – that the part is greater than the whole, and that, for literary appreciation, one wants not all the Bible but the best of it' (p. xi).

Yet, persuasive as the argument is and good as the result is, it is still something like a heresy, even from a literary point of view. This becomes apparent when, in the same spirit, he observes that 'the reader finds his sense of the events in the life of Jesus confused both by the repetitions and the divergences of the four Gospels' (p. xi). We might class this with the incomprehending objections to the repetitions in biblical poetry, or, in another sphere, with the rewritings of Shakespeare by worthies such as Nahum Tate. The effect of the Gospel story is inescapably fourfold: 'to give the basic biography of Jesus found in ... Mark, the earliest and most authoritative, supplemented by those incidents and teachings not found in Mark but in the other Gospels' (p. xii), is to falsify in the name of improvement. The repetitions and confusions not only between but within the Gospels drive the reader from the texts to a composite truth behind them in a way that rarely happens in other literature. Yet this is a literary effect, and any selective presentation that eliminates it makes the Gospels into something they are not. Reordering the books of the Bible seems unobjectionable; so does the identification of the different parts of Isaiah, because there one is making editorial changes to editorial matters. But to edit and select among individual books can be to interfere at a different level: it can be to change the text. In literary terms this is a heresy.

Some of the Bible's warts come from the authors, some from editors. The latter are fair game, but there is no clear line between the two. Are we rescuing a truer version of Job by omitting Elihu? Or giving a truer version of Ruth by omitting the last five verses? We are certainly making the books read better by our standards of literature, and we may be eliminating later additions to those works. But we are also falsifying the whole experience of the individual works as they have come down to us. The issues cannot be argued to a resolution, and it is not my purpose to impeach Bates. In the end, however much one appreciates what he has done, one has also to read the books in a complete Bible and to reach one's own judgement as to what constitutes each book, what its literary quality is, and what the historical experience of it has been. And, behind these problems, there is of course the question of whether the Bible is a single whole or not. Not everyone would agree that it has become a single whole *only* as the result of a long editorial progress, and some would argue that it can only be read truly (a phrase that might mean many things) as a whole. Bates's 'heresy' is provocative.

One other aspect of Bates's work might be regarded as heretical. Mostly he gives the KJB's text re-presented, but for Job, Ecclesiastes, Proverbs and the Song of Songs he uses the RV because it 'is admittedly far superior' (p. xii). Moulton had used the RV throughout for the same reason. There is another question involved here besides the irresolvable one of relative quality, a historical question. Allowing for the sake of argument that the KJB is sometimes bettered by other translations both older and newer (I have suggested that sometimes Tyndale reads better), do readers want the 'best' version of the individual texts or the version that in literary and linguistic terms has been central for the English-speaking world? Readers, after all, are likely to be readers of both the Bible and literature in English: in the latter capacity they cannot escape a historical and cultural awareness that dictates the use of the KJB. For them, it, but no other version, is the English classic.

Bates's heresies are indeed provocative. One may suggest that there is no such thing as the ideal Bible as English literature, either in theory or practice. A strictly historical view might promote Pollard's facsimile of the KJB as the ideal. This magnificent volume gives exactly and completely what became the Bible of most English literature through the last three centuries. Or, given its unwieldiness and unavailability, one might argue for its smaller reissue

(Oxford: Oxford University Press, 1985), which lacks only the documentary appendix to the introduction. But against either of these choices there lie at least four sets of arguments, those against standard presentation of the text, those against an archaic presentation which few people, relatively speaking, experienced, those for selection and those for the superiority of other versions.

A looser historical view would still insist on the text of the KJB as of paramount importance as the English wording of the text. In this looser view, what is needed is still a complete KJB, but one in which the editorial interference with reading caused especially by verse and chapter divisions and by annotation was eliminated. One editorial rearrangement might be added, namely the presentation of parts generally agreed to be poetic as free verse. In other words, the form of presentation might return to something very like the presentation of Tyndale's 1526 NT. Only his insertion of numbered chapter divisions might be deleted in favour of Bates's natural divisions with titles such as 'The creation of the world', 'The fall of man', 'The first murder', etc. Yet there are dangers in this general reversion to 1526: not everyone will agree as to what is poetry and what not, and the line divisions will always be contentious even if one does not go as far as Moulton and others, and argue that stanzaic arrangement is also necessary.

An illustration of some of the difficulties is readily given. Even if one can determine which is right, which is the best of these three presentations of the beginning of Isaiah 40 as poetry?

<blockquote>

1

Comfort ye, comfort ye my people,
Saith your God.
Speak ye comfortably to Jerusalem,
And cry unto her,
That her warfare is accomplished,
That her iniquity is pardoned:
For she hath received of the Lord's hand
Double for all her sins.
The voice of him that crieth in the wilderness,
Prepare ye the way of the Lord,
Make straight in the desert
A highway for our God.
Every valley shall be exalted,
And every mountain and hill shall be made low:
And the crooked shall be made straight,
And the rough places plain:
And the glory of the Lord shall be revealed,
</blockquote>

And all flesh shall see it together:
For the mouth of the Lord hath spoken it.

2

'Comfort ye, comfort ye my people',
Saith your God.
'Speak ye comfortably to Jerusalem,
And cry unto her,
That her warfare is accomplished,
That her iniquity is pardoned:
For she hath received of the Lord's hand
Double for all her sins.'

The voice of him that crieth in the wilderness,
'Prepare ye the way of the Lord,
Make straight in the desert a highway for our God.
Every valley shall be exalted,
And every mountain and hill shall be made low:
And the crooked shall be made straight,
And the rough places plain:
And the glory of the Lord shall be revealed,
And all flesh shall see it together:
For the mouth of the Lord hath spoken it.'

3

'Comfort ye, comfort ye my people', saith your God.
'Speak ye comfortably to Jerusalem, and cry unto
                her,
That her warfare is accomplished,
That her iniquity is pardoned:
For she hath received of the Lord's hand double for
                all her sins.'

The voice of him that crieth in the wilderness,
                'Prepare ye the way of the Lord,
Make straight in the desert a highway for our God.
Every valley shall be exalted,
And every mountain and hill shall be made low:
And the crooked shall be made straight,
And the rough places plain:
And the glory of the Lord shall be revealed,
And all flesh shall see it together:
For the mouth of the Lord hath spoken it.'

There is an obvious lack of agreement as to what the length of the poetic line is. The first version opts for consistently short lines, with the result that attention is drawn to details of parallelism that are apparent more subtly in the longer lines of the third version. A strong analytical awareness is achieved at the expense of making the text staccato. Moreover, the desire for consistency in line length produces breaks in the text that do nothing more than interfere with the flow of the sense, as in 'For she hath received of the Lord's hand / Double for all her sins.' In a short passage such differences may appear to be of minimal importance, but in the long run they are likely to have a real effect on readers' sense of the pace and rhythm of the writing. The addition of quotation marks in 2 and 3 obviously aids perception of the structure of the passage. Version 2 is from Bates, and 1 is from Roland Mushat Frye's more recent selection; this uses headings as Bates does but also includes chapter and verse numbers; unhappily, in the prose parts the verse numbers are included within the text.

In spite of these difficulties, let us assume that the advantages of signalling to the reader that some parts of the Bible are poetic outweigh the disadvantages of leaving too much to the fancy of an individual editor and of leaving these parts unmarked, that is, leaving them as prose, as did W. L. Courtney's popular *The Literary Man's Bible: A Selection of Passages from the Old Testament, Historic, Poetic and Philosophic, Illustrating Hebrew Literature* (London: Chapman and Hall, 1907).[31] The stranger to the Bible whom I pictured at the beginning of volume 1 entering a religious bookshop would not find this ideal KJB – complete, freed of verse and chapter divisions, and visually signalling that some parts are poetry – among the books in print. It is occasionally to be found among the second-hand books and is of course the third of the modern literary presentations most worth hunting for. Except that it retains chapter divisions, *The Reader's Bible* (London: Cambridge University Press, Oxford University Press, Eyre & Spottiswoode, 1951) is exactly the edition I have described. It is from this that the third presentation of the passage is taken. Its presentation of the beginning of Luke is, from an editorial point of view, almost exactly Tyndale's (see volume 1, plate 2). The chapter divisions are marked with centred titles, but there are no verse numbers or annotations. Paragraphs and poetic lines are used, and the only differences from Tyndale are that 'and Mary said' is not distinguished, and the line division in the poetry is not always the same.

The Reader's Bible is the nearest there has been to an ideal complete KJB for the two kinds of readers mentioned earlier, readers of English literature and literary readers of the KJB. If the KJB is an acceptable Bible for religion, then

---

[31] Courtney is conservative to the extent of reproducing the italics of the original KJB, but he does omit the verse numbers, and the result is perfectly tolerable.

one might also call this an ideal Bible for a third group of readers (not necessarily to be distinguished from the other two), religious readers, because it throws them back to the contextual reading which so many people, along with Tyndale, would see as a necessity for true understanding. It is an obvious indicator of the way the Bible is normally used that *The Reader's Bible* is long since out of print while the full variety of standard religious editions of the KJB continue to be printed. A complete reading version of the KJB is an aberration on the market because the Bible is still read – or used – as the book of religion. Distinctively religious presentation remains far more marketable than literary presentation, and the utility of verse division seems to be inescapable.

The disadvantages of complete Bibles are well rehearsed by Bates, and the practice of selecting from an author has an ancient lineage. Comprehensive reading may be a necessity if one is to aim at a complete understanding, but for most readers selection is a normal, unobjectionable fact of life. It is better to read *Hamlet* twice than *Hamlet* and *The Merry Wives of Windsor* once each, better to know the best of Keats than to half-know all of Keats. The function of selection is to open what is best opened and to invite to the rest. Ideal presentations of the complete KJB are for readers who have already come to the Bible. For readers seeking to discover the pleasures of reading the Bible, selection is an ideal. And from this point of view, Bates's *The Bible Designed to be Read as Living Literature*, though sadly out of print, is still the best edition.

Following his introduction, Bates gives two pages to quotations 'in praise of the Bible'. Rather than pursuing a survey of modern reading editions too far and necessarily running into praise of such beautiful but recondite productions as Ruth Hornblower Greenough's *The Bible for my Grandchildren: Arranged from the King James Version* (privately printed, 1950), it will be better to take Bates's opening two quotations as a way in to a final point. First comes Goethe: 'the greater the intellectual progress of the ages, the more fully will it be possible to employ the Bible not only as the foundation but as the instrument of education'; next is Robert Louis Stevenson: 'I believe it would startle and move any one if they could make a certain effort of imagination and read it freshly like a book, not droningly and chillily like a portion of the Bible' (p. xiii). These indicate two central aspects of *The Bible Designed to be Read as Living Literature*, its connection with education and its attempt to freshen the Bible by making it like any other book in appearance. Literary presentations of the Bible descend directly from editions such as the Irish *Extracts from the Old and New Testaments* and from the work of critics such as Halsey and Arnold. A further connection is visible if we place Stevenson's remark in context. It comes from an article entitled 'Books which have influenced me', and is preceded and followed by these sentences:

'The next book, in order of time, to influence me was the New Testament, and in particular the Gospel according to St. Matthew'; and 'Any one would then be able to see in it those truths which we are all courteously supposed to know and all modestly refrain from applying.'[32] Literary presentation of the Bible may be more than an attempt to bring fresh readers to the Bible – it may also be an attempt to revive the freshness of response that was so common a childhood experience in the nineteenth century. It is no accident that so many of these presentations come from men who grew up in a time when the Bible was an inescapable and widely remarked childhood experience, but who then lived their adult life in a time of declining faith. There is a significant change between Bates's edition and Frye's volume: the last part of Frye's subtitle is 'for study as literature'. The realm of childhood love (and reaction) has been left behind: in its place is modern academic study.

Freshness can be a dangerous ideal when it becomes mere novelty, but we may use the same passage from Isaiah at slightly greater length to illustrate one last variety of presentation:

The Lord	Comfort my people –
Isaiah (with flourish)	Says our God.
The Lord	Comfort them! Encourage the people of Jerusalem. Tell them they have suffered long enough and their sins are now forgiven. I have punished them in full for all their sins.
Isaiah	A voice cries out:
Voice	Prepare in the wilderness a road for the Lord Clear the way in the desert for our God! Fill every valley; level every mountain. The hills will become a plain, and the rough country will be made smooth. Then the glory of the Lord will be revealed and all mankind will see it. The Lord himself has promised this.
Isaiah	A voice cries out:
Voice	Proclaim a message!

---

[32] *The Works of Robert Louis Stevenson*, Swanston edition, 25 vols. (London: Chatto, Heinemann and Longmans, 1912), XVI: 274.

Isaiah	What message shall I proclaim?
Voice	Proclaim that all mankind are like grass;
	they last no longer than wild flowers.
	Grass withers and flowers fade,
	when the Lord sends the wind blowing over
	them.
	People are no more enduring than grass.
Isaiah	Yes, grass withers and flowers fade,
	but the word of our God endures for ever.
	(PAUSE)

I chose Isaiah 40 because it confronts readers with real difficulties in following what voice they are hearing – difficulties very like those faced by a reader of a modern poem in the prophetic mode, T. S. Eliot's 'The Waste Land'. An editorial arrangement of this sort is not merely fresh, but is also elucidatory in quite as admirable a way as some of Moulton's arrangements. The words themselves are from the Good News Bible, the arrangement, unsurprisingly, from *The Dramatised Bible*.[33] Perry, the editor, argues that there is OT precedent for dramatic presentation: 'it does appear that the Hebrew people in temple worship used drama to rehearse the acts of God in their history – notably the crossing of the Red Sea and their deliverance from the slavery of Egypt. Such dramatic presentations were not entertainment – though they would have been marvellously *entertaining*' (p. ix), and he goes on to argue in detail from Psalm 118. However, Isaiah 40 is sufficient to make the point: some parts of the Bible not only respond well to dramatic presentation but are best presented in that form because it best reveals the nature and meaning of the text.

The Dramatised Bible makes no mention of the Bible as literature and is, as the little I have already quoted shows, from a religious rather than a literary source. It explicitly claims descent from 'generations of ministers and teachers or youth and children's leaders' who have 'turned the Bible text into drama so that worshippers or students can become actively involved in its teaching', but points out that it is the first edition to give such a presentation to the whole Bible narrative (p. ix).[34] The purpose, then, is evangelical rather than literary, which takes us back to the origins of ideas of the Bible as literature. Perry's preface concludes:

[33] Ed. Michael Perry (London: Marshall Pickering and The Bible Society, 1989).
[34] It is not quite a complete Bible. Passages judged unsuitable for dramatic treatment, notably from the Epistles, are omitted. The Good News Bible and the New International Version are drawn on, and some of the Psalms are given in a new translation.

Much of the work of the Jubilate group [to which he belongs] has been in the interests of a clearer presentation of the facts of the faith in worship. Centrally within this context, *The Dramatised Bible* brings the text of Scripture to life. Using *The Dramatised Bible* means involving people in the recalling and recounting their salvation-history...

Those who listen to *The Dramatised Bible* are drawn into the presentation. As the story moves from voice to voice it is very difficult for attention to wander... Even young children, who naturally grow restive during a long and uneventful reading, find their interest and imagination caught up in the narrative as the scriptures are presented in dramatised form.

We confidently commend this book to churches, youth groups, schools, study groups and all who work in the area of education... We happily anticipate that *The Dramatised Bible* will enrich our worship by granting us a clearer vision of God and a surer knowledge of the revelation of the eternal purpose for our world in Jesus Christ.   (Pp. x–xi)

The linking of education, imagination and salvation is exactly the same linking that produced *Extracts from the Old and New Testaments* back in 1814, and the result is a fresh, particular, literary presentation. Just as Frazer and Inge produced remarkably similar anthologies from different points of view and with different final intentions, *The Dramatised Bible*, developed for religious purposes, is a new literary version of the Bible.

CHAPTER 8

The later reputation of the KJB

Testimonies from writers

In considering the reputation of the KJB over the century since the RV, it may be best to start with a somewhat amorphous collection of testimonies from writers to their experience of the KJB and, sometimes, its influence on their work.

Interest in the KJB as a literary influence helped to shape some of the chorus-books referred to earlier (above, p. 186). One such was by the American Baptist minister and professor, author of *The Religious Influence of Wordsworth*, T. Harwood Pattison (1838–1904). His *The History of the English Bible* (1894) begins ordinarily enough but goes on to chapters on 'the Bible in English literature' and 'the Bible and the nation'. An observation he attributes to the American Presbyterian minister Charles Henry Parkhurst sums up the motivation for this development: '"I am interested in the people who made the Bible, but I am more interested in the people whom the Bible makes, for they show me the fibre and genius of Scripture as no mental studiousness or verbal exegesis can do"' (p. 222). So in these chapters Pattison moves beyond opinions of the literary excellence of the Bible to testimonies from writers that their work was shaped by the Bible. His aim is to show that, 'from John Bunyan to John Ruskin ... we owe more than we can ever tell to our early training in the English of the Bible. The character of our national tongue has been tempered by it; and to it our great writers are largely indebted for the sobriety, the strength and the sweetness which distinguish their best efforts' (p. 185). He by no means confines himself to style, but the question, Where did a writer get his style? recurs. The following passage is characteristic of what he wants to know and the kind of answer he wants, even if the answer does not come directly from the author of *Through the Dark Continent*:

[The Bible's] influence upon a style originally deficient in the essentials of distinction has been illustrated within a few years in the experience of Mr Stanley, the African explorer. Of him a competent writer asks: 'Where did he get his present style?' and then proceeded to answer his own question, thus: 'A clue may be found in his own story of the Bible which Sir William Mackinnon gave him at starting. He read it through, he tells us, three times ... He has read, I will venture to guess, the greater Prophets of the Old Testament and the Epistles in the New Testament till his mind has become saturated with them. There is no imitation of any of these writers, or no conscious imitation ... But they have modified his habits of thought and his methods of expression. He has brooded over them in the recesses of his awful forest till they have become part of his spiritual and part of his intellectual life.'[1]

Not every writer discusses his formative reading – literary autobiography is, if not exactly post-Wordsworthian,[2] nevertheless a fairly modern phenomenon – and only a few of those who do discuss their reading think to remark on the Bible. Moreover, it is only after Petty, McCulloch and Seiss had begun to establish the subject that people would ask writers where they got their style, hoping that they would say as Charles Dickens is supposed to have done, 'Why, from the New Testament, to be sure'.[3] Such answers, even when obtained, may not be genuinely informative. If Dickens did indeed make such a statement, we

---

[1] Pp. 200–1. Pattison refers to the *New York Tribune* (28 May 1890).

[2] Franklin, for instance, was interested in influences on himself and, though it is not quite the same thing, gave a detailed account of how he used the *Spectator* as a model for prose composition (*Autobiography*, pp. 61–2).

[3] Pattison (p. 191) cites this as the answer to Walter Savage Landor's question, but I have been unable to authenticate Pattison's report. Reverently, Dickens had written a version of the Gospel story for his children (*The Life of Our Lord* (1934)). He recalled it in an 1868 letter to his youngest son, who was leaving home for Australia:

> I put a New Testament among your books for the very same reasons, and with the very same hopes, that made me write an easy account of it for you when you were a little child. Because it is the best book that ever was, or will be, known in the world; and because it teaches you the best lessons by which any human creature who tries to be truthful and faithful to duty can possibly be guided. As your brothers have gone away, one by one, I have written to each such words as I am now writing to you, and have entreated them all to guide themselves by this Book, putting aside the interpretations and inventions of man.
>
> (John Forster, *The Life of Charles Dickens* (1872–4); 2 vols., ed. B. W. Matz (London: Chapman and Hall, 1911), II: 421)

While searching for confirmation of Pattison's report I came across the following observation: 'Ben Jonson I have studied, principally for the purity of his English. Had it not been for him and Shakespeare, our language would have fallen into ruin.' The writer is Landor (John Forster, *Walter Savage Landor*, 2 vols. (London, 1869), II: 525). It is a reminder that interest in the purity of English did not necessarily coincide with admiration for the KJB.

might well ask what spirit it was said in, what he might have had in mind, and whether a New Testament quality can be seen in his style. It may be that the same spirit prompts the answers as prompts Pattison's interest, a spirit of automatic reverence for the KJB as a model of language: few of the testimonies which might be gathered from authors are anything more than harmonious contributions to the pious chorus.

Like the passage on Stanley, a good many of Pattison's examples are indirect, not really testimony at all. He cites, for instance, a fairly well-known story about Thomas Carlyle: in the course of conducting family worship, he began to read Job and continued through all forty-two chapters because he thought there was 'nothing written ... in the Bible or out of it, of equal literary merit'.[4] Similar pieces of loose evidence are easily found. Pattison might have cited, say, Walt Whitman, who wrote with extreme enthusiasm of 'the Bible as poetry',[5] or Herman Melville, whose long poem *Clarel* (1876) is dense with biblical allusion. However, the examples that really make the Stanleyesque kind of statement that Pattison is looking for tend to postdate his book. George Bernard Shaw (1856–1950), for example, declared, 'that I can write as I do without having to think about my style is due to my having been as a child steeped in the Bible, *The Pilgrim's Progress* and *Cassell's Illustrated Shakespeare*'.[6]

A third of a century after Pattison, another American, Robert T. Oliver, set out to test the truth of what he took to be commonplace remarks, that 'the

---

[4] Pattison, p. 204. *On Heroes, Hero-Worship and the Heroic in History* (1841), lecture 2; ed. Israel Gollancz (London: Dent, 1901), p. 60.

[5] *The Critic* 3 (3 February 1883), 39–40.

[6] *Everybody's Political What's What* (London: Constable, 1944), p. 181. Shaw, normally independent, provocative and dogmatic, is unexceptional in his view of the KJB's literary qualities, but his independence reasserts itself when he considers some of the content:

> the English Bible, though a masterpiece of literary art in its readable parts and, being the work of many highly gifted authors and translators, rich in notable poems, proverbs, precepts and entertaining if not always edifying stories, is yet a jumble of savage superstition, obsolete cosmology and a theology which, beginning with Calibanesque idolatry and propitiatory blood sacrifices (Genesis to Kings), recoils into sceptical disillusioned atheistical Pessimism (Ecclesiastes); revives in a transport of revolutionary ardor as the herald of divine justice and mercy and the repudiation of all sacrifices (Micah and the Prophets); relapses into sentimentality by conceiving God as an affectionate father (Jesus); reverts to blood sacrifice and takes refuge from politics in Other-Worldliness and Second Adventism (the Apostles); and finally explodes in a mystical opium dream of an impossible apocalypse (Revelation): every one of these phases being presented in such an unbalanced one-sided way that the first Christian Catholic Church forbad the laity to read the Bible without special permission. (P. 357)

Bible, as a force to be reckoned with in writing, is dead', and that 'the old conception that the King James translation of the Bible is the best monument to English prose style is hopelessly out of date' (p. 350). He leaves these remarks unattributed, and I have only come across one passage of this sort from this time.[7] Nevertheless, they have the appearance of a perfectly normal reaction of one generation against the truths of its forebears. That they should have been uttered at about the time of that quintessential essay in A Volatry, Lowes's 'The noblest monument of English prose', is but one more example of the ready co-existence of contrary views, especially when one of those views is a matter of inherited truth.

Rather than relying on published material, Oliver wrote to 'a group of prominent American writers, frankly asking them their impressions of the situation' (p. 351), and gathered a selection from the replies into a unique and neat little article. As he observes, the responses are individualistic and not subject to easy generalisation beyond the observation that there were then still 'many contemporary writers who find the King James Bible as powerfully moving as it has been in any age' (p. 355); in other words, the responses show the co-existence of contrary views just remarked on. Few of the 'prominent' respondents are now household names, but some of their responses have a familiar ring, while others come as a much-needed splash of fresh water on the face. Hendrick Willem van Loon noted that 'the King James version means very little in my life because it was not until my twentieth year that I discovered that God had not written the Bible originally in the vernacular of the delegates to the Synod of Dordrecht' (p. 351). He added, 'why waste your time on this sort of thing? You know that everyone will tell you that they loved their King James version.' Indeed a good many did just that, giving simplistic answers which are vulnerable to the kind of contempt Carl van Doren gave voice to:

---

[7] E. M. Forster's 1944 lecture, 'English prose between 1918 and 1939', moves from a general observation of the KJB's influence to a comment on Bates's *The Bible Designed to be Read as Literature*:

> Its publication gave some of us a shock and caused us to realise that the English of the Authorised Version had at last become remote from popular English. This was well put in a review by Somerset Maugham. The English of the Bible, he agreed, is part of our national heritage, but it is so alien to our present idiom that no writer can study it profitably ... there is now an unbridgeable gulf between ourselves and the Authorised Version as regards style, and the gulf widened about 1920 ... Quotations from the Bible still occur, but they support my contention: they are usually conventional and insensitive, introduced because the author or speaker wants to be impressive without taking trouble.
>
> (*Two Cheers for Democracy* (1951; Harmondsworth: Penguin, 1965), pp. 277–89; p. 283)

'most prose writers who say they have studied the Bible and modelled their style on it are, I believe, liars' (p. 352). Simple statements deserve such simple contradictions.

The remarks become interesting and begin to escape from van Doren's condemnation when they give reasons for the love, and comment on both use and influence. Edwin Markham seems to have gone to school with Stanley. He studied biblical style, especially that of the Prophets, and was certain that 'the remarkable simplicity and directness of those masters of speech helped greatly to fashion my style in both prose and verse' (p. 355), but, if he knew how it had fashioned his style, he does not say. Lew Sarett, a poet, also studied the KJB for its literary beauty, yet, unlike Markham, 'never tried to use the elements of its style. But I respond so deeply ... that perhaps unconsciously I have been influenced' (p. 352). Hamlin Garland's grandparents knew the KJB almost by heart; he himself not only knew it well but 'as I grew toward manhood I heard much talk of its noble simplicity'. From this background he makes a suggestion a shade more precise than Sarett's: 'I doubt if it influenced me directly, but indirectly it undoubtedly served as a corrective to the vernacular of my neighbours and the slovenly English of the press' (p. 353).

Only one of Oliver's respondents, Bess Streeter Aldrich, goes much beyond this, and she is best seen in company with some other more detailed accounts. The most interesting writer from this point of view is the British novelist, poet and miscellaneous writer D. H. Lawrence (1885–1930), not just because of the detail he gives and the insight he shows, but because he is similar to Charlotte Brontë in the way he both uses and is shaped by the KJB. He is arguably the most biblical major writer of the twentieth century, and one might devote a book to showing ways in which this is true. At the simple level of direct use of the Bible, his work includes commentary on the Bible (*Apocalypse*), an adaptation of part of David's story for the stage that retains much of the language of the KJB (*David*),[8] a rewriting of the last part of Jesus' life (*The Man Who Died* or *The Escaped Cock*), and novels which make substantial use of biblical imagery and language such as *The Rainbow*. More complex is the question of his language, which is often, though not always, strikingly

---

[8] One incident in *Women in Love* reflects a literary use of biblical stories that I have only found in one other place. Gudrun and Ursula take part in a balletic performance of Ruth at Breadalby (ch. 8). Charades and invented plays were a common recreation in H. G. Wells's household from the late 1890s onwards. The subjects were frequently biblical and the story of Noah a particular favourite. On one such occasion Charlie Chaplin created 'a marvellous Noah' (*H. G. Wells in Love*, ed. G. P. Wells (Boston, Mass.: Little, Brown, 1984), pp. 30–2).

parallelistic. The problem of how much and how deliberately this is biblical cannot be solved here. One might attribute this parallelism in part to the tendency of a spontaneous speaking voice to move forward by amplifying repetition. Nevertheless, it is difficult to imagine that Lawrence's use of parallelism would have developed in the way it did had he not been intimate with the KJB. He once defended his use of 'continual, slightly modified repetition' with the remark that 'it is natural to the author . . . every natural crisis in emotion or passion or understanding comes from this pulsing, frictional to-and-fro, which works up to culmination'.[9] We might recognise a similarity (no doubt accidental) to Herder's description of parallelism: 'so soon as the heart gives way to its emotions, wave follows upon wave, and that is parallelism' (above, p. 201). The *prima facie* case these observations establish that Lawrence was influenced unconsciously as well as consciously by the KJB gives his comments on it a special interest.

He characterises Jack, the hero of his co-authored novel *The Boy in the Bush*, as knowing

> the Bible pretty well, as a well-brought-up nephew of his aunts. He had no objection to the Bible. On the contrary, it supplied his imagination with a chief stock of images, his ear with the greatest solemn pleasure of words, and his soul with a queer heterogeneous ethic. He never really connected the Bible with Christianity proper, the Christianity of aunts and clergymen. He had no use for Christianity proper: just dismissed it. But the Bible was perhaps the foundation of his consciousness.[10]

This biblical foundation of consciousness is so strong that in one place Jack responds like Bunyan in *Grace Abounding* (see volume 1, p. 311): 'Jack was always afraid of those times when the mysterious sayings of the Bible invaded him. He seemed to have no power against them' (ch. 12, p. 173).

Jack represents Lawrence's sense of the Bible in a nutshell. Lawrence himself turns straightforwardly autobiographical in his final work, *Apocalypse*:

> From earliest years right into manhood, like any other nonconformist child I had the Bible poured every day into my helpless consciousness, till there came almost a saturation point. Long before one could think or even vaguely understand, this Bible language, these 'portions' of the Bible were *douched* over the mind and consciousness, till they became soaked in, they became an influence which affected all the processes of emotion and thought. So that today, although I have 'forgotten' my Bible, I need

---

[9] 'Foreword to *Women in Love*', *Phoenix II*, ed. Warren Roberts and Harry T. Moore (London: Heinemann, 1968), p. 276.

[10] D. H. Lawrence and M. L. Skinner, *The Boy in the Bush* (1924; Cambridge: Cambridge University Press, 1990), ch. 10, p. 141. See also ch. 1, p. 8, and the sequence of quotations in ch. 12, pp. 173–8.

only begin to read a chapter to realise that I 'know' it with an almost nauseating fixity. And I must confess, my first reaction is one of dislike, repulsion, and even resentment. My very instincts *resent* the Bible.

The reason is now fairly plain to me. Not only was the Bible, in portions, poured into the childish consciousness day in, day out, year in, year out, willy nilly, whether the consciousness could assimilate it or not, but also it was day in, day out, year in, year out expounded, dogmatically, and always morally expounded, whether it was in day-school or Sunday School, at home or in Band of Hope or Christian Endeavour. The interpretation was always the same, whether it was a Doctor of Divinity in the pulpit or the big blacksmith who was my Sunday School teacher. Not only was the Bible verbally trodden into the consciousness, like innumerable footprints treading a surface hard, but the footprints were always mechanically alike, the interpretation was fixed, so that all real interest was lost.

The process defeats its own ends. While the Jewish poetry penetrates the emotions and the imagination, and the Jewish morality penetrates the instincts, the mind becomes stubborn, resistant, and at last repudiates the whole Bible authority, and turns with a kind of repugnance away from the Bible altogether. And this is the condition of many men of my generation.[11]

The depth of influence is persuasively shown. The claim that 'this is the condition of many men of my generation' is large but perhaps not excessive: a divided response, and the consequent need to see the Bible in different aspects is a common feature of ideas of the Bible as literature. Lawrence writes from a non-conformist – specifically, a Congregationalist – background and from the generation that suffered the First World War. It may well be that the Congregationalism he grew up in was especially vigorous; certainly the war was a crucial destroyer of faith. As George Orwell (1903–50) remarks in his 1939 state-of-England novel, *Coming up for Air*, 'it would be an exaggeration to say that the war turned people into highbrows, but it did turn them into nihilists for the time being' (2: 8; p. 127).

Though Orwell was almost a generation younger than Lawrence and from a background of India and Eton, he gives a similar sketch of response to the Bible, also in *Coming up for Air*. George Bowling, the lower-middle-class middle-aged narrator whose typicality Orwell stresses, recollects the church of his youth:

You took it for granted, just as you took the Bible, which you got in big doses in those days. There were texts on every wall and you knew whole chapters of the OT by heart. Even now my head's stuffed full of bits out of the Bible. And the children of Israel did evil again in the sight of the Lord [Judg. 3: 12, etc.]. And Asher abode in his

[11] 1931; ed. Mara Kalnins (Cambridge: Cambridge University Press, 1980), pp. 59–60.

breaches [Judg. 5: 17]... And all mixed up with the sweet graveyard smell and the serge dresses and the wheeze of the organ.

That was the world I went back to ... For a moment I didn't merely remember it, I was *in* it.   (1: 4; pp. 30–1)

Bowling concludes the first part of his story with a summary of this lost world of 1900 (Bowling is his creator's senior by a decade; I omit the preceding sentence, 'the drunks are puking in the yard behind the George', to get rid of Orwell's pervasive note of disenchantment, and so, like other collectors of testimonies, to produce the desired effect):

> Vicky's at Windsor, God's in heaven, Christ's on the cross, Jonah's in the whale, Shadrach, Meshach, and Abednego are in the fiery furnace, and Sihon king of the Amorites and Og the king of Bashan are sitting on their thrones looking at one another...
>
> Is it gone for ever? I'm not certain. But I tell you it was a good world to live in. I belong to it. So do you.   (1: 4; p. 31)

In a sense it does not matter if we take this as autobiographical (as I suspect it is) or as Orwell's idea of the typical experience of the generation that fought in the trenches, for both have a validity, and the final, characteristic, challenge, 'I belong to it. So do you', if it does not define an intellectual history, helps to create one.

Later in the novel Orwell gives two clearly autobiographical accounts of Bowling's reading. Although his 'father had never read a book in his life, except the Bible and Smiles's *Self Help*', he himself did not read 'a "good" book till much later' (2: 6; p. 91). Indeed, the significant thing is that Bible reading does not figure at all in Bowling's reading. He knew parts of the Bible well, and had some of its language and events embedded in his mind, but this somewhat literary experience happened independently of his personal reading and belongs with the sentimental warmth of childhood. This is much the same picture as we get from Lawrence, but whether there is any suggestion that the KJB had a literary influence on Orwell is a different matter. The testimony is to familiarity, not influence.[12]

Orwell thought that 'within the last generation the Bible reading which used to be traditional in England has lapsed. It is quite common to meet with young people who do not know the Bible stories even as *stories*.'[13] In general terms this

---

[12] One might mount an argument for influence from the way he uses Ecclesiastes 9: 11 as a model of good writing in 'Politics and the English language', but that would be to press too little evidence too far (Sonia Orwell and Ian Angus, eds., *The Collected Essays, Journalism and Letters of George Orwell*, 4 vols. (London: Secker & Warburg, 1968), IV: 133–4).

[13] 'The English people' (written 1944); *Collected Essays*, III: 7.

may be true, but there are too many exceptions for it to be useful. Lawrence and Orwell were, I suggest, writing of an experience of the Bible that continues to occur, even if not to so many as it used to. Two generations after Lawrence, a continent away and brought up in a different faith, the Canadian Jewish novelist Mordecai Richler (b. 1931) tells engagingly of much the same experience:

> Torah was literally banged into me and seven other recalcitrant boys in a musty back room of the Young Israel Synagogue, our *cheder*, by a teacher I'll call Mr Feinberg. If I got anything wrong, or if I was caught with an Ellery Queen paperback or, say, a copy of the Montreal *Herald* on my lap open at the sports pages, Mr Feinberg would rap my knuckles with the sharp end of his ruler or twist my ear. However, what all of us feared even more than his blows was his bad breath. Grudgingly we attended Mr Feinberg's classes after regular school was out – while other boys, who weren't lucky enough to come from such good homes, were playing street hockey or snooker or just hanging out, smoking Turret cigarettes, five cents for a pack of five.
>
> ('Deuteronomy', Rosenberg, p. 51)

It's quickly apparent that the tone is different – reminiscent comedy as against Lawrence's metaphorical description of the sensibility being formed – but the nature of the experience is similar, from the link between a 'good home' and religious education to the child's resistance and inattention. Lawrence as a thirteen-year-old was only 'fair' at Scripture (11th out of 17), whereas he was 'very satisfactory' at everything else except Science.[14] Canadian or English, Christian or Jewish (to say nothing of more local sectarian differences), 1890s or 1930s – none of these differences seem to weigh much set in the scales against an intensity of biblical education. Moreover, for all the generalisations about the present being a secular age, with not only God but religion having died, churches and families that insist on biblical learning are far from extinct.

To return now to Oliver. The most interesting response to his questioning came from a contemporary of Lawrence, the popular and sentimental novelist of mid-west pioneer days, Bess Streeter Aldrich (1881–1954). It is something of a companion piece to the Lawrence, the Orwell and the Richler:

> Born of a pioneer mother who was deeply religious, I have no earlier recollection than her deep-throated voice intoning the majestic lines of the Psalms ... The lilting words meant more to me as poetry than as any statement of religious fervour.
>
> She seemed to half sing the verses – they accompanied my whole childhood as a deep-toned organ accompanies a service. This – more than any study of the Bible on my own part – has had its influence on my writing. Sometimes as I work, if perchance

---

[14] Ada Lawrence and G. Stuart Gelder, *Young Lorenzo* (1931; New York: Russell and Russell, 1966), p. 60.

there comes a musically turned sentence, it seems in some queer way to be connected with that long-silenced intonation of the Psalms. One hesitates to set down in cold and often cruel black and white the experiences of the heart. But something about my mother's sincere religious nature, the rhythm of the verses she recited from memory, the majesty of the biblical language as she repeated it, has never left me. Does this early influence help me write? I do not know. All I know is that when I have agonised over a clumsy sentence and have finally turned it into something satisfying, for the brief fraction of a moment I have a feeling of oneness with the deep-throated singing of the Psalms.

This, more than any study of the stylistic qualities of the Bible, has influenced me.

(P. 354)

There is no resistance here because the literary experience, of which the Psalms are a part, is part of the dearly loved mother–daughter relationship. It may be that the experience recorded here is entirely a product of the way the mother read and the way the child felt, and so has little to do with actual qualities in the KJB. So, when Aldrich turns to Oliver's question about the effect of the Bible on her, it is to identify a quality of satisfaction in the process of writing: turning a clumsy sentence into something satisfying seems to be a pleasure of the same sort as listening to the mother, which in turn is of the same sort as being held in the mother's arms. The depth and genuineness of emotion associated with the Psalms is not in doubt. What is in doubt is whether it is possible to say anything more than '*associated with* the Psalms', in other words, to say that specific qualities of the Psalms produce the emotion. Aldrich herself thinks it is the 'feeling of oneness' rather than 'the stylistic qualities of the Bible' that counted.[15]

A second recent Jewish account of response to the Bible, like Richler's, solicited for Rosenberg's *Congregation*, suggests how the Bible might have a similar effect on narrative. The account is of special interest because it comes from one of the great masters of the art of the short story, Isaac Bashevis Singer (1904–91).[16] And, as one would expect from Singer, it is a delight in itself. He

---

[15] George Eliot, writing a decade before Aldrich was born and setting her writing still earlier in the century, describes a similar kind of response in one of her characters, Caleb Garth: 'whenever he had a feeling of awe he was haunted by a sense of biblical phraseology, though he could hardly have given a strict quotation' (*Middlemarch* (1871–2), ch. 40).

[16] By a disturbing coincidence, this was written on the day Singer died. It is impossible to write a book as omnivorous as the present without constantly feeling the effects of chance. So, selecting a volume of his to reread as a tribute, I came across this comment in connection with translating his stories into English:

I have been a translator all my adult life and I consider translation the greatest problem and challenge of literature. The 'other' language in which the author's

tells of his childhood study of Genesis, of his 'enlightened' brother Joshua's rational attitude to it and his own consequent scepticism about the science Joshua espoused:

> While I became as skeptical about science and scientists as I was about God and His miracles, I acquired a great love and admiration for the stories told in the Book of Genesis. They were more believable and made more sense than many of the books my brother gave me to read. The description of Noah's ark and the way he rescued all the animals and kept them alive in the time of the Flood was a story I never got tired of reading. It kindled my imagination...
>
> I could see before my eyes the people who in later generations had built the Tower of Babel... I was wandering with Abraham... I walked with Jacob... I was there when the brothers sold Joseph... I lived these tales.   (Rosenberg, pp. 6–7)

This is Orwell's 'I was *in* it' writ beautifully large. But Singer has one more thing to add about this sense of the present aliveness of biblical narrative:

> Whenever I take the Bible down from my bookcase and I begin to read it, I cannot put it down. I always find new aspects, new facts, new tensions, new information in it. I sometimes imagine that, while I sleep or walk, some hidden scribe invades my house and puts new passages, new names, new events into this wonderful book. It is the good luck of the Jewish people, and also of all people, that they were given a book like this.[17] It is God's greatest gift to humanity.   (Pp. 7–8)

This has taken us beyond youthful response, but what Singer is describing is the prime quality he associates with biblical narrative. Just as Aldrich tried to create the kind of feeling she associated with the Psalms in her writing, so Singer took the Genesis narratives as an ideal: 'there is perfection in these stories written by a single genius, from whom all writers can and should learn... I am still learning the art of writing from the book of Genesis and from the Bible generally' (p. 7).

Such accounts suggest ways the Bible may have influenced language and narrative, but testimonies to the influence of the Bible on writers would not be complete without a reminder of something so obvious that it is likely to be forgotten, that the Bible may influence a writer through its effect on his beliefs

----

work must be rendered does not tolerate obscurity, puns and linguistic tinsel. It teaches the author to deal with events rather than with their interpretation and to let the events speak for themselves.
  (Author's note to *A Friend of Kafka* (Harmondsworth: Penguin, 1975))

This suggests another reason for Singer's love of the stories of Genesis: they come from a work that seems to have survived translation better than any other major work, in part because it lets the events speak for themselves in a way achieved by few literary works.

17 The KJB – and the PB – had already been described in these terms (see below, p. 436).

or perceptions. The Roman Catholic poet, best known for *The Hound of Heaven*, Francis Thompson (1859–1907), responded late in life to what he thought of as 'the whole content and soul' of the Bible. So he thinks he was influenced in a different way from most writers:

> My style being already formed could receive no evident impress from it: its vocabulary had come to me through the great writers of our language. In the first place its influence was mystical. It revealed to me a whole scheme of existence and lit up life like a lantern. Next to this, naturally, I was attracted by the poetry of the Bible, especially the prophetic books.
>
> But beyond even its poetry, I was impressed by it as a treasury of *gnomic* wisdom. I mean its richness in utterances of which one could, as it were, chew the cud. This, of course, has long been recognised, and biblical sentences have passed into the proverbial wisdom of our country. But the very finest, as too deep for popular perception, have remained unappropriated. Such is that beautiful saying in Proverbs: 'As in water face answereth to face, so the heart of man to man' [27: 19] . . . None of the eastern and other heathen 'sacred volumes' sometimes brought into comparison with it have anything like the same grave dignity of form or richness of significance in their maxims. Upon this single quality, I think, I finally would elect to take my stand in regard to the Bible; and by this it has firmest hold of me.[18]

In the end this tells nothing about the working of influence, and it could be set down as a better than average piece of appreciation. Nevertheless, it does suggest that the Bible can affect a writer in non-technical areas, and that one may be influenced at any time of life.

The influence of the KJB on literature – and on language – becomes the subject for books in its own right. Here we can go little further than noting both the personal variety of response and the way the KJB has gone on being felt as a significant presence. Making due allowance for the particularly developed literary sensibility of writers, the experiences these passages record suggest something of the general impact of, usually, the KJB on young minds who could not avoid it even if they wished to. The passages also form a background to the occasional discussions of the literary influence of the KJB.

For a final example of a writer's sense of his childhood encounters with the Bible, we may turn back to the nineteenth century, to the very writer Pattison named as his latest example of a writer who owed much to the KJB, John Ruskin (1819–1900). The Bible was inescapably present in his childhood, as he recalls in his autobiographical *Praeterita* (1885–9):

---

[18] 'Books that have influenced me' (1900); *Literary Criticisms*, pp. 542–4. Though the title has the plural, only the Bible is discussed.

After our chapters (from two to three a day, according to their length, the first thing after breakfast . . .), I had to learn a few verses by heart, or repeat, to make sure I had not lost, something of what was already known; and, with the chapters thus gradually possessed from the first word to the last, I had to learn the whole body of the fine old Scottish paraphrases, which are good, melodious and forceful verse; and to which, together with the Bible itself, I owe the first cultivation of my ear in sound.

It is strange that of all the pieces of the Bible which my mother thus taught me, that which cost me most to learn, and which was, to my child's mind, chiefly repulsive – the 119th Psalm – has now become of all the most precious to me, in its overflowing and glorious passion of love for the law of God.   (P. 31)

The punctiliousness of this learning extended as far as a three-day struggle over the stressing of a particular phrase (p. 32), and, though the intention was not in the least literary, the general result was:

From Walter Scott's novels I might easily, as I grew older, have fallen to other people's novels; and Pope might, perhaps, have led me to take Johnson's English, or Gibbon's, as types of language; but, once knowing the 32nd of Deuteronomy, the 119th Psalm, the 15th of 1st Corinthians, the sermon on the mount and most of the Apocalypse, every syllable by heart, and having always a way of thinking with myself what words meant, it was not possible for me, even in the foolishest times of youth, to write entirely superficial or formal English; and the affectation of trying to write like Hooker and George Herbert was the most innocent I could have fallen into.
                                      (P. 6)

Though Ruskin has no doubt that the KJB was the chief influence on his writing, he does not claim that he wrote like it; rather, he sees it as a restraining influence and a basis for his taste. Such an influence must often be impossible to demonstrate: one can see the positive effect of an influence – this writing or this element in it is the way it is because of an influence – but how can one show that something would have been written differently had the influence not existed? This makes Ruskin's testimony peculiarly useful, for the kind of moderating influence he describes must have been common – and not only undemonstrable but also something of which many authors would not have been conscious.

Fundamentalists and the God-given translation

The appearance of the RV spurred rather than checked AVolatry. It helped to drive apart literary and scholarly approaches to the Bible, forcing many critics to choose between the beauty and the truth of holiness, and challenging future translators to the apparently impossible task of producing a generally acceptable new reconciliation of the two. This is not to say that there was an absolute separation between the literary and the scholarly, or between the Bible as literature and the Bible as religion. As we have seen, so-called literary approaches are often thinly disguised and diluted presentations of the results of theological and textual scholarship. While for some the appearance of the RV (and the subsequent destabilisation of the biblical text through the accumulation of quasi-authoritative versions) changed the KJB from being the book of truth to being a literary monument, for others it cemented the KJB's position as the only book of truth.

This latter movement may be dealt with immediately. It is the last manifestation of what, for most Christians, has ceased to be an issue at all, the question of the KJB's accuracy. Though this is not a literary movement, it tells much about that central force in changing literary attitudes, love for the established. Some of the more fundamental Protestant sects refused, in Myles Smith's phrase, to have their religion meddled with and so developed arguments to justify their continued use of the KJB. The Textus Receptus, essentially Estienne's Greek NT of 1551, is defended against all later textual criticism. Because none of the more modern Bibles return to this, but instead use the discredited fruits of 'naturalistic criticism',[19] the KJB is consequently defended: it is the truest and latest representative of the true original text. One caricature presentation of this view – I take it from a comic magazine[20] – has the original Greek (every word of which is direct from God) preserved first by John of Patmos, then by the true Christians in Antioch, then by the Waldensians. When 'the greatest scholars the world had ever seen' (p. 28), the KJB translators, gathered together NT manuscripts, 98 per cent of the evidence came from Antioch. Meantime, Satan, through the Roman Catholic Church (a form of Baal worship disguised as Christianity), made every effort to corrupt the true Bible, and eventually succeeded through Westcott and Hort, 'who secretly supported the Roman Catholic Church' (p. 29). The result has been a total undermining of confidence in the Bible and destruction of true religion. One

---

[19] See, e.g., Hills, ch. 4. The alternative is 'consistently Christian, Bible-believing' textual criticism. None of the books I have seen which argue along these general lines postdate the New King James Bible (1979), so I cannot report whether its appearance has significantly altered the arguments.

[20] Jack T. Chick, *Sabotage* (Chino, CA: Chick, 1979). Chick makes particular use of Hills, J. J. Ray, *God Only Wrote One Bible* (Junction City, Oreg.: Eye Opener, 1970), and David Otis Fuller, ed., *Which Bible?* (Grand Rapids, Mich.: Grand Rapids International, 1970). Much of Fuller's book comes from Benjamin G. Wilkinson, whose work is noted briefly below. Fuller, a Baptist, founded the Which Bible? Society, Inc. He also established and, for thirty-three years, chaired 'The children's Bible hour' on some 600 radio stations.

must return to the true Word, as given in the KJB. That this picture is accompanied by violent anti-Catholicism and anti-Ecumenism goes without saying, nor does it need saying that many of the proponents of the KJB and the Textus Receptus would be far from happy with so simplistic a picture.

The desire – even, the need – for absolute certainty underlies these attitudes. But the arguments that support them are circular: they begin from the premise of the infallible inspiration of the Scriptures (are we not saved by faith?), and this premise becomes their conclusion. Two further premises support the argument, those of the eternal origin of the Scriptures and of their providential preservation – an idea we have already seen in Scholefield's claim that the KJB translators 'were raised up by the providence of God' (above, p. 189). The God who inspired the original Scriptures would not have allowed them to be corrupted. Implicitly (more often than explicitly), this means the KJB is the inspired translation. For Chick it is 'the God honoured text'. Edward F. Hills is fuller, but just as simple:

> the King James Version is the historic Bible of English-speaking Protestants. Upon it God, working providentially, has placed the stamp of His approval through the usage of many generations of Bible-believing Christians. Hence, if we believe in God's providential preservation of the Scriptures, we will retain the King James Version, for in so doing we will be following the clear leading of the Almighty.
>
> (P. 214)

In short, because the KJB has been generally used, it should go on being used.

Tradition is God-given truth, hence the slogan for the KJB, 'the Bible God uses and Satan hates'. An earlier proponent of this way of thinking, Benjamin G. Wilkinson, though he does not claim direct inspiration for a translation, nevertheless makes the essentially inspirationist claim for the KJB that 'when the Bible was translated in 1611, God foresaw the wide extended use of the English language; and, therefore, in our Authorised Bible, gave the best translation that has ever been made, not only in the English language, but as many scholars say, *ever made in any language*'.[21] This differs from the familiar attribution of artistry to the KJB translators only in that the artistry and the foresight that produced perfection are now God's, but the crucial point is that literary AVolatry and conservative fundamentalism share ways of thinking. There is no difference between the traditional (which is the word one would use in a religious context) and the familiar (the word I have used in a literary context) except in the shade of temperamental response made to them.

The fundamentalist, of course, is not much concerned about beauty. His

---

[21] *Our Authorized Bible Vindicated* (Washington, D.C.: the author, 1930), p. 256.

world is a desperate battleground between God and Satan, and belief is the most precious thing. The language of the KJB matters only for reasons that are felt to be religious. Just as the language of the Greek NT 'was biblical rather than contemporary', so 'the language of the Bible should be venerable as well as intelligible, and the King James Bible fulfils these two requirements better than any other Bible in English' (Hills, pp. 208, 212). Moreover, the KJB's English encourages memorisation, especially by children, and memorisation places the word of God in the heart (Hills, p. 213), whereas the unstable text produced by the plethora of modern-language versions discourages memorisation.

One cannot admire or even respect argument built on a rigid position in order to prove that position (the 'proof' is there only to make the believer more comfortable). This is especially so when one of the consequences is a rigid intolerance of other positions, another the failure to realise that sincerity and a conviction of truth are not confined to a single group of people, and a third the rejection of rational argument. Yet the desire for stability and certainty is very real, and veneration of the familiar lies at the heart of many critics' love for the KJB as literature. Such simplism on the religious side of AVolatry may make us more sceptical of literary AVolatry, and it certainly helps to show AVolatry's major negative aspect, its tendency to produce condemnation of the new. The rampant traditionalism of a Hills or a Chick condemns all modern Bibles as the work of Satan. Similarly, though less dangerously, literary AVolatry condemns modern Bibles as lacking literary quality because they are not the KJB. Time has made it the beautiful Bible, and time might possibly do the same for another version – if one could imagine any Bible in the future obtaining the monopoly on consciousness that the KJB had for so long. Such a development is at best unlikely. Christianity is no longer an inescapable national institution, and within Christianity the single verbal form of the Scriptures in translation has been so broken down that it is never likely to be restored.[22]

Modern AVolatry

AVolatry reached its peak in the first half of the twentieth century. Thereafter, with major variations from community to community, the plethora of competing versions and the declining force of institutional Christianity have weakened its hold. Nevertheless, they have not changed its essential nature much beyond giving it something of the deadness that is the usual fate of

---

[22] Chick would see this as the final triumph of Satan, while Hills would deny the triumph by reasserting the principle of the providential preservation of Scripture, for that principle guarantees that God's truth will never be lost.

clichés: we are the inheritors of AVolatry even if we are not true believers. It will be enough now to survey a few of the more memorable or characteristic expressions, then some of the dissenting voices before taking a closer look at modern critical discussions that focus specifically on the KJB.

Grandiose claims that often fly in the face of historical evidence or scholarly attention to the subject, and repetition of received opinions are two of the foremost characteristics of AVolatry. So Francis Bowen repeats much of the praise of the KJB's language that is already so familiar and allows his enthusiasm to carry it still further:

> but beside them all [Shakespeare etc.], and above them all, is the prose of our Common Version. It is more sustained than any of them, more uniformly strong and melodious in its flow ... And it has largely contributed to the fixation of the language at this its best estate, since the number of words in it the meaning of which has become obsolete in the course of nearly three subsequent centuries is so small that they may almost be counted on the fingers.[23]

True, one occasionally finds sample lists of obsolete words of the kind of brevity suggested here, but they are never presented as full lists; only the desire to approve coupled with ignorance and the existence of an authoritative predecessor could produce such a claim.

Vagueness, repetition and exaggeration show clearly in a pair of works. Albert S. Cook is superbly vague in his *The Bible and English Prose Style* (1892), proclaiming that the main characteristics of Bible diction 'may be summed up in a very brief phrase. Whatever their number or variety, I think they may all be comprehended under a single term, noble naturalness' (p. xvi). Unhelpfully, he explains that by 'natural' he means 'conformable to human nature'. Edgar Whitaker Work picks this up in a typical book, *The Bible in English Literature* (New York: Revell, 1917): 'the characteristics of biblical style are in fact quite familiar – they are such as simplicity, directness, concreteness, picturesqueness, and withal a certain dignity and stateliness, a grandeur and elevation – in short a kind of "noble naturalness" that makes the Bible the easy companion of our inmost thought and need' (p. 196). Though this is nothing but cliché, his next point might be suggestive if there were even the slightest trace (or possibility) of demonstration to give it substance:

> the style and tone of English conversation ... no doubt represent a compound of effects, such as racial temperament, lingual inheritance, environment, even climate. It

---

[23] *A Layman's Study of the English Bible, Considered in its Literary and Secular Aspect* (New York, 1885), pp. 10–11. The concluding exaggeration is lineal from Halsey's claim that very few of the KJB's words 'have ever become obsolete, and even these are in portions seldom read' (p. 40).

is impossible, however, to avoid the conclusion that the English Bible has had a very pronounced influence upon the prose style of conversation. The simplicity and directness of English talk are the natural sequence of long conversance with the English Bible. Men do not learn a stilted style from the Bible – rather they learn to speak simply and correctly.   (P. 197)

As this stands (almost too strong a word for a house of straw that needs no huffing and puffing to bring it down), it is no more than a late variation on the idea of the KJB as a standard for language, and is slightly reminiscent of Coleridge's idea that the Bible had affected the passionate expression of the people (above, p. 154).

Another strand of AVolatry goes beyond Bryan Walton's 1659 judgement that the accuracy of the KJB was such that it might 'justly contend with any now extant in any other language in Europe' (volume 1, p. 219). It is a variation on the idea already noted from Jowett and Eckman, that the KJB is more inspired than the originals (above, p. 191). From Europe, and therefore more impressive had it been generally known, came the opinion that 'that which marks the English Bible more especially is the wonderful force and solemnity of its language. In this respect the English version ranks higher than any other, including the Luther Bible.'[24] Then, in the sort of book that gives a bad smell to the phrase, 'the Bible as literature', by twaddle such as characterising 'Tyndale's peculiar contribution to the English Bible [as] that indefinable something we call charm', Charles Allen Dinsmore declared that the KJB 'is a finer and nobler literature than the Scriptures in their original tongues'.[25] In an openly second-hand but, for all that, much better book, Wilbur Owen Sypherd was of the same opinion. The context he puts it in is thoroughly familiar: 'a towering monument marks the highest point of perfection to which English-speaking people have yet attained in the expression of their deepest thoughts and noblest emotions. The King James version has a rare distinction. As a translation from two great languages of antiquity . . . it has given to the world a literature greater than that of the original tongues.'[26] If we think of such remarks in the context of the widespread belief in the perfection of the original Scriptures, it is indeed a monumental claim. That original perfection came from God, and we have seen that the common tendency to attribute artistry to the translators sometimes went as far as attributing divine inspiration to the translation. Another

---

[24] Johan Storm, *Englische Philologie* (Leipzig, 1896), ii: 995. As translated and given in Rosenau, p. 42.
[25] *The English Bible as Literature* (London, 1931), pp. 83, 78.
[26] *The Literature of the English Bible* (New York: Oxford University Press, 1938), p. 40.

expression of the idea of the KJB's literary superiority unashamedly links providence and the time of the KJB:

> It is true that the Greek of the New Testament is common Greek and in many of the books destitute of literary embellishment. But why should we not rejoice in the fact that the Bible in our mother tongue excels the original as literature? If the New Testament was written in the silver age of Greek and the King James in the golden age of English, is it not all Providence? The apostolic Christians worshipped in crypts and sand pits. Should we then tear down our cathedrals and seal up our organs?[27]

A good deal of the general sense of the KJB's reputation comes from John Livingston Lowes's 'The noblest monument of English prose' (1930). This is quintessential AVolatry. The title phrase itself is much repeated, yet it was not new to Lowes. It was anticipated by Pratt's phrase, 'the noblest composition in the universe' (above, p. 117). Spring had come close in describing the KJB as 'a noble monument of the integrity, fidelity and learning of its venerable translators' (p. 63), as had Arnold in calling it 'a great national monument' (*Complete Prose*, VII: 66), Henley had it almost pat in 'a monument of English prose' (above, p. 290), and there were other anticipations. The essay is packed with declarations such as this: 'the English Bible has a pithiness and raciness, a homely tang, a terse sententiousness, an idiomatic flavour which comes home to men's business and bosoms'; or this: 'utter simplicity, limpid clearness, the vividness of direct, authentic vision – these are the salient qualities of the diction of the men who wrote the Bible' (pp. 48, 54). Nothing more than rhetoric, such claims are just as derivative as the title. 'Business and bosoms', for instance, comes from Robert Louis Stevenson by way of Eckman (Eckman, p. 43). Here from 1901 is one of Lowes's sources, part of another typical piece of AVolatry that, in its turn, leans heavily on Faber:

> regarded as the greatest of English classics and the most venerable of the national heirlooms, it is as Englishmen that we have learned to love it ... It is hallowed and endeared to many a heart by memories of the old home days. It has quickened, moulded and sustained what is best and strongest in our individual and corporate life. Bone of our literary bone and flesh of our literary flesh, it has exercised upon English character an influence, moral, social and political, which it is not possible to measure. Unique in dignity, unique in grandeur, unique in stately simplicity, it is the noblest monument that we possess of the genius of our native tongue.[28]

[27] Paul K. Jewett, 'Majestic music of the King James', *Christianity Today* 1: 4 (26 November 1956), 13–15; p. 13.

[28] H. W. Hoare, *The Evolution of the English Bible* (London: Murray, 1901), pp. 3–4.

One would expect a critic who writes like this to admire Harwood, not the KJB. And surely that arch-student of literary sources, Lowes, knew he was borrowing his title just as surely as he must have known that many of the generalisations he filled his essay with were diluted from the work of one of his predecessors at Harvard, John Hays Gardiner (1863–1913).

In some respects Gardiner's *The Bible as English Literature* (1906) is the closest there is to a substantial good study of the KJB as a work of English literature. Yet, for all that it does have some stimulating insights and, *faute de mieux*, is still worth reading, it is not a good book. The mixture of vagueness and repetition is lamentable, and AVolatry, as usual, blinkers the critical faculty. In a general way the book is interesting because it is the first to come out of a university course on the Bible offered within a department of English, and it is hardly surprising that it comes from an American university. Interest in the Bible as literature has always been stronger in America than England, and many of the major figures in developing the subject have been American. In spite of all that had gone before, as late as 1918 Quiller-Couch was arguing that the Bible should be part of literary studies in English universities, and it is an argument that has only been partially accepted.

Gardiner presents his work as being 'a study in English literature' (p. vi), but follows this statement with the worrying comment that he has kept to the KJB for quotations. It is as if he is studying the originals as they happen to be represented in English, rather than confining his study to the KJB. The distinction is important: it is one thing to study the KJB as an autonomous work of literature, another to study the Bible and sometimes to bring into consideration qualities peculiar to the KJB. The uneasy ground taken by the study is reflected, perhaps accidentally, in the change made between the title and the running head: the latter is 'the Bible as literature', which is truer to much of the book than 'the Bible as English literature'. Two more worrying notes appear in the next paragraph of the preface:

> In all my discussion I have assumed the fact of inspiration, but without attempting to define it or to distinguish between religious and literary inspiration. The two come together in a broad region where everyone who cares for a delimitation must run his line for himself. It is obvious, however, that no literary criticism of the Bible could hope for success which was not reverent in tone. A critic who should approach it superciliously or arrogantly would miss all that has given the book its power as literature and its lasting and universal appeal.   (Pp. vi–vii)

The vagueness is characteristic, and the dangers of assuming inspiration hardly need rehearsing. The explicitness of the identification of 'religious and literary inspiration' is new, but the result is the old one: just as the Bible is the supreme book of religion, so it is the supreme literary work. This is Gardiner's fundamental point, that the Bible – as far as English is concerned, in the form of the KJB – is supreme as literature. This leads at last to the seemingly odd yet inevitable position of setting the KJB up in opposition to all other literature. The real emphasis is less on the Bible *as* literature than on the Bible *against* literature. At bottom, the reasoning is again straightforward and familiar: the Bible is the best literature; all other literature must be measured by its standard, and, so measured, is found wanting. 'Much reading in the Bible', Gardiner writes, 'will soon bring one to an understanding of the mood in which all art seems a juggling with trifles and an attempt to catch the unessential when the everlasting verities are slipping by' (pp. 382–3). After many repetitions, he develops the cliché that the KJB is a standard of the language just this far: 'one can say that if any writing departs very far in any way from the characteristics of the English Bible, it is not good English writing' (p. 388), and he concludes that 'it remains true, therefore, in a broad way with the substance of English literature as with the style, that the English Bible stands as the norm about which all the rest can be arranged and as the standard by which it is not unreasonable to estimate it' (pp. 394–5).

He frequently lapses into the weakest of generalisations, such as naming the general qualities of English prose style, as measured by the KJB, 'simplicity and earnestness' (p. 389). Nevertheless, there is a larger idea in the background. In part it grows out of his sense of the characteristics of Hebrew (taken from Renan), principally that Hebraic thought 'knew only the objective and solid facts of which man has direct sensation, and the simple and primitive emotions which are his reaction to them' (p. 86). By contrast, almost all other literature, and modern literature in particular, is essentially abstract and never free from 'the restless egotism that is the curse of the artistic temperament' (p. 384). So if Shakespeare had tried to write a play on a biblical subject,

> His interest would have been in the characters of the play, in their humanity, in the tangled web of their fate, and in the tragedies wrought by their weaknesses and their conflicting desires. It is only in the most shadowy way that the great forces which dominate Job and the Psalms and St Paul's Epistles and Revelation come into his pages. And when one puts even his greatest plays beside these books of the Bible one finds the modern writing almost trivial and ephemeral beside the old. (P. 382)

Gardiner allows that in other literature there is a greater subtlety and ability to develop thought, but with these gains there are greater losses, namely of the power to move directly and of the trust in intuition which arrives 'at glimpses of the verities which lie behind the mask of experience' (p. 170). 'It is only', he preaches, 'by virtue of the deep infusion of feeling which always goes with knowledge attained by intuition that the human mind can soar to the eternal and the infinite' (p. 207). 'Abstract and therefore pale' (p. 120) sums up his judgement on the weakness of modern literature against the strength of the Bible.

With these general arguments goes an essentially familiar view of 'the crowning monument of English literature' (p. 357). The 'large and noble qualities' of the originals 'not only survived the process of translation, but in our English Bible almost gained new power' (p. 278; here he is a touch more cautious than his successors, Dinsmore and Sypherd, yet one suspects the 'almost' is modest rather than meaningful). The KJB has 'unequalled vitality and freshness of expression ... it not only gives us the denotation of the books which it translates, but it clothes its own language with the rich connotation of the original and with the less definable but no less potent expressive power of sound' (p. 283). The strength comes in part from the period, but Gardiner does not resort to the simple argument of the KJB's contemporaneity with Shakespeare. He draws out with often good detail the contributions of the various translators from Tyndale – 'one of the great heroes of the English race' (pp. 315–16), the man who 'fixed the style of the English Bible' (p. 324) – to the King James translators, and adds to this the most persuasive aspect of his argument against modern abstraction: he notes how Tyndale had written (in his prologue to Genesis) of 'sucking out the sweet pith of the Scriptures', and comments that

> we today should probably have written 'extract the essence', and thereby with what is to us the quaintness we should have lost also the eagerness and delight which colour Tyndale's words with their halo of feeling. The language of this sixteenth century was lacking in many of our commonest general words, and as a result men used figures of speech more naturally ... all the men who worked on our English Bible ... must sometimes have adopted figurative forms of expression for the reason that the abstract word had not yet been assimilated in the language.   (Pp. 358–9)

This is but part of a more detailed argument, but it is sufficient to show that Gardiner's vagueness and anti-literary AVolatry do at times cohere into detail that gives a cogency to what in other hands had been the easy cliché of putting AVolatry with bardolatry. One-eyed as it is, his denigration of modern literature has some real insight to it. If Gardiner's excesses and weaknesses contribute to the bad odour of AVolatry, his strengths remind us that AVolatry has some truth to it. The history of AVolatry may be largely a history of human critical weakness, but that in itself is illuminating, and it has never been proof that a view is wrong because it is widely held or stupidly repeated.

The Shakespearean touch

AVolatry made the question of the source of the KJB's perfection very real. One product of that question needs following here, if only as a relief from so much parrotting. Among the respectable contributors to AVolatry was the magisterial egoist George Saintsbury (1845–1933), Professor of Rhetoric and English Literature at Edinburgh University. He could generalise with the best:

> So long as a single copy of the version of 1611 survives, so long will there be accessible the best words of the best time of English, in the best order, on the best subjects – so long will the fount be open from which a dozen generations of great English writers, in the most varying times and fashions, of the most diverse temperaments – libertines and virtuous persons, freethinkers and devout, poets and prosemen, laymen and divines – have drawn inspiration and pattern; by which three centuries of readers and hearers have had kept before them the prowess and the powers of the English tongue. (*English Prose Rhythm*, pp. 157–8)

Yet there is a vital difference: such generalisation is accompanied by close demonstration. Saintsbury is neither a parrot nor a chorister: he may reach conclusions that from other pens are raucous clichés, but he has manifestly reached them for himself and can show his readers why they too should reach them. In a footnote to the passage just given he considers an objection to his scorpion attacks on the RV, that similar objections were made to the KJB, and concludes that 'the sole real question is, "can *we prove our* charges?"'. At the least, he makes a good case.

Saintsbury is an out-and-out aesthete. He presents parts of the KJB as among 'the highest points of English prose', as triumphs of 'ornateness', of which 'rhythm is the chief and the most difficult form or constituent' (p. 142). He rests his case primarily on Isaiah 60, secondarily on 1 Corinthians 13, 'perhaps the finest passage, rhythmically, of the New Testament, as "Arise, shine" is not far from being the finest of the Old ' (p. 152). With no hesitation or embarrassment he raises the ensign of aestheticism, declaring that to compare Isaiah 60 in the KJB 'with the same passage in other languages is a liberal education in despising and discarding the idle predominance of "the subject"' (p. 142). The subject and the imagery are common to all versions, 'but "oh! the difference to *us*" of the expression!' (p. 150). And, having declared his competence to judge rhetorical value in a sufficient range of languages (barring Hebrew), he asserts in the vein that Dinsmore and Sypherd were to mine: 'that any one of the modern languages (even Luther's German) can vie with ours I can hardly imagine anyone who can appreciate both the sound and the meaning of the

English maintaining for a moment' (p. 143), and he proceeds to scan several verses – as prose, using Latinate quantitative scansion – from the KJB, the Septuagint and the Vulgate. This leads to a virtuoso comparative discussion of the three and then an equally detailed discussion of the development of the English through the versions from Coverdale onwards that curious readers may well wish to read for themselves, for there is no comparative discussion of qualities of sound and rhythm like it to be found anywhere else, and brief quotation cannot properly represent it. Writ large, this is the consciousness that produced Nathaniel Scarlett's comments on his prose rhythms (above, p. 104). Out of it emerges a picture of the process of translation as a matter of achieving not a perfect presentation of meaning – the meaning is in all the versions – but a perfect sound. 'The noblest stuff is worthy of the noblest fashion' (p. 157), Saintsbury declares (but we know what happens when translators try to make this their principle), and to read him is to see the successive translators acting not at all as scholars but as artists, with the KJB translators collectively the greatest artists.

Out of this vision of the translators as artists comes the discussion's one real lameness. Given the lack of 'very distinguished men of letters as such' (p. 158) among the translators, where did the artistry come from? All Saintsbury can offer is the old idea of the period, 'the literary tact shown must have been due to an extraordinary diffusion of it among the men of the time': he reminds his reader of some of the great prose artists of the time, including Shakespeare and Bacon, and wonders in a parenthetical return to his best sarcastic mode, 'why has no one contended that Andrewes and the rest were merely "Rosicrucian masks" for' Bacon? The allusion of course is to the long-running attempt to prove that 'the Stratford clown' could not possibly have written the plays attributed to him and that the true author was Bacon. It seems, though, that a quasi-Baconian attempt was made to prove that Shakespeare was the real genius behind the KJB. Shakespeare was forty-six in 1610, and the KJB was receiving its final rubbing and polishing. The forty-sixth word of the forty-sixth Psalm is 'shake', and the forty-sixth word from the end of the same Psalm is 'spear'. It was on just such ingenious observations within Shakespeare's plays that their Baconian authorship was 'proved'.[29] The key thing about Baconianism for us,

---

[29] Newton (p. 32) cites this example but sadly does not give a reference to the labyrinthine depths of Baconianism. I confess to having attended the same Cambridge college as one of its most vehement proponents, Edwin Durning-Lawrence, whom I recollect as the author of the phrase, 'the Stratford clown', possibly in one of his letters to A. W. Ward still to be found in the Peterhouse library tucked inside his *Bacon in Shake-speare*.

though, is that it reflects a preoccupation with the artist that did indeed affect thought about the KJB as literature in this period of high AVolatry.

The rhythms and assonances of the KJB were a likely source of conversation among literary men, and in one such conversation the novelist and future governor-general of Canada, John Buchan, made Saintsbury's point, saying 'it was strange that such splendour had been produced by a body of men learned, no doubt, in theology and in languages, but including among them no writer. Could it be, he wondered, that they had privately consulted the great writers of the age, Shakespeare perhaps and Jonson and others?'[30] Hearing this, Rudyard Kipling remarked, '"that's an idea" and away he went to turn it over'. The result was his fine short story, '"Proofs of Holy Writ"' (1934). In it Shakespeare, reclining in a Stratford orchard in the company of Ben Jonson, receives from Myles Smith some proofs of Isaiah 'for a tricking-out of his words or the turn of some figure' (pp. 345–6). Glancing at Smith's proofs and the earlier versions, Shakespeare, with help from the erudite but not entirely sober Jonson, follows his genius and revises the very verses that Saintsbury had scanned and discussed. The result is a beautifully suggestive imagining of the process of artistic revision and creation. Kipling necessarily takes some artistic licence such as having the work done from the Latin, but he nevertheless captures the essence of this side of AVolatry.

Kipling, who knew Saintsbury well, acknowledged that worthy's help in the writing of the story,[31] and many of the comments are Saintsbury dramatised. But near the end of the story, Shakespeare boasts:

'But, Ben, ye should have heard my Ezekiel making mock of fallen Tyrus in his twenty-seventh chapter. Miles sent me the whole, for, he said, some small touches. I took it to the Bank – four o'clock of a summer morn; stretched out in one of our wherries – and watched London, Port and Town, up and down the river, waking all arrayed to heap more upon evident excess. Ay! "A merchant for the peoples of many isles" . . . "The ships of Tarshish did sing of thee in thy markets"? Yes! I saw all Tyre before me neighing her pride against lifted heaven . . . But what will they let stand of all mine at long last? Which? I'll never know.' (P. 354)

Read carefully, this is more than a suggestion of another passage where a reader

---

[30] Hilton Brown, prefatory note to the *Strand Magazine* (1947) reprint of Rudyard Kipling's '"Proofs of Holy Writ"'. As given in Philip Mason, '"'Proofs of Holy Writ'": an introduction', *Kipling Journal* 62 (March 1988), 33. What follows is dealt with more fully in my '"'Proofs of Holy Writ'"', myths of the Authorised Version: Kipling and the Bible', *Kipling Journal* 63 (December 1989), 18–27.

[31] *Something of Myself* (London: Macmillan, 1937), p. 86.

may care to find Shakespearean quality in the KJB. It is also a question mark placed against the unremitting admiration of the AVolaters, for the first of the two phrases Shakespeare claims as his own is not the KJB's more awkward 'a merchant of the people for many isles'. His final questions, especially the 'which?', have real point: the KJB did not always produce results the imagined perfect artist would have done. The same point is implicit but less obvious in some of the suggestions Shakespeare makes for the verses from Isaiah. This gives the story a quiet undercurrent of criticism of AVolatry. It at once wittily imagines the nature of artistic revision and suggests that AVolatry can go too far.[32]

Dissenting voices

There were much more explicit attacks on AVolatry and related ideas. On 30 April 1918, Thomas Hardy, aged seventy-seven, made this note:

> By the will of God some men are born poetical. Of these some make themselves practical poets, others are made poets by lapse of time who were hardly recognised as such. Particularly has this been the case with the translators of the Bible. They translated into the language of their age; then the years began to corrupt that language as spoken and to add grey lichen to the translation; until the moderns who use the corrupted tongue marvel at the poetry of the old words. When new they were not more than half so poetical. So that Coverdale, Tyndale and the rest of them are as ghosts what they never were in the flesh.[33]

In a sense this belongs with Buchan's search for an alternative explanation of the KJB's quality, but it has a quality of scepticism to it that suggests a reaction against the AVolatrous attribution of supreme artistry to the translators.

The note probably never became well known – it was not published until

---

[32] When a poet was indeed consulted on a translation, the results were not what Kipling had imagined. Philip Larkin recounts:

> Some years ago I had the honour to serve briefly as a literary adviser to the NEB. What I think the panel of translators had in mind was that occasional cruces should be referred to a literary adviser who would suggest a felicitous way of expressing the point in question, but I found it virtually impossible to work like this: the whole text seemed to me lacking in vitality, rhythm, distinction and above all memorability, and I found myself revising almost every sentence – not, I hasten to say, in the direction of poetic prose, but simply, as I thought, into something more forceful. Very likely I was deluding myself: in fact after about a year they quietly stopped sending me anything, so I presume I had been weighed in the balance and found wanting.

(*PN Review* 13 (1979), 15)

[33] Thomas Hardy, ed. Michael Millgate, *The Life and Work of Thomas Hardy* (London: Macmillan, 1984), p. 416.

1930, and only one book on the KJB mentions it, and then it is in order to refute it[34] – so its significance is not as an influence but as an indicator of a small, or at least, rarely expressed, undercurrent of reaction. The critic John Middleton Murry (1889–1957), now unfairly remembered only for his less than glorious role in the lives of Katherine Mansfield and D. H. Lawrence, was thinking along similar lines. In *The Problem of Style* (1922) he raises some crucial issues, for a moment even tackling AVolatry head-on. To him it is 'the dogma of the infallibility of the style of the English Bible', and should not be allowed to go unchallenged (p. 120). So he says (the work was originally a series of lectures):

> It is difficult to object when we are told – as we very frequently are told – that there are two supereminent works of literature in English – the Bible and Shakespeare; but I always feel uneasy when I hear it. I suspect that the man who says so does not appreciate Shakespeare as he ought; and that he is not being quite honest about the Bible. The reason why it is difficult to object is that there is a sense in which it is true that the style of the Bible is splendid. (P. 121)

But his sense of what is splendid about it is a complex one, and he refuses to allow that the style of the whole Bible is splendid: indeed, 'it seems to me scarcely an exaggeration to say that the style of one half of the English Bible is atrocious' (p. 121). This, he knows, may be thought heresy, but he has gone out of his way to say it because 'the superstitious reverence for the style of the Authorised Version really stands in the way of a frank approach to the problem of style' (p. 122).

These frank heresies emerge from a consideration of the way the 'emotional susceptibility' (p. 114) of an audience affects its judgement of style. The point is important, so it will be worthwhile to quote it at length, especially as it will take us back to Sir Thomas Browne's comments on the Bible and the Koran (see volume 1, p. 265):

> But there are certain realms of experience in which the level of emotional susceptibility of the audience is much higher than in others. There is, for instance, the realm of religion. Any deeply religious man is habituated to thoughts and feelings of a kind utterly remote from those which are the accompaniment of his practical life. A man who really believes in a just and omnipotent, a merciful and omniscient God has for his familiar companion a conception and an emotion which are truly tremendous. No suggestion of the poet or the prose-writer can possibly surpass them in force or vehemence. When an old Hebrew Prophet wrote: 'and the Lord said', he had done everything. The phrase is overwhelming. Nothing in *Paradise Lost* can compare with it.

[34] Gustavus S. Paine, p. 171.

> When the most High
> Eternal Father from his secret cloud
> Amidst, in thunder uttered thus his voice

is almost trivial by its side. 'And they heard the voice of the Lord God walking in the garden in the cool of the day.' Two thousand years of Christian civilisation bend our minds to these words; we cannot resist them. Nor can we refuse to them the title of great style. All that we have, as critics of literature, to remember is that style of this kind is possible only when the appeal is to a habit of feeling and thought peculiar to religion. Possibly that very phrase 'and the Lord said' might seem even ridiculous to one brought up in one of the transcendental religions of the East, just as some of the poignant verses of the New Testament are said to be grotesque to an educated Mohammedan.   (Pp. 114–15)

Seemingly by accident, Murry slides from this by way of comments on the variety of underlying styles in the KJB to something that becomes a major point. He observes 'two masterly effects – I hardly know whether to call them effects of style' in Matthew 26, 'then all the disciples forsook him, and fled', and, of Peter after his denials, 'and he went out and wept bitterly'. Initially he links these with 'and the Lord said', 'in the sense that the emotional suggestion is not in the words themselves', but then makes the crucial distinction: 'the reserves of emotion which Matthew's simple statements liberate in us have been accumulated during the reading of the narrative ... The situation given, the force of the words is elemental' (pp. 115–16). As he says of his next example, Matt. 11: 28–30, 'in whatever language that sentence was spoken to you, your depths would be stirred' (p. 116). What Murry is developing is essentially the distinction between content and style. The effect is in the KJB but not of it. The literary quality of the Bible is not necessarily a matter of style. He could not be further removed from Saintsbury's scorn for 'the idle predominance of "the subject"'. Yet Saintsbury was able to show literary quality, and Murry is just as convincing.

Murry prefers to develop the point through a contrast between language which creates its own meaning and statements whose effect is created by the context. The force of these latter

> is supplied by the previous narrative; we have formed in our mind a picture of the circumstances; we know from his own words the nature of the man who has been denied. If we were to adopt, as one critic has done, the distinction between 'kinetic' and 'potential' language, we might say that the half-dozen words describing Peter are merely 'potential'.

> 'And the Lord said' is an example of potential speech where the charge comes wholly from the mind of the audience. 'Come unto me all ye that labour' is partly

kinetic – the actual beauty of the words has a positive effect – partly potential: the longing to which the appeal is made is universal in mankind ... I suppose that the sentence, 'but the iniquity of oblivion blindly scattereth her poppy' [Browne, *Religio Medici*], is almost wholly kinetic; that is to say, it completely creates its own emotion. You need no context, and you bring no emotion to it.   (P. 120)

The distinction is helpful, and may, in its idea of 'potential' language, remind one of Gilfillan's idea of seed poetry (above, p. 212). Murry has one further thought to add to it as part of his attack on 'the superstitious reverence for the style of the Authorised Version'. He suggests that in the Gospels there are

only two elements that can possibly lay claim to be considered creative literature; the actual words of Christ reported, such as 'come unto me...' and 'my God, my God...', and the dramatic effects, such as, 'then all the disciples forsook him and fled'. The first do not belong to the Gospels, but to their author, and the second are not really effects of style at all. It is not the authors of the Gospels who have given us the imaginative realisation of the character of Jesus on which these dramatic effects depend. Take away the words of Jesus which they reproduce and nothing of that character remains. The written evidence of an honest police-constable would give us as much. The most elementary conditions of the presence of style are lacking.

(P. 122)

Here Murry has gone too far without going far enough. To deny stylistic effect wholesale to the narratives is to dismiss much in the words of Jesus – to look no further – that is clearly indebted to the style of the individual Gospel-writers, for the words are not reported identically in each Gospel. It is quite possible to place together, say, the two versions of the houses built on rock and sand or earth (Matt. 7: 24–7 and Luke 6: 47–9), and show not only that they have what he calls a 'kinetic' effect but that the effect is different in kind and quality between the two versions, even though the basic meaning remains unchanged. Moreover, it is possible to distinguish effects of style which belong to the original reporter (Murry's identification of Christ as 'the author' will not do: we only know how his words were reported or recreated, not what, verbatim, he said), and also effects which belong specifically to the translation. Matthew's 'sand' is more evocative than Luke's 'earth', for one is blatantly a fool to build a house on sand, whereas houses are commonly built on the earth; moreover, the exact verbal repetition between the two parts of the image in Matthew draws sharper attention to the differences between the two (which is the point of the image) than Luke's less patterned rendering. These contrasts belong to the original Greek. And one quality in Matthew belongs in part to the original and in part to the KJB, which is not quite identical with any of its predecessors or successors. Rhythm and image unite in the description of the storm in a way that is marvellously kinetic if hardly surprising, since cadence of course invokes falling: 'and the rain descended, and the floods came, and the winds blew, and beat upon that house; and it fell: and great was the fall of it'. The quick, emphatic rhythm of 'and beat upon that house' detaches the previous phrase, 'and the winds blew', from the first two phrases, dividing the four phrases into pairs in terms of both meaning and rhythm, evoking the force of the storm. Then the two cadences do their work, especially because the stress in the last phrase falls on 'great'. By contrast, the NEB has, 'down it fell with a great crash', with equal stresses on the final words: the meaning of the words is left to work unaided. Though much of the KJB's effect in this passage is clearly the result of literal translation, the final cadence marks a departure from the word order of the Greek, so we may set it down as an artistic effect created by Tyndale and preserved by the KJB in spite of alternative suggestions from Geneva and Rheims.

Such discussion undermines much of Murry's point: there very obviously are effects of style of the sort he denies both in the originals and in the translation. But his 'honest police-constable' is not entirely to be dismissed: much of what we read in the Gospels does appear as incompetent narrative and, paradoxically, may be the more effective for so appearing, since the reader is often driven through the text to the thing-in-the-text. To attribute this effect to 'potential language' is at once to break the bonds of received ideas and to start an insight.

With greater vehemence and less insight, an entirely forgotten critic, E. E. Kellett, also took up the cudgels against AVolatry. His opposition to literal translation need not concern us, nor even his argument that, in its archaism and (a point Murry also makes) in its uniformity of style, the KJB seriously misrepresents the original variety and modernity of the Greek. More importantly, like Murry he too protests against the idea of the perfection of the whole of the KJB: 'a little leaven leaveneth the whole lump; and the beauty of some parts of the Version has made many people imagine that the whole is beautiful'.[35] Most importantly, he develops the hint found in Hardy and uses the idea of familiarity to account for the beauty of the KJB, suggesting that 'there is in fact every reason to believe that the "beauty" of the Authorised Version is, to a greater extent than we imagine, the creation of our intimacy with it' (p. 97); tellingly, he cites Selden's evidence. This is his counter to the prevailing admiration for the rhythms of the KJB:

> Often the 'rhythm' is merely another word for 'familiarity' ... the 'rhythms' of the

---

[35] 'The translation of the New Testament', *Reconsiderations: Literary Essays* (Cambridge: Cambridge University Press, 1928), pp. 77–104; p. 98.

Prayer Book version of the Psalms are usually preferred by churchmen; those of the Authorised Version by nonconformists of equal taste and culture: and the difference is due solely to the fact that churchmen are familiar from their childhood with the one, and nonconformists with the other. (P. 96)

This is fair enough, but it does not make that rhythm any the less real and valuable to those Churchmen and non-conformists. Kellett opens up but does not explore the questions of time and subjectivity, and simply to raise the questions is not, as the whole tenor of his article suggests, to prove that the KJB is bad.

Much of the scepticism about prevailing attitudes comes to a head in what is still the best of the dissenting articles, 'The literary impact of the Authorised Version' (1950), by C. S. Lewis (1898–1963).[36] The primary target of Lewis's scepticism is the idea that the KJB has been a great influence on English literature, but he allows himself to range more widely than this. Beginning somewhat in Murry's spirit, he directs attention away from the KJB and towards 'the Bible in general' as represented in 'any good translation' (unlike Kellett, he does not enter on the question of what makes a translation good). So his opening proposition is that 'the literary effect of any good translation must be more indebted to the original than to anything else. This is especially true of narrative and of moral instruction.' And he quickly adds to this an interest in the subject of the present book, 'the literary fortunes of our English Bible'. Appropriately, he warns against 'our dangerous though natural assumption that a book which has always been praised' – here he suggests an ignorance that some of his evidence contradicts – 'has always been read in the same way or valued for the same reasons' (p. 26). After surveying a few of the early literary comments on the Bible, he turns to the English translations, which he insists must be seen in their European context, and he offers the view of translation that has been argued for in this book:

when we come to compare the versions we shall find only a very small percentage of

---

[36] Lewis's *Fern-Seed and Elephants* also has dissenting opinions to offer. However, as Prickett has pointed out (pp. 81–2), he is at cross-purposes with those he is dissenting from. Reasonably warning that biblical critics – specifically Higher Critics – may not be trustworthy as literary critics, Lewis somewhat undermines the point by commenting that 'if [a biblical critic] tells me that something in a Gospel is legend or romance, I want to know how many legends and romances he has read, how well his palate is trained in detecting them by the flavour; not how many years he has spent on that Gospel' (*Fern-Seed and Elephants*, ed. Walter Hooper (Glasgow: Fontana, 1975), pp. 104–25; p. 107). It is one thing to observe that a narrative may not be factual, another to claim that it belongs with, say, Arthurian romance. Yet both points may be made with one word, 'legendary'.

variants are made for stylistic or even doctrinal reasons. When men depart from their predecessors it is usually because they claim to be better Hebraists or better Grecians . . .

It is not, of course, to be supposed that aesthetic considerations were uppermost in Tyndale's mind when he translated Scripture. The matter was much too serious for that; souls were at stake. The same holds for all the translators.   (Pp. 32, 34)

The desire to correct AVolatry is clear here, and it also informs his next topic, the question of the KJB's influence as an English book. With very English understatement, he remarks of this that 'there has been misunderstanding . . . and even a little exaggeration' (p. 35), and he sets about trying to correct the picture.

Distinguishing between a source and an influence – 'a source gives us things to write about, an influence prompts us to write in a certain way' (p. 35) – he admits that the KJB has been a source 'of immense importance', but argues that this has little to do with the particular qualities of the KJB and has 'no place in an account of the influence of the Authorised Version considered as an English book' (p. 36). He will not even allow embedded quotations to be taken as signs of influence, because they depend for their effect on their difference from their context:

our embedded quotations from the Authorised Version are nearly always in exactly this position. They are nearly always either solemn or facetious. Only because the surrounding prose is different – in other words, only in so far as our English is not influenced by the Authorised Version – do they achieve the effect the authors intended.   (P. 38)

As a generalisation, this is fair enough, but it will not sufficiently account for passages such as the one from *Jane Eyre* (above, p. 173) where embedded and open quotations mix with signs of influence, nor will it account for those biblical phrases which have become so much a part of the language as to be generally unrecognisable as quotations. What Lewis does allow – and it bears a close relation to the unrecognised quotations – is the influence of the KJB on vocabulary. He has in mind words such as 'beautiful', 'long-suffering', 'peacemaker' and 'scapegoat', as distinguished from words kept alive by the KJB but only available for poetic or archaic use. These latter he would class as very short embedded quotations. The brevity of his remarks here betrays a desire to diminish the idea of the KJB's influence: AVolatry has produced an excessive reaction.

A similar excess is visible in his remarks on the influence of the rhythm of the KJB, for he treats rhythm as nothing more than stress pattern. Of course his reader will agree that 'at the regatta Madge avoided the river and the crowd' has the same stress pattern as 'in the beginning God created the heaven and the earth', but to leave the point at that is cheap and destructive. We might agree that 'the influence of rhythm, isolated from imagery and style, is perhaps an abstraction' (p. 39), but this is to leave out of account not only the effect of the rhythm but also the fact that the Bible has rhythms of meaning – we have seen how parallelism affected *Jane Eyre* – and structural rhythms, most notably rhythms of repetition. A corrective to AVolatry was certainly needed, but not one that tries to dismiss the question of influence. A similar dismissiveness is present even when Lewis admits influence, as he does when he supposes that imagery has had a great effect but confesses that he has been unable to invent a method of checking it.

Lewis gives most attention to whether the KJB has influenced 'the actual build of our sentences' (p. 40), and here he is more persuasive. Consistently diminishing AVolatry, he proposes that the influence is not what it is generally thought to be, and takes two telling examples. One is Ruskin's passage claiming that the Bible influenced him (above, p. 313); the other is Bunyan. With the Ruskin, Lewis prefers to go the opposite way from mine and emphasise that it is indeed Johnsonian and ultimately indebted to Latin:

> A structure descending from Cicero through the prose of Hooker, Milton and Taylor, and then enriched with romantic colouring for which Homer and the Bible are laid under contribution – that seems to me the formula for Ruskin's style. If you could take away what comes from the Bible it would be impaired. It would hardly, I think, be crippled. It would certainly not be annihilated. This is real influence, but limited influence. (Pp. 41–2)

The little that he does allow as influence is visible in embedded quotations and imagery. I would not dissent from this: Ruskin's style does belong to the essentially Latin tradition in English prose, but this does not answer the question that Ruskin himself raises, what would his prose have been like if he had not been steeped in the KJB?

Murry makes a point that is useful here. For all its purity ('a very arbitrary conception when applied to language'), the vocabulary of the KJB is far less useful as an instrument than Shakespeare's: 'I can conceive no modern emotion or thought – except perhaps some of the more Hegelian metaphysics – that could not be adequately and superabundantly expressed in Shakespeare's vocabulary: there are very few that would not be mutilated out of all recognition if they had to pass through the language of the Bible' (p. 121). As far as the Bible is concerned – and in spite of Macaulay's grand assertion to the contrary (above, p. 179) – this is obviously true, and, following Gardiner, we may make the same point about sentence-structures: the Bible's largely unsubordinated range of structures would not be adequate for the modern awareness of complex interrelationships. The Latin heritage of structure and vocabulary has added more to the expressive power of the native language than any other single source. In relation to it, the Bible has contributed little and acts as a conservative and moderating force, as Ruskin suggested in a part of his passage that Lewis chooses to omit. This suggests that the Bible remains an influence in a way that Latin (and its Romance descendants) are not: they have created the standard form of the language, but the Bible may continue to influence by tempering that form.

In the case of Bunyan, Lewis argues that much of the apparent similarity to the style of the Bible is superficial, the result of both seeming now rather archaic and simple in syntax. After giving a passage he suggests that the appropriate 'question is not how much of this might occur in the Authorised Version, but how much might be expected to occur in Bunyan if he had not read it' (p. 42). This dodges the real question, how much of the style could only have been as it is because Bunyan had read the KJB, but the dodge has its uses. It allows Lewis to suggest that 'his prose comes to him not from the Authorised Version but from the fireside, the shop and the lane', and so 'might have been much the same without the Authorised Version' (pp. 43, 44). This knocks down the idea that Bunyan's prose is essentially biblical, but it does not actually confront the question of influence.

Such discussion is salutary but less than satisfactory. Excess has been corrected, but replaced only with tangential insights. Rather than developing an account of how the influence has worked, Lewis attempts to explain why the KJB's 'strictly literary influence has mattered less than we have often supposed' (p. 44). He suggests two reasons, changing taste and, recognising that it will sound paradoxical, familiarity. Citing Harwood, 'no doubt ... by our standards, an ass' (p. 44), he suggests that the ancient perception of the Bible's lack of elegance persisted longer than generally recognised and that the change in attitude to it is to be associated with the romantic 'taste for the primitive and the passionate which can be seen growing through nearly the whole of the eighteenth century' (p. 44). It was the development of this taste that made the Bible an attractive model and which changed the way it was heard. Rather than being inelegant, to this taste the Bible was sublime if it was admired, or florid or inflated if it was disliked. Given that much of the admiration of the Bible is admiration for its once-despised simplicity, whatever the admirer understands by that, this may seem strange, but it picks up the admiration for the oriental aspect of the Bible. A rather different dissenting voice, Somerset Maugham, confirms Lewis's point:

> To my mind King James's Bible has been a very harmful influence on English prose. I am not so stupid as to deny its great beauty. It is majestical. But the Bible is an oriental book. Its alien imagery has nothing to do with us. Those hyperboles, those luscious metaphors, are foreign to our genius... Those rhythms, that powerful vocabulary, that grandiloquence, became part and parcel of the national sensibility. The plain, honest English speech was overwhelmed with ornament. Blunt Englishmen twisted their tongues to speak like Hebrew Prophets... English prose has had to struggle against the tendency to luxuriance.[37]

Familiarity Lewis treats in a teasingly different way from the way I have treated it. The Bible was so familiar, he suggests, that it could only be echoed 'with conscious reverence or with conscious irreverence, either religiously or facetiously', and he cites Boswell's observation that 'a scripture expression may be used like a highly classical phrase to produce an instantaneous strong impression'.[38] He concludes that 'an influence which cannot evade our consciousness will not go very deep' (p. 46). The illogic is transparent: conscious use producing instant response does not prove that the language of the Bible does not also live in one's subconscious.

If the Bible is not an influence when it is so well known, Lewis wonders if it will become more of a literary influence 'now, when only a minority of Englishmen regard the Bible as a sacred book' (p. 46), and this leads him to perhaps the most stimulating part of the lecture. At the beginning, he had warned that 'there is a certain sense in which "the Bible as literature" does not exist' because of the heterogeneous nature of the originals and the non-literary reasons for gathering them together; but where Kellett makes this a ground for condemning the K JB, Lewis points the paradox that, 'for good or ill', 'when we turn from the originals to any version made by one man, or at least bearing the stamp of one age, a certain appearance of unity creeps in', and so the Bible is read as a single book. Nevertheless, it is still a single book 'read for almost every purpose more diligently than for literary pleasure' (p. 27).

This will become his final point, a challenge to the whole idea of the Bible as literature in the sense that that idea seems to ignore the fact that the Bible is religion. Some fifteen years earlier one of the century's foremost poets and critics, T. S. Eliot (like Lewis, an eminent Christian), had vented his spleen on this idea:

[37] *The Summing Up* (London: Heinemann, 1938), p. 36.
[38] Boswell, *Life*, p. 510. Boswell's other account of this point is given above, p. 137.

> I could fulminate against the men of letters who have gone into ecstasies over 'the Bible as literature', the Bible as 'the noblest monument of English prose'. Those who talk of the Bible as a 'monument of English prose' are merely admiring it as a monument over the grave of Christianity ... the Bible has had a *literary* influence upon English literature *not* because it has been considered as literature, but because it has been considered as the report of the Word of God. And the fact that men of letters now discuss it as 'literature' probably indicates the *end* of its 'literary' influence.[39]

Lewis, more temperately, makes the same insistence on the religious character of the Bible:

> Unless the religious claims of the Bible are again acknowledged, its literary claims will, I think, be given only 'mouth honour' and that decreasingly. For it is, through and through, a sacred book ... It is, if you like to put it that way, not merely a sacred book but a book so remorselessly and continuously sacred that it does not invite, it excludes or repels, the merely aesthetic approach. You can read it as literature only by a *tour de force* ... It demands incessantly to be taken on its own terms: it will not continue to give literary delight very long except to those who go to it for something quite different. I predict that it will in the future be read as it always has been read, almost exclusively by Christians.   (Pp. 48–9)

The importance of this argument can hardly be overestimated even if it is not a final truth. Familiarity is a basic reason for the love of the Bible, and that familiarity is founded on its religious position. But still more important are the twin perceptions of a tendency to falsity in attempts to see the Bible as something which may be read as literature alone, and of elements in the text which repel such reading. These elements have never, I think, been properly analysed, and the lack of such analysis is part of a greater lack that supports Lewis's views. The idea that the KJB is a classic of English literature has been oftener proclaimed than acted on. In spite of calls to do so, the KJB has never really been studied as if it were a classic like the other classics of English literature. The fullest studies of it are those which take it as a translation and seek to illuminate its qualities as such. It is still often used as the form of the text to illustrate discussions that are really discussions of the originals or of what is common to most versions, for it is difficult to take what is really a fictional step, and treat it as if it is an autonomous work of English literature. In England it has never become an integral part of the curriculum of English literature. In America, where courses on the Bible as literature are more common, they

---

[39] 'Religion and literature' (1935); *Selected Prose*, ed. John Hayward (Harmondsworth: Penguin, 1953), pp. 31–42; pp. 32–3. I have not seen Eliot's unpublished address to the Women's Alliance at King's Chapel, Boston, 1932, 'The Bible as scripture and literature'.

occupy an uneasy ground between literary and theological studies, and they do not necessarily use the KJB. Until now the Bible's critical heritage has not received more than the most glancing attention, whereas the critical heritages of all the major authors and a vast number of the minor authors of English and American literature have received detailed attention. In brief, the profession of literature has never properly acted on the idea of the KJB as an English classic. This supports Lewis's contentions that there is an insincerity in the idea of the Bible as literature and that there are elements in the Bible that refuse to become part of literature because they are too inescapably something else.

The Hebrew inheritance and the virtues of literalism

The best modern insights into the KJB come from discussions of its relationship with the original Hebrew. Gardiner, ignorant of Hebrew, relied on the great French scholar Ernest Renan, but I focus on him rather than Renan because he develops Renan's points and directs them, in the end, towards the KJB.[40] Renan identifies the essential difference in structure between Hebrew and modern languages as Hebrew's lack of 'one of the degrees of combination which we hold necessary for the complete expression of the thought. To join the words in a proposition is as far as they go; they made no effort to apply the same operation to the propositions.'[41] Gardiner elaborates:

> In consequence of this poverty in connectives the Hebrew language could not express swiftly and compactly the relations of facts and ideas to each other; and it was wholly incapable of expressing most of the subtle modulations which give variety and flexibility to modern writings. It was a language in which solid fact followed solid fact in hardly changing sequence.   (Pp. 68–9)

Moreover, since Hebrew has only two tenses, one signifying an uncompleted or imperfect act, the other a completed act, each of them past, present or future, Renan observes that

> Perspective is almost entirely lacking in the Semitic style ... One must even allow that the idea of style as we understand it was wholly lacking among the Semitic people. Their period is very short; the extent of discourse which they embrace at a time never passes one or two lines. Wholly preoccupied with the present thought,

---

[40] Sadly, I too am ignorant of Hebrew, and must follow Gardiner in his reliance on the learning of others. If their learning is deficient, it may prompt other Hebraists to correct and supplement their work, for the books I deal with here are the main contributions to an understanding of Hebrew in relation to the KJB available to the English reader.

[41] *Histoire générale et système comparé des langues sémitiques* (1855); 7th edn (Paris, n.d.), p. 21. As given in Gardiner, p. 68.

they do not construct in advance the mechanism of the phrase and take no thought of what has gone before or of what is coming.[42]

Gardiner adds that 'down to the end of the third Gospel there is no narrative in the Bible which departs from' the unpremeditated simplicity described by Renan (p. 70). He demonstrates the point first by contrasting an OT with an NT narrative (1 Sam. 17: 38–43 and Acts 28: 1–6), and then by making a contrast with Bunyan's description of Christian resting in the arbour half way up the hill Difficulty, and losing his roll in his sleep (*Pilgrim's Progress*, p. 173). The latter contrast sounds a real warning to all over-simple claims for influence:

> In this passage the clauses run to three and four and even five lines; and instead of all the clauses being co-ordinate and of equal value, every sentence shows subordination of one idea to another ... Such writing as this is of another kind from that of the Bible narrative. Like the speeches ascribed to St Paul in Acts, Bunyan's writing belongs to a mode of thought and of style which are unknown in the Old Testament.   (P. 76)

Still following Renan's characterisation of the Semitic languages, Gardiner moves to his own explanation of 'the permanent expressive power of the Bible narratives' (p. 86). It comes out of a simplicity made universal by direct contact with the world and the self. So Hebraic thought 'was essentially simple. It knew only the objective and solid facts of which man has direct sensation, and the simple primitive emotions which are his reaction to them' (p. 86). This limitation is fundamental strength, for the narratives 'are an unbroken stream of objective realities. Their whole texture is composed of the things which men can feel and see and hear' (pp. 86–7). In the same vein, he describes 'the distinguishing characteristic of the poetry [as] its absolute objectivity: it knew only facts which are concrete and which mean always the same to all men' (p. 88), and so 'gives the impression of being born in the very heat of joy or grief or triumph' (p. 96). The opening of Psalm 69, used so powerfully by Bunyan and Brontë, makes the point:

> Save me, O God; for the waters are come in unto my soul. I sink in deep mire, where there is no standing: I am come into deep waters, where the floods overflow me. I am weary of my crying: my throat is dried: mine eyes fail while I wait for my God.

There is neither characterisation nor abstraction here. Gardiner invites us to 'notice the number of sensations which are named' (p. 116); physical sensations and the elaborated natural metaphor of flooding do indeed create a universal image of the abstract idea, despair.

---

[42] Renan, *Histoire*, p. 20; Gardiner, pp. 69–70.

Behind this lies Renan's point that all Hebrew words 'went back immediately[43] to things of sense, and in consequence even their everyday language was figurative in a way which we can hardly imagine. The verb "to be jealous" was a regular form of the verb "to glow", the noun "truth" was derived from the verb meaning "to prop", "to build" or "to make firm". The word for "self" was also the word for "bone"' (pp. 113–14; cf. Renan, p. 23). Now, thus far there is nothing that is specific to the KJB, but it will be obvious that the drift of the discussion is to give substance to the familiar idea of the translatability of the Bible: content, it seems, is unusually present in the Bible, form unusually absent. Part of the discussion's effect is to alert the reader to characteristics of the KJB.

An earlier work, evidently unknown to Gardiner, takes the subject further, William Rosenau's *Hebraisms in the Authorized Version of the Bible* (1902). Rosenau has that rare qualification among writers on the KJB of a good knowledge of Hebrew, and he uses this to assemble very detailed listings of words, phrases and constructions in the KJB that are literal reproductions of the Hebrew rather than what was natural English. They lead him to conclude

> that the AV is an almost literal translation of the M[asoretic] text, and is thus on every page replete with Hebrew idioms. The fact that Bible English has to a marvellous extent shaped our speech, giving peculiar connotations to many words and sanctioning strange constructions, is not any less patent. The AV has been – it can be said without any fear of being charged with exaggeration – the most powerful factor in the history of English literature. Though the constructions encountered in the AV are oftentimes so harsh that they seem almost barbarous, we should certainly have been the poorer without the AV. (Pp. 164–5)

This is far from AVolatry. It is an evidenced claim for significance rather than an assertion of quality.

The value of Rosenau's book does not lie in its discussion, which is scanty and often unsatisfactory. For instance, only one passage is given as a whole, and the reader is left to infer the extent to which it is Hebraic rather than English by working through an unconvincing standard-English rendering given in

---

[43] 'Immediately' is the most debatable word here, for what Gardiner and Renan are touching on is a commonly made point about language. They suggest that in Hebrew there was a special intensity to the figurative link. No one, to my knowledge, has considered this idea about Hebrew in relation to the general idea that abstract language has a metaphorical origin. Useful starting-points might be Owen Barfield's essay, 'The meaning of "literal"', in *The Rediscovery of Meaning and Other Essays* (Middleton, Conn.: Wesleyan University Press, 1977) pp. 32–43, and Prickett's discussion of Barfield and others in *Words and the Word*, pp. 86ff.

parallel. Rather, it lies in the quantity and suggestiveness of the evidence, though even here there are difficulties. Not all the examples are convincing, sometimes because they can be shown to antedate the English translations, sometimes (and these are inescapable difficulties) because one's sense of English is different or because one may feel that the Hebraism is not the necessary source of the English phrase.[44] A larger difficulty lies in the limitations of scope. A Saintsbury might well retort that we know the KJB contains Hebraisms: what of the rhythmic superiority of the KJB to its predecessors, which were also literal translations to the degree that Rosenau shows the KJB to be literal? For Rosenau had only Wyclif of the earlier translations available to him and never ventures on judgements of quality. At the least we must put this minor qualification on Rosenau's evidence, that it applies to the tradition of translation as embodied in the KJB. It does not in itself negate the aesthetic view of the translation: rather, it provides a wealth of material for further study of how the KJB came to be and how it influenced English.

Rosenau divides Hebraisms into two classes, lexicographical and syntactical. Syntactical Hebraisms preserve Hebrew forms that are alien to English. Here are some of them (selected from chapter 8, with some additional comments of my own). The plural may be used where a singular is expected, for instance 'heavens' or 'rivers' (as in 'by the rivers of Babylon'). The Hebrew use of apposition sometimes produces phrases such as 'Nathan the Prophet' where the natural English order would be 'the Prophet Nathan' (yet such constructions have become so familiar as often to pass unnoticed). Hebrew cognate accusatives produce phrases such as 'to dream a dream'. Similarly, the superlative form, 'king of kings' or 'song of songs' is alien to English yet has become sufficiently familiar to produce phrases not found in the Bible such as 'heart of hearts', and to allow such biblically orientated writers as Lawrence to coin phrases such as 'workman of workmen' ('Fanny and Annie'). Genitives are often used differently, as in 'altar of stone' for 'stone altar' or 'men of truth' for 'honest men'. Again, some of these genitives have become so familiar a part of English that they pass unnoticed, as in 'man of war'. Prepositions with nouns are often used instead of adverbs, as in 'eat in haste' for 'eat hastily'. Pronouns are sometimes used redundantly as in 'the Lord your God, he shall fight for

---

[44] For example, one may take one's choice whether 'went down to buy corn in Egypt' (Gen. 42: 3) has led to 'go down town' and 'go down to Washington' as used in Baltimore (p. 103), or whether such phrases, including 'go up to town', are the natural result of topography or the imagining of north on a map as up. Rosenau classes 'down' as a superfluous preposition, and his general point is that Hebrew sometimes uses prepositions that are unnecessary in English.

you'. Verbs are often co-ordinated where English would subordinate one, as in the familiar but still obviously biblical 'answered and said'. And so we may go on, noting that the pervasive use of 'and' in the KJB is Hebraic rather than natural written English.

Such itemising of grammatical points is not easy to read: it is no different from starting to learn a new language, but even so abbreviated a list is sufficient to suggest that the extent of Hebraic elements surviving in the KJB because of literal translation is large, and that this is not generally realised for two reasons, one minor, one major: ignorance of Hebrew and acquired familiarity with the idioms. As observed before, what was so harsh and strange to the translators and their early readers is now substantially familiar. The same is true with lexicographical Hebraisms, that is, literal English renderings of words or phrases which give the English an abnormal sense, as in 'heard the voice of your words'. Some very familiar words have an unusual range of meaning as they appear in the KJB, a range that English would normally distinguish by a variety of words. So 'flesh' may signify muscles, meat, body, kinsman, creatures, mankind or pudenda; 'blood', blood, murder, blood-guilt, innocent person, bloodstains, relative or juice; 'hand', hand, power, leadership, supervision, possession, blow, violence, external influence, or may be used for a personal pronoun; and 'heart' may signify breast, wish, judgement, motive, mind, spirit, desire, courage, excitement, affections or middle, or may be used instead of personal or reflexive pronouns. Though these are not standard synonym-lists, it is clear that the relatively limited vocabulary of Hebrew has contributed to the range of meaning of some English words.

Such insight is of real importance for an understanding of the history of English vocabulary and constructions, and for the real rather than the apparent meaning of some of the KJB's language. Rosenau makes but does not stress the point that his examples also help to show how far Hebraisms have become naturalised in English. Such evidence goes along with that from the lists of obsolete words given in the previous two centuries. From them it was apparent that the KJB rescued some words from obsolescence, and this said much about the KJB's power over English as the most familiar book in the language. Rather than confining ourselves to Rosenau's Hebraisms, it is worth extending the point here. A substantial number of phrases and images have become so naturalised that we are often unaware that they are biblical in origin. Other staples of English literature have made such contributions – we might recognise 'groves of academe' as going back to Milton, but not 'all hell broke loose' – but none so substantial as the Bible and related works. By related works I mean, say, Handel's *Messiah*, or Bunyan's *The Pilgrim's Progress*, or *Paradise Lost*, or the PB, or even earlier translations, or the Sternhold and Hopkins Psalter. This last, for instance, is the now unrecognised origin of the phrase, 'for ever and a day',[45] while 'take him at his word' goes back to Coverdale (1 Kgs. 20: 33), but is not found in the KJB. Here are some naturalised Hebraisms: 'a drop in a bucket' (making sense of Isa. 40: 15, 'a drop of a bucket'), 'the last gasp' (2 Macc. 7: 9), 'the skin of my teeth' (also making sense of a Hebraism, 'with the skin of my teeth', Job 19: 20), 'lick the dust' (Ps. 72: 9), 'fell flat on his face' (Num. 22: 31), 'to set one's face against' (Lev. 20: 3), 'a man after his own heart' (1 Sam. 13: 14), 'heart-searching' (from Judg. 5: 16), 'pour out one's heart' (Lam. 2: 19), 'heap coals of fire upon his head' (Prov. 25: 22), 'die the death' (Num. 23: 10), 'far be it from me' (1 Sam. 20: 9), 'from time to time' (but meaning 'at set times', Ezek. 4: 10), 'gird one's loins' (Exod. 12: 11 etc.), 'the land of the living' (Ps. 27: 13), 'put words in his mouth' (Exod. 4: 15), 'sick to death' (from 'sick unto death' meaning 'almost dead', 2 Kgs. 20: 1), 'rise and shine' (from 'arise, shine', Isa. 60: 1, but also Handel's *Messiah*), 'go from strength to strength' (Ps. 84: 7), 'sour grapes' (Ezek. 18: 2), 'a lamb to the slaughter' (Isa. 53: 7), and 'stand in awe' (Ps. 4: 4). From the NT: 'a thorn in the flesh' (2 Cor. 12: 7), 'kick against the pricks' (Acts 9: 5), 'a house divided' (Mark 3: 25), 'den of thieves' (Mark 11: 17), 'labour of love' (1 Thess. 1: 3), and 'no respecter of persons' (Acts 10: 34).

This is not a complete listing, and perhaps no such listing is possible,[46] but to extend it much further would be to begin to give examples where a phrase is only based on the Bible, as 'a fly in the ointment' ('dead flies cause the ointment of the apothecary to send forth a stinking savour', Eccles. 10: 1) or 'the [hand]writing on the wall' (based on Dan. 5: 5 and sometimes used as a page heading in later editions of the KJB), or examples that are more likely to be recognised as biblical, such as 'pride goeth before a fall' (Prov. 16: 18) or 'babes and sucklings' (Ps. 8: 2) or 'cast thy bread upon the waters' Eccles. 11: 1), or examples where one cannot be sure that the phrase really comes from the Bible: 'the twinkling of an eye' comes in 1 Cor. 15: 52 but had been used as early as 1303; was it a native idiom or a translation of the Vulgate's 'in ictu oculi'? Given

---

[45] 'What is his goodness clean decayed / for ever and a day' (Ps. 77: 8, trans. John Hopkins). This may be a variation on the older 'for ever and ay'.

[46] One major difficulty is the question of individual judgement of familiarity, another the sheer size of the undertaking. The *OED* frequently records Hebraisms, and any casual browsing in it would show up a large number of instances where the first recorded use of a word in a particular sense is in a version of the Bible. But even a full search of the *OED* would not be the end of the matter if one were seeking for that illusory and indigestible ideal of comprehensiveness, for it does not deal with all the phrases one would be interested in, nor, treasure house though it is, is it always reliable, especially where Tyndale is concerned. It may be worth remembering that the *OED* dates from the period of highest AVolatry.

the size of the Bible, the list may seem brief, but the familiarity of the examples and the fact that they come from all parts of it including the Apocrypha give an undeniable impression of depth of influence. Naturalisation of this sort is the most striking evidence of the familiarity with the KJB that is so essential to the turnaround in its literary fortunes. It tells us more of the penetrative power of the Bible's language and imagery than do all the assertions of familiarity (true as they may be), or the multitudinous demonstrations of individual writers' and speakers' deliberate use of quotation and allusion.

The third book to explore such connections is a recent one, Gerald Hammond's *The Making of the English Bible* (1982). Hammond writes from the unique position of an intimate knowledge of both Hebrew and the English translations. Though his book is essentially about translation rather than the English Bible as literature, it develops independently the kinds of insights that have been gleaned from Rosenau, Renan and Gardiner in ways not to be found in any of the multitudinous histories of translation. It is a detailed study of the practice of translation, illuminating 'the stylistic relationships between the original and its translation' (p. 14). The KJB, in part because 'its word order is for many verses at a time the word order of the original and [because] it translates the great majority of Hebrew idioms literally' (p. 3), emerges as the most powerful of the English translations. Hammond unashamedly connects literalness and power, and the discussions of the Hebraic qualities of the original OT that we have been following provide an immediate reason for accepting that the connection is valid. But it is not literalism alone which produces the power: in Hammond's view 'the Renaissance Bible translator saw half of his task as reshaping English so that it could adapt itself to Hebraic idiom' (p. 2). In making this point he draws telling contrasts with the practice of modern translators as exemplified in the New English Bible. In effect, there is artistry in the literalism, and much of the discussion brings out ways this faithful artistry worked. This is not to say that Hammond takes a blinkered view of the KJB or its predecessors: he judges for himself where strength and weakness lie, and is candid that there is weakness in the KJB. He resists synthesising his observations into a reductive overview of the stylistic qualities of the KJB, observing that 'no label will properly describe the variety of biblical English'. This is a slap in the eye for the AVolaters and their grandiosely repetitive labellings. Hammond continues: 'I do not want to end up with a demonstration that the style can be categorised and understood in certain highly specific ways: less ambitious than that, I aim to analyse the kinds of decisions which we might judge the translators to have made, and the kinds of principles they might be considered to have held' (p. 14).

After discussion of the earlier translators, Hammond looks in his last two chapters at how the KJB handles words and sentences. He shows that, perhaps in order to keep uniformity between companies, the KJB translators adopted a word-for-word policy in dealing with repetitive patterns and formulaic synonyms while remaining responsive to context and so not aiming for complete consistency (pp. 198–9). So, for instance, 'the past and future forms of the Hebrew verb "to be" . . . are normally rendered as "and it came to pass" and "and it shall come to pass" – almost *ad nauseam*. The hope is, of course, that the English formula will become as natural as the Hebrew one was to the Bible's original readers' (p. 194). By contrasting the KJB's Isa. 7: 21–3 with Coverdale's 1535 rendering, and its Gen. 38: 27–9 with Tyndale's, Hammond shows that the gain in accuracy of signalling to the reader an identity in the original can result in stilted writing, in the first instance, or may lose 'the rough urgency of the narrative' in the second (p. 195). Sometimes this practice produces gains but for the most part it leads to a 'featurelessness' (p. 193) characteristic of committee work.

However, it is more interesting to follow strengths. Here is an instance of how Hammond takes us beyond Rosenau and Gardiner through illustrating the translators' practice:

> The number of verbs in biblical Hebrew is severely limited. This fact encouraged the English translators to use common English verbs in figurative senses. The Hebrew verb *'achaz* gives us examples. Its meaning is 'to grasp, take hold of, take possession', and it is often used with an abstract subject such as pain or fear. In this usage the Geneva Bible prefers to render it as 'come upon', while the Authorised Version has the more vivid – and more literal – 'take hold of'. Two places in the Psalms show the contrasting effects. In 48: [6] Geneva's 'fear came there upon them' becomes, in the Authorised Version, 'fear took hold upon them there'; and in 119: 53, Geneva's 'fear is come upon me' becomes 'horror hath taken hold upon me' (the subjects are different words, hence the Authorised Version's different renderings, 'fear' and 'horror').
>
> (Pp. 202–3)

Hammond takes five more examples, comparing the KJB's treatment of this verb in figurative uses with two other Latin and two other English Bibles, showing that where the other translations 'vary their renderings in their attempts to find the exact shade of meaning', the KJB 'uses a verb form containing the word "hold"' (pp. 203–4). There can be no doubt of the strength produced here by greater literalism, or that the strength is inseparable from the highly physical nature of the Hebrew verb.

Against this example, which is a relatively rare verb, Hammond sets the contrasting example of the verb 'to know', and shows extensive variation in the KJB's rendering. He concludes that 'there is ... no all-pervading attempt to create a word-for-word equivalence in the Authorised Version, although its consistency is measurably greater than that found in any of its predecessors, or in a modern version like the New English Bible' (p. 206). This is a comedown after the previous discussion even if one reminds oneself that Hammond's subject is the practice of translation. Is this 'extensive variation' simply an example of variation for its own sake, or can one detect a deeper motive? Is it artful variation or mere inconsistency? No clue is given. Hammond is at his most illuminating when he shows the results of consistency: examples of inconsistency round out the picture of practice but do not generate insight into the KJB's qualities as English.

Hammond returns to the matter of consistency when he comes to sentences. He shows that it was one of the translators' 'great priorities ... to keep as close as possible to the original's word order' (p. 228), and he analyses some of the results. His discussion of the treatment of the Hebrew infinitive brings out what he calls the KJB's 'neatnesses of rendering' (p. 218):

> The infinitive is often used in tandem with a finite verb, so that its sense is essentially adverbial. The Authorised Version's treatment of it shows a greater care than in any of its predecessors to give it a grammatical status different from the finite verb – usually by means of a participle or gerund ... where [the examples] become important is when we consider their accumulative effect upon English biblical style as it came to be set in 1611. Put simply, it means that the participle becomes a typical part of this style. (P. 218)

He instances Isa. 31: 5 which ends, in his literal translation, 'to-defend he-will-deliver to-pass-over he-will-save'. Coverdale, and the Bishops after him, use four equal finite verbs, 'keep, save, defend, and deliver', while Geneva uses participles divided into pairs (could this division have been made for stylistic reasons? Hammond does not say), 'by defending and delivering, by passing through and preserving it'. It is the KJB that reflects the Hebrew most closely by using a participle before a finite verb, and we recognise that this is peculiar English, the Hebraic English of the Bible:

> As birds flying, so will the Lord of hosts defend Jerusalem: defending also he will deliver *it, and* passing over he will preserve it.

In the sense that this reflects the Hebrew without wasting words, it is indeed a neat rendering; whether it is also felicitous is a different matter. Most important, though, is that it is a characteristic rendering: Hammond goes on to show some other uses of participial forms to render infinitives and observes that the KJB uses them to a greater extent than previous English versions. A particular quality of the KJB's language is thus identified.

Hammond concludes his study with an examination of the way the KJB deals with two more Hebraic constructions, the *casus obliquus* and the *casus pendens*. In the latter the subject or object is separated from the main body of the sentence and then repeated in some pronominal form, producing either emphasis or something like a cadence (p. 225). So we get structures such as this in the KJB's rendering: 'and the Levite that is within thy gates, thou shalt not forsake him' (Deut. 14: 27). But the KJB's most characteristic way of dealing with this structure is to use 'as for', for example, 'as for his judgements, they have not known them' (Ps. 147: 20). The *casus obliquus* is more complex. It is a form of repetition in which a pronoun implicit in the verb form is also given separately. Hammond instances Gen. 27: 34, which, in his literal rendering, reads 'bless-me also-I my-father' (p. 229). The KJB, following Geneva, renders this, 'bless me, *even* me also, my father', and Hammond argues that '"even" turns out to be the best weapon in the Authorised Version's armoury for reproducing Hebraic repetition' (p. 232). Other methods are also used, and, as so often, Hammond notes that the KJB does not always reproduce the construction literally, 'probably reflecting the triumph of the aesthetic over the accurate'. On the other hand, sometimes accuracy triumphs only to produce 'a stubborn, pedantic fidelity to the Hebrew idiom', as in, 'is it time for you, O ye, to dwell in your ceiled houses' (Hag. 1: 4; p. 232). But what is perhaps most interesting is the number of instances he gives of the KJB replacing a natural form of English in its predecessors with a Hebraic form. So the Geneva Bible uses a natural English word order for Isa. 1: 7, 'your land is waste, your cities *are* burnt with fire; strangers devour your land in your presence'. The KJB, however, marks the *casus pendens* in the second part, so reproducing the Hebraic word order: 'your country *is* desolate, your cities *are* burned with fire: your land, strangers devour it in your presence' (pp. 228–9). In such examples Hammond not only alerts us to peculiarities of the KJB but shows that it did indeed give a higher priority to fidelity than to the requirements of natural or artistic English. Without denying that aesthetic considerations affected the translation, he, like Rosenau, shows just how misleading the AVolatrous ideas of the KJB's English are. He concludes that the ways the KJB treats the three grammatical forms he has discussed.

> give us accessible paradigms for understanding the essentially formulaic tendency of the translation. Individual examples mean little until their cumulative effect is registered. Match them to the practices of the earlier translators which the

Authorised Version happily inherited, like the reproduction of a consecutive narrative syntax and the use of the noun plus 'of' plus noun form to translate the Hebrew construct form, and we can grasp the integrity and consistency of English biblical style – and understand why it kept so powerful a hold over English minds for the next three hundred and fifty years.   (P. 233)

Strictly, Hammond's is no more a book about the KJB as English literature than Rosenau's: both are books about translation that show the range of Hebraic qualities in the KJB's English. Especially for readers with no Hebrew, the insight is invaluable. Yet it is strange that these two books, so widely separated in time, should represent the bulk of what the twentieth century has contributed to an understanding of the KJB as literature. Much has been and still is being written about the KJB, but if one takes away the histories of translation and the effusions of AVolatry, one is left with three things: occasional internal examinations of translation, books about the Bible as literature that use the KJB for quotations but which are not really books about the KJB, and dissenting essays such as Lewis's. In other words, given the claims for the KJB as a great, or even as the greatest, work of English literature, there is a void where one would expect plenitude: there are no substantial, good studies of the KJB as a work of English literature. Books like Hammond's and Rosenau's are on one edge of the void, the studies of the Bible as literature on the other edge. The simplest explanation lies in the fact that the KJB is a translation. Good discussions of it as a translation must illuminate its literary qualities, but they go no further than examining the way the original is represented. And discussions of the Bible as literature, for good reasons, tend to concentrate on qualities that are general to the originals and all reasonably close representations of them. A second and somewhat less simple explanation is that the claim for the KJB as great English literature is really a quite narrow claim, that its language is great English, and that scholars are not willing to treat the KJB as a whole, because that would mean pretending that it is an autonomous work of English literature whereas it is obviously but one representation of a body of foreign literature. There may well also be a more complex explanation that lies in the often peculiar relationship of the Bible's language to its content. To a degree that is highly unusual for the great works of English literature, there is a separation between the Bible's content and its words. The KJB translators' image, inherited from Tyndale, of translation as a process 'that breaketh the shell, that we may eat the kernel' is helpful here, for the Bible text itself constantly implies that it too is a shell and so invites its reader to create or discover the kernel as something separate. To give but one obvious example, the multiple narrative of the Gospel story (even without accumulated tradition that makes much of it familiar apart from any text) invites the reader to synthesise an independent version. The Bible text, then, is often a text which, peculiar as it may seem, drives the reader beyond itself. It tends to evade the traditional, text-centred method of literary discussion. Discussion that separates language and content is encouraged.

Whatever the explanation, there is a void, and it remains a challenge to literary criticism to fill it. Close discussion of the range of the KJB's literary qualities in all their aspects is needed not just because such discussion does not exist, but, much more importantly, because it will illuminate our understanding of the most important book in the English cultural heritage, both for what it still offers its readers and for what it has contributed to that heritage.

CHAPTER 9

Narrative and unity: modern preoccupations

Schweitzer, Strauss and the discovery of fiction

As H. Wheeler Robinson wrote in 1940, 'books about the Bible have legion for their name (and some of them deserve a Gadarene destiny)'.[1] There have been well over 400 new versions of part or all of the Bible published so far this century; one survey of twenty of these published in 1975 runs to over 200 pages; another covering eleven versions is nearly twice as long.[2] John H. Gottcent's *The Bible as Literature: A Selective Bibliography* (Boston: Hall, 1979) is over 150 pages long. I have noted not far short of 1,500 — a figure that, like a crocodile, never ceases growing — books, articles and stray comments from the present century that have some relevance to the story, and many of them deserve a far from Gadarene destiny. In short, there is not just the obvious difficulty of writing a history of the present: the comprehensiveness that was the unattainable ideal for some parts of the story becomes an impossibility in a work already so long. This is not wholly a matter for regret. It is the development of ideas rather than their repetition that is of primary interest, and most of the patterns of thought that have been observed continue to show themselves in the modern dress of the last hundred years.

The most interesting work in the last quarter of a century has concentrated on the narrative qualities of the Bible and on the question of whether or not it is a literary unity. Yet, even narrowing the focus this much, and then narrowing it further to only a few of the very many critics who have contributed to understanding of these issues, one has to backtrack immediately. Krister Stendhal has suggested that narrative has taken over from history as a focus of

[1] *The Bible in its Ancient and English Versions* (Oxford: Oxford University Press, 1940), p. v.
[2] Sakae Kubo and Walter Specht, *So Many Versions? Twentieth Century English Versions of the Bible* (1975); revised and enlarged edn, (Grand Rapids, Mich.: Zondervan, 1983); Jack P. Lewis, *The English Bible from KJV to NIV* (Grand Rapids, Mich.: Baker, 1981).

biblical study,[3] but much – not all – of the present study of narrative is the old study of history in a new guise. Albert Schweitzer devoted a fascinating book, *The Quest of the Historical Jesus*, to lives of Jesus through to the end of the nineteenth century. At first sight *The Quest* is a history of a branch of Higher Criticism that has nothing to do with literature and which, besides, was pursued almost entirely in Europe. German scholars led the attempt to form a historical conception of the life of Jesus, and Schweitzer, opening his discussion of 'the problem', remarks that 'the greatest achievement of German theology is the critical investigation of the life of Jesus'; this 'has laid down the conditions and determined the course of the religious thinking of the future' (p. 1). Yet one does not have to read far to suspect that there is a literary side to this historical and theological achievement. The suspicion might begin with Schweitzer's observation that 'there is no historical task which so reveals a man's true self as the writing of a Life of Jesus' (p. 4), for this directs us towards the writer and the character of his writing. The suspicion might be strengthened when he discusses the problem that 'the life of Jesus has no analogue in the field of history' (p. 6). He notes that 'every ordinary method of historical investigation proves inadequate to the complexity of the conditions' (p. 6), and so he describes what we might see as a literary problem. By comparison with Socrates, Schweitzer claims, 'Jesus stands much more immediately before us, because He was depicted by simple Christians without literary gift' (p. 6), a claim which suggests the paradox of literary effect being achieved without literary intention or talent on the part of the Gospel-writers. Yet the Gospels are contradictory – one must choose between the synoptics and John – and there is no 'thread of connection in the material which they offer us' (p. 7). Consequently 'we can only get a Life of Jesus with yawning gaps', gaps to be filled 'at the worst with phrases, at the best with historical imagination' (p. 7). The largest of these gaps is that 'the sources give no hint of the character of His self-consciousness. They confine themselves to outward facts. We only begin to understand these historically when we can mentally place them in an intelligible connection and conceive them as the acts of a clearly defined personality' (p. 7). Readers familiar with some of the recent discussion of biblical narrative, especially that of Meir Sternberg, will realise that Schweitzer has reached a key

---

[3] 'The shift in contemporary biblical and theological work from history to story is obvious and well substantiated by a perusal of the program for the annual meeting of our Society of Biblical Literature and of our sister, the American Academy of Religion' (Presidential Address to the Society of Biblical Literature, 18 December 1983; 'The Bible as a classic and the Bible as Holy Scripture', *Journal of Biblical Literature* 103/1 (1984), 3–10; p. 4).

modern literary idea. Even without this knowledge, the literary aspect of what he is describing should be apparent. What Schweitzer calls the historical imagination is no different from the imagination employed by readers of fiction, bringing the more or less complete information of the text into an imaginative whole. The reason for his suggestion that 'there is no historical task which so reveals a man's true self as the writing of a Life of Jesus' is now apparent: a life of Jesus calls for more from the reader and the recreator than other lives. Implicitly the creative imagination must be used not only to read the life of Jesus but also to create some aspects of it.

Such implications become clear in Schweitzer's lucid summaries and criticisms of the lives. But we may turn to two of the major authors he considers, David Friedrich Strauss (1808–74) and, fleetingly, Ernest Renan (1823–92), to develop the points. Both were major scholars, and both were translated into English and so might have been discussed earlier for their understanding of the Bible as fiction. However, there is little sign that Strauss contributed to the English-speaking world's literary ideas of the Bible, and Renan's influence is most visible in the 1930s, nearly three-quarters of a century after his work began to appear. Their real interest here is that they reveal a convergence between literary studies and Higher Criticism.

Strauss's *Das Leben Jesu* (1835–6) is now known only as a name to most literary scholars, for it was translated as *The Life of Jesus Critically Examined* (1846), anonymously, by a young lady later to achieve fame as George Eliot.[4] As a major work of literary insight, it deserves better. Strauss subjected the Gospels to minute 'scientific'[5] examination in order to determine what in them was historical and what mythical. He saw the work as an attack on the easy assumption of historical fact, not on eternal truth (p. xxx). Whatever the effect of his work might be on the minds of the faithful, this sense that 'eternal truth'

---

[4] George Eliot already knew *An Inquiry Concerning the Origin of Christianity* (1838) by the theist Charles C. Hennell. Schweitzer dismisses this as a poor, largely plagiarised piece (p. 161). Strauss, however, thought well of it and contributed a preface to the German translation. Many of the points made from Strauss and Renan might be made, though less effectively, from Hennell. Moreover, a reader of Hennell might be struck by connections back to deism, of which he writes with some sympathy in the preface to the second edition: there is a fine line between Christian and anti-Christian rationalism. An account of Hennell, the origins of *An Inquiry*, and his connections with George Eliot can be found in Gordon S. Haight, *George Eliot: A Biography* (Oxford: Oxford University Press, 1968), pp. 38ff.

[5] Strauss distinguishes science from fanaticism, and makes a point of his refusal to adopt religious presuppositions: 'if theologians regard this absence of presupposition from his work as unchristian, he regards the believing presuppositions of theirs as unscientific' (p. xxx).

was not denied makes it quite different from the work of deists such as Paine with which it otherwise has much in common.[6] Nevertheless, what Strauss means by 'myth' is more often than not simply fiction. He identifies three different kinds of myth, but it is characteristic of his work that he refers the identification to other critics: for all that *Das Leben Jesu* stands as a major creative work of biblical criticism, it is no sudden outcrop and there are many works to which it is beholden. He takes from OT critics

> the following general definition of the myth.[7] It is the representation of an event or of an idea in a form which is historical, but, at the same time characterised by the rich pictorial and imaginative mode of thought and expression of the primitive ages. They also distinguished several kinds of myths.
>
> 1st. *Historical myths*: narratives of real events coloured by the light of antiquity, which confounded the divine and the human, the natural and the supernatural.
>
> 2nd. *Philosophical myths*: such as clothe in the garb of historical narrative a simple thought, a precept, or an idea of the time.
>
> 3rd. *Poetical myths*: historical and philosophical myths partly blended together, and partly embellished by the creations of the imagination, in which the original fact or idea is almost obscured by the veil which the fancy of the poet has woven around it.
>
> (P. 53)

In each case there is an emphasis on a creative process that develops or even transforms original events or ideas. This creative process belongs to the fictional imagination, and Strauss, leaning on his predecessors, frequently refers to fiction. For instance, he remarks that 'there is always a preponderance of the fictitious' in historical myths (p. 61), and he identifies two aspects of myth: 'in the first place it is not history; in the second, it is fiction, the product of the particular mental tendency of a certain community' (p. 87). His readers are left in no doubt that 'myth' and 'fiction' mean, indifferently, unhistorical, and that most of what we have in the Gospels is indeed unhistorical.

There are two differences between unhistorical and untrue, both significant for ideas of the Bible as literature. Something may be unhistorical, that is, a myth, and yet be imaginatively true. Or, something which is demonstrably not historical truth may be presented as such without any intention to deceive: it is then untrue but not a lie. The first of these ideas gives a large sense of how the Bible may be regarded as literary; the second gives insight into the processes that led to, especially, the composition of the Gospels.

---

[6] Schweitzer observes that a life of Jesus can be written out of hate, and that Strauss's was one such life. But the hatred 'was not so much hate of the person of Jesus as of the supernatural nimbus with which it was so easy to surround Him' (p. 4).

[7] I have anglicised George Eliot's 'mythus' and 'mythi'.

In a general sense, Strauss's idea of religion is based on imaginative truth. So he suggests that 'religion be defined as the perception of truth, not in the form of an idea, which is the philosophic perception, but invested with imagery'. Consequently myth is an integral, even a definitive, part of religion: 'the mythical element', he continues, 'can be wanting only when religion either falls short of, or goes beyond, its peculiar province' (p. 80). Consequently Strauss can view the Gospel narratives favourably as what we would call sacred fiction and what he calls 'sacred poetry'. And this phrase, 'sacred poetry', he uses to link with the other distinction between unhistorical and untrue, for 'what to us can appear only sacred poetry was to Paul, John, Matthew and Luke fact and certain history' (p. 776). This distinction exists in the first place because 'in ancient times, and especially amongst the Hebrews, and yet more when this people was stirred up by religious excitement, the line of distinction between history and fiction, prose and poetry, was not drawn so clearly as with us' (p. 85). Second, what is presented as history but which appears untrue might be written not only without the intention to deceive but even in the conviction that it was true. Such writing is unconscious fiction. Strauss finds it throughout the Gospels, not only where imagination fills up the blanks – what Schweitzer called gaps – in tradition (p. 54), but also in the use of philosophical myths, as when Messianic myths are attached to Jesus:

> many of the legends respecting [Jesus] had not to be newly invented; they already existed in the popular hope of the Messiah, having been mostly derived with various modifications from the Old Testament, and had merely to be transferred to Jesus, and accommodated to his character and his doctrines. In no case could it be easier for the person who first added any new feature to the description of Jesus to believe himself its genuineness, since his argument would be: such and such things must have happened to the Messiah; Jesus was the Messiah; therefore such and such things happened to him.   (P. 84)

One well-known contradiction in the Gospels shows this kind of faithful application of Messianic legend to Jesus. According to Mark, Luke and John, only one animal is involved in Jesus' triumphal entry into Jerusalem, but Matthew makes the strange statement that the disciples 'brought the ass, and the colt, and put on them their clothes, and they set him thereon' (21: 7). Not only are there two animals, but Jesus appears to perform a kind of circus trick. After surveying a number of proposed explanations, Strauss explains the detail as coming from a misreading of Zech. 9: 9, which Matthew quotes two verses earlier. There 'it was the accumulated designations of the ass ... which occasioned the duplication ... for the "and" which in the Hebrew was intended in an explanatory sense, was erroneously understood to denote an addition, and hence instead of: "an ass, that is, an ass's foal" was substituted: "an ass together with an ass's foal"' (p. 554). Since the strange detail depends on misreading the Prophet, Strauss concludes that the mistake must 'have been made by one whose only written source was the prophetic passage, out of which, with the aid of oral tradition, he spun his entire narrative, i.e. the author of the first Gospel; who hereby ... irrecoverably forfeits the reputation of an eye-witness'.[8] Such writing is 'fiction .. without any fraudulent intention' (p. 83).

The tendency of Strauss's work is clear: it is to show the pervasive presence of fiction in the Gospels and, undermining the general sense of their historicity, to direct attention to the imaginative processes by which they were created – for 'the existence of a myth respecting some certain point shows that the imagination has been active in reference to that particular subject' (p. 90). One of the more striking examples of the way Strauss perceives the workings of the imagination is his discussion of 'a man of the Pharisees, named Nicodemus, a ruler of the Jews' (John 3: 1), who appears three times in John's Gospel only. First Nicodemus questions Jesus at night, later he publicly defends Jesus, and finally he helps to bury Jesus; each of the latter occasions is given with a reminder of the first (John 3: 1–21, 7: 50–1 and 19: 39). Reflecting on why a man so distinguished within the story should not be so much as named within the synoptic Gospels, Strauss observes:

[8] P. 554. One consequence of this kind of arguing is to create a desire for a return to the apparent certainty of an eye-witness. This has sparked some fictional treatments, including Irving Wallace's bestseller, *The Word*, a novel full of such information as that at least 70,000 biographies of Jesus have been produced in the last 100 years (p. 89). A new Gospel appears to have been discovered, 'the lost source for the Synoptic Gospels, the so-called Q-document, a fifth but actually the first and original Gospel ... written by James, James the Just, the younger brother of Jesus' (pp. 73–4). Establishing 'the irrefutable historicity of Christ' (p. 79), it leads enthusiasts to imagine a total restoration of faith:

'To people of our time, who are biography and history educated, Jesus has become unreal, the fictional figure of a folktale, like Hercules or Paul Bunyan.'
'And now, with the new Bible, you feel their doubts will be put to rest.'
'Forever', said Dr Evans finally. 'With the advent of the new Bible, universal skepticism will cease. Jesus the Messiah will be fully accepted. The proof will be as strong as if He had been preserved in photographs or on film. Once it is known that Jesus had a brother who anticipated doubt by taking care to set down firsthand facts about His life, once it is known that shreds of manuscript have survived that bear an eyewitness account of His Ascension, the world will be thrilled and unalloyed belief restored everywhere.'   (Pp. 84–5)

This is a thoroughly materialistic conception of the historical Jesus as a basis for faith, but it is essential to Wallace's plot that what is taken as eye-witness truth should have redemptive power.

It is so difficult to conceive that the name of this man, if he had really assumed such a position, would have vanished from the popular evangelical tradition without leaving a single trace, that one is induced to inquire whether the contrary supposition be not more capable of explanation: namely, that such a relation between Nicodemus and Jesus might have been fabricated by tradition and adopted by the author of the fourth Gospel without having really subsisted.   (Pp. 365–6)

And so a chain of supposition starts. It seemed a reproach to the early Church that none of the rulers or the Pharisees followed Jesus:

yet so soon as [the early Church] was joined by men of rank and education, these would lean to the idea that converts like themselves had not been wanting to Jesus during his life. But, it would be objected, nothing had been hitherto known of such converts. Naturally enough, it might be answered; since fear of their equals would induce them to conceal their relations with Jesus. Thus a door was opened for the admission of any number of secret adherents among the higher class ... But, it would be further urged, how could they have intercourse with Jesus unobserved? Under the veil of the night, would be the answer; and thus the scene was laid for the interviews of such men with Jesus ... This, however, would not suffice; a representative of this class must actually appear on the scene: Joseph of Arimathea might have been chosen, his name being still extant in the synoptical tradition; but the idea of him was too definite, and it was the interest of the legend to name more than one eminent friend of Jesus. Hence a new personage was devised, whose Greek name Νικόδημος ['victory of the people'] seems to point him out significantly as the representative of the dominant class.   (P. 366)

'It was the interest of the legend': this is the key phrase, for it is as if the thing being created has its own needs and in effect dictates its own nature. Strauss has shifted from a highly conscious rationalising of what must have been a subtle process, if it happened at all, to a sense of the creative demands of art. A role was needed within the story, so 'a new personage was devised', and in turn given a name that reflects (to some degree) his role within the story.

Such a way of understanding creative forces within the Gospel narratives could be – and was – applied to their central figure, Jesus. Here the seminal figure is Strauss's contemporary Bruno Bauer. Schweitzer traces Bauer's path from the recognition, through criticism of John's Gospel, 'that a Gospel *may* have a purely literary origin' (p. 140) to the idea that all the Gospels were literary in origin:

What if the whole thing should turn out to be nothing but a literary invention – not only the incidents and discourses, but even the Personality which is assumed as the starting-point of the whole movement? What if the Gospel history were only a late imaginary embodiment of a set of exalted ideas, and these were the only historical reality from first to last?   (P. 145)

Eventually the answer is that 'Jesus Christ is a product of the imagination of the early Church', and 'there never was any historical Jesus' (p. 157). It would have given Paine grim satisfaction to see theological scholars tardily catching up with him (see above, p. 132). Schweitzer, surveying the results of a century of critical study of the life of Jesus, concludes that they are thoroughly negative: 'the Jesus of Nazareth who came forward publicly as the Messiah, who preached the ethic of the kingdom of God, who founded the kingdom of heaven upon earth, and died to give His work its final consecration, never had any existence. He is a figure designed by rationalism, endowed with life by liberalism, and clothed by modern theology in an historical garb' (p. 396). Out of this arises the truth that 'it is not Jesus as historically known, but Jesus as spiritually arisen within men, who is significant for our time and can help it' (p. 399). This brings us squarely back to a theological issue, but a theological issue that obstinately insists on retaining a literary element unless one can make a final distinction between the idea of being 'spiritually arisen within men' and the idea of being imaginatively alive and true.

Renan, aesthetic and often sentimental in his treatment of the Gospels, shared many of Strauss's ideas. He too expresses the idea of story begetting character. For him the life of Jesus is traditional, and 'tradition is in its essence a ductile and extensible matter' (*The Gospels*, p. 44). Moreover, it is in effect written in advance in the OT through the Messianic prophecies as they had come to be understood. 'The whole tissue of the life of Jesus was thus an express fact, a sort of superhuman arrangement intended to realise a series of ancient texts reputed to relate to him. It is a kind of exegesis which the Jews call *Midrash*, into which all equivoques, all plays upon words, letters, sense are admitted.' Such exegesis through myths, songs, legends, and so on 'is the work of that great imposter who is called the crowd. Assuredly every legend, every proverb, every spiritual word has its father, but an unknown father. Someone says the word; thousands repeat it, perfect it, refine it, acuminate it; even he who first spoke it has been in saying it only the interpreter of all' (pp. 48–9).

Though the last remark seems no more than a rhetorical flourish to end a chapter, the emphasis it places on creation as an interpretative act is important. Moreover, because 'we supplement our imperfect knowledge by anecdotes invented after the event', we find that in Matthew 'the legend of Samuel begot that of John the Baptist, that of Jesus and that of Mary herself' (pp. 100, 99). Later Renan notes the development of Mary's role in Luke and remarks, 'the legend wants her and allows itself to be led away to speak of her at length' (p. 146). Though this lacks the rigour of Strauss's argument about Nicodemus, it represents the same way of thinking. Again, story creates character.

We may leave Renan and Strauss at this point – enough has been pinned up for later likenesses to be seen – but Schweitzer has a last word to offer. Reflecting on the general progress of the question of the historical Jesus, he observes an element of recurrence:

> A series of experiments are repeated with constantly varying modifications suggested by the results furnished by the subsidiary sciences. Most of the writers, however, have no suspicion that they are merely repeating an experiment which has been made before. Some of them discover this in the course of their work to their own great astonishment... If old Reimarus were to come back again, he might confidently give himself out to be the latest of the moderns. (P. 9)

Strauss, born again, might equally have judged of himself 'to be the latest of the moderns', and yet, to read modern literary criticism of the Bible is to discover that modern critics have little sense of how much they are repeating past experiments. More than that, they have created a myth of their own, that respectable literary criticism of the Bible is a modern invention.

Erich Auerbach

Here, from an authoritative source, is a view of the modern situation of literary discussion of the Bible:

> Over the past couple of decades ... there has been a revival of interest in the literary qualities of [the biblical] texts, in the virtues by which they continue to live as something other than archaeology. The power of the Genesis narratives or of the story of David, the complexities and refinements of the Passion narratives, could be studied by methods developed in the criticism of secular literature. The effectiveness of this new approach – or approaches, for the work has proceeded along many different paths – has now been amply demonstrated. Professional biblical criticism has been profoundly affected by it; but, even more important, the general reader can now be offered a new view of the Bible as a work of great literary force and authority, a work of which it is entirely credible that it should have shaped the minds and lives of intelligent men and women for two millennia and more.
>
> (Alter and Kermode, pp. 1–2)

Even without evidence of the parallels with Strauss and Renan, readers who have followed me thus far and at such length may be amused at such claims of novelty for literary approaches to the Bible at the beginning of *The Literary Guide to the Bible* (1987); they may also have a sense of déjà vu, for claims of novelty have been common enough in English works ever since Husbands set out to fling together his loose remarks. Well, one sympathises with the need to appear new and with the difficulties of mastering the full heritage of literary discussion. Robert Alter and Frank Kermode are doing nothing worse than overstating some valid points. They are distinguishing between literary criticism and the historical scholarship that had been dominant (whence the allusion to archaeology that seems so strange in the first sentence). They are also identifying the new emphasis in literary discussion of the Bible, emphasis on narrative: although they are introducing a volume that tries to cover all literary aspects of the Bible, their three examples of 'literary interest' are all narrative. Poetry had been at the heart of critical interest for a long time, but narrative dominates attention in the last two decades.

No doubt modern critics want to believe that the art or – a minor parallel with Strauss – the science of literary discussion, especially discussion of narrative, is a modern creation. Add to this desire the quantity and difficulty (or, sometimes, wilful obscurity) of recent work on both literary theory and the Bible, to say nothing of the need to set limits in order to get any work done at all: the result is a line of demarcation before which nothing worth a modern critic's attention was published. Though in reality little that is over twenty years old merits more than a reference to prove that one is sufficiently well read, the line is drawn at 1946. This allows for the identification of a suitable father figure, Erich Auerbach, whose *Mimesis*, written during the Second World War, was published in this year. Alter, as if permitting the choice, remarks specifically of Auerbach's first chapter that it 'could be taken as the point of departure for the modern literary understanding of the Bible' (Alter and Kermode, p. 23). Gabriel Josipovici moves from describing the kind of pleasure he found in coming to the Bible as an adult to his disappointment with biblical scholarship for its failure to deal with the Bible's literary dimension, and thence to wondering whether the Bible's mode of narration had contributed to its status. With the easy freedom that characterises his work, he writes that

> Forty years ago one would have looked in vain for even an awareness that this might be a genuine issue. Today, however, it's a different matter. In the years following the publication of Erich Auerbach's *Mimesis* ... the academic world in America and England seemed to have woken up with a start to the fact that the Bible was, among other things, a book which could be explored and examined, and whose special qualities could be brought to light, in the same way as one could examine and bring to light the qualities of *The Canterbury Tales* or *King Lear*.   (P. xi)

The academic world was not necessarily as sleepy – nor is it necessarily as wide awake now – as this implies. But, in so far as it needed waking, Augustine and Lowth, or many of the more recent figures from this history, might have sounded the reveille. Nevertheless, *Mimesis* has some particular qualities that make it a natural starting-point for a sketch of some of the characteristics and achievements of contemporary academic literary discussion of the Bible.

Subtitled *The Representation of Reality in Western Literature*, *Mimesis* explores two contrasting traditions of representation, one dominated by ideas of decorum, the other free of them. In the former, decorum would be broken by any attempt to mix high style with low, and as a consequence high seriousness and ordinary everyday reality could not meet. This was the classical doctrine of the separation of styles. Modern realism, however, finds the serious, even the tragic, in the everyday – a point that might well lead an English reader to think of, say, George Eliot and *Middlemarch*. Well aware of origins of this realism in Stendhal and Balzac, Auerbach, European rather than English, realised that theirs was not the first revolution against the classical doctrine of separation, that there were older kinds of 'serious realism', and that 'the first break with the classical theory had come about [with] the story of Christ, with its ruthless mixture of everyday reality and the highest and most sublime tragedy' (p. 555). So in *Mimesis* he set out to trace two contrasting literary traditions (or styles, as he prefers to call them) which had a 'determining influence upon the representation of reality in European literature' (p. 23). By placing a biblical narrative at the head of one of these traditions, Auerbach ensures that it will be treated not only on the same terms as other narrative, whether fictional or historical, but as a primary element in a literary study that is not confined to the Bible as literature. Moreover, he gives biblical narrative an importance in literary history at least equal to that of the classics.

There are familiar elements here, the conflict between classical and biblical, and the claim of treating the Bible like any other literature. Now, most treatments of the Bible as literature focus on the Bible alone and so can be set on one side by the world of literary criticism, but there was no setting *Mimesis* on one side: it was a marvellously wide-ranging and civilised discussion that challenged thought about literature and reality.

'Wide-ranging and civilised': such qualities are perhaps old-fashioned, and *Mimesis* certainly does seem old-fashioned in its constant generalisation. But there is a more important old-fashioned quality to it, the very idea of a literary text representing reality. Moreover, the reality represented may be historical or fictional: Auerbach slides easily between the two, aware of the legendary or fictional or historical background of what he is discussing, but indifferent to the distinctions. This helps to break down the sense of difference between biblical narrative and fiction without challenging belief in the historicity of the biblical story as so much of both Higher Criticism and discussion of the art of the Bible have done. Biblical narrative is now brought within range of Homer or Petronius: passages may be pinned up for comparison. And pinning-up followed by acute discussion of the texts and then by generalisation constitutes Auerbach's characteristic method. So his first chapter sets an example of 'the genius of the Homeric style', the episode from the *Odyssey* book XIX in which Odysseus is recognised by his old nurse, against 'an equally ancient and equally epic style from a different world of forms' (p. 7), the story of the sacrifice of Isaac (Gen. 22).

After drawing attention to some of the extraordinary qualities of the narrative, quoting the KJB (no doubt a convenient decision by the translator) but referring to the Hebrew, he sums up the contrast between Homer and Genesis:

> The two styles, in their opposition, represent basic types: on the one hand [Homer] fully externalised description, uniform illumination, uninterrupted connection, free expression, all events in the foreground, displaying unmistakable meanings, few elements of historical development and of psychological perspective; on the other hand [Genesis], certain parts brought into high relief, others left obscure, abruptness, suggestive influence of the unexpressed, 'background' quality, multiplicity of meanings and the need for interpretation, universal-historical claims, development of the concept of the historically becoming, and pre-occupation with the problematic.
>
> (P. 23)

The essence of the contrast lies in the foreground quality of Homer and the background quality of Genesis. So the Homeric narrative seems completely present and fully realised, whereas the Genesis story seems only fragmentarily – but yet sufficiently – present: it challenges the reader to imagine what the full reality must have been (the discussion of the omissions from the narrative is excellent). Much that seems essential for the reader to realise the story in full is not told and so remains in the background, calling 'for interpretation' (p. 11). Auerbach's key phrase for this is 'fraught with background' (p. 12 etc.), that is, carrying with it more than it expresses. What he has in mind as 'interpretation' is essentially the allegorical or typological – he notes how Homer, by contrast, 'cannot be interpreted': any attempt to allegorise him remains 'forced and foreign' (p. 13). We, however, can take 'interpretation' more widely. Auerbach, more than any other critic, has made recent critics aware of the degree to which biblical narrative might provide a field in which they could exercise their skills and develop their theories. One of its key attractions as a field is precisely that it invites the critic to deal with what is not in the text. Auerbach stresses the link between mysteriousness – or background or darkness or incompleteness – and the demand for investigation and interpretation (p. 15): together they generate a sense of rich existence that gives the characters, for instance, a fuller reality than the Homeric characters, and the 'stories a historical character, even when the subject is purely legendary and traditional' (p. 18). Mysteriousness and the demand for interpretation are essential issues in considering biblical narrative: Auerbach's prime strength, from the point of view of literary insight into the Bible, is that he identifies and links them. Here Strauss, Renan and Schweitzer's awareness of gaps and the role of imaginative interpretation in the creation of biblical narrative begins to be a part of literary criticism's awareness of power in the Bible.

'Surely the New Testament writings are extremely effective' (p. 45): this, the heart of Auerbach's perception, does no more than place him with the majority of the figures who have been considered here. What is important is his attempt in his second chapter to account for this by developing the insights of his first chapter. The power of Mark's account of Peter's denial (Mark 14: 66–72), taken as representative of the power of the Passion narrative, is 'of such immediacy that its like does not exist in the literature of antiquity' (p. 45). Why, asks Auerbach, does the Passion 'arouse in us the most serious and most significant sympathy'? This is his answer:

> Because it portrays something which neither the poets nor the historians of antiquity ever set out to portray: the birth of a spiritual movement in the depths of the common people, from within the everyday occurrences of contemporary life, which thus assumes an importance it could never have assumed in antique literature. What we witness is the awakening of 'a new heart and a new spirit'. (Pp. 42–3)

Moreover, the central issue involves every man – 'it sets man's whole world astir – whereas [the classics] always directly concern simply the individual' (p. 43). This is old-fashioned generalising such as few modern critics would dare attempt. The literary quality of the narrative is directly related to the values incorporated in it, and, as so often in the past, our agreement or disagreement with the critic's assertion will depend on our own values.

It is time to add a last word to this question of belief-based aesthetic. It is the nature of belief that it is compelling for the individual but not for his neighbour. The appeal to faith can never prove a point to a person who does not share the faith. Nevertheless – and in spite of many blatantly simplistic leaps from belief to literary conclusions – judgement of literary quality almost always involves some kind of ethical or religious values. Humanity (whether in relation to something beyond itself or not) is the essential subject of literature. Literature tells what it is like to be human, and this inevitably involves one's values as a human being. So, however difficult it may be to maintain the appearance of logic or to persuade the reader who does not agree in advance, judgement of literature that depends in part on belief is inescapable. Where one is entitled to be sceptical is where the judgement depends on beliefs alone, as when one bases one's literary judgement solely on a belief in divine inspiration.

Auerbach's explanation for the power of the Passion narrative appears to rest on faith and might well be found unconvincing by non-Christian readers. Yet Auerbach himself was Jewish: the sympathy with which he writes of things Christian is testimony that belief or background need not blind one to the human interests of other faiths. His fundamental criterion that good literature 'sets man's whole world astir' should work across faiths. In general terms, 'a spiritual movement in the depths of the common people' ought to be profoundly interesting, for, no matter how much we may think of ourselves as aristocrats of the spirit or as followers of the one true faith, we are all common people. But if the spiritual movement is one which we feel is part of our heritage and lies at the heart of our 'whole world', the interest will be greater. Auerbach's generalisations have obvious limitations, but they do suggest literary as well as religious matters.

The praise Auerbach gives to the biblical tradition and the fact that he gives it the concluding position in each of his first two chapters suggest a valuation, but he sensibly stops short of judging between the biblical and the classical. Rather, he raises a crucial issue. The effect of biblical narrative is achieved if not totally without artistic intent, then with the intent severely circumscribed. So, generalising from the story of Abraham's sacrifice, he observes that the biblical narrator's 'freedom in creative or representative imagination was severely limited; his activity was perforce reduced to composing an effective version of the pious tradition' (p. 14). And he has this to say in the second chapter:

> the story of Peter's denial, and generally almost the entire body of New Testament writings, is written from within the emergent growths and directly for everyman. Here we have neither survey and rational disposition, nor artistic purpose. The visual and sensory as it appears here is no conscious imitation and hence is rarely completely realized. It appears because it is attached to the events which are to be related, because it is revealed in the demeanor and speech of profoundly stirred individuals and no effort need be devoted to the task of elaborating it.   (P. 47)

No effort on the author's part, that is: the reader is spurred to considerable effort. For Auerbach, part of the effectiveness of the biblical narratives depends on their verity for both author and reader. Because both take the narrative as true, the reader can (and must) do what the unartistic author does not, complete the story. Auerbach goes no further than echoing what we have noted from Schweitzer (above, p. 350), the paradox of unartistic effectiveness. If one accepts his general view, it has a similarity to the suggestion made in this book that much of the power of the KJB's language arises because the translators did not try to make the KJB an artistic translation. Auerbach pictures the biblical narrators doing their utmost to be true to their originals, to people and events that were, to them, real; I have pictured the major biblical translators similarly, as expending every effort to be faithful to their originals. In both pictures there is a clear realisation that artistic intent and artistic effect need not belong together.

Making the Bible into art, or the Bible as fiction

Frank Kermode and artful obscurity

A third of a century later comes a particularly suggestive work, Frank Kermode's *The Genesis of Secrecy* (1979). This is directly in line with Auerbach in its concern with 'the need for interpretation' and its 'pre-occupation with the problematic' (above, p. 360), but makes a significant contrast in two connected areas, historicity and transparency. For the most part, Kermode reads biblical narrative (Mark is his prime example) as artful, fictional narrative. Auerbach was happy to see in Mark an effective artlessness, and he remained committed to the historicity of the story. For Kermode historicity is unimportant:[9] historical or imagined events are the same thing to the writer, the fable that he artfully interprets – or, often, misinterprets – and develops. The historical becomes submerged in fiction as it is worked on by successive imaginations, those of the narrator – or of the first narrator and subsequent retellers – and of exegetes. Here suddenly, rather than thinking in terms of descent from Auerbach, we are back with Strauss and the world of scholarship revealed by Schweitzer.

Now, though Kermode acknowledges a debt to Higher Criticism, he might well want to draw a distinction. A Strauss or a Renan sought to understand the early history and literature of Christianity. He, though he pursues the same material in similar ways, does so as part of his general interest in hermeneutics, that is, in the interpretative ways of the imagination as it both creates and responds to what has been created. So Kermode reverses traditional priorities to stress 'what is written at the expense of what it is written about' (p. 119). This

---

[9] Approvingly, he cites Kant's declaration 'that the historical veracity of these accounts was a matter of complete indifference' (p. 72).

move, so characteristic of modern criticism, underlies his difference from Auerbach. His interest is in writing as an autonomous structure of signs emitting occasional radiances, not in the 'transparency' of the text.

'Transparency' is a key word. It is a metaphor for the effect of the text, implying that one sees through the text to the thing contained in the text. The text is therefore, like glass, more or less invisible. Now, it is a statement of admiration for the power of a text to say that the character or the event or the truth shines through it. So effective is the text in creating this thing that one loses all sense of there being a text and believes the thing has become real. One forgets that the text exists, yet it is, usually, the text that has created this sense of reality. 'Transparency' is a dangerous metaphor because it implies that one has an either/or choice, either the text or the reality behind the text. And it is the more dangerous because it leads one to think of a single thing contained in the text, a thing that is the same to all people. Critics have felt called upon to reassert the importance of the text and, in so doing, have found themselves, caught by the implications of the metaphor, dismissing the existence of a reality behind the text. But a text is not like glass. If one has to take a visual simile, the old one of a picture will do: the closer one examines a picture and understands it, the more one will appreciate what it represents and the more one will become aware of its qualities as a work of art. One cannot choose between representer and represented (or signifier and signified, to use a more popular pair of words): one can only choose the degree of stress one gives to one part and the other.

In spite of its dangers, 'transparency' is a useful image. Kermode uses it, and it is central to some of his conclusions. And, in the subsequent discussion of Alter's work, I shall continue to use it because it is necessary for an exploration of how some contemporary critics think about the Bible.

In Kermode's view, a story is created through one or more acts of interpretation by its narrator or narrators. Reading is similarly an act of interpretation. So he necessarily writes of both creation and reading – of both the genesis and the interpretation of the secret or obscure – as if one cannot understand the text without attending to both. Consequently parts of his work read like a new Higher Criticism, for Kermode too reveals literary methods and sources.

The title of his fourth chapter, 'Necessities of upspringing', is taken from Henry James's discussion, in the preface to *The Portrait of a Lady*, of how things grow in an artist's imagination. For James growth comes from an idea of the main characters: he looks down on authors who see the fable first and thereafter make out the character or 'agents'. Kermode, however, suggests that this latter process takes place in the Gospels, and he takes Judas as his prime example for an argument that is redolent of Strauss's discussion of Nicodemus. Building on Joachim Jeremias's analysis of the Passion story which suggests that in the earliest version of the story Judas was not mentioned and that gradually Judas came to be named and to have his story filled out, Kermode argues that this development is characteristic of the way, through interpretation, narrative moves 'from fable to written story, from story to character, from character to more story' (p. 98). Indeed, he suggests that 'there was originally no Judas at all' (p. 94), but that he was invented through the demands of the story: betrayal implies a betrayer. Imagination, working on and interpreting the story, creates the betrayer. And then, as Matthew retells Mark (and also as later tellings are made), the history of the betrayer develops. So Matthew adds dialogue to Mark's bare fact that Judas went to the chief priests. Now Judas asks, 'what will ye give me, and I will deliver him unto you?' (Matt. 26: 15). The question must have an answer if the narrative is not to be left incomplete, and so it comes, 'thirty pieces of silver'.

For Kermode as for Strauss and Renan,[10] this is a fictional invention dictated by Matthew's respect for messianic prophecies in the OT, in this case Zech. 11: 12. The detail is a midrash, a narrative interpretation or retelling of an earlier piece of narrative. From a rational point of view it is clear that the understanding of what happened is being shaped by something other than what happened, and so the account has an element of fiction in it (Kermode writes that 'parts of the narratives were generated from Old Testament texts, and are therefore interpretations of those texts, and so fictive' (p. 110)). Now, Kermode is only following a host of Higher Critics in pointing out the element of midrash. His interest is to show how it is part of the way the creative imagination works in this text, and to suggest something not found in Higher Criticism, that such midrash creates a narrative link between two distant parts of the Bible. The link becomes part of the superhuman plot of the Bible, and Kermode suggests that it is akin to connections between early and late parts of a novel, wherein the early pages contain seeds, some of which are grown to fruition in the later pages.

Later Matthew completes Judas' story. Judas repents, returns the money, and hangs himself (27: 3–5). 'Nothing but an interest in character can account for these narrative additions', Kermode roundly declares. 'There was an original need of narrative, and it was supplied by narrative interpretation of the testimony. But narrative begot character, and character begot new narrative. In

[10] See Renan, p. 95. Renan also anticipates the key image of Kermode's chapter when he remarks of Matthew's narration of Jesus' baptism that 'the germ of the doctrine of the Trinity is thus deposited in a corner of the sacred page, and will become fertile' (p. 103).

the course of these developments, new gaps may be inevitable. This is how interpretation works in fiction' (p. 91). This may be persuasive as an account of how the imagination works – indeed, it is exactly Schweitzer's point noted earlier (above, p. 350) – but it arouses suspicion. When an incompleteness is felt in a story – whenever one asks a question such as how? or who? – there are two possible sources of answers, the original facts and invention. Each satisfies the need to know, but one produces some sort of historiography, the other some sort of fiction. This need to know is not peculiar property of fiction, even if fiction typically gives the fullest illusion of satisfying it through the ability to supply all the necessary 'facts'. It belongs just as much to the past. When the events of that past are thought to be of supreme importance, the need to know is extraordinarily pressing. Schweitzer and Kermode, like Strauss, Renan and a host of others, do not even consider the possibility that information given in a later version might be the result of some sort of investigation, even if it is only investigation into the author's memory. Thirty pieces of silver, like Matthew's ass and colt, is unquestionably fictive, even if written down in all good faith. But Matthew's midrash is also evidence that the Scriptures have been searched in order to recover what the author believed must have happened. There was investigation: the fictive is only one of its results.

If anything, Kermode is cautious in his treatment of Judas. He then turns more briefly to Pilate – clearly not an invention to fill a role demanded by the fable but a historical character, testified to outside the Bible. Yet he too has a role, that of judge: 'as Betrayal needs a Betrayer, so Trial needs a Judge'. Consequently there begins 'his life in narrative interpretation' (p. 96), and this life is unhistorical. The historical figure becomes a fictional character, and one is left in no doubt that this is meant to make a statement about Judas: clearly a fictional character in his development, *he* never was a historical figure. What was presented as conjecture is intended as conviction, and Kermode later writes of 'Matthew's invention of the Judas narrative' (p. 111). But the persuasiveness of the argument that Pilate was fictionalised does not prove that any or all of the information given about Judas, including his name, was not supplied from memory of the facts as demanded by the need to know. I make this point not to prove Kermode wrong (his text is suitably qualified) but to stress that the present desire is to think of the biblical narratives as fiction, as if they are more responsive to the desires of the literary critic if they are fiction than if they are history.

Kermode wants these narratives to be fiction, not history, because he is interested in them as writing, self-contained and self-referential, not something that is transparent on another thing. The content and form division that has been the basis of so many people's thought is rejected because there is no content apart from the writing itself. This major element in modern critical thought is, as Kermode recognises, untrue to the way most people read. 'We are so habituated to the myth of transparency', he writes, 'that we continue ... to ignore *what is written* in favour of *what it is written about*. One purpose of this book is to reverse that priority.'[11]

The emphasis is not limited to seeing the narratives as fiction. They are artful; they may even be deliberate additions to Scripture. Here is another part of Kermode's discussion of Matthew's creation of Judas, again with allusion to Henry James: 'it cannot have seemed to [Matthew], as he wrote his midrash on Mark's Judas story, that he was simply inventing. There was the image of Judas, *en disponibilité*; intense suggestions as to its disposal were already present in the book to which he was adding. It was all part of the business of being a writer' (p. 89). By 'the book to which he was adding', Kermode means the OT, for that is the book that contains the prophecies which he refers to as suggestions. Preoccupied with the art of fiction, he has imagined that Matthew thought of himself as deliberately writing Scripture. This seems unlikely. Scripture becomes what it is through the process of time and canonisation. In this process it comes to seem unlike the writing of mere mortals: no man conscious of his mortality can believe himself to be writing Scripture – unless, that is, he believes himself to be inspired by God, in which case it is not he but God who is writing.

Kermode's preoccupation with the art of fiction also shows in the way he deals with Matthew perhaps thinking that he was inventing: Kermode is aware of the consequences of faith for writing, but prefers to think in other ways. Just as one may write something other than factual truth while believing one is writing the truth, so one may write something that seems like art without ever thinking of writing literature, perhaps, even, without possessing anything beyond literacy that would be ordinarily recognisable as literary ability. The tendency of literary discussion of the Bible is to imply that it is artful; in this respect Mark is particularly challenging, for no book in the NT seems to have less of the literary graces – except, perhaps, for the supreme grace that Kermode

---

[11] Pp. 118–19. Kermode's insistence on fictive qualities is not an absolute denial of historical qualities; rather, it is an emphasis for purposes of insight, and one should not set him down, as one might set down so many critics of the Bible from the last century and a half, as a covert Tom Paine, bent on subverting the faithful's belief in the truth of the Bible. For Paine the Bible was fiction, and bad fiction at that; for Kermode the Bible is especially interesting if viewed in the same way that he views fiction. There can be a large difference between reading the Bible as if it were fiction and saying that the Bible is fiction.

calls radiance. Several times Kermode puts what he acknowledges are simplistic alternatives, that Mark is either enigmatic or clumsy. He remarks, for instance, 'that Mark is never more enigmatic, or never more clumsy, than at the end of his Gospel' (p. 65), and later rephrases the point, 'the conclusion is either intolerably clumsy; or it is incredibly subtle' (p. 68). We know it is good to be subtle, therefore it is good to be enigmatic. Secrecy is being made into a prime literary quality. Central to Kermode's interest in Mark is his description of it as 'a text so full of obscure relations, so rich in secrecy' (p. 137).

Obscurity seems to have this primacy in part through professional necessity. Kermode remarks at the outset that 'interpreters usually belong to an institution, such a guild as heralds, toastmasters, thieves and merchants' – the list is a good one – 'have been known to form; and as members they enjoy certain privileges and suffer certain constraints. Perhaps the most important of these are the right to affirm, and the obligation to accept, the superiority of latent over manifest sense' (p. 2). Does this not imply that obscure works are better than clear ones, even that the ability to hide meaning is preferable to the ability to convey meaning? In spite of the way the question returns to the idea of a separation between word and meaning, such thinking ought to be self-evident nonsense. But the fact that a good many people do think in this way is testimony to our humility before what we cannot understand – a humility that of course disappears the instant we become convinced that what we fail to understand is, in reality, nonsense. Nothing is so scorned as detected rubbish, nothing more awesome than the mystery one believes to be meaningful, and nothing more frail than the line between them.

The most direct challenge, however, is to one's sense of the role of literary criticism: is it not, fundamentally, to show what there is to be seen, to show the obvious as much as the hidden, so long as one is true to the balance between them which the text maintains? If Kermode's position reminds one of the Roman Catholic Church before the Reformation, my question might remind one of the reformers. The modern university has usurped many of the functions of the Church, and with them many of its characteristics, not least of which is the painstaking emphasis on initiation into mysteries. The power of any priesthood lies in the preservation of mystery. In so far as the discipline of literature has taken over the functions of religion, it seems eminently logical that it should take over the central book of religion, and just as logical that it should stress truth and mystery at the same time. And, just as the Church had its occult language, the possession of which marked initiation into the mysteries, so literary criticism and theory are developing a language whereby the initiates can recognise each other even if they cannot yet communicate efficiently in it –

as Catherine Morland says in Jane Austen's *Northanger Abbey*, 'I cannot speak well enough to be unintelligible'; Henry Tilney, the hero, calls this 'an excellent satire on modern language' (ch. 16). It is not in this kind of way, as a new mystery religion, that Kermode (and others) want to bring literary and biblical criticism together, but obfuscation for the initiated too often seems to be the result.

A good deal of this is not so much criticism of Kermode as development of points he makes with more subtlety, even a certain element of satire. His final two pages are a meditation on the issues just considered.

Kermode's subject is acts of interpretation and what we may learn about interpretation from a study of Mark. The part of the book given to narrative as a creative act of interpretation is particularly close to Strauss and Renan. But when he deals with critical interpretations – reading and exegesis – there is at once a major similarity with, and a major difference from, Schweitzer. One of the most striking aspects of the way Kermode discusses exegesis is a sense of despair such as has afflicted much of the twentieth century. This despair emerges particularly in the way he uses his immediate source for the idea of radiance, Franz Kafka's parable in *The Trial*, commonly called 'Before the Law'. Kermode summarises it:

> It is recounted to K by a priest, and is said to come from the scriptures. A man comes and begs admittance to the Law, but is kept out by a doorkeeper, the first of a long succession of doorkeepers, of aspect ever more terrible, who will keep the man out should the first one fail to do so. The man, who had assumed that the Law was open to all, is surprised to discover the existence of this arrangement. But he waits outside the door, sitting year after year on his stool and conversing with the doorkeeper, whom he bribes, though without success. Eventually, when he is old and near death, the man observes an immortal radiance streaming from the door. As he dies, he asks the doorkeeper how it is that he alone has come to this entrance to seek admittance to the Law. The answer is, 'this door was intended only for you. Now I am going to shut it.'
> (P. 27)

This is what seems to Kermode most significant in the parable and the ensuing discussion:

> it incorporates very dubious interpretations, which help to make the point that the would-be interpreter cannot get inside, cannot even properly dispose of authoritative interpretations that are more or less obviously wrong. The outsider has what appears to be a reasonable, normal and just expectation of ready admittance, for the Law, like the Gospel, is meant for everybody, or everybody who wants it. But what he gets is a series of frivolous and mendacious interpretations. The outsider remains outside, dismayed and frustrated. To perceive the radiance of the shrine is not to gain access to

it; the Law, or the Kingdom, may, to those within, be powerful and beautiful, but to those outside they are merely terrible; absolutely inexplicable, they torment the inquirer with legalisms. This is a mystery; Mark, and Kafka's doorkeeper, protect it without understanding it, and those outside, like K and us, see an uninterpretable radiance and die.   (P. 28)

Radiance is the best the reader, the interpreter, can hope for. It is like the light that blinded Saul on the road to Damascus without the divine voice. This sense of the secrecy of narrative has an intense pessimism to it. Where one might once have been illuminated, now one is dazzled. It is a meagre reward for a lifetime of waiting.

Against this pessimism there is Schweitzer's conclusion to *The Quest of the Historical Jesus*. In keeping with the declaration that it is 'Jesus as spiritually arisen within men who is significant for our time' (above, p. 356), Schweitzer's final, rhetorical paragraph reads:

> He comes to us as One unknown, without a name, as of old, by the lake-side, He came to those men who knew Him not. He speaks to us the same word: 'Follow thou me!' and sets us to the tasks which He has to fulfil for our time. He commands. And to those who obey Him, whether they be wise or simple, He will reveal Himself in the toils, the conflicts, the sufferings which they shall pass through in His fellowship, and, as an ineffable mystery, they shall learn in their own experience Who He is.
>
> (P. 401)

The Gospels finally are – not history but – kerygma, proclamation. They proclaim the truth of Jesus for the spiritual life. This religious declaration of faith is also a literary declaration of faith. The voice *is* there, in the light: narrative, this narrative at least, contains meaning. One kind of content, history, has been allowed to depart, but the greater content, meaning, remains. Kermode and Schweitzer, one writing of 'uninterpretable radiance', the other of 'ineffable mystery', are so close. But from this proximity one leaps to unbelief and death, the other to belief and life. The Gospels have come to stand for all texts, Jesus for meaning. And it seems that the sense that literature has meaning is a kind of religious sense, if only because in discovering meaning one seems, aroused, to move beyond the text into experiencing something that, for 'the moment of its indwelling', appears to be true.

The phrase I have just quoted comes from E. M. Forster's *A Passage to India* (ch. 33; p. 282). It is part of Forster's somewhat bemused account of 'a most beautiful and radiant expression' on the face of the Indian villagers as they experience a kind of mystical ecstasy. Set against this radiance and Godbole's Hindu achievement in developing 'the life of his spirit' (ch. 33; p. 287) is the experience Mrs Moore has in a Marabar cave. Forster's description of her reaction to the experience has become a central English expression of the failure of faith and meaning. Aptly employing biblical phrases, it fits well with Kermode's sense of exegesis. The echo in a Marabar cave undermines Mrs Moore's hold on life by suggesting to her that

> if one had spoken vileness in that place, or quoted lofty poetry, the comment would have been the same – 'ou-boum' . . . But suddenly, at the edge of her mind, Religion appeared, poor little talkative Christianity, and she knew that all its divine words from 'Let there be light' to 'It is finished' only amounted to 'boum'. Then she was terrified over an area larger than usual; the universe, never comprehensible to her intellect, offered no repose to her soul.   (Ch. 14; pp. 160, 161)

Later Forster describes Mrs Moore as having 'the cynicism of a withered priestess' (ch. 23; p. 212). Now here is Kermode, using 'meaning' for 'what is written' and 'truth' for 'what it is written about' (p. 119):

> All modern interpretation that is not merely an attempt at 're-cognition' involves some effort to divorce meaning and truth. This accounts for both the splendours and the miseries of the art. Insofar as we can treat a text as not referring to what is outside or beyond it, we more easily understand that it has internal relationships independent of the coding procedures by which we may find it transparent upon a known world. We see why it has latent mysteries, intermittent radiances. But in acquiring this privilege, the interpreters lose the possibility of consensus and of access to a single truth at the heart of the thing. No one, however special his point of vantage, can get past all those doorkeepers into the shrine of the single sense. I make an allegory, once more, of Kafka's parable; but some such position is the starting point of all modern hermeneutics except those who are consciously reactionary. The pleasures of interpretation are henceforth linked to loss and disappointment, so that most of us will find the task too hard, or simply repugnant; and then, abandoning meaning, we slip back into the old comfortable fictions of transparency, the single sense, the truth.
> (Pp. 122–3)

Modern interpretation seems scarcely worth while if this is a true picture of it: one wonders if the occasional radiances it offers may not be simply a momentary surge of hope against the overwhelming despair that is the real condition of mankind. At all events, they are private, for the possibility of consensus is lost. The radiances offer pleasure, but the pleasure is in spite of everything.

The pessimism, if not despair in this, applies not just to literary criticism. The world also is a text. Interpreters try to find coherence and meaning in it too, and the result is much the same (p. 126). As so often, Kermode seems to me to be double-edged, pushing contemporary positions so far as to make them repelling, but at the same time reminding one of alternatives, even if the alternatives are demeaningly termed 'reactionary' and 'comfortable'. 'Recognition' has been devalued by much modern criticism: the effort to understand either the original truth or the original picture in the imagination seems old-fashioned or fruitless or even a distraction from the true object of attention, that is, from the text which Kermode has so misleadingly called the 'meaning'. One understands this position in relation to fiction – fiction is no more than the written text – but it loses its obviousness in relation to writing that claims to be history.

An anthropological aside

We have just seen Kermode trying to escape from the idea that works of art are coded presentations of 'a known world', and acknowledging that one result is the loss of a sense of 'a single truth at the heart of the thing'. Before moving on to look at an aspect of the claim to be history, it may be helpful to look at the work of a scholar who has an overriding sense of the biblical narratives as encoded messages, the British anthropologist Sir Edmund Leach. He is the more interesting because he has some significant elements in common with Kermode. Moreover, setting aside some displays of diagrammatic incomprehensibility, his writing has a challenging clarity. With perhaps aggressive understatement, he claims in one essay that his 'analysis reveals only a patterning of arguments about endogamy and exogamy, legitimacy and illegitimacy as operative in the thought processes of Palestinian Jews of the third century BC'.[12] But 'thought processes', later phrased in quotation marks as '"unconscious operations of the human mind"' (*Genesis as Myth*, p. 41), suggests a link with Kermode that, in spite of the narrowness and confessed reductiveness of Leach's interests, turns out to be instructive.

Leach makes several assumptions. First, 'the Bible is a much edited compendium of a great variety of ancient documents derived from many different sources, but the end product is a body of mythology, a sacred tale, not a history book'.[13] The dismissal of history is familiar, and the only difference from Kermode in the idea of the text as a body of mythology is that a sense of artistry is missing. Nevertheless, there is a sense of purpose that might pass for artistry: Leach's second assumption is that 'the editor-compilers ... knew what they were up to' (*Structuralist Interpretations*, p. 36). In keeping with this, he makes the Rabbinic assumption that no detail is accidental. Leach suggests that 'if the Bible is a mythology it conveys its meaning as a totality, rather after the fashion

---

[12] 'The legitimacy of Solomon', *Genesis as Myth*, p. 26.
[13] 'Why did Moses have a sister?', *Structuralist Interpretations*, p. 35.

of a novel by a major novelist; no detail of the plot is there by accident; everything ties in with everything else' (p. 35). Seemingly contradictory to this is another assumption, 'that sacred texts contain a religious message which is other than that which can be immediately inferred from the manifest sense of the narrative. Religious texts contain a mystery; the mystery is somehow encoded in the text; it is decodable' (p. 2).

The idea that texts do not say what they are intended to say is an old one. Charlotte Brontë, prefacing the 1850 edition of *Wuthering Heights*, observes, very possibly from her own experience, that 'the writer who possesses the creative gift owns something of which he is not always master – something that at times strangely wills and works for itself'. Lawrence puts the idea most challengingly: 'the artist usually sets out – or used to – to point a moral and adorn a tale. The tale, however, points the other way, as a rule ... Never trust the artist. Trust the tale. The proper function of a critic is to save the tale from the artist who created it.'[14] Kermode, more circumspectly, identified as the primary characteristic of interpreters 'the right to affirm, and the obligation to accept, the superiority of latent over manifest sense' (above, p. 368). Leach pushes the idea one stage further. Brontë, Lawrence and Kermode all leave open the possibility that the writer may sometimes be master, that the tale may sometimes say what the artist intended it to, but Leach makes it a condition of the kind of writing he is interested in that its message is never what was intended. He does not say that this is so of all art, but even in his chosen territory this attitude leads to a revealing contradiction – as if, perhaps, the critic is as vulnerable as the artist to saying something other than he intends to say.

Almost contemporary with Kermode's book, which began as a series of lectures at Harvard, is Leach's 'Why did Moses have a sister?', also originally a prestigious lecture. Since all details are purposeful, he asks why Miriam should be mentioned at all since she 'seems to be a quite unimportant, almost redundant, figure' (*Structuralist Interpretations*, p. 36). The question presumes that her existence has a purpose, and that the purpose is essentially the artistic one of contributing to the meaning of the story. The very phrasing of the question, 'Why did Moses have a sister?', denies the possibility of a historical explanation. We are in the world of fictional creations like Strauss's Nicodemus or Kermode's Judas. Leach asks the question in the same way as he states that 'Joseph of Arimathea has clearly been introduced into the story so that Jesus should have a tomb appropriate to his divine king status' (p. 50), or, in a caricature of typology, that the early Christians' 'divine law-giver was called

---

[14] *Studies in Classic American Literature* (1924; Harmondsworth: Penguin, 1971), p. 8.

Jesus (Joshua) because, like his Old Testament namesake, he was the successor and replacement of Moses' (p. 35). Only an author working with his own creations can do this – and Leach is not thinking in terms of a divine author. He notes elsewhere yet one more of his assumptions, 'that there are really very few … "principal roles" though, in the course of a sequence of stories, the same role may be filled by different individually named characters' (*Genesis as Myth*, p. 65). Women certainly have few possible roles. They 'may be introduced in order to act as sacred mothers to sacred heirs … or to suffer dishonour and thereby cause a feud … or to play an heroic role … or a manifestly evil role … or for a variety of other role-playing reasons' (*Structuralist Interpretations*, p. 45). In other words, they can exist only because the story wants them.

Leach's question becomes this: why does the story want Miriam when she 'hardly seems to have any role at all' (p. 45)? He has proposed that the story is analogous with that of Osiris, Isis and Horus. Therefore Miriam must be the goddess-queen. Moses has a sister because there is a particular logic to mythology which demands 'that the divine king-prophet shall be both married and unmarried, fertile and infertile, born of woman but not begotten of man' (p. 56). Leach reveals the logic through a scintillating comparison of the structures of various myths,[15] but I will not spoil his denouement: the exact solution he provides does not matter here. What does matter is the way his ending reveals an attitude to literature. Leach makes much of a mural found at Dura-Europos in Syria that depicts the discovery of Moses. At the end, referring to the paradoxes just given, he comments: 'I have tried to exhibit some of the ways in which biblical mythology seeks to resolve these puzzles, but, as I have indicated by my reference to the Dura murals, I find that artists make a much better job of it than theologians' (p. 57). It is a curious comment, prompted, I suspect, by the professional rivalry of an upstart discipline. The real point seems to be that pictures come closer to revealing the true meaning of the myth than its biblical telling. Seemingly the closer a work of art comes to revealing the particular truth that the interpreter has detected, the better it is. The biblical stories would say what Leach says they say if they could, and if they were good art. But this contradicts his premise that the real meaning of a work of art is never its apparent meaning. The art might be perfect if the two were the same, but then either the interpreter would be left with nothing to do or he would have to accept that his way of reading is now impossible except as a falsification of the truth. Committed to the idea that the stories are encoded

---

[15] To say nothing of some cheating: in spite of several statements in the Gospels that Jesus had sisters (Matt. 13:56 etc.), Leach bases part of his argument on the complementary question, 'why did Jesus not have a sister?' (p. 35).

messages, he conceives of the interpreter's task not as rescuing the tale from the artist but as rescuing the meaning from the tale. The encoding itself – a hideous word for a pernicious image – has ceased to be of interest.

It is here that the unliterary mind, whatever its manifest cleverness, reveals itself. In his pursuit of the message, Leach has let the work of art go: he is, finally, at the opposite, even less acceptable, extreme to Kermode, a user rather than a reader of literature. This is consistent with one other aspect of his work, his lack of concern with the particularity of the text. 'For the most part', he declares, 'I am concerned with stories not with texts' (*Genesis as Myth*, p. 32). The words that create the story hardly matter. No more does the individuality of the figures matter. Indeed, in his view their individuality, which is what ordinarily would give them human interest, is a distraction from their significance as incarnations of mythical patterns.

Kermode writes with a flavour of irony; Leach does no such thing. Rather, he seems to jut out his jaw and challenge one to hit him. His fist is more than ready to give a return blow. In using him to suggest the unliterary obverse of some of Kermode's points I have responded to the jut of the jaw and caricatured him. There is much in his essays to modify the caricature and make them among the livelier contributions to discussions of biblical narrative.

How many children had Mary?

Within the narrow yet fragmented world of literary studies Kermode's stress on 'what is written at the expense of what it is written about' (above, p. 363) is not a new one. We may discover more about why it is not obviously right for writing such as the Bible by going back to a pioneering essay. In 1933 L. C. Knights debunked character criticism of Shakespeare's plays because it endowed the characters with a life outside the texts that created the characters, rightly reminding us that there is nothing more to the characters than the evidence in the text. He called his essay 'How many children had Lady Macbeth?', and part of his point was the wrongness of asking the question: the text establishes no more than that she knows what it is to have given suck (1: 7). But it is another matter to ask, how many children had Mary? The textual situation is similar – we are told the names of four of Jesus' brothers and that he had sisters[16] – but Mary is taken by most readers to be a historical character, so interest in her as a character only partially reflected in the Gospel narratives is not only natural but reasonable. The texts may be the sum total of knowledge about her that survives, but they obviously are not all that she was.

---

[16] James the less, Joses, Simon and Judas or Juda. See Matt. 12: 46–7, 13: 55–6, Mark 6: 3, 15: 40 and Gal. 1: 19.

Knights touches on the contrast between historical and fictional characters. One of his key examples, Maurice Morgann's *Essay on the Dramatic Character of Sir John Falstaff* (1777), includes this comment: 'if the characters of Shakespeare are thus *whole*, and as it were original, whilst those of almost all other writers are mere imitation, it may be fit to consider them rather as historic than dramatic beings'. Knights's response is instructive:

> It is strange how narrowly Morgann misses the mark. He recognised what can be called the full-bodied quality of Shakespeare's work – it came to him as a feeling of 'roundness and integrity'. But instead of realising that this quality sprang from Shakespeare's use of words ... he referred it to the characters' 'independence' of the work in which they appeared, and directed his exploration to 'latent motives and policies not avowed'.   (P. 12)

A great deal of fiction attempts to feel like history – indeed, is often distinguishable from history by its greater appearance of veracity[17] – so the illusion of a character's independence is a natural one. But in history the character *is* independent. Morgann, and so many critics into this century, treated Shakespeare as if what he wrote was history. A reaction was bound to come and bound to have an element of overstatement. For instance, Knights suggests that the main reason for the eighteenth century's approach to Shakespeare through characters was its 'inability to appreciate the Elizabethan idiom and a consequent inability to discuss [his] plays as poetry' (p. 13). These inabilities existed, but they do not explain why character criticism is so natural and persistent.

When Knights brought attention back to the text, he effected a change like that which Kermode tries to make in relation to the Bible. But the Bible resists the change. Even if one were to grant for the sake of argument that it is fiction, one would have to admit that a great deal of it is unlike most fiction we know, and that the Gospel stories are especially unlike. A prime characteristic of fiction is that it is told once, of history that it is told many times.[18] Essential to

---

[17] The temptation to quote Oscar Wilde's 'The decay of lying' in this connection is a large one. Wilde explores the reality of fiction with his usual provocative brilliance.

[18] Leach appears to make the same point about myths, declaring that 'it is common to all mythological systems that all important stories recur in several different versions' (*Genesis as Myth*, p. 7). However, the distinction is that in history it is apparently the same story that is retold, whereas in mythology apparently different stories are told. Leach fails to make such a distinction in elaborating his statement: 'Man is created in Genesis (1: 27) and then he is created all over again (2: 7). And, as if two first men were not enough, we also have Noah in chapter 8. Likewise in the New Testament, why must there be four Gospels each telling the "same" story yet sometimes flatly contradictory on details of fact?' (pp. 7–8). Adam and Noah are different figures even though each 'becomes a unique ancestor of all mankind' (p. 19); Jesus appears as one person.

Knights's call for a return to the text is an idea of a Shakespeare play as 'a precise particular experience, a poem' (p. 17). But essential to the nature of the Gospels is, as I have suggested before, the fact that they tell what we take to be the same story four different ways. Their very literary form is a statement that there is a truth apart from the text, for that truth can be expressed through at least four different texts. If texts were not conceived of as transparent – if we did not think of form and content as separable – there could not be four Gospels. Nor could there be translation, with its implicit sense of a single content being carried from one form to another.

The Gospels do not appear to us as an artful exploration of the effects of point of view, or as successive retellings of each other. They appear as four different attempts to reveal or preserve a particular body of truth that is not *in* them but only indicated *by* them. This appearance makes it difficult to think of them as fiction: the only reality that can exist apart from the reality of the text is reality itself. The Gospels appear to refer to the actual. Their literary form is anti-fictional. This is not a qualitative judgement – it does not make them good or bad writing – but it does distinguish them. They are not immediately subject to the kind of criticism Knights makes of the way Shakespeare's plays have been discussed, nor are they truly amenable to the Bible as fiction approach of Kermode. Some of their basic literary nature has to be ignored to enable this extreme form of discussion of the Bible as literature to proceed. Through failure to heed a major fact of the form of the Gospels – that their fourfold nature implies a reality beyond the text – literary criticism seems to be overreaching itself.

Robert Alter

The kind of reading that, in the Shakespearean context, aroused Knights's opposition might be illustrated from many critics of the Bible. Percy Cooper Sands, for instance, thinks 'the first great feature . . . of Mark's Gospel is that the narrative has allowed the personality of Jesus to shine clearly through the facts, and has not obscured or dimmed it'.[19] For him Mark is perfectly transparent on the historical reality of Jesus, and he earlier writes of 'the faithful reproduction of scenes where the disciples watched Jesus at work' (p. 8). He is so persuaded by the text that he believes he knows exactly what that original reality was. There is a circularity here because the faithfulness of the Gospel can only be judged by one's conviction of its truth. Sands is conflating the persuasiveness characteristic of fiction with historical verity.

---

[19] *Literary Genius of the New Testament* (London: Oxford University Press, 1932), p. 23.

But is there much difference in attitude to the text (there is an obvious difference in specificity) in the following from a discussion of the story of the assassination of obese King Eglon by the left-handed Ehud (Judg. 3: 15–25)?

> The left-handed Benjaminite warriors were known for their prowess, but Ehud also counts on his left-handedness as part of his strategy of surprise: a sudden movement of the left hand will not instantaneously be construed by the king as a movement of a weapon hand. Ehud also counts on the likelihood that Eglon will be inclined to trust him as a vassal bringing tribute and that the 'secret' he promises to confide to the king will thus be understood as a piece of intelligence volunteered by an Israelite collaborator ... Eglon's encumbrance of fat will make him an easier target as he awkwardly rises from his seat, and perhaps Ehud leaves the weapon buried in the flesh in order not to splatter blood on himself, so that he can walk out through the vestibule unsuspected and make his escape.

This is almost entirely supposition, as the 'perhaps' towards the end indicates. The text says none of these things. We might take it as an illustration of Kermode's observation that once the point is reached 'where interpretation by the invention of new narrative is halted ... interpretation thereafter usually continues in commentary' (p. x), for a change of tense will make it into narrative: 'Ehud *counted* on his left-handedness as part of his strategy of surprise', and so on. It is at one with ideas of the text as transparent, that is, as a faithful reproduction of original events and character because it builds up a complete picture of the event and the character's motivation. In the end this is testimony to the workings of the imagination, inventing possibilities to make sense of the skeletal information of the original. Literary criticism is, as Kermode puts it, 're-cognizing' the original event.

The passage is from *The Art of Biblical Narrative* (pp. 38–9) by Robert Alter, later to become Kermode's fellow-editor of *The Literary Guide to the Bible*. It is especially useful to be able to take such an example from Alter's work not only because he is one of the best contemporary literary critics of the Bible but also because his work allows one to consider further the issues of history and fiction and of the artfulness of biblical narrative.

Alter, Jewish and confining himself to the OT, argues that literary art plays a crucial role 'in the shaping of biblical narrative ... determining in most cases the minute choice of words and reported details, the pace of narration, the small movements of dialogue, and a whole network of ramified interconnections in the text' (p. 3). Later he writes that 'fiction was the principal means which the biblical authors had at their disposal for realising history' (p. 32). His old-fashioned 're-cognizing' of the slaying of Eglon is part of the argument for this general position. Having taken some stories in which a literary artfulness is relatively easy to demonstrate, he turns to this story because it is one of 'that long catalogue of military uprisings, the Book of Judges, where no serious claims could be made for complexity of characterisation or for subtlety of thematic development'. Nevertheless, he argues, it shows 'the modalities of prose fiction in what is told and how it is told'. Assuming for the sake of argument that the story is true, he poses the question, 'where, then, in this succinct political chronicle, is there room to talk about prose fiction?' (p. 37). What I have quoted of the discussion is from near the beginning of his answer to this question. Prefacing it is the observation 'that the detailed attention given here to the implement and technique of killing, which would be normal in the *Iliad*, is rather uncharacteristic of the Hebrew Bible' (p. 38). Because it is uncharacteristic, it draws attention to itself. One presumes it was done for effect, and analysis of the effect shows that each detail contributes to a picture that is much fuller than the brevity of the narrative would lead one to expect. This is to follow Alter's reasoning as he applies it elsewhere, but what he actually writes here is rather different; 'one may assume that Ehud's bold resourcefulness . . . was remarkable enough for the chronicler to want to report it circumstantially. Each of the details, then, contributes to a clear understanding of just how the thing was done' (p. 38). This is, for Alter, unusually lame, but the source of the lameness is significant. Wanting to keep open the premise that the event was historical, he argues that it was so striking as to demand detailed reporting, and that therefore every detail is artistically effective. The horse and the cart have got themselves into a muddle, and it is a familiar muddle. All the details are effective because the author is presumed to be a good one. But at this point in his discussion Alter has established no credentials for the chronicler of Judges; rather, he is seeking to show that, even in this kind of narrative, artistry such as belongs to fiction can be found. The argument can easily be turned around, and the horse may readily pull the cart, but it is striking that this failure of logic, so reminiscent of the argument from inspiration, should accompany writing that explores the life given to the text by the recognitive imagination in a context which accepts the historicity of the event and therefore is committed to seeing the text as transparent.

Lack of detail, what Auerbach sees as the background the text is fraught with and Meir Sternberg calls gapping, may be similarly expressive, and it may also contribute to the sense of transparency by taking the reader through the text into his own reconstruction of what is only partially recorded. Observing that

David's speeches prior to Uriah's death are public and 'properly diplomatic', Alter makes various suggestions as to what David is thinking or feeling when he replies to Saul or his spokesmen. He concludes that

> The narrator leaves these various 'readings' of David hovering by presenting his public utterance without comment, and in this way is able to suggest the fluctuating or multiple nature of motives in this prime biblical instance of man as a political animal. One or all of these conditions might explain David's words; precisely by not specifying, the narrator allows each its claim.   (P. 119)

Now, for this to be a valuable point, we need to be able to say why it cannot be made about any text from Hansard to *Hamlet* that relies on direct speech. And it seems that the only thing that might make the biblical text different is the extent of the reader's interest in the speeches and their situation. If this is so, what must first be accounted for is that interest, which may be a matter of one of three things: the way the story is told (what *is* there must make what is *not* there interesting), the special interest of the story, or the reader's predisposition to be interested in whatever he can find out of the story. What I have been calling 'interest' here really means the degree to which the reader is drawn to recreate the story in his imagination.

Alter's discussions include much sophisticated examination of detail which, for the sake of focussing on the problematic, I have not illustrated. Their large aim is not too far from Kermode's, but far enough to change what seems to be the satirical edge for an appearance of good sound sense. As Alter writes at the conclusion of his discussion of the Ehud and Eglon story, 'it is perhaps less historicised fiction than fictionalised history – history in which the feeling and the meaning of events are concretely realised through the technical resources of prose fiction' (p. 41). The fundamental difference from Kermode is that 'fiction' and 'history' are used in two ways, that is, as both technique and genre.[20] 'Historicised fiction' is fiction using techniques that make it look like history; 'fictionalised history' is history using the techniques of fiction. Kermode would have us think of biblical narrative as belonging to the genre, fiction, but Alter

---

[20] Sternberg also detects confusion here. He analyses it in this way. 'History' and 'fiction' can refer to both world and word, 'to the source and to the discourse'. Consequently, 'history-writing is wedded to and fiction-writing opposed to factual truth'. Sternberg escapes this problem by coming back to the nature of the writing, that is, to the characteristics of genre: 'history-writing is not a record of fact – of what "really happened" – but a discourse that claims to be a record of fact. Nor is fiction-writing a tissue of free inventions but a discourse that claims freedom of invention. The antithesis lies not in the presence or absence of truth value but in the commitment to truth value' (pp. 24–5). Unfortunately, the vagueness of 'truth value' raises more problems than it solves.

allows us to think of some of these narratives as historical yet using techniques usually associated with fiction.[21] The resources of fiction can be used to recreate an original that may be historical or imaginary. What's more, exactly as in Sands's remarks on Mark, it seems that this is a true recreation, for it produces 'a clear understanding of just how the thing was done' (p. 38). Fully aware of the unfashionableness implicit in such statements, Alter declares in his concluding chapter, 'I certainly reject the contemporary agnosticism about all literary meaning' (p. 179). He could hardly do otherwise: to find things other than just the words in a text is to be committed to transparency, and 'meaning' signifies transparency – the word leading through to an idea or object. From apparent closeness on the issue of the Bible as fiction, Alter and Kermode suddenly appear in opposing positions, the one affirming the presence of meaning, the other, in spite of the suspicion of satire, denying it. The divergence stems from the question of transparency: it seems that if one conceives of language as having a relational or referential aspect, one will believe that meaning exists, whereas if, in a kind of excess of aestheticism, one tries to see language as an absolute thing in itself, meaning, though not necessarily beauty, disappears.

Transparency and art are involved in another area that Alter discusses stimulatingly, the vexed matter of repetition and contradiction. This is something like biblical narrative's equivalent of the problem of Hebrew verse form. Repetition is essential to both, and in each case commonly accepted literary standards are violated. In this century the narrative contradictions and repetitions are as much a problem as the apparent tautology of the poetry was in past centuries.

One of the assumptions that Alter, viewing the narratives as artful fiction, shares with Kermode is 'that the text is an intricately interconnected unity' rather than the 'patchwork of frequently disparate documents, as most modern scholars have supposed'.[22] It is a view that leads to a good deal of stimulating reading, not least because of its insistence on the artistry of the redactors who have been so maligned by Higher Criticism, but it also leads to some difficulties. Alter is particularly rewarding in his discussion of what appear as contradictory

---

[21] Even so, there are occasions when he writes as if the genre of biblical narrative were fiction, for instance, the remark that 'all fiction, including the Bible, is in some sense a form of play' (p. 46). Later he writes of 'a closer *generic* link ... between Genesis and *Tom Jones* than between Genesis and the *Summa Theologiae* or the cabbalistic *Book of Creation*' (p. 156).

[22] Alter, p. 11. He gives no attention to the fact that different strands of material remain identifiable in the stories. A full account of the issue (which is not what he is attempting) would deal with the elements that tend to make one perceive the text as fragmented as well as showing what is to be gained by viewing it as a unity.

redundancies in OT narratives. One of these concerns the discovery by Joseph's brothers of the money hidden in their sacks. First, we read that, after leaving Joseph, 'as one of them opened his sack to give his ass provender in the inn, he espied his money', and then told his brothers (Gen. 42: 27–8). Seven verses later we read that after their return to Jacob 'it came to pass as they emptied their sacks, that, behold, every man's bundle of money was in his sack'. The contradiction is fairly obvious,[23] and the traditional Higher-Critical explanation is that two different sources have been preserved by the redactor with no attempt at reconciliation. Alter takes a different route:

> The contradiction ... is so evident that it seems naive on the part of any modern reader to conclude that the ancient Hebrew writer was so inept or unperceptive that the conflict between the two versions could have somehow escaped him. Let me suggest that, quite to the contrary, the Hebrew writer was perfectly aware of the contradiction but viewed it as a superficial one. In linear logic, the same action could not have occurred twice in two different ways; but in the narrative logic with which the writer worked, it made sense to incorporate both versions available to him because together they brought forth mutually complementary implications of the narrated event, thus enabling him to give a complete imaginative account of it.
>
> (P. 138)

He develops this suggestion with a subtle and illuminating reading of the effects of each narration, showing the complementary ways they fit into the whole story. In the first version of the discovery, for instance,

> the emphasis is on [the brothers'] sense of the strange ways of destiny: 'what is this God has done to us?' The J version in this way is crucial for the writer because it ties in the discovery of the money with the theme of Joseph's knowledge opposed to the brothers' ignorance that is central to both meetings in Egypt and, indeed, to the entire story. When the brothers ask what is it *'Elohim* – God, fate, and even judge or master in biblical Hebrew – has done to them, we as readers perceive a dramatic irony continuous with the dramatic ironies of the previous scene in the viceregal palace: Joseph in fact is serving as the agent of destiny, as God's instrument, in the large plan of the story; and the very brothers who earlier were shocked at Joseph's dream of

---

[23] It is possible to argue that there is no contradiction, that one brother found his money while on the journey, and the rest of them did the same only after arriving back with Jacob. But if this was so one would expect the later narrative to contain some recognition of the first discovery, such as including reference to it in the summary account given to Jacob, and then making a small change such as, 'it came to pass as *the others* emptied their sacks ...'.

Such a reading is just about tenable using the KJB text, but Alter takes the reader back to the Hebrew where the different sources (J and E), and with them the sense of contradiction, are much more obvious.

having the sun and moon and eleven stars bow down to him now unwittingly say 'God' when we as readers know that they are referring to that which Joseph has wrought. (Pp. 138–9)

Such attentiveness to the text is persuasive. We see how well the first account works in the context of the whole story, and Alter is similarly persuasive with his reading of the second account. The contradiction is left unresolved, but his point is that the redactor 'was prepared to include the minor inconvenience of duplication and seeming contradiction in his narrative because that inclusion enabled him to keep both major axes of his story clearly in view at a decisive juncture in his plot' (p. 140).

What looks to us like a fault of repetition is thus the product of different, alien, lost literary standards. Alter has done as Lowth did with parallelism, discarded standard ideas of literary propriety, accepted the text on the page and teased out its effect. As with the repetition in parallelism, the narrative repetition shows that there is further insight to be gained from saying or narrating a thing twice, even if the thing narrated changes its nature in the process.

For all the quality of the reading that goes to make up this argument, it remains an argument rather than becoming a truth. Here is another way of responding to these contradictory repetitions that also allows that the narrator knew what he was doing. They may be a reflection of the uncertainty of historical narrative, a deliberate rejection of the idea that the text can be a final and true statement of what actually happened. In this instance the narrator does not know which of his sources tells what actually happened, but he does know that the money must have been discovered. The reader also knows it, and the writer in effect says, this happened, and it may have happened in either of these two ways: I don't know. What is missing is the explicit statement of narrative purpose. Nevertheless, the implication that the event did happen is very, very strong, as is the invitation to the re-cognising imagination to work on the story. In short, the narrative repetition appears simultaneously as a rejection of narrative omniscience, a statement of the problem of historical knowledge and an affirmation of historicality.

Alter takes the biblical narrator (singular and, a decade prior to Harold Bloom's fiction about the sex of J, male) as being 'all-knowing and also perfectly reliable' (p. 184). He makes a brief comparison with omniscient narrators such as Fielding, and we may follow his example. Fielding certainly isn't perfectly reliable – he will deliberately lead his reader into misinterpretation of events – but he is obviously in total control of, say, *Tom Jones*, omnipotent if not always omniscient. Here he does something a little like the contradiction of the discovery of the money: 'now, whether Molly in the agonies of her rage pushed this rug with her feet: or, Jones might touch it; or whether the pin or nail gave way of its own accord, I am not certain; but . . . the wicked rug got loose from its fastening . . .' (5: 5). There is an element of contradiction in that the rug cannot get loose both 'of its own accord' and because it was touched or pushed. For the story all that matters is that the rug did get loose. Fielding as 'historian' knows that it did; by pretending not to know how it happened he can leave these various possibilities in the reader's imagination and, what is much more useful to him, create a sense of both Molly's and Tom's movements. Seeming to concentrate on a detail of how something happened, he creates a vivid picture of the whole scene. The difference (for present purposes) from the biblical example lies in the Bible's lack of sense of authorial presence and its lack of explicit awareness of the contradiction. The biblical example looks omniscient but isn't; the Fielding gives the opposite impression.

The largest test of Alter's points about omniscience and contradiction is the Gospels. The frequency of multiple tellings that are often incompatible in detail yet consistent in outline makes the issues important. Though the narratives are told in a way that appears to us as omniscient, the repetitions and inconsistencies imply the fallibility of the historian in the face of the unrecoverable details of the grand plot of history. The biblical narrator, then, is only omniscient from certain points of view; in one major way, whether deliberately or no, he can be seen as undermining that sense of omniscience.

Alter, taking the omniscience to be self-evident ('every biblical narrator is of course omniscient' (p. 126)), finds a major significance in it. 'The assurance of comprehensive knowledge', he writes,

> is . . . implicit in the narratives, but it is shared with the reader only intermittently and at that quite partially. In this way the very mode of narration conveys a double sense of a total coherent knowledge available to God (and by implication, to His surrogate, the anonymous authoritative narrator) and the necessary incompleteness of human knowledge, for which much about character, motive and moral status will remain shrouded in ambiguity.   (P. 184)

So the manner of writing is part of a theological outlook, and the paradox of a narrator who appears to know everything but will not tell all that he knows becomes an essential part of the art.

The reticence (or even, following Kermode, the secrecy) in presentation of character is also meaningful. This is how Alter interprets the narrator's 'drastic selectivity' in the display of this omniscience where character is concerned:

> He may on occasion choose to privilege us with the knowledge of what God thinks of a particular character or action – omniscient narration can go no higher – but as a

rule, because of his understanding of the nature of his human subjects, he leads us through varying darknesses which are lit up by intense but narrow beams, phantasmal glimmerings, sudden strobic flashes. We are compelled to get at character and motive, as in Impressionist writers like Conrad and Ford Madox Ford, through a process of inference from fragmentary data, often with crucial pieces of narrative exposition strategically withheld, and this leads to multiple or sometimes even wavering perspectives on the characters. There is, in other words, an abiding mystery in character as the biblical writers conceive it, which they embody in their typical methods of presentation. (P. 126)

Consequently the characters who are treated at length appear more changeable than we are used to in fiction, for they develop in and are transformed by time. There is therefore, as Alter puts it in a nice phrase, 'a sense of character as a centre of surprise ... unknowable and ... unforeseeable' (pp. 126–7).

This is a part of the contrast between the author's (and the creator's) omniscience and man's limited understanding. Just as Kermode moved from a sense of the difficulties and disappointments of reading literary texts to the same difficulties and disappointments in reading the world, so Alter connects his sense of the world and his sense of the art of the OT narrators:

these ancient writers, like later ones, wanted to fashion a literary form that might embrace the abiding complexity of their subjects. The monotheistic revolution of biblical Israel was a continuing and disquieting one. It left little margin for neat and confident views about God, the created world, history and man as political animal or moral agent, for it repeatedly had to make sense of the intersection of incompatibles – the relative and the absolute, human imperfection and divine perfection, the brawling chaos of historical experience and God's promise to fulfil a design in history. The biblical outlook is informed, I think, by a sense of stubborn contradiction, of a profound and ineradicable untidiness in the nature of things, and it is toward the expression of such a sense of moral and historical reality that the composite artistry of the Bible is directed. (P. 154)

It is here, I think, that the most important difference from Kermode emerges. It is not a matter of the contrast between their attitudes to the historicality and fictionality of the text – for Kermode the text *is* fiction, for Alter it uses techniques of fiction and may be profitably read as if it were fiction; rather, it is a matter of their attitudes to the expressiveness of texts. Kermode appears uninterested in the text as expression, whereas Alter, like Schweitzer, is. For all that they have much in common through their interest in fiction, their assumption that the Bible is artful, and their responsiveness to words artfully used, they are basically divided. Alter's approach accommodates belief, Kermode's does not. They belong with different tendencies of criticism, and the essential difference between them is religious. Kermode is inimical to the Bible as a book of belief whereas Alter is not. Alter's belief may only be of the sort that one draws from any literary text – he draws inferences about the Bible's outlook as he might draw inferences from many a literary text – but the acceptance that there is an outlook is crucial.

Meir Sternberg

Some of the issues that have been raised here may be taken further through a glance at the longest recent work on biblical narrative, Meir Sternberg's *The Poetics of Biblical Narrative*. But first his book may be used to make a general point. Poetics – 'the systematic working or study of literature', as Sternberg grandly but not entirely helpfully defines it – assumes that there are 'well-defined rules of poetic communication' (p. 2) within the work or the literature in question, and it aims to discover these rules. Once discovered, they will enable the reader to read the work or literature fully. Now, Sternberg, like Alter, keeps to the OT, so we might rephrase his title, apparently so like Alter's, as 'the secret of Hebrew narrative'. Narrative is to modern critics what poetry was to their pre-Victorian predecessors, and Sternberg's quest for the secret of Hebrew narrative is like the old quest for the secret of Hebrew poetry. He is far from alone on the quest, and one might maliciously conclude from a casual reading of his or Kermode's or Alter's or Josipovici's work that modern critics are as ingenious in finding narrative art as Gomarus was in establishing his scheme of Hebrew versification. If God had written a telephone directory, Gomarus would have proved it metrical and they would prove it readable.

Behind the attempts to discover the secret of Hebrew poetry lay the religious conviction that, having God for author, it was the perfection of poetry. Among modern critics of the Bible there is remarkably little admission that the Bible might have imperfections – one has to go back to T. R. Henn's *The Bible as Literature* (1970) for any regular acknowledgement of their existence. In part this is the necessary reaction against the failure of Higher Criticism to recognise that apparent faults in the text might be not only deliberate but artful.[24]

In part it may also indicate that the premise of inspiration is, though unfit to be mentioned in polite company, nevertheless alive and well. It hovers on the edge of Alter's discussion of omniscience, but Sternberg is bold enough to

---

[24] Alter writes 'that elements like disjunction, interpolation, repetition, contrastive styles, which in biblical scholarship were long deemed sure signs of a defective text, may be perfectly deliberate components of the literary artwork, and recognised as such by the audience for which it is intended. There is a distinctive poetics informing both biblical narrative and biblical poetry, and an understanding of it will help us in many instances to make plain sense of a puzzling text instead of exercising that loose and derivative mode of literary invention that goes under the scholarly name of emendation' (Alter and Kermode, p. 27).

bring it into the open. The essence of his position is this, that one must accept the idea of inspiration in order to read the Bible properly:

> Across all doctrinal boundaries, inspiration simply figures as an institutional rule for writing and reading; and it is no more liable to questioning than the Bible's rules of grammar (or the reality of *Hamlet*'s ghost). To make sense of the Bible in terms of its own conventions, one need not believe in either, but one must postulate both. And to postulate inspiration is to elevate the narrator to the status of omniscient historian, combining two otherwise irreconcilable postures or models: the constrained historian and the licensed fiction-maker. (P. 81)

In short, one should willingly suspend one's disbelief in inspiration while reading the Bible. And this is the more necessary because only thus will the historical and the fictional elements be reconciled and correct reading be made possible.

This way of thinking involves a sense of opposition between the historical and the fictional in the text that one need not share. Since the narrative never discusses what it is doing, it appears neither constrained nor licensed: the practical reader remains sublimely unaware of the issue that looms so large to the theoretician. But behind the theory there is belief. Like Alter, Sternberg takes the biblical narrator as omniscient. He brings a number of his arguments together in the observation that 'however far from omnicommunicative, the Bible's narration yet remains omniscient and authoritative and intelligible on different levels of reading. The narrator may play games with the whole truth for the pleasure and benefit of the cunning few, but he must communicate the truth in a fashion accessible to all' (p. 235). The lack of full communication and the games played with the truth are part of what Sternberg sees as the Bible's 'overarching principle of composition, its strategy of strategies, namely, manoeuvering between the truth and the whole truth' (p. 51). This is exactly consistent with Alter. However, the reference to the cunning few and to the need to 'communicate in a fashion accessible to all' is part of another of Sternberg's leading ideas, that of the 'foolproof composition' of the Bible. By this he means 'that the Bible is difficult to read, easy to underread and overread and even misread, but virtually impossible to ... counterread', because 'the essentials are made transparent to all comers: the story line, the world order, the value system' (p. 50). At this late stage in our history a phrase such as 'foolproof composition' must set more than one kind of bell ringing. Besides being a restatement of the old belief that nothing is hidden in the Bible which is not also revealed in a form that the simplest can understand, it is yet one more form of the familiar belief, so closely associated with ideas of inspiration, in the perfection of the text. For Sternberg inspiration is more than a matter of hypothesis, and we see him at last as a reader whose would-be faithful reading of the text is indeed made through the eyes of faith.

This appears as a negative criticism. Implicit is an ideal of clear-eyed reading, reading, that is, that responds without bias or blindness to exactly what is in the text. Most critics who do not belong to a school which sets out to use texts for its own purposes would probably claim that this is their aim. One perpetual lesson of this history is that reading is shaped by one's biases towards or against the text. Such a lesson is particularly likely to emerge in relation to a text that has a central place in religion: not only is one likely to know something about the text before one reads it, but one is also likely to have a particular attitude to the text. This can hardly be so with a text which one discovers at random, never having heard of it or its author (though even then there will be predisposing factors such as one's sense of the genre to which it belongs or one's sense of the quality of its manufacture). Now, it is one of the common premises of biblical criticism that the Bible is a book of this sort. So when Sternberg writes that 'the most startling thing about the Bible's opening words, "When God began to create heaven and earth", is that God comes on stage with a complete absence of preliminaries' (p. 322), he is writing not only as if one has never begun to read Genesis before but also as if one has no prior knowledge of God. This is indeed what critics usually do, but it may be misleading in connection with the Bible. Sternberg asserts that 'the narrator does not in practice assume even sketchy knowledge of the reader's part' (p. 261), but surely the writing points in the opposite direction. God is not a surprise in the first sentence of Genesis because the writer takes it for granted that we know who or what God is. And the same presumption is present in all the stories. As soon as one conceives of them as memoranda of what is known, such qualities fit into place. Moreover, to take them as memoranda fits with the perception that a good deal of their power comes from the reader not reading the words as creators of the story but instead as reminders of it. Then indeed the reader *recognises* the story, and one has no need to insert Kermode's hyphen into that word.

A book or a ragbag?

Small-scale unity and fragmentation

Bates proclaimed it as the final heresy, 'that the part is greater than the whole' (above, p. 292). Alter, apparently contradictory, insisted that 'even if the text is really composite in origin ... it has been woven into a complex artistic whole' (p. 20). Northrop Frye appears to be saying the same thing when, as roundly as Bates, he proclaims that 'the unity of the Bible as a whole is an assumption underlying the understanding of any part of it' (p. 62). And Gabriel Josipovici seems to define the issue in asking, 'is the Bible the repository of some marvellous stories and poems, or is it a whole, perhaps a narrative or a poetic whole? Is it, in short, a book or a ragbag?' (p. xii). The appearances deceive, for more than one question is involved according to the scale on which one is thinking. It is Josipovici's 'marvellous stories' that Alter is describing as 'a complex artistic whole', and these stories are some of the parts that Bates declares to be greater than the whole. Frye, on the other hand, is thinking in terms of the whole Bible, and Josipovici, framing the question as he does, is thinking in the same terms.

Sternberg identifies the poles between which the issues range when he notes that 'by the law of reaction, the old and self-defeating extreme of exegetical and/or genetic atomism makes the opposite extreme of holism doubly attractive' (p. 439). Critics like Kermode and Alter make much of their opposition to the fragmentation of the text produced by Higher Criticism, but they work on a scale usually no larger than an individual book. They never tackle the question of the unity of the whole. Theirs is micro-unity (or, worse still, micro-holism) as against Frye's macro-unity. The question Josipovici poses is one of macro-unity.

The idea of micro-unities – Bates's 'final heresy', descended from collections of gems from the Bible – dominates present-day literary thinking about the Bible. But it is open to challenge from both sides. So far the most significant response to the dismissal of Higher Criticism's fragmentation of the text has come in David Damrosch's *The Narrative Covenant*. Working against Sternberg's holism, he proposes that assumptions of 'difficult coherence' are

> plausible if the text really is a fully unified and self-consciously artful composition, the work of a single author like Henry James or James Joyce. Suppose, however, that the cataclysm of the First World War had left us with only fragments of [*The Portrait of a Lady* and *A Portrait of the Artist as a Young Man*], with no clear memory of their original nature. Suppose that a later editor, finding the fragments and believing them to be versions of a single story, had pieced together the *Portrait of a Lady as a Young Man*, by someone known only as 'James', or 'J'. No doubt, a sufficiently skillful editor might put together a text that later scholars could read in a unified fashion. Even the hero-heroine's frequent changes of sex could to some extent be thematically justified by reference to the theme of androgyny in 'James's' oeuvre, and further understood by comparison to other modernist literature, such as Woolf's *Orlando*. All the same, there can be little doubt that various problems in the text could best be solved by unravelling the two strands of 'J', distinguishing the Henry James contributions from those by James Joyce. (P. 26)

This is a splendid fancy: obviously the reader's ingenuity at putting two and two together does not prove either that they belong together or that they are best read together. Sometimes modern literary discussion of biblical narratives does seem like an attempt to wrestle an effective unity out of such disparate texts. Is it any greater a contradiction to call one's leading character sometimes Isabel and sometimes Stephen than to call Him sometimes Jehovah and sometimes Elohim?

But it is also argument by parody. Damrosch tackles the problem of micro-unity in his conclusion. First he points out the simplification involved in being made to choose between 'our literary notions of intricate design' and 'a crazy quilt of ancient traditions' (p. 299, quoting Alter, p. 132). Historical study is rarely so atomistic, and 'there has been a broad movement toward the rehabilitation of the later stages of the biblical texts and an increasing interest in relating source study to the context of the overall text' (p. 300). Such study can bring out tensions that are in the text as well as showing how easy it is to fall in with reading one of the strands of composition at the expense of another. Damrosch shows how Alter's analyses sometimes do this. So Alter's reading of 1 Sam. 17 does not properly take account of the different sources and as a result creates an idea of composite artistry that is true neither to the final redactor's intentions nor to all the material that he has presented. Historical criticism, Damrosch observes, 'can help to guard against over-reading', and can also help 'keep us from under-reading the complex internal dialogue of the text' (p. 307).

Alter invites us to choose between 'confused textual patchwork' and 'purposeful pattern'. Damrosch wants a middle road, suggesting, though with unease because the image is too simple, that we think of the text as 'a purposeful patchwork' (p. 325):

> To do full justice to the dynamics of biblical narrative, we must often read a passage three or even four ways at once.
>
> This is not quite possible, of course, and at any given moment we may entertain the reading fostered by one of the authors at work in the text; then, in a reversal of figure and ground, another reading becomes uppermost. It is difficult for Eli to be both kindly and evil; we can read him one way or the other, in each case following one of the authors of the text; or we can construct a temporary amalgam in which we correct each author in the light of the other, a solution that might be, but probably is not, what the later author intended us to do in this instance. Historical criticism both helps us to recover authorial intentionality and also forces us to see our distance from it, in the many cases where the intentions of the different authors do not easily harmonise. This may represent a loss of meaning for those readers who are committed to the

ideology of tenth-century Yahwism, or fifth-century Priestly thought, but for most readers an awareness of the multiplicity of biblical narrative should enrich the reading process it destabilises. (P. 325)

Such argument does not directly confront the issue of the quality of the text, but we normally take contradictoriness to be a weakness as against the strength of unity. Damrosch, like the other critics discussed here, aims at the best possible close reading of the text. That best possible reading comes out of a mix of historical and literary awareness of the text, and it is not necessarily easy or simple. Kermode led us away from our desire for fulfilment into a no man's land of occasional glimmerings. Damrosch too leads us away from fulfilling reading, but only in order to remind us that what we might take as fulfilment in the reading – our sense of the composite but finally unified artistry of the text – can be our own unfaithful creation, unfaithful, that is, to the whole text. There is a healthy caution and scepticism in this position.

Large-scale unity

Caution and scepticism have no place in ideas of the large-scale unity of the Bible. This is the territory of grandiosity and belief. The difficulties a critic faces in formulating such ideas show why such qualities are inevitable. Foremost is a problem we have not had to face before. Up to this point the Bible we have been considering as literature is, through all its changes, the Bible that has come down into the English Protestant tradition. It is, once we reach the Reformation, the Bible of literature in English, and it has one chief form, the KJB without the Apocrypha. The OT of Roman Catholic tradition is somewhat different in that the Apocryphal books are mixed in, but both OTs end with the twelve minor Prophets, the last of whom is Malachi. Outside Christianity there is the Tanakh, the Bible of Judaism. Not only does this not have the NT, but it also presents the books of the OT in a different order, first the Torah or Law, that is, the Pentateuch, then the Prophets (Nevi'im) and lastly the Writings (Kethubim, Hagiographa). This 'OT' finishes with Chronicles.

As long as attention is confined to the qualities of individual books or stories, such differences matter little. But the arrival on the English-speaking scene of Jewish critics such as Alter and Sternberg signals the need to face the issue. The most radical (though by no means unreasonable) observation in Alter's whole book is that, in spite of

> certain literary as well as theological continuities between the Hebrew Bible and the New Testament . . . the narratives of the latter were written in a different language, at

a later time, and, by and large, according to different literary assumptions. It therefore does not seem to me that these two bodies of ancient literature can be comfortably set in the same critical framework.   (P. ix)

If we are to think of a Bible as a whole rather than as a collection – as a book rather than as *ta biblia*, the little books – then it is a matter of literary importance what individual books we read and what order we read them in. Yet few critics have any difficulty solving this problem – because the answer is dictated not by literary considerations but by faith and culture. This is the primary reason why discussions of large-scale unity appear to be expressions of belief.

Gabriel Josipovici's *The Book of God* is largely an attempt to determine whether the Bible of Protestant tradition has a large unity. The answer emerges early and instructively. It depends on the existence of the NT, on Malachi being the last book of the OT, and on there being no interruption of the Apocrypha between Malachi and Matthew. Each Testament, Josipovici declares, has four parts. In the OT these are the Pentateuch, the historical books, the poetic books and the prophetic books, and, correspondingly, in the NT the Gospels, Acts, the Epistles and Revelation. Focussing on Malachi's vision of the lapse of the chosen people and of the coming of a new Elijah preparing the way for the day of the Lord, he comments, 'so this section and with it the entire Old Testament ends, with a vision of the terrible Day of Judgement, but also with a reminder that, as Moses saved Israel from the Egyptian bondage, so Elijah will return, heralding the final reconciliation of God and Israel'. Here he quotes the final chapter, with its stirring mixture of warning and promise – 'for, behold, the day cometh, that shall burn as an oven; and all the proud, yea, and all that do wickedly, shall be stubble ... But unto you that fear my name shall the Sun of righteousness arise with healing in his wings' (4: 1–2). Josipovici notes that 'thus the end looks back to the beginning, and forward into the future'. 'The New Testament', he writes, 'follows immediately after this' (p. 40), and he goes on to sketch a few of the links the Gospels have with, particularly, Genesis and Malachi. At last he exclaims:

> It's a magnificent conception, spread over thousands of pages and encompassing the entire history of the universe. There is both perfect correspondence between Old and New Testaments and a continuous forward drive from Creation to the end of time: 'It begins where time begins, with the creation of the world; it ends where time ends, with the Apocalypse, and it surveys human history in between, or the aspect of history it is interested in, under the symbolic names of Adam and Israel.' Earlier ages had no difficulty in grasping this design, though our own, more bookish age, obsessed with both history and immediacy, has tended to lose sight of it. Neither

theologians nor biblical scholars have stood back enough to see it as a whole. Yet it *is*
a whole and quite unlike any other book.[25]

A number of questions may be put against this vision of the book. What
happens to it if Malachi does not precede Matthew? Could other books have
been placed at the end of the OT to equally good effect? Is the order of the other
books in either Testament the best possible – would it not be more appropriate,
for instance, to begin the NT with the words that match the beginning of the
OT, the opening of John? Or, would it not be better to have Mark before
Matthew, and, having removed the interruption of John, to have Luke
followed directly by Acts? Why should we think of each Testament as dividing
into four rather than, say, the tripartite division of the Hebrew Bible, or the
seven-part division that Frye divines, giving five parts to the OT and two to the
NT?

There is, in short, a seeming arbitrariness or an act of faith involved in any
conception of the Bible as a unity. Some of that arbitrariness comes from the
variable constitution and ordering of the Bible, and some from the multiple
possibilities of interrelationship. The act of faith that might be involved is a
variant on the familiar one, inspiration. Essentially God dictated not only the
books but which should be held canonical and what order they should come in.
Josipovici's leap into rhetorical exclamation – 'it's a magnificent conception ...
perfect correspondence' – is the sort of leap we have seen made so many times
by believers. It leaves out of account the distance there may be between
continuities and unity.

Alter willingly concedes that there are literary as well as theological
continuities between the two Testaments. The primary continuity is typological, which is at once a theological and a literary way of perceiving. Jesus saw
himself as the living fulfilment of the Law and the Prophets, and the Gospels, as
they themselves proclaim and as a host of commentators have taught us, are full
of connections, explicit and implicit, with the OT. These connections are not
just like references backwards and forwards in the plot of a novel but also like
poetic echoes and patterns of similarity, and they all serve to express the belief
that Jesus is the promised Messiah. Christian belief thus gives new meaning to
the OT, and it shapes the NT so that it connects back to this new understanding
of the OT.

Frye, who regards typology as both a form of rhetoric and a mode of
thought, describes it as 'a figure of speech that moves in time: the type exists in

[25] P. 42, quoting Frye, p. xiii.

the past and the antitype in the present, or the type exists in the present and the antitype in the future' (p. 80). It is not only the basis of connection between the two Testaments; it is also the shaping force behind his vision of the unity of the Protestant Bible:

> The content of the Bible is traditionally described as 'revelation', and there seems to be a sequence or dialectical progression in this revelation, as the Christian Bible proceeds from the beginning to the end of its story. I see a sequence of seven main phases: creation, revolution or exodus (Israel in Egypt), law, wisdom, prophecy, gospel and apocalypse. Five of these phases have their center of gravity in the Old Testament and two in the New. Each phase is not an improvement on its predecessor but a wider perspective on it. That is, this sequence of phases is another aspect of biblical typology, each phase being a type of the one following it and an antitype of the one preceding it.   (P. 106)

This is a grand invitation to the imagination rather than a persuasive analysis – and if that remark sounds dismissive, it is worth remembering that nothing in literature can be good that does not please and involve the imagination. Frye spends some time exploring how the scheme works, but gives no attention to why the parts should come in the order they do, or any indication of why we should think in terms of these divisions rather than others. So, unless we are disciples, we remain unbelievers in the quality of this unity and even in its existence.

One of the characteristics of unity is a sense of necessity – a sense that all the parts are necessary for the whole and that not one of them could be removed without detracting from or even destroying the whole. In other words, if one believes the Bible to be a perfect literary unity, one would find, say, Leviticus necessary to the whole. And indeed Leviticus has spurred some extraordinary literary ingenuity. Damrosch, writing on that book for *The Literary Guide to the Bible*, broaches a key issue in estimating the quality and nature of the literary unity of the Bible, 'the fact that so much of the Bible is not literature at all' (p. 66). This is the other side of Bates's heresy. Damrosch cheerfully acknowledges that most readers will find Leviticus 'an unappetising vein of gristle in the midst of the Pentateuch', and that their natural reaction 'is simply to push it quietly off the plate' – in other words, to say that the Bible is better read without it. It is one of the 'frequent eruptions of intractably nonliterary, even antiliterary, material' in the Bible.[26] Yet he shows that it is written with

---

[26] P. 66. Much of this article is given in chapter 6 of *The Narrative Covenant*. Bates and Roland Mushat Frye each allow three pages of Leviticus into their selections. Many other selections ignore Leviticus altogether. A recent addition to the legion of books on the Bible is Philip Rosenbaum's *How to Enjoy the* Boring *Parts of the Bible* (Brentwood, Tenn.: Wolgemuth and Hyatt, 1991).

considerable finesse, and even argues that chapters 11–25 are 'not a nonnar-rative but an *anti*narrative whose purpose is to complete the transformation of history inaugurated in chapters 1–7' (p. 73).

Josipovici picks out Damrosch's argument as 'a salutary reminder of how much damage we do to this book by focusing on isolated portions of it without regard to the rest', and goes on to look at another bit of gristle, the description of the tabernacle in the second half of Exodus. It is, he notes, a description that is given twice, as if once were not bad enough:

> Reading the instructions once is difficult enough; reading them twice seems to be beyond the powers of even the most dedicated reader. But is this not perhaps the very point the text is making? May it not be that if we ask, not What is the text saying? but What is happening to me as I read? we may be able to understand the function of the descriptions? (P. 93)

After detailed and enlightening comparisons with other descriptions of making in the Bible, he offers this conclusion:

> The episode of the making of the Tabernacle mirrors our own reading of it. We cannot get beyond and above the elements of the unfolding description, for we are only human, with a limited memory and an even more limited capacity for concentrating and imagining. Better in such circumstances to concentrate on the detail of the work in hand than to try and see the whole shape. And when we do this we discover that it is we too who have been the makers of this most elaborate tent. And at each rereading we remake it. It is quite other than we could ever have imagined had we tried to invent it ourselves, and yet without us it would not exist. (Pp. 106–7)

This is at once ingenious, engagingly simple, and wise in its sense of human capacity, but it is a suggestion as to how to swallow the gristle rather than demonstration that the gristle was good lean meat. And, on any moderately strict sense of what unity entails, that is what needed to be demonstrated.

Josipovici's tussle with the tabernacle seems to me a noble effort to confront a major problem in reading the Bible as a unified work. It gives incidental insight without succeeding in its large aim. Yet the tussle is part of a long effort that is often suggestive, even if it lacks the perfection of fully convincing insight. The suggestiveness comes in part because he is asking some of the right questions. Nowhere is this more obvious than when he discusses Judges. He refers to Alter's discussion of Ehud and Eglon as a fine example of 'subtle and sensitive treatment . . . of individual episodes', and then notes the key point distinguish-ing Alter's interest in the micro-artistry of the text from his own interest: Alter does not address 'the question of why these stories should be where they are in the book or how they function within the larger economy of the whole'. This is how Josipovici goes on:

> But a critic of such an approach might argue, how can one talk of a larger whole in this instance? Is it not obvious to every reader that the book of Judges is in fact only a collection of disparate stories and completely lacks the organisation and patterning so obvious in the book of Genesis or in Samuel? My response to this would be that the book of Judges is indeed oddly fragmented and jagged, even by the standards of the Bible, but that this is part of what it is about, not something to be condemned. To put it in the terms we have been using so far, I would want to argue that in this book the underlying rhythm, which was established in the very first chapter of Genesis, which was developed in the stories of the Patriarchs and given a new dimension in the account of the building of the Tabernacle and the giving of the laws, here comes under such a strain that it almost collapses. I would want to argue further that it is important for the larger rhythm of the whole book that this should occur, and that it prepares us for a re-establishment of the rhythm, after a stutter under Saul, when David appears on the scene, and for its eventual disintegration under the Kings of Israel and Judah. In other words, I want to argue that the sense of fragmentation, sometimes of parody and absurdity, which recent scholars have detected in many of the episodes of the book of Judges, is not the result of confusion on the part of authors and redactors, but has to be taken seriously as the central feature of what the book itself is about. (P. 110)

We are, therefore, to trust the authors: if they frustrate or confuse, that is essential to their vision of that time. We must have faith in the text and in our own responses: in that way we will experience the visionary truth of the text.

If this is a fair inference, the inextricability of the literary and the religious in Josipovici's sense of the Bible is clear. This is not to say that the religious aspect is Christian but that he writes out of a faith in the value of reading (a faith such as one suspected Kermode had lost) and a faith in the quality of the Bible as a book to be read. It is, in short, a faith in the value of literature.

In an age so burdened with academic literary theory it is positively indecent to set down in two sentences why literature is valuable. It is because it presents life with a luminousness that is otherwise hidden from us. At its best it engages our minds, our imaginations and our experience of humanity in insight, which is both a way of knowing and an experience of meaningfulness.

Kermode linked the problem of literary interpretation with the problem of interpreting the world. Josipovici makes a similar link in a striking passage which sums up his view of the Bible:

> There is then a unity to this book, which runs all the way from the ubiquitous use of the particle *wa*, 'and', to the inclusion within it of disparate and sometimes conflicting material. It is the unity of disjunction, at the same time as it is an assertion of conjunction. How and why the parts hold together is not, primarily, a subject for scholars delving into the history of manuscript traditions, but for the reader, from the

first sentence to the last. The disjunctions, in other words, are not dark patches in our understanding which are waiting for the light of scholarship to shine upon them, or even for the blinding flash of a once-and-for-all understanding. They are the very fabric of this book ... the peculiarity of the Bible is that it keeps calling into question our ability to make sense of our past, and of stories to explain ourselves or describe the world. There is, it is true, a strong tendency in Christianity, already evident in the New Testament, to search for the single story that will give shape to the world; but that tendency exists in tension with the sense, present in the Gospels as well as in much of the Hebrew Bible, that if there is such a story it is not one we will ever be able to know or tell.

Perhaps, instead of thinking about the Bible as a book to be deciphered or a story to be told, we should think of it as a person. We do not decipher people, we encounter them. And the closer we are to a person the more certain we will be that we cannot tell his story. Yet we also know that we will never be likely to confuse that person with anyone else, even a close relative ... Looked at in this way, the Bible can be seen to be unique not because it is uniquely authoritative but because it is itself and not something else.   (Pp. 306–7)

Essentially he is reading the Bible as he reads the world, as having a 'unity of disjunction'. It denies what Christianity wishes to assert, an overall meaningfulness and singleness of purpose in history. It takes us back from the search for truth to the experience of encountering without knowing. This means being content merely to read. At the last, then, Josipovici's reading is, from an orthodox point of view, a subversive one, and the sense of a lack of fully convincing insight is explained. He does not want such insights. The paradox is that this is the somewhat empty insight he is offering.

Frye too links word and world. As he continues his description of typology, he sees it as generative of a world-vision:

What typology really is as a mode of thought, what it both assumes and leads to, is a theory of history, or more accurately of historical process: an assumption that there is some meaning and point of history, and that sooner or later some event or events will occur which will indicate what that meaning or point is, and so become an antitype of what has happened previously. Our modern confidence in historical process, our belief that despite apparent confusion, even chaos, in human events, nevertheless those events are going somewhere and indicate something, is probably a legacy of biblical typology: at least I can think of no other source for its tradition.

(Pp. 80–1)

This is a fair enough description of typology itself, though some might want to be more precise and specify Jesus as the meaning or point of it all. But what is most interesting is what this sense of typology leads Frye to. Typology is, as I have suggested, a way of creating unity that is at once theological and literary.

Now it seems that we can slide from 'unity' to 'meaning': seeing things in combination with each other is what makes up both unity and meaning. Man, to generalise as largely as Frye, is always seeking to understand the world around him, is always searching for meaning and so presuming, until evidence to the contrary becomes overwhelming, that there is a unity to things. One does not need to posit biblical typology as a source for this: it is inherent in human nature.

Frye's description of typology suggests that he may belong with Kermode and Josipovici as a critic who does not find shape and meaning in the world. At all events, he seems to suggest that he does not share what he calls 'our modern confidence'. This may be the reason behind the final step he takes on the question of the Bible's unity. More than most other critics, Frye is prepared to admit fragmentation and weaknesses into his view of the Bible, even to allow that there is a sense in which the Bible is as fragmentary a work as it is possible to have. It is 'a mosaic: a pattern of commandments, aphorisms, epigrams, proverbs ... and so on almost indefinitely' (p. 206), so it does not have the kind of unity associated with individual authorship. What's more, to pick a phrase out of context, 'anything that can go wrong with a book has gone wrong with the Bible' (p. 228). Finally, there is a real sense in which the Bible works through the unit of the verse, so that 'every sentence in it is a kind of linguistic monad ... as epiphanic and discontinuous as Rimbaud' (p. 209). So, along with the unifying elements there are disintegrative ones. Frye therefore offers this observation:

> It is remarkable that the Bible displays as much interest as it does in unifying its material ... But unity, a primary principle of works of art since Plato's time, also indicates the finiteness of the human mind, the *care* that works towards transforming the 'imperfect' or continuous into the 'perfect', the form achieved once and for all. The Bible, however unified, also displays a carelessness about unity, not because it fails to achieve it, but because it has passed through it to another perspective on the other side of it. We have now to try to get a glimpse or two of that wider perspective.
>
> (P. 207)

'The finiteness of the human mind' may, through contrast, invoke an idea of the infinite mind of God. Unity and perfection belong to the limited human mind, but there is something beyond that. Rather than approaching an area where faith fails, we may here be witnessing another step taken by faith. Frye attempts to give a glimpse of this further step, but it proves elusive. The closest he comes is the suggestion 'that faith has its dialectical opposite ... and must somehow combine with it. Doubt then ceases to be the enemy of faith and becomes its complement, and we see that the real enemy of faith is not doubt but merely the mental insensitivity that does not see what all the fuss is about' (p. 230).

This is very like Josipovici's final position, that we must read the Bible. For reading is the exercise of mental sensitivity, and it is this sensitivity that all these critics have been trying to foster as they encourage their readers to read the Bible. Whether in the end they write from despair or acceptance or faith – and whether indeed we can tell the three apart – this remains constant. It may seem a poor bottom line to religious believers, for, though there are faith-like qualities involved in reaching this position, there is precious little agreement on anything except that one should read. No common understanding of what one is reading emerges. The Bible may have a grand unity or may be made of local unities or may be a random pile of stones, some of them very diamonds. Critics do not tell us. Even if we take those who agree, for instance, that there is a grand unity, they do not agree as to how to describe it. For all that criticism is a faith-like activity, in the end it is a method of promoting and sharing sensitivity and insight. The nature of the insight is dictated not by the criticism but by the thing read.

CHAPTER 10

This (spiritual) treasure in earthen/earthenware/clay vessels/pots/jars

Introduction: two kinds of translations

'This treasure in earthen vessels' (2 Cor. 4: 7) served as the title for my opening chapter. It indicated the division between form and content in biblical thought. The content was of God, and we might read the form as the text of the Bible. The form was so much dross, setting off the divine beauty of the content. As Robert Gell, echoing Jerome, put it, 'such must the captive maid be . . . who must have her head shaven and her nails made to grow . . . and all means used to make her ugly and deformed . . . that the divine truth alone may be fair and beautiful in our sight' (volume 1, p. 262). Now, the division of form and content has proved to be one of the most constant ideas through this history, but the Pauline anti-aesthetic has not often been encountered since patristic times. In any period when it was possible to believe that the form of the Scriptures was beautiful, most of the faithful held that faith. Only when the form of the Bible was manifestly inadequate by contemporary aesthetic standards did people try to justify that inadequacy along the lines suggested by Paul. There have been three periods when the current form (or forms) of the Bible has appeared inadequate, the early Christian centuries when the standards of Athens and Rome reigned imperious, the Reformation, when the lowly vernaculars struggled not only to replace the Vulgate but to forge themselves into an acceptable single form, and the present.

Whatever differences there may be between the faiths of the two periods, as far as the history of the Bible is concerned the Reformation and the present are alike in that an old standard has ceased to command allegiance from a large range of sects, but has yet to be replaced by a new standard. The Vulgate was

400

archaic to the point of being arcane, and Christianity was a mystery religion. Moreover, the Vulgate was thought by its defenders to be truer than the Greek and Latin originals, and by its opponents to be inferior to them. The parallels with the KJB are obvious. The main difference, that the KJB is in a form of the still current language, is a matter of degree. In relation to contemporary Bibles, the KJB stands as the Vulgate stood in relation to the vernacular translations of the sixteenth century.

As in the Reformation, none of the new Bibles commands general, unreserved approval. There has never been a period like the present in terms of the variety of Bibles generally available and the lack of consistent ecclesiastical backing for any one version. In the large view the text has been totally destabilised, leaving a modernistic mélange like the title of this chapter. It is no wonder that literary critics have become coy of referring to any version.

One further parallel between the Reformation and the present is worth noting. From Tyndale onwards (with minor exceptions) the Protestants translated from the Hebrew and the Greek, and they tended to avoid language that sounded too like the Vulgate. The Catholics translated from the Vulgate and did their best to preserve its vocabulary. All the modern versions pretend to represent some form of the Hebrew and Greek originals, but they divide into two groups according to whether or not they show an allegiance to the modern equivalent of the Vulgate, that is, to the KJB. From the Revised Version through the American Standard Version, the Revised Standard Version, and the New King James Version to the New Revised Standard Version, there has been a sustained effort to retain the linguistic (and sometimes more than the linguistic) character of the KJB. Against this there has been a deliberate effort to avoid the language of the KJB and to translate or paraphrase into some form of contemporary English. Various kinds of translations contribute to this group. There are the numerous independent efforts, and a much smaller but growing number of versions made with substantial institutional support, beginning with the New English Bible (NEB), and including the Jerusalem Bible, the New Jerusalem Bible, the Good News Bible, the New International Version and the Revised English Bible. Some of these profess to be translations, some paraphrases.

The NEB, as the most revealing of the major contemporary-language translations, will be the focus of much of this chapter, but first, without intending any disrespect to several very important versions, we need to examine the use advertisers have made of the KJB's reputation in marketing a new form of the Bible, the electronic Bible, and one particular Bible, the New King James Version.

A commercial break: the New King James Version

The hero of Irving Wallace's *The Word* is the head of a public relations business. Personally in need of redemption, he turns out to be more honest than most of the characters in the novel. He is hired by Mission House – 'number one in the Bible publishing field. Way out in front of Zondervan, World, Harper and Row, Oxford, Cambridge, Regnery and all the rest' (p. 61) – to publicise the 'International New Testament'. Despite huge efforts to make Bibles freely available,[1] as Black's *Cambridge University Press* makes abundantly clear, money and the Bible have long gone together. Wallace narrates that 'when the firm of Thomas Nelson & Sons had brought out the Revised Standard Version in 1952, $500,000 had been spent on advertising alone. With his International New Testament, [the publisher] planned to spend double that amount' (p. 67). If we turn now to a few samples of the advertiser's art as it is currently employed, some light is shed on the present sense of the Bible as literature.

The most obvious development in Bible publishing in the last few years has been Bibles for personal computers. These began to be readily available in 1990. In this age of the hand-held electronic game, it was inevitable that there should also be what was advertised as 'the world's first hand-held electronic Bible', the Franklin Holy Bible (1989). The puff continues: 'Now, the poetic, inspirational qualities of the King James Bible combine with the latest linguistic technology. The result is a hand-held electronic unit which provides a new level of access to the most influential literature in the western world.' In short, technology meets poetry. The Franklin Holy Bible is more than a toy but less than a way of reading. It is a tool for searching the Scriptures somewhat more easily than with a concordance, a tool that nevertheless has to be sold on its miraculous technology and the aesthetic merits of the KJB. Perhaps the most significant fact about this twentieth-century answer to the man described as 'a living concordance', Henry Jessey, is that it has a 'large, four-line, 214-character LCD screen'. It can display a single verse at a time. So it presents the text of the Bible in a form almost as fragmentary as the one-line citations in a concordance. For all that the popular idea of the literary qualities of the KJB are used to sell this Bible, real reading is made impossible.

More useful are the variety of text-searching programs for personal

---

[1] In the fiscal year to 1990 the Gideon Society alone distributed 29 million Bibles to 147 countries. John Maxwell Hamilton uses these figures to support his claim that 'the Bible is clearly *the* most stolen book, an all-time favourite that people can't resist lifting' ('Is there a klepto in the stacks?', *New York Times Book Review*, (18 November 1990), 48).

computers. MacBible,[2] for instance, states on its packaging that it 'will revolutionise the way you study the Scriptures'. Study is indeed the point. Without making a good concordance such as Strong's obsolete,[3] macBible takes over most of its functions and not only makes them far easier to perform but allows one to search the text in new ways. Moreover, the user can now choose the text from a range that includes the Hebrew and the Greek, the KJB, the New International Version, the RSV and the New Revised Standard Version. This is what a theological or literary student of the text wants. Yet, like the Franklin Holy Bible, it places the emphasis on the fragmented text, isolated words and verses. From a literary point of view it would be irrelevant were it not that, like the old printed form of the Bible that Locke inveighed against, it tempts one away from continuous, contextual reading.

One of the most substantial and revealing of recent advertising campaigns has been mounted on behalf of the New King James Version (NKJV; NT 1979, OT 1982). It tells of AVolatry and the present state of popular ideas of the Bible as literature. The publisher is a later, fundamentalist incarnation of the one that spent half a million dollars on promotion of the RSV, Thomas Nelson Inc., of Nashville, Tennessee,[4] and the key element both in the making of the version and the campaign to sell it is the claim that, for all the improvements it makes, it *is* the KJB. This is implicit in the title, and one might take that as no more than a clever gimmick. Elsewhere it becomes explicit. Some editions of the complete NKJV have a dedication which begins, 'This edition of the Authorised Version of the Bible . . .'.[5] 'Edition', as in several places in the prefaces, is substituted for 'revision'.

The prefaces constitute the kind of evidence we have so frequently examined in the past. This time little more than a glance is necessary. The original introduction to the NT is presented as being by the publishers – in the light of Wallace's novel, a significant contrast with the KJB. It is a sometimes shrewd, sometimes plainly muddled combination of modernising principles and AVolatry. Following an apt opening reference to the KJB preface's claim not

---

[2] Grand Rapids, Mich.: Zondervan Electronic, 1990.
[3] One programme goes so far as to incorporate Strong's links to the Greek and the Hebrew.
[4] Jack P. Lewis gives a brief history of the NKJV's publishing background (*The English Bible from KJV to NIV: A History and Evaluation* (Grand Rapids, Mich.: Baker, 1981), pp. 329ff.).
[5] The designation and spelling 'Authorised Version' suggests this is peculiar to the British-usage text, first published as the Revised Authorised Version by Bagster (London, 1982). I take it from a Bible Society of Australia edition (Canberra, 1987).

'to make a new translation ... but to make a good one better', the publishers write:

> After nearly four hundred years, the King James is still deeply revered among English-speaking peoples throughout the world. This is in part due to the majesty of the form of the work, but also because it has been the mainspring of the religion, language, and legal foundations of our civilization. For these reasons the publishers have felt obliged to follow the method of the original translators – to produce a revised English edition which will unlock the spiritual treasures found uniquely in the King James Version of the Holy Scriptures.   (P. iii)

This is as slippery as wet soap. The KJB is *uniquely* a container of spiritual treasures, yet they are locked up, so a revision must be made. The revision is identical, so the unique character is retained, but different so that the treasures are unlocked. Moreover, they are unlocked by pursuing the same method as the original KJB translators followed. Were this not mere vagueness, seeking, like the title, to give the new the nimbus of the old, one might ask a series of questions, the first being whether the rules of translation laid down for the KJB were actually followed. But what is most important is the character of the AVolatry. The KJB is presented first as a classic, majestic in form (though what is meant by form is indeterminable) and fundamental to religion, language and the law. In short, it is the KJB's cultural character that is given first place, as it might be by secular literary people and historians. One would therefore expect the language of the KJB to be the shaping principle of the 'edition', as if, perhaps, the KJB were more inspired than the Greek originals.

This turns out not to be the shaping principle. The preface slithers around until at last it arrives fairly in the camp of such luminaries as Wilkinson, Hills and Chick. First, all the 'competent scholars' who worked on the NKJV 'have signed a document of subscription to the plenary and verbal inspiration of the original autographs of the Bible' (p. v). Second, 'of greater importance than the beauty of the language in the King James Version is the textual base from which that work was translated' (p. v). So it seems that, as with most versions, accuracy precedes beauty.

Such a preface might wisely have been scrapped. The complete NKJV does the next best thing: it rewrites it with some intelligence. The confusions are diminished. Here is part of its revision of the paragraph just quoted:

> For nearly four hundred years, and throughout several revisions, the King James Bible has been deeply revered among the English-speaking peoples of the world. The quality of translation for which it is historically renowned, and its majesty of style, have enabled that monumental version of the Word of God to make a unique contribution to the religion and language of the English-speaking world.   (P. iii)

'Several revisions' ought to arouse suspicion, but the crucial change is that 'quality of translation' has been placed ahead of the old cliché, 'majesty of style'. The preface continues:

> The King James translators were committed to producing an English Bible that would be a precise translation, and by no means a paraphrase or a broadly approximate rendering. On the one hand, the scholars were fully familiar with the original languages of the Bible and were especially gifted in their use of their native English. On the other hand, their reverence for the divine Author and his Word assured a translation of the Scriptures in which only a principle of utmost accuracy could be accepted.
>
> In 1786 the Catholic scholar, Alexander Geddes, said of the King James Bible, 'if accuracy and strictest attention to the letter of the text be supposed to constitute an excellent version, this is of all versions the most excellent'... Therefore, while seeking to unveil the excellent *form* of the traditional English Bible, special care has also been taken in the present edition to preserve the work of *precision* which is the legacy of the 1611 translators. (P. iii)

We might first exclaim at the use of Geddes as an authority, not merely because there has been so much biblical scholarship since his day, but because it was his judgement 'that James's translators have less merit than any of their predecessors' (*General Answer*, p. 4); if one reads the quoted commendation in context (*Prospectus*, p. 92), it is much less than it seems. 'Accuracy and strictest attention to the letter' were not Geddes's priorities as a translator. But the main point is the changed sense of the KJB. The primary characteristic of its legacy is now its literalness. Even in the translation which most blatantly seeks to preserve aesthetic qualities, in the end accuracy, however conceived, is placed first. AVolatry now acclaims literalness as the KJB's primary quality, with the extraordinary result of implying that the KJB is still a totally accurate translation.

The blurb on the unlovely orange dustjacket of the NT concludes that the NKJV 'makes the King James even better for twentieth century readers'. Four endorsements elaborate on this. Here is one:

> In my humble opinion, it was the providence of the elective purpose of God that drew together those scholars who produced the King James Version of the Bible in 1611. God knew that the English world needed one great common denominator. The New King James Bible takes the King James Version and brings it up to this present moment. It is still the great authoritative, fundamental book that we have used for centuries.   Dr W. A. Criswell, Pastor, Dallas, Texas

If one can swallow the combination of inspiration, oldness and newness that this depicts, then here is the perfect Bible. And it is precisely the aim of the NKJV's publicists to convey this impression.

A 1989 brochure from Nelson explains 'Why the New King James is the World's Fastest Growing Translation'. Under that caption a freckled, gap-toothed child in pyjamas grins unconvincingly as he holds up a Precious Moments Bible. Inside one reads, 'The New King James Version Is: Accurate. Faithful to the words and structures of God's message contained in the original language'. 'Language', singular, is amusing. Beneath this, a greying man, in jacket and tie, a gold band on his ring finger, holds 'the New King James Version Open Bible, one of the world's best-selling study Bibles'. On the next panel a charming oriental girl in a peplum jacket displays what looks like a handbag in matching blue: 'Beautiful. Contemporary language is set forth in the literary style of the classic King James. Shown here is our attractive New King James Version Shoulder Strap Bible, ideal for today's active Christian woman.' 'Set forth' as 'contemporary language' is also amusing. On the third panel, headed 'Complete', a grandparental couple (he also in jacket and tie, she in another blue jacket) seem to be sharing amusement at something in 'our Family Reference Bible, in which you'll find study references, a family register, family devotions, illustrated stories for children, much more!'

Opening out the last fold, one finds the gap-toothed boy again (his pyjamas are light blue). A blonde girl in a blue dress holds 'the Reader's Companion Bible, which helps youngsters learn more about the Scriptures through the eye-catching graphics of its colorful, information-packed "Reader's Companion" section'. A blond teenage boy chats happily to an Afro-American girl; she carries 'the colorful New King James Version Textbook edition', he 'The Transformer, the best-selling youth Bible that features guidance from top youth evangelists'. The pictures say it all: this is the all-American, middle-American, Bible. It comes in all forms for all ages.

The further explanations of 'accurate', 'beautiful' and 'complete' confirm the sense of perfection. 'If you believe the original Greek texts were given by the Holy Spirit Himself, then you will feel comfortable with the New King James Version. The NKJV is a complete translation based on these texts, thus it presents the entire message contained in the words and structures of the original language.' So 'accuracy' (not an obvious quality of the words just quoted) means no more than translating from inspired originals. Middle America's fundamentalism is a key to selling this Bible.

This is how the miracle of being in the language of the KJB and yet modernised is conveyed:

> Some Bible readers and church congregations are concerned that perhaps the archaic language of the old King James turns off younger Christians, yet many congregations still wish to memorise God's word and read it aloud together, as is traditional with the King James. The New King James answers these concerns by making use of contemporary language presented in elegant literary style. It is clear yet retains the dignity and beauty of the classic King James. Therefore it is ideal for public speaking and church use.

The miracle is to be at once old and new, yet is not this a perpetual aim of religion? It has to be eternal truth, the truth we have always known, even if, perchance, we happen to say 'mumpsimus'. Yet is has also to be revelation, and revelation always feels new.

One last thing might catch our eye, the claim that the NKJV 'preserves words that are basic to our Christian vocabulary – words like righteousness, redemption, atonement, sanctification'. The list may be only four words long, but it is in the identical spirit to the list of words which Bishop Stephen Gardiner in 1542 'desired for their germane and native meaning and for the majesty of their matter might be retained as far as possible in their own nature' (see volume 1, p. 115). For all that the NKJV comes from fundamentalist sources, it represents the same conservative desire for the old truth and the old beauty that was so strong in the Roman Catholic resistance to the Reformation. Yesterday's Catholics are indeed today's Protestants. Times change, and names change with them, but human nature keeps a remarkable consistency.

According to the brochure, 'the world's fastest growing translation comes in over 35 editions, from the new Precious Moments Baby Bible to the Transformer Bible for youth to the New Scofield Study Edition'. One of these, the New Open Bible: New King James Version, is pushed so hard that a sampler booklet is available which includes the whole of John. But the cover says all that we need to attend to: 'The study edition that speaks for itself. A personal Study Bible that provides a sweeping overview of Scripture and pinpoints the answers you seek'. The greatest publicity effort for this perfect version is reserved for its incarnation as a study Bible. And one realises that among the 'over 35 editions' there is no NKJV 'designed to be read as literature'. In the end it is not merely a case of accuracy triumphing over beauty: the thought that anyone might want a straightforward reading text is, if considered at all, rejected as uncommercial. The literary qualities of the Bible are all very well for a publisher so long as they help to sell a version, but he has no other interest in them if the public, while happy to believe that what it is reading is great literature, does not want to read it in a literary way. In spite of continuing claims, and in spite of a flourishing industry of academic literary commentary on the Scriptures, the Bible remains firmly enshrined in the world of religion.

The New English Bible

Aims

The most interesting of the independent translations for the purposes of this study is the NEB. In the larger historical context created by the appearance in 1989 of the Revised English Bible it now appears as a stage in an outstanding process of translation sustained over nearly half a century. But it is as a pioneering translation that it commands attention, for it shows certain problems at their most acute and, as a result, aroused more heated debate than any other modern version. That debate focussed modern literary argument about the Bible in English and so is the inevitable culmination of many of the major themes of this history.

Though the NEB was an ecumenical translation, it was made entirely by British scholars. Moreover, the most important discussion of its literary and religious value took place within a specifically Anglican context. As a result there is a narrowing of national and sectarian focus in taking it as the last translation for study. Most of the narrowing is superficial, for the ideas themselves are neither national nor sectarian. Even so, one may detect something like a high-church idea of religion shaping the arguments of those hostile to the NEB, and to that extent the focus is unavoidably narrowed.

In his valuable but too brief account of the making of the NEB, Geoffrey Hunt begins his description of 'the object in view' thus: 'it goes without saying that a translation – especially of the Bible – must be faithful to the original. The first duty of translators, therefore, is to understand the meaning of the original as completely as they can' (p. 19). The tone rightly suggests that this is not the most important point about the NEB. It was indeed a step forward in terms of scholarship: textual advances produced by, among other things, the Dead Sea Scrolls and advances in understanding of the original languages, helped by discoveries of a large number of contemporary manuscripts, were fully utilised. But the same might be said of the RSV before, and of a number of versions after. What made the NEB unique as an ecclesiastical committee translation was its linguistic aim. All the previous mainstream versions from the Great Bible through the KJB and the RV to the RSV had been revisions within an established linguistic framework. The NEB set out to be a completely new translation. It went back to Tyndale's aim of writing for the 'boy that driveth the plough' (volume 1, p. 96) in that it sought to be an ordinary-language version. Its origin lay in the feeling that the language of the K JB had become a barrier to the communication of the Bible to the people.

Archbishop Donald Coggan's preface to the NEB notes that, prior to the Second World War, Oxford and Cambridge University Presses had contemplated a revision in the K JB tradition, but that a new, independent suggestion was made as the war drew to a close:

> In May 1946 the General Assembly of the Church of Scotland received an overture from the Presbytery of Stirling and Dunblane, where it had been initiated by the Reverend G. S. Hendry, recommending that a translation of the Bible be made in the language of the present day, inasmuch as the language of the Authorised Version, already archaic when it was made, had now become even more definitely archaic and less generally understood.   (P. v)

A large number of churches recommended 'that a completely new translation should be made ... and that the translators should be free to employ a contemporary idiom rather than reproduce the traditional "biblical" English'. Hunt gives some further explanation of these decisions:

> The experience of many British pastors, chaplains, teachers and youth leaders in the War of 1939–45, when they were trying under difficult conditions to expound and convey the message of the Bible, was that very frequently the language of the Authorised Version was not a help but a hindrance. It was beautiful and solemn, but it put a veil of unreality between the scriptural writers and the people of the mid-twentieth century who needed something that would speak to them immediately. 'Whenever we have a certain time to teach a particular Bible passage', was the complaint, 'we have to spend half that time giving an English lesson, "translating" the Bible English into the current language of today. We need a Bible translation in which this is already done for us; then we can start from where people actually are and give them the Bible message in language they understand.'   (Pp. 9–10)

At times the stress varies. C. H. Dodd sounds more traditional in writing that the intention was to provide 'English readers, whether familiar with the Bible or not, with a faithful rendering of the best available Greek text into the current speech of our own time, and a rendering which should harvest the gains of recent biblical scholarship' (introduction to the NT, p. v). Faithful scholarship seems here to have the priority, as it did in previous ecclesiastical versions. No doubt this reflects the thinking of most of the scholars who worked on the translation. Yet their scholarship was serving a purpose: it was not an end in itself. And that purpose, dictated by the original suggestion and the war experience, was linguistic.

The growth of AVolatry had made the language of an English translation a major issue. Up to this point it had also settled the issue: Bibles should be in Bible English. As long as this was to be the outcome, the work of revision could – as Bois's and Wright's notes have shown – concentrate on matters of scholarship. The NEB's change of language shifted the balance, with the result that it belongs with the large group of maverick translations, including Harwood's and Jordan's, in which a linguistic purpose shapes the work. This at first sight is odd company, especially when Harwood's name is invoked. Most of these translations were made with the intention of achieving some sort of appropriate beauty of translation. They put beauty ahead of literal faithfulness. But now that beauty had become so associated with the KJB, to choose to translate into a new idiom could be an anti-aesthetic move.

A good many reviewers thought that the translators had deliberately set out to destroy the beauty of the Bible. Certainly they set out as far as possible to avoid the English of the KJB, but ideas of the literary beauty of the Bible were inescapable. This is clearest in Dodd's memorandum, written at an early stage of the work in his capacity as General Director, entitled 'Purpose and intention of the project'. Dodd first distinguishes three kinds of reader, those outside the Church who are put off by the language of the KJB, the young, 'for whom the Bible, if it is to make any impact, must be "contemporary"', and those for whom it is too familiar to engage their minds.[6] The language appropriate for reaching such an audience is clearly of more importance than scholarly faithfulness. This is how Dodd goes on to describe it:

> With this tripartite public in view, we aim at a version which shall be as intelligible to contemporary readers as the original was to its first readers – or as nearly so as possible. It is to be genuinely English in idiom ... avoiding equally both archaisms and transient modernisms. The version should be plain enough to convey its meaning to any reasonably intelligent person (as far as verbal expression goes), yet not bald or pedestrian. It should *not* aim at preserving 'hallowed associations'; it *should* be without pedantry. It is to be hoped that, at least occasionally, it may produce arresting and memorable renderings. It should have sufficient dignity to be read aloud. Although it is not intended primarily to be read in church, we should like to think that it may prove worthy to be read occasionally, even at public worship ... We should like to produce ... a translation which may in some measure succeed in removing a real barrier between a large proportion of our fellow-countrymen and the truth of the Holy Scriptures.

---

[6] Hunt gives part of this memorandum, pp. 22–3. In contrast with the RV, the full text of this and other relevant documents such as the Joint Committee's statement of principles have not been published.

Hunt, writing with the authority of an Oxford University Press staff member concerned with editing religious books during the whole period of work, takes this as expressing 'an objective which had been in the minds of many of those concerned with the translation', and adds: 'how far it was carried out, for the Bible as a whole, the reader of the NEB can now begin to judge'.[7] Nevertheless, the more ambitious aesthetic aims – 'arresting and memorable renderings' and 'sufficient dignity to be read aloud' – are omitted from the prefaces. If this is not just a case of sensible modesty, it may be that the translators were not confident that the aims had been achieved. In that case there is no real contradiction in the later statements that the version was not intended for reading aloud.

The closest the prefaces come to implying aesthetic ambitions is Coggan's phrase in the general preface, 'a delicate sense of English style' (p. v). This comes in connection with a major innovation in the method of translation. There was a Joint Committee and three panels, one for each part of the Bible, and a literary panel. Coggan explains: 'apprehending, however, that sound scholarship does not necessarily carry with it a delicate sense of English style, the [joint] committee appointed a fourth panel, of trusted literary advisers, to whom all the work of the translating panels was to be submitted for scrutiny'. Taking the words of the KJB preface as they appear to a contemporary reader rather than as they were intended, this panel was to rub and polish the translation. It was to do what Kipling envisaged Shakespeare doing for the KJB. Rule 8 for the making of the RV, that literary men among others should be referred to for their opinions, is elevated into a major part of the whole process.[8] Thus the long growth of literary ideas of the Bible is inescapably formalised in the making of a new translation. Moreover, for good or ill, the separation between form and content which is to be found in the Bible and which makes translation possible is, for the first time, reflected in the formal process of translation.[9] One committee dealt with the content, one with the form, and one with the combined result.

---

[7] P. 23. Hunt's own statement of the aim is that 'what was wanted was a Bible combining the highest scholarly authority with an English style which would not put it at a disadvantage when set beside the classic English Bible' (p. 15).

[8] The revisers, it will be remembered, did no more than consult with the First Sea Lord for nautical terms in Acts 27. The NEB translators are said to have been advised by an amateur yachtsman for the same passage (above, p. 221n; Nineham, p. 109). This might be an emblem of the democratising tendency some critics find in the translation.

[9] Few critics have noticed this point, and none have made it favourably. Ian Robinson implies a negative judgement (e.g., p. 41). Prickett, in an article that has much in common with Robinson, is blunt. He sees it as a 'disastrous distinction' reflecting a 'kind of naivety about language' ('What do the translators think they are up to?', *New Universities Quarterly* 33 (1979), 259–68; p. 259).

If we were to judge from Philip Larkin's account of his experiences as a member of the literary panel,[10] we might conclude that this panel was no more than a pious gesture to the religion of beauty, and therefore that, as in the other major revisions, aesthetic matters, if granted any importance at all, were of least importance. However, the published accounts of how the panel operated give a different picture. The literary panel was an integral part of the project, and every bit of the translation had to receive not only its consideration but its approval. Dennis Nineham's is the best summary of how the panel fitted into the whole process:

> The seven members of the [NT] translators' panel divided the various books ... between them and each one produced a draft translation of the books assigned to him. These drafts were then circulated to all the members, who worked on them at a series of residential conferences until a version had been arrived at on which all could agree. In this form it was passed on to the literary panel, whose members, without necessarily claiming any expert knowledge of the original language, were equipped to judge the translators' work from the point of view of its English style. They could say, in effect: 'this may be what the Greek means, but it is not good current English; we suggest such and such amendments'. To which the panel of translators was free to reply: 'the amended version may be good English but it is not what the Greek means' – and so the dialogue between the two panels would go on until a version was reached which satisfied the members of both. At this stage a book was ready for the comments of the joint committee and if passed by them, was filed to await the process of final revision when all the books had passed both panels and could be reviewed together.
>
> (P. xi)

The one moderately detailed account of the working of the literary panel only corrects this in one minor respect. The author, Basil Willey, a much-respected English don, was a member of the literary panel through the full period of the work. Much of the dialogue between the translators and the literary panel took place within the meetings of the literary panel. The convener of the appropriate translation panel attended the literary panel's meetings to ensure, as Willey recalls, 'that, in our zeal for English style, we did not depart from the true meaning of the text' ('On translating', p. 12).

---

[10] Above, p. 326n. Larkin's account has only a tenuous relationship to the other accounts, and it is clear that his involvement was indeed brief. The NEB dispensed with the services of the one poet of stature originally involved in the project. His name does not appear in Hunt's list of members of the panel, though he was later a literary adviser to the Revised English Bible. Some of the panel are still remembered as critics; few are now remembered as writers. They were: Professor Sir Roger Mynors, Professor Basil Willey, Sir Arthur Norrington, Mrs Anne Ridler, the Rt Rev. A. T. P. Williams, the Rev. Canon Adam Fox, Dr John Carey, Sir Herbert Grierson, Mr F. H. Kendon, the Very Rev. E. Milner-White and Mr W. F. Oakeshott.

Willey's article divides in two. Much of it is an exceptionally perceptive and lucid account of the KJB and some of the issues involved in the making of the NEB. He notes, for instance, that 'the old translators achieved literary distinction largely because they were not self-consciously aiming at it ... Like all good style, theirs was a by-product; aiming at truth, they achieved beauty without effort or contrivance' (p. 2). It is a neat formulation. He goes on to remark 'how fortunate it was that the accepted English translation was made when it was, and not (for instance) in the eighteenth century' (p. 3), as he shows by some judicious specimens from Harwood. What he does not note is that Harwood aimed at literary distinction through effort and contrivance. Indeed, Harwood's aims sound in part like those of the NEB, to 'clothe the genuine ideas and doctrines of the apostles with that propriety and perspicuity in which they themselves ... would have exhibited them had they *now* lived and written in our language' (above, p. 86). Nevertheless, Willey recognises that the NEB might be an effort of the same sort: 'should we perhaps be producing something which, *mutatis mutandis*, might appear later as absurd as Dr Harwood's version now appears to ourselves?'.[11] Some critics would answer in the affirmative: for better or worse, everyday English for the man in the street, that is, proper, perspicuous English, is as much the fetish of the present day as neo-classical elegance was to the Augustans.

Having so praised the KJB, Willey tackles the question of the need for a new translation. This leads him to dispraise. He is one of the few critics to produce examples of bad English in the KJB. He sees the main reason for such failures as the KJB's tendency, especially in obscure passages, to rely on word-for-word translation. After examples such as 'the noise thereof sheweth concerning it, the cattle also concerning the vapour' (Job 36: 33),[12] he comments:

> Those who exalt Bible English as the grandest and noblest in our literature ignore this kind of thing. And there is something else they overlook, namely the constant

[11] P. 4. One critic has indeed hinted that the NEB produced Harwood-like revisions. Commenting on the change from 'his own soul' to 'his true self' in Mark 8: 36, Patrick Cruttwell notes 'that just as Harwood's eighteenth-century language changed the Lord of Hosts into the "great governor and parent of universal Nature", so this change transmutes the Redeemer and Messiah into a platitudinous psychiatrist' ('Fresh skins for new wine', *Hudson Review* 23 (1970), 546–56; p. 551).

[12] Ronald Knox, the Roman Catholic translator, chooses Mark 7: 3 as an example of bad English: 'For the Pharisees, and all the Jews, except they wash their hands oft, eat not, holding the tradition of the elders' (*On Englishing the Bible* (London: Burns Oates, 1949), p. 4). Nineham cites 2 Cor. 6: 11–13: 'O ye Corinthians, our mouth is open unto you, our heart is enlarged. Ye are not straitened in us, but ye are straitened in your own bowels. Now for a recompense in the same, (I speak as unto my children,) be ye also enlarged' (p. xiin). And surely a literary panel would never have approved Zech. 2: 6, 'Ho, ho, come forth, and flee from the land of the north, saith the LORD.'

failure of the old translators to translate, i.e. to render Hebrew or Greek idioms, constructions and modes of speech by English counterparts. Too often they simply transliterate and give us mongrel English which we tolerate only because we are accustomed to hearing it in church.   (Pp. 6–7)

'Mongrel English': this is intended as a condemnation, yet it identifies one of the sources of the KJB's strength. One begins to suspect that Willey's brief, to care for the English of the translation as good modern English, has blinded him to strengths in the originals, strengths which the KJB has reflected. Indeed, it seems that the members of the panel felt that, as well as avoiding the language of the KJB, they should avoid reflecting any characteristics of the originals that were not also characteristics of contemporary English. So Willey's most curious revelation is that the literary panel at first tried, like Blackmore (see above, p. 23) and many another paraphraser before it, to get rid of parallelism:

This method of poetic utterance is foreign to the English mind and language, and the NEB translators at first struggled hard, whenever they could, to make one statement out of the two without losing whatever was significant in either. In the end, however, they were forced to give up and admit defeat; there was far too much of this kind of thing for even their patience and ingenuity to cope with – it was like trying to change the colour of the Ethiopian's skin.   (P. 8)

The last image, biblical of course, slips in too easily. Throughout, Willey writes (as did Harwood) in terms that separate form from content: it is clear that the panel would, if possible, have changed the Ethiopian's skin and the leopard's spots in order to do good. But there have to be limits, and translators in the end have not the freedom of the paraphrasers to make an absolute separation between meaning and expression.

Willey's remarks on parallelism may suggest some naivety about translation that a judicious reading of Lowth might have cured (see above, p. 69) – though naivety, as I observed in connection with Tyndale, is often a valuable aid in the accomplishment of a major task. But eighteen years of active involvement in translation must eventually have left the literary panel with a highly practical sense of the possibilities of its task. The latter part of Willey's article is a fascinating glimpse of the panel at work. He calls it 'a few dramatised passages from a typical Old Testament session' (p. 12). It seems to belong somewhere between Kipling's '"Proofs of Holy Writ"' and Bois's notes on the KJB or Wright's notes on the RV, but, in the key matter of authenticity, it belongs with Bois and Wright. In the absence of other such evidence, Willey's account is most useful if taken in the way he suggests, 'as representative rather than actual' (p. 13).

Not being free to mention names, he identifies the speakers by letters. Only one of them, 'R' for Rabbi, the representative of the OT panel, is identifiable, Godfrey Driver. One might guess at some further identities from the following reminiscence by Michael Black, who attended the NEB literary panel and was later one of the literary advisers for the Revised English Bible:

> The Literary Panel was ... preponderantly Anglican, and what's more Oxford-dominated. The two most powerful personalities were Roger Mynors and Driver (who attended as translator, but often swayed the argument). Old Canon Fox was literary in some way I don't remember, and AVolatrous. Anne Ridler was a poet (ex-secretary to T. S. Eliot). Frank Kendon was at CUP – also a poet. In one way or another, all the members were keenly sensitive to language, and the discussions – as Willey's reminiscence shows – were quite subtle. But the result was as it was.
>
> Dodd came sometimes. I remember him saying, 'Of course, what we'd all say *now* is...', and then he'd come out with some very 1930ish upper middle class English idiom, already pretty faded. I felt it was characteristic of the general tone of the translation: what the critics seized on. I also remember wanting to argue for 'tares', but refraining. The argument would have been that nobody would recognise a tare if they saw one, but some people *did* know that these were weeds which an enemy planted in your corn. Nobody knew what 'darnel' was either, but it didn't have the sanctified association ['darnel' was substituted for 'tares'] ... I suppose my general point is: this was another world, not ours, and our unaltered language won't do insofar as it reflects our world only (our thought-world, to use Lawrence's term).
>
> (Letter to the author)

'As in all human discussions of whatever kind', Willey notes, 'we had a right-wing and a left; the radicals, who wanted down-to-earth "contemporary" language, and the conservatives who stood out for dignity, and often preferred closeness to the AV. A good many of the discussions centred upon the questions: "What *is* 'contemporary' English?" and "What *is* obsolete?"' (p. 13). The notations in square brackets are Willey's, the passage is from 1 Samuel 19. Given the uniquenes of this account, I quote it at some length:

The Rabbi reads aloud:

R. 'Saul spoke to Jonathan his son and all his servants about killing David. But Saul's son Jonathan was (much attached to (very fond of)) David, and said to him, "My father Saul is seeking to kill you. Be careful tomorrow morning, and stay quietly in hiding. Then I will come out and join my father ... and if I find anything amiss I will tell you." Jonathan spoke well of David to his father Saul, and said to him, "Sir, do not sin against your servant David, for he has not sinned against you; his conduct towards you has been exemplary. He risked his life and slew the Philistine . . . why should you sin against an innocent man and put David to death for no reason?'''

Pause

A. What about 'servants'? Is that the right shade of meaning?

R. No, not really; it means his entourage, his personal attendants at court. 'Retinue'? No, that suggests a procession.

A. 'Household'? [*Agreed*]

B. In the next sentence, do we need to say 'Saul's son' again?

R. Well, it's in the Hebrew, but I agree: let's leave it out.

C. I don't like either of the alternatives 'much attached to' and 'very fond of'; the first suggests offhand and the second commonplace. I suggest 'devoted to'. [*Agreed*] And 'be careful' is so colourless.

R. Yes, and the Hebrew means 'look after yourself'. Why not 'be on your guard'? [*Agreed*]

D. I'm not happy about 'sin against'. 'Sin' isn't a contemporary idea anyway, but quite apart from that the phrase is archaic. 'Do not wrong your servant David'? [*Agreed*]

C. 'His conduct . . . has been exemplary' – I feel that this phrase is out of a different sort of book, or perhaps a school report. 'Blameless' would be better, I think. [*Agreed*][13]

B. I'm not sure about 'for no reason'. The question begins with 'why', which means 'for what reason', so you're really saying 'for what reason should you . . . put David to death for no reason?' 'Without cause' would perhaps still be open to the same objection, but less so, I think.

C. Oh dear, aren't we getting rather hyper-subtle? Still, 'without cause' is all right, and rhythmically a much nicer concluding phrase than 'for no reason'. [*Agreed*]

Chairman. Shall we go on?

C. Just one little point, my lord. I think we're in danger all the time of becoming flat and prosy. So much that was picturesque and vigorous in the AV has to be sacrificed that we should neglect no chance of putting a bit of life into our version. Here, for instance: 'He risked his life and slew the Philistine' – if we put this in the form of a rhetorical question it would at once enliven the passage: 'Did he not take his life in his hands and slay the Philistine?'

R. Oh yes, that's all right. It's not a question in the Hebrew, but I'm sure the OT panel will accept that.
                                                          (Pp. 13–14)

A discussion of whether 'slay' is archaic follows. To *C*'s sorrow, the committee decides that it is and adopts 'kill' instead. His rhetorical question, born out of a

---

[13] The NEB reads 'beyond reproach'.

desire to enliven the text, became 'Did he not take his life in his hands when he killed the Philistine?'

So far Willey has shown the translators leaving the literary panel a choice of phrases – 'much attached to' or 'very fond of' – and the panel working in a variety of ways. The members scrutinise shades of meaning, and it quickly becomes apparent that the translators were not necessarily precise in the choice of phrases offered to the literary panel: 'be careful' is not only colourless but a weak representation of the Hebrew. Archaism, register and rhythm are all considered, and then comes the revelation in the acceptance of *C*'s rhetorical question, that the translators, collectively, felt themselves free to rewrite the original. If grammar can be altered even when a correct representation of the original grammar makes satisfactory English, the line between translation and improvement would seem to have been crossed. Literary considerations override faithfulness, and, for a moment, the translators are placed firmly in Harwood's camp.

Soon afterwards Willey gives an example that most readers would probably agree stays on the translation side of the line. The translators proposed the following verses 9–10:

> An evil spirit from the Lord came upon Saul; he was sitting in the house holding his spear and David was playing the harp. Saul tried to pin David to the wall, but he broke away from Saul's presence so that Saul drove the spear into the wall.
>
> (Pp. 14–15)

Among the comments are these by *E*:

> 'Sitting in the house holding his spear' – I don't like two '-ings' so close together; and besides, doesn't this suggest that 'holding his spear' was (so to speak) Saul's whole-time occupation just then? I suggest 'with his spear in his hand'. And aren't there too many 'Saul's' in this passage? Why not say 'he broke away from the King's presence and Saul drove...'. etc.
>
> (P. 15)

The objection to the '-ings' starts as a perhaps pedantic matter of style but suddenly transforms itself into a sharp perception of the implications of the phrasing. 'With his spear in his hand' changes the grammar (Willey does not indicate how the proposed versions relate to the Hebrew), and so avoids potentially risible implications while giving an appropriate sense of the importance of the observation. However, the substitution of pronoun for noun that follows is a matter of changing the Ethiopian's skin exactly as Purver had done (above, p. 78).

Willey reports that the panel agreed to both these suggestions. But what finally appeared was this (the changes from the draft are italicised):

> An evil spirit from the Lord came upon Saul *as* he was sitting in the house *with his spear in his hand*; and David was playing the harp. Saul tried to pin David to the wall *with the spear*, but he *avoided the king's thrust* so that Saul drove the spear into the wall.

Not all the suggestions agreed to in the literary panel were adopted, which is no more than one would expect. 'Avoided the king's thrust' is a change of sense made by the translators at a later stage. Similar inconsistencies in Kipling's story implied a quiet criticism of the KJB, but here the implication is that Willey worked from his own authentic record of what the literary panel said and decided, for he has not attempted to make his account consistent with what eventually appeared.

The next part of the discussion again concerns archaism. *C*, the real conservative on the panel, suggests that the translation may preserve fine words that are on the verge of obsolescence. *A* suggests this is 'rather a dangerous argument', and Willey notes, 'prolonged wrangle sets in' (p. 16). The conservative line loses, and the implication is that the NEB rejected the idea that it had a duty to preserve language.

The last part of Willey's dramatisation concerns poetry, part of David's lament over Jonathan and Saul (2 Sam. 1: 19–20). Again *C*, playing the part Dean Stanley played in the RV (above, p. 231), is the central figure:

The Rabbi reads from David's lament over Jonathan and Saul

R.   The flower of the nation lies slain upon your
            heights, O Israel!
        Fallen are the warriors.
        Do not tell it in Gath,
        Do not proclaim it in the streets of Ashkelon!

C. (*warming to a congenial opportunity*) Now of course this is *poetry*, and different canons of translation must be applied. We're allowed a more elevated diction and various rhetorical devices; and this makes an appeal to everyday modern usage irrelevant. So let's begin:
        O flower of the nation lying slain!
        The men of war are fallen;
        Fallen they lie upon your heights, O Israel!   [*General approval*]
Well then, if we're allowed so much – if we're allowed such a departure from prose order as the inversion 'Fallen they lie', why not go on:
        Tell it not in Gath,
        Publish it not in the streets of Ashkelon?

G.   B-b-but this is pure AV! Just the sort of thing we've been directed to avoid!

C. I know, I know; but what is the alternative? 'Do not tell it in Gath' – could anything be more utterly banal and hopeless? It's terrible how much the English language has lost in ceasing to use 'not' after an imperative, and putting in 'do'. How much finer is 'Fear not', or 'Judge not', than 'Do not fear', 'Do not judge'! I think in this poetic context 'Tell it not' is permissible. And as for its being an AV phrase, 'Tell it not in Gath' is so familiar as to have become an English saying; and any re-wording will appear as just what it is – a mere attempt *not* to use an AV phrase.

G. Hm. It's arguable. Very well, I'll agree – but not without misgiving.

(Pp. 16–17)

C's trap is neatly laid. He does not try to preserve 'how are the mighty fallen', but sets a style that leads to direct quotation from the KJB. He has proved this to be *the* style for poetic translation. And in this instance he almost wins the day: 'publish' was later changed to 'proclaim'. The normal deliberate avoidance of KJB language is set aside. Willey takes us no further. Moreover, there is nothing in the article to indicate which of the speakers he himself might be except that he probably is not *C*. He concludes as any one of this group of translators might, making a clear separation between medium and message and reminding his reader of a point he has made several times, that for many the KJB is no more than a 'numinous rumble' (p. 5):

> Those who talk of 'loss' – loss of mystery, awesomeness, ceremony and so on – should make very certain that they themselves, in responding to the AV, have not mistaken a sort of liturgical trance for true understanding and spiritual discernment. Much of the Bible has an enduring message and admonition for every age; and it is hoped that readers, seeing clearly at last what it is saying, may find their consciences disturbed at points formerly protected by the comfortable sonorities of the old version. The translation was made in the belief that the Bible's message had for too long been embalmed in beautiful or familiar archaism, and that it was high time to let it speak home to our condition.
>
> (P. 17)

Reception

Willey's dramatisation is, as I suggested, closer to Bois's or Wright's notes than to Kipling's story in that it is more nearly authentic than fictional. But in another sense the dramatisation is as much the counterpart of Bois's notes as Kipling's story is. In Bois's notes there was every indication of concern for correctness of understanding and accuracy of rendering, but minimal concern for aesthetic qualities. Willey's dramatisation, though representing only part of the process, takes us almost as far in the other direction. Like the very existence of the literary panel whose activity it recreates, it is eloquent testimony to the change in attitude to the nature of the Bible that has taken place. Even if the intention is as narrow as to make the Bible's message 'speak home to our condition', a literary awareness of the Bible pervades the business of translation. The NEB may be the first ecclesiastical translation in modern dress, but it is as much dominated by the literary success of the KJB as the RV and its successors. *They* reflect that domination by preservation; the NEB reflects it by reaction.

The NEB's reception similarly reflects the changed spirit. All there was of contemporary reaction to the KJB was Broughton's disconsolate anathematising. Nineham was able to fill a book with responses to the NEB, and yet leave much unrecorded. From the point of view of this history the most interesting responses are the hostile ones, for they are the ones most concerned with literary questions. Nevertheless, a brief sample of the favourable responses to the NT, taken from Nineham's collection, will be useful, not least because it is a new sight to see a major version received with substantial applause.

G. B. Caird exclaimed: 'into the new version of the New Testament have gone the accumulated learning and wisdom of a century of scholarship, and what a magnificent and exciting achievement it is! The translators have aimed at accuracy and clarity and have achieved dignity and beauty as well' (p. 32). Now, Caird was a member of the Apocrypha panel, but he voices the sentiments of many reviewers. With a generosity and sympathy uncommon among rivals and literary scholars, the popular translator J. B. Phillips declared the NEB NT 'a magnificent and memorable accomplishment' (p. 135). For him this was the word of God reborn in English. He continues:

> There is an evenness of texture which runs through the whole volume – not, of course, the evenness of style which is so evident in the version of 1611, but a kind of common spiritual authority which binds the various authors together. They obviously have access to the same living God. If they speak in different ways they speak with one voice, and that voice speaks unerringly to the innermost heart of man.
>
>   All in all I see no loss of spiritual potency in this rendering of the New Testament into the English of today; indeed, I see great gain. Striking and priceless truths, which have lain dormant for years in the deep-freeze of traditional beauty, spring to life with fresh challenge and quite alarming relevance to the men of the jet age. There is no need to argue about inspiration, for the word of God is out of its jewelled scabbard and is as sharp, as powerful and as discerning as ever.   (P. 135)

In short, the NEB NT is all the translators hoped it might be, and more. Already the suggestion of inspiration hovers close to the translators. And one notes a novel turning of the idea of language as the dress of thought in the idea of the KJB as scabbard for the sword of truth.

From the other side of the Atlantic, Frederick W. Danker observed: 'because it communicates in timely idiom and yet with timeless phrase it merits classification with the choicest products of *English* literary art' (p. 40). Although writing in a theological journal, Danker suggests that 'the first test of a work which claims to be a new translation is whether it communicates in contemporary terms without erasing to the point of illegibility the historical gap' (p. 41). Accuracy seems so much to be taken for granted that it is forgotten about. Danker appears to think in the very way the translators themselves are accused of thinking by another American, Ernest C. Colwell: 'in this new translation, style is king, and whenever accuracy or clarity interfere with style, they are sacrificed' (p. 37). But, if style is indeed king, Danker finds it magnificent:

> Felicitous expressions meet one everywhere in astounding prodigality. There is the rasp of desert sand in words like these, 'No bullying; no blackmail; make do with your pay!' (Luke 3: 14), that captures the man who dared to take the path to greatness through the obscure way. The social game of petty character sniping comes to a halt at words like these:
>
>> Why do you look at the speck of sawdust in your brother's eye, with never a thought for the great plank in your own? How can you say to your brother, 'My dear brother, let me take the speck out of your eye', when you are blind to the plank in your own? You hypocrite! First take the plank out of your own eye, and then you will see clearly to take the speck out of your brother's [Luke 6: 41–2] ...
>
> The watchful and sensitive ears of a special committee of experts on the English language have insured this version against the banal and pedestrian ... Many of its cadenced phrases will become a part of tomorrow's literary expression. 'do not feed your pearls to pigs' (Matt. 7: 6) ... All one-syllable words, cleanly hewn. Here is modern speech, tomorrow's idiom and liturgical rhythm in rare combination ... In this 350th anniversary year of the publication of the [KJB] we can pay our British cousins no higher tribute than to say: You have done it again! (Pp. 41, 57, 59)

The praise could not be higher, and the examples give one some opportunity to form one's own opinion. This is just as well, since the identical examples are given by the elder statesman of poetry, T. S. Eliot. Citing Matthew's version of the saying about the plank (7: 4), 'Or how can you say to your brother, "Let me take the speck out of your eye", when all the time there is that plank in your own?', he suggests it 'may be literally accurate but will certainly, if it is read in church, raise a giggle among the choirboys' (Nineham, pp. 97–8). It may indeed, but only because the meaning has become inescapable. The KJB avoids risibility by chance misunderstanding: common sense knows that one cannot have a roof-beam in one's eye, but 'beam' sounds like 'gleam', which is something one can have in one's eye. Eliot's objection looks like fear of the real meaning of the Bible, Danker's praise like welcome for the meaning.

Eliot gives more detailed attention to 'do not feed your pearls to pigs', chosen as a version of a familiar phrase. He tries it against the KJB:

> We notice, first, the substitution of 'pigs' for 'swine'. The Complete Oxford Dictionary says that 'swine' is now 'literary' but does not say that it is 'obsolete'. I presume, therefore, that in substituting 'pigs' for 'swine' the translators were trying to choose a word nearer to common speech, even if at the sacrifice of dignity.
>
> I should have thought, however, that the word 'swine' would be understood, not only by countryfolk who may have heard of 'swine fever', but even by the urban public, since it is still applied, I believe, to human beings as a term of abuse.
>
> Next, I should have thought that the sentence would be more in accordance with English usage if the direct and indirect objects were transposed, thus: 'Do not feed pigs upon your pearls' . . .
>
> The most unfortunate result, however, is that the substitution of 'feed' for 'cast' makes the figure of speech ludicrous. There is all the difference in the world between saying that pigs do not *appreciate* the value of pearls, and saying, what the youngest and most illiterate among us know, that they cannot be *nourished* on pearls.
>
> (P. 97)

For three paragraphs this looks like nit-picking, but the last paragraph convicts the translators, and Danker for admiring the phrase. Later editions of the NEB revert to the sense of the KJB, 'do not throw your pearls to the pigs'. It looks as if some critics admired the NEB because it was not the KJB, and others for the same reason reviled it. Certainly the same thing may produce opposite responses, and the dispassionate judge is likely sometimes to sympathise with one side, sometimes with the other.

Some of the hostile responses were as intemperate as Broughton's. But there is a telling difference. With the exception of some fundamentalist reviews such as Terence H. Brown's (Nineham, pp. 143–51), almost all the hostility was directed at the NEB's language. Broughton despaired because the KJB appeared to him a compendium of scholarly errors. The modern reviewers, like Eliot, despaired because of the language of the NEB.

Worthy Bishop Beveridge spoke for millions when he declared that 'it is a great prejudice to the new that it is new, wholly new; for whatsoever is new in religion at the best is unnecessary' (above, p. 43). Moreover, the KJB translators knew well that 'he that meddleth with men's religion in any part meddleth with their custom, nay, with their freehold' (preface, p. 2). Were the hostile moderns mere new-born Beveridgeans? Were they protesting because their religion had been meddled with? And, since some of the protesters were not Churchmen, were they protesting because their religion was not Christianity but AVolatry? All these questions might be answered in the affirmative, and conclusions reached about mankind's ineradicable fidelity to the familiar.

Since it was published in two parts, the NEB was subject to two sets of reviews. It also became involved in the controversy that surrounded the Church of England's revision of the Liturgy. This controversy came to a head with the presentation of three petitions to the General Synod of the Church of England on 5 November 1979. These petitions were published in the *PN Review*, and there was substantial correspondence in the *Daily Telegraph* and then, after it resumed publication a week later, *The Times*. This mass of material may be taken together, for there is no significant change of views to be registered over the decade.

Beveridge was a bishop, and one might well expect his spirit to live on in his modern successors, members of that General Synod that approved so much change, and a more adventurous, forward-looking spirit to be found in leading intellectuals of the day. The Reverend Michael Saward, Vicar of Ealing, member of General Synod and Church Commissioner, makes a key point about the Synod in a letter to *The Times* (17 November 1979):

> Why is it that the present Synod and its predecessor, both relatively conservative bodies, have pursued liturgical change together with the authorisation of modern Bible translations for liturgical use with such dedication?
>
> Anyone who knows the Synod with real intimacy will recognise that it cannot possibly be because of a love for change for its own sake. No, the issue is far more fundamental than that. What is at stake is the whole future of Anglican Christianity in this country. Put at its starkest, the choice in the next 30 years lies between a jewelled corpse or a living pilgrim... What is at stake is the *truth* of Christianity and its capacity to save and transform men and women. If that be not true and demonstrable, then all the cultural and literary beauty of Tudor English is nothing more than the cosmetic mask of a Hollywood cadaver.

Just what this last rhetorical flourish means I am uncertain, but the main point is important and also familiar. The revisions were being made not for the sake of change but because, as in the Reformation, souls (and institutions) were at stake. Not much of the protest at the revisions comes from the clergy because the point made at the inception of the NEB holds good, that the KJB had ceased to speak to large numbers of the people the Church wanted to speak to.

It may also be true – here again there is a parallel with the Reformation – that the KJB had ceased to speak with sufficient meaning to some of the clergy. S. G. Hall, Reverend Professor of Ecclesiastical History, suggests this in another letter to *The Times* (29 November 1979). He castigates a group of the protesters 'as outsiders meddling irrelevantly and irreverently in matters of no concern to them', and declares that 'the ordinary earnest clergyman is deeply concerned to generate warm, spontaneous, directly expressed and intelligent worship from a congregation which knows what it is saying and doing'. The KJB and the PB often get in the way of this, and Hall goes on to look at the clergy's preference for a version about which he is scathing, the Good News Bible. 'They favour it', he suggests, 'because they themselves can understand it, and so can the lay people who are invited to participate by reading parts of the service. Many of the clergy themselves do not read the Authorised Version intelligibly, perhaps because they do not understand it enough to give the words the right emphasis and punctuation.' In other words, the clergy's literacy has been weakened to the point where they are in danger of saying 'mumpsimus' rather than 'sumpsimus'. Hall does does not blame the clergy for this; rather, it is – he does say 'in part' – the fault of 'the leaders of the national and educational establishment who by their indifference or contempt have forced the confession of God in Christ out of national and university life into the sectarian backwater of private belief, personal taste and gathered congregations'. The fault, then, lies largely with the very people who signed the petitions to the Synod, though Hall decently refrains from sending the shaft that far home. And, as Peter Mason, Vicar of Writtle, simplistically observes, 'it is difficult to find any suggestion in the New Testament that the Church's task includes that of preserving a cultural and literary heritage' (letter to *The Times*, 21 November 1979).

One other shaft is worth recording. It comes from the Reverend Douglas Bean, Vicar of St Pancras. He suggests that the clamour for the old forms is 'purely academic':

> Two per cent of the population of Great Britain attend Holy Communion on Sundays. The percentage who attend the divine offices of Mattins and Evensong is even less. How the linguistic heritage of the Authorised Version of the Bible and the Book of Common Prayer can be influential on the people of this country when the great majority of them are not present at the services of the Church is a question I would like to be answered.   (Letter to *The Times*, 21 November 1979)

This is fair enough, but his final point is truly barbed: 'This church is a hundred yards or so from the centre of London University and there are several halls of residence within the parish. I have not noticed professors of English or students attending in any numbers to appreciate the beauties of the Liturgy, nor, as a matter of fact, at any other of the main churches of the country.' Athens and Jerusalem, it seems, still have nothing to do with each other.

Yet Athens has taken upon itself to be the defender of traditional religion because the language of the NEB and the new liturgy is as abhorrent to it as, say, that of the Old Latin Bible was to Ciceronians such as Jerome, whose skin crawled at the uncultivated language of the Prophets (see volume 1, p. 32). This is the main petition that was presented to the General Synod:

> We, the undersigned, are deeply concerned by the policies and tendencies which decree the loss of both the Authorised Version of the English Bible and the Book of Common Prayer. This great act of forgetting, now under way, is a tragic loss to our historic memory and an impoverishment of present awareness. For centuries these texts have carried forward the freshness and simplicity of our language in its early modern splendour. Without them the resources of expression are reduced, the stock of shared words depleted, and we ourselves diminished. Moreover, they contain nothing which cannot be easily and profitably explained.
>
> We ask for their continued and loving use in churches as part of the mainstream of worship and not as vestiges indulged intermittently. We welcome innovation and experiment, but hope that changes will take place alongside the achievements of the past. The younger generation in particular should be acquainted as far as possible with their inheritance.
>
> Clearly this is not an issue confined only to the churches or communities of faith. Some of us do not claim religious belief. Yet we hope that steps are taken to ensure a lively pleasure in the Authorised Version of the Bible in the nation at large. If humane education means anything it includes access to the great renderings of epic and wisdom, prophecy and poetry, epistle and gospel. *(PN Review*, p. 51)

The 600-odd signatories to this are an awe-inspiring gathering, so much so that it would be invidious to single out anyone: it is as representative as could be of the intellectual and cultural leaders of the time. Concern for the cultural heritage embodied in the KJB and the PB was general among the literati. And it is essentially a concern for the Bible as literature.

Some of the signatories, like C. H. Sisson, were quite candid that 'familiarity and continuity are what are at stake' (*PN Review*, p. 8). Now, one readily admits the value of familiarity and continuity – only a rampant anarchist would not. Humanity has made itself what it is through its ability to combine memory of the past with innovation. Without continuity we would still be reinventing the wheel. But without innovation, the wheel would never have been invented in the first place. Sitting back and surveying the literary ruckus over the appearance of the NEB, one sees it as an expression of the fear that all continuity will be lost in the face of innovation: so innovation is attacked. Yet, in the field of biblical translations it seems that all innovations (apart from the legendary

Septuagint) have needed decades if not centuries to gain acceptance. No generation has made the same judgement on its own work as subsequent generations.

Familiarity and continuity were not all that were at stake. There is also the question of the appropriate language for religion – and here it is perhaps a pity that revision of the liturgy became mixed up with revision of the Bible as an issue. Liturgy, being sacramental and ceremonial, would seem naturally to demand a liturgical quality of language. But is it so obvious that a Bible should be in biblical style? To some extent the argument against the NEB rode on the back of the argument against the revision of the liturgy, and most of the arguers seemed to believe that the Bible had to be in what they recognised as biblical style. The educationalist and philosopher Mary (later Baroness) Warnock put the matter most carefully. There is, she argues, another ground besides the cultural for retaining the KJB and the PB. It is that their particular language, and the particular contexts in which it is used, has a particular suggestiveness to which the imagination responds. 'It is not only the clarities of language', she reminds her readers, 'that are significant, but the obscurities, the ambiguities, the suggestions. And these may suggest to us things which we cannot, indeed could never, fully grasp or express more clearly, though we may try' (*PN Review*, p. 16). Religious truth is not religious truth without this imaginative quality:

> Religious truths cannot be adequately or precisely stated. There must in the nature of the case be something ambiguous, paradoxical, even mysterious in their proper expression. No religious writer, no philosopher of religion has ever denied this. Thus the effort to clean up the language of the Bible and the prayer book, to sanitise it, to render it exact, up-to-date and unambiguous is itself an anti-religious effort. The ideas of religion ... are for ever just beyond the scope of language.   (P. 17)

In a letter to *The Times*, she and some other notable Oxford figures put the matter even more simply: 'the full meaning of the Bible cannot be conveyed in a strictly non-poetic language' (14 November 1979). This is a reasoned challenge to the linguistic rationale of the NEB. Though it sounds rather like John Dennis 275 years earlier (above, p. 4), one only begins to suspect this when one observes the company it keeps and sees how it comes out from less diplomatic pens. Then it begins to be subject to the reservation the editor of the *Daily Telegraph* voiced about the whole *PN Review* collection, that 'here is the spectacle of a collection of outsiders making points about language which are aesthetic rather than religious' (6 November 1979, p. 18).

Here is one example of the AVolatrous company these careful arguments keep:

I find it difficult to describe in temperate language my feelings regarding the current tendency to reject the Jacobean translation of the Scriptures to say nothing of the Book of Common Prayer in favour of recent versions of these masterpieces.

Whether one is a believer or not, it is surely not open to question that, with Shakespeare, these works are the main background of our literary heritage. To substitute for their marvellous cadences and deep spiritual and poetic appeal, these supreme examples of literary insensibility ... seems to me an outrage which, if it were not a real danger, one would never believe to be possible ... What would [the young] – or we – say of an attempt to rewrite one of Hamlet's soliloquies in modern English? All eyes would be dry. How much more so to be condemned is this forcing the adoption of such parodies of the greatest literary manifestations of one of the great religions of the world. (*PN Review*, p. 17)

Missing the point that the NEB is not a revision of the KJB but a new translation of the originals, this implies that 'marvellous cadences and deep spiritual and poetic appeal' are what matter most. It is as if cadences were the key to religion (and the old the key to culture and education). Moreover, the implication that the KJB, rather than the unconsidered originals, is the true word of God hovers in the background. Passages such as this undermine the credibility of the petition, and one suspects that it was only included because of the prestige of the author, Lord Robbins, economist and chairman of the English Committee on Higher Education that produced the *Higher Education Report* to parliament (1963) commonly known by his name.

Several critics developed arguments similar to Mary Warnock's.[14] The fullest and most vehement came from a lecturer in English language at the University College of Swansea, Ian Robinson. The piece, for all that it has important things to say, is marked by outspoken criticism, a total lack of sympathy for the NEB's aims and a scorn for the judgements of others; Broughtonian is a suitably ugly adjective for it. Robinson asks, for instance, 'why the translators can't write English at all (and why so glaringly obvious a fact was generally missed by the literary critics who reviewed the version)' (p. 24). His case against the NEB is based on the idea that the division between content and form which has persisted in asserting itself throughout this history is false. 'The way "things" are said affects the "things"' (p. 46). This should be obvious if it were not so absolutely stated: if 'can affect' were substituted for 'affects', the statement would be so true as to be hardly worth making. But Robinson's belief is that meaning exists only in form. It is a belief that stretches common sense into

---

[14] For example, Prickett, 'What do the translators think they are up to?', and Geoffrey Strickland, 'The Holy Bible: translation and belief', both in *New Universities Quarterly* 33 (1979), 259–68 and 269–82.

absurdity. Yet the absurdity is rarely apparent because it is so close to common sense and because the belief is fairly generally held within the academic community.

Robinson's sense of the inextricability of language and meaning is closely linked to something highly prized in literary discussion, the ability to show what is good in a piece of writing. A comparison between the KJB's and the NEB's renderings of the first four verses of Genesis leads him to this:

> The 1611 version is so good here because its translators command the style for the subject. The slow, measured rhythmic sentences, one for each step in creation, convince one in a poetic way as well as being, I am told, closer to the procedure of the Hebrew ... Look at the different use of 'and' – the difference made to the rhythm of the passage, its pace, phrasing and stressing. That was, at least, done by people who were masters of the craft of writing English.   (P. 26)

Though this is not in the same class as Boileau's observation on verse 3 (above, p. 8), it is a reasonable suggestion that the repeated 'and's help to bring home to the reader a ritualistic sense of the stage-by-stage quality of the action, and that therefore the form of the passage contributes to the perception of the meaning. Robinson, however, would not accept such a formulation. When he returns to the passage, it is to use it as a dogmatic demonstration of the Saintsburyan point (see above, p. 323) that the rhythm of the passage is its meaning:

> To say that the Bible's mastery of language is primarily a question of rhythm, the careful and strong rhythms of the individual phrase controlled by the tempo of a whole passage, is not to reduce it to 'orotundity' or 'resonant opacity', but to discuss the meaning and credibility of what is said. That is why it was insufficient, though true, to say that the 1611 opening of Genesis was done by masters of the craft of writing. The old translators were religious artists, the truth of whose utterance depended on their grasp of their language.   (P. 58)

A contributing element has been made into the whole. We might well accept that the meaning is not so well created in the NEB, even that the meaning is not quite the same, but it is nonsense to imply that the whole meaning disappears if the phrasing is changed. If that were true then 'the meaning and credibility of what is said' would not be there in the original Hebrew, or in any other language, or in any other English version. All that is true is that the precise character of phrasing that produces a particular character of response in a particular individual would be missing. The particular character of the response may be very important, and it may be shared by a large number of people, but there is a dogmatism about the way Robinson has moved from commentary to assertion. We have reached literary fundamentalism rather than insight.

Robinson goes almost as far as proclaiming outright what I have just suggested is self-evident nonsense, that the meaning and credibility are not there in the original language. The preface to the NEB OT observes that the Greek of the NT 'is indeed more flexible and easy-going than the revisers were ready to allow, and invites the translator to use a larger freedom'. To this he retorts: 'Only if [the translator] is radically confused about the purpose of his translation, which is in this case to produce a New English Bible, not a modern replica of an easy-going first-century text. The intended fidelity is *not* to whatever it is that allowed the text to become the Bible' (p. 44). The stress is not mine but his. Apparently the original Greek was not the Bible. And it was not the Bible because a key characteristic of a Bible is that it should be in religious language and have a sense of tradition behind it. He sums up this part of his ideas thus:

> Religious English is the style of our common language that makes religion possible (or not, as the case may be). Religious English can only make religious seriousness possible to the individual, in whom any religion is not restricted or standardised but perpetually new, unique and his own; it could not do so, however, without the many generations whose lives have expressed themselves in our language, in the context of the many Christian languages, in *their* context of history and human nature.
>
> (Pp. 55–6)

All this flows from the dogma that meaning and expression are inseparable. It might as well be a belief in the divine inspiration of the K JB, for the end result, reached by a different route but with equal vehemence, is no different from the position held by fundamentalists such as Hills and Chick.

One other aspect of Robinson's argument reaches, challengingly, something like this position. He characterises the style of the NEB as journalism, and incompetent journalism at that (pp. 22, 39). 'Its one consistent effect', he adds, 'is that it cheapens' (p. 22). Consequently, 'the NEB miracles all seem gross impostures, superstitions as reported by the modern journalist' (p. 37). It will be useful to follow some of the development of this point in detail, not least because it will correct the impression that Robinson is not worth attending to:

> In the NEB the story of the resurrection, the central miracle of Christianity, is simply nonsense.
>
> > The angel then addressed the woman: 'You', he said, 'have nothing to fear. I know you are looking for Jesus who was crucified. He is not here; he has been raised again, as he said he would be. Come and see the place where he was laid, and then go quickly and tell his disciples: "He has been raised from the dead and is going on before you into Galilee; there you will see him." That is what I had to tell you.' (Matt. 28: 5–7)

The angel is obviously an imposter: he speaks far too much like a usually reliable source, flustered by an impossible brief. To take a miracle so much as a matter of course ('He has been raised from the dead and is going...') is a sign either of extraordinary stupidity or a wide credibility gap. So it is hardly surprising that Matthew's continuation of the story would convince no dispassionate reader.

> After meeting with the elders and conferring together, the chief priests offered the soldiers a substantial bribe and told them to say, 'His disciples came by night and stole the body while we were asleep.' They added, 'If this should reach the Governor's ears, we will put matters right with him and see that you do not suffer' [28: 12–14].

A likely tale! Roman soldiers expected to put out the story that they had been asleep on duty but yet knew what happened. Even so, in this version some sort of body-snatching seems the most likely solution to a question which almost puts the book into the genre of detective novel.

The Jerusalem Bible's angel is similarly unangelic and even chatty. The 1885 version is ... the only one of the three I could in any sense believe in:

> And the angel answered and said unto the women, Fear not ye: for I know that ye seek Jesus, which hath been crucified. He is not here; for he is risen, even as he said. Come, see the place where the Lord lay. And go quickly and tell his disciples, He is risen from the dead; and lo, he goeth before you into Galilee.   (P. 38)

This is not quite as persuasive as it appears at first sight, for Robinson resorts to assertion just when close discussion is most needed. Declaring the RV the only one of the three fairly modern versions he 'could in any sense believe in', he probably expects his reader to agree that it positively escapes his Paine-like condemnation of the NEB and Jerusalem.

If one takes the whole of what he quoted from the NEB in the RV, or, better still, in the KJB with the few differences from his quotation italicised, the comparison can begin to be fairly made:

> And the angel answered and said unto the women, Fear not ye: for I know that ye seek Jesus, which *was* crucified. He is not here: for he is risen, *[ ]* as he said. Come, see the place where the Lord lay. And go quickly, and tell his disciples *that* he is risen from the dead; and, *behold*, he goeth before you into Galilee; there shall ye see him: lo, I have told you ... And when they were assembled with the elders, and had taken counsel, they gave large money unto the soldiers, Saying, Say ye, His disciples came by night, and stole him away while we slept. And if this come to the governor's ears, we will persuade him, and secure you. So they took the money, and did as they were taught: and this saying is commonly reported among the Jews until this day.
>
> (Matt. 28: 5–7, 12–15, KJB)

Is this angel also an imposter? The answer depends most on 'lo, I have told you'. Does this have the impressiveness of an annunciation, created by a combination of the archaic trumpet-call[15] of 'lo' and a stress on 'I', implying, 'I, an angel'? Or does it have something of the worldly Rosamond Vincy confessing to Dorothea that everything had been her own fault and that Will Ladislaw had been telling her he loved Dorothea: she adds, beginning to return to her characteristic self-righteousness, 'But now I have told you, and he cannot reproach me any more' (*Middlemarch*, ch. 81)? Both readings are possible. Nevertheless, if the annunciatory quality is something of what convinces Robinson, then we must agree with him that it is not possible in the NEB's version. But it is also true that the quality in the KJB is created by a combination of archaism, sound and the reader's collusion, that is, the reader's willingness to find the appropriate stress in 'I'.

Does the KJB's angel 'take a miracle as a matter of course'? He says, 'he is risen from the dead; and, behold, he goeth...'. It is the pause, followed by 'behold' (or 'lo' in the RV), that makes the difference: statement is turned into exclamation, so the miracle is indeed wondered at. With the evidence to be seen if they will go and look, the angel convinces his hearers of the miraculous, as if saying, 'look, there He is! Believe!'

Robinson dismisses verses 12–15 in the NEB as 'a likely tale', but does not show how any other version might appear more likely. The information in the KJB is the same and there is nothing in the manner of telling that makes much difference except for a vagueness that comes from an odd use of familiar words in 'we will persuade him, and secure you'. Here I think Robinson shows what dangerous ground he is treading on: the denial of credibility to the NEB can in a moment slip into rationalistic denial of the story told. He joins company with Strauss, even, perhaps, with Paine. But he differs from them in that his grounds for criticism, the convincingness of the style, is not only subjective but passes over a range of questions. Is he asserting that the versions are convincing or otherwise as truth or as fiction? If the former, does he accept the miraculous and the existence of angels?

Such questions matter. They leave one uneasy over what appears initially as a reasonable but not fully persuasive piece of comparative discussion. The unease suddenly becomes a major worry as Robinson gives his version of Mary Warnock's claim that making the Bible's language 'exact, up-to-date and unambiguous is itself an anti-religious effort' (above, p. 426):

[15] Doubtless I am less sensitive than Saintsbury, who wrote of the 'clarion sound' of the 'i's in 'Arise, shine.' One should imagine what Saintsbury might have written of this passage.

The failure of style here *is* a failure of belief. How can the new translators have felt right, in those words? How can they have felt they have said what the Bible says? By satisfying themselves with incompetent journalism they have branded their own religion as shallow and chaotic. In that sense they have published work that is not sincere.   (Pp. 38–9)

This is a drastic charge, distasteful to read and, one hopes, distasteful to make. Yet surely it stems from an excessive equating of style and meaning. Paul knew how false the equation was. Now we are being asked to accept that sincerity will produce writing that is good or convincing, and that poor writing is a sign of insincerity and shallowness.

Robinson sees the NEB as a sign of the times (p. 22). Others too take it as a sign, usually of the decline of the present age in both moral and linguistic terms. The very thing Swift feared, that English will 'at length infallibly change for the worse' (above, p. 40), has happened. T. S. Eliot, finding the NEB far below the level of dignified mediocrity, asked in alarm, 'what is happening to the English language?' (Nineham, p. 96). Henry Gifford, in a review which Robinson applauds (p. 27), claims that 'over the past hundred years literature has been steadily losing ground' (Nineham, p. 107), and, pithily, that 'the English language is becoming a dustbowl, the deposits of centuries blown away, and a thin temporary soil remaining' (p. 108). He shows the version's tendency to cliché, and comments that 'translators are perhaps bound to mediate the world of their own time. Here we can recognise the grey, anonymous, oatmeal-paper forms, the ill-phrased regulations, the barren communiqués and reassuring statements from which there is no escape' (p. 109). A tellingly chosen collage of phrases from the NEB follows. The case is powerfully suggested, but what is perhaps most significant is that it is the exact reflex of reverence for the time of Shakespeare and the KJB. A great time produced a great Bible – or did a great Bible bespeak a great time? Now a shallow, faithless time produces a Bible that is both its symptom and its image.

A princely epilogue

English royalty has had an important, if occasional, role in this story. A scholar king gave the nod to the work of revision that became the KJB. A scholar prince may be allowed the last word on versions old and new. Charles, Prince of Wales, revived the debate about the merits of the PB, the KJB and their modern revisions with a speech on the occasion of the 500th anniversary of the birth of Archbishop Cranmer, 19 December 1989.[16] He was presenting a prize commemorating the occasion and designed to encourage familiarity with the PB among secondary-school pupils. The sentiments are authentic Prince Charles, but one witty reference to speech-writers might lead us to a Baconian heresy. It is certainly a good speech. Yet we may also see it as a series of echoes.

Beginning with a reflection on the dangers of speaking out about the importance of the British heritage, the Prince places himself firmly in the company of Bishop Beveridge:

> The fear of being considered old-fashioned seems to be so all-powerful that the more eternal values and principles which run like a thread through the whole tapestry of human existence are abandoned under the false assumption that they restrict progress. Well, I'm *not* afraid of being considered old-fashioned, which is why I am standing here at this lectern wearing a double-breasted suit and turn-ups to my trousers, ready to declaim the fact that I believe the Prayer Book is a glorious part of every English-speaker's heritage and, as such, ought to be a grade I listed edifice!

This is essentially the view of all the signatories to the petition to the General Synod. Like Sisson, the Prince believes in 'the profound human need for continuity and permanence'. Like Robinson, he believes that 'the words *are* the thoughts'. Not yet titular head of the Church of England, he can take the unclerical, Athenian view 'that for solemn occasions we need exceptional and solemn language: something which transcends our everyday speech. We commend the "beauty of holiness", yet we forget the holiness of beauty. If we encourage the use of mean, trite, ordinary language we encourage a mean, trite and ordinary view of the world.' So he comments that he 'would have liked to begin with a ringing phrase from the King James's Version of the Bible: "hearken to my words"'. However, the NEB 'translates the phrase in less commanding terms: "give me a hearing". It might seem more humble but it also sounds less poetic.' As Robinson or Saintsbury would tell us, there is indeed an authority to the rhythm of 'hearken to my words' that comes from opening and closing the phrase with stresses. But what is most important is the clear identification between beauty, poetry and religious feeling. So, if we lose the liturgy and the Bible as literature, we lose religion.

This leads the Prince to reflect on the issue that concerned Eliot, Gifford and Robinson, the decline of 'the world's most successful language'. It 'has become so impoverished, so sloppy and so limited – that we have arrived at such a dismal wasteland of banality, cliché and casual obscenity'. As if inspired by

---

[16] The full text may be found in the *Daily Telegraph* (20 December 1989), 14.

Lord Robbins's reflection on what the young would make of a Hamlet soliloquy in modern English, the Prince gives a version of 'to be or not to be': 'Well, frankly, the problem as I see it at this moment in time is whether I should just lie down under all this hassle and let them walk over me, or whether I should just say OK, I get the message, and do myself in.' This is light relief, but it shows a danger. Hamlet saying, 'well, frankly . . .', is no prince but one of the illiterate mob portrayed in *2 Henry VI*,[17] or one of the groundlings Hamlet himself is so scornful of, 'the groundlings, who for the most part are capable of nothing but inexplicable dumb-shows and noise' (3: 2). The modern prince condemns the present by the groundlings and reveres the past through the old prince. It is the age of Shakespeare against the age of Nick Cotton in *EastEnders*.

Prince Charles makes an earnest plea 'to uphold standards amid the general spread of mediocrity', and concludes:

> Ours is the age of miraculous writing machines but not of miraculous writing. Our banalities are no improvement on the past; merely an insult to it and a source of confusion in the present. In the case of our cherished religious writings, we should leave well alone, especially when it is better than well: when it is great. Otherwise we leave ourselves open to the terrible accusation once levelled by that true master of the banal, Samuel Goldwyn: 'You've improved it worse.'

Not surprisingly, there were ruffled feathers among the clergy, for the Prince had brought together most of the arguments being used against the clergy's innovations without consideration of any religious matters except the relation between poetry and religion:

> Astonishment was not confined to the Church of England. Roman Catholics, for example, are unlikely to be amused by the Prince's choice of a passage to illustrate the 'crassness' of the [Alternative Service Book]. Exactly the same words occur in the modern Roman missal.

For the Church of England, of course, the future Defender of the Faith's distaste

---

[17] For instance, when the Clerk of Chatham is brought before Jack Cade:

> Weaver. The Clerk of Chatham – he can write and read and cast account.
> Cade.   O, monstrous!
> Weaver. We took him setting of boys' copies.
> Cade.   Here's a villain.
> Weaver. He's a book in his pocket with red letters in it.
> Cade.   Nay, then he is a conjuror! . . . (*To the Clerk*) Dost thou use to write thy name? Or hast thou a mark to thyself like an honest plain-dealing man?
> Clerk.   Sir, I thank God I have been so well brought up that I can write my name.
> All Cade's Followers. He hath confessed – away with him! He's a villain and a traitor.
> Cade.   Away with him, I say, hang him with his pen and inkhorn about his neck.
>   (4: 2)

for the ASB is embarrassing. Even the stoutly traditionalist Bishop of London uses the new prayer book; some observers thought he looked distinctly uncomfortable sitting next to the Prince yesterday.

At least one supporter of the ASB has already resolved to try to change the Prince's mind. Canon Donald Gray of Westminster Abbey, one of the volume's authors, told me: 'I'd like to talk it over with him and put the other side. Knowing him, I think he might give us the chance.' ('Peterborough', *Daily Telegraph* (20 December 1989))

If the Prince is on the side of Athens, the other side is of course Jerusalem. Tertullian asked rhetorically what Athens had to do with Jerusalem: for him the answer was nothing. But the two have remained as closely linked as form and meaning. Athens has taken on much of the form of Jerusalem, and much of the meaning of Jerusalem is now to be found in Athens. To speak plainly, culture, in the form of higher education, has taken on many of the characteristics of religion. Moreover, religion has been so long a part of the culture of everyman that it is still difficult to admit it could lose that place.

A history of the Bible as literature turns out to be an examination of the shifting interrelationships between religion and culture. It does not reach a conclusion because the interrelationships continue to shift and because one becomes convinced that ways of thinking are perennial. The commonest way of thinking seems to be what so often issues as fundamentalism, an adherence to the past and a dread of the new. Bishop Beveridge is the representative figure, easily made into a figure of fun because we none of us like to be behind the times, but yet a figure whom we should all see something of ourselves in. His most recent incarnation is Prince Charles, complete with double-breasted suit and turn-ups to his trousers. One of his earlier incarnations was the old Catholic priest who chanted 'quod in ore mumpsimus'. They represent the desire for religious feeling and the inability to distinguish that feeling from a love of the past and a sense of beauty. It is they, more even than the great line of translators from Tyndale to Myles Smith, who created the beauty of the English Bible. And it is because they are creators as well as representative of something deep within ourselves that I choose to end with them.

But a consequence of ending with such conservative figures is that condemnation of the NEB, representative of the new effort at translation, is left ringing in our ears. We have seen enough of contemporaries' judgements of new translations – always excepting the Septuagint – to be thoroughly sceptical of our own judgements. Too many factors independent of the intrinsic qualities of a translation are involved in its eventual fate and reputation. However, it seems to me likely that no translation will ever become what the KJB has been to the English-speaking world. I do not suggest this as a judgement on either the quality or the quantity of modern translations, but as a reflection on the decline of Christianity to effective non-existence for the majority of English-speaking people. No Bible can become a classic if it is not perpetually and inescapably encountered by all of us. It was the KJB's good fortune to be inescapable for centuries; many would add that it was the good fortune of the English-speaking peoples that they had such a Bible to live with. Iris Murdoch, novelist, philosopher and signatory to the petition to the Synod, may speak for them: 'the Bible and the Prayer Book were great pieces of literary good fortune, when language and spirit conjoined to produce a high unique religious eloquence. These books have been *loved* because of their inspired linguistic perfection. Treasured words encourage, console and save' (*PN Review*, p. 5).

Appendix

The passages given in the appendix to volume 1 showed work by most of the translators discussed in that volume. The two main translations discussed in this volume, the RV and the NEB, are easily found, and the dialect versions have already been sufficiently illustrated. So only three passages are given to fill out the sense of eighteenth-century prose and verse translation. Finally, as a curiosity, Franklin's spurious chapter of Genesis is included for readers who might like to try the great American's trick of reading it aloud as a 'genuine' passage.

Again Isaiah 60 and Matthew 7 are used, so comparisons with some of the translators from volume 1 are possible. Again the KJB has been given with modernised spelling but the original 1611 punctuation. Only the italics are omitted. The eighteenth-century passages are given with original spelling and punctuation.

Isaiah 60. The KJB, Robert Lowth and John Husbands

Husbands implies admiration of this chapter both by choosing to translate it and by placing it first in his anthology. He must, one guesses, have thought particularly highly of his own effort, or the chapter as it appears in the KJB. Lowth is more explicit. His notes on the passage begin with an indication of literary admiration: it 'is set forth in ... ample and exalted terms ... in the most splendid colours, under a great variety of images highly poetical'.

Several of Lowth's notes explain variations from the KJB on grounds of scholarship. For instance, his change from 'then shalt thou see, and flow together' (v. 5) to 'then shalt though fear, and overflow with joy' is made on the basis of forty manuscripts, ten of them ancient. That it is 'the true reading' is 'confirmed by the perfect parallelism of the sentences: the heart "ruffled" and "dilated" in the second line answering to the "fear" and "joy" expressed in the first'. The other scholarly variations which he notes are: 'shall be carried at the side' for 'shall be nursed at thy side' (v. 4); 'praise' for 'praises' (v. 6); 'like doves upon the wing' for 'as the doves to their windows' (v. 8); 'among the first' for 'first' (v. 9); and 'nor by night shall the brightness of the moon enlighten thee' for 'neither for brightness shall the moon give light unto thee' (v. 19). Some, at least, of his other changes seem to show a tug in the direction of literary improvement.

KJB 1611	*Robert Lowth 1778*
Arise, shine, for thy light is come, and the glory of the LORD is risen upon thee.	Arise, be thou enlightened; for thy light is come; And the glory of JEHOVAH is risen upon thee.
For behold, the darkness shall cover the earth, and gross darkness the people: but the LORD shall arise upon thee, and his glory shall be seen upon thee.	For behold, darkness shall cover the earth; And a thick vapour the nations: But upon thee shall JEHOVAH arise; And his glory upon thee shall be conspicuous.
And the Gentiles shall come to thy light, and kings to the brightness of thy rising.	And the nations shall walk in thy light; And kings in the brightness of thy sun-rising.
Lift up thine eyes round about, and see: all they gather themselves together, they come to thee: thy sons shall come from far, and thy daughters shall be nursed at thy side.	Lift up thine eyes round about, and see; All of them are gathered together, they come unto thee: Thy sons shall come from afar; And thy daughters shall be carried at the side.
Then thou shalt see, and flow together, and thine heart shall fear, and be enlarged, because the abundance of the Sea shall be converted unto thee, the forces of the Gentiles shall come unto thee.	Then shalt thou fear, and overflow with joy; And thy heart shall be ruffled, and dilated; When the riches of the sea shall be poured in upon thee; When the wealth of the nations shall come unto thee.

KJB	Robert Lowth
The multitude of camels shall cover thee, the dromedaries of Midian and Ephah: all they from Sheba shall come: they shall bring gold and incense, and they shall show forth the praises of the LORD.	An inundation of camels shall cover thee; The dromedaries of Midian and Epha; All of them from Saba shall come: Gold and frankincense shall they bear; And the praise of JEHOVAH shall they joyfully proclaim.
All the flocks of Kedar shall be gathered together unto thee, the rams of Nebaioth shall minister unto thee: they shall come up with acceptance on mine altar, and I will glorify the house of my glory.	All the flocks of Kedar shall be gathered unto thee; Unto thee shall the rams of Nebaioth minister: They shall ascend with acceptance on mine altar; And my beauteous house I will yet beautify.
Who are these that fly as a cloud, and as the doves to their windows?	Who are these, that fly like a cloud? And like doves upon the wing?
Surely the isles shall wait for me, and the ships of Tarshish first, to bring thy sons from far, their silver and their gold with them, unto the Name of the LORD thy God, and to the Holy One of Israel, because he hath glorified thee.	Verily the distant coasts shall await me; And the ships of Tarshish among the first: To bring thy sons from afar; Their silver and their gold with them: Because of the name of JEHOVAH thy God; And of the Holy One of Israel; for he hath glorified thee.
And the sons of strangers shall build up thy walls, and their kings shall minister unto thee: for in my wrath I smote thee, but in my favour have I had mercy on thee.	And the sons of the stranger shall build up thy walls; And their kings shall minister unto thee: For in my wrath I smote thee; But in my favour I will embrace thee with the most tender affection.

KJB

Therefore thy gates shall be open continually, they shall not be shut day nor night, that men may bring unto thee the forces of the Gentiles, and that their kings may be brought.

For the nation and kingdom that will not serve thee, shall perish, yea those nations shall be utterly wasted.

The glory of Lebanon shall come unto thee, the Fir tree, the Pine tree, and the Box together, to beautify the place of my Sanctuary, and I will make the place of my feet glorious.

The sons also of them that afflicted thee, shall come bending unto thee: and all they that despised thee shall bow themselves down at the soles of thy feet, and they shall call thee the city of the LORD, the Zion of the Holy One of Israel.

Whereas thou hast been forsaken and hated, so that no man went through thee, I will make thee an eternal excellency, a joy of many generations.

Robert Lowth

And thy gates shall be open
    continually;
By day, or by night, they shall not
    be shut:
To bring unto thee the wealth of
    the nations;
And that their kings may come
    pompously attended.

For that nation, and that kingdom,
Which will not serve thee, shall
    perish,
Yea, those nations shall be utterly
    desolated.

The glory of Lebanon shall come
    unto thee;
The fir-tree, the pine, and the box
    together:
To adorn the place of my
    sanctuary;
And that I may glorify the place,
    whereon I rest my feet.

And the sons of thine oppressors
    shall come bending before
    thee;
And all, that scornfully rejected
    thee, shall do obeisance to the
    soles of thy feet:
And they shall call thee, The City
    of JEHOVAH;
The Sion of the Holy One of
    Israel.

Instead of thy being forsaken,
And hated, so that no one passed
    through thee;
I will make thee an everlasting
    boast;
A subject of joy for perpetual
    generations.

KJB	Robert Lowth
Thou shalt also suck the milk of the Gentiles, and shalt suck the breast of kings, and thou shalt know that I the LORD am thy Saviour and thy Redeemer, the mighty One of Jacob.	And thou shalt suck the milk of nations; Even at the breast of kings shalt thou be fostered: And thou shalt know, that I JEHOVAH am thy saviour; And that thy redeemer is the Mighty One of Jacob.
For brass I will bring gold, and for iron I will bring silver, and for wood brass, and for stones iron: I will also make thy officers peace, and thine exactors righteousness.	Instead of brass, I will bring gold; And instead of iron, I will bring silver: And instead of wood, brass; And instead of stones, iron. And I will make thine inspectors peace; And thine exactors, righteousness.
Violence shall no more be heard in thy land, wasting nor destruction within thy borders, but thou shalt call thy walls salvation, and thy gates praise.	Violence shall no more be heard in thy land; Destruction and calamity, in thy borders: But thou shalt call thy walls, Salvation; And thy gates, Praise.
The Sun shall be no more thy light by day, neither for brightness shall the moon give light unto thee: but the LORD shall be unto thee an everlasting light, and thy God thy glory.	No longer shalt thou have the sun for a light by day; Nor by night shall the brightness of the moon enlighten thee: For JEHOVAH shall be to thee an everlasting light, And thy God shall be thy glory.
Thy Sun shall no more go down, neither shall thy moon withdraw itself: for the LORD shall be thine everlasting light, and the days of thy mourning shall be ended.	Thy sun shall no more go down; Neither shall thy moon wane: For JEHOVAH shall be thine everlasting light; And the days of thy mourning shall be ended.
Thy people also shall be all righteous: they shall inherit the	And thy people shall be all righteous;

KJB	*Robert Lowth*
land for ever, the branch of my planting, the work of my hands, that I may be glorified.	For ever shall they possess the land: The cion of my planting, the work of my hands, that I may be glorified.
A little one shall become a thousand, and a small one a strong nation: I the LORD will hasten it in his time.	The little one shall become a thousand; And the small one a strong nation: I JEHOVAH in due time will hasten it.

John Husbands 1731

See! from the Empyrean height descends
Glory divine; See! the collected Rays
Center in Thee; rise, happy *Zion*, rise,
Supreme in Brightness; and to distant Worlds
Diffuse the blessings of thy heav'n-born Light.

Distinguisht Care of Heav'n! behold around
The chearless Nations wrapt in silent Night,
Shadow of Death; where Sorrows, and Despair,
And Fears sit brooding o'er the cold Obscure.
Whilst Thou with Glory never-fading crown'd
Lookst from thy Throne of Brightness, like the Sun
O'er the benighted World, dispensing round
Life-giving Heat, and Joy ineffable.
The Gentiles hail the new-born vital Day,
And Eastern Kings thy rising Beams adore.

From far the thronging Multitudes advance,
Thy future Sons, and Daughters yet unborn.
To Thee the Islands, like their mighty Tides
High-rolling hasten, and far-distant Lands
Sever'd in vain by interposing Seas.
Then thy divided Heart shall ebb and flow,
And feel a strange Vicissitude of Thought,
Distrustful Fear concomitant of Joy.

Hither slow-pacing o'er the Sun-burnt Plains,
Patient of Thirst, a num'rous bunch-backt Drove
Camels and Dromedaries shape their Way,
Fraught with the riches of fam'd Eastern Lands
Epha and *Midian*: for Thee *Araby*
Breaths all its Sweets: to Thee *Sabean* Kings
Adoring offer tributary Gifts,
Gold, Frankincense, and Aromatick gums.

For Thee well-pastur'd *Kedar*, Nurse of Flocks,
Feeds many a Sacrifice; with all her Rams
Nebaioth serves Thee, on thy Altars bleed
The dedicated Victims, while the Steam
Of smoking Holocausts ascends to Heav'n
Sweet-smelling. Thus the World's Magnificence
Adorns the Seat of Sanctity divine.

Say, who are Those, that, like wind-driven Clouds,
Fleet thro' the Air, still growing on the Sight,
Various, unnumber'd? – Or say, who are Those
That close-embody'd urge their trembling Flight
Like Doves returning to their peaceful Cells,
Safe from the Horrors of tempestuous Air.

I view the Ships of *Tarshish*, like in show
To floating Islands: deep-embosom'd Sails
Whiten the Waves, and flutter in the Wind.
Hither They fly, and leave the Western World
Unpeopled, and exhausted. See thy Sons,
Mother of Nations, with their votive Gifts,
Silver and Gold, in splendid Piety,
Adoring thy *Jehovah*, dreaded Name!
Monarchs shall wait in humbled Majesty
Proud of thy Service; unknown, foreign Hands
Thy Walls re-edify, and bid Thee rise
More glorious from thy Ruins. Wrath divine
Now softens into Pity: O belov'd
Rise, and enjoy the blest Vicissitude.

Nor Day nor Night shall shut thy crowded Gates;
But th'ever-open hospitable Space

Shall widen to admit the thronging Hosts
Of Gentile Kings, thy Vassals: happy They
And free in Servitude! Ye Rebel Thrones
Beware, and tremble at impending Doom.

For Thee the Woods their verdant Honours wear;
The Box, Th'aspiring Firr, and spreading Pine,
And fragrant Cedar, fav'rite Plant of Heav'n,
And all the shady Trees that flourish fair
On *Lebanon*'s high Brow, assume new Forms
Taught to reflourish by the Artist's Hand:
In smooth-shav'd Plane, or bossy Sculpture bold
Add beauty to the Place of Holiness.

Ye Sons of Violence, once dreaded Powers,
Where's now your Pride? how impotent, how chang'd,
Abject, and crest fall'n! now in humble Plight
Bow the stiff Neck, and bend the stubborn Knee,
To kiss the hallow'd Feet of *Zion* – Hail
Heav'n-favour'd, Seat of *Israel's Holy-One*.

Once scorn'd and desolate, how art Thou chang'd
O Mother City of th'admiring Earth,
And Queen of Nations, Throne of Excellence
Eternal, Joy of Ages yet unborn!
Thee Kingdoms, proud of such Relation, claim
Their Foster-child with emulating Love.
Hail Thou adopted Charge of Gentile Kings,
Thy nursing Fathers! Thy strange happiness
Speaks its great Author, Me, the *Mighty One*
Of *Jacob, thy Redeemer*. –

See! how improv'd by Change all nature feels
My Love in Signs miraculous exprest.
Thy Trees forget their vegetable Life
Ascending, and into metallick Ore
Harden condens'd, and yellow into Brass.
Thy Stones that moulder in their Beds, unpriz'd,
Base Fossils, chang'd in texture Iron grow,
Solid and ductile ferrugineous Mass.
Thy Iron brightens into Silver Form,

Pale-shining Glory: and thy Brass impure
Glows into yellow-ruddy-tinctur'd Gold,
Supreme of Metals, fit to bear imprest
The Majesty portray'd of Scepter'd Kings.

Nor in the Moral World the sudden Change
Less marvellous. The Noise of Violence
Lies husht in Peace: succeeding Plenty smiles,
Filling the waste of Rapine: Specious Fraud
Shrinks from the Light: Each bold Oppressor proves
A Minister of Justice: Equity
Enthron'd the even-poised Balance holds,
Guardian of publick Good; and on thy Walls
Peace and Salvation in bright Triumph reign.

No more the Sun, Source of material Light,
Shall shine diurnal: Nor the waning Moon,
Making Night chearful, shed her borrow'd Rays:
The Light of Lights shall rise, *Jehovah*'s self
Shall Thee illumine with eternal Day.
See! the faint Sun hides his diminish'd Head,
The Moon, opacous Globe, in Darkness sets;
But God on Thee in gracious Brightness shines
Unclouded, never-fading, heav'nly Light,
Presence divine, thrice-hallow'd *Shechinah*.

Hail Rising *Sun of Righteousness* serene,
Chearing the Face of Day! The mournful Gloom
Fleets off before the cloud-dispelling Beams,
And in bright order sprightly Joys succeed.

Behold! The *Branch* planted by Hand divine,
Shall by thy Influence auspicious rise
High-shadowing, and round the Nations spread
His far-stretcht Honours. Wonderful to Sight!
Behold a Point swell to Infinitude;
One growing into People numberless.
Miraculous Increase! which future Times
Shall see accomplisht. – Thus th'Almighty wills.

Job 41. The KJB and Anthony Purver

Purver's annotations explain some of his continual variations from the KJB. Typical is his note to 'lion' in the final verse:

> He being counted King of the Brutes. It is thus rendered 28: 8 in which two places only the word occurs. Castellio translates, 'omne genus ferarum, every kind of wild beasts'; Tremellius and Junius, 'omnes feras, all the wild beasts', Broughton, 'all the wild kind'. It would have been tiresome to remark how often, as here, the common English Translation was made from the wretched old corrupt Latin instead of the Hebrew in this book.

Such annotations are eloquent of the Quaker's industry.

Care for his language appears in his explanation of 'put' in the beginning of v. 8: 'elegantly for "shouldest thou put"', and literary awareness as well as wide reading appear in his note to 'as the eyelids', v. 18:

> Young in a note to his *Paraphrase on Job*, supposes that this gives as great an image of what it expresses as can enter the thought of man; and Quarles expresses it,
>
> – his moving Eye
> Shines like the glory of the morning sky.

KJB 1611	*Anthony Purver 1764*
Canst thou draw out Leviathan with an hook? or his tongue with a cord which thou lettest down?	Canst thou draw out the Whale with a Hook, and his Tongue with a Line thou makest sink down?
Canst thou put an hook into his nose? or bore his jaw through with a thorn?	Wilt thou put a Rush into his Nose, and pierce through his Jaw with a Thorn?
Will he make many supplications unto thee? will he speak soft words unto thee?	Will he multiply Supplications to thee? Will he sooth thee with soft Things?
Will he make a covenant with thee? wilt thou take him for a servant for ever?	Will he make an Agreement with thee? Wilt thou take him for a Servant continually?
Wilt thou play with him as with a bird? wilt thou bind him for thy maidens?	Wilt thou play with him as a Bird, and tie him for thy Girls?
Shall the companions make a banquet of him? shall they part him among the merchants?	Shall the Companions make a Feast upon him? Shall they part him in the midst between the Dealers?

KJB

Canst thou fill his skin with barbed
irons? or his head with fish-spears?

Lay thine hand upon him,
remember the battle: do no more.
Behold, the hope of him is in vain:
shall not one be cast down even at
the sight of him?
None is so fierce that dare stir him
up: who then is able to stand
before me?
Who hath prevented me, that I
should repay him? whatsoever is
under the whole heaven, is mine.
I will not conceal his parts, nor his
power, nor his comely proportion.

Who can discover the face of his
garment? or who can come to him,
with his double bridle?
Who can open the doors of his
face? his teeth are terrible round
about.
His scales are his pride, shut up
together as with a close seal.

One is so near to another, that no
air can come between them.

They are joined one to another,
they stick together, that they
cannot be sundered.
By his neesings a light doth shine,
and his eyes are like the eye-lids of
the morning.
Out of his mouth go burning
lamps, and sparks of fire leap out.

Anthony Purver

Wilt thou fill his Skin with
Grappling-hooks, and his Head
with Fish-spears?
Put thy Hand upon him; remember
the Combat, do not proceed.
Lo the Hope of him is false: will
he also be cast down at the Sight
of any one?
There is not a fierce one that will
rouse him up: who is it then will
stand before me?
Who would prevent me? and I will
recompense; what is under the
whole Heaven being mine.
I will not be silent with his Limbs,
the Matter of Powers, and Grace
of his Disposition.

Who shall discover the outside of
his Cloathing? With his double
Bridle who shall come?
The Doors of his Face who shall
open? His Teeth round about
being terrible.
Excellent is the Strength of the
scaly Shields, each shut with a
close Seal.

One to another they come so nigh,
that the Wind does not enter
between them.

They cleave to each other; take
hold of, and do not separate,
themselves.
With his Sneezings the Light
shines; and his Eyes are as the
Eye-lids of the Morning.
Lamps go from his Mouth, Sparks
of Fire escape.

KJB

Out of his nostrils goeth smoke, as out of a seething pot or caldron.

His breath kindleth coals, and a flame goeth out of his mouth.
In his neck remaineth strength, and sorrow is turned into joy before him.
The flakes of his flesh are joined together: they are firm in themselves, they cannot be moved.
His heart is as firm as a stone, yea as hard as a piece of the nether mill-stone.
When he raiseth up himself, the mighty are afraid: by reason of breakings they purify themselves.

The sword of him that layeth at him cannot hold: the spear, the dart, nor the habergeon.
He esteemeth iron as straw, and brass as rotten wood.
The arrow cannot make him flee: sling-stones are turned with him into stubble.

Darts are counted as stubble: he laugheth at the shaking of a spear.

Sharp stones are under him: he spreadeth sharp pointed things upon the mire.
He maketh the deep to boil like a pot: he maketh the sea like a pot of ointment.

Anthony Purver

Smoak goes out of his Nostrils, like a Pot that is blowed under, or a Caldron.
His Breath kindles Coals, and a Flame goes out of his Mouth.
Strength lodges in his Neck, and Sorrow triumphs before him.

The Muscles of his Flesh cleave together; are firm upon him, cannot be moved.
His Heart is firm like a Stone, nay firm as a Piece of the lower one *of a Mill.*
The Strong are afraid by reason of his Excellency, they purify themselves by reason of the Breakings.
The Sword that comes nigh him shall not rise up, the Spear, the Dart, or the Breast-plate.
He reckons Iron for Straw, Steel for rotten Wood.
The Offspring of the Bow does not make him flee: the Stones of the Sling are turned into Stubble to him.
Those of the Cross-bow are counted as Stubble; and he laughs at the Shaking of the Lance.
Sharp Shells are under him; he makes a Bed with broken Things upon the Dirt.
He causes the Deep to boil as a Pot, makes the Sea like Ointment.

KJB	Anthony Purver
He maketh a path to shine after him; one would think the deep to be hoary.	He makes a Path light after him; the Gulf is reckoned to be grey. There is none upon the Land
Upon earth there is not his like: who is made without fear.	comparable to him: he is made without Dread.
He beholdeth all high things: he is a king over all the children of pride.	He can look on every one, he is a King above all the Lion's Breed.

Matthew 7. The KJB and Edward Harwood

Harwood's rendering of the last two verses makes this an especially appropriate demonstration of his conception of the 'propriety and perspicuity' (p. iii) with which he thinks Jesus would have spoken had he been an English Augustan. 'He taught them as one having authority, and not as the Scribes' is changed into a comment on the divine eloquence of the chapter.

Harwood's verbosity and discomfort with the KJB's imagery are obvious. So he changes 'give not that which is holy unto the dogs, neither cast ye your pearls before swine' into 'Let your admonitions be ever dictated by prudence – for to rebuke those, whom you have reason to believe are obstinate and incorrigible, is unnecessarily exposing your person to insult, and your instructions to contempt.' This might have come from many an eighteenth-century moralist. Fielding, for instance, in his capacity as narrator of *Tom Jones*, writes, 'prudence and circumspection are necessary even to the best of men. They are indeed as it were a guard to Virtue, without which she can never be safe. It is not enough that your designs, nay that your actions, are intrinsically good, you must take care they shall appear so also' (3: 7).

KJB *1611*	Edward Harwood *1768*
Judge not, that ye be not judged.	Be not prone to censure others, lest you provoke God to judge you with the like severity.
For with what judgement ye judge, ye shall be judged: and with what measure ye mete, it shall be measured to you again.	For the same measures that you keep in your treatment of others, the same measures will God, at the last day, strictly observe in his conduct towards you – for according as you judge men with

KJB

Edward Harwood

And why beholdest thou the mote that is in thy brother's eye, but considerest not the beam that is in thine own eye?

lenity or cruelty, so will supreme justice retaliate it with like mercy or rigour.

Why is thine eye fixed upon thy brother's conduct with a penetration, that the slightest fault and foible cannot escape – while at the same time thou thyself art guilty of most heinous enormities? With what face canst thou reprove, and exhort others to reformation and amendment, when thine own life is a notorious satyr upon thine instructions?

Or how wilt thou say to thy brother, Let me pull out the mote out of thine eye, and, behold, a beam is in thine own eye?

Thou hypocrite, first cast out the beam out of thine own eye: and then shalt thou see clearly to cast out the mote out of thy brother's eye.

First leave off, hypocrite, thy shameful courses – and then gravely remonstrate against the venial imperfections of thy neighbours.

Give not that which is holy unto the dogs, neither cast ye your pearls before swine: lest they trample them under their feet, and turn again and rent you.

Let your admonitions be ever dictated by prudence – for to rebuke those, whom you have reason to believe are obstinate and incorrigible, is unnecessarily exposing your person to insult, and your instructions to contempt.

Ask, and it shall be given you: seek, and ye shall find: knock, and it shall be opened unto you.

These are the duties which the gospel requires of you, but in order to the discharge of them invoke divine assistance – which will not be denied to your sincere and virtuous endeavours to obtain it.

For every one that asketh, receiveth: and he that seeketh, findeth: and to him that knocketh, it shall be opened.

For the fervent prayers of every good person to the father of wisdom to aid and strengthen his imperfect virtue will not be rejected.

KJB

Edward Harwood

Or what man is there of you, whom if his son ask bread, will he give him a stone?

Learn from parental tenderness the indulgent disposition of the supreme father towards his dependent creatures – For is there any man, however abandoned and depraved, who, when his son asks him for the necessaries of life, will give him something that is useless or hurtful? for example, when his child cries for bread, will give him a stone,

Or if he ask a fish, will he give him a serpent?
If ye then being evil, know how to give good gifts unto your children, how much more shall your Father which is in heaven, give good things to them that ask him?

or a serpent – when he desires a fish.
If, therefore, parents of the very worst characters give to their children what is proper and useful for them – how much more will the most kind and compassionate Father of all, impart suitable favours and blessings to his supplicants.

Therefore all things whatsoever ye would that men should do to you, do ye even so to them: for this is the Law and the Prophets.

In fine, make the condition of your fellow creatures your own, – and behave to others in the same manner, as you would expect, if you were in their circumstances, and they in yours – In this one moral maxim is virtually comprehended the whole system of duty in the law and the prophets.

Enter ye in at the strait gate, for wide is the gate, and broad is the way that leadeth to destruction, and many there be which go in thereat:

Enter into the strait gate of virtue and christianity – for the gate is wide, and the road spacious and easy that conducts to perdition – and the generality of mankind travel it.

Because strait is the gate, and narrow is the way which leadeth

For the gate is narrow, and the road rough and difficult that leads

KJB

Edward Harwood

unto life, and few there be that
find it.

to the gospel and to life – and such
is the degeneracy of Jews and
Gentiles, that there are but few
who will discover it.

Beware of false prophets which
come to you in sheep's clothing,
but inwardly they are ravening
wolves.

Be ever cautious of being
deluded by false teachers, who will
practise every art to impose upon
you, and assume the harmless
innocence of the lamb to cover the
inward treachery and rapacity of
the wolf.

Ye shall know them by their fruits:
Do men gather grapes of thorns,
or figs of thistles?

But the infallible criterion of their
characters is this – Inspect their
lives and actions, and you cannot
be deceived. The fruit discovers
the true nature of the tree. Thorns
produce not the generous grape –
the thistle bears not the luscious
fig.

Even so, every good three bringeth
forth good fruit: but a corrupt tree
bringeth forth evil fruit.
A good tree cannot bring forth
evil fruit, neither can a corrupt tree
bring forth good fruit.
Every tree that bringeth not forth
good fruit, is hewn down, and cast
into the fire.

A good tree bears good fruit – a
bad tree, bad fruit.

In the same manner, a good heart
produces good actions – a bad
heart, wickedness.
And as the tree that bears
worthless fruit, however fair its
form and beautiful its leaves, is cut
down and burnt, – such will be the
fatal destruction to which God will
consign the specious hypocrite and
incorrigible sinner.

Wherefore by their fruits ye shall
know them.

So that a man's actions are the true
index of his heart, and the sole
infallible test of the goodness, or
badness of it.

Not every one that saith unto
me, Lord, Lord, shall enter into

It is not an outward profession of
the christian religion that will

KJB

the kingdom of heaven: but he that doth the will of my father which is in heaven.

Many will say to me in that day, Lord, Lord, have we not prophesied in thy name? and in thy name have cast out devils? and in thy name done many wonderful works?

And then will I profess unto them, I never knew you: Depart from me, ye that work iniquity.

Therefore, whosoever heareth these sayings of mine, and doeth them, I will liken him unto a wise man, which built his house upon a rock:

And the rain descended, and the floods came, and the winds blew, and beat upon that house: and it

Edward Harwood

entitle men to future happiness, but a sincere obedience to the divine will, and an uniformly pious and virtuous conduct.

Many at the day of judgement will thus address me – Lord! did we not embrace thy religion – did we not preach and instruct others in the doctrines and duties of it – did we not in consequence of our profession, perform the most stupendous miracles, and work the most astonishing cures. Are we not, therefore, thy true disciples – and wilt not thou bestow upon us those blessed rewards thou art now going to dispense?

But to these I will reply – Notwithstanding your former persuasion of the truth of my religion, and the zeal you have showed in asserting and vindicating its doctrines – yet you have disgraced it by an immoral life. Such as you I will never approve as my genuine disciples – Ye sinful and abandoned creatures depart!

These are the religious and moral instructions of my gospel – whosoever, therefore, shall cordially embrace and practise them, may be compared to a prudent and intelligent person, who built his house upon a rock: which, when assaulted by the raging tempest, the impetuous torrent, or the furious whirlwind,

KJB	Edward Harwood
fell not, for it was founded upon a rock.	sustains the shock — for it is founded on the unshaken basis of a rock.
And every one that heareth these sayings of mine, and doeth them not, shall be likened unto a foolish man, which built his house upon the sand:	But him, who is persuaded of the truth of christianity, and yet lives in the open practice of the vices it condemns, I will compare to a foolish man, who builds an house upon the sand.
And the rain descended, and the floods came, and the winds blew, and beat upon that house, and it fell, and great was the fall of it.	So that whenever the storms rage, or the floods rush, or the blasts assail it; it sinks, and falls in most dreadful ruins.
And it came to pass, when Jesus had ended these sayings, the people were astonished at his doctrine.	Here Jesus ended his discourse — and the multitude stood fixed with admiration at the sublimity of his doctrines:
For he taught them as one having authority, and not as the Scribes.	for these instructions were delivered not in the cold and negligent manner of the Scribes — but with a dignity and authority that spoke their divine original.

Benjamin Franklin: 'A Parable against Persecution' (c. 1755)

Chap. XXVII

And it came to pass after these Things, that Abraham sat in the Door of his Tent, about the going down of the Sun.

And behold a Man, bowed with Age, came from the Way of the Wilderness, leaning on a Staff.

And Abraham arose and met him, and said unto him, Turn in, I pray thee, and wash thy Feet, and tarry all Night, and thou shalt arise early on the Morrow, and go on thy Way.

And the Man said, Nay, for I will abide under this Tree.

But Abraham pressed him greatly; so he turned, and they went into the Tent; and Abraham baked unleavend Bread, and they did eat.

And when Abraham saw that the Man blessed not God, he said unto him, Wherefore dost thou not worship the most high God, Creator of Heaven and Earth?

And the man answered and said, I do not worship the God thou speakest of; neither do I call upon his Name; for I have made to myself a God, which abideth always in mine House, and provideth me with all Things.

And Abraham's Zeal was kindled against the Man; and he arose, and fell upon him, and drove him forth with Blows into the Wilderness.

And at Midnight God called unto Abraham, saying, Abraham, where is the Stranger?

And Abraham answered and said, Lord, he would not worship thee, neither would he call upon thy Name; therefore have I driven him out from before my Face into the Wilderness.

And God said, Have I born with him these hundred ninety and eight Years, and nourished him, and cloathed him, notwithstanding his Rebellion against me, and couldst not thou, that art thyself a Sinner, bear with him one Night?

And Abraham said, Let not the Anger of my Lord wax hot against his Servant. Lo, I have sinned; forgive me, I pray Thee:

And Abraham arose and went forth into the Wilderness, and sought diligently for the Man, and found him, and returned with him to his Tent; and when he had entreated him kindly, he sent him away on the Morrow with Gifts.

And God spake again unto Abraham, saying, For this thy Sin shall thy Seed be afflicted four Hundred Years in a strange Land:

But for thy Repentance will I deliver them; and they shall come forth with Power, and with Gladness of Heart, and with much Substance.

Bibliography

Abington School District v. *Schempp. United States Supreme Court Reports.* Lawyers' edition. Second series. 10: 844–914.

Ackerman, Robert. *J. G. Frazer: His Life and Work.* Cambridge: Cambridge University Press, 1987.

Allen, Alexander V. G. *Life and Letters of Phillips Brooks.* 2 vols. London: Macmillan, 1900.

Alter, Robert. *The Art of Biblical Narrative.* New York: Basic Books, 1981.

Alter, Robert and Frank Kermode, eds. *The Literary Guide to the Bible.* London: Collins, 1987.

Arnold, Matthew. *The Complete Prose Works of Matthew Arnold.* Ed. R. H. Super. 11 vols. Ann Arbor: University of Michigan Press, 1960 etc.

Ashton, Thomas L. *Byron's Hebrew Melodies.* London: Routledge, 1972.

Auerbach, Erich. Trans. Willard R. Trask. *Mimesis.* Princeton: Princeton University Press, 1953.

Barr, David L. and Nicholas Piediscalzi, eds. *The Bible in American Education.* Philadelphia: Fortress; Chico, Calif.: Scholars, 1982.

Bates, Ernest Sutherland. *The Bible Designed to be Read as Living Literature.* New York: Simon and Schuster, 1936. *The Bible Designed to be Read as Literature.* London: Heinemann, 1937.

Beveridge, William. *A Defence of the Book of Psalms.* London, 1710.

The Bible in the Public Schools. Arguments in the case of John D. Minor et al. versus the Board of Education of the City of Cincinnati et al. Cincinnati, 1870.

Black, M. H. *Cambridge University Press 1584–1984.* Cambridge: Cambridge University Press, 1984.

Blackmore, Richard. *Essays upon Several Subjects.* London, 1716.
A Paraphrase on the Book of Job. 1700. Second edn. London, 1716.

Blackwall, Anthony. *An Introduction to the Classics.* London, 1718.
The Sacred Classics Defended and Illustrated. 2 vols. London, 1725, 1731.

Blaikie, William Garden. *David Brown . . .: A Memoir.* London, 1898.

Blake, William. *Blake Records.* Ed. G. E. Bentley, Jr. Oxford: Oxford University Press, 1969.
The Complete Writings of William Blake. Ed. Geoffrey Keynes. London: Oxford University Press, 1966.

Bloom, Harold and David Rosenberg. *The Book of J.* 1990. New York: Vintage, 1991.

Boileau-Despréaux, Nicolas. *Œuvres complètes de Boileau.* Ed. A. C. Gidel. 4 vols. Paris, 1872–3.

Boles, Donald E. *The Bible, Religion, and the Public Schools.* 1961. New, revised edn. New York: Collier, 1963.

Boswell, James. *Boswell's Life of Johnson.* Ed. R. W. Chapman. London: Oxford University Press, 1953.

Brontë, Charlotte. *Jane Eyre.* 1847. Oxford: Oxford University Press, 1973.

Burges, George. *A Letter to ... the Lord Bishop of Ely on the subject of a new and authoritative translation of the Holy Scriptures.* Peterborough, 1796.

Burgon, John William. *The Revision Revised.* London, 1883.

Burke, Carl. *God is for Real, Man.* London and Glasgow: Fontana, 1967.

Byron, George Gordon, Lord. *Byron's Letters and Journals.* Ed. Leslie A. Marchand. 12 vols. London: John Murray, 1973 etc.

The Cambridge History of the Bible. Vol. III: *The West from the Reformation to the Present Day.* Ed. S. L. Greenslade. Cambridge: Cambridge University Press, 1963.

Campbell, George. *The Four Gospels.* 2 vols. London, 1789.

   The Philosophy of Rhetoric. 1776. Ed. Lloyd F. Bitzer. Carbondale: Southern Illinois University Press, 1963.

Chambers, Talbot W. *A Companion to the Revised Old Testament.* New York and London, 1885.

   'The English Bible as a classic'. In *Anglo-American Bible Revision.* By members of the American Revision Committee. New York and London, 1879. Pp. 37–42.

Coleridge, Samuel Taylor. *Aids to Reflection and The Confessions of an Inquiring Spirit.* London, 1884.

   Collected Letters of Samuel Taylor Coleridge. Ed. Earl Leslie Griggs. 6 vols. Oxford: Oxford University Press, 1956–71.

   The Collected Works of Samuel Taylor Coleridge. Princeton: Princeton University Press; London: Routledge, 1971 etc.

   The Notebooks of Samuel Taylor Coleridge. Ed. Kathleen Coburn. 3 vols. London: Routledge. 1957–73.

   The Poems of Samuel Taylor Coleridge. Ed. Ernest Hartley Coleridge. Oxford: Oxford University Press, 1912.

Collins, Anthony. *A Discourse of the Grounds and Reasons of the Christian Religion.* London, 1724.

Cook, Albert S. *The Bible and English Prose Style: Selections and Comments.* Boston, 1892.

Cowper, William. *Poetical Works.* Ed. H. S. Milford. 4th edn, corrections and additions by Norma Russell. London: Oxford University Press, 1967.

Cruttwell, Clement. *The Holy Bible ... with notes by Thomas Wilson.* 3 vols. Bath, 1785.

Damrosch, David. *The Narrative Covenant.* San Francisco: Harper & Row, 1987.

Day, Henry Thomas. *Bible and Ritual Revision.* London, 1858.

Dennis, John. *The Grounds of Criticism in Poetry.* 1704. In Elledge, I: 102–42.

Dwight, Timothy. 'A dissertation on the history, eloquence and poetry of the Bible'. 1772. Facsimile in *The Major Poems of Timothy Dwight.* Intro. William J.

McTaggart and William K. Bottorff. Gainesville, Fla.: Scholars' Facsimiles & Reprints, 1969. Pp. 545–58.

Eckman, George P. *The Literary Primacy of the Bible*. New York: Methodist Book Concern, 1915.

Elledge, Scott, ed. *Eighteenth-Century Critical Essays*. 2 vols. Ithaca, New York: Cornell University Press, 1961.

Ellicott, Charles John. *Addresses on the Revised Version of Holy Scripture*. London: SPCK, 1901.

Erskine, Thomas. 'The speeches of the Hon. Thomas Erskine . . . on the trial of the King versus Thomas Williams for publishing *The Age of Reason*'. 2nd edn. London, 1797. Facsimile in *The Prosecution of Thomas Paine: Seven Tracts*. New York and London: Garland, 1974.

Felton, Henry. *A Dissertation on Reading the Classics*. London, 1713.

Forster, E.M. *A Passage to India*. 1924. Ed. Oliver Stallybrass. Harmondsworth: Penguin, 1979.

Franklin, Benjamin. *The Autobiography of Benjamin Franklin*. Ed. Leonard W. Labaree et al. New Haven and London: Yale University Press, 1964.

Frazer, James George. *Passages of the Bible Chosen for their Literary Beauty and Interest*. 1895. 2nd edn. London: Macmillan, 1909.

Frye, Northrop. *The Great Code*. London: Routledge, 1982.

Frye, Roland Mushat, ed. *The Bible: Selections from the King James Version for Study as Literature*. Princeton, N.J.: Princeton University Press, 1965.

Gardiner, John Hays. *The Bible as English Literature*. London: Fisher and Unwin, 1906.

Geddes, Alexander. *General Answer to the Queries, Counsels and Criticisms that have been communicated to him since the publication of his proposals for printing a new translation of the Bible*. London, 1790.

Prospectus of a New Translation of the Holy Bible. Glasgow, 1786.

Gildon, Charles. *The Complete Art of Poetry*. 2 vols. London, 1718.

The Laws of Poetry Explained and Illustrated. London, 1721.

Gilfillan, George. *The Bards of the Bible*. 1851. 4th edn. Edinburgh, 1856.

Guardian, The. Ed. John Calhoun Stephens. Lexington: University Press of Kentucky, 1982.

Halsey, Le Roy J. *The Literary Attractions of the Bible; or, A Plea for the Word of God Considered as a Classic*. 1858. 3rd edn. NY, 1860.

Hammond, Gerald. *The Making of the English Bible*. Manchester: Carcanet, 1982.

Harwood, Edward. *A Liberal Translation of the New Testament*. 2 vols. London, 1768.

Hatch, Nathan O., and Mark A. Noll, eds. *The Bible in America*. New York and Oxford: Oxford University Press, 1982.

Hazlitt, William. *The Complete Works of William Hazlitt*. Ed. P.P. Howe. 21 vols. London: Dent, 1931–4.

Hemphill, Samuel. *A History of the Revised Version of the New Testament*. London: Elliot Stock, 1906.

Herbert, A.S. *Historical Catalogue of Printed Editions of the English Bible, 1525–1961*. Revised and expanded from the edition of T.H. Darlow and H.F. Moule, 1903. London: The British and Foreign Bible Society; New York: The American Bible Society, 1968.

Herder, Johann Gottfried von. *The Spirit of Hebrew Poetry.* Trans. James Marsh. 2 vols. Burlington, Vt.; also Boston, Mass., 1833. Rpt. Naperville, Ill.: Alec R. Allenson, 1971.

Hills, Edward F. *The King James Version Defended!.* 1956. Des Moines, Iowa: Christian Research, 1973.

Home, Henry (Lord Kames). *Elements of Criticism.* 1762. 11th edn. London, 1840.

Hunt, Geoffrey. *About the New English Bible.* Cambridge: Oxford University Press and Cambridge University Press, 1970.

Husbands, John. *A Miscellany of Poems by Several Hands.* Oxford, 1731.

Huxley, Thomas Henry. 'The School Boards: what they can do, and what they may do'. 1870. *Collected Essays.* 1893. London: Macmillan, 1910. III: 374–403.

Jebb, John. *Sacred Literature.* London, 1820.

Johnson, Samuel. *A Dictionary of the English Language.* 2 vols. London, 1755. *Lives of the English Poets.* 2 vols. London: Dent, 1925.

Johnston, David. *Plea for a New English Version of the Scriptures.* London, 1864.

Jordan, Clarence L. *The Cotton Patch Version of Matthew and John.* Piscataway, N.J: New Century, ?1970.

Josipovici, Gabriel. *The Book of God.* New Haven and London: Yale University Press, 1988.

Kermode, Frank. *The Genesis of Secrecy.* Cambridge, Mass., and London: Harvard University Press, 1979.

Kipling, Rudyard. '"Proofs of Holy Writ"'. *The Sussex Edition of Kipling's Works.* London: Macmillan, 1937–9. XXX: 339–56.

Knights, L. C. 'How many childen had Lady Macbeth?'. *Explorations.* London: Chatto & Windus, 1945. Pp. 1–39.

Knox, Vicesimus. *Essays, Moral and Literary.* 1778. Vol. 1 of *The Works.* 7 vols. London, 1824.

Kugel, James L. *The Idea of Biblical Poetry.* New Haven and London: Yale University Press, 1981.

Leach, Edmund. *Genesis as Myth and Other Essays.* London: Cape, 1969.

Leach, Edmund, and D. Alan Aycock. *Structuralist Interpretations of Biblical Myth.* Cambridge: Cambridge University Press, 1983.

Le Clerc, Jean. 'An essay upon critics, wherein it is endeavoured to show in what the poesy of the Hebrews consists'. *The Young Student's Library.* London: The Athenian Society, 1692. French version in *La Bibliothèque universelle* 9. Paris, 1688. Latin original reprinted in Blasio Ugolino, ed., *Thesaurus Antiquitatem Sacrarum,* XXXI. Venice, 1766. Cols. 991–1020.

Lehmann, William C. *Henry Home, Lord Kames, and the Scottish Enlightenment.* The Hague: Nijhoff, 1971.

Lewis, C. S. 'The literary impact of the Authorised Version'. 1950. *They Asked for a Paper.* London: Bles, 1962. Pp. 26–50.

Lightfoot, Joseph Barber. *On a Fresh Revision of the English New Testament.* London and New York, 1871.

Locke, John. *A Paraphrase and Notes on the Epistles of St Paul.* London, 1707.

Longinus. *Dionysius Longinus of the Height of Eloquence.* Trans. John Hall. London, 1652. *Dionysius Longinus on the Sublime.* Trans. William Smith. London, 1739.

On the Sublime. Trans. T. S. Dorsch. *Classical Literary Criticism.* Harmondsworth: Penguin, 1965.

A Treatise of the Loftiness or Elegancy of Speech. Trans., from the French, J. Pulteney. London, 1680.

Lowes, John Livingston. 'The noblest monument of English prose'. *Of Reading Books.* London: Constable, 1930. Pp. 47–77.

Lowth, Robert. *De Sacra Poesi Hebraeorum Praelectiones.* London, 1753.

Isaiah: a New Translation. 1778. 10th edn. London, 1833.

Lectures on the Sacred Poetry of the Hebrews. Trans. George Gregory. 2 vols. London, 1787.

A Short Introduction to English Grammar. 1762. Facsimile of Philadelphia, 1775 edn. Intro. Charlotte Downey. Scholars' Facsimiles & Reprints: Delmar, New York, 1979.

McCulloch, John Murray. *Literary Characteristics of the Holy Scriptures.* 1845. 2nd edn, with additions and supplementary notes. Edinburgh, 1847.

Macpherson, James. *Fragments of Ancient Poetry.* Edinburgh, 1760.

Marsh, George P. *Lectures on the English Language.* Ed. William Smith. London, 1862.

Moulton, Richard Green. *The Literary Study of the Bible.* Boston, 1895. 2nd edn. Boston, 1899.

The Modern Reader's Bible. 1895 etc. New York: Macmillan, 1907.

Murry, John Middleton. *The Problem of Style.* London: Oxford University Press, 1922.

Newcome, William. *An Attempt towards an Improved Version ... of the Twelve Minor Prophets.* London, 1785.

An Historical View of the English Biblical Translations. Dublin, 1792.

Newton, A. Edward. *The Greatest Book in the World.* London: Lane, 1926.

Nineham, Dennis, ed. *The New English Bible Reviewed.* London: Epworth, 1965.

Oliver, Robert T. 'The Bible and style'. *Sewanee Review* 42 (July 1934), 340–5.

Orwell, George. *Coming up for Air.* 1939. London: Secker & Warburg, 1986.

Paine, Gustavus S. *The Men Behind the King James Version.* Baker Book House: Grand Rapids, Michigan, 1977. Originally *The Learned Men.* 1959.

Paine, Thomas. *The Complete Writings of Thomas Paine.* Ed. Philip S. Foner. 2 vols. New York: The Citadel Press, 1945.

The Theological Works of Thomas Paine. London, 1819.

Pattison, T. Harwood. *The History of the English Bible.* London, 1894.

Petty, William Thomas (later FitzMaurice), Earl of Kerry. *An Essay upon the Influence of the Translation of the Bible upon English Literature, which Obtained the Annual Prize at Trinity College.* Cambridge, 1830.

Pilkington, Matthew. *Remarks upon Several Passages of Scripture.* Cambridge, 1759.

PN Review 13: *Crisis for Cranmer and King James.* Ed. David Martin. 6: 5 (1979).

Pollard, A. W. *The Holy Bible. A Facsimile in a Reduced Size of the Authorized Version Published in the Year 1611.* Oxford: Oxford University Press, 1911.

Pope, Alexander. *The Twickenham Edition of the Poems of Alexander Pope.* General ed., John Butt. 11 vols. London: Methuen; New Haven: Yale University Press, 1961–9.

Pratt, Samuel Jackson. *The Sublime and Beautiful of Scripture.* 2 vols. London, 1777.

Prickett, Stephen. *Words and the Word.* Cambridge: Cambridge University Press, 1986.

Purver, Anthony. *A New and Literal Translation of all the Books of the Old and New Testament.* 2 vols. London, 1764.

Quiller-Couch, Arthur. *On the Art of Reading.* Cambridge: Cambridge University Press, 1920.

Renan, Ernest. *The Gospels.* Vol. v of *The History of the Origins of Christianity.* 7 vols. London, 1888–9.

Robinson, Ian. *The Survival of English.* Cambridge: Cambridge University Press, 1973.

Rosenau, William. *Hebraisms in the Authorized Version of the Bible.* 1902. Baltimore: Friedenwald, 1903.

Rosenberg, David, ed. *Congregation.* San Diego: Harcourt Brace Jovanovich, 1987.

Ross, Hugh. *An Essay for a New Translation of the Bible.* London, 1701.

Roston, Murray. *Prophet and Poet: The Bible and the Growth of Romanticism.* London: Faber, 1965.

Ruskin, John. *Praeterita.* 1885–9. Ed. Kenneth Clark. London: Hart-Davis, 1949.

Saintsbury, George. *A History of Criticism.* 1900–4. 5th edn. 3 vols. Edinburgh and London: Blackwood, 1929.

A History of English Prose Rhythm. London: Macmillan, 1912.

Schaff, Philip. *The Revision of the English Versions of the Holy Scriptures.* New York, 1873.

Schweitzer, Albert. *The Quest of the Historical Jesus.* Trans. W. Montgomery. London: Black, 1910.

Seiss, J. A. 'The influence of the Bible on literature'. *Evangelical Review* XVII (July 1853), 1–17.

Shaftesbury, Anthony, 3rd Earl of. *Characteristics of Men, Manners, Opinions, Times, etc.* 1711. Ed. John M. Robertson. 2 vols. 1900. Gloucester, Mass.: Peter Smith, 1963.

Shelley, Percy Bysshe. *The Complete Works of Shelley.* Ed. Roger Ingpen and Walter E. Peck. 10 vols. New York: Gordian, 1965.

Sidney, Philip. *An Apology for Poetry.* 1580. London, 1595.

Smart, Christopher. *The Poetical Works of Christopher Smart.* Ed. Karina Williamson. 4 vols. Oxford: Oxford University Press, 1980–7.

Spring, Gardiner. *The Obligations of the World to the Bible.* New York, 1839.

Stennett, Joseph. *A Version of Solomon's Song of Songs.* London, 1700.

Sternberg, Meir. *The Poetics of Biblical Narrative.* Bloomington: Indiana University Press, 1985.

Sterne, Lawrence. Sermon XLII. 1769. In James P. Browne, ed., *The Works of Lawrence Sterne.* 4 vols. London, 1885. IV: 413–20.

Strauss, David Friedrich. *The Life of Jesus Critically Examined.* Trans. George Eliot. 1846. 5th edn. London: Swan Sonnenschein, 1906.

Strong, James. *The Exhaustive Concordance of the Bible.* 1894. London: Hodder & Stoughton, 1974.

Symonds, John. *Observations on the Expediency of Revising the Present English Version of the Four Gospels and of the Acts of the Apostles.* Cambridge, 1789.

Tate, Nahum. *An Essay for Promoting Psalmody.* London, 1710.

Taylor, John (Hebrew lexicographer). *A Scheme of Scripture-Divinity ... With a vindication of the Sacred Writings.* London, 1762. In Watson, *Tracts,* 1: 4–219.

Temple, William. 'An essay upon the ancient and modern learning'. 'Of poetry'. 1690. *Five Miscellaneous Essays by Sir William Temple*. Ed., with an introduction, Samuel Holt Monk. Ann Arbor: University of Michigan Press, 1963.

Thompson, Francis. *Literary Criticisms*. Ed. Terence L. Connolly. New York: Dutton, 1948.

Trench, Richard Chenevix. *On the Authorised Version of the New Testament*. London, 1858.

Wallace, Irving. *The Word*. London: Cassell, 1972.

Watson, Richard, ed. *An Apology for the Bible*. 1796. 3rd edn. London, 1796.

A Collection of Theological Tracts. 6 vols. Cambridge, 1785.

Webster, Noah. *The Holy Bible ... in the Common Version. With Amendments of the Language*. New Haven, 1833.

Westcott, Brooke Foss. *A General View of the History of the English Bible*. 1868. 3rd edn, revised by William Aldis Wright. London: Macmillan, 1905.

Some Lessons of the Revised Version of the New Testament. London, 1897.

Westerhoff, John H. 'The struggle for a common culture: biblical images in nineteenth-century schoolbooks'. In Barr and Piediscalzi, pp. 25–40.

White, Joseph. *A Revisal of the English Translation of the Old Testament Recommended*. Oxford, 1779.

White, Newman Ivey. *Shelley*. 2 vols. New York: Knopf, 1940.

Whittaker, John William. *An Historical and Critical Inquiry into the Interpretation of the Hebrew Scriptures, with Remarks on Mr Bellamy's New Translation*. Cambridge, 1819.

Willey, Basil. 'On translating the Bible into modern English'. *Essays and Studies*, new series (1970), 23: 1–17.

Wordsworth, William. *The Prose Works of William Wordsworth*. 3 vols. Ed. W. J. B. Owen and Jane Worthington Smyser. Oxford: Oxford University Press, 1974.

Wright, David F., ed. *The Bible in Scottish Life and Literature*. Edinburgh: Saint Andrew Press, 1988.

Wright, William Aldis. 'Proposed alterations in the Authorised Version'. Hectographic reproduction of manuscript notes. Cambridge University Library, Adv C 100 17[1].

General index

Biblical index

Books of the Bible are listed in alphabetical order of their name: hence 1
Corinthians is to be found in the Cs. All references to the original Scriptures or to
the Bible in general are listed under 'Scripture'.

poetic appeal', 427; 'mongrel English', 414; 'more definitely archaic and less generally understood', 409; 'noble naturalness', 317; 'noble simplicity', 305; 'noble simplicity . . . energetic bravery', 90; 'noblest and purest English', 188; 'noblest monument', 117, 319, 336; 'numinous rumble', 419; 'obsolete and harsh expressions', 76; 'obsolete phraseology', 177; 'obsolete words and uncouth ungrammatical expressions', 79; 'perfection of English', 181; 'perfection of our English language', 177; 'preserved a purity of meaning to many of the plain terms', 154; 'primarily a question of rhythm', 428; 'pure English words', 121; 'pure well of English undefiled', 186; 'purest standard of the English language', 98; 'remarkable simplicity and directness' of the Prophets, 305; 'resonant opacity', 428; 'severe beauty', 178; 'simple and natural', 96; 'simplicity and earnestness', 321; 'slovenly and vulgar phrases', 153; 'standard of style', 205; 'standard of the purity of our language', 205; 'strong and close', 17; 'style of one half of the English Bible is atrocious', 327; 'superstitious reverence', 327, 329; 'subject of highest commendation', 185; 'this venerable relic has involuntarily made our language warm', 90; 'too foul to be uttered in decent society', 246n; 'unbridgeable gulf between ourselves and the [KJB] as regards style', 304n; 'uncommon beauty and marvellous English', 183; 'uncouth and obsolete words and expressions', 76; 'unequalled vitality and freshness of

expression', 322; 'variety of expression' criticised by RV, 226; 'venerable as well as intelligible', 316; 'very harmful influence on English prose', 335; 'wonderful force and solemnity', 318; appropriate source for the language of theology, 58; attacked, 76–81; attacked for unintelligibility, 78, 424; beautiful, solemn and unreal, 409; became remote from popular English about 1920, 304n; becoming familiar, 40; criticised by *Critical Review*, 89; criticised by Wynne, 88–9; English 'acquired new dignity by it', 98; faults ignored because it is the appropriate language, 79; gave English 'a perennial beauty and majesty', 178; has raised English 'above common use and has almost sanctified it', 90; helped preserve words, 85; inadequate tool for expressing modern emotion and thought, 333; inconsistent vocabulary criticised, 121, 226, 239–40; influence on English conversation, 317–18; lists of obsolete words, 77, 80–1, 83n, 89n, 243n, 244; lists of offensive passages, 247n; may turn off younger Christians, 407; merits which 'cannot be augmented', 179; obscenity, **244–8**; Old Testament better than New, 153; passages 'not adapted to modern views of propriety', 246n; shows the whole extent of English's beauty and power, 179; so enthusiastically praised as to prevent rational discussion, 177; statistics on vocabulary and comparison with Shakespeare and Milton, 179n; superior to Shakespeare and all other English writers, 317; the norm by which to judge English

Matthew, 298, 392–3
3: 4-17, 99
5: 'a beautiful specimen of English composition', 269
5–7, 313
5: 22: translated by Purver, 75
6: 28, 169
6: 28–9: paraphrased by Doddridge, 87: paraphrased by Harwood, 87; translated by Wynne, 89n
7: paraphrased by Harwood, 449–54
7: 1–5, 142–3; paraphrased by Smart, 143
7: 4: KJB and NEB compared, 421
7: 6: KJB and NEB compared, 422; NEB version praised, 421
7: 24–7: KJB compared with Luke 47–9 and NEB, 329–30
10: 29, 141
11: 28, 83
11: 28–30, 328–9
12: 46–7, 375n
13: 55–6, 374n, 375n
16: 13–26: translated by Jordan, 259, 261
16: 20: translated by Lorimer, 260
21: 7: shows Matthew was not an eyewitness, 353–4
21: 12: harsher but better in RV, 235
21: 16, 85n
22: 21: translated by Scarlett, 104
26: 15, 365
26: 56 and 75: 'masterly effects', 328–9
27: 3–5, 365
27: 46, 329
28: 5–7: NEB version condemned, 429–30
28: 5–7 and 12–15: KJB version compared with NEB, 430–1
28: 11, 232n
28: 12–14: NEB version condemned, 430
28: 19: superiority to RV shown by Westcott, 234
Fictional development of story of

Judas, 364–7
Micah, 292
1: 8, 245
Midrash, 356, 365–7
Mill's Greek Testament, 58
Miriam: reason for her existence discussed by Leach, 373–4
Modern Roman missal, 434
Moffatt Bible, 54n
Moses, 91, 115, 130, 134, 216, 373–4, 392
'Astonishing poetry', 164

Nahum 2: 7: KJB incomprehensible, 78
Nehemiah, 213
Nevi'im, 391
New English Bible, 218, 326n, 343, 345, 401, **408–32**, 437
'Felicitous expressions meet one everywhere in astounding prodigality', 421
'Magnificent and exciting achievement', 420
'Magnificent and memorable accomplishment', 420
'Not sincere', 432
Another KJB, 421
Matt. 7: 27 compared with KJB, 330
Style: 'failure of style . . . a failure of belief', 432; journalistic, 429
New International Version, 229n, 401, 403
New Jerusalem Bible, 401
New King James Version, 401, **403–8**
New Revised Standard Version, 401, 403
New Testament, 48, 298, 392–4, 397
'Best book that ever was, or will be, known in the world', 302n
'Farce of one-act', 132
'Supremely effective', 361
'Thousand latent beauties', 87
Attacked by Paine, 132–3
Greek: 'biblical rather than contemporary', 316; 'flexible and easy-going', 429
Greek classic, 86